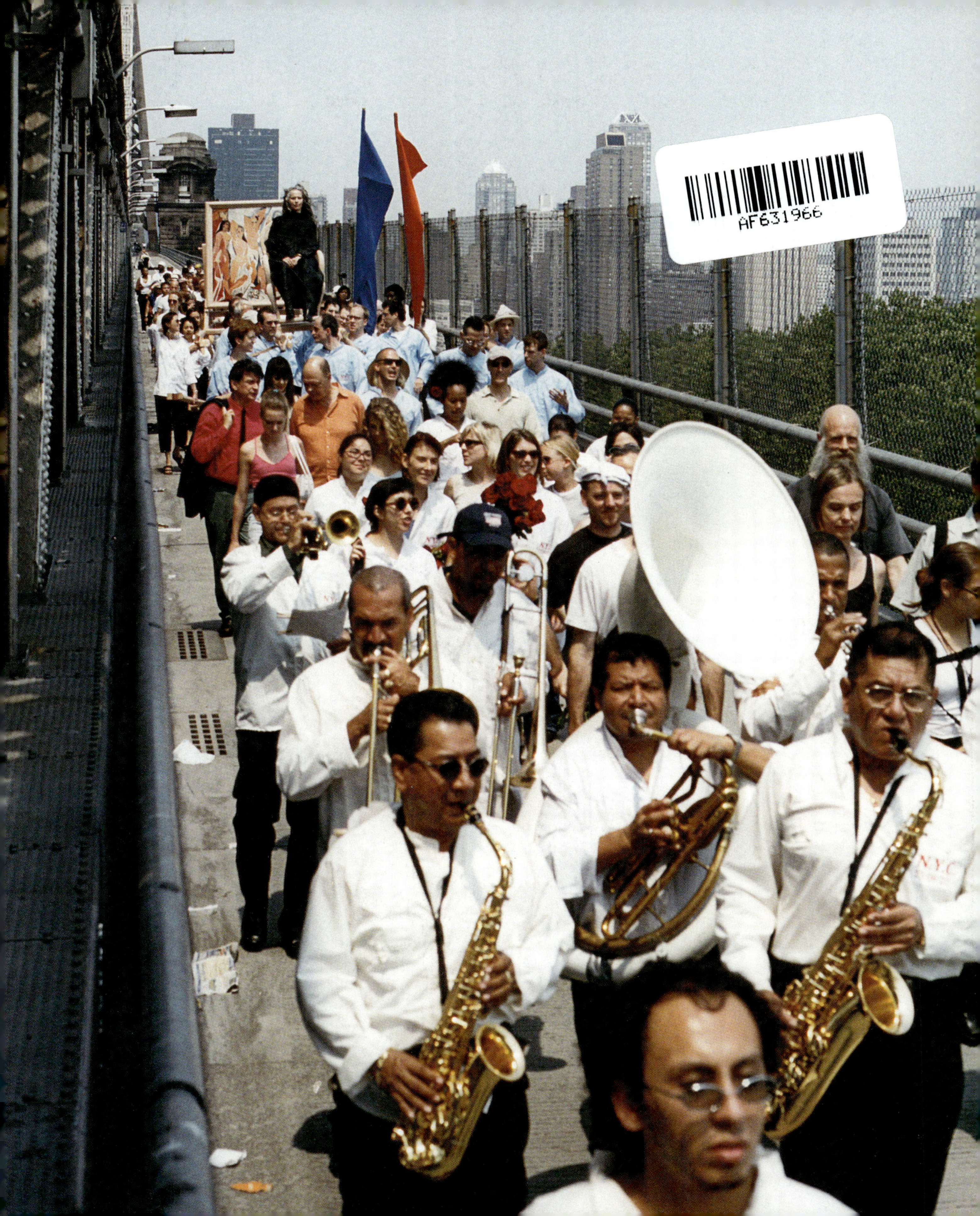
N.Y.C

DIE PARKETT-REIHE MIT GEGENWARTSKÜNSTLERN / THE PARKETT SERIES WITH CONTEMPORARY ARTISTS

Book Series with contemporary artists in English and German, published three times a year. Each volume is created in collaboration with artists, who contribute an original work specially made for the readers of Parkett. The works are reproduced in the regular edition and available in a limited and signed Special Edition.

Buchreihe mit Gegenwartskünstlern in deutscher und englischer Sprache, erscheint dreimal im Jahr. Jeder Band entsteht mit Künstlern oder Künstlerinnen, die eigens für die Leser von Parkett einen Originalbeitrag gestalten. Diese Werke sind in der gesamten Auflage abgebildet und zusätzlich in einer limitierten und signierten Vorzugsausgabe erhältlich.

PARKETT NR. 70 ENTSTEHT IN COLLABORATION MIT • **CHRISTIAN MARCLAY, WILHELM SASNAL, GILLIAN WEARING** • WILL BE COLLABORATING ON PARKETT NO. 70

JAHRESABONNEMENT (DREI NUMMERN) / ANNUAL SUBSCRIPTION (THREE ISSUES) SFR. 116.– (SCHWEIZ), € 78 (BRD), € 82 (ÜBRIGES EUROPA), US$ 80 (USA AND CANADA ONLY)

ZWEI- UND DREIJAHRESABONNEMENTPREISE SIEHE GELBE BESTELLKARTE IM HEFT / FOR TWO & THREE YEAR RATES, PLEASE CONSULT YELLOW ORDER FORM.

Zürichsee Druckereien AG (Stäfa) Satz, Litho, Druck/Copy, Printing, Color Separations

PARKETT-VERLAG AG ZÜRICH DEZEMBER 2003 PRINTED IN SWITZERLAND ISBN 3-907582-19-5 ISSN 0256-0917

HEFTRÜCKEN / SPINE 67–69: FIONA BANNER

Cover & flap / Umschlag & Klappe: ANISH KAPOOR, MARSYAS, 2002, Tate Modern Turbine Hall, Unilever Series, detail / Ausschnitt. (PHOTO: JOHN RIDDY/TATE GALLERY, LONDON)
Inside cover / Innere Umschlagseite: FRANCIS ALŸS, THE MODERN PROCESSION, NEW YORK CITY, JUNE 23, 2002, drawing & collage for MoMA brochure / Zeichnung und Collage. (PHOTO: DAVID ALLISON/PUBLIC ART FUND & THE MUSEUM OF MODERN ART)
Page 1 / Seite 1: FRANCIS ALŸS, THE MODERN PROCESSION, NEW YORK CITY, JUNE 23, 2002, photograph / Photographie.
Back cover / Rückseite: ISA GENZKEN, EMPIRE/VAMPIRE, WHO KILLS DEATH, 2003, detail. (PHOTO: GALERIE DANIEL BUCHHOLZ, KÖLN)
All images slightly cropped / Alle Bilder leicht beschnitten.

PARKETT Zürich New York

Bice Curiger Chefredaktorin/Editor-in-Chief; **Jacqueline Burckhardt** Redaktorin/Senior Editor; **Cay Sophie Rabinowitz** Redaktorin USA / Senior Editor US; **Suzanne Schmidt** Textredaktion und Produktion / Editing and Production; **Hanna Koller · Simone Eggstein** Graphik / Design, **Trix Wetter** (beurlaubt / on temporary leave); **Catherine Schelbert** Englisches Lektorat / Editorial Assistant for English; **Claudia Meneghini Nevzadi** Korrektorat/Proof Reading

Beatrice Fässler Vorzugsausgaben, Inserate/ Special Editions, Advertising; **Nicole Stotzer** Buchvertrieb, Administration / Distribution, Administration; **Mathias Arnold** Abonnemente / Subscriptions; **Ali Subotnick** Redaktion USA / Associate Editor US **Monika Condrea** Vorzugsausgaben, Inserate und Abonnemente USA/Special Editions, Advertising, and Subscriptions US; **Cliff Borress** Praktikant USA/Intern US; **Adrian Koerfer** Deutsche Verlagsvertretung/German Representative

Jacqueline Burckhardt – Bice Curiger – Dieter von Graffenried Herausgeber/Parkett Board;
Jacqueline Burckhardt – Bice Curiger – Dieter von Graffenried – Walter Keller – Peter Blum Gründer/Founders

Dieter von Graffenried Verleger/Publisher

www.parkettart.com

PARKETT-VERLAG AG, QUELLENSTRASSE 27, CH-8031 ZÜRICH, TEL. 41-1-271 81 40, FAX 41-1-272 43 01
PARKETT, NEW YORK, 155 AV. OF THE AMERICAS, N.Y. 10013, PHONE (212) 673-2660, FAX (212) 271-0704

EDITORIAL

Diese Ausgabe von Parkett präsentiert drei eigenwillige Positionen, welchen eines gemeinsam ist: das kühne Durchkreuzen und Umstülpen von Raumvorstellungen. Dies geschieht etwa bei Francis Alÿs allein schon durch seine Spaziergänge in einer Stadt wie Mexico City. Durch die Art und Weise, wie er diese unternimmt und wie in der Folge darüber erzählt und wieder erzählt wird, erhält die Figur des Künstlers, aber auch die Auffassung vom Kunstwerk, die Beinote des Unterwegsseins und Setzungen wie jene von Zentrum und Peripherie werden verwischt (wie Saul Anton auf S. 43 ausführt). Als Edition für Parkett realisiert Francis Alÿs einen mit Magneten gefüllten Blechhund, genannt «Ghetto Collector», der auch unsere Leserinnen und Leser zu Spaziergängen verführen soll, und zwar zu solchen, die – in geeigneter Umgebung – ganz sichtbar einen materiellen «Mehrwert» schaffen, akkumuliert in Form von auf der Strasse herumliegenden Metallteilen, die sich unweigerlich an den magnetischen Hundeleib heften werden. Der Künstler hat sich auch schon daran versucht, mit vereinten Kräften den sprichwörtlichen Berg zu versetzen (vgl. S. 18/19); oder er hat den temporären Umzug des Museum of Modern Art in den Stadtteil Queens zum Anlass genommen, eine wahre Prozession mit einigen quasi zu profanen «Heiligenbildern» erhobenen Meisterwerken zu organisieren.
Bleiben wir innerhalb dessen, was gemeinhin als «Kunstraum» bezeichnet wird, so beschreibt Jörg Heiser (S. 62 ff.) die mentale Reise eines fiktiven «Betrachters» der nach dreissig Jahren aus dem Koma erwacht und über Isa Genzkens Werkphasen ins Staunen gerät. Genzken hat Skulpturen geschaffen, die wie okkulte Präzisionsinstrumente den Namen «Hyperbolo» tragen, andere, die «Weltempfänger» heissen. Später bringt sie an Gebäuden gigantische Haare oder an Fassaden enorme Photos eines menschlichen Ohrs an, hängt Flugzeugfenster an die Wand einer Galerie und bietet in ihrer neuen Werkserie «Empire/Vampire» eine wie im Kinderspiel in Fluss geratene, doch vom Raffinement des kollektiven Kunstkönnens wieder in Form gebrachte Welt an; als ein «Justierungssystem der Wahrnehmung», ein «Scharfstellen», das mit dem «Vergleich von Skulptur und Körper, Architektur und Mensch» erst beginnt (Heiser, S. 67).
Wenn Anish Kapoor die Betrachter in Situationen befördert, die ihre Wahrnehmungsfähigkeit auf noch unbekannte Weise herausfordern, geschieht dies in der Art, wie es Norman Bryson beschreibt: «Unser Dasein dehnt sich bis zur Grösse des Universums aus oder schrumpft zu einem einzigen Quantenteilchen Lebensenergie.» (S. 115)
Alle drei Künstler machen in ihrer Arbeit eines deutlich: mit welcher Konsequenz sowohl die statischen Vorstellungen von Skulptur und Malerei verabschiedet werden, aber auch die Bezugnahmen auf vergangene Bewegungen wie Konzept- und Aktionskunst, Land-Art oder Minimal Art, obsolet geworden sind. Diese machen lediglich die Freiheit, die Abgelöstheit ihrer Kunst spürbarer. Und so fragt denn unsere neueste Parkett-Umfrage in dieser Ausgabe nach dem Publikum, nach jenem Gebilde, das Menschen kurzfristig vereinigt und Einigkeit, Konsens (auch im Schein) abzubilden vermag.

Wir möchten an dieser Stelle Mario Merz', 1925–2003, gedenken, seiner unvergesslichen Anwesenheit, seiner Gabe der poetischen Sprache, welche Energien und Vorstellungskraft zu durchdringen und als starke Vektoren in den Raum zu setzen verstand.

EDITORIAL

The three idiosyncratic positions presented in this issue of Parkett share common ground: they all boldly frustrate and invert received notions of space. Francis Alÿs achieves these objectives quite simply by strolling through a metropolitan area like Mexico City. The way he does this, how he talks about it and reports on it invests not only the figure of the artist but also the concept of an artwork with the flavor of being on the road, which in turn blurs positionings like center and margin (as analyzed by Saul Anton, p. 36). In his Edition for Parkett, Alÿs has created a tin dog filled with magnets, a "Ghetto Collector," thereby inviting our readers to take walks that will yield a highly visible added value–in suitable surroundings–inasmuch as the wheeled creature attracts all the stray metal lying around on the streets. The artist has also joined forces with others in the attempt to move the proverbial mountain (see pp. 18/19), and has used the Museum of Modern Art's temporary move to Queens as an excuse to organize a very real procession of masterworks, of profane "sacred images."

Staying within the boundaries of what is conventionally called the "space of art," Jörg Heiser (from p. 68) describes the mental journey of a fictional "viewer" who wakes up out of a coma after 30 years and is astonished to discover the phases of Isa Genzken's oeuvre. Genzken has created sculptures that she calls "Hyperbolo," like occult precision instruments, and others called "World Receiver." Subsequently, she placed gigantic hairs on buildings or enormous photographs of the human ear on facades and mounted aircraft windows on gallery walls. Her latest series, "Empire/Vampire," explores a world in flow, as if in a child's game, to which form is restored through the refinement of collective artistry as a "calibration of perceptions," a "focusing" that replaces the "comparison of sculpture and form, architecture and the human being" (Heiser, p. 73).

Anish Kapoor places viewers in situations that challenge perception in hitherto unknown ways. Norman Bryson tellingly describes the consequences: "Your being expands to the size of the universe, or shrinks to the compass of a single quantum of life energy" (p. 110).

These three artists make one thing clear: undeniably archaic is the concept of sculpture and painting as static phenomena, and obsolete the reference to past movements like Conceptual, Aktion, Land, or Minimal art. They merely make the freedom and detachment of their art more tangible. Logically, therefore, Parkett's latest inquiry examines the question of the public, an entity that fleetingly unites people and mirrors (the appearance of) agreement or consensus.

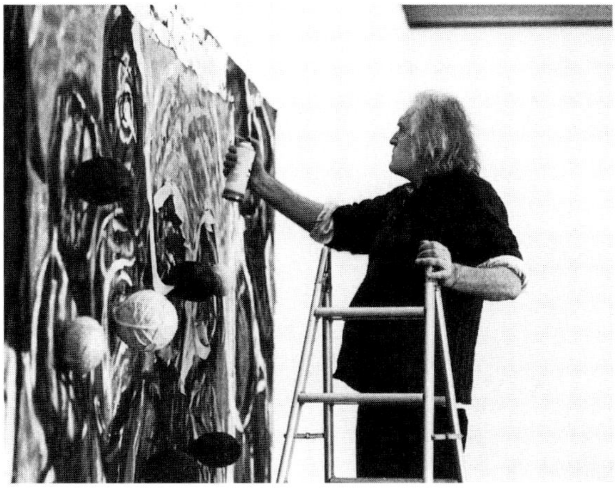

(Photo: Walter Drayer)

We take this opportunity to commemorate Mario Merz, 1925–2003, his unforgettable presence, the energy and imaginative power of his poetic language, and the powerful vectors that he placed in the space of art.

BICE CURIGER

PHILIPP KAISER

Amelie von Wulffen

Bruchstücke

Wohl aber habe ich an diesem Abend mein Zimmer und mein Bett mir eingeprägt wie man sich einen Ort genauer merkt, von dem man ahnt, man werde eines Tages etwas Vergessenes von dort holen müssen.[1] An jenem Abend erfährt der fünfjährige Walter Benjamin, wie er in *Berliner Kindheit* schreibt, vom Tode seines Vetters, den er mit kindlicher Gleichgültigkeit vernimmt.

Wir kennen diese zentralen und vermeintlich einmaligen Momente in unserem Leben, in denen sich alle Aufmerksamkeit auf die Gegenwart im Hier und Jetzt konzentriert, um nicht eines Tages vergessen zu müssen. Der verzweifelte Versuch, das unerbittliche Fliessen des Lebens anzuhalten und die eigene Geschichte oder wenigstens Teile davon immer wieder rekonstruieren zu können, mag daher nahe liegen. Gerade die Verbreitung der Photographie ist Zeuge für diesen Umgang mit individueller und kollektiver Erinnerung. Amelie von Wulffens Collagen, die virtuos die unterschiedlichen Repräsentationssysteme Photographie und Malerei fast nahtlos ineinander übergehen lassen, finden hier ebenfalls ihren Ausgangspunkt. Photographien eines aufgeräumten, bieder bürgerlichen Esszimmers mit dunkelbraunen Möbeln, Zimmerpflanzen, Stehlampen, Perserteppich, Kerzenständern, Ölbildern an der Wand und einem seltsamen Plexiglaskasten mit Plattenspieler und Nippes zeigen menschenleere Interieurs. Die Innenräume kleben auf der papiernen Oberfläche und geben vor, trotz ihres reproduktiven Charakters gewissermassen einzigartig zu sein. Wenngleich diesen unterbelichteten Bildern eine historische Dimension im Sinne der Vergewisserung des «So ist es gewesen» zukommt, kondensiert sich Erinnerung in Amelie von Wulffens Collagen nur partiell in photographischen Dokumenten. Erinnerung setzt vielmehr an den Rändern an, da, wo die Photographie aufhört und die malerische Imagination anfängt. Die Rekon-

PHILIPP KAISER ist Kurator am Museum für Gegenwartskunst Basel.

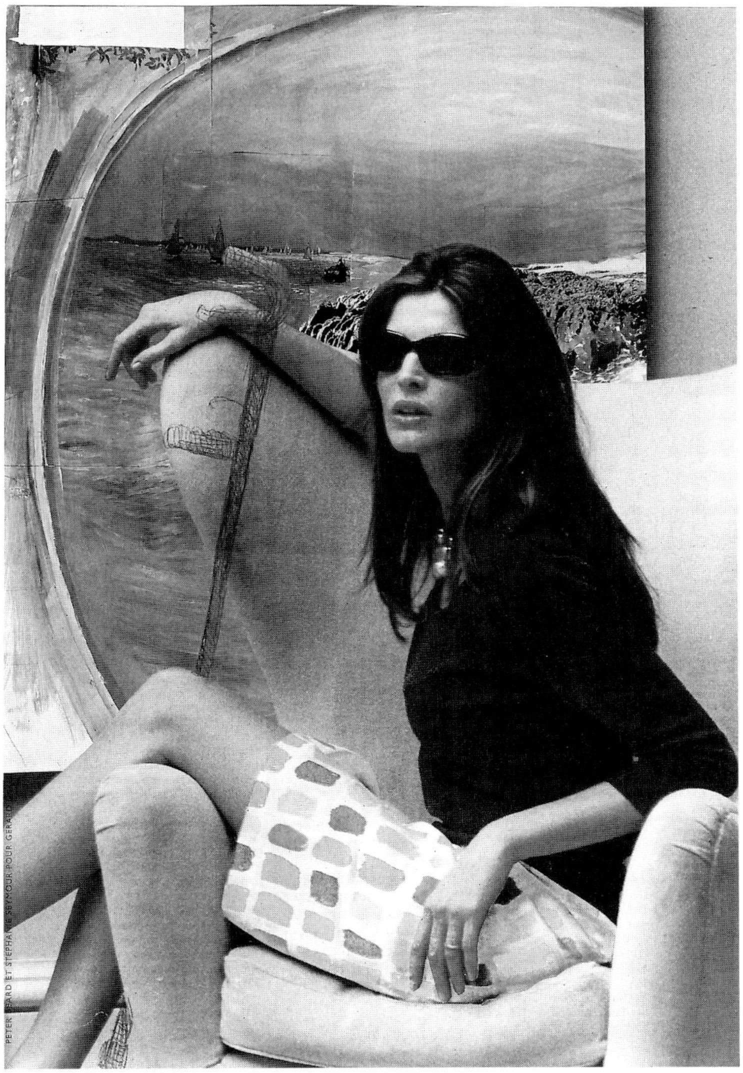

AMELIE VON WULFFEN,
COMPUTERCOLLAGE 2000–2002, 40 x 30 cm /
COMPUTER COLLAGE, 15 3/4 x 11 13/16".
(PHOTO: GALERIE ASCAN CRONE, BERLIN & HAMBURG)

struktion des Vergessenen und Verdrängten ist bei Amelie von Wulffen eine physische Tätigkeit, deren gestische Spuren ablesbar bleiben. Das Nebeneinander der einzelnen Photographien von Elternhaus, Museen, Schwimmbädern, Innenräumen und neuerdings auch Landschaften ist Ausdruck der durch die Photographie atomisierten Wirklichkeit, denn durch sie wurde die Welt zu einer Aneinanderreihung beziehungsloser, frei schwebender Partikel.[2)]

Amelie von Wulffens Collagen sind Montagen, die nicht dem naiven Glauben anheim fallen, Erinnerungssplitter in einem dumpfen Kontinuum einebnen zu können. Die Montage als avantgardistisches Gestaltungsprinzip ist vielmehr selber Bruchstück, da sie nicht an Totalität glaubt. Bereits die Photocollagen spätmodernistischer, zumeist osteuropäischer Architektur lassen in der kubistischen Zersplitterung der Häuser eine sequenzielle Ordnung erkennen, in der das dynamische Moment der Moderne vielleicht ein letztes Mal aufkeimt. Die filmische Qualität der Raumabwicklung und die montierte Mehrfachperspektive erinnern dabei an Darstellungsweisen konstruktivistischer Architekturutopien, und wenn am Himmel gar ein Zeppelin auftaucht, wähnt man sich tatsächlich in den 20er Jahren. War die Montage in den früheren Arbeiten als Sequenz organisiert, so vermochte sie später unterschiedlichste Erinnerungsfetzen miteinander in Verbindung zu bringen. Die Montage ist bei Amelie von Wulffen ein Bruchstück von Bruchstücken und kann im Sinne von Walter Benjamins Geschichtstheorie als Ruine beschrieben werden. Sie

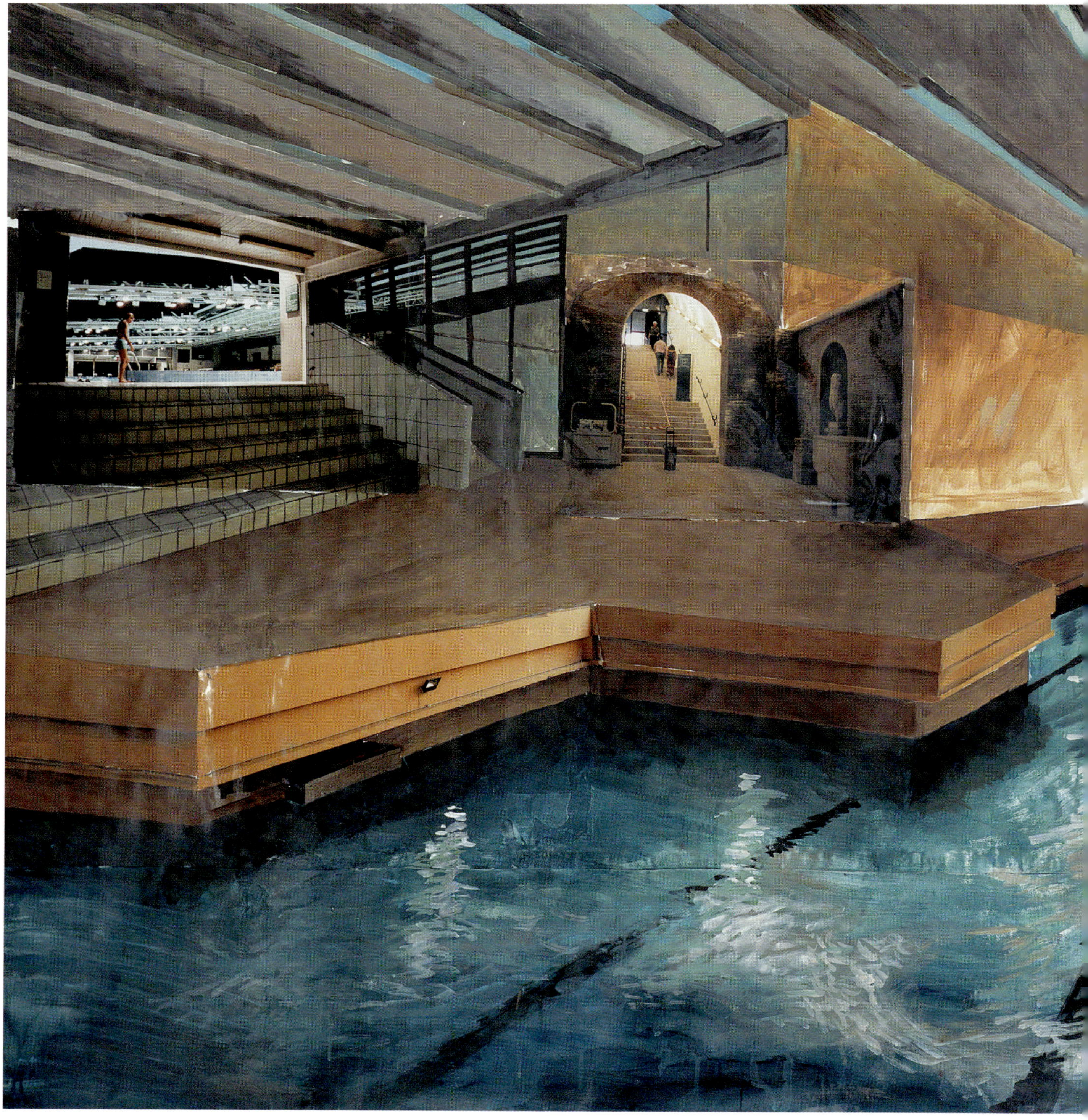

AMELIE VON WULFFEN, OHNE TITEL, 2000, Photographie und Acryl auf Papier,
126 x 184 cm / UNTITLED, photograph and acrylic on paper, 49 5/8 x 72 7/16".

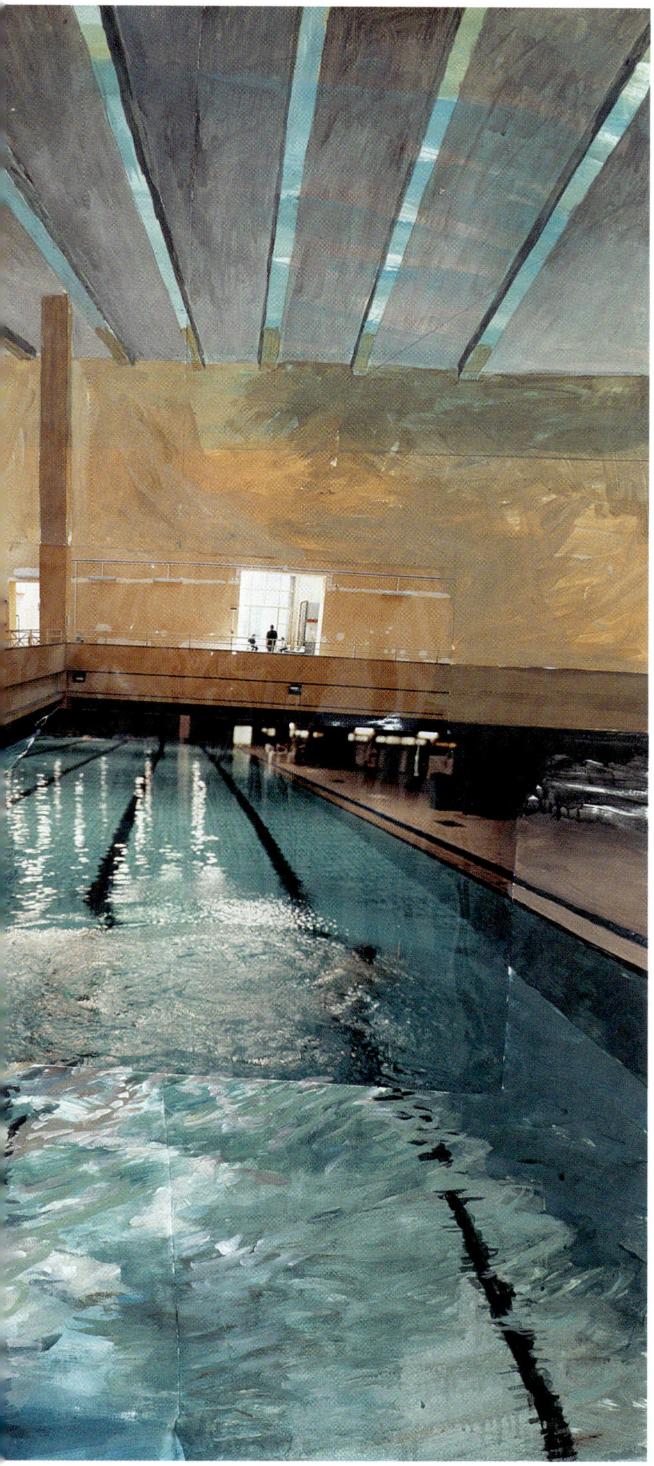

vereint Disparates, wie bekanntlich auch die Allegorie nach Benjamin eine Domäne des Willkürlichen ist. Auch sie ist dem Fragmentarischen und Unvollständigen zugeneigt – eine Affinität, die ihren umfassendsten Ausdruck schliesslich in der Ruine findet, die für Benjamin das allegorische Emblem schlechthin ist.[3)]

Als Geschichtszeichen spricht die Ruine in erster Linie von Verlust, doch entwirft sie als Verfallsmoment gleichzeitig eine Vergegenwärtigung des Vergangenen. In Amelie von Wulffens Photocollagen tauchen überall Ruinen auf, und zwar als Motiv und Metapher. Die klaustrophobische Verschachtelung von Abgründen und Klippen korrespondiert mit einer Archäologie traumatischer Erfahrung.[4)] Erinnerung meint bei Amelie von Wulffen demnach Re-Konstruktion, da Räume so etwas wie ständige Begleiter sind, die sich ans Denken heften.[5)]

Bereits vor einigen Jahren hat sich die Künstlerin mit Architektur als lebensweltlich bestimmender Kraft auseinander gesetzt. Nach ihrem ersten Animationsfilm, *Pedigree* (1996–99), in dem eine ganze Stadt aus Papphäusern aufgebaut und mit Knetfiguren eine wundersame Beziehungsgeschichte inszeniert wurde, zeigte *Die Krumme Pranke* (1997) – eine Zusammenarbeit mit Alice Creischer, Andreas Siekmann und Josef Strau – die euphorische Baupolitik Berlins in den 90er Jahren. Die *Low-Budget*-Produktion verstand sich als politisch kritische Auseinandersetzung mit spätkapitalistischen Investorenphantasien und den dazugehörigen Ohnmachts- und Allmachtsgefühlen der aktivistischen Szene.[6)] Wir befinden uns im Jahre 2005: Derrick und sein ewiger Assistent Harry Klein versuchen in kriminalistischer Manier die Skandale um den Potsdamer Platz und die Spekulationen lokaler Baulöwen aufzudecken.

Gänzlich frei vom architektonischen Paradigma scheinen hingegen Amelie von Wulffens Zeichnungsserien zu sein, die zur gleichen Zeit wie die Photocollagen entstanden. Gleichwohl sind auch sie Rekonstruktionen; bloss handelt es sich hier nicht um konstruktivistische Akte, sondern um eine langwierige Auseinandersetzung mit dem photographischen Erinnerungsvermögen. In *Die graue Partizipation* (2001) wurden Schnappschüsse, die während eines Sommers nachts in Berliner Clubs und Konzertlokalen entstanden sind, am nächsten Morgen mit Bleistift abgezeichnet. Die zeichnerische Wiederaneignung eines ephemeren und eigentlich unsichtbaren Momentes nimmt Zeit in Anspruch. Amelie von Wulffen protokolliert urbanes Grossstadtleben, richtet ihren Fokus jedoch ausschliesslich auf das Spektakel heutiger Freizeitkultur. Mit nüchternem Geist werden die Empfindungen des Vorabends analytisch seziert, etwa beim Warten auf die Goldenen Zitronen[7)], auf die wir vermutlich alle schon einmal irgendwo gewartet haben. Zigarettenrauch, Biergeruch, fettige Haare und rasierte Glatzen; doch die Künstlerin scheint sich einsam und mit leiser Melancholie ausserhalb des Geschehens zu positionieren. In einer anderen Zeichnungsserie, *Ohne Titel* (2001), präsentierte Amelie von Wulffen in installativer Hängung dreizehn gerahmte Zeichnungen ihrer Grossmutter. Der graue Hintergrund vermochte die einzelnen Blätter in eine kohärente Erzählung einzubinden, obwohl er sich selber in seiner Funktion zu erkennen gab, da er nämlich noch nicht zu Ende gemalt war. Die einzelnen Bleistiftzeichnungen zeigen immer wieder die Grossmutter der Künstlerin, einmal zu Pferde, dann mit verklärtem Blick, in fremdländischer Tracht oder mit einem Käuzchen auf dem Balkon. Sowohl ihre Körperhaltung als auch Schmuck und Frisur lassen unschwer die soziale Herkunft erkennen, wie auch rasch klar werden dürfte, dass die abgezeichneten Photographien aus den 30er und 40er Jahren des zwanzigsten Jahrhunderts stammen. Amelie von Wulffen unternimmt hier den Versuch, über ihre Grossmutter, eine begeisterte Naturlyrikerin, eine autobiographische Recherche zu betreiben, indem sie sich und ihre Arbeit in die familiären, aber auch historischen Parameter einschreibt. Die Verflechtung von kollektiver Geschichte und individuellen Geschichten steht auch in einer neuen Zeichnungsserie mit Alexander Solschenizyn und John Travolta im Mittelpunkt. Ein Doppelporträt zeigt die Männer mit nacktem Oberkörper, als wären sich die beiden einmal begegnet. Doch nur in dieser Zeichnung verschmelzen die Idole: ein Schwarm adoleszenter Mädchenträume und der seinerzeit prominenteste politische Widersacher der Sowjetunion. Ausgewiesen und verbannt mutierte Solschenizyn nicht allein im Hause der von Wulffens zum antikommunistischen Vorbild der 80er Jahre.

Auf einigen wenigen Photocollagen ist die Künstlerin selbst zu sehen. Der Photoapparat erfasst ihr Spiegelbild im Zugabteil oder im Bus, auf jeden Fall unterwegs, wohin auch immer. Amelie von Wulffens Rekonstruktionen sind keine Autobiographismen mit authentischem Ausdruck. Erinnerung findet bei ihr im Gegenteil immer im Angesicht der Historizität eigener Erfahrung statt. Neben Solschenizyn und John Travolta treten deshalb auch Zitate Albrecht Dürers oder ein Bild Eduard Zimmermanns, des Verbrecherjägers aus *Aktenzeichen XY ungelöst*, auf, um sich mit der gelebten Erfahrung zu überblenden und als nationalistische und xenophobe Dispositive dekonstruiert zu werden. Das Selbstporträt im Zug, das aus dem malerischen Riss in der Collage als Spiegelung seinen Weg an die Oberfläche sucht, ist also nicht Ausdruck narzisstischer Privatgespräche.[8)] Es ist vielmehr eine Spiegelung im gesellschaftlichen Feld, die Amelie von Wulffens Arbeit fernab von subjektivistischen und essenzialistischen künstlerischen Positionen verortet.

1) Walter Benjamin, *Berliner Kindheit um neunzehnhundert,* Giessener Fassung, Suhrkamp, Frankfurt am Main 2000, S. 58.
2) Susan Sontag, «In Platos Höhle», in: *Über Photographie,* S. Fischer Verlag, Frankfurt am Main 1980, S. 28.
3) Craig Owens, «The Allegorical Impulse: Toward a Theory of Postmodernism», in: *Beyond Recognition. Representation, Power, and Culture,* University of California Press, Berkeley 1992, S. 55.
4) Zur Psychoanalyse des Raumes vgl. Anthony Vidler, *UnHEIMlich. Über das Unbehagen in der modernen Architektur,* Edition Nautilus, Hamburg 2002.
5) Isabelle Graw, «In die Enge getrieben», in: *Amelie von Wulffen,* Ausstellungskatalog, Museum der Römischen Kultur, Kunstverein Braunschweig, 2001, S. 17.
6) Heike Munder, «Geknetete Allmachtsphantasien – Berlin im Jahre 2005», in: *Texte zur Kunst,* März 1998, S. 130–133.
7) Die Goldenen Zitronen sind eine politisch ausgerichtete Punkrockband aus Deutschland. Sie sind Gegenstand des gleichnamigen Roadmovies von Jörg Siepmann (2003), das während ihrer zweiwöchigen Amerikatournee als Begleitband von Wesley Willis gedreht wurde.
8) Georg Schöllhammer: «Privatgespräche», in: *Springerin,* Bd. II, Heft 2, 1996, S. 18–21.

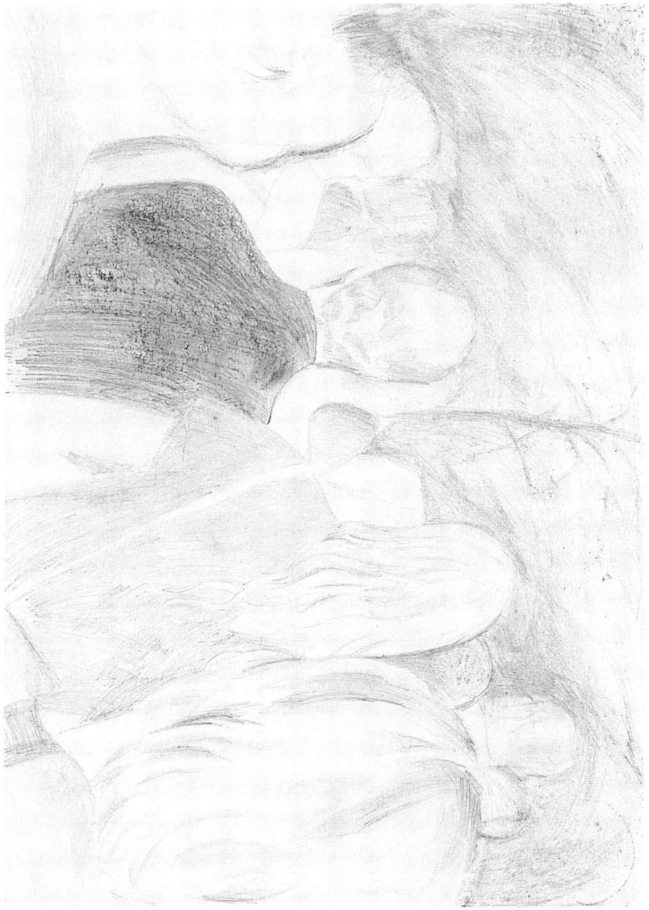

AMELIE VON WULFFEN, WARTEN AUF DIE GOLDENEN ZITRONEN, 2001, Bleistift auf Papier, 43 x 60 cm / WAITING FOR "THE GOLDEN LEMONS," pencil on paper, 17 x 23$^5/_8$". (PHOTO: GALERIE BORGMANN NATHUSIUS)

AMELIE VON WULFFEN, OHNE TITEL, 2002, Bleistift auf Papier, 44$^1/_2$ x 63 cm / UNTITLED, pencil on paper, 17$^1/_2$ x 24$^{13}/_{16}$". (PHOTO: GALERIE ASCAN CRONE, BERLIN & HAMBURG)

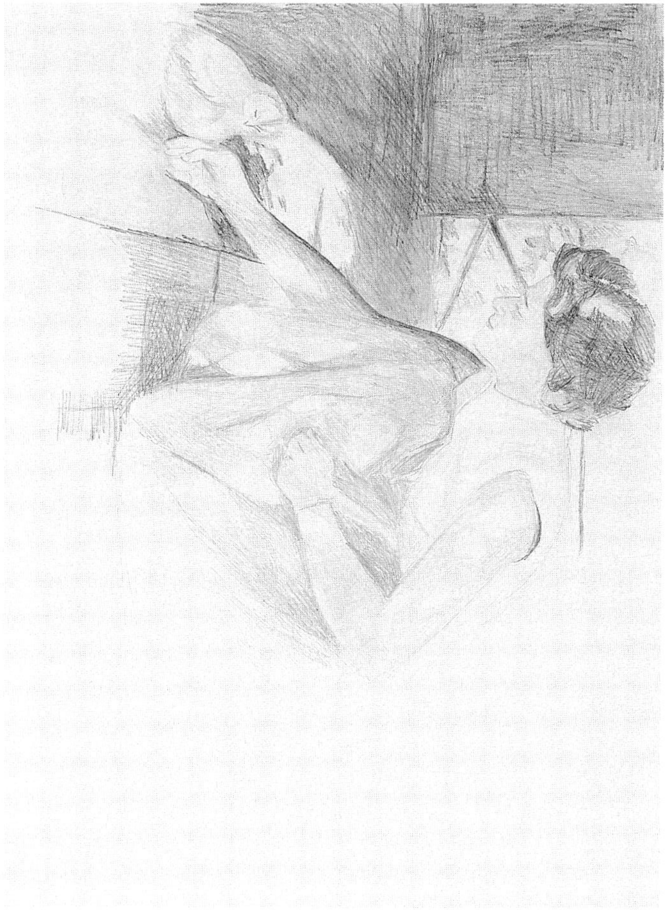

Amelie von Wulffen

PHILIPP KAISER

Ruins Present

But that evening I did impress on my memory my room and my bed, the way you look at a place carefully, sensing that you will have to go there one day to fetch something you have forgotten.[1)] Walter Benjamin thus describes how he reacted on being told at the age of five that his cousin had died; he responds with the indifference of childhood.

We have all experienced such crucial and supposedly unique moments in our own lives when mind and body focus exclusively on the present, on the here and now, in order to prevent memory from ever fading. Desperately, we attempt to arrest the inexorable flow of life in order to retain the ability to reconstruct our own history or at least parts of it. The popularity of photography bears witness to this means of dealing with individual and collective memory. Amelie von Wulffen's collages with their virtuoso and almost seamless blend of two different systems of representation, photography and painting, take that potential of photography as their point of departure. Pictures of a deserted but tidy, respectable upper-class dining room show dark brown furniture, potted plants, floor lamps, a Persian carpet, candleholders, oil paintings on the wall, and a curious Plexiglas case containing a record player and knickknacks. The interiors cling to their paper support, pretending to be more or less unique despite their character as reproductions. Although a historical interpretation can be assigned to these underexposed pictures as evidence of Barthe's "that-has-been," Amelie von Wulffen's collages effect only a partial condensation of memory in photographic documents. Memory only kicks in at the edges, where photography stops and the painterly imagination begins. For Amelie von Wulffen the reconstruction of what has been forgotten

---

PHILIPP KAISER is the curator of the Museum für Gegenwartskunst Basel.

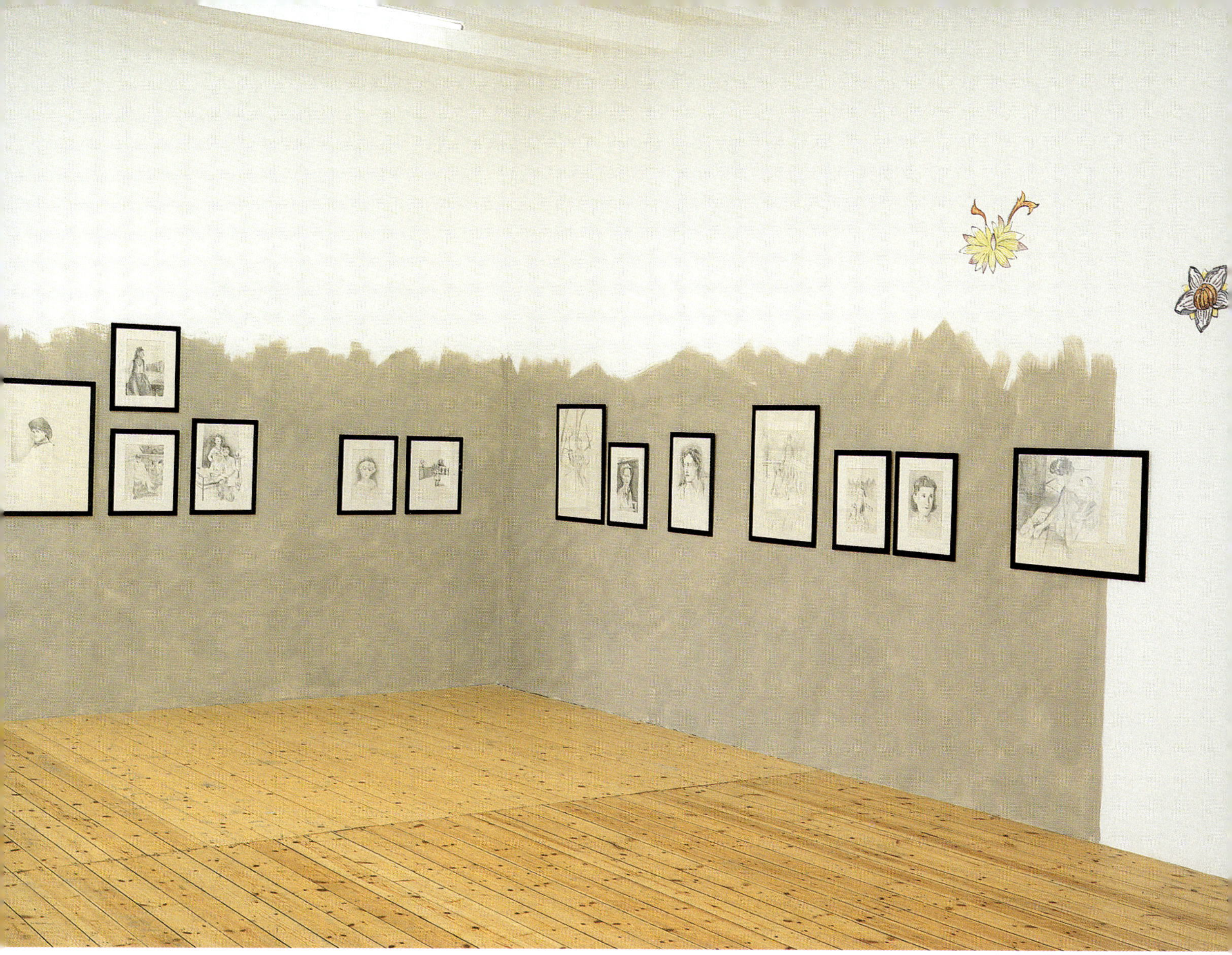

AMELIE VON WULFFEN, Installationsansicht (Wandmalerei und 13 Zeichnungen), Galerie Ascan Crone, Hamburg, 2001 / installation view (wall painting and 13 drawings).(PHOTO: GALERIE ASCAN CRONE, BERLIN & HAMBURG)

and repressed is a physical activity whose gestural traces remain legible. Single photographs show her parents' house, museums, swimming pools, interiors, and, more recently, landscapes. Placed side by side, they demonstrate photography's inherent ability to turn the world into "a series of unrelated, freestanding particles ... The camera makes reality atomic."[2)]

Amelie von Wulffen's collages do not succumb to the naïve conviction that bits of memory can be leveled out into an indeterminate continuum. Montage as an avant-garde principle of design is itself a fragment since it does not believe in totality. The Cubist fragmentation of the buildings in Wulffen's photocollages of late Modernistic, largely eastern European architecture signal a sequential order in which the dynamics of Modernism flare-up, possibly for the last time. The cinematic quality of the progression of rooms and the multiple perspectives of the montages

AMELIE VON WULFFEN, OHNE TITEL (BUNDESKANZLERAMT), 2002,
Photographien und Acryl auf Papier, 113 x 141 cm /
UNTITLED (OFFICE OF THE FEDERAL CHANCELLOR), photographs and acrylic on paper, 44 1/2 x 55 1/2".

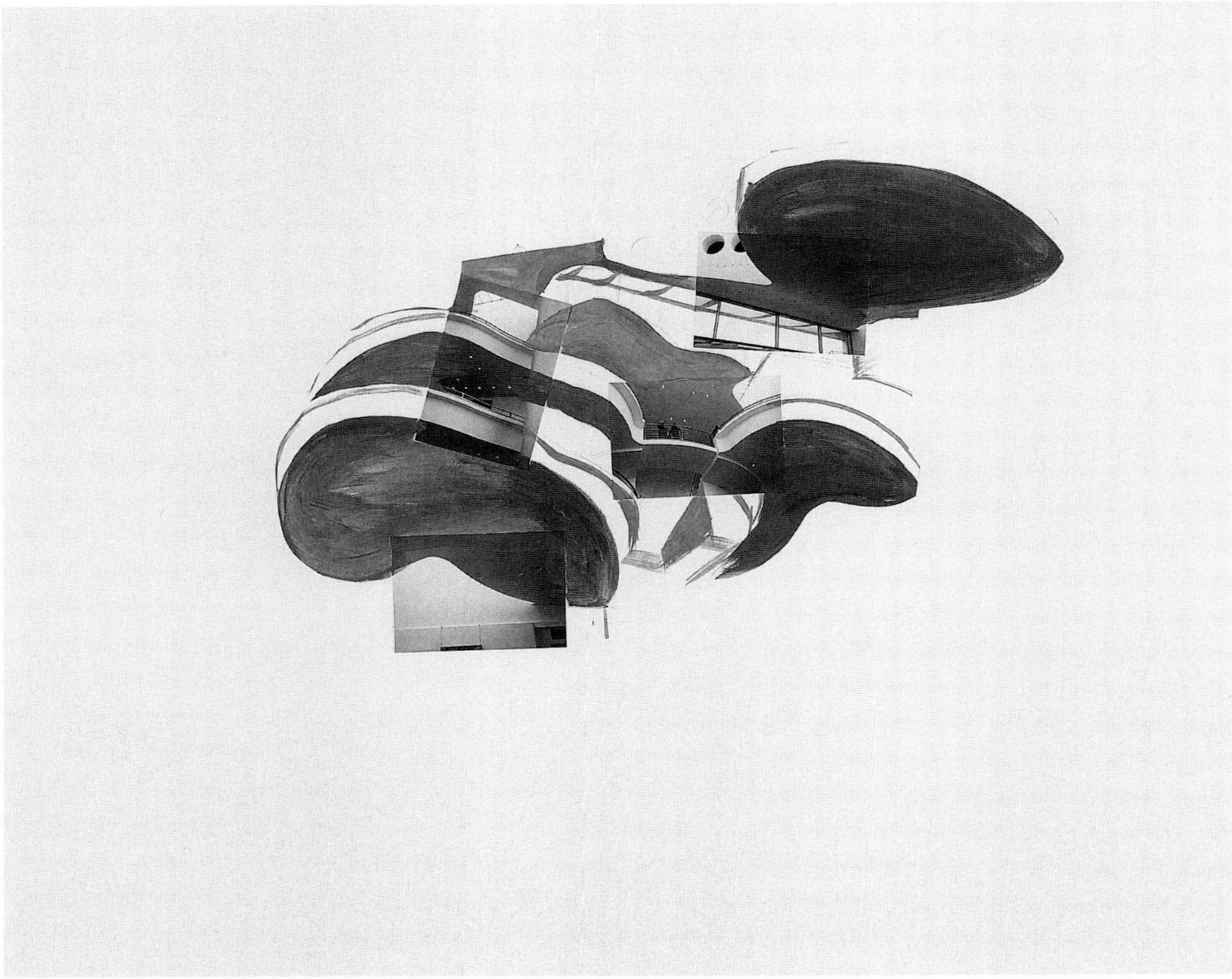

AMELIE VON WULFFEN, OHNE TITEL, 2000, Photographien und Acryl auf Papier, 70 x 100 cm /
UNTITLED, photographs and acrylic on paper, 27 9/16 x 39 3/8". (PHOTO: GALERIE ASCAN CRONE, BERLIN & HAMBURG)

recall the architectural utopias of Constructivism and when a Zeppelin crops up overhead we feel transported back to the twenties. The sequential order of the montage in the earlier works has given way to combinations of diverse scraps of memory. In Amelie von Wulffen's oeuvre, montage, as a fragment of fragments, can be described as a ruin of the kind elaborated by Walter Benjamin in his theory of history. It is a method that unites disparate aspects and thus resembles what Benjamin postulates as the arbitrariness of the allegory. Allegories are "consistently attracted to the fragmentary, the imperfect, the incomplete—an affinity which finds its most comprehensive expression in the ruin, which Benjamin identified as the allegorical emblem par excellence."[3)]

Ruins are signs of history that primarily evoke loss but their state of decay also draws the past into the present. Ruins crop up everywhere in Amelie von Wulffen's photocollages, both as motifs and as metaphors. Claustrophobically intertwined abysses and cliffs correspond to an archeology of traumatic experience.[4)] Memory in Amelie von Wulffen's work therefore entails reconstruction since rooms may be seen as the constant companions of thought.[5)]

Some years ago, the artist already addressed architecture as a life-determining force. After her first animation film *Pedigree* (1996/99), in which she built a cardboard city and staged a curious story with figures molded out of clay, Wulffen collaborated with Alice Creischer, Andreas Siekmann, and Josef Strau on *Die Krumme Pranke* (The Crooked Fist, 1997), a film about Berlin's runaway building euphoria of the nineties. The low-budget production took a critical look at the fantasies of late capitalist investors, pitting them against feelings of both helplessness and omnipotence amongst political activists.[6)] We are in the year 2005: Detective Derrick and his trusty side-

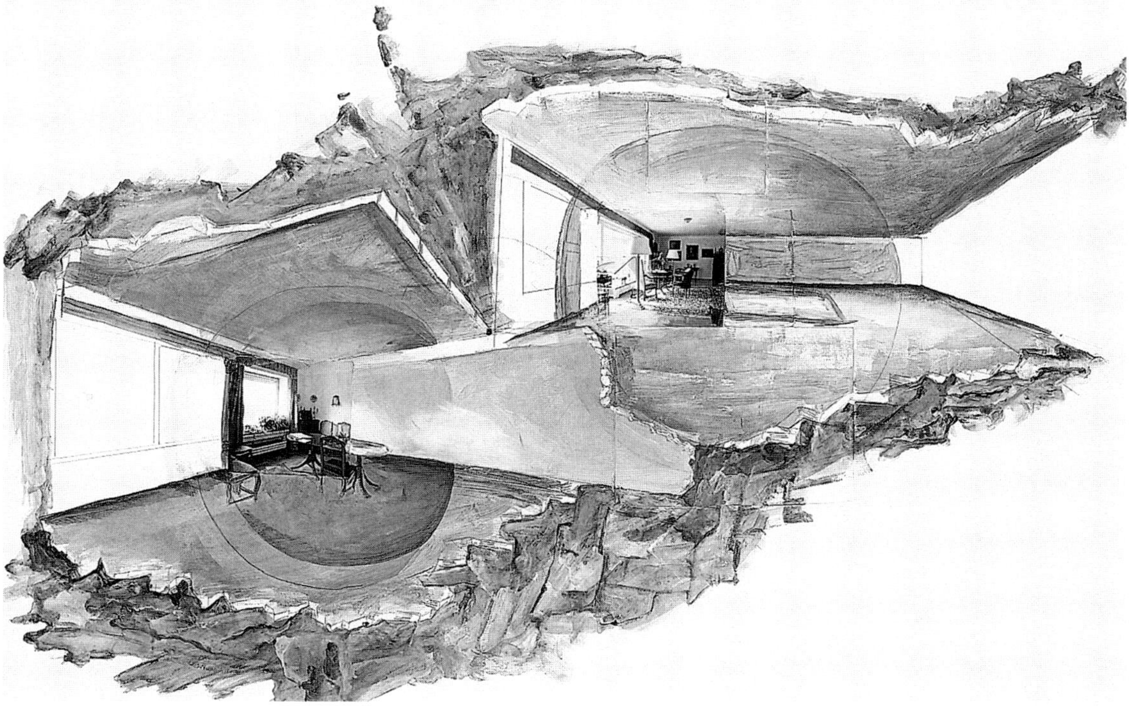

kick Harry Klein are trying to expose the scandalous dealings and speculative excesses of the local building tycoons who were involved in developing Potsdamer Platz.

The series of drawings produced at the same time as the photocollages make no reference at all to the architectural paradigms of contemporary art although they, too, are reconstructions. Instead of dealing with Constructivist acts, however, they engage in a protracted investigation of photographic memory. For *Die graue Partizipation* (Gray Participation, 2001), Wulffen took snapshots one summer night in bars and concert halls in Berlin, which she then copied in pencil the following morning. Reappropriating ephemeral and essentially invisible moments in the act of drawing takes time. Amelie von Wulffen's record of metropolitan life focuses exclusively on the spectacle of today's leisure culture. Her matter-of-fact analysis dissects the previous evening's sensations, for instance while waiting for The Golden Lemons,[7)] something we've probably all done at some point or other. We see and smell the cigarette smoke, the stench of beer, the greasy hair, and shaved heads, even though the artist seems to position herself with a touch of melancholy, alone and segregated from the events. Another series, *Ohne Titel* (Untitled, 2001), presents thirteen framed drawings of the artist's grandmother as an installation. The gray background gives the individual drawings the unity of a coherent narrative although it betrays its own function by being unfinished. The pencil drawings all depict the artist's grandmother: mounted on a horse, gazing enraptured, wearing a foreign folk costume, or on a balcony with a small owl. Posture, jewelry, and hairstyle reveal her social status; several clues indicate that the copied photographs probably date from the thirties and forties. Through the medium of her grandmother, an ardent writer of nature poetry, Amelie von Wulffen embarks on an experimental foray into autobiographical research by inscribing herself and her work into the parameters of her own family history and history in general. The conflation of collective history and individual stories also informs a new series of drawings that picture Alexander Solzhenitsyn and John Travolta. A double portrait shows the two men, bare-chested, as if they had been photographed together; it is the only drawing in which the two idols converge: Travolta, the idolized object of girlish adolescent dreams; Solzhenitsyn, the most prominent political dissident in the Soviet Union. Expatriated and exiled, Solzhenitsyn became anti-Communism incarnate in the eighties—and not only in the home of the von Wulffens.

On a few of the photocollages we see the artist herself. The camera captures her mirror image in the compartment of a train or on a bus, always traveling from one place to another. Her reconstructions are not authentically expressed renditions of autobiographical memory. On the contrary, her study of memory takes place within the setting of the historicism of her own experience into which she weaves not only Solzhenitsyn and John Travolta, but also references to Albrecht Dürer or Eduard Zimmermann, host of the German criminal-stalking television program *Aktenzeichen XY ungelöst.* The resulting fabric deconstructs them as nationalist and xenophobic scenarios. Thus, the self-portrait in the train, a mirror image that seeks to surface out of the painterly crack in the collage, does not emerge as an expression of narcissistic monologues.[8)] Rather, the reflection is mirrored in a social context that locates Amelie von Wulffen's work at a clear remove from subjectivist and essentialist artistic positions.

(Translation: Catherine Schelbert)

1) Walter Benjamin, *Berliner Kindheit um neunzehnhundert,* (Frankfurt am Main: Suhrkamp, 2000), p. 58.
2) Susan Sontag, "In Plato's Cave," in *On Photography* (London: Penguin, 1979), p. 23.
3) Craig Owens, "The Allegorical Impulse: Toward a Theory of Postmodernism," in *Beyond Recognition. Representation, Power, and Culture* (Berkeley: University of California Press, 1992), p. 55.
4) On the psychoanalysis of space, see Anthony Vidler, *The Architectural Uncanny. Essays in the Modern Unhomely* (The MIT Press, 1994).
5) Isabelle Graw, "In die Enge getrieben," in *Amelie von Wulffen,* ex. cat. (Kunstverein Braunschweig: Museum der Römischen Kultur, 2001), p. 17.
6) Heike Munder, "Geknetete Allmachtsphantasien – Berlin im Jahre 2005," in *Texte zur Kunst,* March 1998, pp. 130–133.
7) A politically oriented punk band from Germany and subject of the eponymous documentary road movie (2003), filmed by Jörg Siepmann during The Golden Lemons' two-week tour of the United States as the support band for Wesley Willis.
8) Georg Schöllhammer, "Privatgespräche," in *Springerin,* vol. II, no. 2, 1996, pp. 18–21.

FRANCIS ALŸS

BORN 1959 IN ANTWERP, BELGIUM,
LIVES AND WORKS IN MEXICO CITY /
GEBOREN 1959 IN ANTWERPEN, BELGIEN,
LEBT UND ARBEITET IN MEXICO CITY.

ISA GENZKEN

GEBOREN 1948 IN OLDESLOE, DEUTSCHLAND,
LEBT UND ARBEITET IN BERLIN /
BORN 1948 IN OLDESLOE, GERMANY,
LIVES AND WORKS IN BERLIN.

ANISH KAPOOR

BORN 1954 IN BOMBAY, INDIA,
LIVES AND WORKS IN LONDON /
GEBOREN 1954 IN BOMBAY, INDIEN,
LEBT UND ARBEITET IN LONDON.

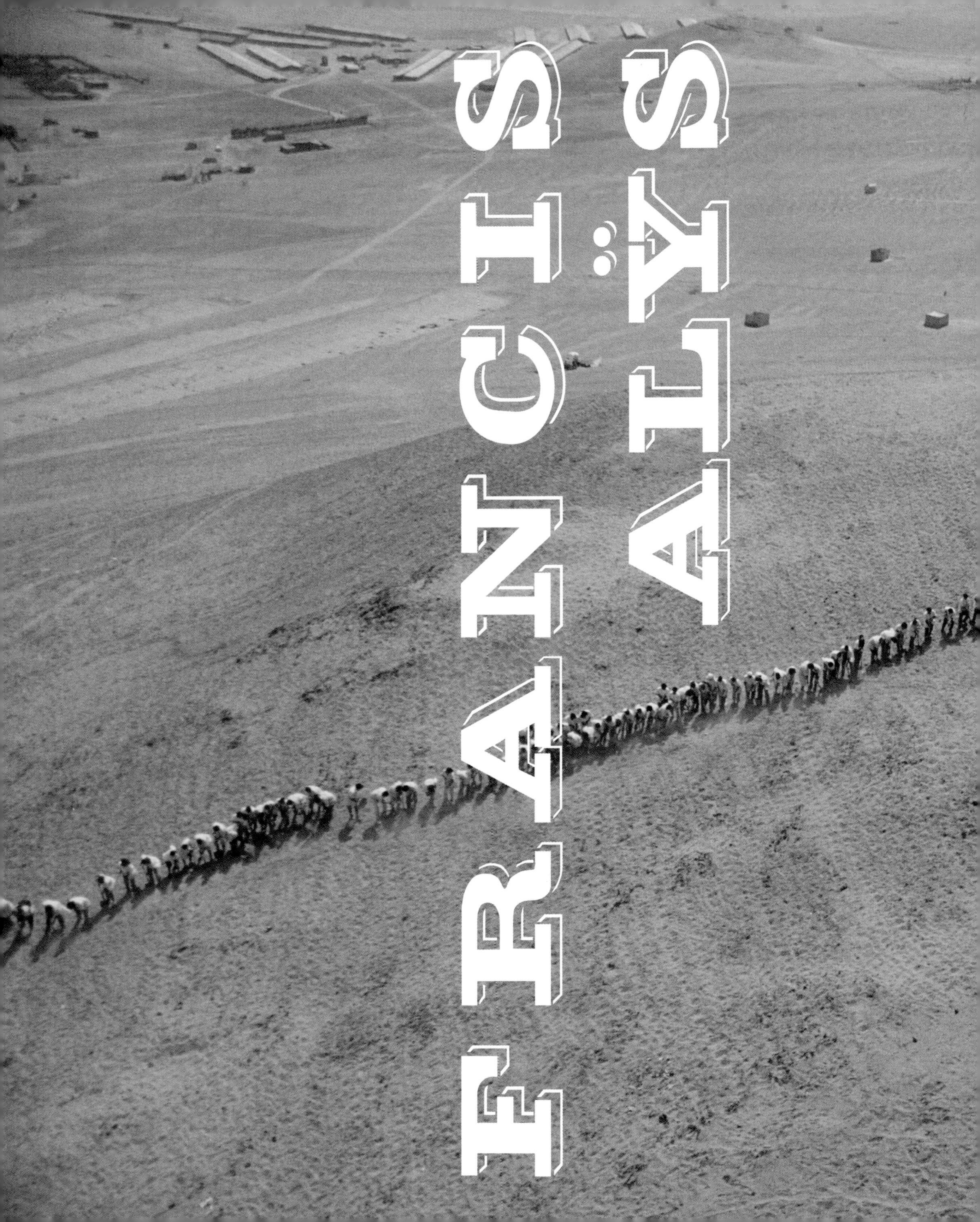
FRANCIS ALŸS

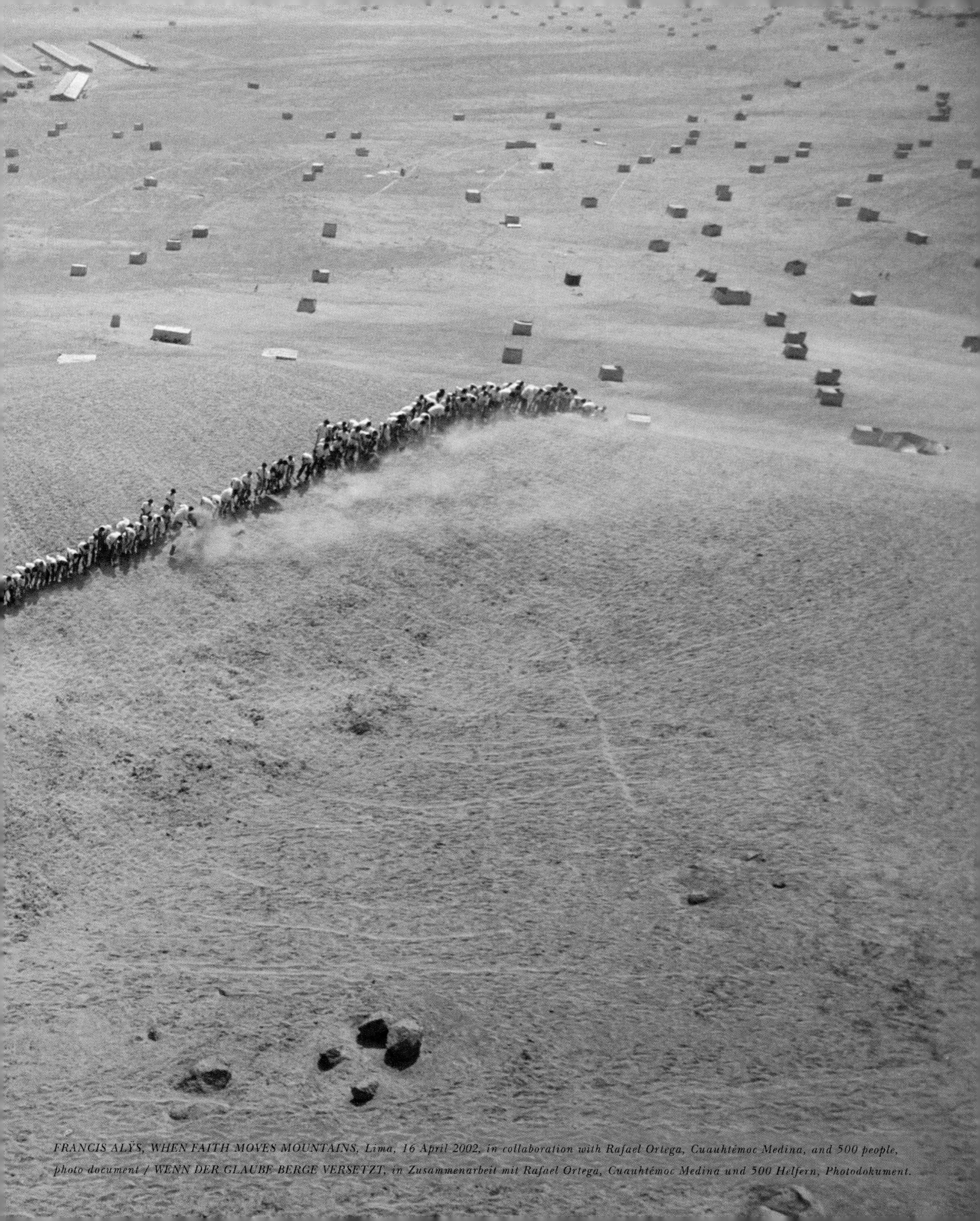

FRANCIS ALŸS, WHEN FAITH MOVES MOUNTAINS, Lima, 16 April 2002, in collaboration with Rafael Ortega, Cuauhtémoc Medina, and 500 people, photo document / WENN DER GLAUBE BERGE VERSETZT, in Zusammenarbeit mit Rafael Ortega, Cuauhtémoc Medina und 500 Helfern, Photodokument.

PORTRAIT
Francis Alÿs

KITTY SCOTT

It is a hot day in mid-June 1995 and Peter Sprunt is driving his old black Audi through the pine-dotted hills crowned by a brilliant blue sky with the occasional cloud. Francis Alÿs is in the front, pencil in hand, jotting down phrases in his little Chinese notebook that he takes everywhere. Jodi Carson, the Administrative Assistant for Site Santa Fe[1] and Peter's partner, is in the back, and from time to time, she imparts her knowledge of this conflicted place. We are traveling north, en route from Santa Fe to Chimayó, listening to Johnny Cash's *American Recordings*. One sorrowful tune follows another. Francis arrived in New Mexico a few days ago for the opening of the inaugural Site Santa Fe Exhibition "Longing and Belonging: From the Faraway Nearby."[1] At the behest of Francis, we are searching for a sometime portrait painter named Randy Martinez.

The artist has made two works for the exhibition, one of which is a handcrafted multiple, UNTITLED (SNOWGLOBE) (1995)—the first and only existing snow globe to feature symbols of, and buildings from, Mexico City. These representative elements were chosen through a "democratic" process involving a questionnaire with 100 respondents. Rumor has it that he also made a version with tequila and cocaine instead of water and synthetic snow. The other work, THE PORTRAIT (Mexico City, 1995), is a huge mural-sized painting of a bird's-eye view of Mexico City. It was executed in the typical sign-painter format using auto-enamel on metal. To produce THE PORTRAIT, Francis adapted a collaborative painting project he was working on in Mexico City.

KITTY SCOTT is Curator of Contemporary Art at the National Gallery of Canada, Ottawa.

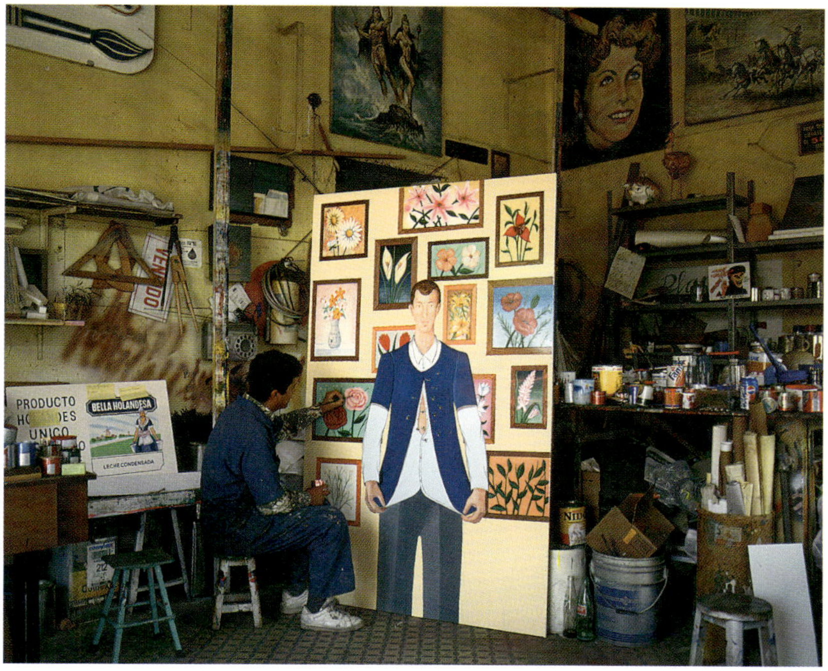

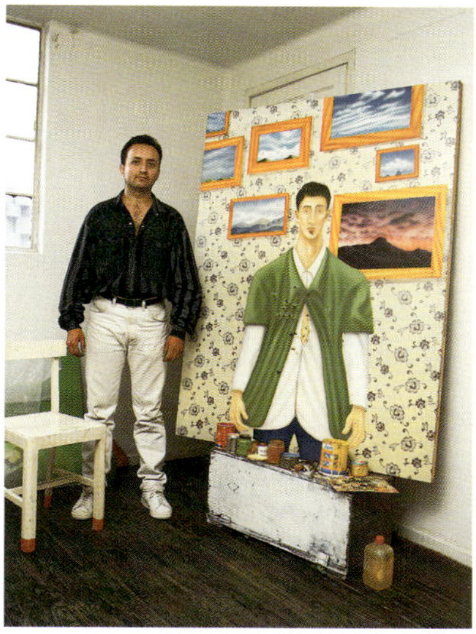

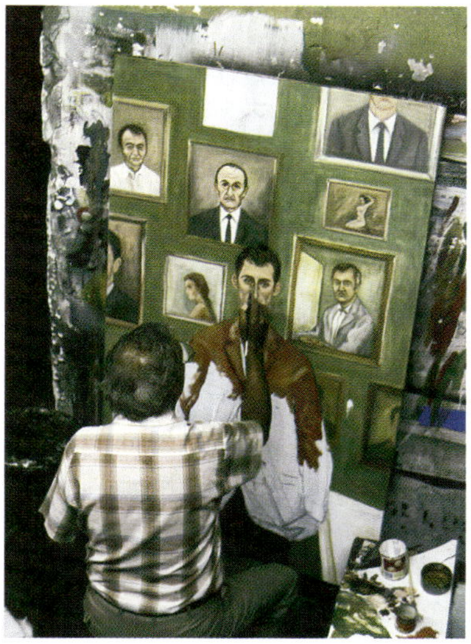

FRANCIS ALŸS, EL SOPLON (THE PROMPTER), 1995, work in progress / DER SOUFFLEUR, Enrique Huerta (top left / oben links); Emilio Rivera (top right / oben rechts); Juan Garcia (bottom / unten).

In an effort to resolve sculptural proposals, the artist was painting small "originals," based on situations, or in his own words, "feasible experiments" where the protagonist, usually a suited man, engages with props or his physical surroundings, for some obscure and apparently irrational, but believable reason. Francis has been painting these small "originals" and passing them to *rótulistas* (sign painters), who would repaint their own versions of these paintings. Francis would then generate a new "original" based on the copies. The nature of collaboration, questions concerning authorship, as well as the idea of a painting as a unique object were foremost in his mind.

Francis wanted to make a billboard-size sign painting for the façade of the Site Santa Fe warehouse, advertising the snow dome and ultimately New Mexico's relationship with Mexico City. In the spirit of his current painting projects, the artist decided to collaborate with *Hispanos* painters Denis, Nolan, and Randy Martinez, specialists in traditional low-rider car culture. After discussions with the Martinezes, it was decided that they would portray their fantasy version of Mexico City—a place these artists were connected to socially and historically, but had never visited.

As the collaborative process with the sign painters was challenging and questioning notions of authorship, Francis had been tempted to test the genre of self-portraiture within the larger experiment. With THE PORTRAIT, he devised a project with a built-in contradiction that could alternately be called "Self-Portrait Made by Others." To realize this idea, the artist

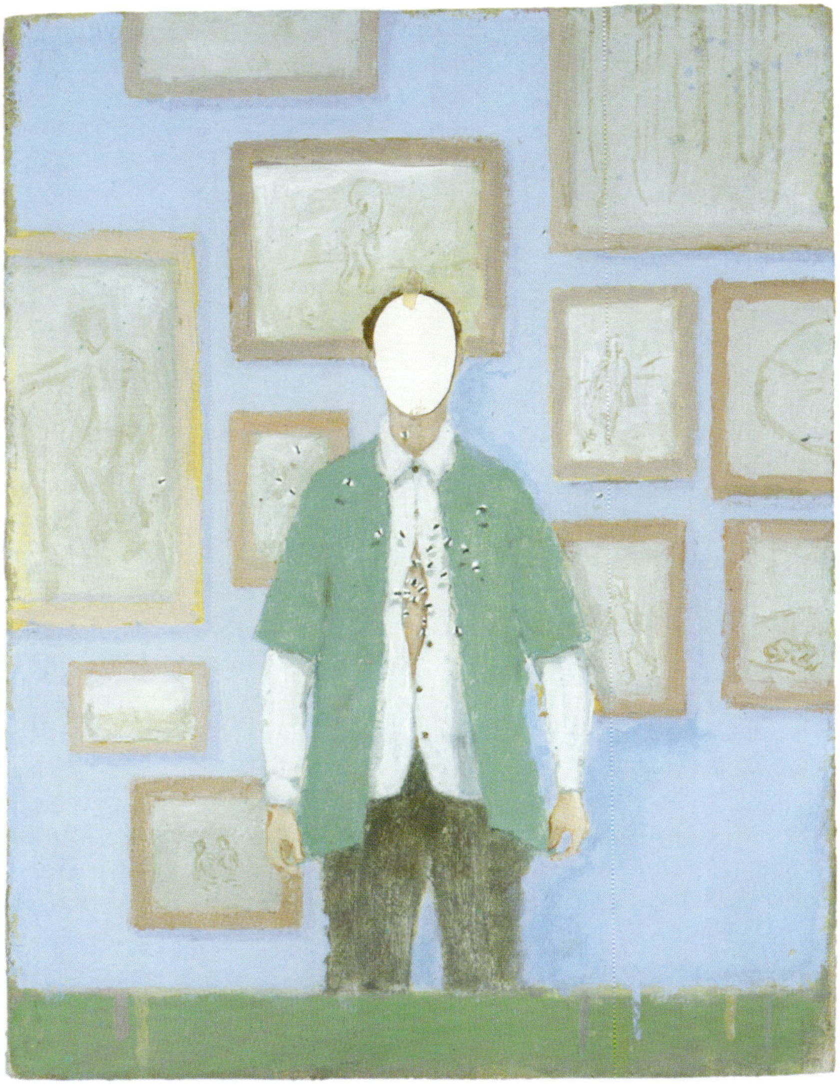

FRANCIS ALŸS, EL SOPLON (THE PROMPTER), 1995–2002, oil, encaustic, and collage on canvas on wood, 5 7/8 x 7 7/16 x 3/8" / DER SOUFFLEUR, Öl, Enkaustik und Collage auf Leinwand auf Holz, 15 x 19,6 x 1,7 cm.

commissioned portraits from Enrique Huerta, Juan García, and Emilio Rivera, three Mexican sign painters that he worked with regularly. Francis asked each of therm to make a likeness of him and to depict in the background a series of paintings of their choice and specialty. In this way, each portrait of Francis would portray the signature styles of each painter. He also modeled for each sign painter.

Paralleling this activity, Francis developed his own small distinct self-portrait of a three-quarter-figure wearing a smock buttoned only at the neck and underneath, a white shirt partly open to reveal his chest. A swarm of flies hovers near the artist's heart, having escaped from the fissure. Miniature paintings reminiscent of Francis's own cityscapes hang on the wall behind. An oval-shaped piece of paper taped onto the surface obscures the artist's face. He did not share this picture with the sign painters.

During an earlier research visit to Santa Fe, Francis decided to include Randy Martinez in the project and to commission a self-portrait from him. Martinez accepted, received advance payment and chose to paint the portrait on the hood of a car.

The perpetually incomplete version of THE PORTRAIT was documented in a small catalogue from the now defunct Galeria Carmargo Vilaça. It takes the form of four photographs, three of which depict a sign painter alongside a completed portrait of Francis, and the other is a reproduction of Francis's self-portrait. The three photographs are as much portraits of the sign painters as they are of Francis, and when seen together they emphasize the subjective nature of portrait painting. While the *rótulistas'* visual renderings all bear a likeness to him, none of them is Francis. Each panel presents a version of the artist, however the shape of his face, tone of his skin, style of his hair, look of his hands, and the color of his clothes, change from picture to picture. Not one of the painters is able to capture the medieval quality in his face, his long slender body, or his lightly freckled skin. And like all painted portraits, these pictures are incapable of conveying the grace of a particular walk, the sound of the sitter's voice as well as the small gestures that together give rise to an individual's personality.

By now, it is well known that Francis's early projects originated in his practice of walking through Mexico City. In 1990–91, he was making a series of interventions, usually inserting or withdrawing elements such as pillows and animal puppets into or from the existing architecture and urban fabric of the city. At the same time, he was searching for a way of illustrating these actions, without necessarily representing them directly. Photography seemed to present a fraudulent document in relation to the reality of the moment and place of the intervention. So he started thinking about painted situations that might correspond to these live scenarios and have an equivalent intention, but would not quote them directly. As Francis was not a painter, he looked for a language; the most obvious one was that of the sign painters' billboards just down the street from his studio. It was also the most effective, given that their profession depends on the ability to successfully communicate. Once he began to paint, the temptation to return the images to the ones that inspired them was inevitable.

FRANCIS ALŸS, EL SOPLON (THE PROMPTER), 1995, mixed-media drawing and collage, 11 11/16 x 7 7/8"/ Zeichnung und Collage, diverse Materialien, DER SOUFFLEUR, 30 x 20 cm.

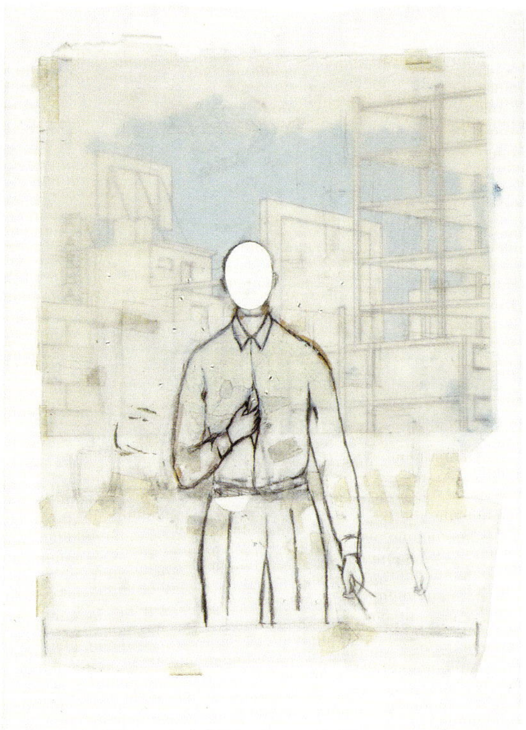

More recently, the artist has increased his number of collaborators exponentially. Where he worked with three or four sign painters previously, he now engages hundreds of people. Francis's ability to work with so many people at once is fitting, considering his original training as an engineer and architect. These professionals, like film directors, realize their visions through the concerted effort of a variety of many skilled workers.

It is often thought that walking is central to understanding Francis's process and oeuvre; arguably writing, although almost invisible in the final product, is an equally significant part of his daily practice. Francis is an artist who aspires to being a sixteenth-century writer. In their initial stages, his projects exist as files filled with sheaves of looseleaf papers covered with the artist's ornate French, Spanish, and English scripts and diagrams. These notes are the means by which he conceptualizes and pinpoints his ideas. In due course, images are introduced, the medium of expression defines itself, and the texts begin to fall away, but not entirely. Sometimes an artwork will exist only as a spoken story or a typewritten text, as with THE RUMOR (Tlayacapan, Mexico, 1998). But often "scripts" or "stories" are an inherent part of the work, be it a painting, postcard, video, walk, sculpture, or other large-scale undertaking. In a recent conversation, Francis described his practice as "nearly writing" and referred to his sketches with fragments of text as "written drawings."

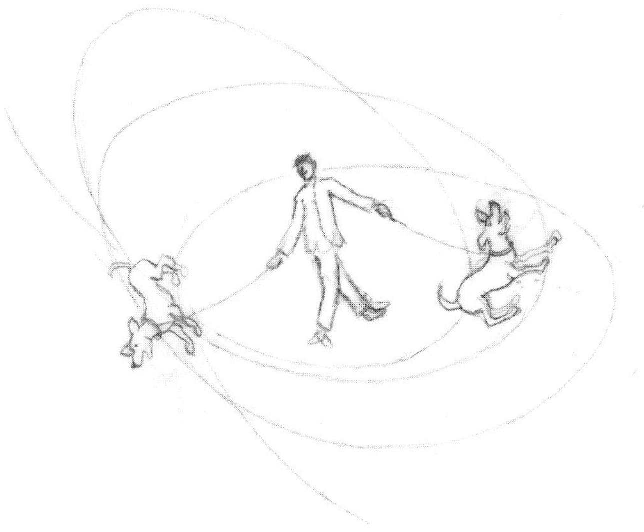

FRANCIS ALŸS, sketch on tracing paper, no date / undatierte Skizze auf Pergamentpapier.

During the research phase of his projects, the artist often enounces ideas, only to contradict them almost instantly. He then spends much time and effort trying to reconcile these two views eventually creating a third, more oblique, unspeakable option, the only one he sees as worthy. His methodology is illustrated by one of those old tin key-wind clockwork toys of a gentleman and his two mischievous dogs tethered by rigid leashes. On winding up the toy, one assumes that the master will simply take his canine friends for a walk. But the dog on the man's right arm lags stubbornly behind, as the dog on his left pulls eagerly ahead and to the right. Acting as a tripod and a pivot, the obstinate animals permit the man to stand vertically and prevent him from falling, but force him to walk in circles.

Francis's attitude, progress by failure, is illustrated in the situation of the man and his animals. To reveal the inertia of a process, the artist will expend the maximum effort ("to move in circles") for the minimum result ("to advance by walking"). The action, or lack thereof, of the dogs and their master also exemplifies "the paradox of praxis"—one of the artist's favorite axioms—PARADOX OF PRAXIS (SOMETIMES MAKING SOMETHING LEADS TO NOTHING), part one, Mexico, D. F., 1997; PARADOX OF PRAXIS (SOMETIMES MAKING NOTHING LEADS TO SOMETHING), part two, 1997–ongoing.

In due course, Peter pulls up to a small white house. Francis gets out of the car and knocks on the door. A woman answers—Randy is not there. She gives Francis another lead as to his whereabouts. We follow her directions and the same thing happens again. And again. There is a snapshot of Francis taken at this moment in the narrative. Framed by the cloudy sky and the surrounding hills covered with short bushy pines and dry, straggly grasses, the artist is leaning on an abandoned vintage car, wearing a baseball cap backwards, an old white T-shirt, loose fitting pants and Converse sneakers. He strikes a match to light the cigarette dangling from his lips; the scene exudes a mythic American quality. After smoking the cigarette, Francis decides to give up the search and we circle back to Santa Fe. Johnny croons, "Why me Lord? What have I ever done to deserve even one of the pleasures I've known and ..."

1) Site Santa Fe is a private not-for-profit contemporary arts organization in Santa Fe, New Mexico, providing an ongoing venue for regional, national, and international exhibitions. Since its inception in 1995 the International Santa Fe Biennial has been a major focus; the fifth biennial (curated by Robert Storr) will take place from 18 July 2004 to 9 January 2005.

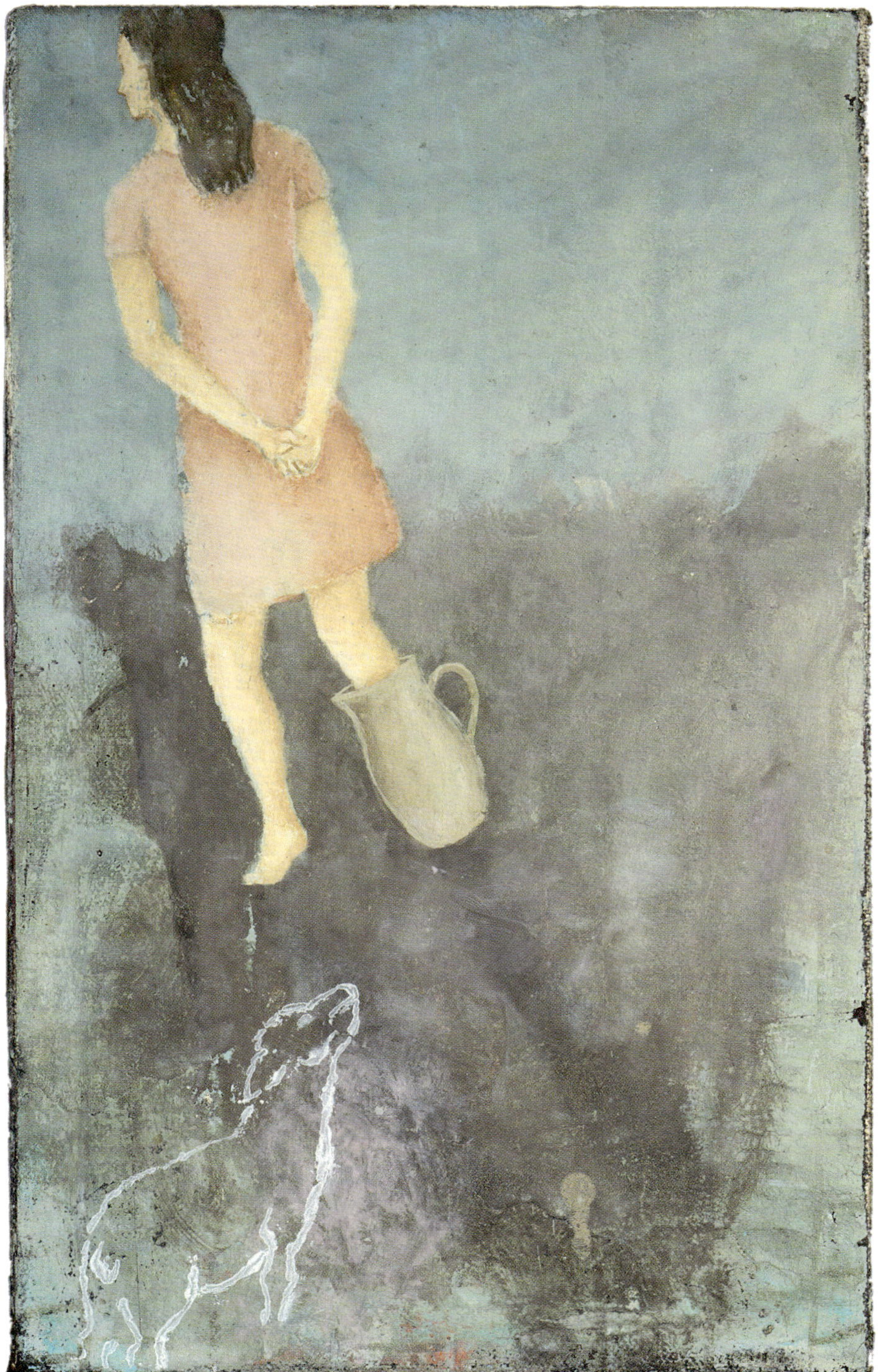

FRANCIS ALŸS, UNTITLED, 2001, oil and encaustic on cloth on wood, $10^{5}/_{8}$ x $6^{3}/_{4}$ x $1^{1}/_{16}$" /
OHNE TITEL, Öl und Enkaustik auf Leinen auf Holz, 27 x 17,1 x 2,7 cm.

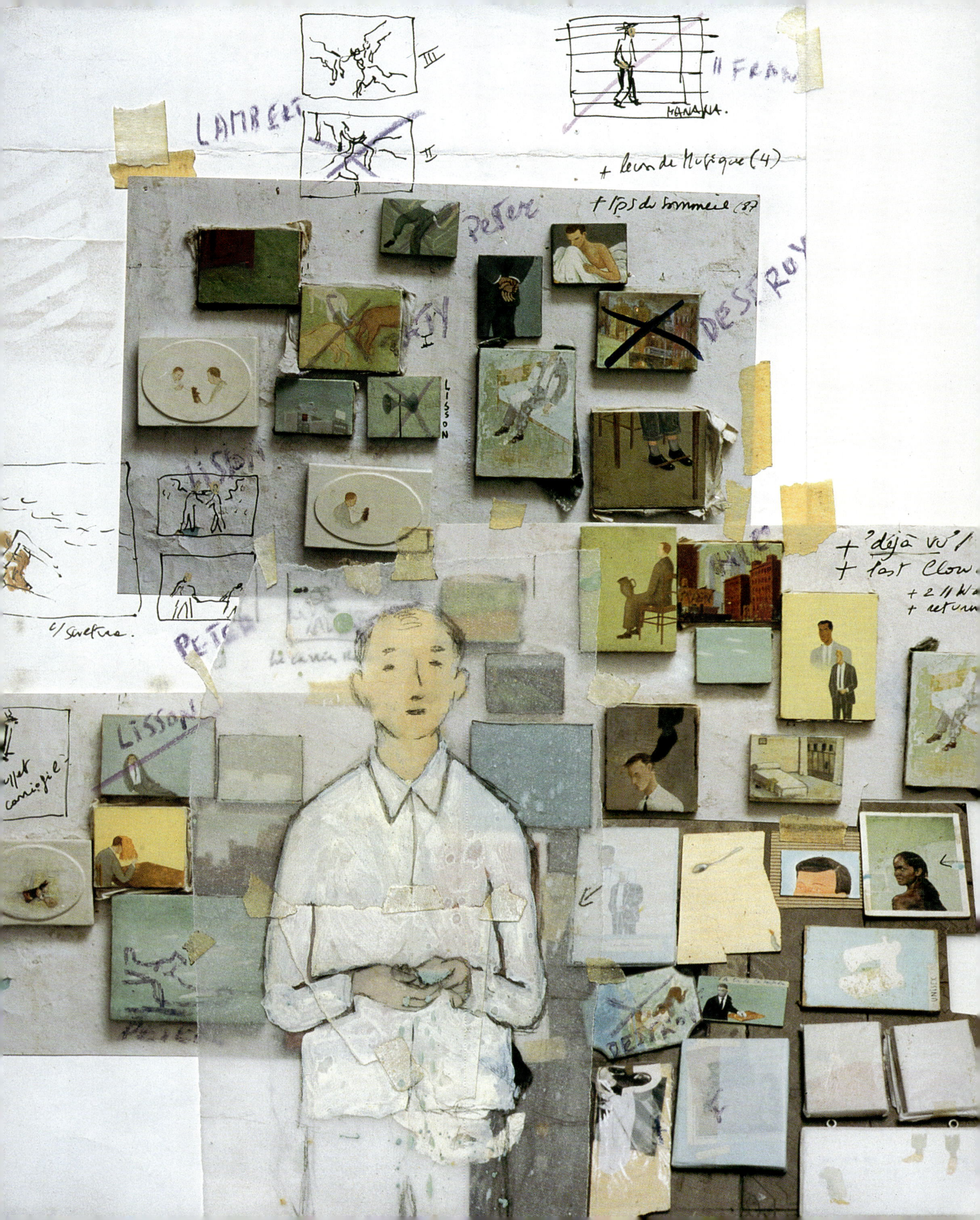

Francis Alÿs

Ein Porträt

KITTY SCOTT

Es ist ein heisser Tag Mitte Juni 1995 und Peter Sprunt fährt seinen alten schwarzen Audi durch die mit Kiefern gesprenkelten Hügel; darüber wölbt sich ein leuchtend blauer Himmel mit vereinzelten Wolken da und dort. Francis Alÿs sitzt vorn mit einem Bleistift in der Hand und kritzelt Sätze in sein kleines chinesisches Notizbuch, das er immer bei sich trägt. Jodi Carson, Peters Partnerin und Verwaltungsangestellte des Site Santa Fe[1)], sitzt hinten und tut hin und wieder etwas von dem kund, was sie über diese widersprüchliche Gegend weiss. Wir fahren nach Norden, *en route* von Santa Fe nach Chimayó, und hören uns Johnny Cashs *American Recordings* an. Eine traurige Melodie folgt der anderen. Francis ist erst vor ein paar Tagen nach New Mexico gekommen, und zwar zur Eröffnungsausstellung des Site Santa Fe, «Longing and Belonging: From the Faraway Nearby». Auf seinen Wunsch sind wir auf der Suche nach einem Gelegenheits-Porträtmaler namens Randy Martinez.

Francis Alÿs hat zwei Werke zur Ausstellung beigesteuert; das eine ist ein handgefertigtes Multiple, UNTITLED (SNOWGLOBE) – Ohne Titel (Schneekugel), 1995 –, die erste und einzige Schneekugel, welche Wahrzeichen und Bauwerke von Mexico City zeigt. Diese typischen Elemente wurden in einem «demokratischen» Prozess ausgewählt, der auch eine Umfrage unter hundert Befragten mit einschloss. Es wird gemunkelt, dass Francis auch eine Version mit Tequila und Kokain anstelle von Wasser und künstlichem Schnee schuf. Das andere Werk, THE PORTRAIT (Das Porträt, 1995), ist eine Ansicht von Mexico City aus der Vogelperspektive, so gross wie ein Wandgemälde. Es ist im klassischen Plakatformat mit Autolack auf Metall ausgeführt. Für dieses Bild stützte sich Francis auf ein Gemeinschaftsprojekt, an dem er in Mexico City arbeitete.

KITTY SCOTT ist Kuratorin für zeitgenössische Kunst in der National Gallery of Canada, Ottawa.

FRANCIS ALŸS, CABINET, 1994, pencil and oil on tracing paper, photo collage (slightly cropped), $11^{13}/_{16}$ x $8^{5}/_{8}$" / KABINETT, Bleistift und Öl auf Pergamentpapier, Photocollage, (leicht beschnitten) 30 x 22 cm.

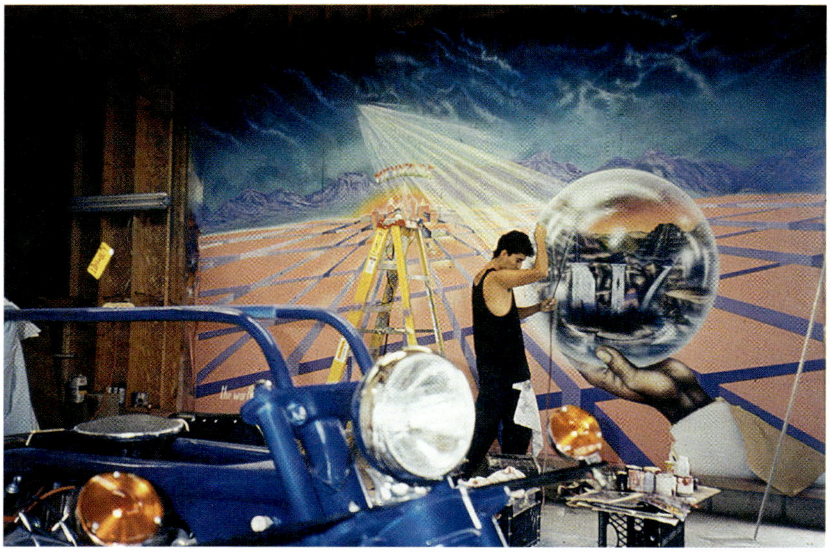

FRANCIS ALŸS, Making of THE PORTRAIT, Santa Fe, New Mexico, 1995: Randy Martinez (left/links); Dennis, Randy, and Nolan Martinez, Francis Alÿs (below/unten).

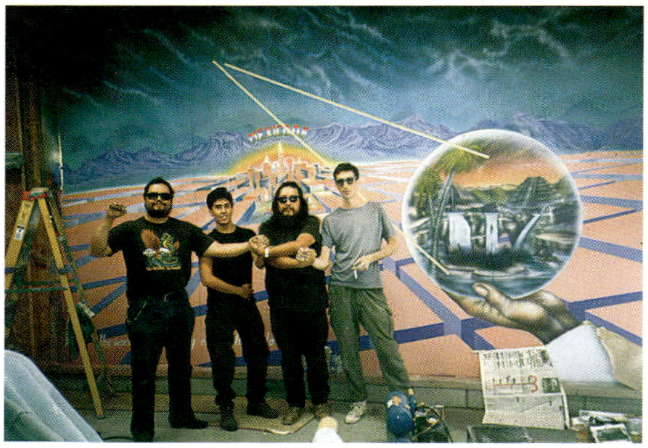

In Auseinandersetzung mit skulpturalen Fragestellungen, malte der Künstler kleinformatige «Originale», die auf Situationen oder, wie er es ausdrückt, «plausible Experimente» Bezug nahmen, in denen der Protagonist, meist ein Mann im Anzug, sich aus irgendeinem unerfindlichen und scheinbar unsinnigen, aber dennoch glaubwürdigen Grund mit Requisiten oder seiner äusseren Umgebung beschäftigte. Francis malte diese «Originale» und gab sie an *rótulistas* (Plakatmaler) weiter, die anhand dieser Vorlagen ihre eigenen Versionen malten. Aufgrund dieser Kopien schuf Francis wiederum neue «Originale». Dabei interessierten ihn vor allem das Wesen der Zusammenarbeit, Fragen der Urheberschaft sowie die Idee, ein Gemälde sei ein einzigartiges Objekt .

Francis wollte ein Bild in Plakatwandgrösse für die Fassade der Lagerhalle des Site Santa Fe anfertigen, das auf die Schneekugel und letztlich auf die Beziehung zwischen New Mexico und Mexico City hinweisen sollte. Im Einklang mit seinen aktuellen Malprojekten beschloss der Künstler, mit den hispanischen Malern Denis, Nolan und Randy Martinez, allesamt Experten der traditionellen *Lowrider*-Kultur, zusammenzuarbeiten. Nach Gesprächen mit den drei Künstlern wurde entschieden, dass sie ihre Phantasieversion von Mexico City darstellen sollten – ein Ort, mit dem diese Künstler durch ihre Herkunft verbunden waren, den sie aber nicht aus eigener Anschauung kannten.

Als im Laufe der Zusammenarbeit mit den Plakatmalern der Begriff der Urheberschaft in Frage gestellt wurde, reizte es Francis, das Genre des Selbstporträts im Rahmen eines umfassenderen Experiments zu untersuchen. Mit THE PORTRAIT entwickelte er ein in sich widersprüchliches Projekt, das man auch als «Selbstporträt durch andere» bezeichnen könnte. Für dessen Realisierung beauftragte der Künstler Enrique Huerta, Juan García und Emilio Rivera, drei mexikanischen Plakatmaler, mit denen er regelmässig zusammenarbeitete, ein

Porträt von ihm zu malen. Francis bat jeden der drei, ein Abbild von ihm anzufertigen und im Hintergrund jeweils einige Bilder seiner Wahl aus dem eigenen Wirkungsbereich zu zeigen. So zeigte jedes Porträt von Francis zugleich auch den charakteristischen Stil jedes einzelnen Malers. Er sass übrigens allen dreien Modell.

Parallel dazu schuf Francis sein eigenes kleines Selbstbildnis; es zeigt ihn als Figur im Dreiviertelporträt, die einen nur am Hals geknöpften Kittel trägt und darunter ein halb offenes weisses Hemd, so dass seine Brust zu sehen ist. Ein aus dem Hemd entwichener Fliegenschwarm, schwirrt in der Herzgegend des Künstlers herum. An der Wand im Hintergrund hängen Miniaturbilder, die an Francis' eigene Bilder von Stadtlandschaften erinnern. Das Gesicht des Künstlers wird von einem ovalen Stück Papier verdeckt, das auf die Bildoberfläche geklebt ist. Dieses Bild entstand ohne Zutun der Plakatmaler.

Bei einem früheren Erkundungsbesuch in Santa Fe beschloss Francis, Randy Martinez in dieses Projekt einzubeziehen und ihn mit einem Selbstporträt zu beauftragen. Martinez willigte ein, erhielt sein Honorar im Voraus und entschied sich, das Porträt auf die Kühlerhaube eines Autos zu malen.

Die für immer unvollständig bleibende Version von THE PORTRAIT ist in einem kleinen Katalog der mittlerweile nicht mehr existierenden Galeria Carmargo Vilaça dokumentiert. Zu sehen sind vier Photographien, von denen drei einen Plakatmaler neben einem fertig gestellten Porträt von Francis zeigen, während es sich bei der vierten um eine Reproduktion von Francis' Selbstporträt handelt. Die drei Photos sind ebenso sehr Porträts der Plakatmaler wie von Francis und insgesamt unterstreichen sie den subjektiven Charakter der Porträtmalerei. Obschon die Bilder der *rótulistas* ihm alle ähnlich sehen, ist keines von ihnen Francis. Jedes Werk zeigt eine Variante des Künstlers, wobei seine Gesichtsform, der Farbton seiner Haut, seine Frisur, die Form seiner Hände und die Farbe seiner Kleider bei jedem Bild anders sind. Keinem der Maler gelingt es, den mittelalterlichen Charakter seines Gesichts, seine hoch gewachsene, schlanke Gestalt oder seine leicht sommersprossige Haut einzufangen. Und wie alle gemalten Porträts sind diese Bilder nicht in der Lage, die Anmut einer bestimmten Gangart, den Klang der Stimme und all die kleinen Gesten zu vermitteln, die zusammen die Persönlichkeit eines Menschen ausmachen.

Mittlerweile ist allgemein bekannt, dass Francis' frühe Arbeiten ihren Ursprung in zahlreichen Spaziergängen hatten, die er in Mexico City unternahm. 1990–1991 unternahm er eine Reihe von Interventionen, üblicherweise indem er Elemente wie Kissen und Tierfiguren in die bestehende Architektur und die urbane Struktur der Stadt einfügte oder aber aus ihr entfernte. Gleichzeitig suchte er nach einer Möglichkeit, diese Aktionen zu dokumentieren, ohne sie unbedingt direkt abzubilden. Die Photographie erschien ihm dabei als zu ungetreue Wiedergabe der Wirklichkeit von Moment und Ort der Intervention. Daher begann er über gemalte Situationen nachzudenken, die diesen Live-Szenarien vielleicht besser entsprächen und in eine ähnliche Richtung wiesen, ohne direkte Zitate zu sein. Da Francis kein Maler war, suchte er nach einer geeigneten Ausdrucksmöglichkeit; die augenfälligste war jene der Reklametafeln ganz in der Nähe seines Ateliers. Angesichts der Tatsache, dass der Erfolg der Plakatmaler von ihrer Fähigkeit erfolgreich zu kommunizieren abhängt, war es wohl auch die effektivste. Als er schliesslich zu malen begann, konnte er der Versuchung nicht widerstehen, die Bilder jenen zurückzugeben, von denen sie inspiriert waren.

In jüngster Zeit hat sich die Zahl der Mitarbeiter des Künstlers sprunghaft erhöht. Während er früher mit drei bis vier Plakatmalern arbeitete, setzt er jetzt Hunderte von Leuten ein. Dass Francis fähig ist, mit so vielen Leuten gleichzeitig zu arbeiten, leuchtet ein, wenn man an seine ursprüngliche Ausbildung als Ingenieur und Architekt denkt. Denn wie Filmregisseure verwirklichen die Vertreter dieser Berufe ihre Visionen nur dank der vereinten Anstrengungen zahlreicher, mannigfach qualifizierter Arbeiter.

Es wird oft gesagt, dass die Spaziergänge für das Verständnis von Francis Alÿs' Schaffensprozess und Werk von zentraler Bedeutung sind, aber das Schreiben, obwohl es im Endprodukt kaum in Erscheinung tritt, macht einen ebenso wichtigen Teil seiner täglichen Arbeit aus. Francis ist ein Künstler, der gern ein Schriftsteller des sechzehnten Jahrhunderts wäre. In der Anfangsphase bestehen seine Projekte jeweils aus Mappen voll loser Blätter, die mit kunstvollen französischen, spanischen und englischen Notizen und Skizzen des Künstlers bedeckt sind. Diese helfen ihm dabei, seine Ideen festzuhalten und einzuordnen. Zu gegebener Zeit kommen Bilder dazu, die geeignete Ausdrucksform kristallisiert sich heraus und die Texte beginnen wegzufallen, aber nie vollständig. Manchmal existiert ein Kunstwerk nur als mündliche Geschichte oder maschinengeschriebener Text, so etwa THE RUMOR (Das Gerücht, Tlayacapan, Mexico, 1998). Häufig aber sind diese «Skripte» oder «Geschichten» integrale Bestandteile des Werks, egal, ob es sich dabei um ein Gemälde, eine Postkarte, ein Video, einen Spaziergang, eine Skulptur oder irgendein grösser angelegtes Unternehmen handelt. In einem Gespräch hat Francis seine Arbeitsweise erst vor kurzem als «beinah Schreiben» und seine Skizzen mit Textfragmenten als «geschriebene Zeichnungen» bezeichnet.

In der Recherchierphase seiner Projekte formuliert der Künstler häufig Ideen, nur um ihnen fast schon im gleichen Atemzug zu widersprechen. Danach verwendet er viel Zeit und Mühe darauf, die beiden Meinungen in Einklang zu bringen, bis schliesslich vielleicht eine dritte, weniger offensichtliche, nicht in Worte zu fassende Variante entsteht – die einzige, die er als angemessen erachtet. Sein methodisches Vorgehen wird durch eines dieser alten Aufziehspielzeuge aus Blech veranschaulicht, das aus einem Herrn und seinen zwei widerspenstigen Hunden besteht, die durch starre Leinen mit ihm verbunden sind. Wenn man das Spielzeug aufzieht, erwartet man, dass der Meister ganz einfach seine Begleiter spazieren führt. Doch der Hund am rechten Arm des Mannes bleibt störrisch zurück, während der Hund links ungeduldig vorwärts und nach rechts drängt. Bei diesem Gebilde, das wie ein drehbares dreibeiniges Stativ funktioniert, sorgen die eigensinnigen Tiere zwar dafür, dass der Mann aufrecht steht und nicht hinfällt, zwingen ihn aber gleichzeitig dazu, sich ständig im Kreis zu bewegen.

In der Situation des Mannes und seiner Tiere spiegelt sich Francis' Prinzip des Fortschritts durch Scheitern. Um die Trägheit eines Prozesses sichtbar zu machen, bringt der Künstler die maximale Anstrengung auf («Drehen im Kreis») und erzielt ein minimales Ergebnis («sich zu Fuss vorwärts bewegen»). Die Bewegung (oder mangelhafte Bewegung) der Hunde und ihres Meisters ist auch ein Beispiel für das «Paradox der Praxis» – eines der Lieblingsaxiome des Künstlers: PARADOX OF PRAXIS (SOMETIMES MAKING SOMETHING LEADS TO NOTHING), (Teil I, Mexico City, 1997) und PARADOX OF PRAXIS (SOMETIMES MAKING NOTHING LEADS TO SOMETHING), (Teil II, seit 1997 laufendes Projekt).

Irgendwann hält Peter vor einem kleinen weissen Haus. Francis steigt aus dem Auto und klopft an die Tür. Eine Frau macht auf – Randy ist nicht da. Sie gibt Francis einen weiteren Hinweis auf Randys Aufenthaltsort. Wir folgen ihrer Wegbeschreibung und erleben noch einmal dasselbe. Und dann nochmals. Es gibt einen Schnappschuss von Francis, der genau in diesem Moment gemacht wurde. Umrahmt von dem wolkigen Himmel und Hügeln, auf

FRANCIS ALŸS, PARADOX OF PRAXIS (SOMETIMES MAKING SOMETHING LEADS TO NOTHING) – ICE, MEXICO D.F., 1997, video still / PARADOX DER PRAXIS (MANCHMAL FÜHRT ES ZU NICHTS, WENN MAN ETWAS TUT) – EIS, Videostill.

denen knorrige, buschige Kiefern und trockenes, struppiges Gras wachsen, steht der Künstler gegen das verlassene Wrack eines Oldtimers gelehnt. Er trägt eine verkehrt herum aufgesetzte Baseballmütze, ein altes weisses T-Shirt, weite Hosen, Converse-Turnschuhe und zündet gerade ein Streichholz an, um die zwischen seinen Lippen baumelnde Zigarette anzustecken. Die Szene verströmt einen Hauch amerikanischen Mythos. Nach beendeter Zigarettenpause beschliesst Francis die Suche aufzugeben und wir fahren zurück nach Santa Fe. Johnny singt mit schmachtender Stimme: «Why me Lord? What have I ever done to deserve even one of the pleasures I've known and ...»

(Übersetzung: Irene Aeberli)

1) Site Santa Fe ist eine private Non-Profit-Institution für zeitgenössische Kunst in Santa Fe, New Mexico. Seit 1995 veranstaltet sie lokale, nationale und internationale Ausstellungen, darunter auch die Internationale Biennale von Santa Fe, die vom 18. Juli 2004 bis 9. Januar 2005 (unter Kurator Robert Storr) bereits zum fünften Mal ihre Tore öffnet.

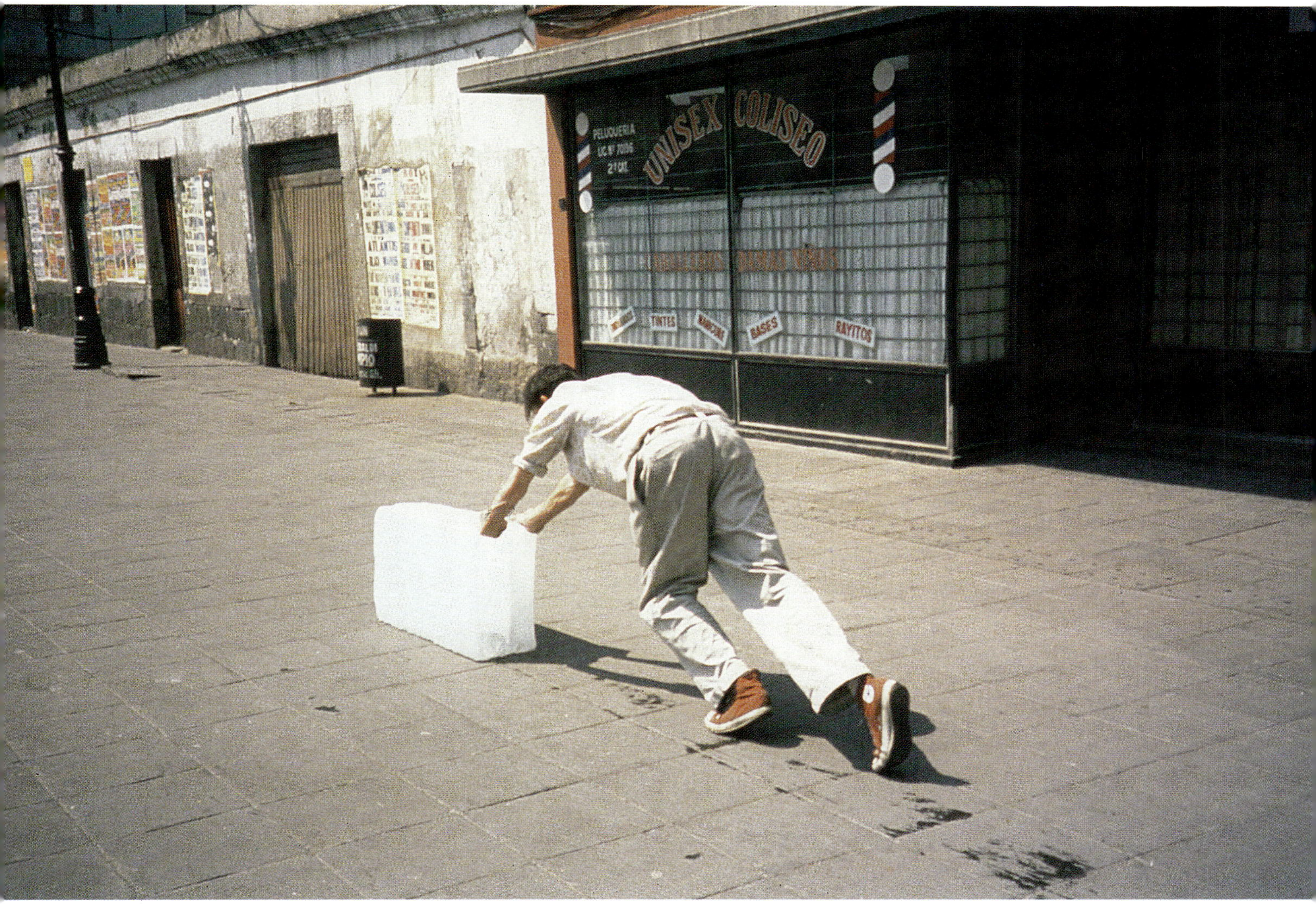

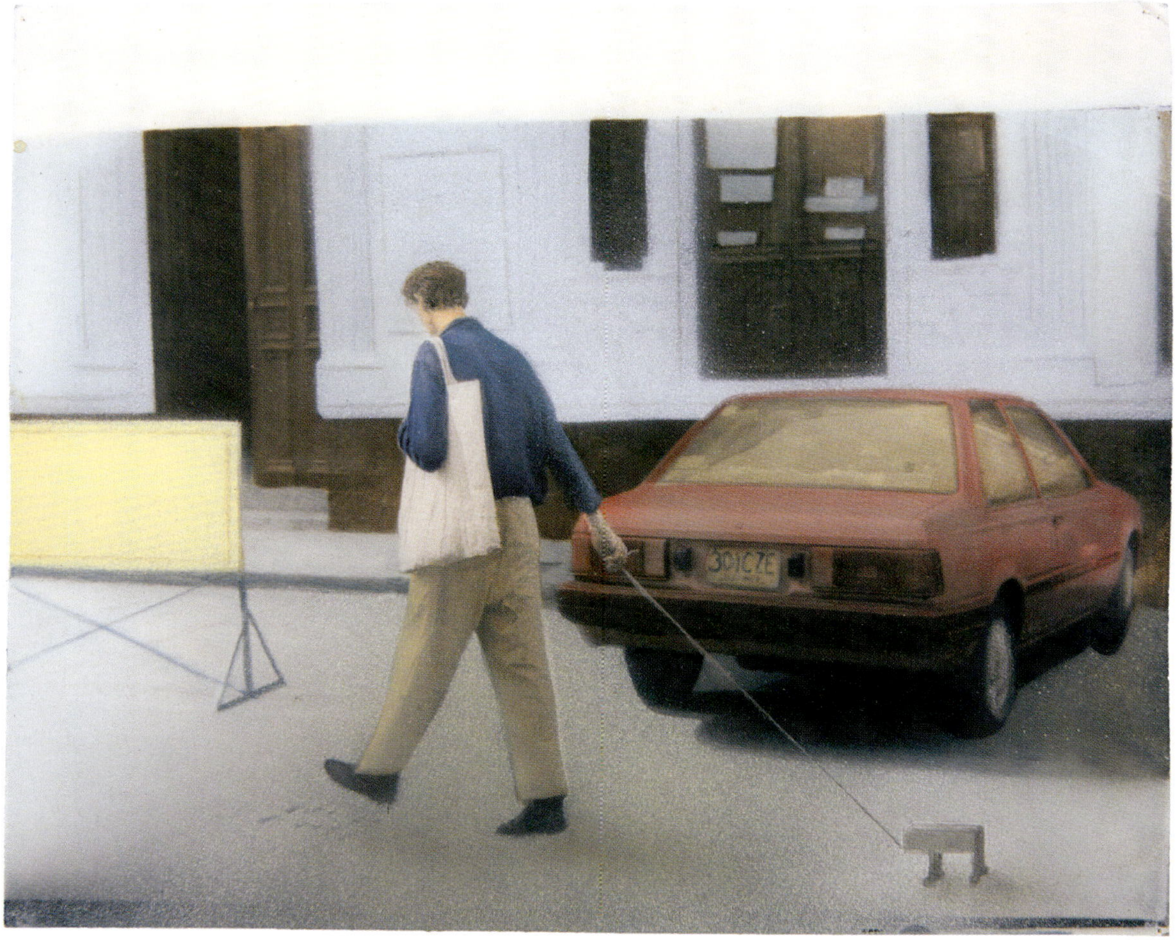

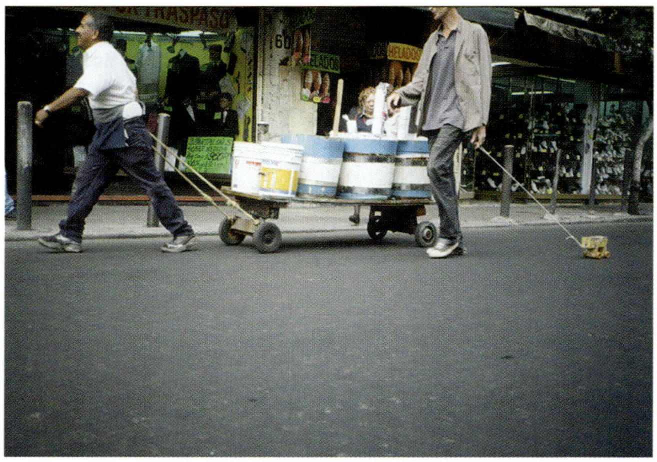

Above / Oben: FRANCIS ALŸS, THE COLLECTOR, 1991, retouched photograph, $7\frac{7}{8}$ x $9\frac{13}{16}$" / DER SAMMLER, retouchierte Photographie, 20 x 25 cm. On the right / Rechts: GHETTO COLLECTOR, 1991–1992, photo document / GHETTOSAMMLER, Photodokument. Righthand page / Rechte Seite: FRANCIS ALŸS, WALKING A PAINTING, 2002, oil and pencil on tracing paper, $13\frac{3}{4}$ x $9\frac{13}{16}$" / EIN GEMÄLDE SPAZIEREN FÜHREN, Öl und Bleistift auf Pergamentpapier, 35 x 25 cm.

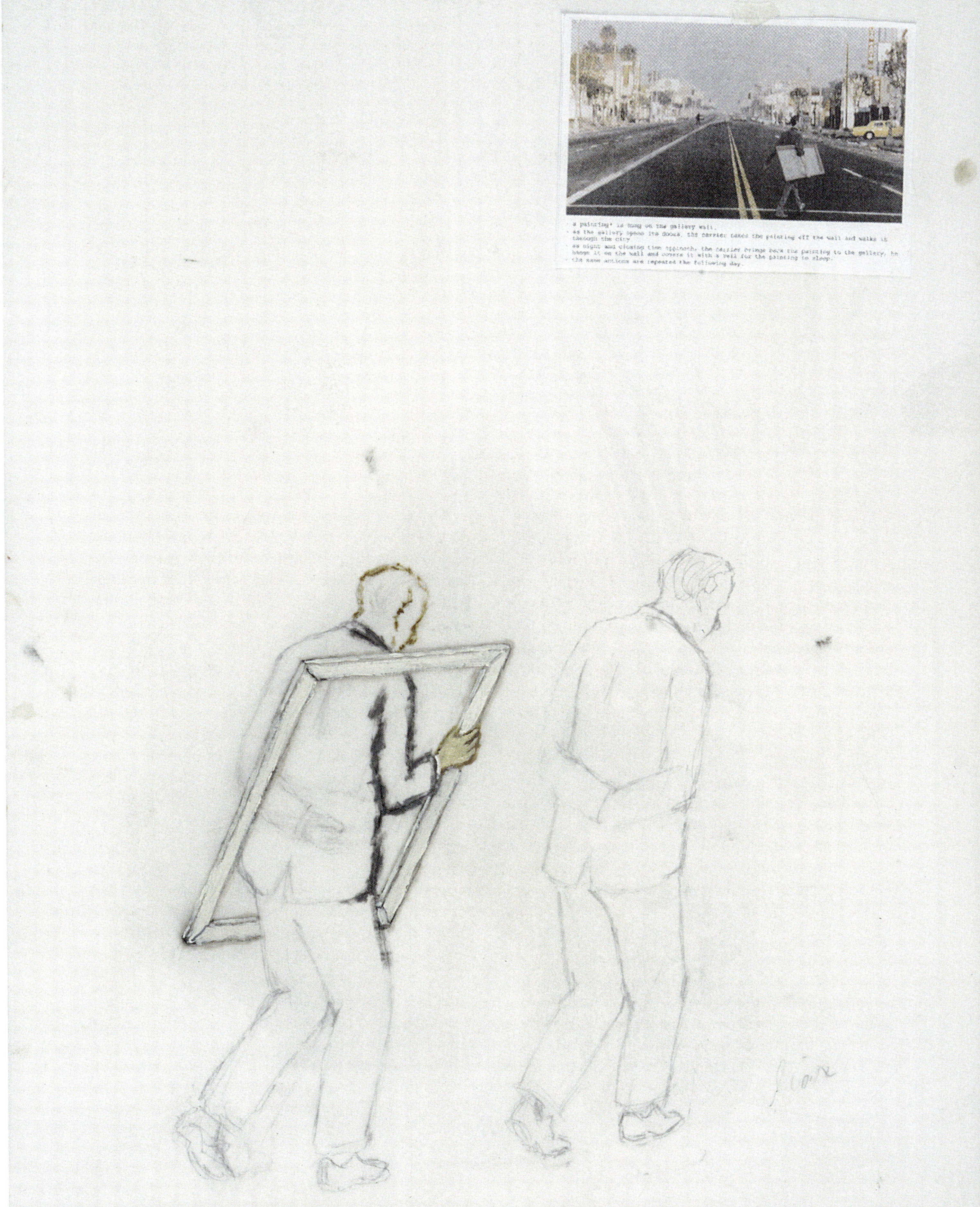
- a painting* is hung on the gallery wall.
- as the gallery opens its doors, the carrier takes the painting off the wall and walks it through the city
- as night and closing time approach, the carrier brings back the painting to the gallery, he hangs it on the wall and covers it with a veil for the painting to sleep.
- the same actions are repeated the following day.

One More Step

SAUL ANTON

It's no secret that when writing about art and artists, critics must turn to metaphors to make their points, especially to tropes of typography, printing, and molds. The work or the artist is said to make an "impression" or a "mark," if not on the critic him- or herself, then on society, or "in history" (one doesn't often hear nowadays that a work has "moved" someone; criticism likes to think of itself as a cognitive activity not as the story of an affective experience). More often, an artist is said to have "cut a new path," or even, in extreme cases, to have "broken the mold." Though such new paths seem to be inevitably connected to the ones art moved on before, and broken molds seem to always magically constitute new ones, we can point to two distinct dimensions of the critical metaphor of imprinting: violence and inscription. At the same time, the work strikes, cuts, or shatters something, it also writes upon it, if only a basic contour line of a form.

I point out this recurrent trope and its double aspect because I was tempted to use it to begin this essay on the work of Francis Alÿs. Alÿs is one of the most singular and incisive (there's the trope of cutting) artists to have emerged in the past decade. At the same time, however—and here's what made me hesitate—there's something in Alÿs's work that undermines the typographical metaphor of criticism and its double character as violence and inscription. I say undermines, but that doesn't mean he rejects or avoids it. It's not that Alÿs is not "impressive," literally and figuratively. Indeed, he is impressive in the way his works impress themselves upon us, but, at the same time, his works are also what is impressed upon and into. If he has made an impact, it's only because he allows his work to be impacted. He is impressive precisely because he is profoundly impressionable.

For example, the 1996 photograph TURISTA shows Alÿs standing in line with a group of unemployed Mexican men who indicate their profession to any potential employer with small handmade signs. Among them are an *electricista* and a *plomero*. Alÿs describes himself rather dryly as a *turista*, in a gesture that points ironically to the dubitable nature of art "work." What does an artist do? For Alÿs, it's not so much that an artist doesn't work or produce, but rather that this work is travel.

What is crucial here is how TURISTA quite brutally includes Alÿs, essentially an outsider, in the group of

SAUL ANTON writes frequently for *Artforum* and other magazines. His fictional dialogue, *Warhol's Dream*, is forthcoming in Spring 2004 from Vel Press, Los Angeles. He has taught at the City University of New York and the Tyler School of Art and is currently a doctoral candidate at Princeton University.

unemployed Mexicans, while at the same time it allows Mexican reality to impress itself upon Alÿs, who now has joined the line of the unemployed. Alÿs takes the moment and place of impression as the starting point and subject of his work, yet he also subjects it—if I may be coy for a minute—to a double gesture. Alÿs impresses himself into a place, and allows that place to impress itself upon him and his work. This double gesture is deliberately not a dialectic of self and other. There is no pretense in it of sovereign subjects in dialogue with each other, for what they have in common is their unemployment. Rather, TURISTA affirms that the relation that constitutes them in the first place—work, or rather, the lack of it—is a mutual destitution of subjectivity. The photograph is only the narration of this *depropriation* rather than auto-appropriation of subjectivity in work, one that Alÿs rehearses in a variety of contexts and ways. This ambivalent double gesture runs counter to the usual way of conceiving the necessary relation between the artwork and its context, in which the artist, through work, imprints his/her subjectivity upon the world. Whereas too often today, this relation takes the form of a merely formal nod to so-called "site-specificity"—as if location were somehow itself an adequate condition of singularity or criticality—and so becomes, in fact, a form of branding, for Alÿs the specificity of the site does not itself confer any essential meaning or value. A singularity does not exist prior to the relation but rather takes shape only in the time that one is in that place. In other words, site-specificity is a relation between a work and its outside

FRANCIS ALŸS, TURISTA, 1996, one of several photographs / TOURIST, eine von mehreren Photographien.

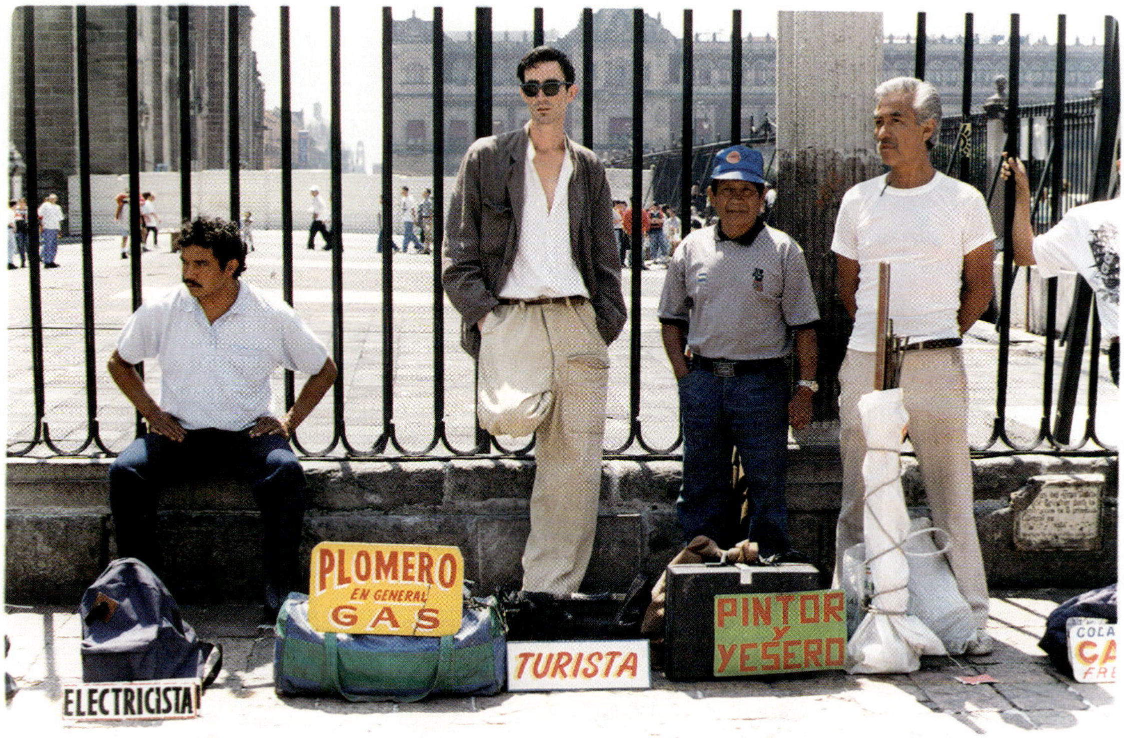

that must be produced each time. If specificity were already there, the artwork would be entirely superfluous at worst, merely a realist representation at best.

This double relation between the artist and the "context" can be traced back to the now well-known genesis of Alÿs's life as an artist. In 1987, Alÿs came to Mexico City as an architect working for a French governmental project, but a few years later he abandoned architecture and the task of building in lieu of what came to be known as his *paseos,* or walks. In this sense, TURISTA is simply a description of his new life in Mexico City. Yet, here again, if architecture can be described as the impression of place through violent incision, then one can say that in abandoning architecture, Alÿs abandoned the violence of building as incision and impression, the stamping of the urban grid onto the earth. In the *paseos* that he has performed since 1991, Alÿs doesn't so much work as he moves through something. He wore magnetic shoes as he wandered around Havana on the occasion of the Biennial (MAGNETIC SHOES, 1994), and for THE LEAK (São Paolo, 1995), he carried a leaking can of blue paint around São Paolo. For Alÿs the *paseo* is never simply the passage through a place, but something that traverses the distance between the violence of inscription and its readability of any form.

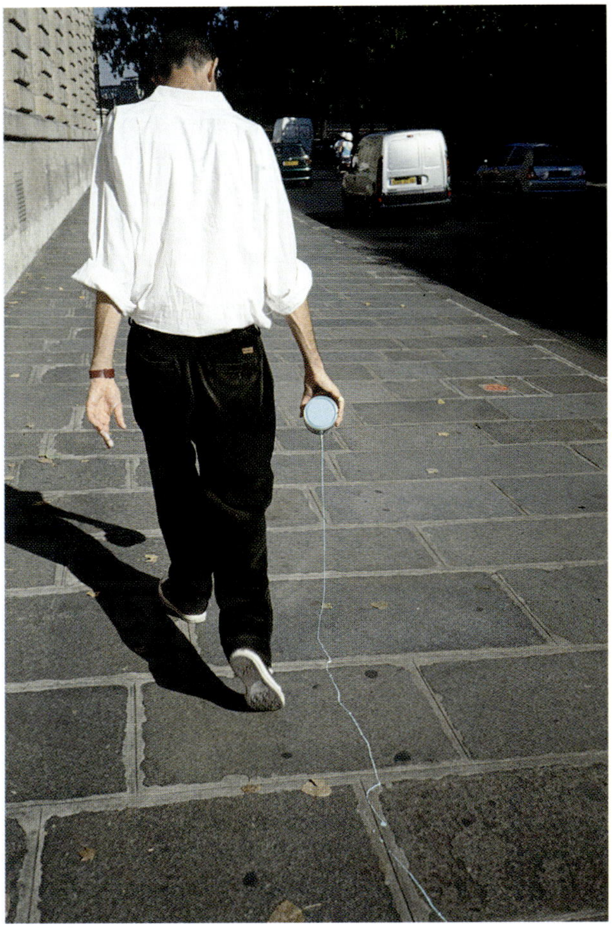

In this sense, you might say the motif of the *paseo* is something like the *trans* in the passage from one language to another in translation. Quite literally, Alÿs is a *transartist* and his art is an art in translation, a *Passagenwerk* in which the aesthetic moment is recast as a movement between two points, a relation rather than an obdurate instant of aesthesis. This recasts the notion of site-specificity as a practice of wandering between sites just as it recasts the dialectical relation between margin and center that has become a cliché of international art. In Alÿs's work, every place is a nowhere except from the point of view of an elsewhere. TURISTA and Alÿs's walks in general imply that the margin, you might say, is inside every place as its center, but because of its plurality and in order to acknowledge its plurality cannot become a site from which a critique of the center is deployed without reifying itself as a center.

What is important to keep in mind here is that the *paseo* as aesthetic paradigm can never be grasped literally as an object since by definition, it is a movement. It is not the opposite of making (an object), because like production, it is an activity (work). On the other hand, it cannot be reduced to a conceptual or Situationist critique of object hood, or attempt to realize social change through the theatricalization of materialist aesthetics. In two versions of PARADOX OF PRAXIS (SOMETIMES MAKING SOMETHING LEADS TO NOTHING, part one, Mexico, D.F., 1997 and SOMETIMES MAKING NOTHING LEADS TO SOMETHING, part two, 1997–ongoing), Alÿs indicates this double condition in the formal terms of a paradox. In the first, Alÿs pushes a block of ice through the streets of Minimalism, re-enacting the reduction of the art to the object, but reminding us that a block of ice is only frozen water, something that lacks a fixed form.

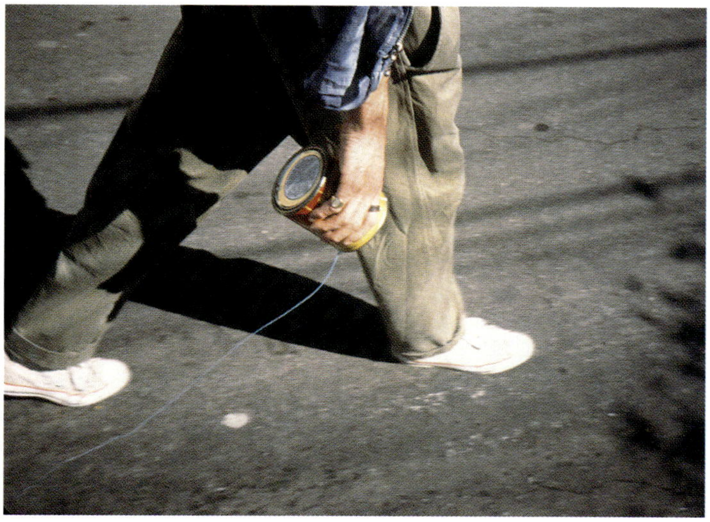

Page/Seite 36:
FRANCIS ALŸS, THE LEAK, Paris, 2003, photo document / DAS LECK, Photodokument.

FRANCIS ALŸS, THE LEAK, São Paulo, 1995, photo document / DAS LECK, Photodokument.

"Sometimes making something leads to nothing," writes Alÿs. Yet, at the same time, "sometimes making nothing leads to something." The second part, SOMETIMES MAKING NOTHING LEADS TO SOMETHING, has produced a considerable amount of notes and sketches, but the process remains a work in progress in which Alÿs has sought to explore what it might mean that "nothing" might lead to "something," an idea which in effect maps the production of art onto the cosmotheological and scientific question of genesis: If there was nothing before the universe, how could a universe arise in the first place? His answer is hardly a theological one in that there is no God in the nothing that produces creation. Rather, the nothing is not static but a spacing, a mere possibility, as it were. In the beginning of art, there is this spacing that isn't a space, a void between two things in which art becomes possible, and it must be marked each time, for it is what art "is," a mere "nothing" that isn't nothing, since it happens. As Alÿs notes, there is "more nothing to come."[1)]

The screensaver that Alÿs designed for the Dia Foundation's website in 1999, (http://www.diacenter.org/alys) shows a window through which a thief escapes. This virtual work, available free online, implies that the very frame of the work—the screen—holds this escape and congeals it. Despite the nothingness of virtuality, its formlessness, there remains, even after the work has escaped, as it were, through the frame of the window, the frame through which one perceives this escape. How then does one describe this frame that remains even after the artwork escapes? In RE-ENACTMENTS (Mexico City, 2000), which presents two versions of Alÿs carrying a gun through the streets of Mexico City until he is noticed and arrested by the police, this unavoidable frame is rendered in explicitly temporal terms. We are shown both an event and its re-enactment. Yet what is the relation between them? I would suggest that it's less the mimetic logic of the relation between original and copy that Alÿs is seeking to examine or undermine, though this is certainly one possible reading, but rather an attempt to simply mark the temporal distance between these two versions as the space of representation itself. Alÿs suggests that every artwork carries the unavoidable burden of time whether it is seen in terms of originality (i.e. as modernism), or as simulacrum (i.e. as postmodernism). Both interpretations of the temporality of the image depend upon this delay or time-gap, which for Alÿs necessarily leads to the production of what he calls fables.

Two recent works—WHEN FAITH MOVES MOUNTAINS (CUANDO LA FE MUEVE MONTAÑAS), Lima, 2002, for which he had hundreds of volunteers "move" a mountain in the poor and arid outskirts of Lima, and his well-documented THE MODERN PROCESSION (New York City, 2002) for the Museum of Modern Art in New York—demonstrate this point. There can be no meaning given to the acts alone in either event. It is only in their wake, as narratives, that these temporal works can achieve duration in the production of storytelling. One day a mountain moved four inches. One day there was a procession from midtown Manhattan to Queens. Meaning as narrative comes afterwards, and it implies that the interval between the event and its re-enactment is infinite, the space of any number of stories to arise.

This temporality is the reason that the critical horizon in which to grasp the work of Alÿs is not that of post-Minimalism, Pop, and the relation between sculpture and painting, but rather that of music. Music's absolute formalism (even opera is ultimately musical, *contra* Wagner) lies in its temporal dimension, the fact that it must be played and replayed. One can never lose sight of the essentially relational form of music that is the minimal condition for anything that isn't simply noise, even so-called ambient music. Reduced to its zero degree, silence, or noise (musically, these are indistinguishable), music will always presume a relation that distinguishes it from any atomistic materialism.

It is something like this *reductio* to silence that Alÿs, along with his longtime collaborator Rafael Ortega, attempted in Panama in March 2003, where, along with 45 young Panamanians, they sought to produce one minute of silence in a variety of cacophonous public situations, not in memoriam to anything in particular, but rather as a space (temporal, but also figurative) in which the fable, or the narrative becomes possible. In this minute of silence—what Blanchot described as "the essential solitude"[2]—arises the very possibility for all sound, talk, and communication that makes up any given public situation. In ZÓCALO (1999) Alÿs insists on the idea that this possibility is the space of his art, by presenting a long video of Mexico City's main square, the very paradigm of public space as an aesthetic, theatrical space of social gathering and intercourse. Yet Alÿs's video reveals that the Zócalo is not so much an intersubjective space where individuals exchange ideas, opinions, and property, but rather a place where a kind of pre-subjective, quasi-instinctual, or quasi-automatic behavior is seen. In effect, he presents this space in its pure state. As the day passes and we see people line up in the shadow of the square's central flagpole, what becomes apparent is that humans can seem more like bees or ants, whose social behavior is hardly rational "communication" in either Habermas's utopian terms or in the terms of liberal capitalist market exchange dynamics. Rather, Alÿs undermines here the notion that the aesthetic space of the square—here identified with the frame of the ZÓCALO video itself—can function as a space for social interaction. In other words, this prototypically "public" space presents what seems to be distinctly extra-subjective group behavior, thereby challenging the notion that art can serve as the space of intersubjectivity, as it is so often claimed today. For Alÿs, art is the space of pure possibility of interaction that generates fables.

If modernity and postmodernity in art have sought to use the aesthetic materiality of the artwork as the "space" of social discourse, Alÿs de-aestheticizes this space and insists that it is a nothing out of which the something that is social discourse arises. This discourse is not what you would call communication—though the media always seek to reduce it to that—but rather, more primordially, fable. The fable is the structural matrix of possibility of all social relation, but de-subjectified and put, as it were, "out of work," as Blanchot writes.[3] This is the allegory of the Zócalo, which, because it is only ever the possibility of fable, reminds us that we always have one more step to take in the direction of meaning, and art is that which permits us to make this step, but also forces us to take one more after that, in the recognition that we cannot arrive there. For art is homeless, a *turista,* not a landowner. There is always "more nothing to come."

1) This and all further quotes by the artist come from an E-mail sent to the author on October 6, 2003.
2) Maurice Blanchot, *L'espace littéraire,* 1. chapt. : "La solitude essentielle" (Paris: Gallimard, 1955), p. 9.
3) Ibid., p. 22.

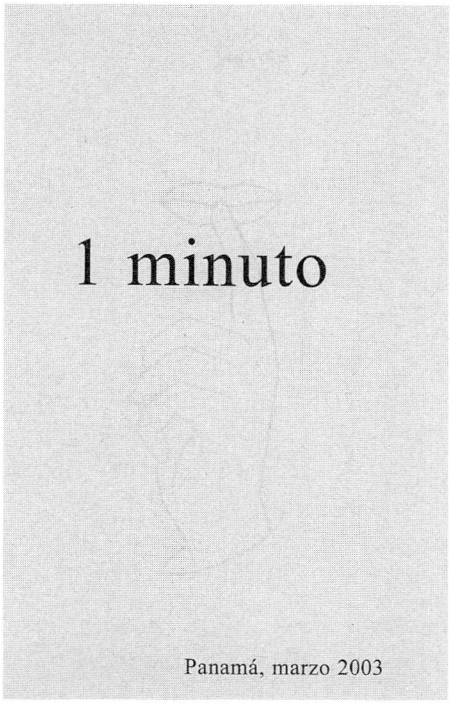

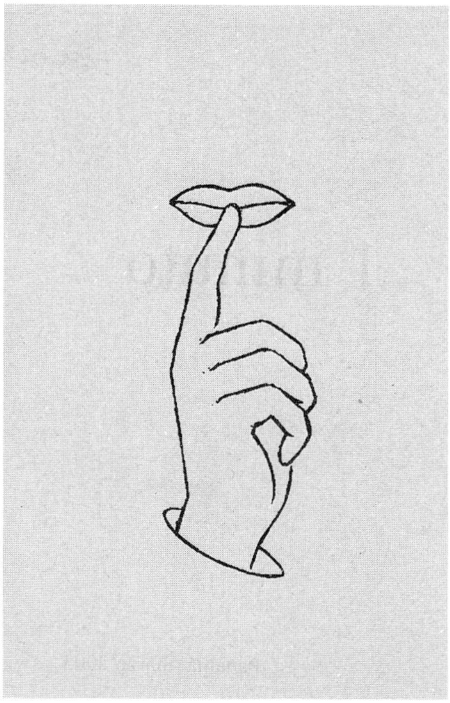

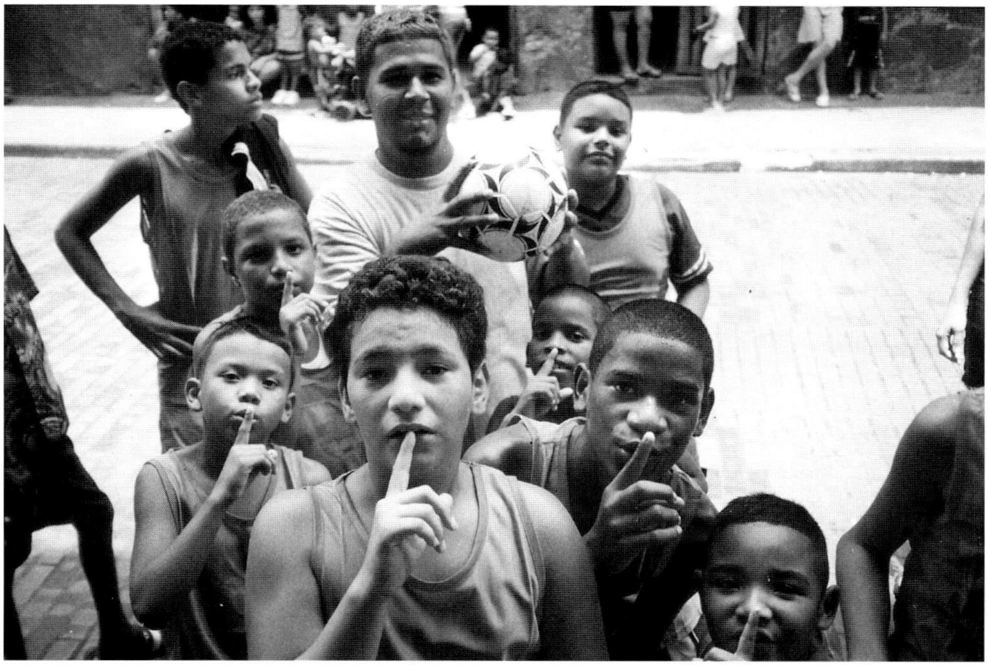

FRANCIS ALŸS & RAFAEL ORTEGA, 1 MINUTE OF SILENCE, Panama, March 2003, flyers and photograph / EINE MINUTE DER STILLE, Flugblätter und Photodokument.

Und noch ein Schritt

SAUL ANTON

Es ist kein Geheimnis, dass Kritiker beim Schreiben über Kunst und Künstler Metaphern zu Hilfe nehmen müssen, um ihren Standpunkt deutlich zu machen, und zwar vor allem Ausdrücke aus dem Bereich der Typographie, des Druckgewerbes und der plastischen Ausformverfahren. Es wird gesagt, das Werk oder der Künstler hinterlasse einen «Eindruck» oder eine «Spur» – wenn nicht beim Kritiker oder der Kritikerin selbst, so doch in der Gesellschaft oder «in der Geschichte» (nur selten hört man noch, ein Werk habe jemanden «ergriffen», denn die Kritik möchte sich als kognitive Aktivität und nicht als affektive Erfahrung verstanden wissen). Häufig heisst es auch, ein Künstler habe «einen neuen Weg eingeschlagen», oder in extremen Fällen gar, er habe «alte Formen gesprengt». Obwohl solch neue Wege unweigerlich mit jenen verbunden zu sein scheinen, auf denen sich die Kunst vorher bewegt hat, und gesprengte Formen auf wunderbare Weise stets neue hervorzubringen scheinen, möchte ich zwei unterschiedliche Aspekte der Druckmetapher besonders hervorheben: das Gewaltsame und den Inschriftcharakter. Immer wenn in einem Werk etwas geschlagen, zerschnitten oder gesprengt wird, bleibt darauf auch so etwas wie eine Inschrift zurück, und seien es nur die elementaren Umrisse einer Form.

Ich spreche deshalb von dieser häufig gebrauchten Metapher und ihrem Doppelsinn, weil es einfach zu verlockend war, einen Essay über das Werk von Francis Alÿs damit zu beginnen. Alÿs ist einer der aussergewöhnlichsten und eindrücklichsten (schon wieder die Druckmetapher) Künstler, die sich in den letzten zehn Jahren einen Namen gemacht haben. Gleichzeitig aber – und das liess mich zögern – haben Alÿs' Arbeiten etwas an sich, was die typographische Metapher in ihrer Zwiespältigkeit von Gewaltsamkeit und Inschrift unterläuft. Ich sage unterläuft, aber das heisst nicht, dass der Künstler sie ablehnt oder meidet. Es ist nicht etwa so, dass Alÿs nicht «eindrücklich» wäre, wörtlich und bildlich gesprochen. Tatsächlich ist er sogar besonders eindrücklich durch die Art, wie seine Arbeiten sich uns einprägen; zugleich aber bestehen seine Werke gerade in dem, was sich *ihnen* auf- und einprägt. Wenn Alÿs uns Eindruck macht, so liegt das allein daran, dass er seine Arbeit äusseren Eindrücken und

---

SAUL ANTON schreibt regelmässig für *Artforum* und andere Zeitschriften. Sein fiktiver Dialog, *Warhol's Dream,* erscheint im Frühjahr 2004 bei Vel Press, Los Angeles. Er unterrichtete an der City University of New York sowie der Tyler School of Art und ist zurzeit Doktorand in Princeton.

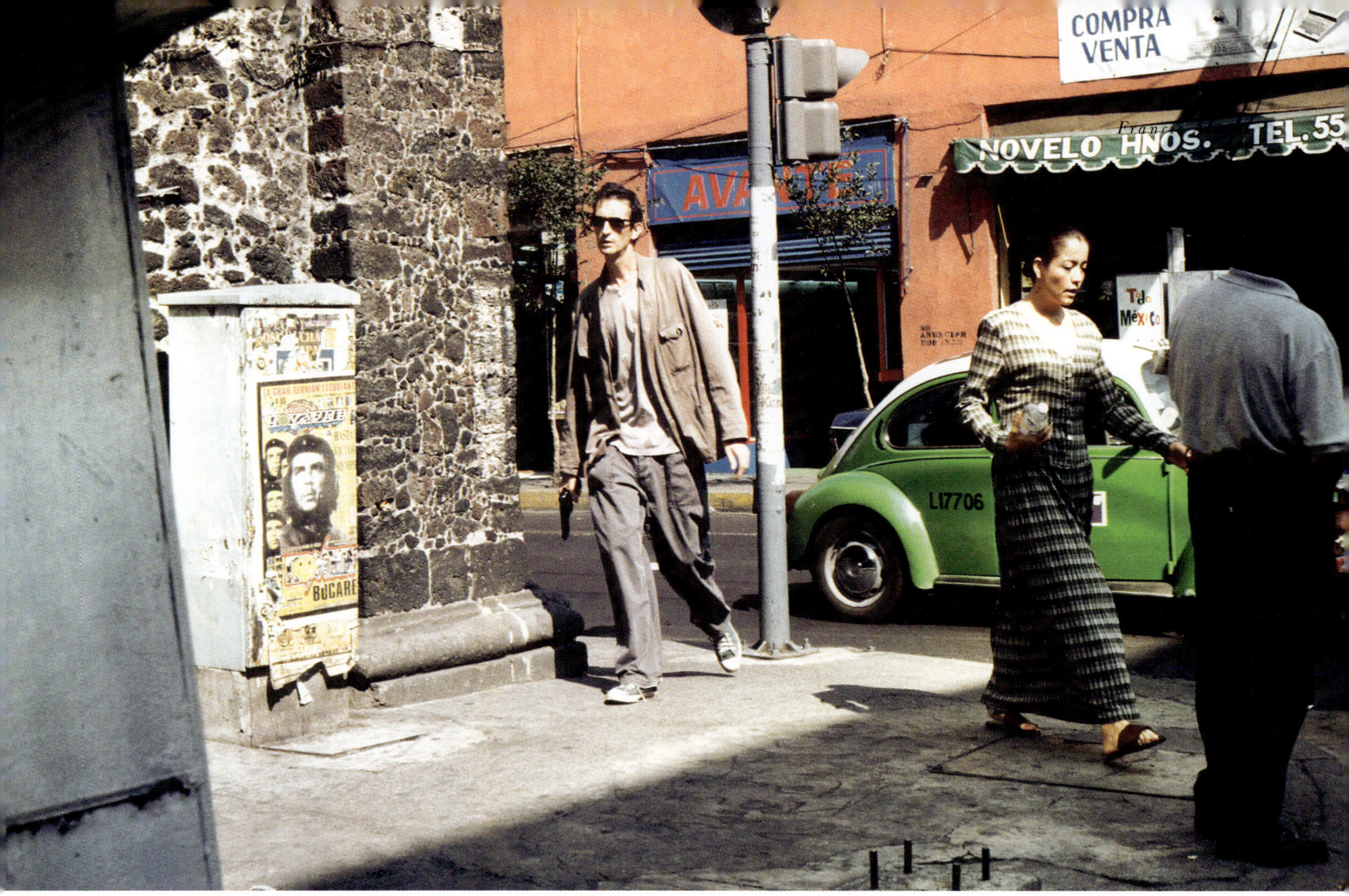

FRANCIS ALŸS, RE-ENACTMENTS, Mexico D.F., 2000, photo document / REINSZENIERUNG, Photodokument.

Einflüssen aussetzt: Er beeindruckt uns, weil er sich selbst beeindrucken lässt.

So zeigt beispielsweise die Photographie TURISTA (Tourist, 1996) den Künstler inmitten einer Reihe von Arbeit suchenden Mexikanern, die kleine handgefertigte Schilder bei sich haben, auf denen sie potenziellen Arbeitgebern ihren Beruf anzeigen. Darunter sind ein *electricista* und ein *plomero*. Alÿs bezeichnet sich selbst trocken als *turista* – eine Geste, die ironisch auf das Fragwürdige künstlerischer «Arbeit» verweist. Was tut denn ein Künstler eigentlich? Alÿs ist nicht der Meinung, dass Künstler nicht arbeiten oder produktiv seien, aber er glaubt, dass diese Arbeit im Reisen besteht.

Dabei ist entscheidend, dass der eigentlich aussenstehende Alÿs sich in TURISTA ziemlich unvermittelt in die Schar arbeitsloser Mexikaner einreiht, so dass er ebenso dem prägenden Einfluss der mexikanischen Realität ausgesetzt ist. Alÿs macht Moment und Ort der Prägung zum Ausgangspunkt und Thema seines Werks, doch er setzt es zugleich einer, man erlaube mir die Koketterie, Wechselwirkung aus. Alÿs prägt sich einem Ort ein und lässt sich und sein Werk zugleich von diesem Ort prägen. Diese Wechselwirkung ist bewusst keine Dialektik von Ich und Anderem. Da gibt es nicht den Anspruch souveräner Subjekte, die miteinander im Dialog stehen, denn ihre Gemeinsamkeit besteht lediglich in ihrer Arbeitslosigkeit. TURISTA zeigt auf, dass die Beziehung, die diese Menschen in erster Linie bestimmt – nämlich ihre Arbeit oder vielmehr deren Fehlen – ein wechselseitiger Subjektivitätsverlust ist. Die Photo-

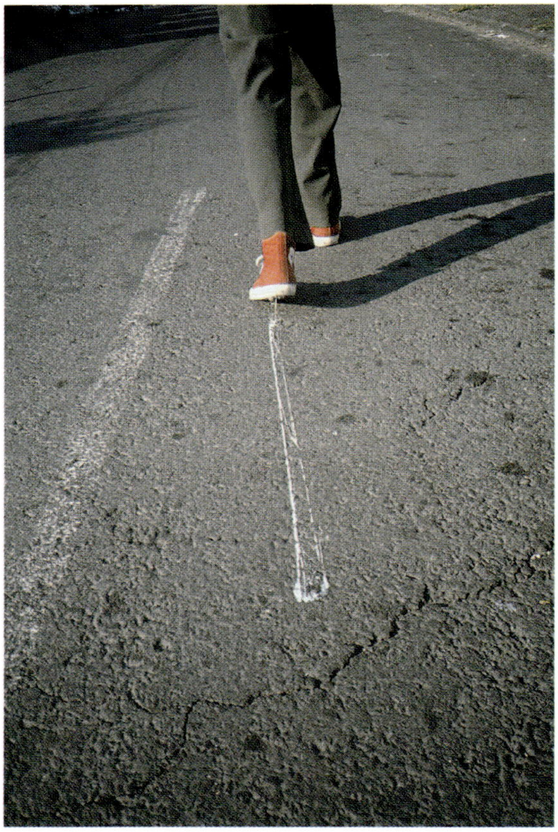

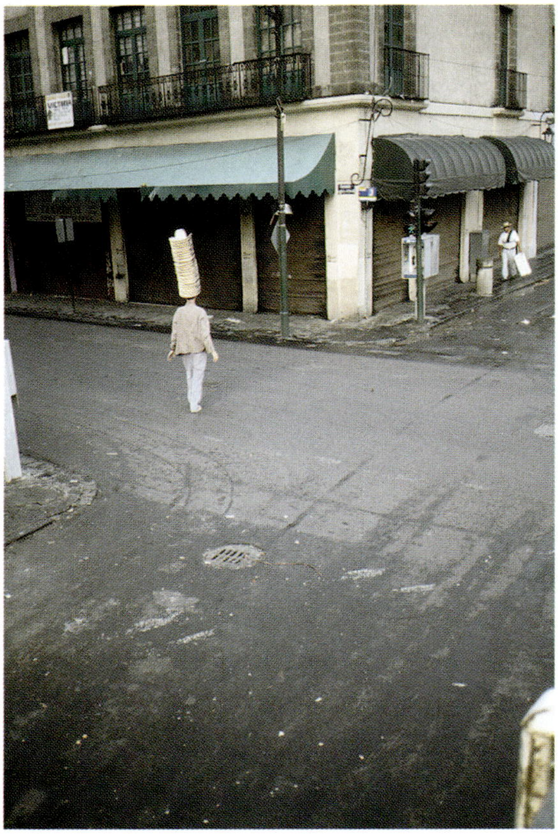

On the left / Links: FRANCIS ALŸS, UNTITLED, Mexico D.F., 1995;
on the right / rechts: UNTITLED, Mexico D.F., 2003; photo documents / Photodokumente.

graphie ist lediglich eine Schilderung dieser Enteignung im Gegensatz zum selbständigen sich Aneignen von Subjektivität durch Arbeit, und zwar eine, die Alÿs in verschiedenen Kontexten immer wieder anders abhandelt.

Die Ambivalenz dieser Wechselwirkung steht im Widerspruch zur üblichen Auffassung der Beziehung zwischen Kunst und Kontext, nach welcher der Künstler der Welt durch seine Arbeit den Stempel seiner Subjektivität aufdrückt. Während diese Beziehung heute allzu häufig in einer rein formalen Aufnahme der so genannten *site-specificity* oder Ortsbezogenheit besteht – als biete der Ort allein schon genügend Gewähr für Einzigartigkeit oder Nachhaltigkeit – und so zu einer Art Markenzeichen wird, vermittelt die Besonderheit des Ortes allein nach Alÿs' Auffassung noch keinen wesentlichen Wert oder Sinn. Die Einzigartigkeit besteht nicht schon vor jeder Bezugnahme, sondern nimmt erst Form an, wenn man Zeit an diesem spezifischen Ort verbringt. Mit anderen Worten: *Site-specificity* ist eine Beziehung zwischen Werk und Umgebung, die stets von neuem erzeugt werden muss. Würde sie bereits bestehen, wäre das Kunstwerk bestenfalls eine realistische Darstellung und schlimmstenfalls vollkommen überflüssig.

Diese besondere Beziehung zwischen Künstler und «Kontext» lässt sich bei Alÿs bis zu den mittlerweile bekannten Anfängen seines Künstlerdaseins zurückverfolgen. 1987 kam Alÿs als Architekt nach Mexico City, um für ein französisches Regierungsprojekt zu arbeiten, doch wenige Jahre später gab er Architektur und Bautätigkeit zugunsten dessen auf, was man heute als seine *paseos* oder «Spaziergänge» kennt. So betrachtet ist TURISTA einfach eine

Schilderung seines neuen Lebens in Mexico City. Doch auch hier: Wenn Architektur als Prägung eines Ortes durch gewaltsame Einschnitte beschrieben werden kann, könnte man sagen, dass Alÿs mit dem Verzicht auf die Architektur auch die Gewalt des Bauens im Sinne von Einschnitt und Prägung aufgab und der Erde nicht länger einen urbanen Raster aufdrücken mochte. Die *paseos,* die Alÿs seit 1991 durchführt, sind weniger Arbeit denn Bewegung. Er trug magnetische Schuhe, als er im Rahmen der Biennale durch Havanna spazierte (MAGNETIC SHOES, 1994), und für THE LEAK (Das Leck, São Paolo, 1995) trug er eine undichte Dose voll blauer Farbe in der Stadt herum. Für Alÿs ist der *paseo* nie einfach das Durchqueren eines Ortes, sondern etwas, was die Distanz zwischen der gewaltsamen Einschreibung und ihrer Lesbarkeit überwindet.

In diesem Sinne könnte man sagen, dass das Motiv des *paseo* etwas Ähnliches ist wie das *trans* in *translation* – der Übersetzung von einer Sprache in eine andere. Alÿs ist buchstäblich ein *transartist,* und seine Kunst ist eine Kunst der Übersetzung, ein «Passagenwerk», in dem das ästhetische Moment neu als Bewegung zwischen zwei Punkten entworfen wird, als Beziehung statt als statischer Augenblick der *aistesis.* Dabei wird *site-specificity* neu als ein Unterwegssein zwischen den Orten begriffen und das dialektische Verhältnis von Zentrum und Peripherie – mittlerweile ein Klischee der internationalen Kunst – erscheint in neuem Licht. Bei Francis Alÿs ist jeder Ort ein Nirgendwo, es sei denn aus der Sicht eines Anderswo. TURISTA und Alÿs' «Spaziergänge» überhaupt implizieren, dass der Rand gewissermassen jedem Ort als dessen Zentrum innewohnt, jedoch aufgrund seiner Pluralität, und um der Anerkennung dieser Pluralität willen, nicht zu einem Ort werden kann, von dem her eine Kritik des Zentrums möglich ist, ohne dass er sich selbst als Zentrum realisiert.

Dabei gilt es zu bedenken, dass der *paseo* als ästhetisches Paradigma nie wirklich als Objekt verstanden werden kann, da er *per definitionem* eine Bewegung darstellt. Er steht nicht im Gegensatz zum Herstellen (eines Objekts), denn wie jede Produktion ist er eine Tätigkeit (Arbeit). Andrerseits lässt er sich weder auf eine konzeptuelle oder situationistische Kritik des Objekthaften reduzieren, noch kann er durch theatralische Inszenierung der materialistischen Ästhetik einen gesellschaftlichen Wandel anstreben. In zwei Versionen seines Werks PARADOX OF PRAXIS (Paradox der Praxis), SOMETIMES MAKING SOMETHING LEADS TO NOTHING (Teil I, Mexico City, 1997) und SOMETIMES MAKING NOTHING LEADS TO SOMETHING (Teil II, seit 1997 laufendes Projekt), bringt Alÿs diese doppelte Bedingtheit als formales Paradoxon zum Ausdruck. In der ersten Version schiebt Alÿs einen Eisblock durch die Strassen der Minimal Art und imitiert so die Reduzierung der Kunst auf das Objekt, während er uns daran erinnert, dass ein Eisblock nur gefrorenes Wasser ist, etwas, was keine feste Form hat. «Manchmal führt es zu nichts, wenn man etwas macht», schreibt Alÿs; aber zugleich gilt auch: «Manchmal führt es zu etwas, wenn man nichts macht». Der zweite Teil, SOMETIMES MAKING NOTHING LEADS TO SOMETHING, hat schon eine beträchtliche Anzahl Notizen und Skizzen gezeitigt, doch der Prozess ist nach wie vor ein *work in progress,* in dem Alÿs der Frage nachgeht, was es bedeutet, dass «nichts» zu «etwas» führen kann, eine Idee, die das Kunstschaffen mit der kosmotheologischen und wissenschaftlichen Frage der Genesis verknüpft: «Wenn es vor dem Universum nichts gab, wie konnte dann das Universum überhaupt entstehen?» Seine Antwort ist kaum theologisch, weil es im Nichts keinen Gott gibt, der die Schöpfung hervorbringt. Das Nichts ist jedoch nicht statisch, sondern ein Zwischenraum, gewissermassen reine Möglichkeit. Am Anfang der Kunst steht dieser Zwischenraum, der kein Raum ist, sondern eine Leere zwischen zwei Dingen, in der Kunst möglich wird; und sie muss jedesmal gekennzeichnet werden, denn sie ist, was Kunst «ist», ein blosses «Nichts», das nicht nichts ist, weil es sich ereignet. Wie Alÿs bemerkt, ist «noch mehr Nichts zu erwarten».[1)]

Der Bildschirmschoner, den Alÿs 1999 für die Website der Dia Foundation gestaltete, zeigt ein Fenster, durch das ein Dieb entflieht – www.diacenter.org/alys. Diese online kostenlos erhältliche virtuelle Arbeit impliziert, dass ihr eigentlicher Rahmen – der Bildschirm – diese Flucht aufhält und einfriert. Trotz der Leere und Formlosigkeit des virtuellen Raums bleibt, selbst nachdem das Werk sozusagen durch den Fensterrahmen «entflohen» ist, der Rahmen zurück, durch den man die Flucht beobachtet hat. Aber wie beschreibt man den Rahmen, der zurückbleibt, wenn das Kunstwerk entschwunden ist? In RE-ENACTMENTS (Reinszenierungen, Mexico City, 2000), das in zwei Versionen zeigt, wie Alÿs mit einer Waffe durch die Strassen von Mexico City geht, bis ihn die Polizei entdeckt und verhaftet, wird das unvermeidliche Grundmuster bewusst zeitbetont abgehandelt. Gezeigt wird sowohl das Ereignis selbst als auch seine Reinszenierung. Aber in welcher Beziehung stehen die beiden zueinander? Ich vermute, dass Alÿs weniger die mimetische Logik der Beziehung zwischen Original und Kopie untersuchen oder unterlaufen will, obschon das sicher eine mögliche Lesart ist, sondern dass er einfach versucht, die zeitliche Distanz zwischen den beiden Versionen und damit den Darstellungsraum selbst sichtbar zu machen. Alÿs deutet an, dass jedes Kunstwerk die unvermeidliche Last der Zeit trägt, ob es nun als Original (und damit als Erzeugnis der Moderne) oder als Nachbildung (und Produkt der Postmoderne) betrachtet wird. Beide Interpretationen der Zeitlichkeit des Bildes basieren auf dieser Verzögerung oder zeitlichen Distanz, die Alÿs zufolge unweigerlich zur Entstehung von «Geschichten» führt.

Dies beweisen auch zwei neuere Werke: WHEN FAITH MOVES MOUNTAINS (CUANDO LA FE MUEVE MONTAÑAS, (Wenn der Glaube Berge versetzt, Lima, 2002), für welches er in den armen, ausgetrockneten Aussenbezirken von Lima Hunderte von Freiwilligen einen Berg «versetzen» liess, sowie die gut dokumentierte Arbeit THE MODERN PROCESSION (Die moderne Prozession, New York City, 2002) für das Museum of Modern Art in New York. In beiden Fällen ergibt die Handlung allein noch keinen Sinn. Erst im Nachhinein, als Erzählung, erlangen diese zeitlich begrenzten Werke durch die produktive Tätigkeit des Erzählens Dauerhaftigkeit. Eines Tages bewegte sich ein Berg zehn Zentimeter. Eines Tages gab es eine Prozession vom Zentrum Manhattans nach Queens. Die Bedeutung in Form einer Geschichte folgt erst später und das heisst, dass der Zwischenraum zwischen dem ursprünglichen Ereignis und seiner Reinszenierung unendlich ist und dass darin unendlich viele Geschichten Platz haben.

Diese Zeitbezogenheit ist der Grund dafür, dass weder Postminimalismus, Pop-Art noch das Verhältnis von Skulptur und Malerei als kritischer Horizont für Alÿs' Werk taugen, und dass die Musik sich da schon eher eignet. Der strenge Formalismus der Musik (entgegen Wagners Meinung ist selbst die Oper letztlich musikalisch) ergibt sich aus ihrer zeitlichen Dimension, aus der Tatsache, dass sie immer wieder von neuem gespielt werden muss. Man kann den Beziehungscharakter von Musik, minimale Voraussetzung für alles, was nicht nur Lärm ist, nie ausser Acht lassen, selbst bei der so genannten *Ambient Music*. Selbst reduziert auf ihren Nullpunkt – Stille oder Lärm (musikalisch gesehen gibt es da keinen Unterschied) – wird Musik immer eine Beziehung voraussetzen, die sie von einem rein atomistischen Materialismus unterscheidet.

Etwas Ähnliches wie diese *reductio* auf die Stille versuchten Francis Alÿs und Rafael Ortega, mit dem Alÿs seit Jahren zusammenarbeitet, im März 2003 in Panama. Zusammen mit 45 jungen Einheimischen wollten sie in verschiedenen kakophonisch anmutenden öffentlichen Situationen eine Schweigeminute initiieren, und zwar nicht als Gedenkminute, sondern als (zeitlicher, aber auch symbolischer) Raum, in dem die Fabel oder Erzählung möglich wird. In dieser Minute der Stille – Blanchot nennt das «la solitude essentielle»[2] – entsteht erst die Möglichkeit zu all den Geräuschen, Worten und Kommunikationsformen, die jede öffentliche Situation auszeichnen. In ZÓCALO (1999) untermauert Alÿs die Idee, dass dieser Möglichkeitsraum der Raum seiner Kunst ist, indem er ein langes Video von Mexico Citys Hauptplatz zeigt, Inbegriff des öffentlichen Raums als ästhetische Arena und Schauplatz von Geselligkeit und Diskussionen. Doch Alÿs' Video enthüllt, dass der Zócalo nicht so sehr ein intersubjektiver Raum ist, wo Individuen ihre Ideen, Meinungen und Waren austauschen, sondern eher ein Ort, an dem eine Art präsubjektives, quasi instinktives oder automatisches Verhalten zu beobachten ist. Er zeigt den Platz ganz unverfälscht: Wir sehen, wie sich die Leute im Laufe des Tages in den Schatten der Fahnenstange in der Mitte des Platzes stellen, und es zeigt sich, dass uns die Menschen eher wie Bienen oder Ameisen anmuten, deren Sozialverhalten kaum als rationale «Kommunikation» im utopischen Sinne von Habermas oder im liberal-kapitalistischen Sinn irgendwelcher Marktgesetze bezeichnet werden kann. Alÿs unterläuft hier vielmehr die Vorstellung, dass der ästhetische Raum des Platzes – hier durch den Rahmen des ZÓCALO-Videos umrissen – als Raum für soziale Interaktion dienen kann. Mit anderen Worten, dieser Prototyp eines «öffentlichen» Raums lässt offenbar ein klar aussersubjektives Gruppenverhalten erkennen und stellt damit die weit verbreitete Vorstellung in Frage, dass Kunst als intersubjektiver Raum zu dienen vermag. Für Alÿs ist die Kunst ein Raum der reinen Interaktionsmöglichkeit, der eben dadurch Fabeln und Geschichten hervorbringt.

Während in der Moderne und Postmoderne versucht wurde, die ästhetische Stofflichkeit des Kunstwerks als «Raum» des sozialen Diskurses zu nützen, entästhetisiert Alÿs diesen Raum und betont, dass das Etwas des sozialen Diskurses aus einem Nichts entsteht. Dieser Diskurs ist nicht, was man gemeinhin Kommunikation nennt – obschon die Medien ihn immer darauf reduzieren wollen –, sondern eher, viel ursprünglicher, eine Erzählung ... Diese Erzählung bildet das Grundmuster aller sozialen Beziehungsmöglichkeit, ist jedoch entsubjektiviert und gleichsam ausser Kraft gesetzt, wie Blanchot sagt.[3] Dies ist das Gleichnis des Zócalo, das uns, weil es immer nur Möglichkeit zur Erzählung bleibt, daran erinnert, dass immer noch ein Schritt in Richtung Bedeutung zu tun bleibt: Die Kunst erlaubt uns, diesen Schritt zu machen, zwingt uns aber auch, danach einen weiteren Schritt zu tun, im vollen Bewusstsein darum, dass wir das Ziel gar nicht erreichen können. Denn die Kunst ist heimatlos, eine *turista,* kein Grundbesitzer. Es ist immer «noch mehr Nichts zu erwarten».

(Übersetzung: I. Aeberli & W. Parker)

FRANCIS ALŸS, *L'IMPRÉVOYANCE DE LA NOSTALGIE,* 6th International Istanbul Biennale, 1999 / THE CARELESSNESS OF NOSTALGIA, *photograph* / DIE UNVORSICHTIGKEIT DER NOSTALGIE, *Photographie.*

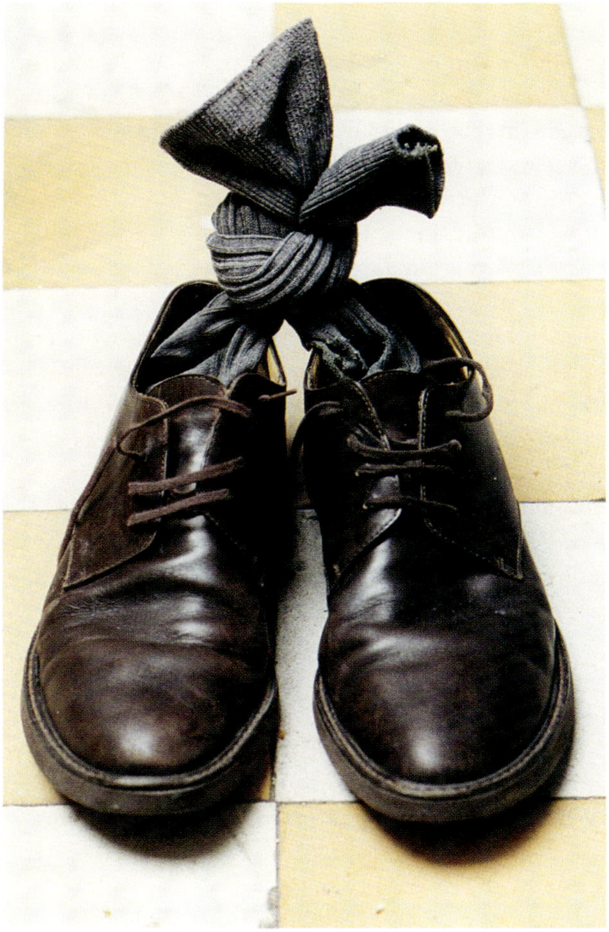

1) Dieses und alle weiteren Zitate des Künstlers stammen aus einer E-Mail an den Autor vom 6. Oktober 2003.
2) Maurice Blanchot, *L'espace littéraire,* 1. Kap., «La solitude essentielle», Gallimard, Paris 1955, S. 9.
3) Ebenda, S. 22.

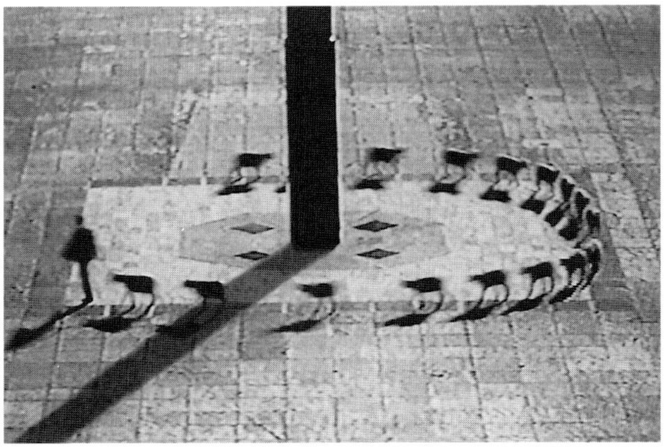

FRANCIS ALŸS, CUENTOS PATRIOTICOS / PATRIOTIC TALES (MULTIPLICATION OF SHEEP), Mexico D.F., 1997, videogram / PATRIOTISCHE GESCHICHTEN (VERMEHRUNG DER SCHAFE), Videogramm.

ROBERT STORR

STRANGE

Compose a graph. Label axis X movement, and the other, axis Y, stasis. Now choose two colors for dots of two distinctive sizes. On the key to the graph, identify the first as referring to groups, or rather members of a group in the appropriate number. The second will refer to individuals, though in reality the plural is a bit misleading since in all cases we will be dealing with the same individual pursuing different regimens. Mindful of the uncertain linkage between signifier and signified, as well as of the dialectical interchangeability of all terms, we will then "fold" and repeat this diagram in the space below the original and inscribe the inverse X axis with the designation non-movement, and the inverse Y axis with the designation non-stasis, thus underscoring the fact that in temporal situations walking is immanent in standing and standing is immanent in walking.

We will call this diagram, "The Expanded Field of Sculpture," or would if the name had not already been branded by another school of post-structuralist criticism. In keeping with the spirit of advanced opinion on such matters, we might alternatively title it "Debord's Delight," or "Delineations of *la Dérive*," in recognition of Situationism's chief theoretician, and the man who transformed meandering into a medium. It is a medium that, to borrow from the current lingo, nicely conflates absolutes of horizontality and verticality, the ground and the person who traverses it on foot or, as may happen, on hands and knees. However, in honor of the patron saint/demon of urban wanderers whose alertness to the interpenetrations of the ephemeral and the essential, the whimsical and rigorous, the splendid and the strange undergirds our appreciation of the ever-widening mesh of Modern art, we will instead call this exercise in nonsensical schematic rendering "Baudelaire's Boardgame." Within this field—which has been overlaid onto a reality characterized by labyrinthine streets and dusty paths more so than by the hard even grid of utopian-planners—you may plot a series of events, divided into the categories cited above.

For example, using the symbols for groups, chart the progressive gathering of a flock of sheep trouping in a perfect oval around the flagstaff at the center of a grand plaza. The actual location is the Zócalo in the heart of Mexico City, which, despite its "folkloric" aspects, is not where you expect to find someone choreographing a geometrical strict livestock ballet. The shepherd is the Belgian-born artist Francis

ROBERT STORR, artist, critic, and independent curator, is the Rosalie Solow Professor of Modern Art at New York University.

ATTRACTOR

Alÿs, who is the organizer of every sequence mapped on the graph and often its protagonist.

Given that time is a factor in MULTIPLICATION OF SHEEP (LA MULTIPLICACIÓN DE LOS BORREGOS, Mexico, D.F., 1997) from the series *Patriotic Tales* (*Cuentos Patrióticos,* Mexico, D.F., 1997), as it is in all the others, we must refine our system and further color-code our dots to record the staggered entrance of the sheep into this ring. To that end, we will modulate the tone of the dots from dark to light to indicate which ones have been there longest. In similar fashion, we must take account of the gradual assembling of people in the lengthening shadow of the same flagpole in ZÓCALO (1999), another video-performance work from the series *Patriotic Tales*. Here the action is spontaneous rather than staged; in this vast expanse of pavement, people seeking protection from the raking sunlight routinely line up in the protective shade of this landmark at the top of which waves a huge banner. Hence, the slyly mocking reference to patriotism since these citizens are not standing proudly to attention under a national emblem but rather pragmatically marshalling themselves to escape the glare.

Now add another long line made up of hundreds of dots that snake irregularly in a contracting crescent. They represent men shoveling sand as they climb a barren hill. Their combined effort displaced a fraction of the mass of the hill by an immeasurably small unit of space. WHEN FAITH MOVES MOUNTAINS (Lima, 2002) is a group enterprise that measures collaboration in spade-fulls of dusty earth. By the same token, it is also an exercise in futility which affirms the status of labor in relation to earthworks. In considering the cultural specificities of movements and styles, remember that in North America the concept of labor was essentially left out of the equation in the seventies (and after) despite a fascination with Nazca Lines and other pre-Columbian precedents. Moreover, although Alÿs's project was executed by volunteers—most of them students—it was undertaken in a place where on a perennial basis "labor is cheap" because unemployment is perpetually high. Thus, along with its positive communitarian dimension, the express futility of the enterprise assumes an explicitly economic and ambiguously political dimension. Moreover, where great temples were once raised by multitudes, the uncanny visual correlation between the hill and the memory of ancient pyramids stirs discomforting thoughts of empires past and present, of industrious—and expendable—masses then and now.

Finally, shifting our grid to a modern environment of more or less consistent verticals and horizontals, we can trace the path of a quasi-religious parade from midtown Manhattan over the East River to Queens. The participating members of the cult consist of art lovers and art professionals. The objects of their devotion are copies of paintings and sculptures by Picasso, Giacometti, and Duchamp, with Kiki Smith, a high priestess of the contemporary scene appearing in person on a sedan chair born aloft by her acolytes. To the sound of a traditional marching band drilled in such ceremonies, THE MODERN PROCESSION (New York City, 2002) simultaneously celebrated and lampooned the migration of the holy icons of Modernism from the Mother Church to its temporary home in exile.

Turning to the second symbol category, we may begin with the simplest proposition, even as we return to the site of our initial mapping of the shepherd and his flock. This time around, and in all that follow, whether in a crowd or on an empty thoroughfare, Alÿs is alone. In this instance, he is standing, or rather leaning, against a fence with other men on either side of him. He is tall and pale. In general, they are shorter and darker skinned. In front of them are toolboxes and hand-lettered cards advertising skills such as plumber and painter. The setting then is an open-air job market in the Zócalo next to the National Cathedral and near other stretches of sidewalk where other men sell effigies of Commandante Zero (Subcomandante Marcos), leader of the popular Zapatista revolt in the Southern province of Chiapas, as well as caricature dolls of the "forward-looking," notoriously corrupt, and widely-despised former President Carlos Salinas de Gortari. In front of Alÿs is a small shoulder bag and a card saying "tourist." They are looking for work; he is there to look. Or so his sign seems to indicate, except that instead of blending in and "going native" as romantic travelers from Richard Burton, T. E. Lawrence, and John Reed have traditionally attempted to do, he has jarringly included himself in the "picturesque" reality of his unemployed cohort, in effect becoming the mirror image to other tourists embedded in the sights they have come to see. Their idleness is detached pleasure; the plumber's and painter's idleness is anxious anticipation, and Alÿs's idleness accents both. The point on the graph that "stands for" TURISTA (Tourist, Mexico City, 1996) is unique and fixed but begs for reiteration within its confines to mark prolonged and uneasy duration.

The incidents devoted to the actions of an individual that remain to be registered on this graph hew to the axis of movement rather than that of stasis. They include: the trajectory of a man walking down the street pulling a boxy steel model of a dog that magnetically picks up bottle caps, nails, and metal scraps in its vicinity (THE COLLECTOR, Mexico City, 1991–1992); that of a man strolling down the street wearing magnetized shoes to much the same effect, (MAGNETIC SHOES, La Habana, 1994); that of a man walking down the street with a paint can that drizzles a liquid thread of violet (THE LEAK, São Paulo, 1995); that of a man trailing a strand of blue yarn from the sleeve of his unraveling sweater (FAIRY TALES, Mexico City, 1992 & Stockholm, 1998); and that of a man pushing a block of ice down the same hot streets until the ice melts away, PARADOX OF PRAXIS (SOMETIMES MAKING SOMETHING LEADS TO NOTHING), part one (Mexico, D.F., 1997). Finally, for RE-ENACTMENTS (Mexico City, 2000), Alÿs performed the same walk twice, starting in a Mexico City gun shop where he purchased a heavy automatic pistol. Proceeding through a congested commercial district, he openly carried the pistol with muzzle aimed toward the ground until one of the many, sometimes oblivious sometimes intimidated, people he passed by reported him and the police arrived, sirens screaming, to arrest him and bundle him into their car. At considerable risk to himself, and implied risk to others, Alÿs set off on the first walk without warning anyone. The second he repeated with police cooperation, but the sense of casual recklessness and unspecified menace heading toward a possibly abrupt *A Bout de Souffle (Breathless)* denouement with Alÿs in the Belmondo role is undiminished.

Each of Alÿs's disturbances in the normal traffic patterns of everyday life spans a portion of the city, most involve a process of accumulation or depletion, all are willful, deadpan, understated, and efficient with regard to their apparent aimlessness. And, whether documented in videos or photos, all are visually memorable. One of them, PARADOX OF PRAXIS, presages the Sisyphusian dynamics of WHEN FAITH MOVES MOUNTAINS. As a solo performance the former aligns the idea of futility with the frustrations of Beckett's existential clowns, but taken together with the latter and its "pointless" expenditure of human resources both may plausibly be viewed through the distorting prism of Georges Bataille's anti-capitalist logic of potlatch ritual and ecstatic, gratuitous waste. Or, as seems more satisfying, the slightly displaced hill may be read as a perversely conceived anti-monument to collective endeavor in a society without appropriate vocations or rewards for which the disappearing block of ice is the anti-sculptural equivalent in the realm of solitary endeavor.

Overall, Alÿs operates in the world by simultaneously drawing attention to and away from himself in order to focus on situations whose latent characteristics he brackets by presence and absence or underlines by his passage. In corresponding polarities between working assumptions and their contextual impact, THE COLLECTOR and MAGNETIC SHOES cast the artist in the role of a benign anarchist—a social particle for which we might borrow the physics-based nomenclature of "strange attractor." However, in RE-ENACTMENTS, Alÿs becomes that anarchic particle's sinister opposite, not so much a "strange repeller" but a potentially violent being who generates fear and draws to itself the force of official violence.

By now, of course, the graph proposed has been covered in points and loops, and lines and zigzagging rays that tend towards mobility or immobility and represent in various codes the artist himself, those he enlists to his purposeless purpose, or those whose curious behavior he observes from his shifting position as an unflappable, undeterrable odd-man-out. The analytic device suggested mimics the rule-bound conceits we have inherited from late formalism. A by-product of the attempt to reconcile prescribed models of the expanding field of sculpture with the actual diversification of sculptural practices epitomized by Alÿs's evolving body of performance work—is he an ambulatory monument or is he ain't?—the parameters set by "Baudelaire's Boardgame" are patently absurd. So too are the pseudo-scientific prototypes that inspired it.

Charming—like his faux-naif paintings—superficially capricious but also deftly disruptive and not infrequently saturnine Alÿs's art is absurd as well, but in a disciplined and revealing way. If you remove the diagram upon which his activities have been configured and resist the temptation to impose another one with better academic credentials, you can readily see that all along he has been overlapping premises and procedures while connecting the dots between the quotidian poetics of the supercharged urban environment—a sleeping dog, a broken window patched with plastic—and the social and cultural tensions that condition whatever freedom the Baudelairian "flaneur" or contemporary nomad still has. There may not be much, but within the tightening coordinates of "global" reality as well as within the rigidifying theoretical matrices of conceptually oriented practice, Alÿs has found room for maneuver.

FRANCIS ALŸS, MAGNETIC SHOES, 1994, 5th Havana Biennale, postcard / MAGNETISCHE SCHUHE, Postkarte.

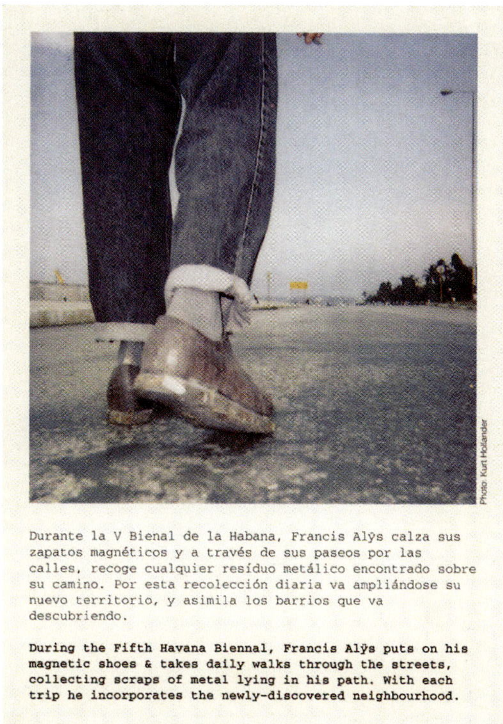

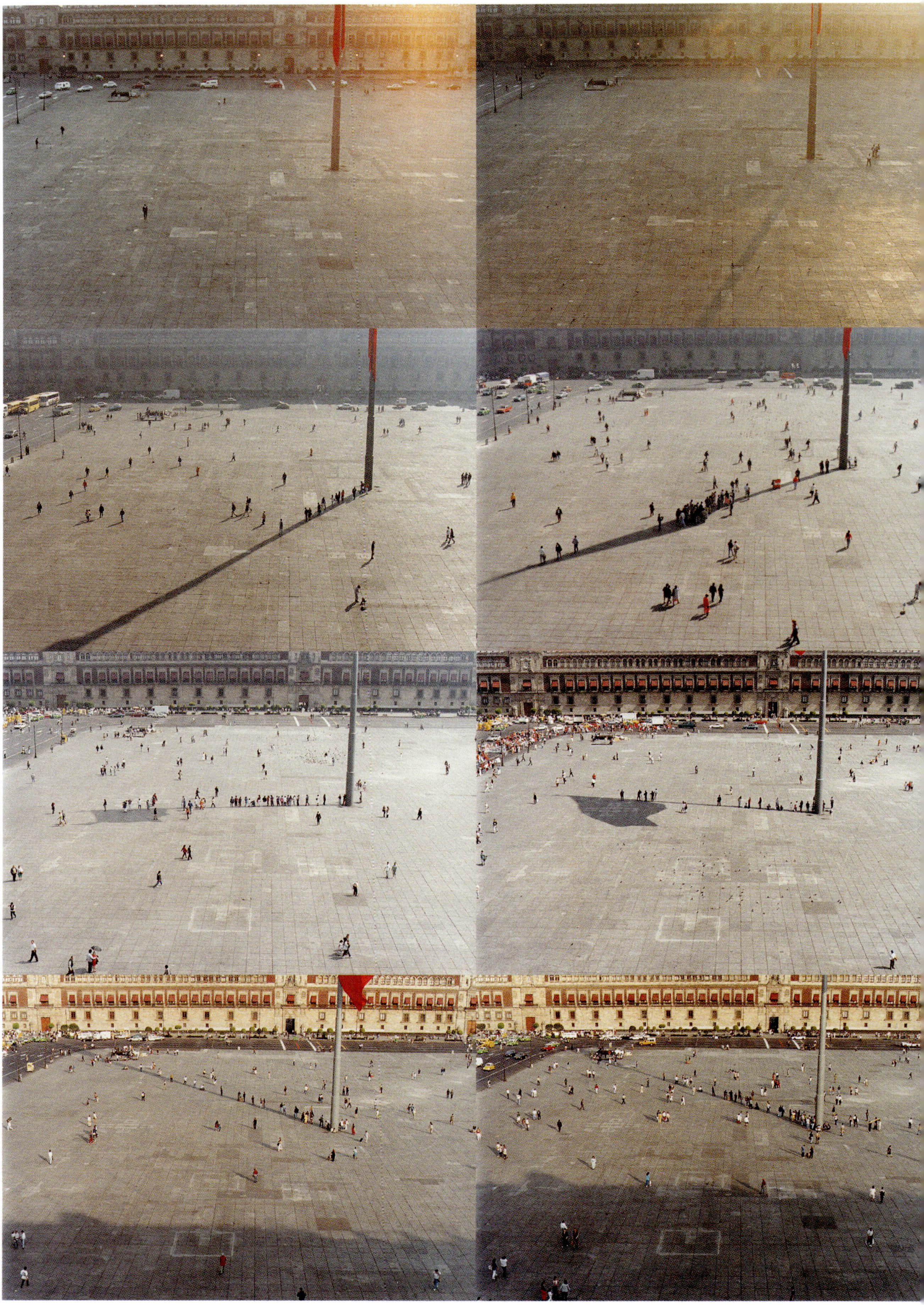

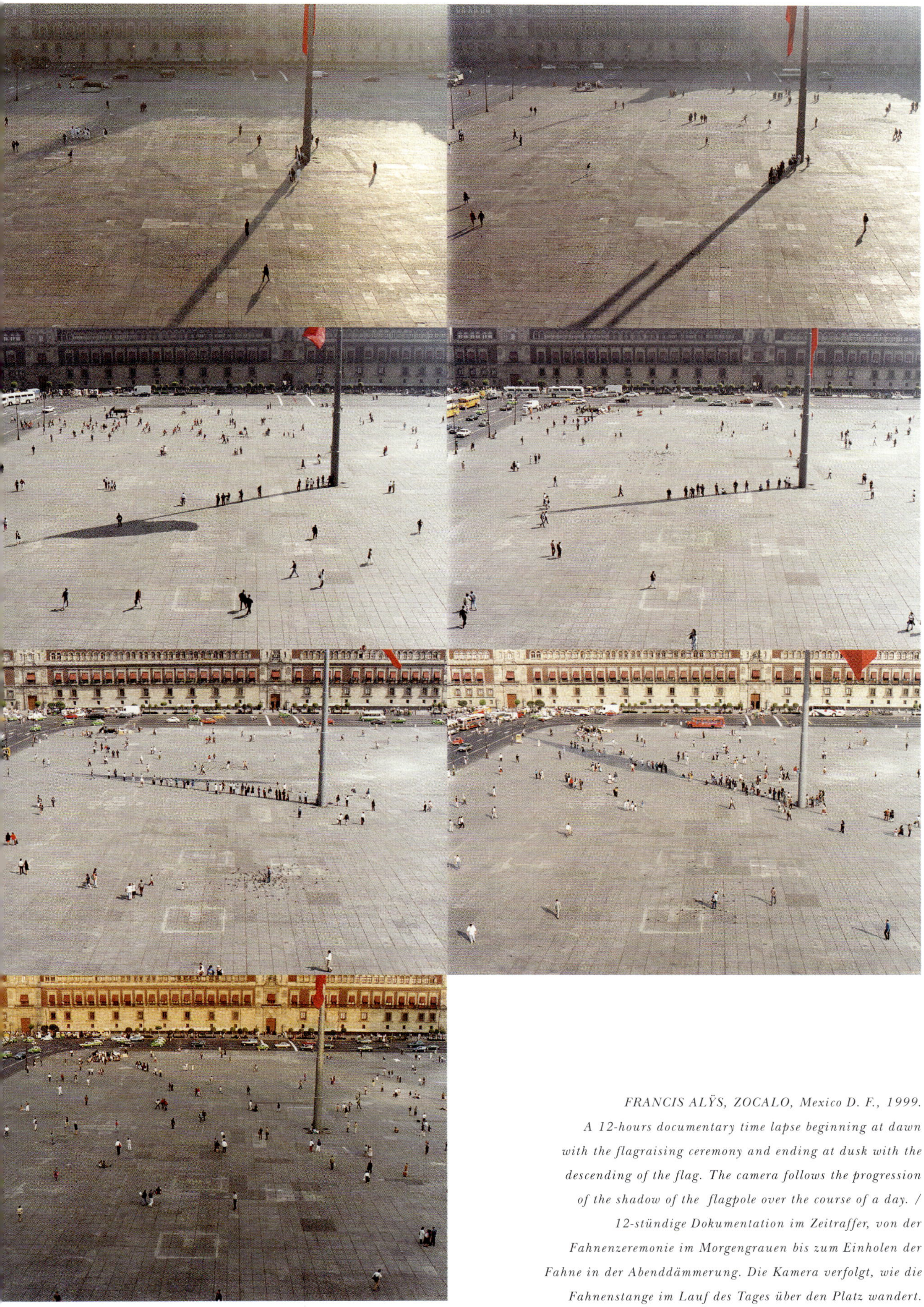

FRANCIS ALŸS, ZOCALO, Mexico D. F., 1999.
A 12-hours documentary time lapse beginning at dawn with the flagraising ceremony and ending at dusk with the descending of the flag. The camera follows the progression of the shadow of the flagpole over the course of a day. /
12-stündige Dokumentation im Zeitraffer, von der Fahnenzeremonie im Morgengrauen bis zum Einholen der Fahne in der Abenddämmerung. Die Kamera verfolgt, wie die Fahnenstange im Lauf des Tages über den Platz wandert.

ROBERT STORR

SELTSAMER

Zeichnen wir ein Diagramm und nennen wir die x-Achse Bewegung, die y-Achse Stillstand. Wählen wir nun zwei unterschiedliche Farben für Punkte zweierlei Grösse und geben wir in der Legende an, dass die Punkte der einen Farbe sich auf Gruppen beziehen, oder besser: auf Angehörige einer Gruppe in entsprechender Zahl, und die der anderen auf Einzelpersonen – obwohl in Wirklichkeit der Plural leicht irreführend ist, weil wir es stets mit ein und demselben Individuum zu tun haben werden, das von Fall zu Fall in unterschiedliche Handlungsabläufe verwickelt ist. Eingedenk der unsicheren Beziehung zwischen Zeichen und Bezeichnetem sowie der dialektischen Austauschbarkeit der jeweiligen Variablen werden wir als Nächstes das Diagramm «umklappen» und in gespiegelter Form darunter nachzeichnen. Die x-Achse des gespiegelten Diagramms versehen wir mit der Bezeichnung Nicht-Bewegung und die y-Achse mit der Bezeichnung Nicht-Stillstand um so die Tatsache zu unterstreichen, dass in zeitlich ablaufenden Situationen dem Stehen das Gehen und dem Gehen das Stehen immanent ist.

Wir werden dieses Diagramm den «Erweiterten Bereich der Skulptur» nennen – das heisst, wir würden es gerne, wäre dieser Begriff nicht bereits von einer anderen Richtung der poststrukturalistischen Kritik zum Schlagwort erhoben worden. Ganz im Geiste der neuesten Sichtweise in Dingen dieser Art könnten wir es auch «Debords Lust» oder «Beschreibung von *la dérive*» nennen, in Anerkennung des wichtigsten Theoretikers des Situationismus und des Mannes, der das Umherschweifen zur Kunstform erhoben hat – einer Kunstform, in der sich, um den derzeitigen Fachjargon zu bemühen, Horizontalität und Vertikalität in ihrer Reinform aufs Wunderbarste miteinander verbinden, nämlich in Gestalt des Bodens und der Person, die zu Fuss oder gegebenenfalls auf Händen und Knien über diesen Boden geht. Stattdessen aber werden wir unser Nonsensdiagramm «Baudelaires Brettspiel» nennen, zu Ehren des Schutzpatrons (beziehungsweise Schutzdämonen) der Grossstadtwanderer, dessen Sinn für die gegenseitige Durchdringung von Ephemerem und Wesentlichem, von Launenhaftem und Exaktem, von Grossartigem und Sonderbarem unserem Verständnis des sich ständig erweiternden Geflechts der modernen Kunst zugrunde liegt. Dieses Koordinatensystem, das über eine Wirklichkeit gelegt wurde, die eher durch ein Gewirr von Strassen und staubigen Wegen gekennzeichnet ist als durch das strenge, regelmässige Strassennetz utopischer Städteplaner, erlaubt es uns, aufgegliedert nach den oben angeführten Kategorien eine Reihe von Ereignissen einzuzeichnen.

So kann man mit den Zeichen für Gruppen die allmähliche Ansammlung einer Herde von Schafen graphisch darstellen, die in einem perfekten Oval um einen Fahnenmast in der Mitte eines weiten Platzes herumtrotten. Der Schauplatz ist, um genau zu sein, der Zócalo (Marktplatz) im Herzen von Mexico City, ungeachtet seiner «volkstümlichen» Seiten nicht unbedingt ein Ort, an dem man jemanden beim Choreographieren eines geometrisch strengen Hammelballetts anzutreffen erwartet. Der Schafhirt ist der aus Belgien gebürtige Künstler Francis Alÿs, Organisator jeder im Diagramm verzeichneten Ereignisabfolge und oft auch deren Protagonist.

Da die Zeit in LA MULTIPLICACIÓN DE LOS BORREGOS (Die Multiplikation der Schafe, Mexico, D.F., 1997) aus der Serie *Cuentos Patrióticos* (Patriotische Geschichten, Mexico, D.F., 1997), wie in allen ande-

---

ROBERT STORR ist Künstler, Kritiker, freier Kurator und Inhaber des Rosalie-Solow-Lehrstuhls für moderne Kunst an der New York University.

ATTRAKTOR

ren Fällen auch, ein wesentlicher Faktor ist, müssen wir unser System weiter ausfeilen und eine zusätzliche farbliche Codierung der Punkte vornehmen, um den zeitlich gestaffelten Eintritt der Schafe in diesen Ring zu erfassen. Zu diesem Zweck werden wir den Tonwert der Punkte je nachdem, wie lange sich die Schafe im Ring aufhalten, von dunkel nach hell abstufen. In ähnlicher Weise wäre die allmähliche Ansammlung von Menschen im länger werdenden Schatten des gleichen Fahnenmastes in ZÓCALO (1999) zu erfassen, einer weiteren Videoperformance-Arbeit aus der Serie der *Cuentos Patrióticos.* Hier ist die Handlung eher spontan als inszeniert: Auf dem weiten gepflasterten Platz reihen sich Menschen, die Schutz vor dem Licht der niedrig stehenden Sonne suchen, gewohnheitsmässig im schützenden Schatten dieses Wahrzeichens auf, an dem zuoberst eine riesige Fahne weht. Daher der unterschwellig spöttische Hinweis auf Patriotismus, da diese Bürger nicht stolz unter einem Symbol ihres Landes strammstehen, sondern sich vielmehr pragmatisch darunter aufstellen, um dem grellen Sonnenlicht zu entfliehen.

Zeichnen wir nun zusätzlich eine weitere lange Linie aus Hunderten von Punkten ein, die sich in einer schrumpfenden Halbmondform unregelmässig schlängeln. Die Punkte sind Menschen, die Sand schaufeln, während sie einen kahlen Hügel hinaufsteigen. Durch ihre vereinte Anstrengung wurde ein winziger Teil der Masse des Hügels um eine unmessbar kleine räumliche Masseinheit verlagert. CUANDO LA FE MUEVE MONTAÑAS (Wenn der Glaube Berge versetzt, Lima 2002) ist ein Kollektivprojekt, das die Zusammenarbeit in Spaten voll staubiger Erde misst. Es ist zugleich eine sinnlose Übung, die auf den Stellenwert der körperlichen Arbeit im Zusammenhang mit Erdarbeiten pocht. Wenn wir Kunstrichtungen und Stilarten in ihrer jeweiligen

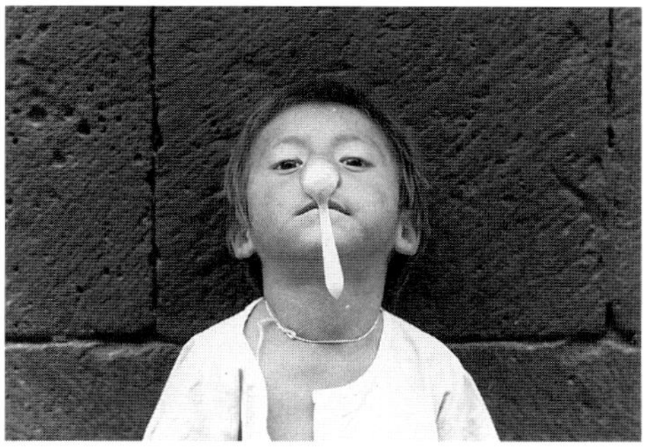

FRANCIS ALŸS, UNTITLED, Mexico D.F., 1991, photograph / Photographie.

kulturellen Eigenart betrachten, erinnern wir uns, dass im Nordamerika der 70er Jahre (und danach) der Faktor Arbeit im Wesentlichen unberücksichtigt blieb, ungeachtet der Faszination, die von den Bodenzeichnungen der Nazca und anderen präkolumbianischen Vorbildern ausging. Hinzu kommt, dass Alÿs' Projekt, obwohl von Freiwilligen – überwiegend Studenten – ausgeführt, an einem Ort realisiert wurde, wo aufgrund der chronisch hohen Arbeitslosigkeit Arbeit allzeit billig ist. So erhält das Unterfangen, neben seiner positiven kommunitaristischen Seite, durch seine ausgesprochene Sinnlosigkeit auch eine ausdrückliche wirtschaftliche und vieldeutig politische Dimension. Wo grosse Tempel einst von Massen errichtet wurden, lässt der unheimliche optische Zusammenhang zwischen dem Hügel und der Erinnerung an alte Pyramiden zudem beunruhigende Gedanken an Reiche der Vergangenheit und Gegenwart, an emsige – und beliebig austauschbare – Massen damals und heute aufkommen.

Schliesslich können wir, wenn wir unser Koordinatensystem auf ein modernes Umfeld aus mehr oder weniger regelmässigen Vertikalen und Horizontalen übertragen, den Weg eines religiös angehauchten Umzugs von Midtown Manhattan über den East River nach Queens nachzeichnen. Die teilnehmenden Anhänger des Kults sind Kunstliebhaber und Vertreter des Kunstbetriebs. Die Objekte ihrer Anbetung sind Kopien von Gemälden und Skulpturen von Picasso, Giacometti und Duchamp, während Kiki Smith, eine Hohepriesterin der zeitgenössischen Kunstszene, höchstpersönlich hoch oben auf einer von ihren Ministranten getragenen Sänfte auftritt. Zu den Klängen einer traditionellen, in Zeremonien dieser Art geübten Kapelle feierte THE MODERN PROCESSION (New York City 2002) den Umzug der sakralen Ikonen der Moderne von der Mutterkirche zu ihrem vorübergehenden Zuhause im Exil und zog ihn gleichzeitig durch den Kakao.

Wenn wir uns der zweiten Kategorie von Zeichen zuwenden, können wir uns zunächst den simpelsten Sachverhalt vornehmen, selbst wenn wir zur Stätte unseres ursprünglichen Studiums des Schafhirten und seiner Herde zurückkehren. Dieses Mal, wie in allen nachfolgenden Fällen, ist Alÿs, ob in einer Menschenmenge oder auf einer leeren Durchfahrtsstrasse, allein. In diesem Fall steht er oder vielmehr lehnt er sich gegen einen Zaun, flankiert von anderen Männern. Er ist gross gewachsen und bleich, während sie, im Grossen und Ganzen, kleiner und von dunklerer Hautfarbe sind. Vor ihnen stehen Werkzeugkästen, und von Hand beschriftete Pappschilder weisen auf ihre Fähigkeiten als Klempner oder Anstreicher hin. Der Schauplatz ist also ein «Markt» für Gelegenheitsarbeiter auf dem Zócalo neben der Nationalen Kathedrale und unweit anderer Gehsteigabschnitte, wo andere Männer Bildnisse von Commandante Zero (Subcommandante Marcos), dem Anführer des populären Zapatisten-Aufstandes in der südlichen Provinz Chiappas, sowie karikaturhafte Puppen des «vorausschauenden», notorisch korrupten und weithin verachteten ehemaligen Präsidenten Carlos Salinas de Gortari feilbieten. Vor Alÿs steht eine kleine Umhängetasche und ein Schild mit der Aufschrift *Turista*. Sie suchen Arbeit; ihn interessiert die Szenerie. So viel scheint zumindest sein Schild zu verstehen zu geben, nur dass er im Unterschied zum klassischen Typus des romantischen Reisenden von Richard Burton und T. E. Lawrence bis John Reed, der sich unter die «Eingeborenen» zu mischen und deren Lebensweise anzunehmen versuchte, sich selbst als Fremdkörper in die «pittoreske» Wirklichkeit seiner arbeitslosen Nebenmänner einreiht und sich damit effektiv zum Spiegelbild anderer Touristen macht, die sich selbst in den Sehenswürdigkeiten «einnisten», die zu besichtigen sie gekommen sind. Deren Müssiggang ist unbeteiligtes Geniessen, die Untätigkeit des Klempners und Anstreichers dagegen banges Warten, und Alÿs' Nichtstun hebt beides hervor. Der Punkt im Diagramm, der «stellvertretend» für TURISTA (Tourist, Mexico City 1996) steht, ist ein einzelner Fixpunkt, der aber innerhalb seiner Grenzen Wiederholung erheischt, um eine längere und quälende Dauer zu bezeichnen.

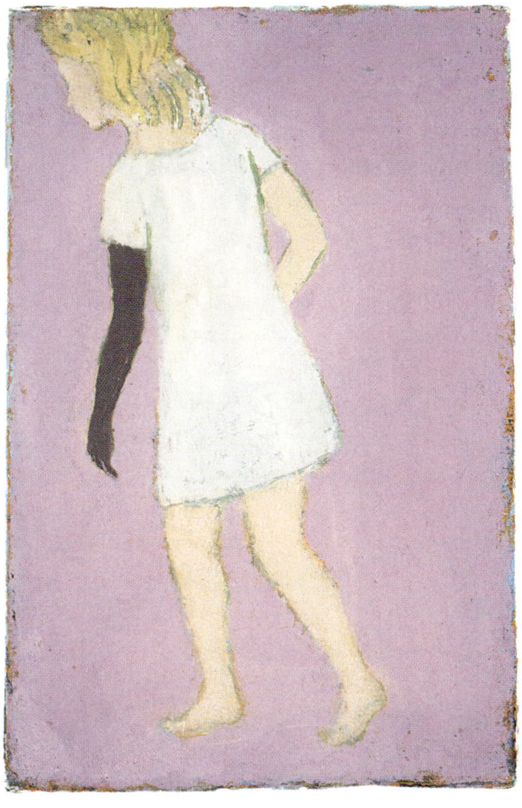

FRANCIS ALŸS, STUDY FOR "TWO SISTERS," 2001, diptych, part II, oil and encaustic on canvas on wood, 11 5/16 x 7 5/8 x 13/16" / STUDIE FÜR «ZWEI SCHWESTERN», Diptychon, Teil II, Öl und Enkaustik auf Leinwand auf Holz, 28,8 x 19,4 x 2,1 cm.

Die die Handlungen einer Einzelperson betreffenden Begebenheiten, die weiterhin ihrer Eintragung in dieses Diagramm harren, halten sich eher an die Achse der Bewegung als an die des Stillstandes. Zu ihnen zählen: der Weg eines Mannes, der eine Strasse entlanggeht und dabei ein kastenförmiges Blechmodell eines Hundes hinter sich her zieht, das Flaschenverschlüsse, Nägel und Metallschrott in seiner Nähe magnetisch aufsammelt (THE COLLECTOR, Mexico City 1991–92); der Weg eines Mannes, der mit magnetischen Schuhen eine Strasse entlangspaziert und dabei mehr oder weniger den gleichen Effekt erzielt (MAGNETIC SHOES, La Habana 1994); der Weg eines Mannes, der die Strasse entlanggeht mit einer Farbbüchse, aus der ein feines blaues Rinnsal träufelt (THE LEAK, São Paulo 1995); der Weg eines Mannes, der einen blauen Faden vom Ärmel seines ausfransenden Pullovers hinter sich her zieht (FAIRY TALES, Mexico City 1992 & Stockholm 1998); sowie der Weg eines Mannes, der einen Eisblock immer dieselben heissen Strassen entlangschiebt, bis das Eis wegschmilzt – in PARADOX OF PRAXIS (SOMETIMES MAKING SOMETHING LEADS TO NOTHING) / Paradox der Praxis (Manchmal führt es zu nichts, wenn man etwas macht), Teil I, Mexico, D.F., 1997. Schliesslich machte Alÿs für REENACTMENTS (Nachinszenierungen, Mexico City, 2000) zweimal denselben Spaziergang: Zunächst kaufte er in einem Waffengeschäft in Mexico City eine schwere Schnellfeuerwaffe, ging dann durch ein überfülltes Geschäftsviertel, wobei er die Waffe, den Lauf nach unten gerichtet, offen mit sich herumtrug, bis schliesslich einer der vielen, teils nichts bemerkenden, teils eingeschüchterten Passanten, die Polizei rief, die mit heulender Sirene eintraf, um ihn festzunehmen und in ihr Auto zu packen. Unter erheblicher Gefahr für seine eigene Person und indirekt auch für andere machte sich Alÿs das erste Mal ohne jede Vorwarnung auf den Weg. Beim zweiten Mal wiederholte er das Ganze unter Mitwirkung der Polizei, doch der Eindruck von Leichtsinn und dunkler Gefahr, die auf ein möglicherweise abruptes Ende à la *A Bout de Souffle (Ausser Atem)* mit Alÿs in der Rolle Belmondos zusteuert, ist unvermindert stark.

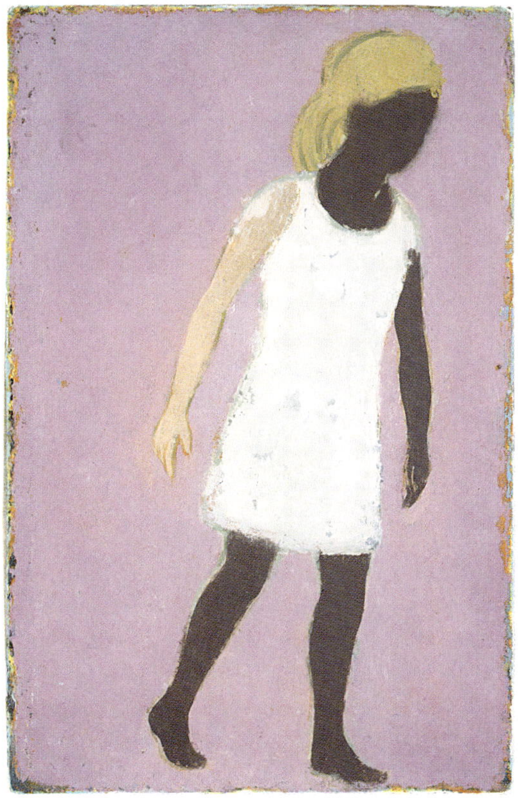

FRANCIS ALŸS, STUDY FOR "TWO SISTERS," 2001, diptych, part I / STUDIE FÜR «ZWEI SCHWESTERN», Diptychon, Teil I.

Die Aktionen, mit denen Alÿs die üblichen Verlaufsmuster des Alltags aufbricht, erstrecken sich jeweils über einen Teil der Stadt und es geht dabei meist um einen Vorgang der Anhäufung oder Verringerung. Sie sind immer vorsätzlich, durch Emotionslosigkeit und Understatement gekennzeichnet und in Anbetracht ihrer offenkundigen Ziellosigkeit überaus effizient. Und ob sie nun durch Videoaufnahmen oder Photos dokumentiert werden, die Bilder prägen sich tief ein. PARADOX OF PRAXIS, zum Beispiel, weist auf die sisyphusartige Dynamik von WHEN FAITH MOVES MOUNTAINS voraus. Während Erstere, eine Einpersonenperformance, für sich gesehen, die Vorstellung von Vergeblichkeit mit den Frustrationen von Samuel Becketts existenziellen Clowns verbindet, ist es im Zusammenhang mit Letzterer und ihrem «sinnlosen» Aufwand an menschlicher Arbeit durchaus vertretbar, beide durch die Zerrbrille von Georges Batailles antikapitalistischer Logik des Potlatschrituals und der ekstatischen, grundlosen Verschwendung zu betrachten. Man kann aber auch, was eher einleuchtet, die minimal verlagerte Düne als ein – von der Idee her perverses – Antidenkmal für das kollektive Streben in einer Gesellschaft ohne geeignete Beschäftigung oder angemessene Löhne verstehen, für die der wegschmelzende Eisblock das antiskulpturale Äquivalent im Bereich des individuellen Strebens ist.

Insgesamt betätigt sich Alÿs in der Welt, indem er die Aufmerksamkeit gleichzeitig auf sich zieht und von sich ablenkt, um Situationen in den Blickpunkt zu rücken, deren latente Besonderheiten er durch An- und Abwesenheit in Klammern setzt oder durch sein Hindurchgehen unterstreicht. Entsprechend ist das Spannungsfeld zwischen Arbeitshypothese und kontextueller Wirkung, wenn der Künstler in THE COLLECTOR und MAGNETIC SHOES in die Rolle eines gutmütigen Anarchisten schlüpft: eines sozialen Elements, für dessen Klassifizierung man den physikalischen Terminus des «seltsamen Attraktors» oder Anziehungspunktes beiziehen könnte. In RE-ENACTMENTS jedoch wird Alÿs zum finsteren Widerpart jenes anarchischen Elements, weniger zu einem «seltsamen Abstossungspunkt» als vielmehr zu einem potenziell gewalttätigen Wesen, das Angst erzeugt und die Gewalt der Hüter des Gesetzes auf sich zieht.

Mittlerweile ist das vorgeschlagene Diagramm natürlich überzogen mit Punkten und Schleifen, Linien und zickzackförmigen Strahlen, die zu Beweglichkeit oder Unbeweglichkeit neigen und in jeweils unterschiedlichen Codes stellvertretend für den Künstler selbst oder für jene stehen, die er für seine zwecklosen Zwecke rekrutiert, beziehungsweise für die, deren seltsames Verhalten er aus der immer wieder wechselnden Warte eines unerschütterlichen, unverdrossenen Aussenseiters beobachtet. Das vorgeschlagene analytische Hilfsmittel imitiert die regelgebundenen Vorstellungen, die wir vom späten Formalismus geerbt haben. Die Parameter von «Baudelaires Brettspiel» – ein Nebenprodukt des Versuchs die vorgegebenen Modelle eines erweiterten Skulpturbegriffs in Einklang zu bringen mit der tatsächlichen Diversifizierung der bildhauerischen Praxis, für welche das Werk von Alÿs das beste Beispiel liefert (ist er nun ein wandelndes Denkmal oder nicht?) – sind offenkundig absurd. Dasselbe gilt für die pseudowissenschaftlichen Vorbilder, die den Anstoss dazu gaben.

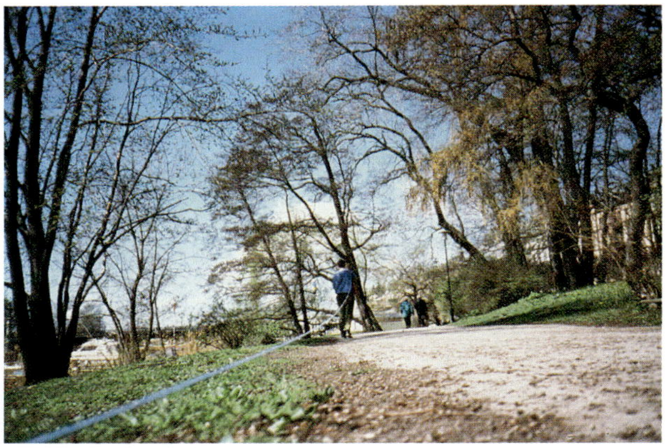

FRANCIS ALŸS, FAIRY TALES, Stockholm, 1998 / MÄRCHEN.

Die Kunst des Francis Alÿs ist bezaubernd – wie seine sich naiv gebenden Gemälde –, auf den ersten Blick kapriziös, aber auch raffiniert verstörend und nicht selten finster; sie ist auch absurd, allerdings auf eine disziplinierte und aufschlussreiche Art. Rückt man das Diagramm, in dem seine Aktivitäten aufgezeichnet sind, etwas weiter weg und widersteht der Versuchung, ein anderes, wissenschaftlich besser abgesichertes darüber zu stülpen, so wird man unschwer erkennen, dass Alÿs immer schon zuliess, dass sich Prämissen und Prozeduren überlappten, während er seine Verbindungslinien schlug, von den poetischen Fixpunkten des Alltags in der überbordenden Grossstadt – ein schlafender Hund, ein mit Plastik notdürftig abgedecktes, zerbrochenes Fenster – zu den sozialen und kulturellen Spannungen, welche die Freiräume bestimmen, die dem Baudelaireschen Flaneur oder modernen Nomaden noch geblieben sind. Viel mag davon nicht übrig sein, aber Francis Alÿs hat zwischen den immer enger geschnürten Koordinaten der «globalen» Wirklichkeit und den zunehmend erstarrenden theoretischen Schablonen der konzeptuell ausgerichteten Kunst seinen Spielraum gefunden.

(Übersetzung: Bram Opstelten)

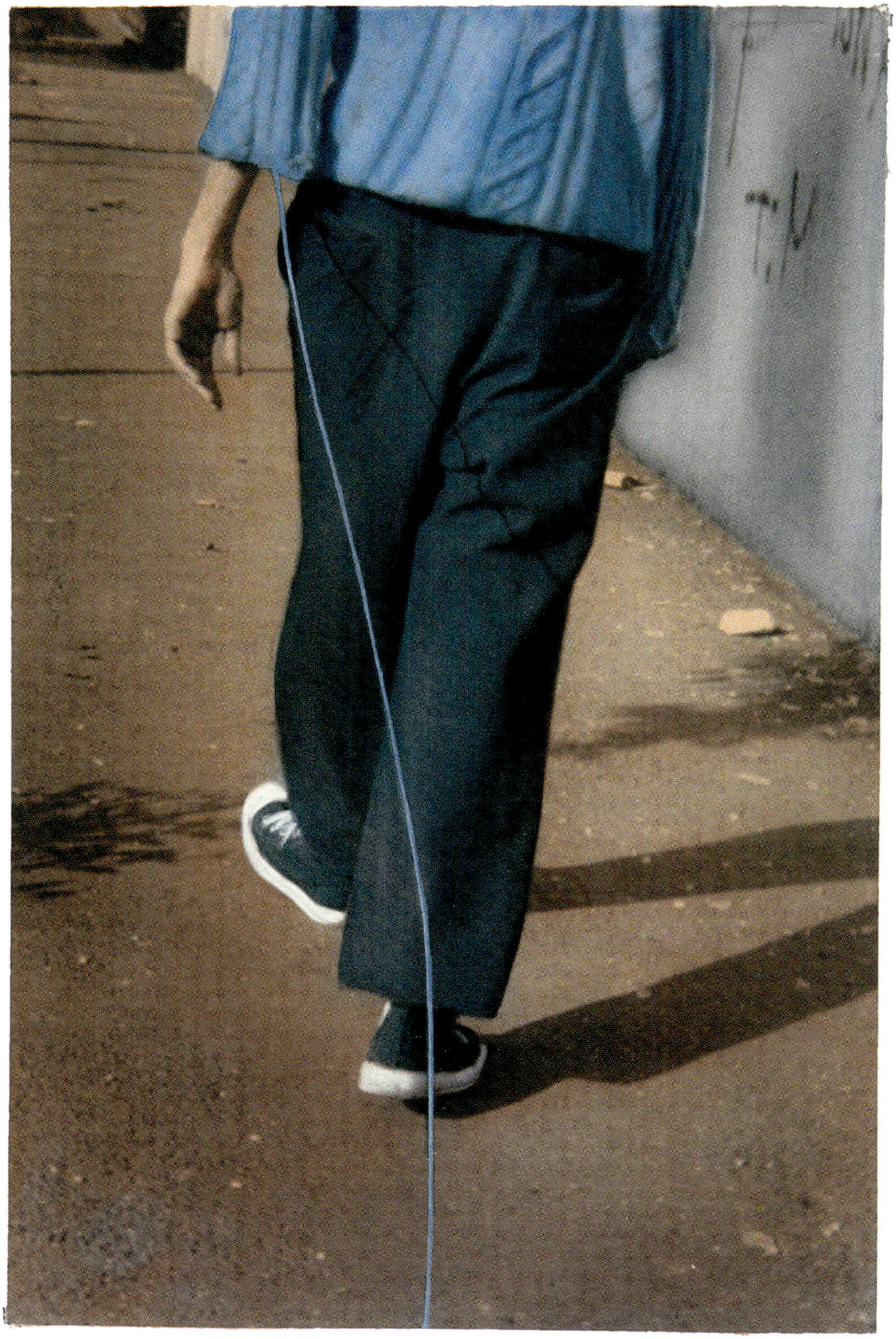

FRANCIS ALŸS, FAIRY TALES, Mexico D.F., 1992, photo document / MÄRCHEN, Photodokument.

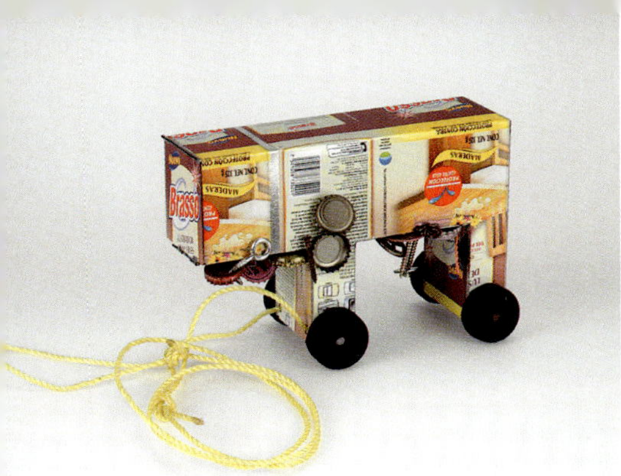

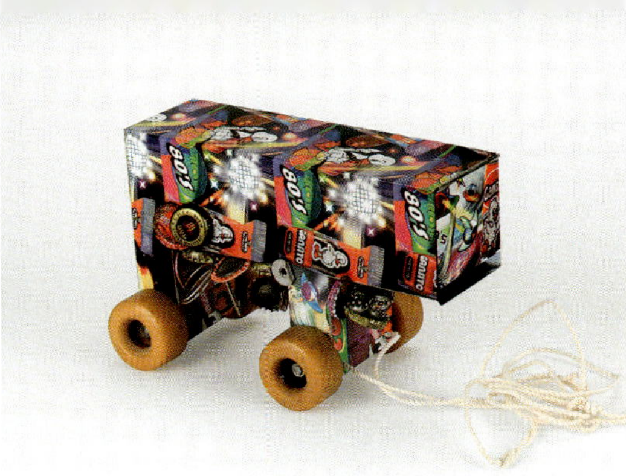

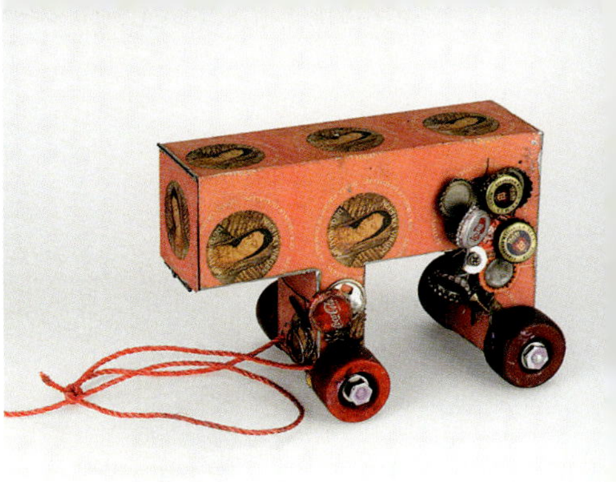

EDITION FOR PARKETT **FRANCIS ALŸS**

GHETTO COLLECTOR, 2003

Tin, magnets, plastic string, rubber wheels, 25 design variations, ca. 6 1/2 x 9 x 5".
Edition of 99, signed and numbered.

Blech, Magnete, Plastikschnur, Gummiräder, 25 Design-Variationen, ca. 16,5 x 23 x 12,5 cm.
Auflage: 99, signiert und nummeriert.

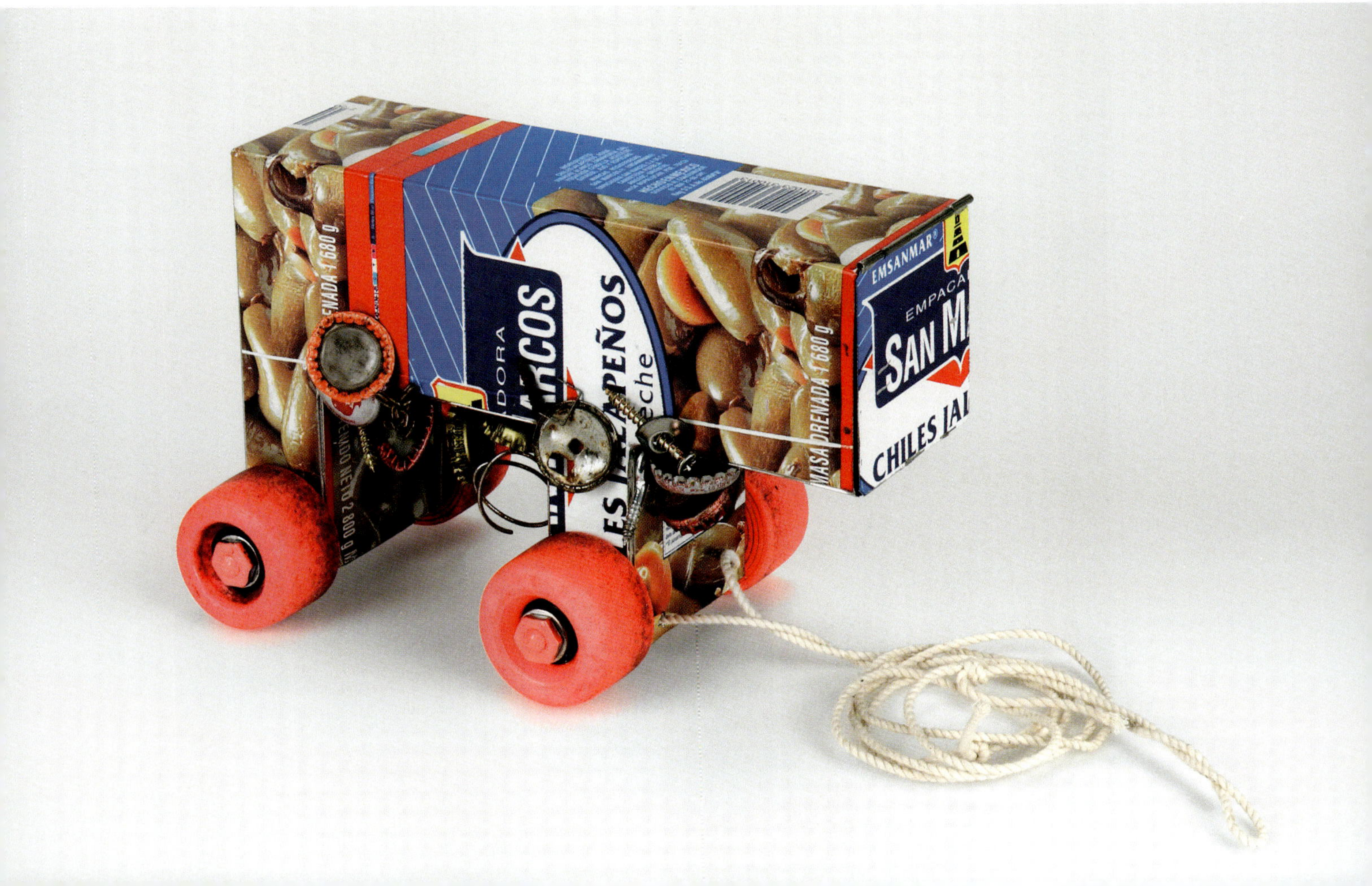

(PHOTOS: MANCIA/BODMER, FBM STUDIO, ZÜRICH)

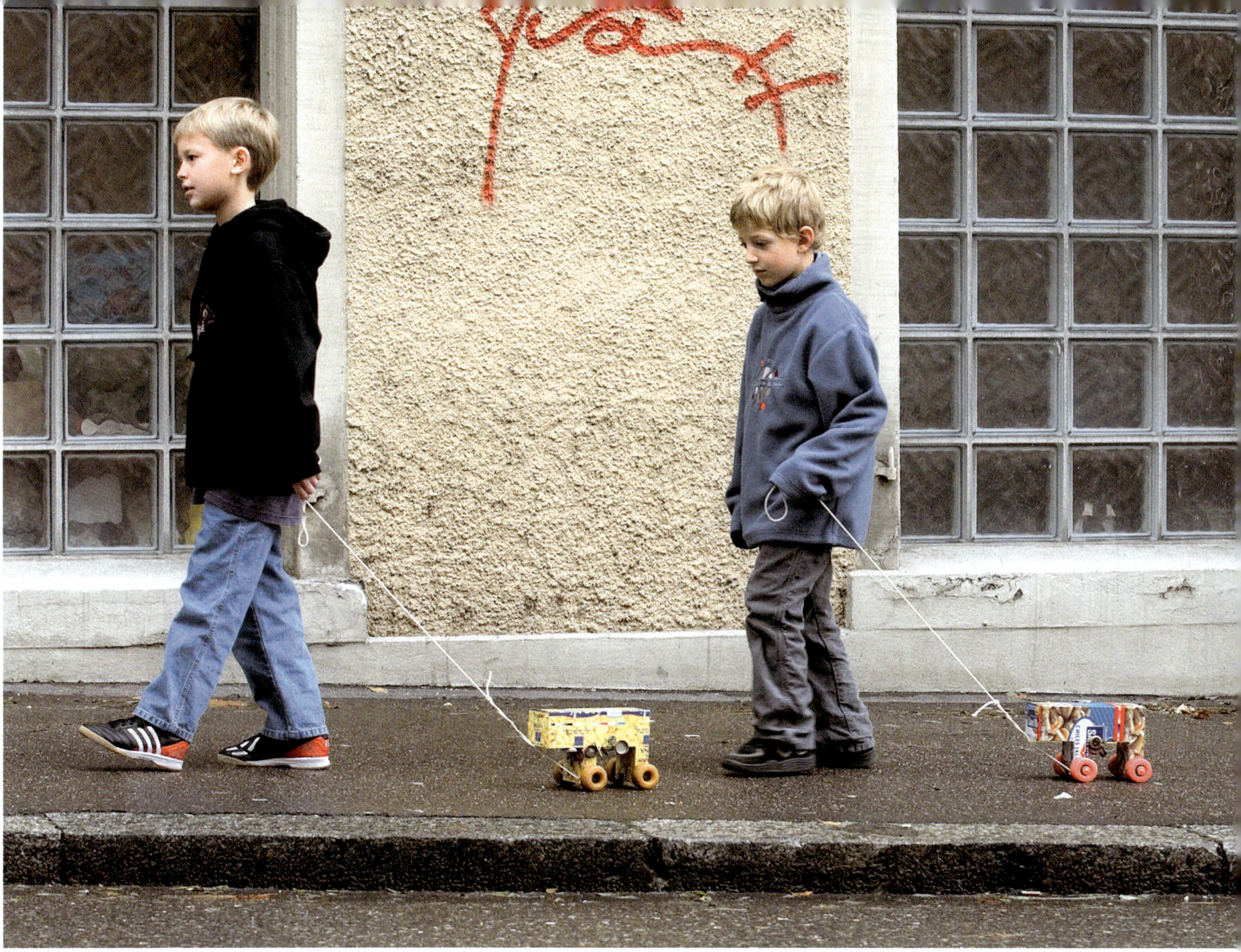

THE COLLECTOR (Mexico City, 1991–1992) ...

... is a toy on rubber wheels made of tin and stuffed with magnets: "For an indeterminate period of time, the magnetized collector takes a daily walk through the streets and gradually builds up a coat made of any metallic residue lying in its path." This urban toy was conceived in 1991 to be mass commercialized, invading the streets of Latin American metropolises. For Parkett, Francis Alÿs revisited the original concept by producing a limited edition. It is 30 percent smaller than the original.

... ist ein mit Magneten gefülltes Blechspielzeug auf Gummirädern: «Für unbestimmte Zeit wird der magnetische Sammler täglich durch die Strassen spazieren geführt und legt sich dabei allmählich einen Mantel aus Metallabfällen zu.» Die Idee zu dem urbanen Spielzeug hatte Alÿs 1991, es sollte in Massenproduktion gehen und die Strassen der lateinamerikanischen Metropolen erobern. Für Parkett hat der Künstler die Idee wieder aufgegriffen und eine limitierte Edition geschaffen. Diese Version ist 30 Prozent kleiner als das Original.

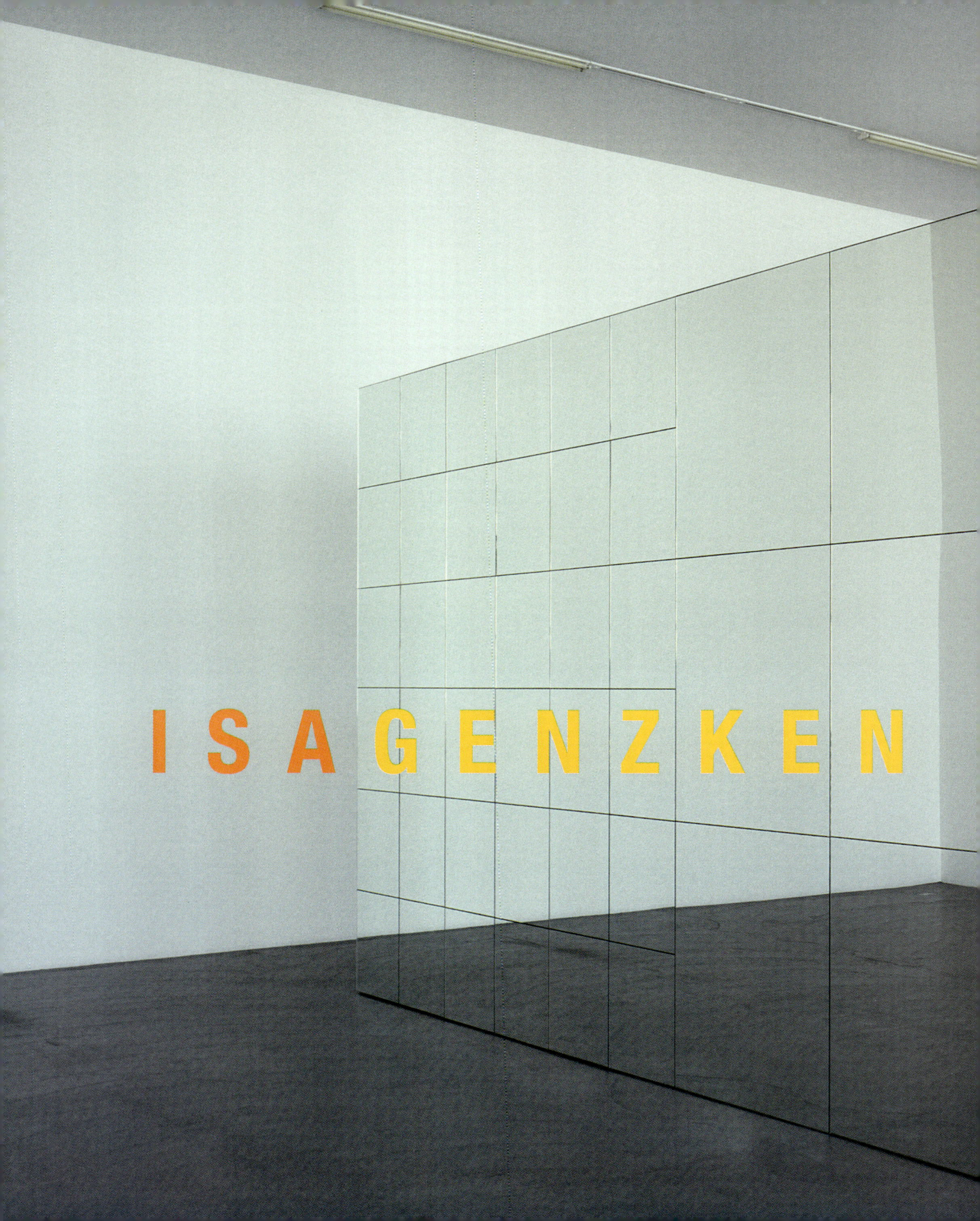

ISA GENZKEN

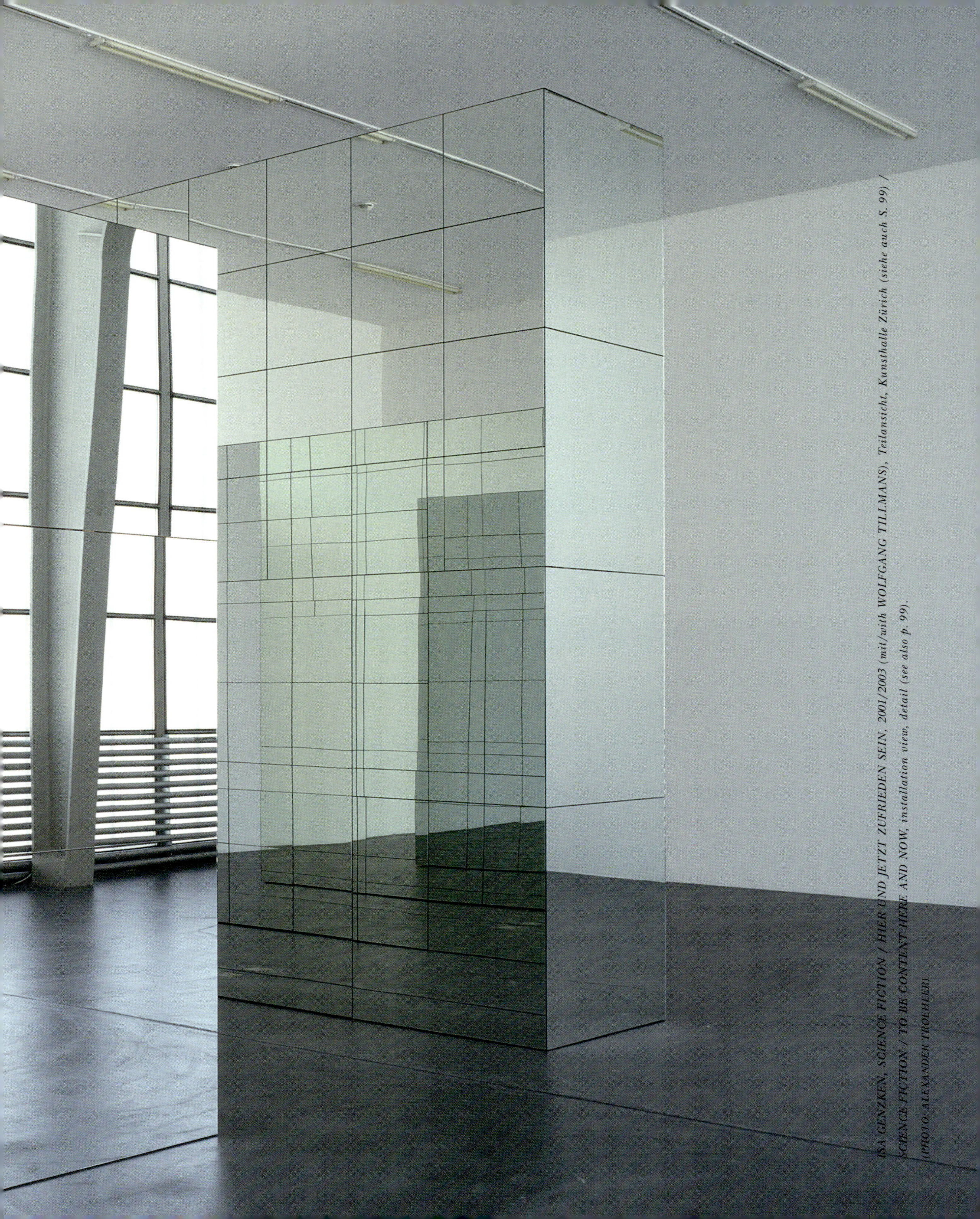

ISA GENZKEN, SCIENCE FICTION / HIER UND JETZT ZUFRIEDEN SEIN, 2001/2003 (*mit/with* WOLFGANG TILLMANS), *Teilansicht, Kunsthalle Zürich (siehe auch S. 99)* / SCIENCE FICTION / TO BE CONTENT HERE AND NOW, *installation view, detail (see also p. 99).*

(PHOTO: ALEXANDER TROEHLER)

DREI DEKADEN, eine Rekonstruktion

JÖRG HEISER

In zahllosen Romanen und Filmen fällt eine Person ins Koma und erwacht nach Jahrzehnten in einer veränderten Welt. Stellen wir uns vor, diese Person wäre nicht aus Fleisch und Blut, sondern der abstrakte «Betrachter» der Kunstkritik. Jener Pappkamerad mit Augenpaar (und bei Bedarf weiteren Sinnesorganen) hätte Ende der 70er Jahre Isa Genzkens erste grosse Werkphase gesehen: extrem lang gestreckte, stereometrische, horizontal am Boden aufruhende Objekte, am Computer berechnet und perfekt in farbig lackiertem Holz gefertigt. Unmittelbar danach wäre der Betrachter in einen tiefen Schlaf versunken, um 2003 inmitten einer Gruppe von über den Raum verteilten schlanken weissen Sockeln aufzuwachen. Auf diesen ruhen, wie Tabletts, spiegelnde rechteckige Platten, auf denen sich wilde Szenen aus wüsten Materialmischungen abspielen: Spielzeugsoldaten, die über silbern besprühte Ruinen aus Sneakers kriechen oder sich hinter Kindergummistiefeln verschanzen, Superhelden, die zwischen Dünen aus Sonnenblumenkernen umherirren oder wie Fliegen in gläserne Kelche zu fallen drohen, Plastiktiere, die an Felsen aus wie verschimmelt grün-silbern gänzendem Brot weiden, Kampfroboter, verharrend vor abgebrochenen Gläsern und Vasen und von Farbspritzern übersäten spiegelnden Flächen, die wie Kriegsfassaden über ihnen aufragen. All das zusammengefügt zu durchtobten szenischen Modellen auf ungefährer Augenhöhe, Miniatur-Panoramen von politischen Kämpfen und ästhetischen Konkurrenzen in Theaterblutrot, Tarnfarbengrün und Technologiesilber.

«Wie kann es sein», hätte unser abstrakter Betrachter sich wohl gefragt, «dass diese Arbeiten von der gleichen Künstlerin stammen?» Doch was rein formalistisch von damals und jetzt her betrachtet so disparat in schreienden Gegensätzen erscheint, ist zwingend verknüpft. Und das nicht nur biographisch, sondern zyklisch ineinander greifend im Werk selbst. Es geht nicht nur um einen roten Faden, der sich notfalls immer spinnen lässt. Es geht ums Ganze.

JÖRG HEISER ist Redaktor der Kunstzeitschrift *Frieze* und lebt in Berlin.

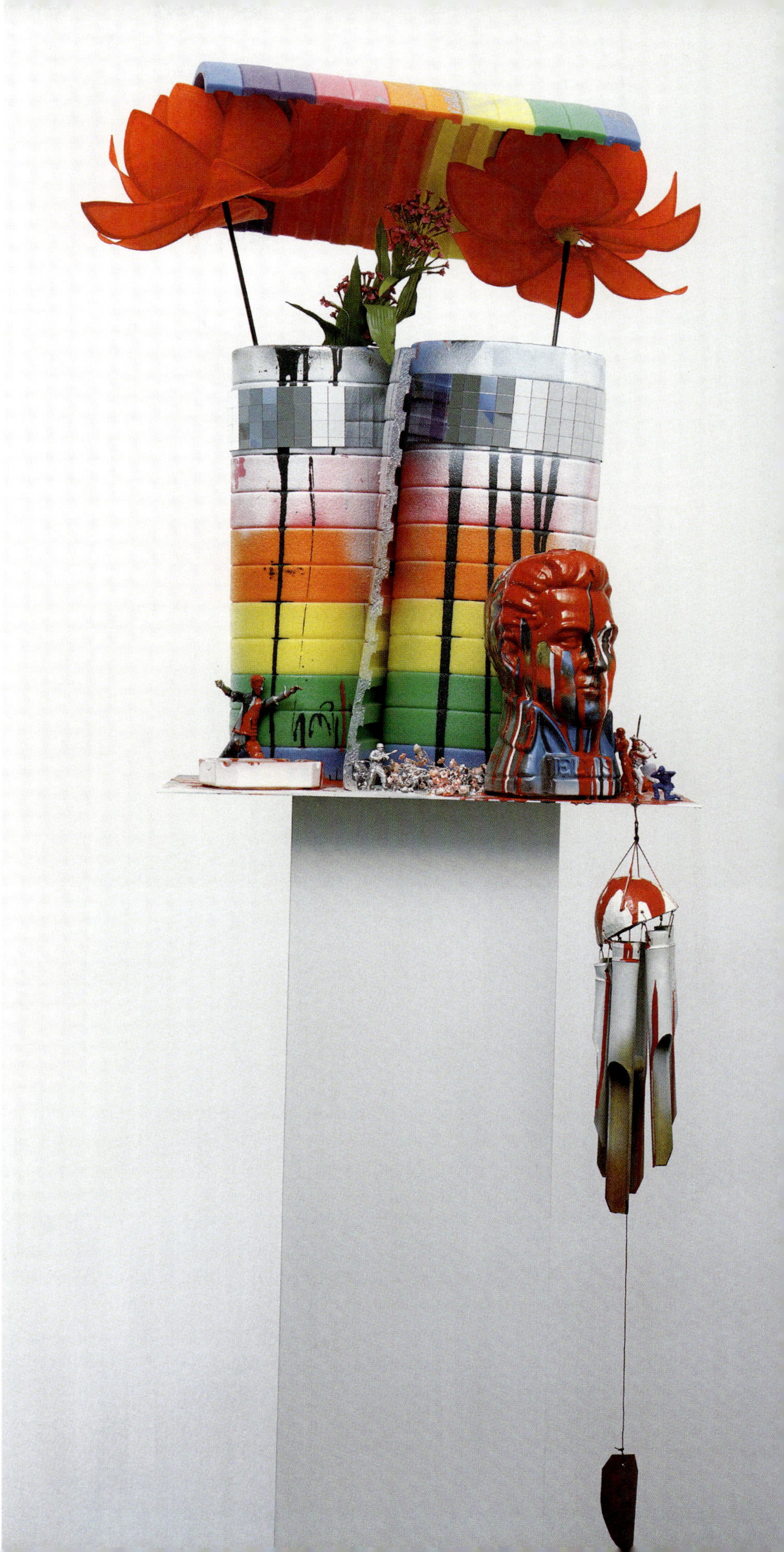

ISA GENZKEN, EMPIRE/VAMPIRE X, 2003,
verschiedene Materialien, Holzsockel.
Aluminiumplatte, 219 x 60 x 45 cm /
mixed media, wooden stand, aluminum panel,
$86\frac{1}{4}$ x $23\frac{5}{8}$ x $17\frac{11}{16}$".

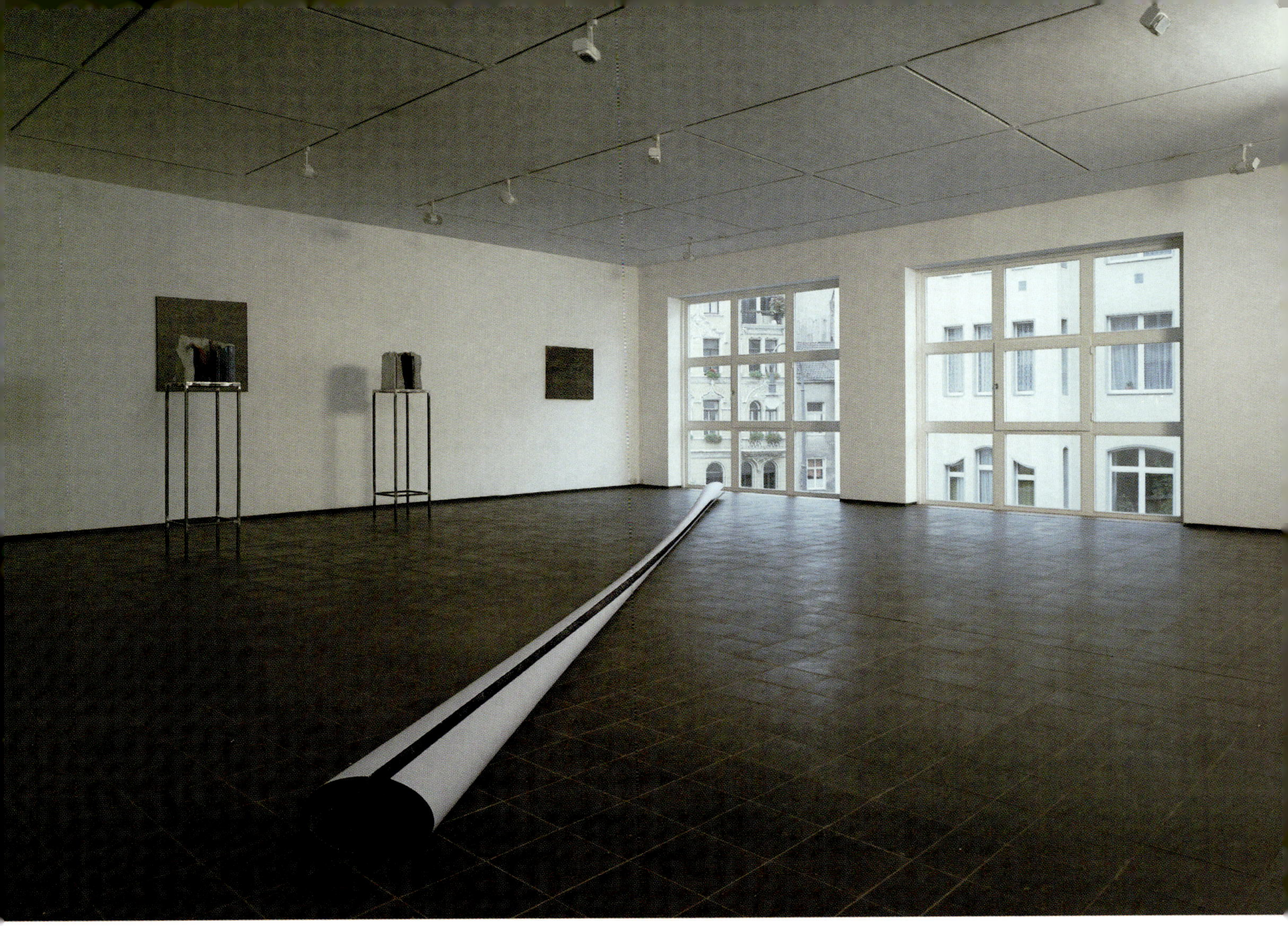

ISA GENZKEN, GRAUSCHWARZES HYPERBOLO «MBB», 1981, Epoxidharz, Länge 1000 cm, Installation in der Galerie Daniel Buchholz, Köln, 1989 / GRAY-BLACK HYPERBOLO "MBB," epoxy resin, length 32 10/12', installation view.

Die Verwunderung unseres abstrakten Betrachters ist verständlich. Die Ellipsoide und Hyperbolos konnte man mit Verrenkungen noch in die Nachfolge der Minimal-Art stellen. Liest man Texte von Donald Judd («Specific Objects», 1965) und Robert Morris («Notes on Sculpture», 1966) als Gospel einer Glaubensrichtung (wie es nicht wenige getan haben), begehen Genzkens Arbeiten von 2003 sämtliche Todsünden. Es werden zwar industriell gefertigte Teile verwendet, sie ordnen sich aber nicht zu einem geschlossenen Volumen. Die Arbeiten sind komponiert, sie bilden keine einheitliche Gestalt im Sinne eines eindeutigen Figur-Grund-Verhältnisses. Sie arbeiten mit gestischem Farbauftrag auf der Oberfläche der Skulptur; sie erzeugen bildlich-räumliche Illusionseffekte. Sie geizen nicht mit Anspielung und Allegorie. Schliesslich zeigen sie sich auch noch frech auf dem Fundament des überkommenen Skulpturbegriffs, dem Sockel. Unser abstrakter Betrachter könnte meinen, dass es Isa Genzken um willkürliche Verwerfung dessen geht, wofür auch ihre frühe Arbeit einmal einstand.

Dem erwachten Koma-Patienten muss man bekanntlich die Wahrheit schonend beibringen. Beginnen wir bei der Annahme, die Ellipsoide und Hyperbolos der 70er Jahre liessen die Minimal-Art intakt. Es sind tatsächlich uniform geschlossene Volumen von einheitlicher Gestalt, theoretisch in einem Blick erfassbar. Doch schon die Schwierigkeit, sie zu photographieren – bei frontaler Perspektive drohen sie im Bild zu verschwinden –, offenbart, dass sie diesen Aspekt wörtlich zerdehnen. Durch die extreme stereometrische Streckung in der Horizontalen – die sich gleichwohl nicht ins Flächige entspannt wie bei Carl Andre – wird die Gestalt extrem unter Druck gesetzt. Die Ellipsoide wirken wie Hybride aus Speeren und Rennbooten, die Hyperbolos erinnern an Rohre oder Pfeifen, die wie von einem Ansaugvakuum in der Mitte zusammengezogen sind. In beiden scheint die Energie physischer Bewegung starr gespeichert. Sie ducken sich an den unteren Rand des Sichtfelds eines Gehenden wie Katzen vor dem Sprung. Wobei all dies figürlich-konkrete Assoziationen sind, die dem orthodoxen Minimal-Diskurs längst zu weit gehen würden: Wie Isa Genzken sich beim Atelierbesuch erinnert, wurde seinerzeit mitunter «ermahnt», derlei Vergleiche zu vermeiden, als gehe es um Benimmregeln.

Die Energie, die in den Skulpturen gespeichert scheint, ist tatsächlich in sie eingegangen in vielen Stunden schwieriger Herstellung aus dem «lebenden» Material Holz. Sie widersprechen so der uniform industriellen Anmutung minimalistischer Objekte (Robert Morris etwa gab Holz als «arbeitendes» Material auf, sobald er ab 1965 mit weiss eingebranntem Email auf Stahl ein industriell makelloses Finish erreichen konnte). Die Ellipsoide und Hyperbolos führen die Logik geschlossener, geometrisch beschreibbarer Volumen mit der Unnachgiebigkeit eines Crashtests an ihre Grenze. Und doch bersten sie nicht. Es gibt Hyperbolos (DIANA, 1983, MÄRZ, 1985), die aufrecht stehen und wie von einem präzisen Blitz in zwei passend-unpassende Teile gespalten sind, so wie Paare mit ihren euphorisierenden Anziehungs- und tragischen Abstossungseffekten (auch das nach minimalistischer Orthodoxie eine schauerliche Bedeutungsebene). Aber nie geht es um die Verabschiedung aller geschlossenen Gestalt ins heterogen Biomorphe, in «Anti-Form». Die Skulpturen hätten sich sonst vom Minimal-Diskurs aus gesehen entsorgen lassen können nach dem Motto: andere Baustelle. Sie wären aus ihrer Verantwortung entlassen gewesen, zugleich Einwand und Entwurf zum Bildhauerischen auf dem jeweils reflektiertesten Stand der Zeit zu sein.

Es musste also einen anderen Weg geben, nach dem Speichern von Bewegung im Geschlossenen die Energie der Bewegung selbst freizusetzen. Die Hi-Fi-Werbeanzeigen-Photos (1979), die Photos von Frauenohren (OHR, 1980) und der WELTEMPFÄNGER (1982) bilden in diesem Moment eine Triade: Sie finden das Skulpturale im Offenen, im Äther von Sendung und Empfang, in Empfindlichkeiten und Feinjustierungen. Hi-Fi-Geräte sind das Nächste, was die säkularisierte Wohnwelt zum Skulpturalen kennt (TV als Kamin, Stereoanlage als Altar). Das Ohr kommt als Sinnesorgan moderner Skulptur am nächsten: Es gibt im Unterschied zur Nase mehr als eins davon, und im Gegensatz zu den Augen ragt es hervor und lässt sich nicht schliessen. Es wirkt intim und bleibt doch anonym – Genzken photographierte Ohren anonymer Passantinnen in New York. Dass es Frauenohren sind, lässt sich so als Warnung an männerdominierte Bildhauerei verstehen: Wir flüstern uns zu, Netzwerke entstehen. Der WELTEMPFÄNGER als Readymade verbindet die Motive von Hi-Fi und Ohr zum utopischen Versprechen. Mit ihm kommt der Sockel ins Werk, denn er ist nun nicht bloss traditionelles Instrument der Abgrenzung von Kunst und Raum, sondern wird Teil der Arbeit selbst: Denn ist der WELTEMPFÄNGER nicht plötzlich ein wahrnehmender Kopf auf einem Sockel-Körper? Es geht nicht um anthropomorphes Stellvertreten, sondern um eine vorsätzliche Verwechslung: Dem WELTEMPFÄNGER als Kopf kommen plötzlich selbst Eigenschaften der «Beseelung», des Psychomorphen zu.

Umgekehrt werden Menschen wie Skulpturen behandelt: Das gilt für die Ohren wie für die Röntgenphotos, die Genzken zu Anfang der 80er Jahre von ihrem eigenen Kopf machte. Das geschlossene Volumen des Schädels erscheint offen, von seiner «Beseeltheit» (um die wir natürlich weiterhin wissen) abstrahiert und zugleich beinahe knirschend physisch konkret. Es ist, als kehre die prämoderne

Trepanation – die physische «Anbohrung» des Kopfes zum Entweichenlassen böser Geister – zurück als allegorische Technik für ein Gegeneinanderhalten von Skulptur und Körper. Das 83er SELBSTPORTRÄT in Ton – eben ein solches Kopf-Volumen mit seltsam verzogenen und schiefen Öffnungen – geht einer Serie von rohen Arbeiten in Gips voraus (1984–1985), die sich zunehmend zu architektonischen Motiven verfestigen. Die Materialien klassischer Plastik können zurückkehren, weil genau einer der Gründe, aus denen sie verworfen wurden, wieder nach ihnen verlangt: Der Vorwurf des Kunstgewerblichen, den industriell geplante und gefertigte Skulptur gegenüber «einfacheren» Techniken implizierte, ist längst auf diese selbst zurückgefallen. Erstarrt im Administrativen des Herstellungsprozesses muss sie wörtlich wieder aufgebrochen werden. Das krude, vom Zufall mitbestimmte «Finish» erzeugt nun tatsächlich das «Bersten» des geschlossenen Volumens. MEIN GEHIRN (1984) – ein kruder Klumpen mit einem einzeln sich keck emporreckenden Draht – ist so das exakte Gegenstück zu den erwähnten Röntgenphotos des Kopfes.

Die gipsernen Bau-Fragmente führen direkt zu den Beton-Arbeiten (1986–1991): Wie hohle Zähne, die nach Goldfüllung verlangen, umreissen sie mit zwei, drei Wänden den leeren Raum, den es zu beleben gilt. Die grobe Fertigung in Beton besetzt die Lücke zwischen «altmodischem» Gips und industriell gefertigten Flächen. Die stelzenhaften Stahlrohrgestelle weisen Richtung Vitrine und Architekturmodell, ohne die Augenhöhe aufzugeben. So sind es Modelle wie Bauruinen, in denen Zukunftsentwurf und morbides Überbleibsel, Gewalt und Verletzlichkeit vexieren. Ihre halb geöffnete Struktur wird in den FENSTERN (1991–1994, erst aus Beton, später Epoxydharz), die wie Paravents frei mit angewinkeltem Scharnier aufgestellt sind, noch einmal emphatisch überboten. In den Vierkant-Säulen (ab 1998), die teils auf Namen von Freunden der Künstlerin «getauft» sind, kehrt zwar das geschlossene Volumen zurück. Aber es ist in die Länge gestreckt wie ein anorektischer Wolkenkratzer. Jedes Albert-Speer-hafte Pathos des Vertikalen (teils sind die Arbeiten über drei Meter hoch) wird aber sofort unterbunden durch kassettenartige Unterteilungen der Oberfläche in Holz, Aluminium, Glas, Photographien und so weiter, die wie affektive Besetzungen und zugeschriebene individuelle Eigenschaften funktionieren. Auch hier geht also die «Verwechslung» von Skulpturen und Menschen wieder über die offensichtlich anthropomorphen Parallelen von Körpern und Gebäuden hinaus.

Die frühen Ellipsoide und Hyperbolos haben quasi die Funktion von Batterien, aus denen sich die Energie der Arbeit bis heute aufbaut. Freigesetzt in der eingangs beschriebenen Serie *Empire Vampire* (2003), wird aus erstarrten Modellen ein szenisches Panorama. Die Rede vom «Film im Kopf» wird wörtlich im Splattereffekt «aufgeplatzten» Innenlebens, das auf einem Sockel als Körper ruht. Dabei geht es nicht um Bricolage des Vorgefundenen, sondern um skulpturale Ökonomie der Mittel: Warum mühsam Spielzeugsoldaten anfertigen, wenn die Firma Revell dieses Problem schon «bildhauerisch gelöst» hat, wie Genzken sagt. Die Sockel, auf denen diese Szenen ruhen, sind dabei zu schlank, um einfach nur Träger zu sein. Sie sind wie Schatten der Körper, deren libidinöses und imaginäres Drama wir gleichsam schockgefrostet vor uns sehen.

Das seltsame Gefühl, inmitten psychomorpher Präsenzen zu stehen, dämmert unserem abstrakten Betrachter. Er beginnt sich wie King Kong beim Blick in die verwüsteten Zimmer im fünfzigsten Stockwerk eines Wolkenkratzers zu fühlen. Zumal bei der Ausstellung in der Galerie Neugerriemschneider (Berlin, Herbst 2003) mit den an der Rückwand angebrachten Flugzeugfenstern (DA VINCI, 2003) eine radikal umgekehrte Grössendimension nahe gelegt wurde. Der Raum wurde ansatzweise zum Innern eines Passagierjets umgedeutet. Die Fensterpaare wirkten dabei – ähnlich wie bei der Photographie FLUGZEUGFENSTER (1992) – zugleich wie Augenhöhlen eines Wesens so gross wie King Kong. Die Sonnenschutzblenden sind wie Lider teils offen, teils halb oder ganz zu. Angebracht wie Tafelbilder und teils mit Lackschüttungen bemalt, verkehren die Flugzeugfenster die klassische Vorstellung des Bildes als Fenster zur Welt: Das Bild schaut zurück. Beinah unnötig zu sagen, dass der Gegenwart Hochhäuser und Flugzeuge unheimlich geworden sind, dass ein tiefer Riss durch die glatten, glänzenden Oberflä-

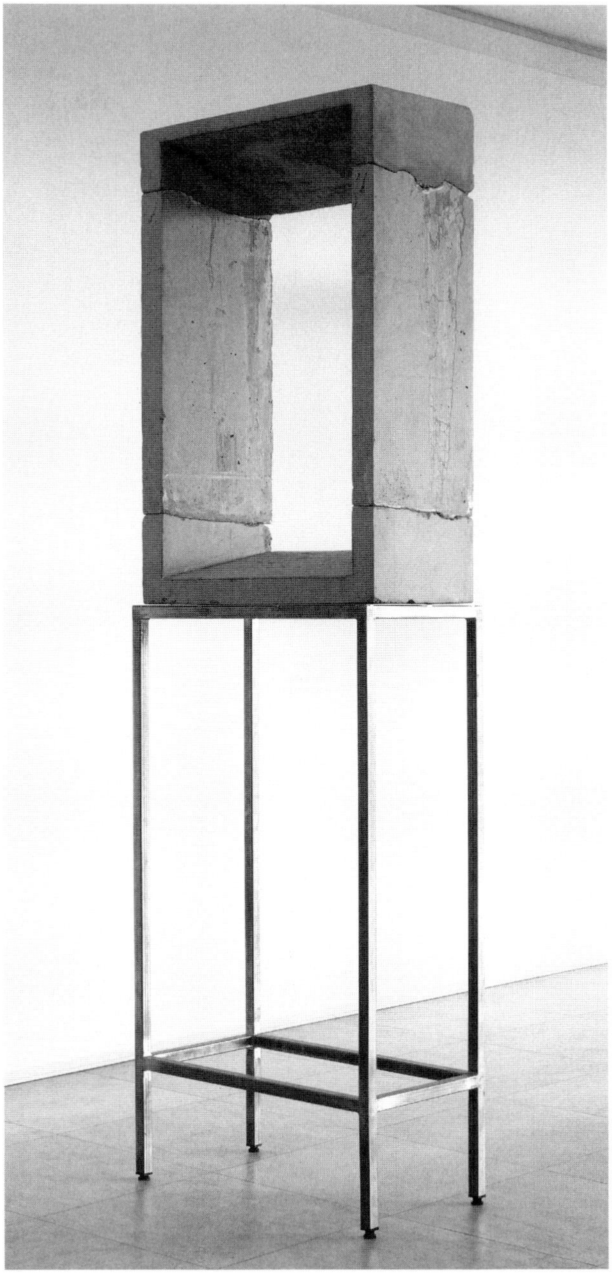

ISA GENZKEN, FENSTER, 1990, Beton, Stahl, 210 x 86 x 38 cm / WINDOW, concrete, steel, $82^{11}/_{16}$ x $33^{7}/_{8}$ x 15".

chen der Hypermoderne geht. Angelegt war das schon in Robert Smithsons früher, subversiver Rede von der «impure-purist surface»[1], die sich aus der Minimal Art entwickelte. *Empire Vampire* spielt das auch im Titel durch: das Empire State Building und sein unheimlicher, gotischer «Schatten», das Chrysler Building; vielleicht auch Warhols Film *Empire* (1964) und Warhols Image als Sozialvampir.

An den Kanten und Scharnieren, Antennen und Fensterrahmen, in der Lücke zwischen den Worten *Empire* und *Vampire,* zwischen grosser weiter Welt und Kunstwelt, Beseelung des «kalten» Konstruierten und Objektivierung des «warmen» Körperlichen, entsteht ein Justierungssystem der Wahrnehmung. Es ist hilfreich und gut wie der Blick zum Horizont für den Seekranken. Es konnte nur entstehen, weil Genzken die Formensprache geometrisch abstrakter Körper nicht einfach zugunsten von «Anti-Form» verworfen, sondern von deren Grenzen und Übergängen her aufgefächert hat. Aus dem essenzialistischen Vergleich von Skulptur und Körper, Architektur und Mensch, wird ein unablässiges «Scharfstellen» zwischen zwei beweglichen, aber sozial und politisch bestimmbaren Orten. Und dieses Scharfstellen lässt schliesslich auch unseren abstrakten Betrachter nicht aus; er wird als Sie, Er, Wir konkret.

1) Robert Smithson, *The Collected Writings,* hrsg. v. Jack Flam, University of California Press, Berkeley/Los Angeles/London 1996, S. 20.

THREE DECADES, a Reconstruction

JÖRG HEISER

In numerous novels and films a person sinks into a coma and wakes up decades later in a changed world. Let's imagine this person were not made of flesh and blood, but that they were the abstract "viewer" of art criticism. Let's imagine our cardboard chum with a pair of eyes (and other sense organs as needed) had seen Isa Genzken's first main body of work in the late seventies: extremely elongated, stereometric objects resting horizontally on the floor, calculated using a computer and perfectly finished in colorfully painted wood. Immediately afterwards the viewer sank into a deep slumber only to wake up in 2003 in the midst of a group of slim white plinths distributed around the room. On these lie reflective, rectangular panels like trays, supporting wild scenarios with weird mixtures of materials: toy soldiers crawling over silver-sprayed ruins that once were sneakers or taking cover behind children's rubber boots, superheroes blundering around amongst sunflower-seed dunes or threatening to drop into glass funnels like flies, plastic animals grazing near rocks made of gleaming, silvery-green moldy bread, fighting robots at a standstill in the face of broken glasses and vases and shiny surfaces spattered with paint that rise up before them like war-torn facades. The sum of the parts is a group of turbulent scenic models roughly at eye level, miniature panoramas of political struggles and aesthetic rivalries in theatrical blood red, camouflage green, and technology silver.

"How can it be," our abstract viewer would no doubt have wondered, "that these works are by the same artist?" Yet what seems—in purely formal terms—so disparate, like a crass contradiction between the way things looked then and now, is in fact crucially connected. Not only through the artist's biography but cyclically interlocking within the work itself. Not simply because of a red thread that can always be spun out as the need arises but because of the work as a whole.

The bewilderment of our abstract viewer is understandable. With a bit of effort, the ellipsoids and hyperbolas could be located within the heritage of Minimal Art. If texts by Donald Judd ("Specific Objects,"

JÖRG HEISER is the associate editor of *Frieze* magazine and lives in Berlin.

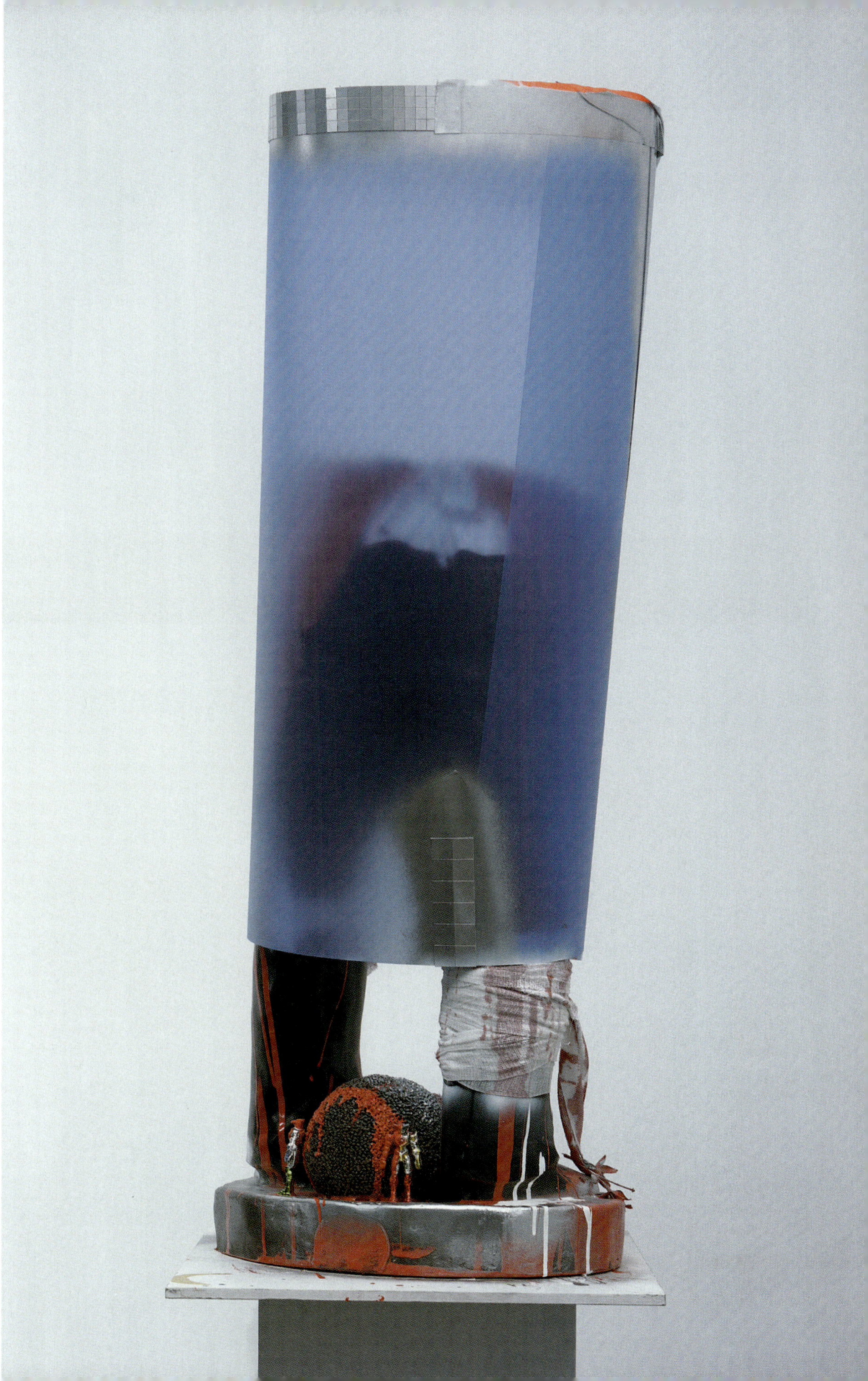

ISA GENZKEN, *EMPIRE/VAMPIRE IX,* 2003, *diverse Materialien, Kunststoff-Folie, Holzsockel, Holzplatte, 248 x 60 x 45 cm / mixed media, plastic foil, wooden stand and plate, 97 5/8 x 23 5/8 x 17 11/16".*

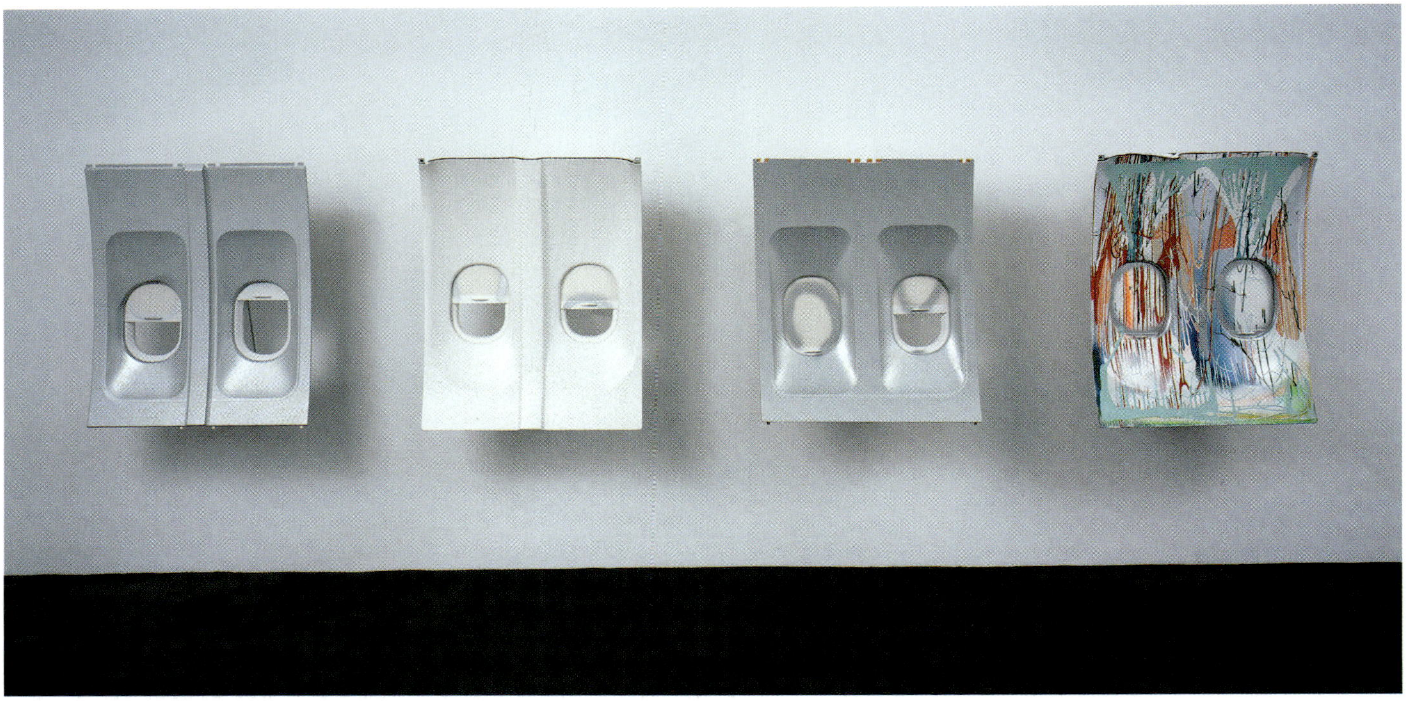

ISA GENZKEN, DA VINCI, 2003, 4 Flugzeugfenster, Metallträger, Lack, je 129 x 105 x 52 cm, Galerie Neugerriemschneider, Berlin / 4 aircraft windows, metal supports, lacquer, 50 3/4 x 41 5/16 x 20 1/2".

ISA GENZKEN, FLUGZEUGFENSTER, 1992, 2 Schwarzweissphotos (Edition), je 30 x 24 cm / AIRCRAFT WINDOWS, 2 b/w photographs (edition), 11 13/16 x 9 7/16" each.

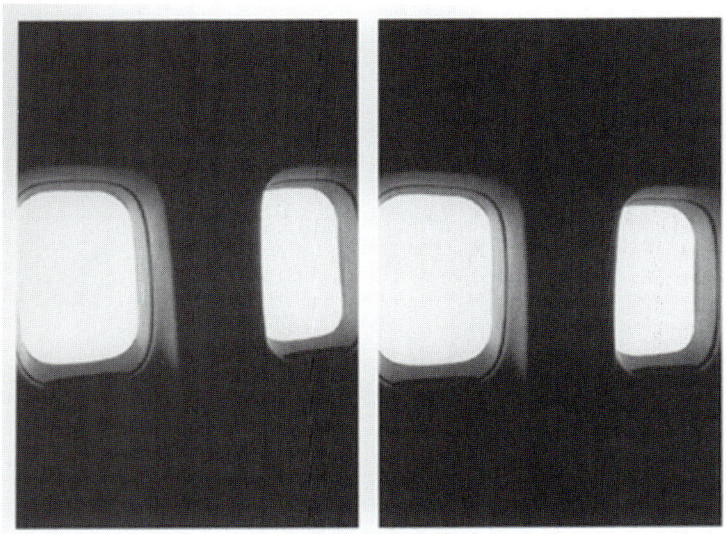

1965) and Robert Morris ("Notes on Sculpture," 1966) are read as the gospel of a particular belief (as more than a few did), then pieces Isa Genzken has made in 2003 are guilty of every last deadly sin. Industrially manufactured parts are used, but the end-result is not a self-contained volume: the works do not constitute a coherent structure along the lines of figure and ground. They are arranged as scenes; they operate with a gestural layer of color on the surfaces of the sculptures; they generate pictorial and spatial illusions; they do not shrink from allusion and allegory; ultimately they even expose themselves, cheekily, on the very fundament of an out-dated notion of sculpture, the plinth. Our abstract viewer might well come to the conclusion that Genzken is willfully setting out to overturn all the things that her earlier work once stood for.

Obviously care has to be taken in the way that the coma patient is acquainted with the truth. Let's start by supposing that Genzken's ellipsoids and hyperbolos from the seventies left Minimal Art unscathed. They are after all uniformly closed volumes of a clearly defined shape, theoretically digestible in one glance. Yet the sheer difficulty of photographing them—they threaten to disappear entirely when shot from the front—shows that they literally over-extend this aspect. Their extreme stereometric horizontal elongation—which never resolves into the planar as in Carl Andre's work—exerts immense pressure on the forms themselves. The ellipsoids look like hybrids of spears and racing boats, the hyperbolas call to mind tubes or pipes that are contracted in the middle by a vacuum. In both forms the energy of physical movement seems to be held tautly in check. They crouch—like cats ready to pounce—at the lower edge of the field of vision of anyone walking by. All of these are figurative, concrete associations, which do, of course, go far too far for orthodox Minimal discourse: as Isa Genzken recalled on a visit by the author to her studio, in those days she was "warned" amongst other things to avoid comparisons of that sort, as though they were some kind of breach of etiquette.

The energy that seems to be pent up in the sculptures has in fact been poured into them in the many hours of hard labor needed to produce them from "living" wood. As such they speak out against the uniform industrial appearance of Minimalist objects (Robert Morris, for one, gave up wood as a "working" material in 1965 as soon as he was able to achieve an immaculate, industrial finish with white enamel burnished on steel). The ellipsoids and hyperbolos take the logic of closed, geometrically definable volume to its limit, with all the ruthlessness of a crash test. And yet they do not shatter. There are hyperbolos (DIANA, 1983; MÄRZ, 1985), that stand upright and which seem to have been riven into two fitting yet not-fitting parts as though struck with great precision by a bolt of lightening, like couples with their euphoric mutual attraction and tragic rejection processes (another horrendous layer of meaning according to the Minimalist orthodoxy). But Genzken's work is not about dismissing all coherent forms into the "anti-form" of heterogeneous biomorphism. Otherwise, in terms of Minimal discourse, they could have been disposed of with the comment: different building site. The sculptures would have been relieved of the responsibility of constituting both an argument and a blueprint for sculpture at the most profoundly reasoned level of its respective time.

So, after having contained energy in closed volumes, there had to be a different way of releasing the energy of movement. The photos of Hi-Fi ads (1979), the photographs of women's ears (OHR, 1980), and the WELTEMPFÄNGER (World Receiver, 1982) together formed a triad: they find the essence of sculpture in openness, in the ether of transmission and reception, in sensitivities and minute adjustments. Hi-Fi equipment is the nearest thing the world of secularized living has to sculpture (the television as the domestic hearth, the stereo deck as an altar). Of our sense organs, the ear gets closest to modern sculpture: unlike the nose there is more than one ear, and unlike the eyes it sticks out and cannot be closed. It seems somehow intimate and yet remains anonymous—Genzken photographed the ears of anonymous female passersby in New York. The fact that these are women's ears can be taken as a warning to the male-dominated world of sculpture. We whisper to each other, networks ensue. The WELTEMPFÄNGER as a readymade turns the combined motifs of the Hi-Fi and the ear into a utopian promise. With this the plinth also enters the scene, for it is no

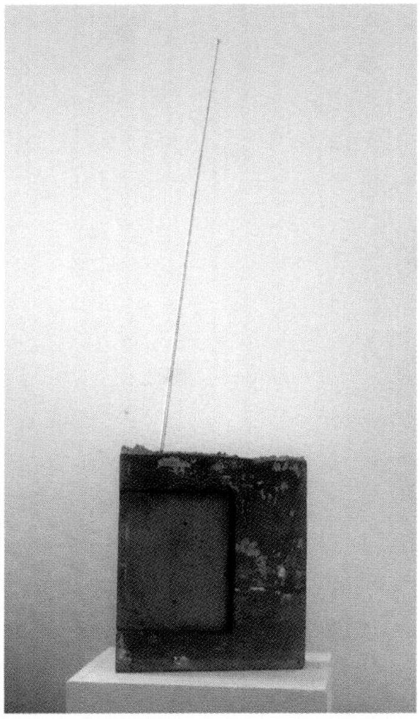

ISA GENZKEN, WELTEMPFÄNGER TORONTO, 1991, Beton, Metall, ca. 25 x 20 x 5 cm / WORLD RECEIVER TORONTO, concrete, metal, ca. $9^{13}/_{16}$ *x* $7^{7}/_{8}$ *x 2".*

longer merely a traditional instrument to separate art from the space around it but becomes part of the work itself. Is not the "world receiver" suddenly a perceiving head on a plinth-body? This is not about anthropomorphic substitution but about an intentional "mistaken identity." All at once the world receiver as a head takes on qualities we associate with the "quickened soul," with the psychomorphic.

By the same token, people are treated as sculptures: both in the case of the ears and in the x-ray photographs that Genzken made in the eighties (X-RAYS, 1981) of her own head. The closed volume of the skull appears to be open, abstracted from its "living soul" (which we of course know about) and at the same time almost gratingly physically concrete. It is as though premodern trepanation—a hole bored into the skull to release evil spirits—had returned as an allegorical technique for contrasting and comparing sculpture and the human body. The 1983 clay SELF-PORTRAIT—just such a headshape with strangely distorted and squint openings—precedes a series of raw plaster works (1984–1985), which increasingly veer towards architectural motifs. The materials of classical sculpture can return precisely because one of the reasons that led to their rejection now requires their presence again: the taunt of craft skills that industrially planned and manufactured sculpture by implication used to direct at "simpler" techniques has long since come home to roost. Locked into administrative processes it literally has had to be broken open again. The crude finish, partly left to chance, has now in fact caused closed volumes to "burst" open. MEIN GEHIRN (My Brain, 1984)—a rough lump with a single wire sticking jauntily upwards—is thus the exact counterpart to the previously mentioned head x-rays.

The plaster fragments of buildings lead directly to the concrete works (1986–1991): like hollow teeth waiting for gold fillings, their two or three walls enclose an empty space yearning to be filled with life. The rough concrete finish closes the gap between "old-fashioned" plaster and industrially manufactured surfaces. The stilt-like tubular steel stands call to mind showcases and architectural models, without relinquishing their eye-level height. The result is models like ruined buildings, in which a possible future tangles with morbid detritus, as do power and vulnerability. Their semi-opened structure is emphatically surpassed in the FENSTER (Windows, 1991–1994, originally in concrete, later in epoxy resin), which are set up like free-standing windbreaks with angled, hinged joints. In the four-sided pillars (1998), which are partly "christened" with the names of friends of the artist, the closed volume does appear to have returned. But it has now been stretched upwards like an anorexic skyscraper. However, any Albert Speerish vertical pathos (some of the works are over three meters high) is immediately prevented by the coffered divisions of the surface into wood, aluminum, glass, photographs, and so on, which function like affective occupation and individually attributed qualities. But here again the "mistaken identity" of sculpture and people goes beyond the apparently anthropomorphic parallels of the human form and buildings.

In a sense the early ellipsoids and hyperbolas have the function of batteries that are still supplying the energy for Genzken's work today. Set free in the series *Empire Vampire* (2003), described earlier here, rigidified models form a scenic panorama. The idea of a "film in your head" becomes true in the splatter effect of an inner life that has "burst open." Yet this

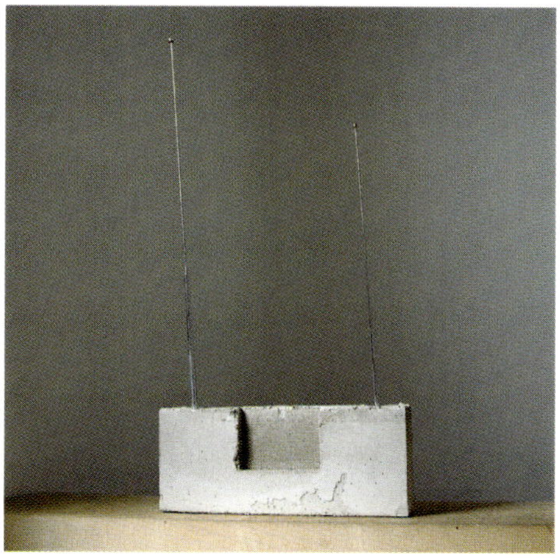

ISA GENZKEN, WELTEMPFÄNGER, 1992, Beton, Metall, ca. 10 x 30 x 5 cm / WORLD RECEIVER, concrete, metal, ca. 4 x 11 13/16 x 2".

is not about bricolage and found objects, but about a sculptural economy of means: why painstakingly construct toy soldiers when the firm of Revell has already found a "sculptural solution" to this problem, as Genzken puts it. At the same time the plinths on which these scenes are placed are too slim to simply be supports. They are like the shadows of the bodies whose libidinous, imaginary drama we see fast-frozen before us.

The strange feeling of standing amongst psychomorphic presences gradually dawns on our abstract viewer who feels like King Kong gazing into wrecked rooms on the 50th floor of a skyscraper. All the more so at the exhibition in the Neugerriemschneider gallery in Berlin (autumn 2003) where aircraft windows were shown on the back wall (DA VINCI, 2003). The space ressembled the interior of a passenger jet. At the same time the pairs of windows—as in the photograph FLUGZEUGFENSTER (1992)—were like pairs of huge eye sockets. The blinds, like eyelids, were open, half-open or completely closed. Fixed to the wall like easel paintings and partly covered with splattered paint, the aircraft windows subvert the classical notion of a painting as a window on the world: here the painting is looking back. It almost goes without saying that the combination of tall buildings and aircraft has become disturbing, that a deep crack has opened up in the shiny smooth surface of the hypermodern. The seeds of that were already sown in Robert Smithson's early subversive talk of the "impure-purist surface,"[1] which developed out of Minimal Art. *Empire Vampire* also plays that out in its title: the Empire State Building and its uncanny, gothic "shadow," the Chrysler Building; Warhol's film *Empire* (1964) and Warhol's image as a social vampire.

On the edges and hinges, the antenna and window frames, in the gap between the words "Empire" and "Vampire," between the big wide world and the art world, between the soul breathed into the "coldly" constructed and the objectification of the "warmly" physical, there is a calibration of perceptions. It is helpful and useful, like the sight of the horizon for those prone to seasickness. It could only arise because Genzken did not simply reject the formal language of abstract geometric bodies in favor of "anti-forms," but worked outwards from its limitations and transitions. The essentialist comparison of sculpture and the human form, architecture and the human being, is replaced by a constant "focusing" between two socio-historically mobile places. And ultimately this focusing does not leave out our abstract viewer who takes shape as a specific She, He, We.

(Translation: Fiona Elliott)

1) Robert Smithson, *The Collected Writings,* ed. by Jack Flam (Berkeley/Los Angeles/London: University of California Press, 1996), p. 20.

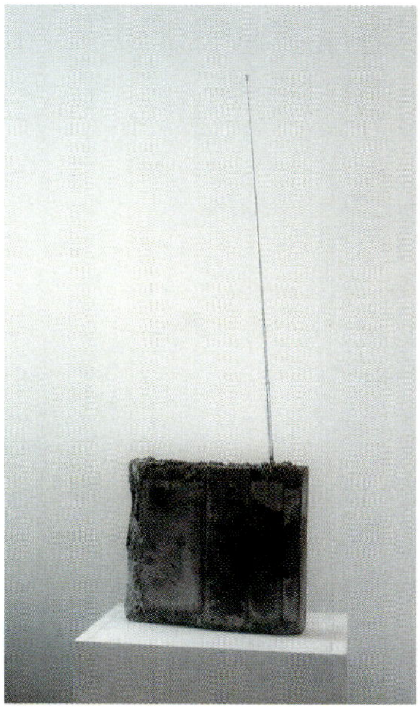

ISA GENZKEN, WELTEMPFÄNGER CHICAGO, 1990, Beton, Metall, ca. 20 x 20 x 5 cm / WORLD RECEIVER CHICAGO, concrete, metal, ca. 7 7/8 x 7 7/8 x 2".

The Skyscraper at Ear Level

The ear is uncanny. Uncanny is what it is; double is what it can become; large of small is what it can make or let happen (as in laisser-faire, *since the ear is the most tendered and most open organ, the one that, as Freud reminds us, the infant cannot close); large or small as well the manner in which one may offer or lend an ear.*

– Jacques Derrida[1)]

PAMELA M. LEE

There's an ear on the side of the building. I wonder what it hears. Set flush against a translucent paneled surface, a monumental ear—or rather, a digital print of one—stands several stories high above the city of Innsbruck, as if eavesdropping on some conversation down below. The fleshy lobe, an arabesque wisp of hair, the shadowed recess spiraling into the depths of the tympanum all stand in marked contrast to the featureless stripped-down side of the building upon which it appears. The ear is visible from inside the new, adjacent hotel with its shopping complex on the ground floor but is more difficult to read outside at street level. But whatever dissonance exists between the ear and the building—the one, a delicate, erogenous zone, the other a chill, inorganic presence—we, as viewers, tend to treat the two together. We see them as indivisible. The ear belongs to the building. Or maybe the building belongs to the ear. We don't read the ear as a surface ornament of the building—like the decorated shed of Robert Venturi's Postmodern architecture—but somehow, as contiguous with our experience of that architecture. We might call this architecture at "ear level": at the threshold where the interior space of mental life represented by the ear—generally conceived as private—is intertwined with the public space of the architectural environment, experienced in stereo. Somewhere between the inside and out is the space occupied by the work of Isa Genzken, the artist who placed the ear on the building in 2002.

Let's admit the ear seems a strange opening into this discussion. It is strange because, as a motif, its appearance seems out of sorts from what we usually think of Genzken's architecturally-inflected sculpture: her brusque concrete fragments of the eighties, the minimalist fenestrations from the early nineties. More lately she has shown fields of "models" on

PAMELA M. LEE is Associate Professor of Art History at Stanford University. She is the author of *Object to be Destroyed: The Work of Gordon Matta-Clark* (Cambridge: The MIT Press, 2000) and *Chronophobia: On Time in the Art of the 1960s* (also published by The MIT Press, 2004). Her writing has appeared in *October, Artforum, Grey Room,* and *Texte zur Kunst.*

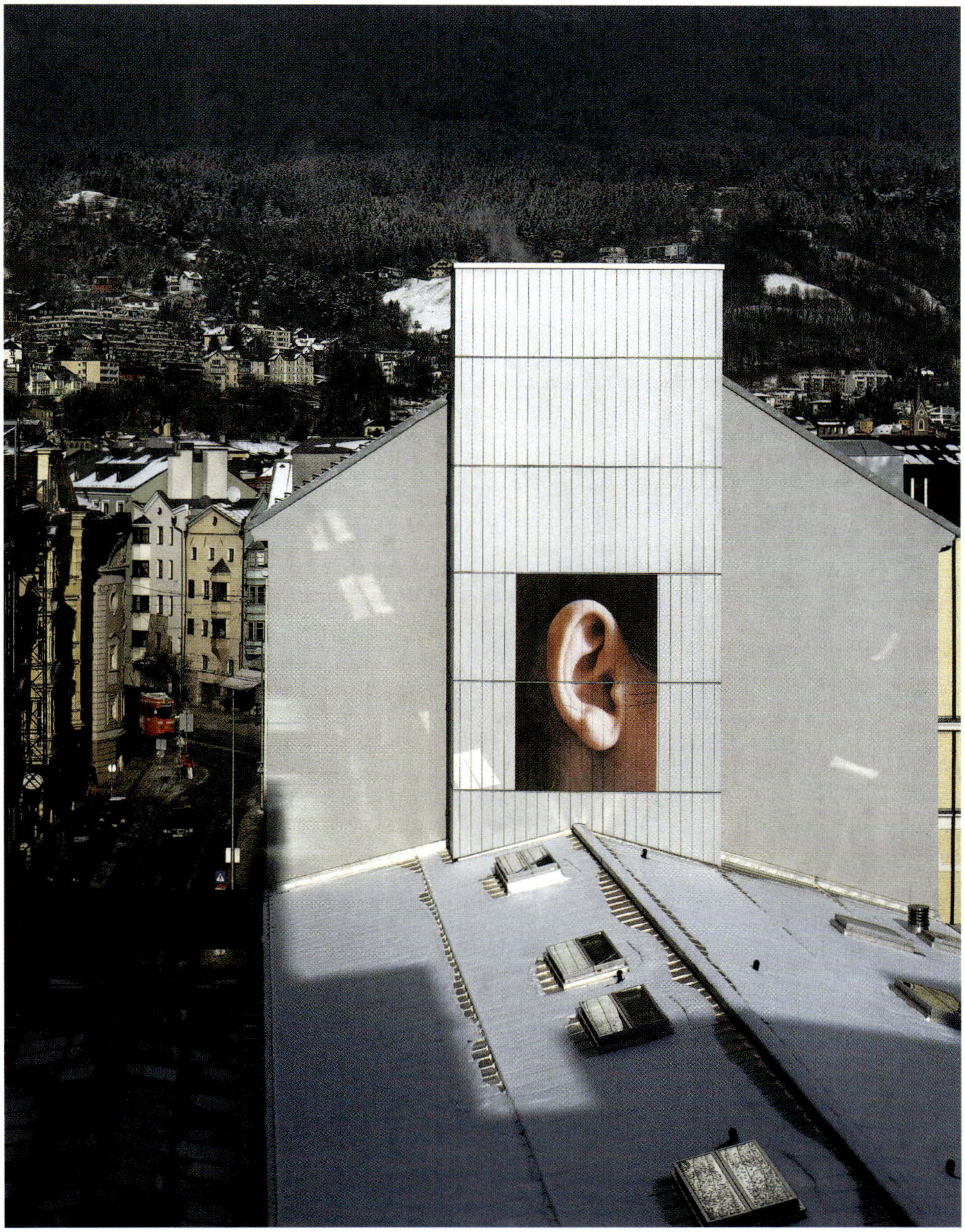

ISA GENZKEN, OHR, 2002, Digitaldruck auf Hochleistungsfolie, 5,8 x 3,9 m, Aussenprojekt Innsbruck / EAR, digital print on high-performance foil, 19 x 12 10/12', outdoor project, Innsbruck.

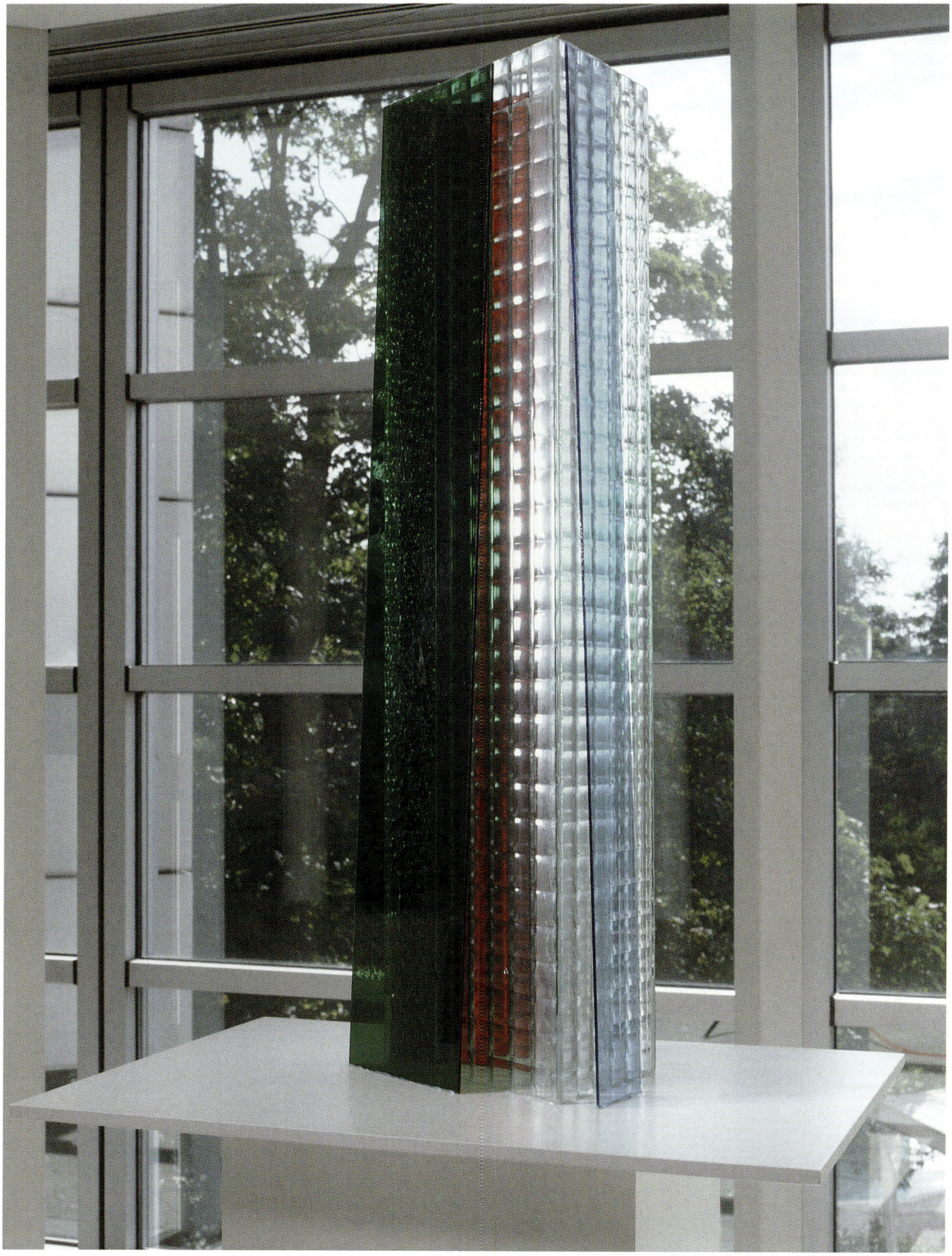

ISA GENZKEN, NEW BUILDINGS FOR BERLIN I, 2002, Glas, Klebeband, Silikon, 220 x 60 x 45 cm / glass, adhesive tape, silicon, 86 5/8 x 23 5/8 x 17 11/16".

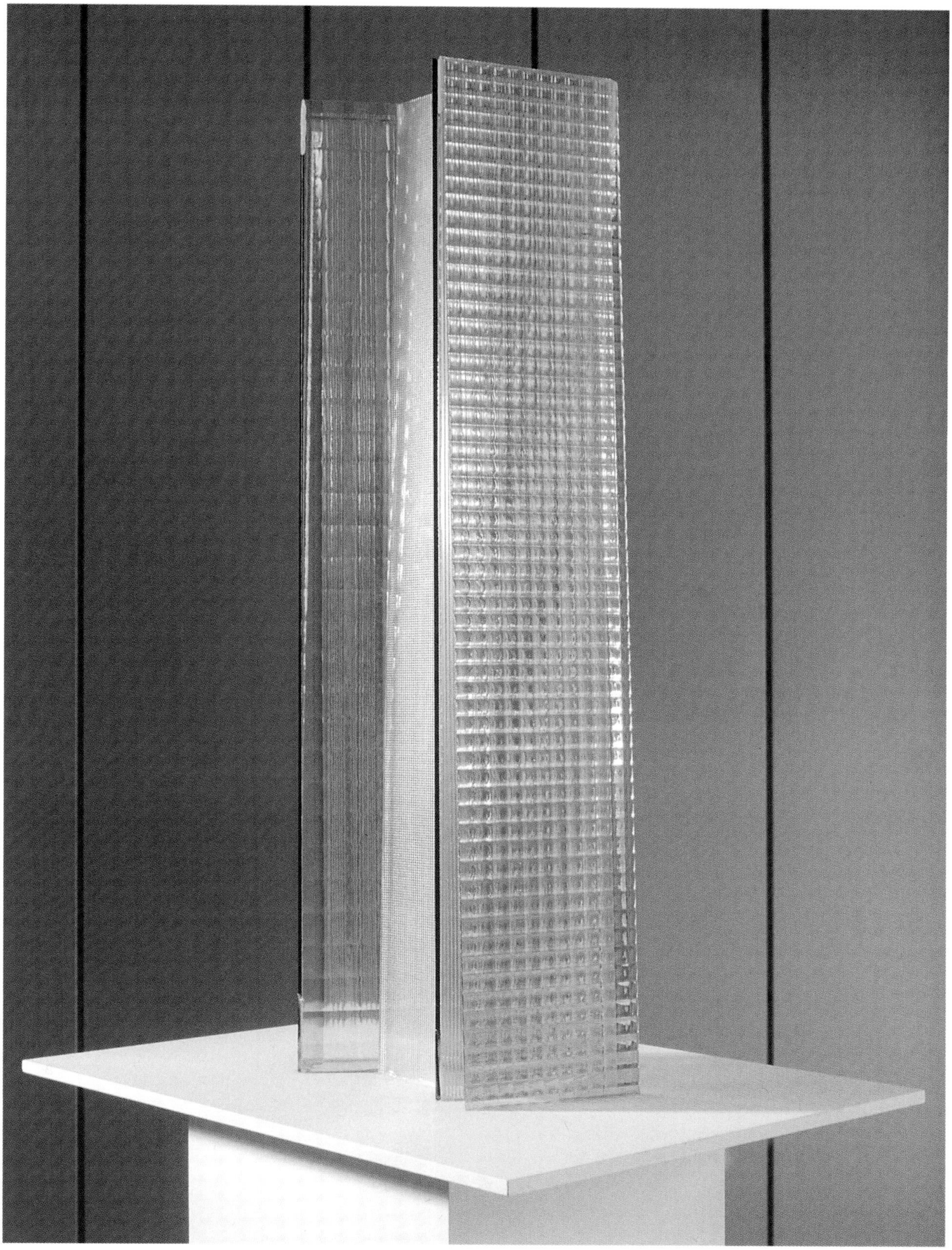

ISA GENZKEN, NEW BUILDINGS FOR BERLIN II, 2002, Glas, Klebeband, Silikon, 220 x 60 x 45 cm / glass, adhesive tape, silicon, 86 5/8 x 23 5/8 x 17 11/16".

plinths: rainbow prisms of glass, foil and tape as in the NEW BUILDINGS FOR BERLIN (2001) or the vacation-home-by-way-of-the-fun-house aesthetic suggested by the works in the exhibition "Urlaub" (2000) or the ersatz skyscrapers, noisy with color and junk, that comprise FUCK THE BAUHAUS: NEW BUILDINGS FOR NEW YORK (2000). And it is the eye, not the ear that we tend to associate with this work. The eye's movement of scanning the horizon of Genzken's sculptural objects seems analogous to the kinesthetic dimensions we bring to our experience of architecture in general. As Beatrix Ruf has persuasively written, "the importance and role of the 'eye level' from which we perceive her sculptures" is that of "a kind of filmic movement of the works themselves."[2] The "eye-level" perspective of Genzken's work, like that of Bruce Nauman's, is the perceptual horizon from which we conceive our individual relationship to architecture.[3]

This is hardly to deny the eye for thinking about Genzken's art, but somehow, in leaving the ear out of the picture, we get only half the story. As Maurice Merleau-Ponty reminds us, it is in the communion and integration of the senses that perception occurs; and the body, as much as it is a seeing body, is also "an object which ... reverberates to all sounds."[4] Attention to the ear might complete an understanding of Genzken's practice. If the eye's relationship to the human sensorium is binocular, facilitating the forward trajectory of our bodies as we move through space, the ear's implication of that space is stereographic, in the round. And because the ear is "the most open organ" as Derrida points out, it is a liaison between the self and the environment that is always porous, always ready to receive. At the same time, Derrida identifies the ear as "the most tendered" organ, suggesting something of the intimacy that it represents. Sensitized to register the external vibrations of the environment, the ear also internalizes the world outside it: it is a figure of the inside out. It is with this kind of perceptual balancing act (as Rita Kersting observed of Genzken's art, the ear is an instrument of balance[5]) that we begin to grasp how Genzken appeals to the gendered dimension of architectural space relative to the mythic divide between public and private.

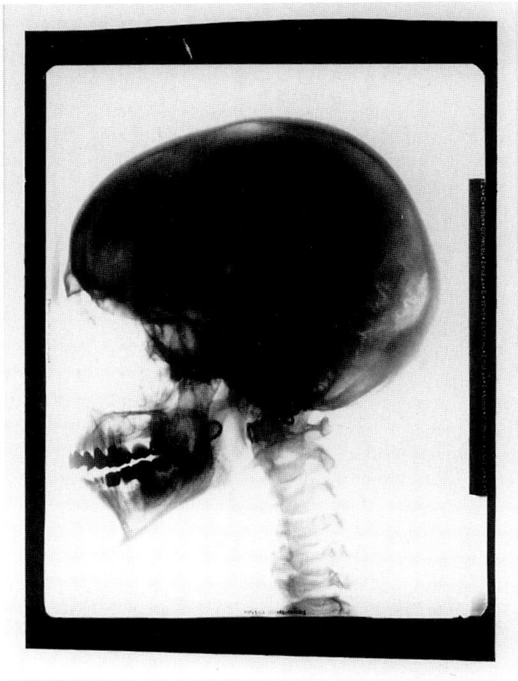

ISA GENZKEN, X-RAYS, 1989, aus einer Serie von 9 Röntgenaufnahmen, Schwarzweissphotos, jeweils je 1 mal in den Grössen 62 x 50 bzw. 108 x 80 cm / from a series of 9 X-rays, b/w photographs, each in 2 sizes: 24 3/8 x 19 11/16 x 31 1/2" and 42 1/2 x 31 1/2".

Making that leap demands a brief review of the ways in which Genzken both inherits and departs from Minimalism and the generalized discourses of phenomenology around which it flourished.[6] Genzken's practice is unambiguous in its engagement with Minimalist sculpture, not just in terms of her works' finish and geometries, but also in how she dramatizes issues of scale and space for the viewer. She does this by rendering explicit that which was inchoate to Minimalism's theory of reception: its references to architecture. Indeed, following Carl Andre's call for "sculpture as place" Minimalism was necessarily an art of location: of the ways in which the body calibrated space as it was shaped by those sculptural objects in the museum or gallery or outdoors. The movement of the body in space served to register

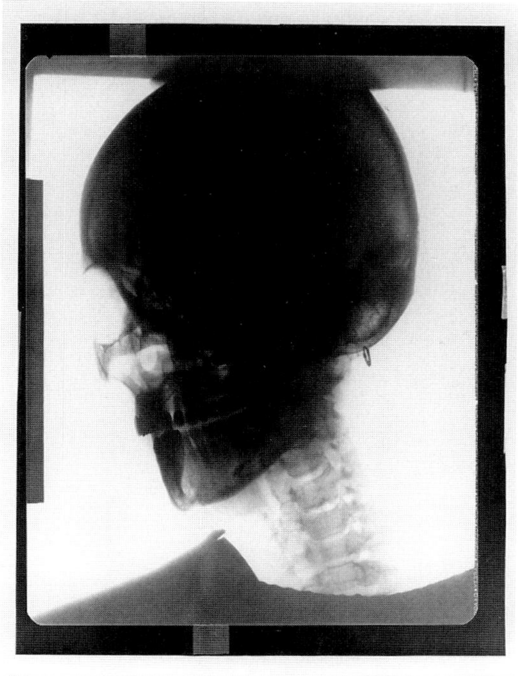

that relationship, which shifted continuously depending on the range of environmental and temporal conditions informing the encounter.

But critics of the Minimalist legacy have argued that the body relating to that space was largely represented as an idealized or neutral (perhaps neutered) body. If spatial perception was contingent on the ever-changing conditions of the environment, the body was nevertheless regarded as socially unmarked, without gender, ethnicity or class. Even still the contemporary criticism around Minimalism pointed the way to that thinking by alluding to the terms of public and private space in the work's reception. Genzken's art insists upon the shifting values of public and private; and the artist advances this critique in thematizing Minimalism's architectural dimensions. An ear-level perspective of her work gains particular access into that space.

Consider, for instance, a few of Genzken's extra-architectural works, the things that don't immediately fall under the rubric of "architecture," or "buildings" or even just plain old "space." These objects, which include chairs, videos, and clothes, constitute a considerable part of her oeuvre and cannot be merely dismissed as one-offs relative to the rest of her practice. This is especially so with her photographs. Genzken's first venture into the medium in 1979 included (and not incidentally) pictures of hi-fi systems appropriated from newspaper advertisements, which she described not only in terms of sound and music but also "their very own strong form."[7] But the photographs that followed in 1980 more pointedly call up the problematic of inside and outside, private and public coextensive with her more architectural work. It was a series of women's ears. Walking down the streets of New York, a city she loves well for its skyscrapers, Genzken would ask random women pedestrians if she might take a picture of their ear. None, she claimed, refused or was offended by the odd request. For Genzken, the images represented "Something organic. Something from the inside out. Coming from the head."[8] The photographs engender a paradox: Genzken asked women strangers to expose their ears, a rather delicate organ, as she encountered them on the highly trafficked, expressly public streets of Manhattan. The identities of the women pictured are anonymous, but there's a certain intimacy in the ears represented: each is different, some sport distinctive earrings, a tendril of hair suggests the pedestrian's overall appearance.

Genzken's ear-level photographs play upon this oscillation between inside and out, or what feminists describe as "the intimate public sphere." These pictures stage the precarious threshold between public and private life, captured on the very streets lined by the architecture Genzken so admires. It's not surprising that Genzken followed this series with "self-portraits" of a kind—x-rays of her head—along with photographs of the facades of New York buildings. Both represent dialectical flipsides of the same spatio-temporal coin: here an image of the head as an internal landscape, a "globe" as she called it, is poised in relation to the blunt frontality, the external surfaces, of New York's architecture.

Much of Genzken's work of the last few years has progressively collapsed these two registers of spatial experience. With the *Urlaub* series, Genzken offers a perspective into the intimate workings of domestic life and its phantasmatic projections; here, the external constructions of vacation homes act as inverted screens or mirrors for psychosexual desire and fantasies of retreat from the world outside. In brilliantly colored sculptural columns named after friends and associates from 1999—Karola, Daniel, Lawrence, Isa herself—Genzken further meshes the social world of the intimate sphere with forms evoking its architectural surround. For Genzken, those spaces are of the same phenomenal and perceptual plane: they are not oppositional but contiguous.

Perhaps this is why one of the ears from 1980 made an uncanny return of sorts, monumentalized on the side of a hotel in Innsbruck. That work, simply called OHR, recalls one of Genzken's most oft-repeated remarks: "Everyone needs at least one window." It's hard not to take this mandate literally as a call to spatial poetics (and even politics) as determined by the accessories of architecture. To treat Genzken's work from the inside out, however, suggests a different vantage point altogether. She lends us a window in the form of an ear.

1) Jacques Derrida, "Otobiographies," in *The Ear of the Other,* trans. by Peggy Kamuf (Lincoln, Nebraska, and London: University of Nebraska Press, 1985), p. 33.
2) Beatrix Ruf, "Contact," in *Isa Genzken: 1992–2003,* ex. cat., Kunsthalle Zurich (Cologne: Verlag der Buchhandlung Walther König, 2003), p. 11.
3) Ibid.
4) Maurice Merleau-Ponty, *Phenomenology of Perception,* trans. by Colin Smith (London: Routledge, 1989), p. 236.
5) Rita Kersting, "Ellipsoids and Grandparents in the Bavarian Forest—Unsuspected Conjunctions," in *Isa Genzken: "Sie sind mein Glück,"* ex. cat., Kunstverein Braunschweig (Ostfildern-Ruit: Hatje Cantz Verlag, 2000), p. 51.
6) Benjamin H. D. Buchloh, "Isa Genzken: From Model to Fragment," in *Isa Genzken: Jeder braucht mindestens ein Fenster,* ex. cat., Renaissance Society at the University of Chicago (Cologne: Verlag der Buchhandlung Walther König, 1992), pp. 135–141.
7) Isa Genzken, "A Conversation with Wolfgang Tillmans," *Camera Austria,* No. 81/2003, p. 17.
8) Ibid.

ISA GENZKEN, FUCK THE BAUHAUS/NEW BUILDINGS FOR NEW YORK, 5, 2000, diverse Materialien, ca. 213 x 70 x 50 cm / mixed media, ca. 83 7/8 x 27 9/16 x 19 11/16".

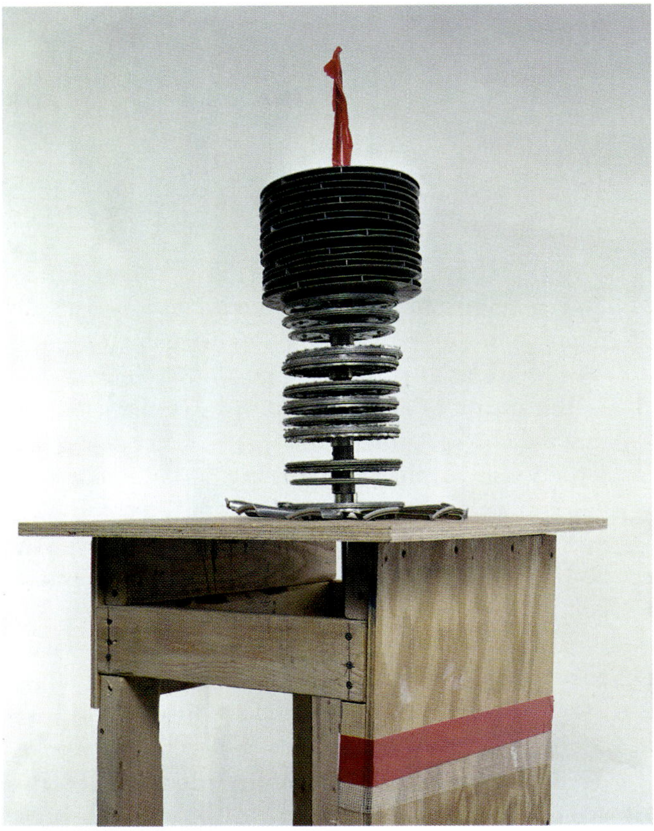

Der Wolkenkratzer auf Ohrhöhe

«Unheimlich» ist das Ohr: was es ist, doppelt; was es werden kann, lang oder klein; was es tun oder lassen kann (lassen, nicht wahr, weil es das offenste und preisgegebenste Organ ist, das der Säugling – Freud erinnert uns daran – nicht schliessen kann), die Art, wie man sein Ohr leihen oder spitzen kann.

– Jacques Derrida[1)]

PAMELA M. LEE

Das Gebäude hat seitlich ein Ohr. Ich frage mich, was es wohl hört. Glatt auf der Fläche aus transparenten Platten anliegend befindet sich ein monumentales Ohr – oder vielmehr der digitale Print eines solchen –, mehrere Stockwerke hoch über der Innsbrucker Innenstadt, als würde es irgendein Gespräch dort unten belauschen. Das fleischige Ohrläppchen, die Arabeske einer Haarsträhne, die schattige Vertiefung, die spiralförmig in die Tiefen des Mittelohrs hinunterführt, all das steht in klarem Kontrast zu dem nichts sagenden, kahlen Gebäude, auf dem es angebracht ist, seitlich gegenüber dem Hotelneubau samt Einkaufszentrum im Erdgeschoss. Vom Hotel aus ist das Ohr gut zu sehen, von der Strasse aus dagegen kaum sichtbar. Aber ungeachtet der Dissonanz, die zwischen Ohr und Architektur bestehen mag – ersteres eine erogene Zone, letztere eine kalte unorganische Sache –, wir, die Betrachter, tendieren dazu, beides als eins wahrzunehmen. Wir betrachten beides als etwas unteilbar Zusammengehöriges. Das Ohr gehört zum Gebäude. Oder vielleicht gehört auch das Gebäude zum Ohr. Wir fassen

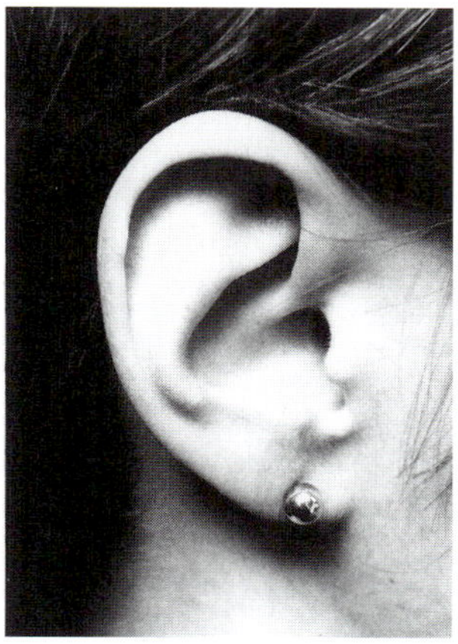
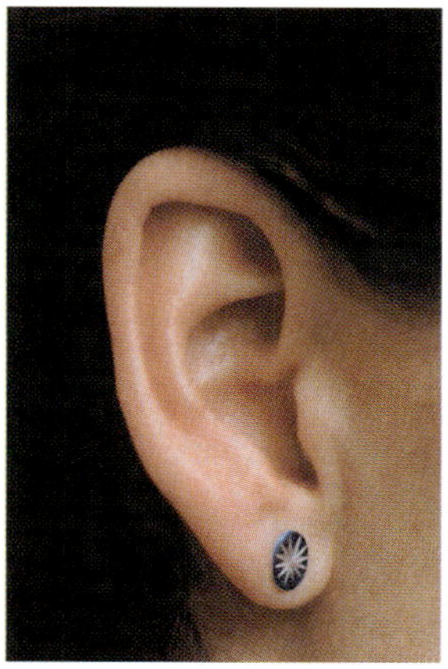

ISA GENZKEN, OHR, 1980, aus einer Serie von 12 Photographien, je 1 mal: 175 x 118 cm; 115 x 80 cm; 70 x 50 cm / EAR, from a series of 12 photographs, each in 3 sizes: 68 7/8 x 46 1/2"; 45 1/4 x 31 1/2"; 27 9/16 x 19 11/16".

PAMELA M. LEE ist Associate Professor für Kunstgeschichte an der Stanford University. Sie ist Autorin von *Object to be Destroyed: The Work of Gordon Matta-Clark* (2000) und *Chronophobia: On Time in the Art of the 1960s* (2004), beide erschienen bei MIT Press, Cambridge, MA, und hat in den Zeitschriften *October, Artforum, Grey Room* und *Texte zur Kunst* publiziert.

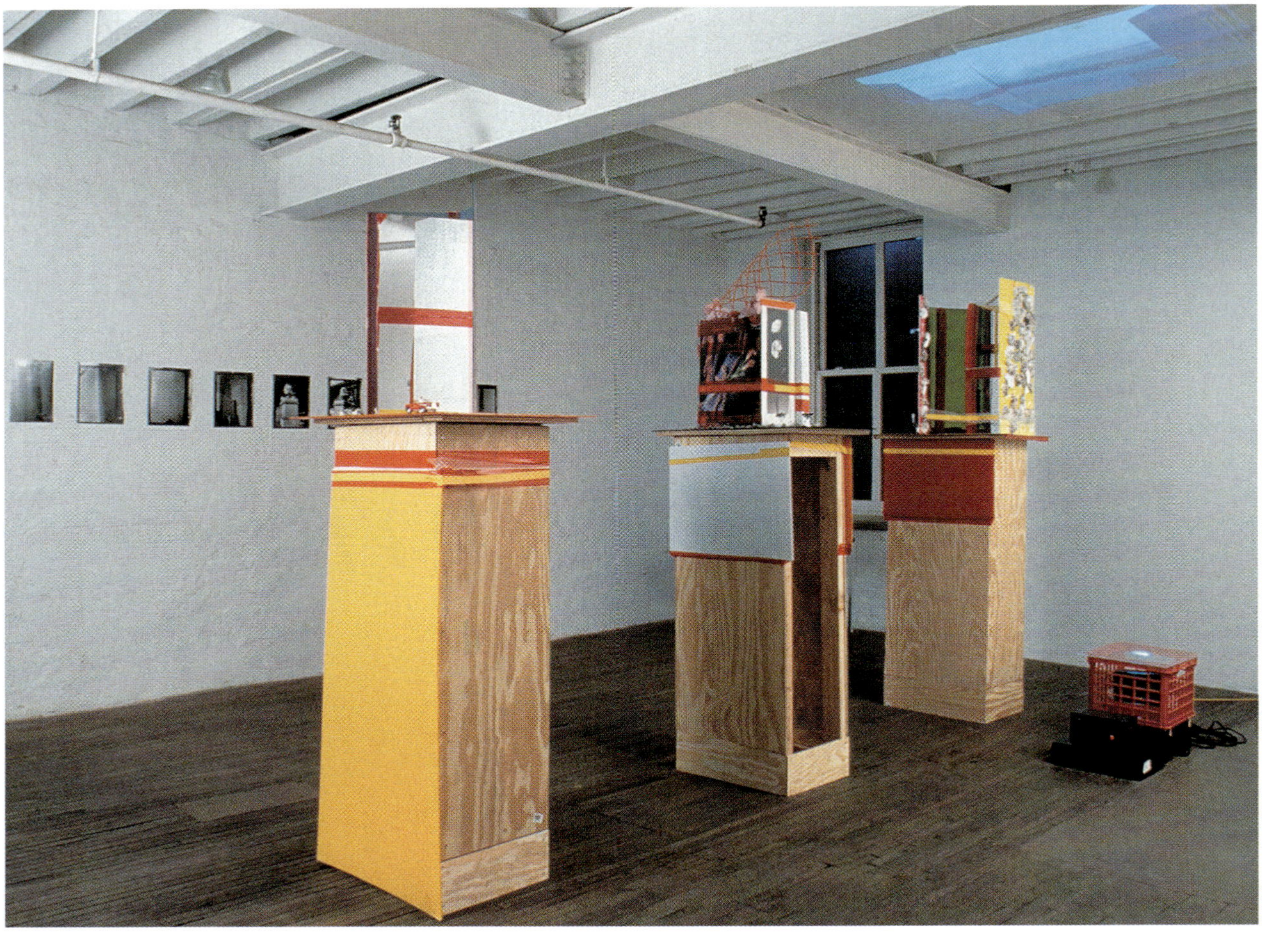

ISA GENZKEN, FUCK THE BAUHAUS / NEW BUILDINGS FOR NEW YORK, 2000, Installationsansicht / installation view, AC Project Room, New York.

das Ohr nicht als Fassadenschmuck auf – wie etwa im Fall der dekorierten Lagerhallen in Robert Venturis postmoderner Architektur –, sondern es scheint irgendwie zu unserem Erleben dieser Architektur zu passen. Man könnte sagen, diese Architektur sei auf Ohrhöhe: auf der Schwelle, wo der Innenraum des Mentalen, für den das Ohr steht – und der allgemein als privat gilt –, sich mit dem öffentlichen Raum der architektonischen Umgebung stereophonisch verknüpft. Irgendwo zwischen diesem Innen und Aussen liegt der Raum, den Isa Genzkens Werk einnimmt. Denn sie ist es, die das Ohr 2002 hier angebracht hat.

Zugegeben, das Ohr mag ein etwas seltsamer Einstieg in diese Diskussion sein. Seltsam, weil es als Motiv irgendwie aus dem Rahmen dessen fällt, was uns im Zusammenhang mit Genzkens architekturbezogenen Skulpturen gewöhnlich einfällt: ihre schroffen Betonfragmente aus den 80er oder die minimalistischen FENSTER aus den frühen 90er Jahren. In jüngerer Zeit hat sie Platten mit «Modellen» auf Sockeln gezeigt: Regenbogenprismen aus

Glas, Folie und Klebeband wie etwa in den NEW BUILDINGS FOR BERLIN (Neue Gebäude für Berlin, 2001) oder die Ferienhaus-Spielhaus-Ästhetik, auf welche die Arbeiten in «Urlaub» (2002) anspielen, oder die Wolkenkratzer-Stellvertreter mit ihren schreienden Farben und den gefundenen Materialien, aus denen FUCK THE BAUHAUS/NEW BUILDINGS FOR NEW YORK (2000) besteht. Und es ist das Auge, nicht das Ohr, das wir mit diesen Arbeiten in Verbindung bringen. Die Bewegung des den Horizont absuchenden Auges in Genzkens skulpturalen Objekten scheint den kinästhetischen Voraussetzungen zu entsprechen, die wir für unsere Erfahrung von Architektur überhaupt mitbringen. Beatrix Ruf verwies sehr überzeugend auf «die Wichtigkeit und Rolle der ‹Augenhöhe›, in der wir ihre Skulpturen wahrnehmen können», und auf «eine Art filmische Bewegung der Arbeiten, die wir entweder als Bewegung der Arbeiten selbst oder als Fiktionalisierung durch unsere eigene Bewegung erfahren».[2)] Die Perspektive der «Augenhöhe» in Genzkens Arbeiten ist – wie bei Bruce Nauman – der Wahrnehmungshorizont, der uns unsere eigene Körperwahrnehmung mit der Raumerfahrung in Beziehung setzen lässt.[3)]

Es kann nicht darum gehen, die Bedeutung des Auges für das Verständnis von Genzkens Arbeit zu schmälern, aber solange man das Ohr vernachlässigt, erfasst man irgendwie nur die halbe Wahrheit. Wie uns Maurice Merleau-Ponty in Erinnerung ruft, finden Empfindungen in einer Kommunion und Kommunikation der Sinne statt; und der Leib ist nicht nur ein sehender Leib, sondern auch ein Leib, der sich der jeweiligen «Schwingung und Raumerfüllung» ausliefert.[4)] Vielleicht verstehen wir Genzkens Kunst besser, wenn wir auf das Ohr achten. Während das binokulare Sehen des menschlichen Sinnesapparates die Vorwärtsbewegung unseres Körpers im Raum erleichtert, nimmt das Ohr denselben Raum stereographisch, das heisst rundum wahr. Und weil das Ohr, wie Derrida betont, das «offenste Organ» ist, stellt es eine Verbindung zwischen Ich und Umgebung dar, die immer durchlässig, immer auf Empfang ist. Gleichzeitig bezeichnet Derrida das Ohr als «das am stärksten ausgesetzte» Organ, das auf die Intimität verweist, für die es steht. Empfindlich genug, um die äusseren Schwingungen der Umwelt wahrzunehmen, verinnerlicht das Ohr auch die Welt ausserhalb: Es ist ein Bild des nach aussen gekehrten Inneren. Und mit diesem Balanceakt der Wahrnehmung (Rita Kersting hat darauf hingewiesen, wie wichtig das Ohr auch als Gleichgewichtsorgan in Genzkens Kunst sei.[5)]) beginnen wir zu begreifen, wie Genzken die von Menschen geschaffene Dimension des architektonischen Raums immer hinsichtlich der mythischen Scheidung zwischen öffentlich und privat befragt.

Um diesen Sprung zu schaffen müssen wir kurz anschauen, wie Genzken die Minimal-Skulptur und die allgemeine Diskussion der phänomenologischen Raumerfahrung, auf deren Boden sie gedieh, sowohl aufgreift wie hinter sich lässt.[6)] Genzkens künstlerische Praxis nimmt ganz offen Bezug auf die Skulptur des Minimalismus, und zwar nicht nur in der Verarbeitung und Geometrie ihrer Werke, sondern auch im gesteigerten Sichtbarmachen von Dingen wie Grössenordnung und Raum. Sie tut das, indem sie explizit ausführt, was in der Rezeptionstheorie des Minimalismus bereits angelegt war: sein Verhältnis zur Architektur. Carl Andres Ruf nach einer «Skulptur als Ort» Folge leistend war Minimal Art notwendig eine Kunst des Standortes: der Art und Weise, wie ein Körper den Raum auslotet, der von den skulpturalen Objekten im Museum, in der Galerie oder im Freien geformt wird. Die Bewegung des Körpers im Raum diente dazu, diese Beziehung zu registrieren, die sich je nach Umweltbedingungen und zeitlich wechselnden Einflüssen laufend veränderte.

Kritiker der Minimal Art führten jedoch ins Feld, dass der Körper im Verhältnis zum Raum weitgehend als idealisierter oder neutraler (vielleicht sogar neutralisierter) Körper dargestellt wurde. Obwohl die räumliche Wahrnehmung von den ständig wechselnden Voraussetzungen der Umwelt abhängig war, wurde der Körper als gesellschaftlich unbeeinflusst, geschlechtslos, ohne Zugehörigkeit zu einer Ethnie oder Klasse betrachtet. Selbst die aktuelle Kritik rund um die Minimal Art weist noch in diese Richtung, wenn sie im Zusammenhang mit der Werkrezeption die Begriffe «öffentlich» und «privat» verwendet. Genzkens Kunst unterstreicht dagegen die schwankende Bedeutung dieser Begriffe. Und sie vertieft diese Kritik, indem sie die architektonischen Aspekte der Minimal Art thematisiert. Gerade eine Betrachtung ihres Werkes auf Augenhöhe gewährt uns Zutritt zu diesem Raum.

Betrachten wir, zum Beispiel, einige von Genzkens nicht direkt architektonischen Arbeiten, Dinge, die nicht sofort unter die Rubrik «Architektur», «Gebäude» oder auch nur «Raum» fallen. Diese Objekte, zu denen Stühle, Videos und Kleidungsstücke gehören, machen einen beträchtlichen Teil ihrer Arbeiten aus und können nicht einfach als Ausnahmefälle innerhalb des Werks behandelt werden. Das gilt insbesondere für die Photographien. Genzkens Einstieg in dieses Medium begann 1979 (und nicht zufällig) mit Bildern von Hi-Fi-Anlagen aus Werbeanzeigen, die sie nicht nur wegen der Tonqualität und Musik interessierten, sondern auch weil sie «eine ganz starke, eigene Form» hatten.[7)] Die Photographien, die 1980 folgten, thematisieren dann – parallel zu den anderen, mehr architektonisch ausgerichteten Arbeiten – die Problematik von innen und aussen, privat und öffentlich schon sehr viel pointierter. Es handelt sich um eine Serie von Aufnahmen, die Frauenohren zeigen. Unterwegs auf den Strassen New Yorks, einer Stadt, die die Künstlerin wegen ihrer Wolkenkratzer liebt, fragte Genzken irgendwelche zufällig vorbeigehenden Frauen, ob sie ihre Ohren photographieren dürfe. Keine Einzige, sagt sie, habe abgelehnt oder sich durch das seltsame Begehren belästigt gefühlt. Für Genzken waren die Bilder «etwas Organisches. Etwas von innen nach aussen. Vom Kopf kommend.»[8)] Diese Photographien stellen ein Paradox dar: Genzken bat fremde Frauen darum, ihr Ohr zu entblössen, ein ziemlich verletzliches Organ, und dies auf den äusserst verkehrsreichen, betont öffentlichen Strassen Manhattans. Die photographierten Frauen bleiben zwar anonym, aber es liegt eine gewisse Intimität in den abgebildeten Ohren: Jedes ist anders, einige zeichnen sich durch besondere Ohrringe aus, eine Haarsträhne lässt Schlüsse auf die Gesamterscheinung der Passantin zu.

Genzkens Photos auf Ohrhöhe spielen mit diesem Oszillieren zwischen innen und aussen, beziehungsweise dem, was Feministinnen als «öffentlichen Intimbereich» bezeichnen. Diese Bilder rücken die heikle Schwelle zwischen öffentlichem und privatem Leben ins Blickfeld, eingefangen auf genau jenen Strassenzügen, entlang derer sich die Architektur findet, die Genzken so bewundert. Es überrascht nicht, dass Genzken dieser Serie eine Reihe von «Selbstporträts» folgen liess – Röntgenaufnahmen ihres Kopfes –, zusammen mit Photos von New Yorker Fassaden. Es sind die zwei dialektischen Seiten derselben raumzeitlichen Münze: Ein Bild des Kopfes als innere Landschaft, ein «Globus», wie sie es nennt, wird der blanken Frontalität, den glatten Aussenfassaden der New Yorker Architektur gegenübergestellt.

In einem grossen Teil von Genzkens Arbeiten der letzten Jahre fallen diese beiden Register räumlicher Erfahrung mehr und mehr zusammen. In der Werkserie *Urlaub* gewährt Genzken Einblick in die intimen Mechanismen des häuslichen Lebens und seine Phantasieprojektionen; hier wirken äussere Ferienhauskonstruktionen als invertierte Projektionsschirme oder Zerrspiegel unseres psychosexuellen Begehrens und unserer Rückzugsphantasien. In leuchtend farbigen Säulenskulpturen, benannt nach Freunden und Weggenossen aus dem Jahr 1999 – Karola, Daniel, Lawrence, Isa selbst –, bringt Genzken einmal mehr die intime Beziehungswelt mit Formen zusammen, die das entsprechende architektonische Umfeld beschwören. Für Genzken sind die beiden Bereiche auf derselben phänomenologischen und perzeptorischen Ebene: Sie sind keine Gegensätze, sondern ergänzen sich.

Vielleicht taucht deshalb eines der Ohren von 1980 noch einmal wie ein unheimlicher Wiedergänger in monumentaler Vergrösserung an einer Fassade seitlich gegenüber einem Hotel in Innsbruck auf. Diese Arbeit, deren Titel einfach OHR ist, ruft einen von Genzkens meistzitierten Sätzen in Erinnerung: «Jeder braucht mindestens ein Fenster.» Es fällt schwer, diese Aussage n i c h t wörtlich zu nehmen, sondern sie als Aufruf zu einer Poesie (ja, einer Politik) des Raumes im architektonischen Sinn zu verstehen. Will man Genzkens Arbeit jedoch von innen heraus verstehen, drängt sich eine ganz andere Perspektive auf: Die Künstlerin öffnet uns ein Fenster in Gestalt eines Ohrs.

(Übersetzung: Wilma Parker)

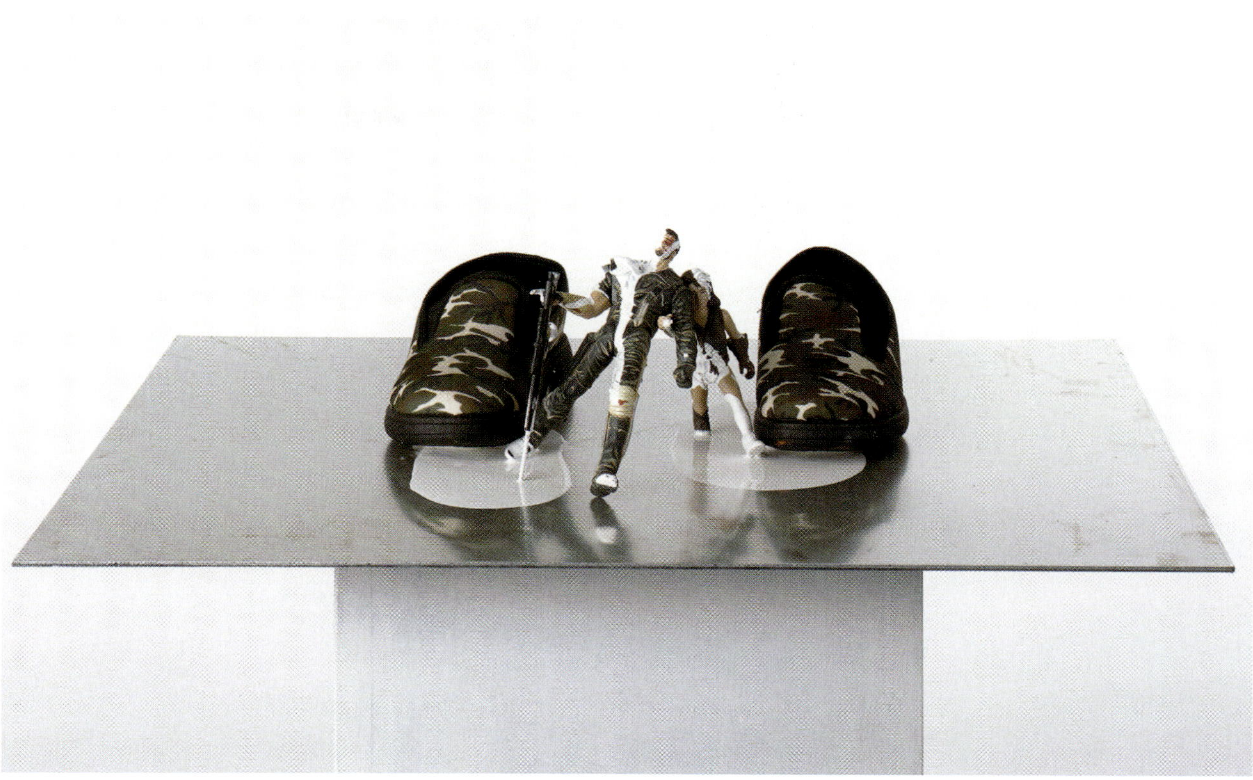

ISA GENZKEN, EMPIRE/VAMPIRE, WHO KILLS DEATH, 2003, Teil der 22-teiligen Installation aus diversen Materialien, Kunsthalle Zürich, 155 x 60 x 40 cm / detail from the 22-part, mixed-media installation, 61 x 23 5/8 x 15 3/4".

1) Jacques Derrida, «Otobiographien,» in: J. Derrida / F. Kittler, *Nietzsche – Politik des Eigennamens. Wie man abschafft, wovon man spricht,* Merve Verlag, Berlin 2000, S. 56.
2) Beatrix Ruf, «Kontakt», in: *Isa Genzken: 1992–2003,* Ausstellungskatalog der Kunsthalle Zürich, Verlag der Buchhandlung Walther König, Köln 2003, S. 8.
3) Ebenda.
4) Maurice Merleau-Ponty, *Phänomenologie der Wahrnehmung,* Walter de Gruyter, Berlin 1966, S. 249.
5) Rita Kersting, «Ellipsoide und Grosseltern im Bayrischen Wald – unerwartete Begegnungen», in: *Isa Genzken: «Sie sind mein Glück»,* Ausstellungskatalog, Kunstverein Braunschweig, Hatje Cantz Verlag, Ostfilder-Ruit 2000, S. 44.
6) Benjamin H. D. Buchloh, «Isa Genzken: vom Modell zum Fragment», in: *Isa Genzken: «Jeder braucht mindestens ein Fenster»,* Ausstellungskatalog der Renaissance Society an der University of Chicago, Verlag der Buchhandlung Walther König, Köln 1992, S. 127–134.
7) Isa Genzken, «Ein Gespräch mit Wolfgang Tillmans», *Camera Austria,* Nr. 81/2003, S. 18.
8) Ebenda.

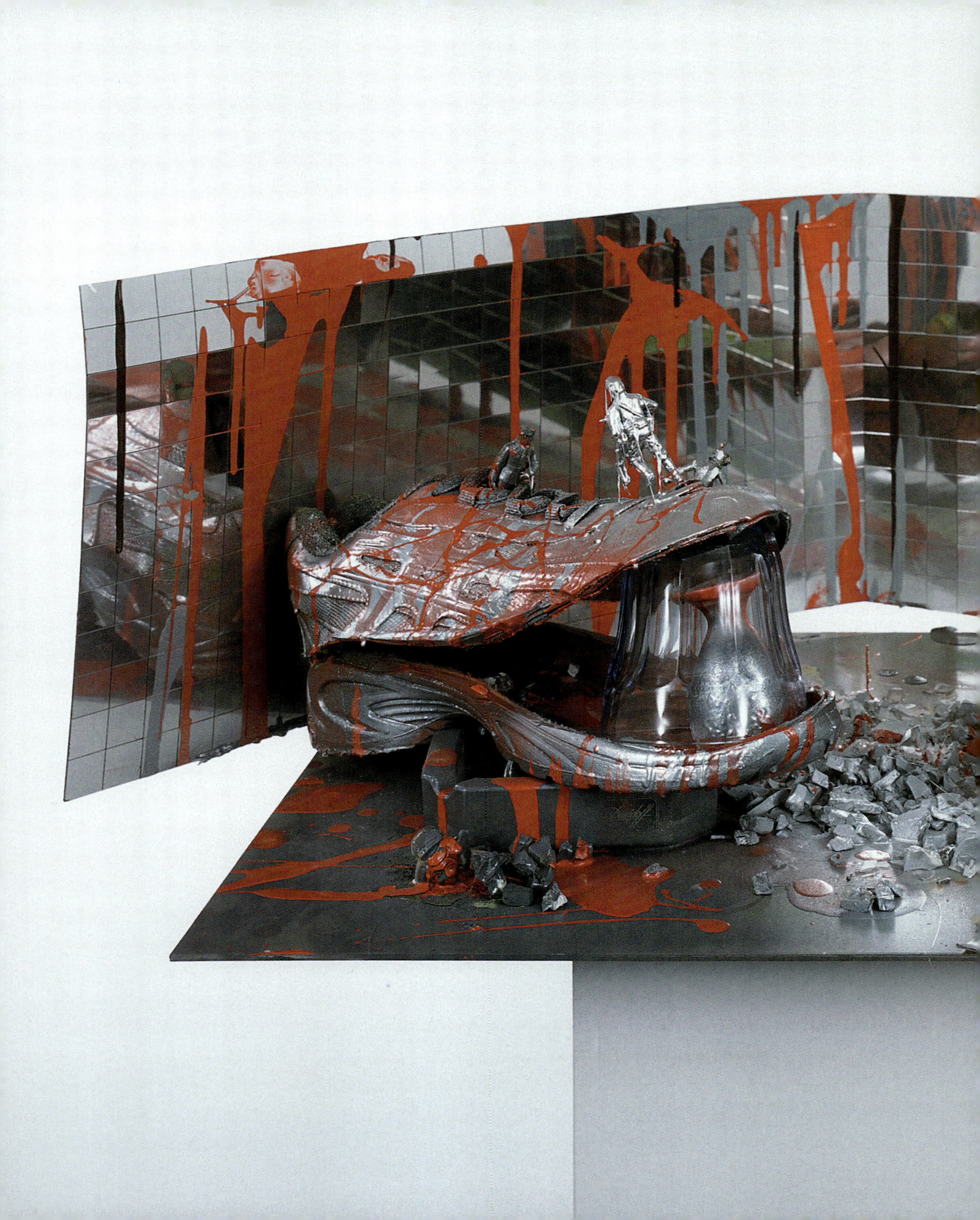

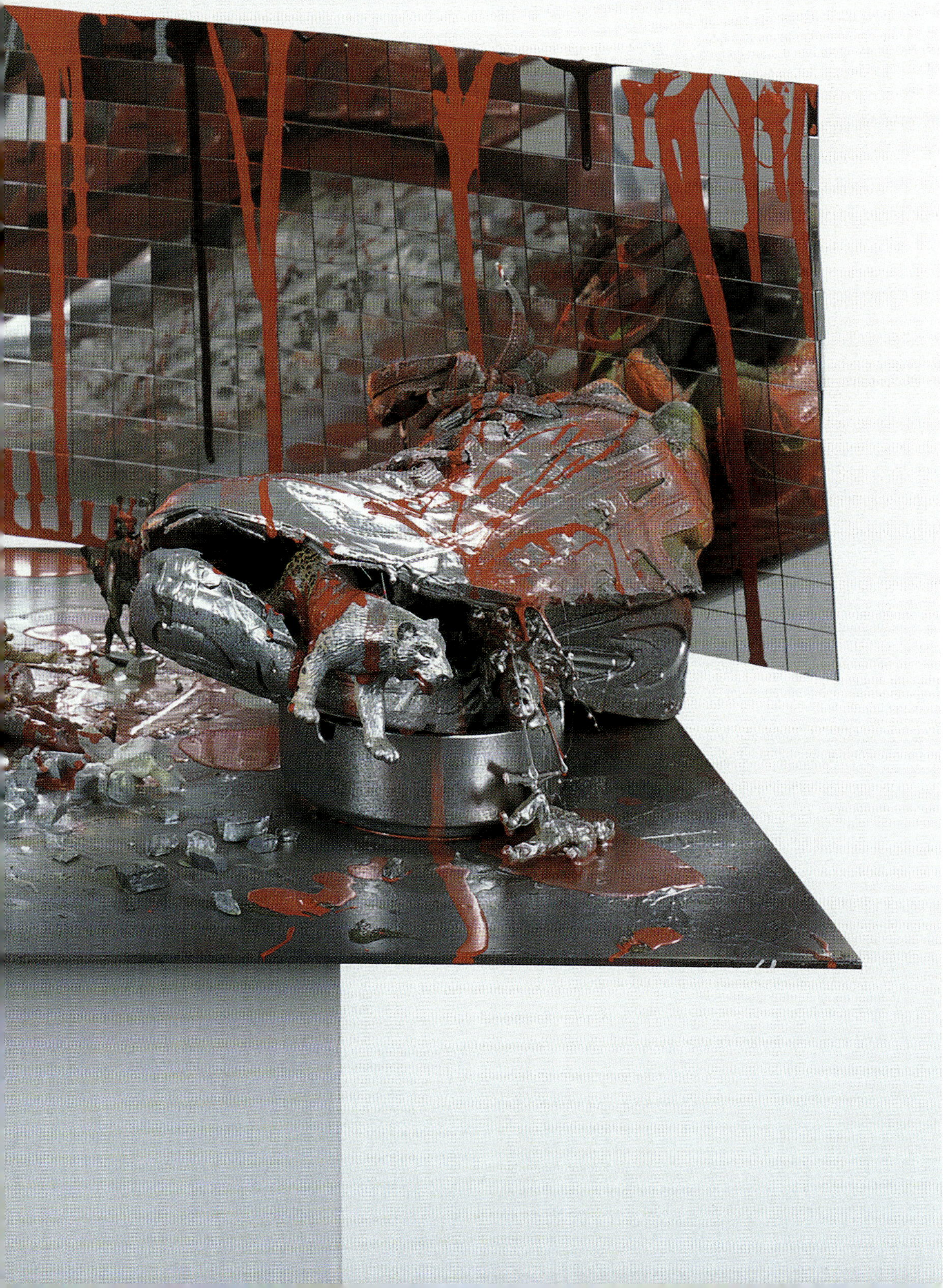

ISA GENZKEN, EMPIRE/VAMPIRE VIII, 2003, Spiegel, Glas und diverse Materialien, Holzsockel, Aluminiumplatte, 163 x 60 x 45 cm / mirror, glass, and mixed media, wooden stand, aluminum panel, $64^{3}/_{16}$ x $23^{5}/_{8}$ x $17^{11}/_{16}$".

«FRAGILITÄT KANN ETWAS SEHR SCHÖNES SEIN»

MICHAEL KRAJEWSKI & ISA GENZKEN

GESPRÄCH MIT ISA GENZKEN AM 28. JULI 2003 IN BERLIN

Michael Krajewski: Du fühlst dich nicht ganz wohl dabei, interviewt zu werden. Warum hast du dich bislang kaum öffentlich geäussert?

Isa Genzken: Ich mache doch seit meiner Jugend Kunst und stelle sie aus. Das ist eine sehr lange Zeit, in der ich mich nicht in Sprache, sondern wirklich in bildnerischer Sprache übe. Es ist schon kompliziert genug, sich im bildnerischen Bereich weiterzuentwickeln, nicht stillzustehen. Das möchte und kann ich eigentlich auch nicht erklären. Ansonsten würde ich Bücher schreiben.

MK: Dennoch scheinen manche Katalogtexte sich auf Gespräche mit dir zu beziehen. Ein Essay von Benjamin Buchloh wird immer wieder zitiert, weil er die frühe Phase deiner Arbeit im Kontext der Minimal Art, der Konzeptkunst und der Kunstszene der 70er Jahre in Düsseldorf analysiert.[1] Ist dieser Text in Absprache mit dir entstanden?

IG: Wir hatten damals ein Gespräch geführt. Als ich anschliessend den Text las, fand ich eigentlich keine meiner Äusserungen wieder – Bezüge zu Eva Hesse etwa –, trotzdem hielt ich ihn für zutreffend. Er war also fähig, was ich meinte, in seine Sprache zu übersetzen.

MK: Er hatte natürlich Hintergrundwissen, die Jahre im Rheinland miterlebt ...

IG: ... ja, auch mich aus nächster Nähe miterlebt. Doch das war kein Interview, ich kann nur betonen: Ich kann keine Seite über meine Arbeit schreiben, wie soll ich denn darüber sprechen?

MK: Das kann man etwa in deinem Gespräch mit Wolfgang Tillmans sehen.[2] Er ist Photograph, fragt dich nach Photographie und hat offensichtlich seine eigene Vorstellung davon, was Photographie ist, es entsteht so fast ein Streitgespräch.

IG: Das war keine Situation, wo ich ausgefragt wurde, sondern ein Gespräch unter Freunden. So was würde ich nicht Interview nennen. Ich weiss überhaupt nicht, wie man darauf kommt, dass Künstler gerne Interviews geben. Ich habe mit anderen Künstlern darüber gesprochen, dass ich es nie wollte, und war überrascht, wie ungern auch andere das tun.

MK: Ein Interview bietet die Möglichkeit, Dinge, die einem nicht passen, zurechtzurücken.

IG: Ich bin doch kein Politiker. Mein Bereich ist das Bildnerische, das kann man mit Worten ganz schwer fassen, wie ich mich fühle, wenn ich eine Skulptur mache, oder warum ich sie mache. Insofern bin ich kein amerikanischer Mini-

---

MICHAEL KRAJEWSKI ist Kunsthistoriker und -kritiker. Er lebt in Köln.

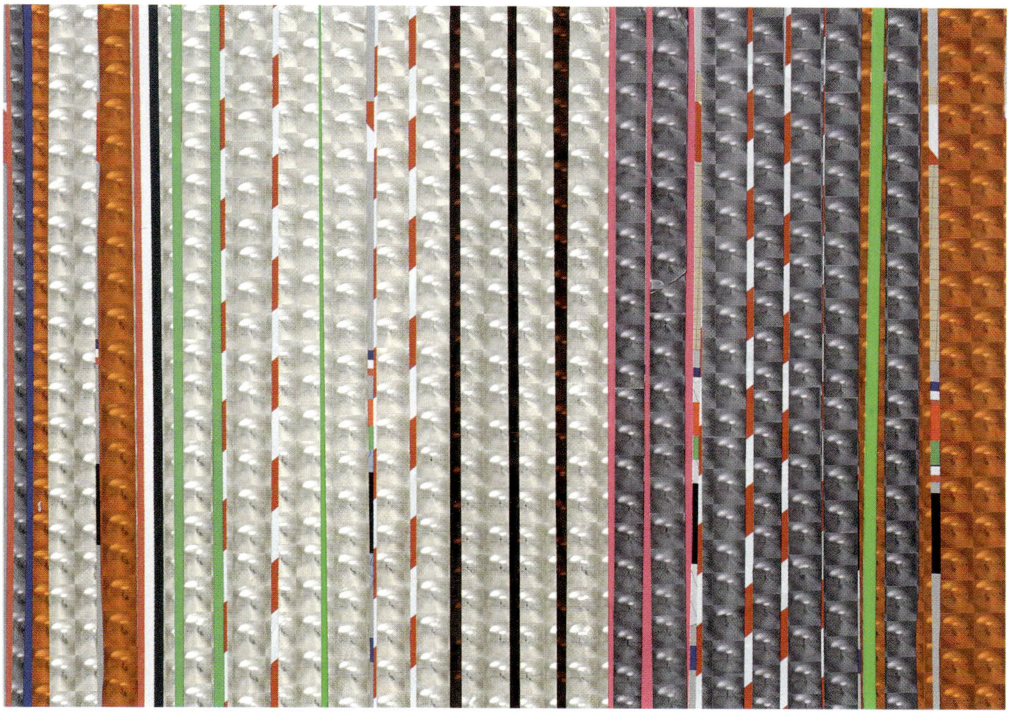

ISA GENZKEN, SOZIALE FASSADE, 2002, Metall, Holz, Metallfolie, Klebeband, 70 x 100 cm / SOCIAL FACADE, metal, wood, metal foil, adhesive tape, 27 9/16 x 39 3/8".

mal- oder Konzeptkünstler; die können das schon eher. Sie sind geübt darin, Interviews zu geben. Lawrence Weiner oder Carl Andre, die wissen ganz genau, wie ihre Arbeiten aussehen müssen, und weichen davon nicht sehr ab.

MK: Das hat wahrscheinlich mit dem Charakter ihrer Kunst zu tun.

IG: Je karger, je reduzierter, desto mehr Erklärung braucht die Kunst. Die gehört praktisch noch mit dazu. Ich kann meine letzten Skulpturen gar nicht erklären, weil ich auch nicht will. Wie gesagt, ist Kunst bildlich und nicht sprachlich! Es ist ja schon viel, wenn ich monatelang an den Skulpturen arbeite, bis ich endlich das Gefühl habe, dass sie in sich stimmig sind.

MK: Warum gibst du deinen Arbeiten dann Titel, was ja bereits ein Hinweis auf Inhaltlichkeit ist.

IG: Na ja, Inhaltlichkeit. Die Titel bestehen manchmal nur aus zwei, drei Worten und erleichtern die Identifizierung. Bei den «Ellipsoiden» und «Hyperbolos» haben die einzelnen Skulpturen noch Titel, damit ich genau weiss, um welche es sich handelt. Heisst eine etwa MIES VAN DER ROHE, erinnere ich mich an diesen Architekten und mit diesem Namen auch an meine Skulptur. Ich habe viele Skulpturen gemacht, deshalb ist es gut, dass sie Titel tragen.

MK: Die Skulpturengruppe EMPIRE/VAMPIRE. WHO KILLS DEATH (2003) hat durchaus etwas Programmatisches: Man denkt bei Empire an die USA. Man hat den Eindruck, auf ein Katastrophenszenario zu sehen.

IG: Der Titel ist schon viel älter: Ich hatte einmal geplant, einen Film, *Empire/Vampire. Who kills*, zu drehen, der auf zwei Gebäude in New York anspielt: das Empire State Building und das Chrysler Building gegenüber, das viel gefährlicher aussieht – also wie ein Vampir. Dieser alte Titel passte nun sehr gut zu den Skulpturen.

MK: Es tauchen figürliche Elemente auf.

IG: Mich interessierten die unterschiedlichen Massstäbe: Es gab ganz kleine kriegerische Figuren, normale und

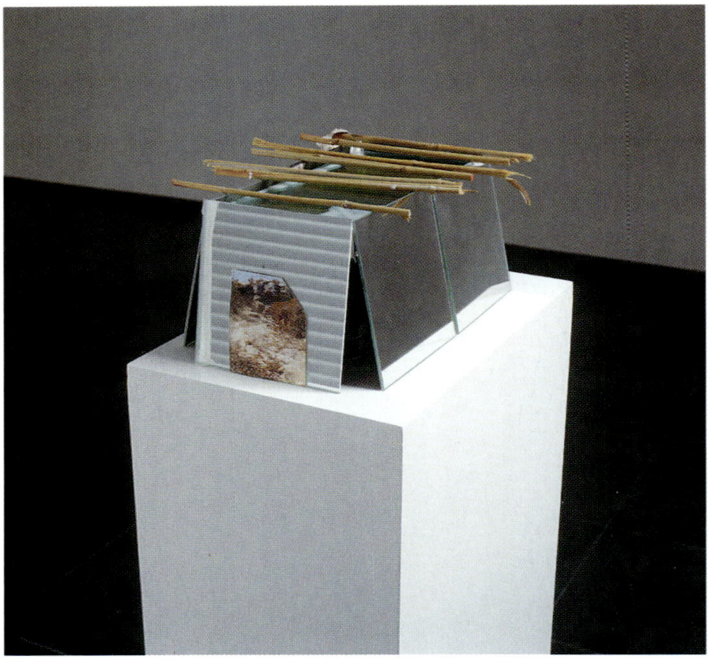

ISA GENZKEN, STRANDHÄUSER ZUM UMZIEHEN, 2000, Spiegel, Bambus, Muscheln, Sand, 155 x 27 x 42 cm / BEACH-HOUSE CHANGING ROOMS, mirror, bamboo, sea shells, sand, 61 x 10 5/8 x 16 1/2".
(PHOTOS: GALERIE DANIEL BUCHHOLZ, KÖLN)

etwas grössere, Bürger, herumsitzende Zeitungsleser, immer aus verschiedenen Epochen. Natürlich hatte die ganze Sache etwas mit der kriegerischen Atmosphäre zu tun, mit der ich gefühlsmässig nicht anders umgehen konnte. Die Bedrohung des Irakkrieges hat damals die Skulpturen ausgelöst. Ich wollte ursprünglich Skulpturen machen, die eine Filmszene darstellen, also Modellcharakter haben, nicht Skulpturen im traditionellen Sinn, sondern in einer Bewegung der Figuren und der Perspektive. Man könnte sich die Szenen in einem Sciencefictionfilm vorstellen. Das fing an mit der Ausstellung «Fuck the Bauhaus» in New York, wo ich schon Modelle mit Figuren und kleinen tanzenden Puppen auf dem Boden gemacht habe.

MK: In der Kunsthalle Zürich waren die Skulpturen gleichmässig im Raum verteilt. Man konnte um sie herumgehen, sie einzeln und von allen Seiten aus der Nähe betrachten.

IG: Ja, auch die grosse Ausdehnung ist wichtig, denn so entsteht ein imaginärer Raum, den man als monumental erlebt. So erzeuge ich Raum, ohne Raum wegzunehmen. Die Installation war aber auch psychisch gemeint. Was da passierte, war lustig, aber teilweise auch drastisch, etwa wenn Soldaten mit einem Gewehr vor einem standen. Als ich daran arbeitete, meinte jeder, der ins Atelier kam: «Was machst du denn hier? Das sieht ja komisch aus.» Und ich sagte: «Das werden Filmszenen.» Wenn ich etwas mache, versuche ich es auf den Punkt zu bringen. Das ist ganz merkwürdig. Ich erzähle das, weil ich oft gefragt werde, wie ich auf diese Ideen komme. Als wäre das etwas Besonderes. Bei mir kommt das so, entsteht intuitiv. Wenn ich versuche etwas Besonderes zu machen, funktioniert das nicht. Ich kann es jetzt nicht anders erklären, aber ich finde das wichtig. Das ist nur so normal, wie der eigene Alltag sein muss.

MK: Bedeutet Alltag für dich Arbeit?

IG: Ich lasse es völlig laufen. Meistens stehe ich auf, koche einen Kaffee und fange an zu arbeiten, meistens ein paar Stunden lang. Dann gehe ich essen, fahre mit dem Fahrrad, mache Dinge, die Spass machen. Oder ich rufe mal jemand an, kriege Besuch, verabrede mich mit meiner Mutter. Ich liebe die Arbeit und ich arbeite regelmässig.

MK: Wie wurde die Ausstellung «Fuck the Bauhaus» in New York (2000) aufgenommen?

IG: Ich hatte das Gefühl, dass es bei den Künstlern ein Aufatmen gab, insbesondere bei den jungen. Es war ja keine kommerzielle Galerie, AC-Project-Room war ein

ISA GENZKEN, STRANDHÄUSER ZUM UMZIEHEN, 2000, Glas, Tapete, Folie, 175 x 40 x 27 cm / BEACH-HOUSE CHANGING ROOMS, glass, wallpaper, foil, 68 7/8 x 15 3/4 x 16 1/2".

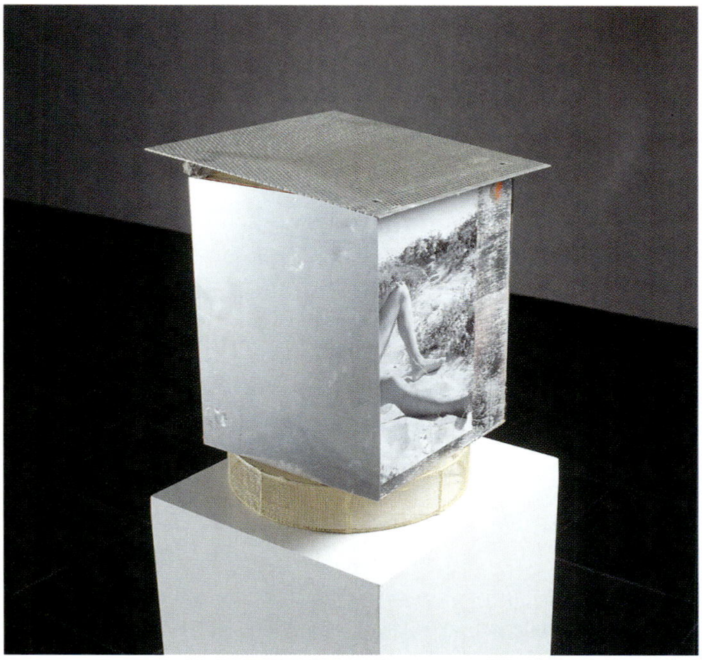

alternativer Raum. Mir sagten viele Leute, dass es die wichtigste Ausstellung in dieser Zeit war. Es gab eine extreme Stimmung für die Ausstellung. Wenn man zu der Zeit durch New Yorker Galerien ging, war alles ein wenig tot, es gab da nichts Neues, Erfrischendes, alles sah erschreckend teuer und tot aus. Meine Materialien waren billig und frech.

MK: Material und Machart weisen in eine andere Richtung.

IG: Im Prinzip ja. Viele Modelle – ich wollte einen Modellcharakter – sind nun einmal fragiler als etwa eine monumentale Eisenskulptur. Und oft ist der Mensch ja sehr erfreut, wenn er noch etwas Altes, als Skizze Gemeintes sehen kann, weil man es erhalten konnte. Fragilität kann etwas sehr Schönes sein, schöner als das eindeutig für immer Gemachte. Mir ist es sehr wichtig, dass die Sachen wirklich von mir sind, und nicht von Assistenten gemacht oder in Auftrag gegeben worden sind. Jedes Stück ist von mir, von meiner Hand. Das mit den Auftragsarbeiten hat sich in den letzten dreissig Jahren durchgesetzt und ist so langweilig geworden. Künstler machen es sich einfach, entwerfen eine Skizze, geben sie weg, dann wird es für teures Geld hergestellt und dann gekauft. Na ja – die Idee ist vom Künstler, aber das Handschriftliche fehlt. Wichtig ist bei dieser Ausstellung, sie ist in New York gemacht. Ich war zwei Monate dort, und dort ist sie entstanden: in der Galerie selbst und aus der Atmosphäre der Stadt heraus. Ich nahm eine Gegenposition, gegen New York, ein. In Berlin hätte ich das nicht machen können.

MK: Der mit Photographien übersäte SPIELAUTOMAT (1999–2000) ist eine der wenigen Arbeiten mit persönlichen Bezügen.

IG: Die Ausstellung im Frankfurter Kunstverein (2000) hiess «Urlaub». Es gab die STRANDHÄUSER, und ich dachte an Strand und Meer. Da sollte auch etwas Spielerisches sein, ein Spielautomat, also ein Pseudonym für ein Spielkasino. Ich wollte am Strand mit all meinen Freunden sein, oder zumindest mit denen, die ich mag: Lawrence Weiner, Kai Althoff, Wolfgang Tillmans, meinem Freund aus New York. Oder einem reichen Filmstar.

MK: Du scheust dich nicht, Persönliches zu zeigen?

IG: Ich denke, dass Freunde das Wichtigste im Leben sind, und es gibt viele Künstler, die ihre Freunde porträtierten. Etwa Gerhard Richter mit den beiden Palermo- und Richter-Büsten, denk an Wolfgang Tillmans. Das ist also nicht so einmalig, das kommt schon öfters vor. Auch den ganzen Säulen gab ich Namen meiner Freunde. Ich finde es schön, wenn Leute das wissen. Das ist ja interessant. Es gab auch mal eine Arbeit, die MEISTER GERHARD hiess. Ich mochte das immer sehr gerne. So, als wäre man eine Familie. Was auch so ist.

MK: Du hast selten mit anderen Künstlern zusammengearbeitet: mit Wolfgang Tillmans bei einer Installation im Museum Ludwig, mit Josef Strau in Berlin hast du einen Pavillon gemacht. Fiel es dir schwer, etwas von deiner künstlerischen Autonomie abzugeben?

IG: Nein. Das darf nur nicht aufgesetzt sein. Zwischen mir und Wolfgang hat sich die Arbeit irgendwie entwickelt. Wir haben vorher nichts festgelegt. Sondern es hat sich irgendwie ergeben. Wie von selber.

Für den Pavillon am Rosa-Luxemburg-Platz habe ich Entwürfe gemacht, und Josef Strau hat die praktischen, statischen und bürokratischen Probleme übernommen. Ich habe das sehr gemocht. Josef hat über unsere Zusammenarbeit einen sehr schönen reflektierenden Text verfasst.[3)] 1982 habe ich mit Gerhard Richter zusammen den U-Bahnhof in Duisburg gestaltet. Er machte mir zuliebe mit, obwohl ihn das überhaupt nicht interessierte. Das war ihm viel zu sozial gedacht – so 'n U-Bahnhof! –, aber ich wollte es unbedingt. Ich finde es sehr schön, wenn man von seinem Ego etwas wegkommt und merkt, dass man mit einer Person, die man als Künstler sehr schätzt, etwas gemeinsam machen kann. Das könnte ich zwar nicht immer, finde es aber ganz gut, wenn es sich ergibt.

MK: Wolltest du schon früh Künstlerin werden?

IG: Immer, immer, immer schon.

MK: Woher stammst du?

IG: Ich bin in Hamburg aufgewachsen. In Oldesloe bin ich geboren, meine Eltern sind gleich nach Hamburg gezogen. Meine Mutter wollte Schauspielerin werden, hat in meiner Kindheit immer Goethe rezitiert. Mein Vater wollte Sänger werden und es gab von morgens bis abends klassische Musik. In dieser chaotischen Atmosphäre bin ich aufgewachsen – als Einzelkind von zwei Kunstbesessenen. Beide sind an ein und demselben Tag geboren, zwei Tage nach Josef Beuys. Das ist doch komisch. Mit Beuys verstand ich mich übrigens immer sehr gut.

MK: Du lebtest damals in Düsseldorf.

IG: Ich kam mit einundzwanzig aus Berlin nach Köln, weil dort mein Freund Benjamin Buchloh lebte und bei Rudolf Zwirner arbeitete. Dann ging ich in die Akademie, zog irgendwann nach Düsseldorf, dann wieder zurück nach Köln, also hin und her. Schliesslich blieb ich zwanzig Jahre lang in Köln und erlebte den Aufstieg dieser Stadt in Sachen Kunst mit. Düsseldorf war vorher wichtiger, wegen Konrad Fischer und seiner amerikanischen Mannschaft. Dann änderte sich die Situation zugunsten Kölns.

MK: Damals hast du zum ersten Mal ausgestellt.

IG: In Düsseldorf hatte ich mit siebenundzwanzig in der Galerie von Konrad Fischer meine erste Ausstellung. Als Studentin war ich schon immer in diese Galerie gegangen, und dort kamen die Künstler persönlich zu den Eröffnungen. Ich fand relativ schnell Kontakt, ich verstand mich gut mit Carl Andre, mit Gilbert & George, Bruce Nauman, Lawrence Weiner. Es war immer so eine Atmosphäre bei Konrad Fischer, dass man etwas essen ging und sich gut kennen lernte. Dann gab es natürlich die Arbeiten, die mich tief beeindruckten.

MK: Diese Künstler waren damals ein wenig älter?

IG: Sie waren alle älter, das war eine ganz andere Generation.

MK: Damals gab es wahrscheinlich schon den Kontakt zu Gerhard Richter?

IG: Der war auch immer da und war zu der Zeit mein Lehrer. Ich lebte mit Benjamin Buchloh zusammen, doch er hatte seinen Job, ich meinen – das war keine ganz symbiotische Verbindung. Ich hatte immer meine Art, mich selbständig zu bewegen. Ich legte dann ja auch in meiner Ehe mit Gerhard Richter darauf immer Wert, wechselte etwa die Galerie und kam in einen ganz anderen Kreis, mit dem er überhaupt nichts zu tun hatte.

MK: Habt ihr auch ästhetische Diskussionen geführt?

IG: Ja, sehr oft. Es gab aber selten Übereinstimmung. Nach der Scheidung ging es 1989 erst einmal nach New York, dann nach Berlin.

MK: Wie lange warst du in New York?

IG: Ein Jahr.

MK: Hast du damals ausgestellt?

IG: Nein, nach dem Bruch der vierzehnjährigen Ehe war ich sehr aufgewühlt und machte die Collagenbücher *I love New York, Crazy City*. Daran arbeitete ich durchgehend und hatte regelmässig Kontakt zu Lawrence Weiner. Er hat sich freundschaftlich und unglaublich rührend um mich gekümmert, damit es mir wieder besser ging.

MK: Sind die Bücher mit dem Hintergedanken entstanden, sie auszustellen oder zu publizieren?

IG: Ja. Deswegen sind sie entstanden. Ich wollte Bücher

über New York für einen Touristen machen, vielleicht auch für einen New Yorker, der auf diese Weise einen anderen Einstieg in die Stadt bekommt, wie verrückt sie halt ist. In normalen Städteführern stehen ja auch Hotels, Preise, Namen, Adressen, Kinos, Bars, Diskotheken ... es sollte ein richtiger Reiseführer mit all diesen Informationen sein, und eben viel mehr.

MK: Es gibt darin Photographien von Hausfassaden, Müll auf der Strasse, von auffälligen Gitterrosten auf dem Fussboden. Das ist auch der Blick der Bildhauerin?

IG: Ja. Es hat mit meinem ganz persönlichen Blick zu tun. Wie New York mir auffiel, wie ich New York sah, was ich liebte. Es sollte eben auch persönlich sein. Jemand, der mich nicht kennt, sollte denken: «Die liegt da mit drei Typen im Bett.» Das passiert da auch. Das passiert in New York viel eher als in Berlin. Man lernt Leute viel schneller kennen und kennt sich dann nicht mehr. Manche geben einem die Telefonnummer, am nächsten Tag ruft man an, und dann tun sie, als hätten sie einen nie getroffen. Als Europäer ist man da überrascht. Und manchmal kennen sie einen und treffen sich mit dir. Das ist ganz anders. Das wollte ich mitteilen.

MK: Du scheust dich auch hier nicht, Persönliches preiszugeben. In einem Brief verbittet sich ein Rechtsanwalt nach einer Auseinandersetzung strikt jeden Kontakt zu dir. Dieses Buch auszustellen bedeutet ja eine Veröffentlichung.

IG: Ich finde es gut, wenn man nicht immer nur das Vorteilhafte von sich zeigt. Warum sollte man? Es kann ja nicht sein, dass ein Mensch nur aus positiven Dingen besteht. Ich finde es mutig, etwas zu zeigen, was für andere interessant ist. Das merkte ich ja, als ich das Buch ausstellte. Die Besucher vertieften sich oft darin und sahen sich alles aufmerksam an. Es hat mich sehr gefreut, dass diese Arbeit nicht umsonst war, und sie werden jetzt alle drei als Faksimile gedruckt. Das habe ich mir immer gewünscht!

MK: Mir fällt ein, dass es doch ein Interview mit dir gibt, mit Lawrence Weiner in einem der Collagenbücher.

IG: Das ist wahr. Ich hatte Lawrence darum gebeten. Das Interview beschäftigt sich mit New York, ich wollte wissen, wie seine Erfahrung mit der Stadt ist. Er redete los, das verschlug mir den Atem und ich konnte überhaupt nichts mehr sagen. Ich habe das Band abschreiben lassen und es ihm so, wie es war, geschickt. Er gab sein Okay, und ich nahm es ohne Überarbeitung hinein. Aber ich sage da nicht viel. Es gibt seit neuestem noch ein anderes Interview mit Kai Althoff aus Köln, mit dem ich seit langem befreundet bin. Ich hatte ihn diesen Sommer gebeten, mich zu befragen, warum ich keine Interviews gebe. So entstand eine Art Anti-Interview. Der zehn Minuten lange 8-mm-Film ist lustig geworden; er war gar nicht vorbereitet, wir hatten nicht geübt, alles geschah spontan. Ich bin sehr glücklich mit dem Ergebnis.

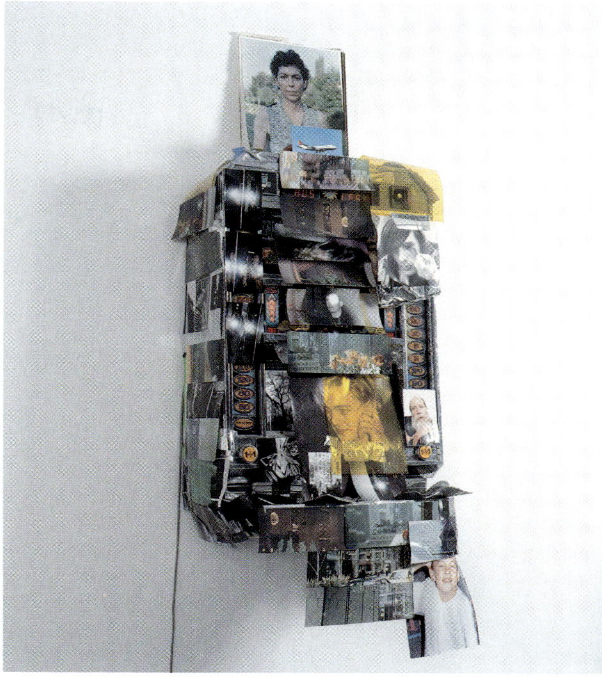

ISA GENZKEN, SPIELAUTOMAT, 1999–2000, verschiedene Materialien, Photographien, 160 x 65 x 50 cm / FRUIT MACHINE, mixed media, photographs, 63 x 25 5/8 x 19 11/16".

1) Benjamin Buchloh, «Isa Genzken. Vom Modell zum Fragment», in: *Isa Genzken*, Ausstellungskatalog der Renaissance Society, Chicago, et al., Verlag der Buchhandlung Walther König, Köln 1993, S. 127–134.
2) «Isa Genzken. Ein Gespräch mit Wolfgang Tillmans», *Camera Austria*, Nr. 81, 2003, S. 7–18.
3) Josef Strau, «Haare wachsen, wie sie wollen», in: *Isa Genzken 1992–2003. Ausstellungen, Arbeiten, Werkverzeichnis / Exhibitions, Works, Catalogue raisonné.* Ausstellungskatalog, Museum Abteiberg, Mönchengladbach/Kunsthalle Zürich, Verlag der Buchhandlung Walther König, Köln 2003, S. 37.

"FRAGILITY CAN BE A VERY BEAUTIFUL THING"

MICHAEL KRAJEWSKI & ISA GENZKEN

CONVERSATION WITH ISA GENZKEN ON 28 JULY 2003 IN BERLIN

Michael Krajewski: You aren't very comfortable being interviewed. Why is it that you have hardly ever commented on your art in public?

Isa Genzken: I've been making art and exhibiting it ever since I was young. That's a very long time during which I've been working on my visual language, not on my language skills. It's complicated enough to go on developing visually, not to stand still. I can't actually explain that, nor would I want to. Otherwise I would have written books.

MK: Yet certain catalogue texts seem to refer to conversations with you. There's one essay by Benjamin Buchloh that's always being cited because he analyzes the early stages of your work in the context of Minimal Art, Conceptual Art and the art scene in Düsseldorf in the seventies.[1] Did he talk to you about that text?

IG: We did have a conversation at the time. When I read the text afterwards, I didn't actually find anything I had said in it—links to Eva Hesse and so on—but still it seemed right to me. Obviously he was able to translate what I had said into his own language.

MICHAEL KRAJEWSKI is an art historian and critic living in Cologne.

MK: Of course he also had the right background information; he had firsthand knowledge of the Rhineland in those days ...

IG: Yes, and firsthand knowledge of me too. But it wasn't an interview, as I said: I can't write even a single page about my work, so how could I speak about it?

MK: Something of that comes through in your conversation with Wolfgang Tillmans.[2] He's a photographer, asks you about photography, evidently has his own ideas about what photography is, and the outcome is practically an argument.

IG: The situation wasn't that I was being asked questions, it was just a conversation between friends. I wouldn't call that an interview. I really don't know why people imagine that artists like giving interviews. I've talked with other artists about the fact that I've never wanted to do that, and I've been surprised how unwilling the others are too.

MK: An interview is an opportunity to rectify things that one doesn't like.

IG: But I'm not a politician. My field is visual art, it's very hard to put into words how I feel when I'm making a sculpture, or why I'm making it. In that sense I'm no American Minimalist or Conceptual Artist; they're better at that.

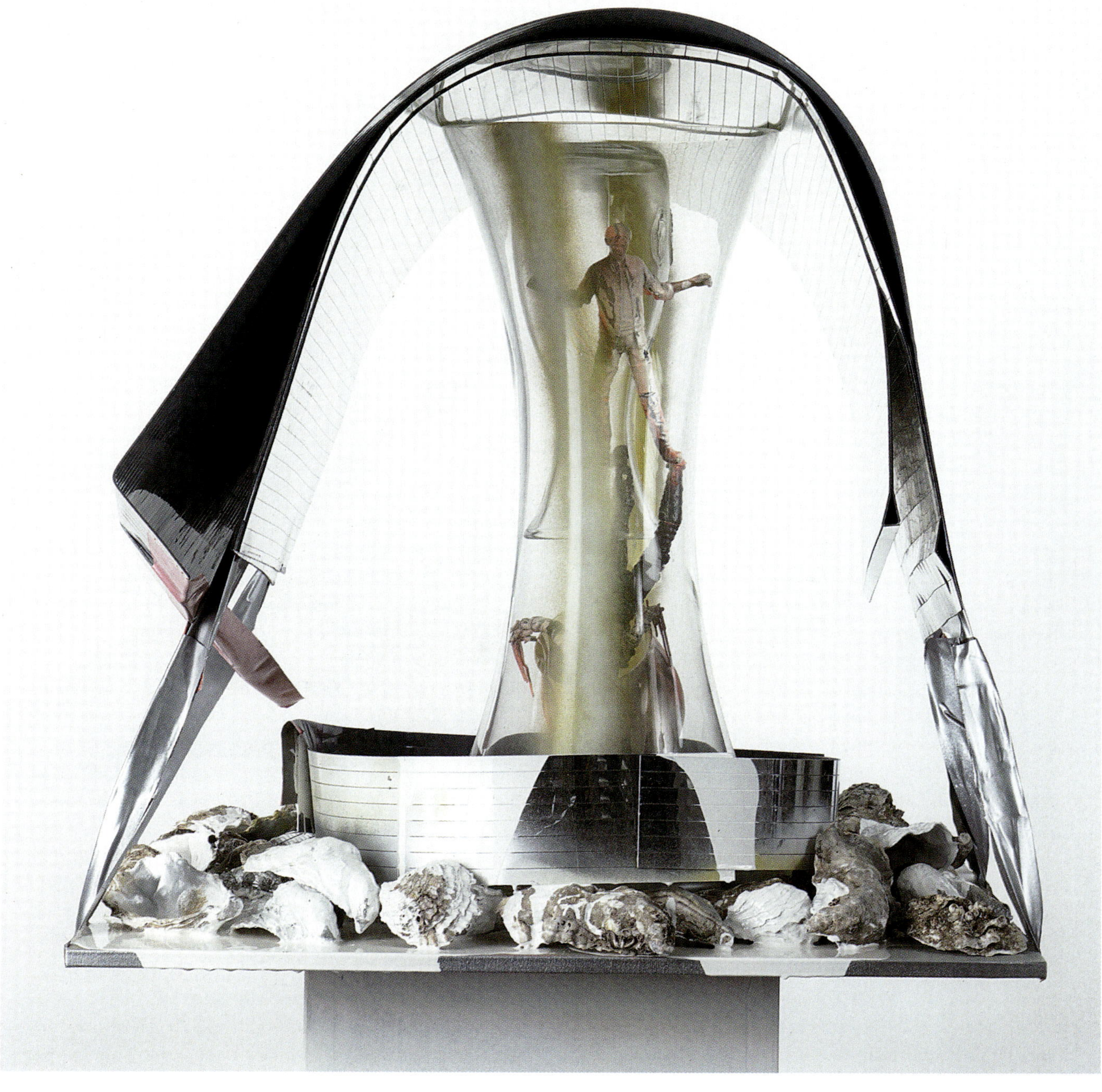

ISA GENZKEN, EMPIRE/VAMPIRE, WHO KILLS DEATH, 2003, Teil der 22-teiligen Installation aus diversen Materialien, Kunsthalle Zürich, 220 x 70 x 45 cm / detail from the 22-part, mixed-media installation, $86^5/_8$ x $27^9/_{16}$ x $17^{11}/_{16}$".

They've practiced giving interviews. Lawrence Weiner or Carl Andre, they know precisely what their works should look like, and they never really depart from that.

MK: That probably has something to do with the nature of their art.

IG: The bleaker, the more reduced art is, the more explanation it needs. The explanation is almost part of the art. I'm completely unable to explain my most recent sculptures; in any case I don't want to. As I said, art is visual, not verbal! It's already something if I work for months on the sculptures until at last I have the feeling that they make sense within themselves.

MK: Then why do you give your works titles, which is already an indication that they are partly about content?

IG: Oh dear, content. The titles sometimes consist of only two or three words, and make the pieces easier to identify. In the case of the "Ellipsoids" or the "Hyperbolos," certain sculptures still have titles, so that I know exactly which one is meant. So if one is called MIES VAN DER ROHE for instance, then I remember that architect and his name reminds me of my sculpture. I've made so many sculptures, that's why it's good that they have titles.

MK: The group of sculptures EMPIRE/VAMPIRE. WHO KILLS DEATH (2003) has something distinctly programmatic about it: "Empire" makes you think of the USA. It feels like looking at the scene of some catastrophe.

IG: The title is much older: At one time I was planning to make a film, *Empire/Vampire. Who kills,* about two buildings in New York: the Empire State Building and the Chrysler Building opposite it, which looks much more dangerous—like a vampire. This old title just fit the sculptures very well.

MK: There are also figurative elements in the sculptures.

IG: I was interested in the different scales: there were little warlike figures, normal and slightly larger ones, citizens, people sitting around reading newspapers, all from different epochs. Of course the whole thing had something to do with the warlike atmosphere that I couldn't deal with, in terms of my feelings, in any other way. It was the threat of the Iraq War that triggered those sculptures. Originally I had wanted to make sculptures portraying a scene from a film, that is, rather like models: not sculptures in the traditional sense but with moving figures and perspective. You could think of them as scenes in a sci-fi film. It started with the exhibition in New York, "Fuck the Bauhaus," (2000) where I already made models with figures and little dancing dolls on the floor.

MK: In the Kunsthalle Zürich the sculptures were distributed evenly around the room. People were able to walk around them, look at them alone and close up from any side.

IG: Yes, and it's also important that they cover a large area, because that generates an imaginary space which you register as monumental. It's a way of creating space without taking up space. But that installation was also supposed to affect people's minds. What happened there was funny, but sometimes drastic too, like when you are faced by soldiers with guns. When I was working on it, people coming into the studio kept saying, "What's this you're making? It looks funny." So I would say, "It's going to be film scenes." When I make something, I really try to get to the point. It's strange. I'm saying that because I'm often asked how I come up with these ideas. As though it was something special. But they just come to me, they're intuitive. If I try to make something particular, it just doesn't work. I can't explain it any other way, but I think it's important. They're just normal, like your everyday life has to be.

MK: Does everyday life mean work for you?

IG: I just let things take their own course. Usually I get up, make coffee, and start working, usually for a few hours. Then I go and eat something, go out on my bike, do things I like doing. Or sometimes I phone someone, have visitors, arrange to meet my mother. I love working and I work regularly.

MK: How did the exhibition "Fuck the Bauhaus" go down in New York?

IG: I had the feeling that the artists breathed a sigh of relief, especially the young ones. It wasn't in a commercial gallery, the AC Project Room is an alternative space. A lot of people told me that it was the most important exhibition at that time. There was an extremely positive response to the exhibition. If you took a walk through the New York galleries at the time, everything was a bit dead, there was nothing new, refreshing, everything looked frighteningly expensive and dead. My materials were cheap and cheeky.

MK: The materials and the methods pointed in two different directions.

IG: In principle, yes. Models—I wanted the pieces to be like models—are usually more fragile than some monumental metal sculpture. And people often find it very pleasing when they can still see something old, intended as a sketch, because it's been preserved. Fragility can be a very beautiful thing, more beautiful than something that's obviously made to last forever. It's very important to me that the things I'm making are really by me, and not made by as-

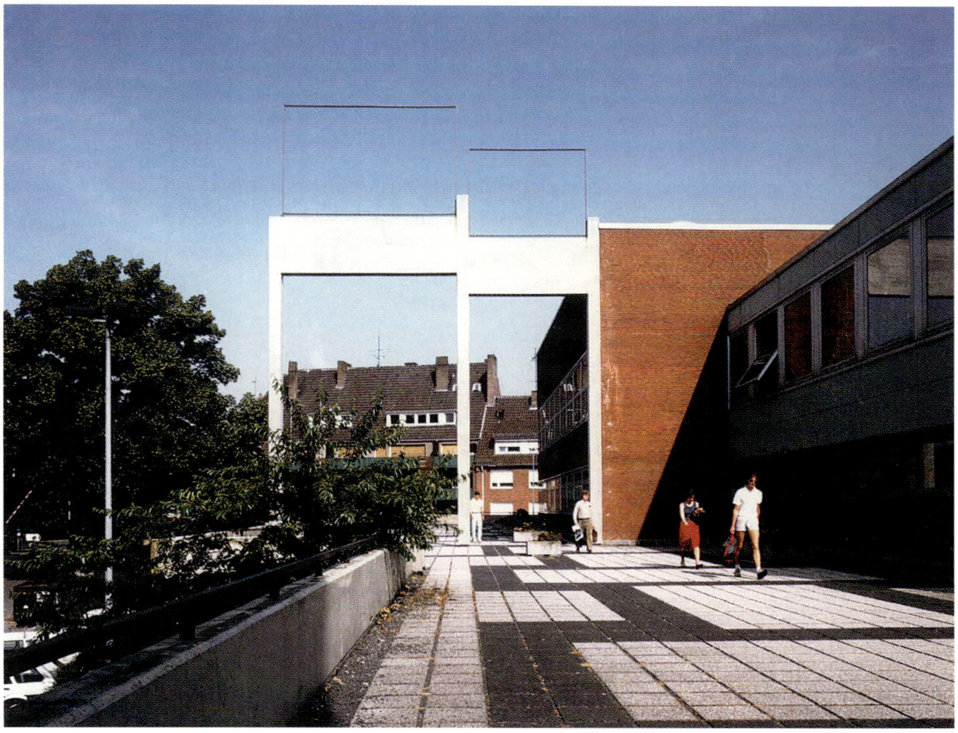

ISA GENZKEN, ABC, 1987, Aussenskulptur, Universitätsbibliothek Münster, im Rahmen der «Skulptur.Projekte Münster 1987», Beton, Stahl, 14,85 x 11,2 x 0,4 m / outdoor sculpture, University Library, Münster, concrete, steel, 48 3/4' x 36 3/4' x 15 3/4".
(PHOTO: GALERIE DANIEL BUCHHOLZ, KÖLN)

sistants or farmed out as commissions. Every piece is by me, made by my own hand. The business of commissioning other people to make things has taken hold in the last thirty years, and has become really boring. Artists take the easy way out, produce a sketch, hand it over to someone else, then the work is made at great expense and finally it's bought. Okay—the idea is the artist's, but their handwriting is missing. The important thing about this exhibition is that it was produced in New York. I was there for two months and that's where it was made: in the gallery itself and breathing in the atmosphere of the city. I adopted a counter-position, against New York. I could never have done that in Berlin.

MK: The SPIELAUTOMAT (1999–2000) covered with photographs is one of the few works with personal references.

IG: The exhibition in the Frankfurt Kunstverein in 2000 was called "Urlaub." The STRANDHÄUSER were in it and I was thinking about beaches and the sea. There had to be something playful as well, a fruit machine, a pseudonym for a casino. I wanted to be at the beach with all my friends, or at least the ones I like: Lawrence Weiner, Kai Althoff, Wolfgang Tillmans, my friend from New York. Or a rich filmstar.

MK: You're not reluctant to show personal things?

IG: I think that friends are the most important thing in life, and there are many artists who have made portraits of their friends. Like Gerhard Richter with his two busts of Palermo and Richter. Or think of Wolfgang Tillmans. It's not that unusual, it often happens. And I gave all the pillars my friends' names. I think it's good if people know that. It's interesting. There was one work that was called MEISTER GERHARD. I always liked it very much. As though we were all one family. Which is how it is.

MK: You've rarely worked with other artists: with Wolfgang Tillmans on an installation in the Museum Ludwig, and you made a pavilion in Berlin with Josef Strau. Was it hard for you to relinquish some of your own artistic autonomy?

IG: No. But it mustn't be imposed on you. The work with Wolfgang somehow just happened. We didn't fix anything in advance. It just turned out as it did. As though of its own accord. As far as the pavilion at the Rosa Luxembourg Platz is concerned, I made designs and Josef Strau dealt with all the practical, statistical and bureaucratic problems. I liked that very much. Josef wrote a very nice, reflective text on our work together.[3] In 1982 Gerhard Richter and I worked together on the subway station in Duisburg. He found it much too social—a subway station like that!—but I absolutely wanted it. I think it's very good when you can get away from your own ego a bit and find that you can do something together with someone who you value very highly as an artist. Of course I couldn't always be doing that, but I think it's pretty good when it turns out like that.

MK: Did you always want to be an artist, from an early age?

IG: Always, always, always.

MK: Where do you come from?

IG: I grew up in Hamburg. I was born in Oldesloe, my parents moved to Hamburg straight afterwards. My mother wanted to be an actress, she was always reciting Goethe when I was a child. My father wanted to be a singer so there was classical music in the house from morning till night. I grew up in that rather chaotic atmosphere—the only child of two arts freaks. Both of them were born on the same day, two days after Joseph Beuys. That's funny somehow. And I always got on very well with Beuys.

MK: You were living in Düsseldorf at the time.

IG: When I was twenty-one I moved from Berlin to Cologne, because my friend Benjamin Buchloh lived there, he was working at Rudolf Zwirner's. Then I went to the Academy, moved to Düsseldorf at some point, then back to Cologne, backwards and forwards. In the end I stayed in Cologne for twenty years, I was there as the city raised its profile on the art scene. Before that Düsseldorf had been more important because of Konrad Fischer and his American team. Then things changed and it was Cologne's turn.

MK: That was when you had your first exhibition.

IG: My first exhibition was when I was twenty-seven, in Konrad Fischer's gallery. As a student I had always gone to that gallery; the artists used to come to the openings in person. I made contact with various people relatively quickly, I got on well with Carl Andre, with Gilbert & George, Bruce Nauman, Lawrence Weiner. There was always a good atmosphere at Konrad Fischer's, people would go for something to eat and get to know each other. Then of course there were also the works themselves, which deeply impressed me.

MK: Those artists were a bit older than you?

IG: They were all older, they were a completely different generation.

MK: You had probably also met Gerhard Richter by then?

IG: He was always around, and he was also my teacher at the time. I was living with Benjamin Buchloh, but he had a job, I mean—it wasn't a very symbiotic relationship. I always had a way of being rather independent. And when I was married to Gerhard Richter, I still valued my independence, moved to another gallery and entered a very different circle that he had nothing at all to do with.

MK: Did you talk about aesthetic issues?

IG: Yes, very frequently. But we rarely agreed. After the divorce I went to New York, in 1989, and then to Berlin.

MK: How long were you in New York?

IG: A year.

MK: Did you have any shows?

IG: No, after my marriage of 14 years collapsed I was very unsettled and made the collage books, *I love New York, Crazy City*. I worked constantly on those and was regularly in touch with Lawrence Weiner. He looked after me in such a friendly, incredibly touching way, helping me to recover.

MK: When you were working on the books, were you intending to exhibit them or to publish them?

IG: Yes. That's why I did them. I wanted to make books about New York for a tourist, perhaps even for a New Yorker who would find a different take on the city, just how crazy it is. In normal city guides there are hotels, prices, names, addresses, cinemas, bars, discotheques ... it was supposed to be a proper guide book with all this information, and a lot more.

MK: There are photographs of the façades of buildings, garbage on the streets, unusual grilles in the ground. Is this also the gaze of the sculptress?

IG: Yes. It does have to do with my own personal gaze. How New York struck me, how I saw New York, what I loved. And it was also supposed to be personal. Anyone who knows me is supposed to think, "There she is, lying in bed with three guys." Which is perfectly possible. More possible in New York than in Berlin. You get to know people much faster and then suddenly you don't know them at all any more. Some people give you their phone number, you call them the next day and they act as though they had never met you. That takes the European by surprise. And then sometimes they do know you and they meet up with you. It's very different. That's what I wanted to put over.

MK: Again, you're not afraid to reveal personal matters. In a letter after an argument a lawyer breaks off all contact with you. Exhibiting this book is a form of publication.

IG: I think it's good if you don't only present your better side. Why should we? It's not possible for a person to have nothing but positive features. I think it's brave to show something that's interesting to other people. And I noticed that when I exhibited the book. The visitors often immersed themselves in it and looked very carefully at everything. It gave me considerable pleasure that this work had not been in vain, and now all three are going to be printed as facsimiles. It's exactly what I always wanted!

MK: I've just remembered that of course there is an interview with you, with Lawrence Weiner in one of the collage books.

IG: That's true. I asked Lawrence to do it. The interview is about New York, I wanted to know what his experience of the city is. He just started talking; I lost my voice and could not say another thing. I had the tape transcribed and sent it to him exactly as it was. He okayed it, and I included it without reworking it in any way. But I don't say a lot there. Very recently, there has been another interview with Kai Althoff from Cologne, who I have been friends with for a long time. I asked him this summer to ask me why I don't give interviews. The result was a kind of anti-interview. The ten-minute 8-mm film is fun; it was not at all prepared, we hadn't rehearsed, it was completely spontaneous. I'm very happy with the way it turned out.

(Translation: Fiona Elliott)

1) Benjamin Buchloh: "Isa Genzken. The Fragment as Model," in *Isa Genzken*, ex. cat., Renaissance Society, Chicago, et al. (Cologne: Walther König, 1993), pp. 135–141.
2) "Isa Genzken. A Conversation with Wolfgang Tillmans," *Camera Austria*, no. 81, 2003, pp. 7–18.
3) Josef Strau, "Hair that grows as it will," in *Isa Genzken 1992–2003. Ausstellungen, Arbeiten, Werkverzeichnis / Exhibitions, Works, Catalogue raisonné*, ex. cat., Museum Abteiberg, Mönchengladbach/Kunsthalle Zürich (Cologne: Walther König, 2003), p. 38.

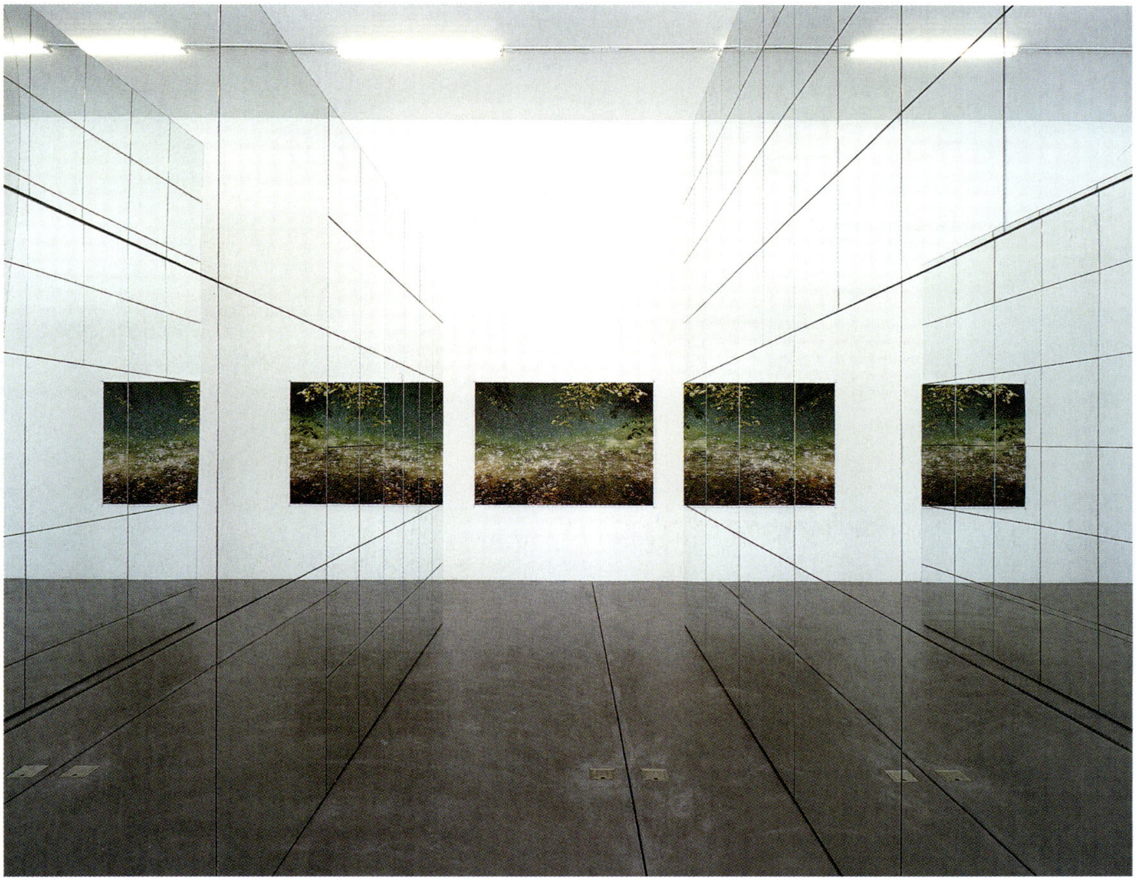

ISA GENZKEN/WOLFGANG TILLMANS, SCIENCE FICTION/HIER UND JETZT ZUFRIEDEN SEIN, 2003, Kunsthalle Zürich. ISA GENZKEN: 2 Elemente, Holz und Spiegelglas, 400 x 100 x 500 cm bzw. 300 x 100 x 500 cm / 2 parts, wood and mirror, 157 1/2 x 39 3/8 x 196 7/8" and 118 1/8 x 39 3/8 x 196 7/8"; WOLFGANG TILLMANS: BLAUTOPF, LANDSCAPE, 2001, Inkjet-Print auf Papier, ca. 137 x 200 cm / ink-jet print on paper, ca. 54 x 78 3/4".

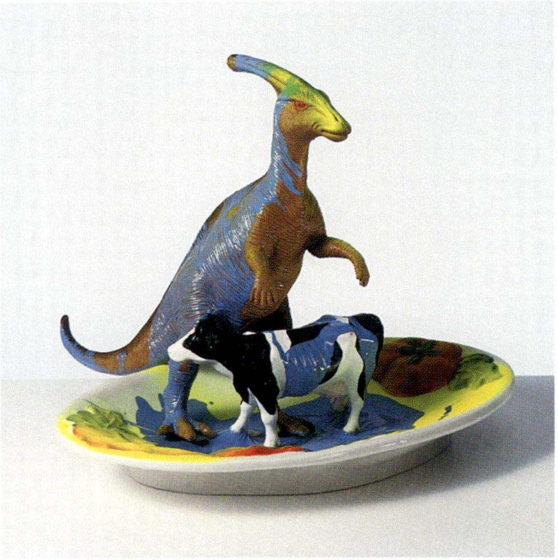

EDITION FOR PARKETT

ISA GENZKEN

AL DENTE, 2003

Italienische Keramik, Lack, Kunststoff.
Je individuell von Hand gestalteter Teller
mit zwei Spielzeugfiguren (Kuh und Dinosaurier),
ca. 30 x 20 x 26 cm.
Auflage: 74, signiertes und nummeriertes Zertifikat.

Italian ceramic, lacquer, plastic.
Plate with two toy figures (cow and dinosaur),
each unique and handmade by the artist,
ca. $11\,^{13}/_{16}$ x $7\,^{7}/_{8}$ x $10\,^{1}/_{4}$".
Edition of 74, signed and numbered certificate.

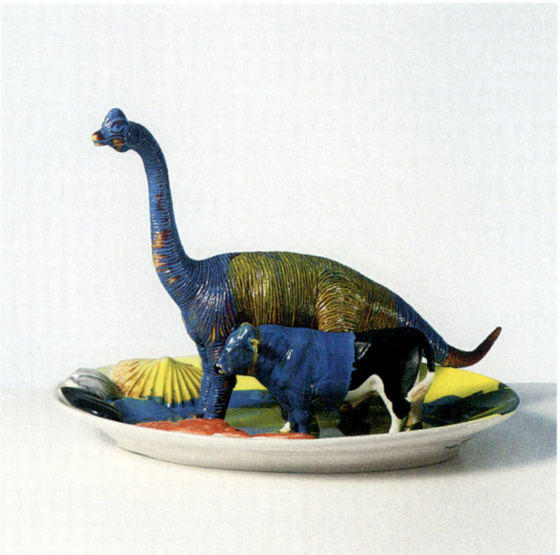

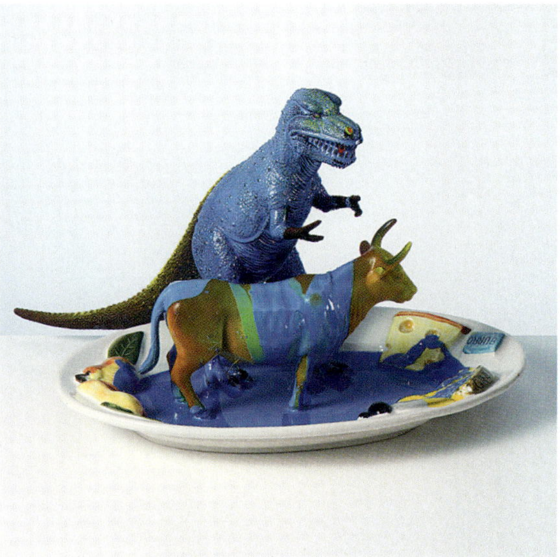

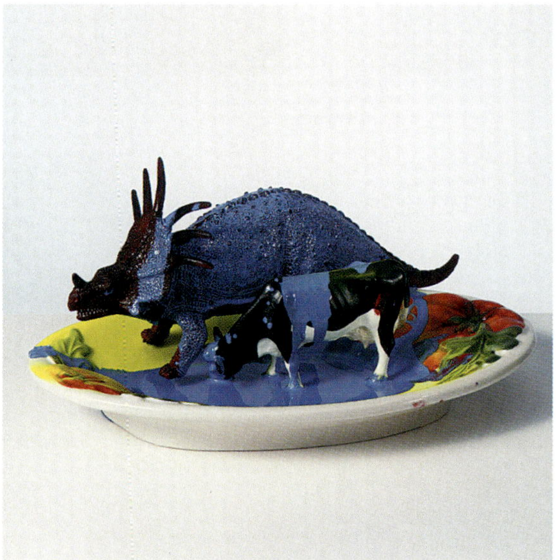

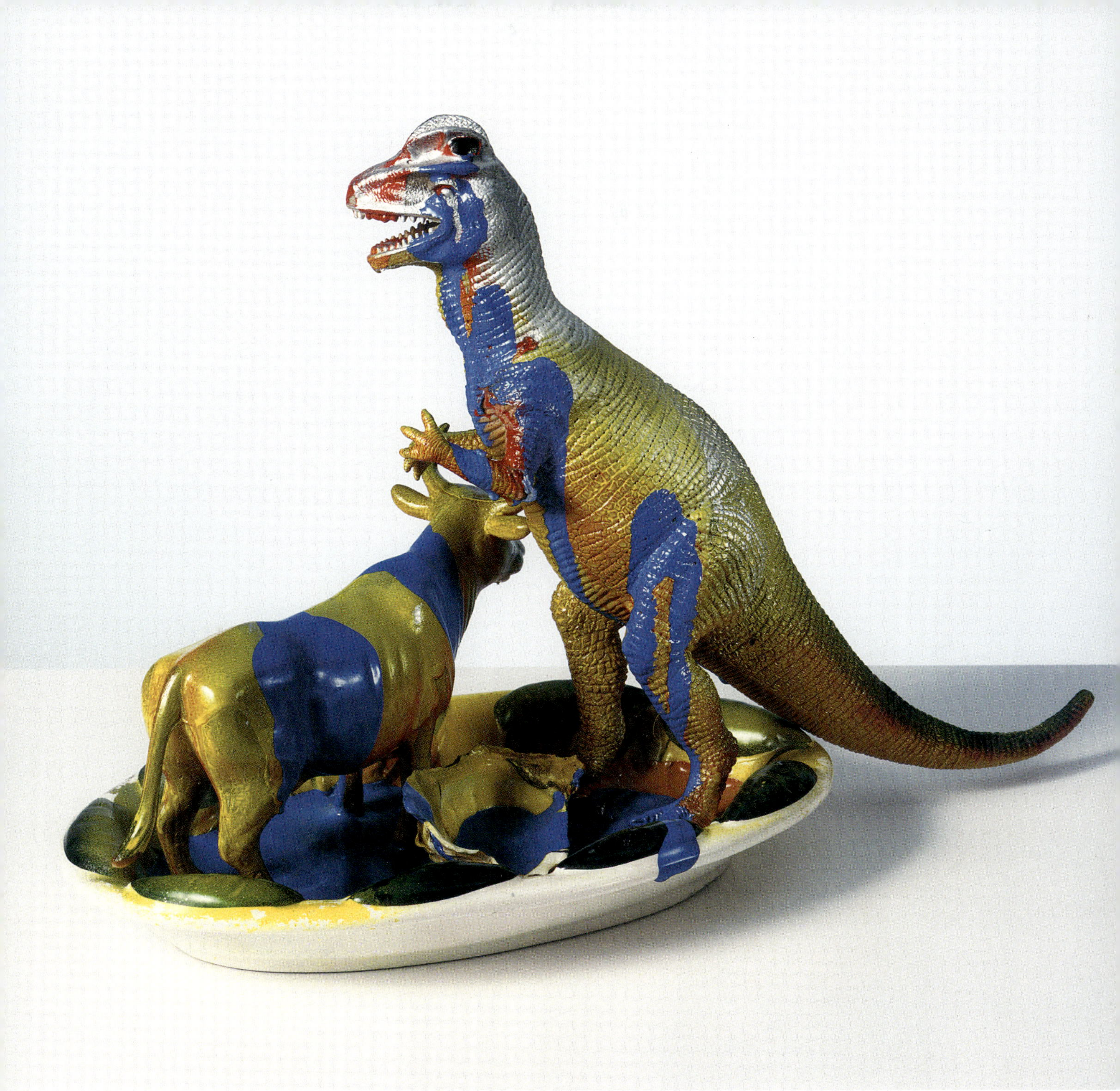

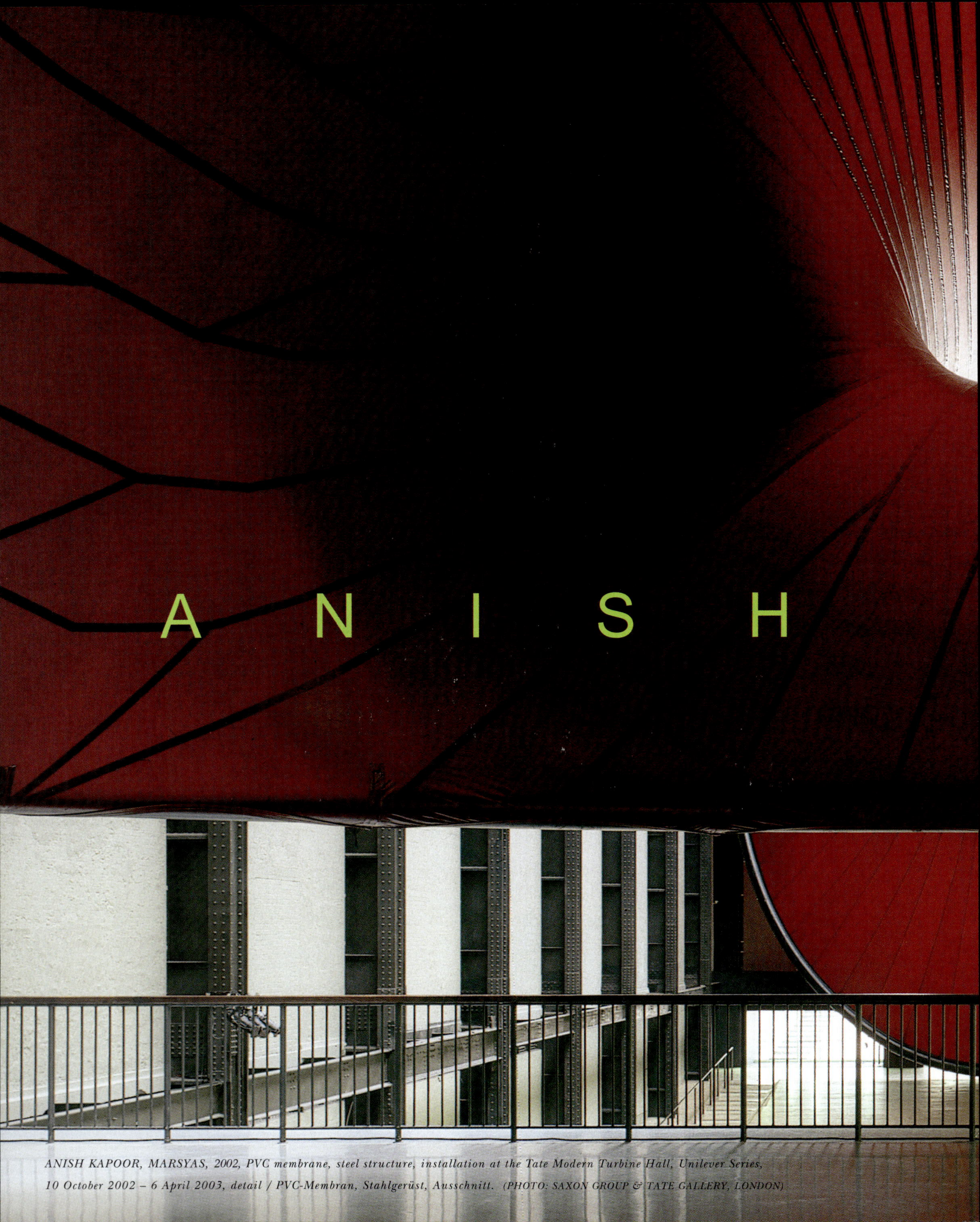

ANISH KAPOOR, MARSYAS, 2002, PVC membrane, steel structure, installation at the Tate Modern Turbine Hall, Unilever Series, 10 October 2002 – 6 April 2003, detail / PVC-Membran, Stahlgerüst, Ausschnitt. (PHOTO: SAXON GROUP & TATE GALLERY, LONDON)

K A P O O R

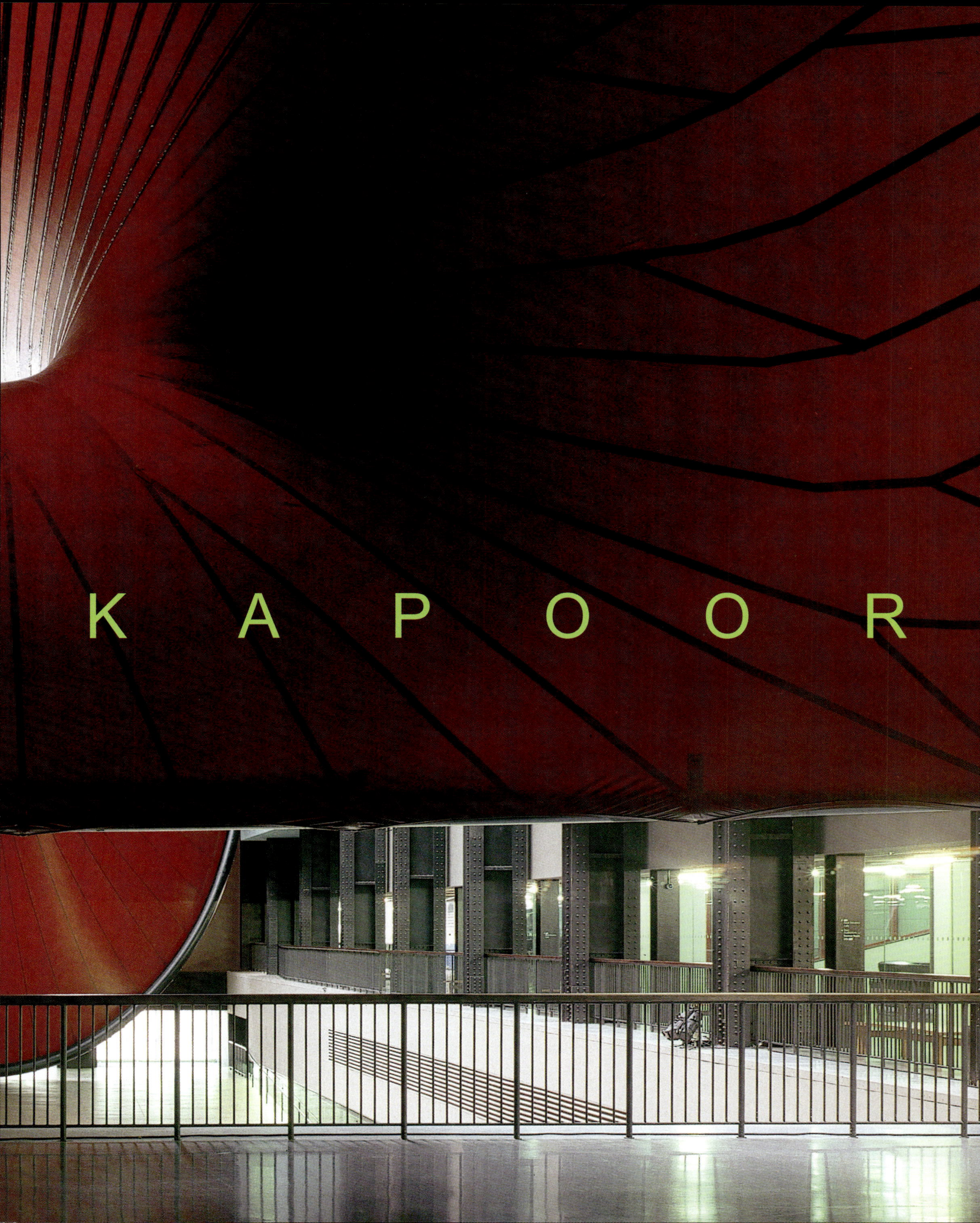

NORMAN BRYSON

KAPOOR'S VERTIGO

"I have always felt drawn," Kapoor has said, "towards some notion of fear in a very visual sense, towards sensations of falling, of being pulled inwards, of losing one's sense of self."[1] Spend time with any work and before long you will feel an unmistakable shift in the coordinates of space and time you take for granted. That shift, that sliding of the ground from under your feet, is not always subtle, something you might miss if your mind is less than fully concentrated on the work before you. Sometimes the effect hits you at levels of intensity approaching a theme park ride. Sensation is stimulated to the point where ideas of where you stand in the world, and what manner of being you might be in the world, are radically disrupted. My suggestion here is that close to the source of this feeling of uncanniness, of losing one's moorings, is Kapoor's discovery of ways of withdrawing the body's normal sense of self-image or ego-image from available experience: the kind of specular definition of the self which, for a long time now, has typically been theorized by way of Lacan's essay on the mirror stage.

There, the ego's sense of self is said to be formed through identification with what emerges in the mirror as an ideal imago: the ego's sense of itself as an entity bounded by the outline of the body as this appears to others. It is an outside view *on* the body, from an essentially exterior viewpoint, and through all of its subsequent elaborations in the social field and in adult life, that is how the sense of self is maintained: *you* are what manifests as the image before other social beings, that image is you.

Kapoor's work, in its moment or moments of vertigo, temporarily blocks our access to this bounded and limited entity; it severs our tie to the template imago, untethers us from it, breaks its spell. For a certain period of time, you are cut loose from this statue or monument in which the ego consists. How? Perhaps one can locate some of Kapoor's means by analogy with similar moments when the fundamental coordinates that fix us in place in the world give way: when, for instance, turning a corner on the road or after an arduous climb, you suddenly see a panorama opening out on all sides, and the small envelope of space you habitually occupy is pried open and spread out flat to the horizon. Or when, in a classical garden in Kyoto, those small boulders you first saw change and yes, unmistakably, they have become mountains, valleys, chasms, gorges, and you are no longer your usual stature, but vast, like a Titan, or else minute, a Lilliputian—or somehow you are both these things. Kapoor's vertigo is like the moment in the planetarium when, as the simulated twilight at last fades out, the

---

NORMAN BRYSON is Professor of Art History at University of California, San Diego.

ANISH KAPOOR, TARATANTARA, 1999, PVC installation, Baltic Center for Contemporary Art, Gateshead, England / PVC-Installation. (PHOTO: JOHN RIDDY, LONDON)

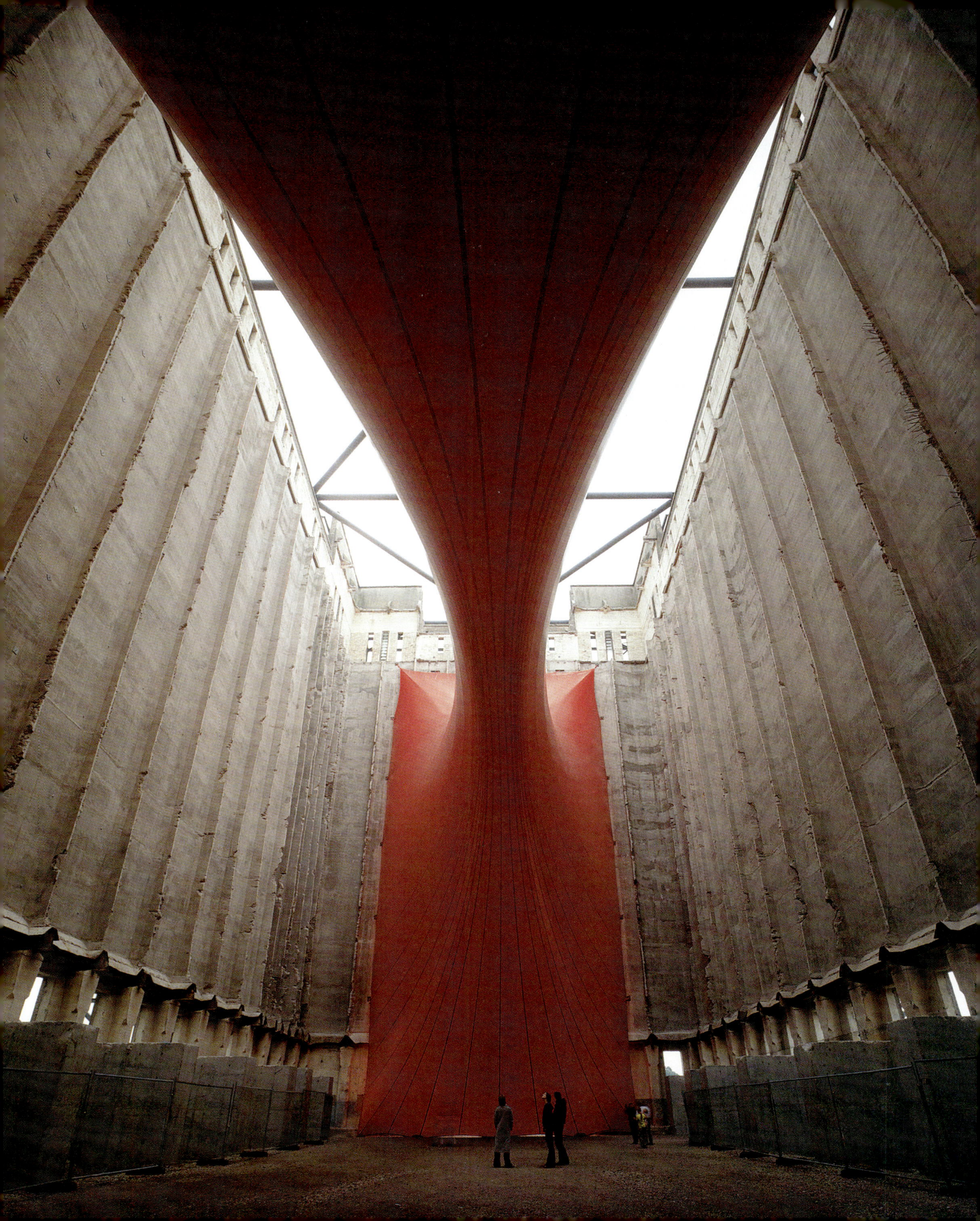

ANISH KAPOOR, AT THE EDGE OF THE WORLD I, 1998, fiberglass and pigment, $16^5/_{12}$ x $26^1/_4$ x $26^1/_4$',
Dobre Espacio, Centro Galego de Arte Contemporanea, Santiago de Compostela / Fiberglas und Pigment, 5 x 8 x 8 m.

projection screen overhead suddenly disappears and the dome vault of heaven, the deep black of the galaxies swings into view around you.

To a lesser or greater extent this kind of effect is always there in Kapoor. Let me trace it in phases—from the early pigment pieces, on to what I want to call the "portal" pieces of the nineties; toward the colossi of recent years, the vast burnished mirrors and the immensities of TARATANTARA (2000), works that seem frankly intent to swallow you up.

It was already clear in 1000 NAMES (1989–1990) that the forms you actually saw operated by withholding more than they revealed. "With the early powder pieces, one of the things I was trying to do was to arrive at something which was as if unmade, as if self-manifest, as if there by its own volition"; "the pigment on the floor defines the surface of the floor and the objects appear to be partially submerged, like icebergs."[2] Perhaps the first disruption of the space of the gallery takes place as the eye tries vainly to locate the planes and curves from which the work's geometries are built, since the particles of brightly colored dust in effect undo the very idea of a solid, bounding outline: the powder, ground from solids yet filled with air, robs the forms of their ideal, Platonic coordinates and replaces them with an edge that is incalculable, made of microscopic peaks and valleys that are at the same time weightless and dematerialized. Each of the forms suggests a manifestation different from its literal appearance, a hidden existence at a quite different scale from the mere centimeters we actually see. What we see is, for example, a small powdery cone, scooped in its center; but before long perception moves into a new gear and it is Fujiyama, or a crater on the moon. It is a tiny pile of powder, cut in steps; but now it is a *mastaba* or a *ziggurat*; similar steps, less than a meter in height, become the ceremonial staircase of a pyramid.

As the forms go through their scalar shifts, a "Kyoto garden" effect sets in: what scale are *you*? You are still in the gallery, in an objective space, finely calibrated; and yet you feel that in other, virtual dimensions each of the forms—and you—touch on the limitless. The level of sensation is intense: these powders have all the exotic appeal of spices in a souk, of turmeric or chili or kohl. Your senses are heightened—yet somehow your normal, bounded body, the one you see in the mirror, the one that was precipitated in the mirror stage, is no longer with you as you experience these sensations. If the word "anthropomorphic" denotes a process whereby things that are not human are appropriated to a human measure, this is the opposite of anthropomorphism: the space of the human, of Vitruvian man, the "measure of all things," is emptied out in such a way that the intensities of bodily sensation—the thrill of the colors, the vertigo—now unfold *in* you, but away from your Vitruvian body, your mirrored body. You are somewhere else, as Kapoor says, "pulled inward ... losing one's sense of self."

Developing the dynamics of this pull has been central to Kapoor's work of the recent past, which has found a unique vocabulary of the inward vortex, of magnetic fields that draw you inside, like a waterfall going down. In work from the nineties a recurring idea is the portal, star gate, gateway to a dark infinity. Before you stands a rough-hewn monolith UNTITLED (1992), and already you are thinking in terms of a different, geological time: the time of stone formation in the earth's crust, or else the dawn of *homo sapiens* and *homo faber*. Kapoor's genial idea is to activate the "resident narrative" that lies potentially within the rocks he carves. Kapoor's limestone comes from myriad deposits over time of minute cellular skeletons, on what was once the seabed; Kapoor's granite is born of volcanic fire, out of magma and immense, diamond-yielding pressures from within the planetary core. Cut into this monolith is

ANISH KAPOOR, 1000 NAMES, 1979–1980, wood, gesso, and pigment, 25 x 20 x 12" / 1000 NAMEN, Holz, Kreidegrund und Pigment, 63,5 x 51 x 30,5 cm. (PHOTO: LISSON GALLERY, LONDON)

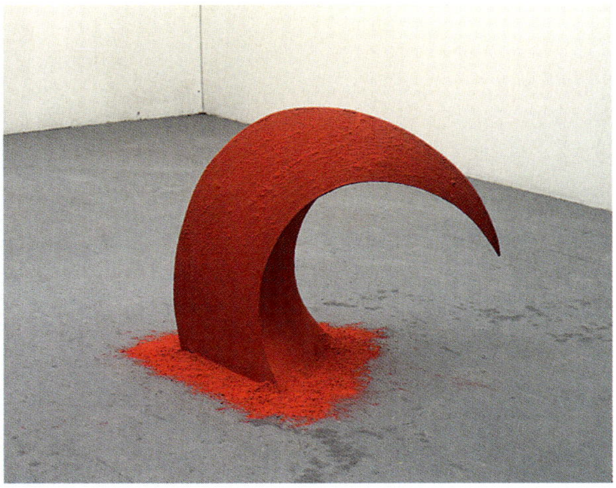

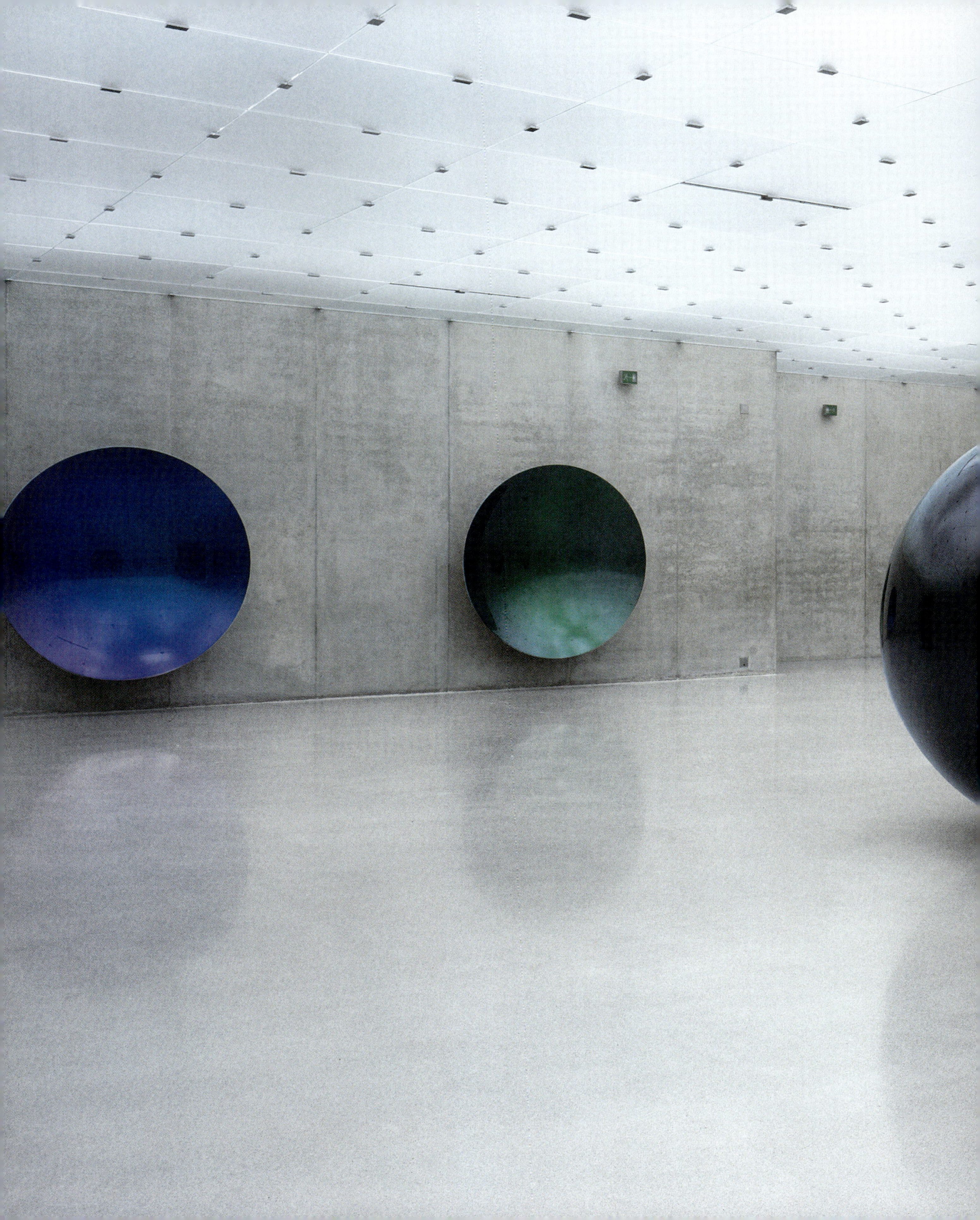

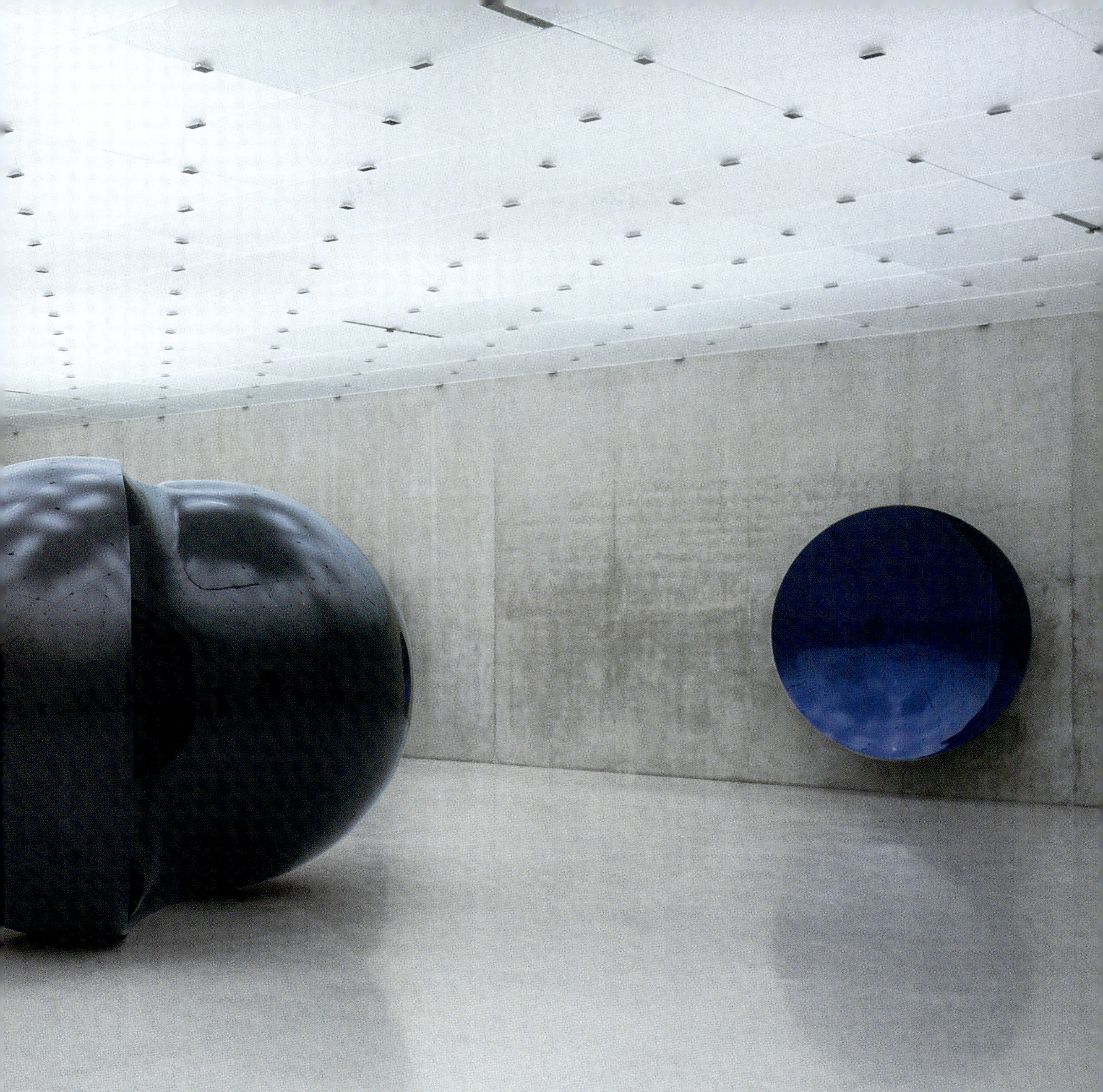

From left to right / Von links nach rechts: ANISH KAPOOR, UNITLED, WAVE, UPSIDE DOWN/INSIDE OUT, EXTREME, all 2003, exhibition "My Red Homeland," Kunsthaus Bregenz, 27 September – 16 November 2003 / OHNE TITEL, WELLE, OBEN UNTEN/INNEN AUSSEN, EXTREM, alle 2003.
(PHOTO: NIC TENWIGGENHORN / KUNSTHAUS BREGENZ & LISSON GALLERY)

an opening, a doorway, evident sign of humanity and history: what happens if you attempt to enter that door? As your head approaches (or passes inside) the lintel, suddenly you are in that geological narrative—on the inside. You are a being that has never altogether broken its connection to the mineral life of the earth from whose elements your own organic body ultimately derives. You are a becoming-rock, a becoming-stone; meaning, acutely, that you lose your place within the bounded body of your ego-image, as part of you travels out of the body, far away. You encounter your actual elasticity as a consciousness: yes, you are still in the real time and space of the gallery, but an aspect of your being twists out of line, torques toward and into a zone of being you did not realize you were somehow already equipped to navigate. Or you stand in front of IT IS MAN (1989–1990), where a strange hollow has been carved whose magical property is that you cannot be sure how deep it goes: is it shallow, a few centimeters only? Does it extend to the far side of the block? Or perhaps—and now the "portal"

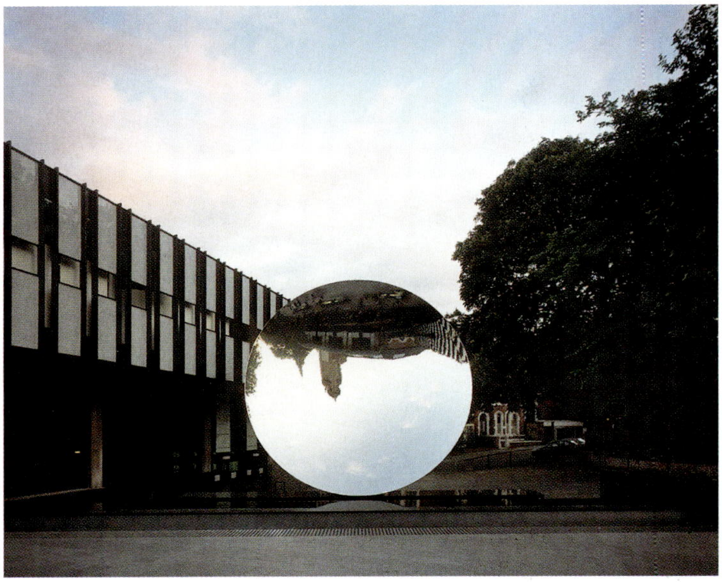

ANISH KAPOOR, SKY MIRROR, 2001, stainless steel, 226 3/8" in diameter, Nottingham, spring 2001 / HIMMELSSPIEGEL, Edelstahl, Durchmesser 575 cm, Nottingham, Frühjahr 2001. (PHOTO: DAVE MORGAN)

really springs into operation—it extends *beyond* the far side of the block, as an opening on to dark infinity, a black hole from which light—and you—cannot escape.

Hence the present direction of Kapoor's work: to maximize the force that pulls you free of your corporeal imago, and sets you in motion as a being of another kind. It is not just that TARATANTARA is the largest sculpture you will ever see (it is that, too): it undoes the scale by which greater and lesser, relative to one's body, are measured in the first place. Your being expands to the size of the universe, or shrinks to the compass of a single quantum of life energy. Standing before his fiery, molten mirrors, you find, then lose yourself again in the shimmering brilliance of a surface that inverts, and then negates what every mirror has ever told you: that the image is "you."

If you are *not* that, what are you?

1) Anish Kapoor quoted in Claire Farrow, "Anish Kapoor: Theatre of Lightness, Space and Intimacy," *Art and Design* no. 33, 1993, p. 53.
2) Quoted in "Anish Kapoor: Interview with Ameena Meer," *Bomb*, Winter 1990, p. 39.

NORMAN BRYSON

SCHWINDEL ERREGENDER SOG

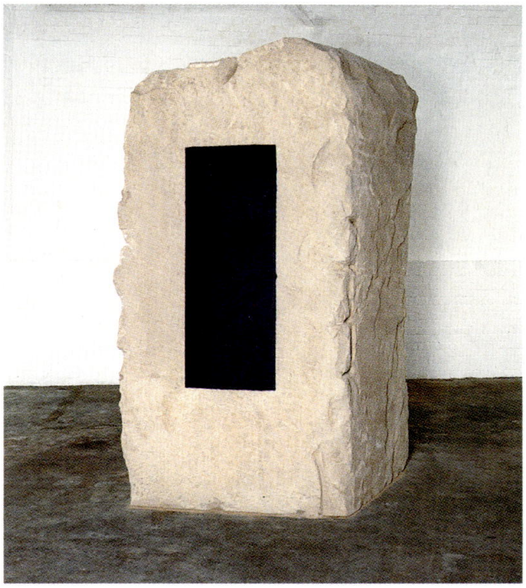

ANISH KAPOOR, IT IS MAN, 1989/90, sandstone and pigment, 84⅞ x 50 x 44⅞" / ES IST DER MENSCH, Sandstein und Pigment, 241 x 127 x 114 cm. (PHOTO: SUSAN ORMEROD AND GARETH WINTERS, LONDON)

«Ich fühlte mich schon immer zu einer sehr bildhaften Vorstellung von Angst hingezogen», meinte Kapoor einmal, «zu dem Gefühl zu fallen, hineingesogen zu werden, sein Ichgefühl zu verlieren.»[1)] Sobald man sich für eines seiner Werke Zeit nimmt, ganz gleich für welches, wird man unweigerlich eine Verschiebung der sonst so selbstverständlich vorausgesetzten Zeit-Raum-Koordinaten erleben. Diese Verschiebung, dieses Wegrutschen des Bodens unter den Füssen ist dabei durchaus nicht immer so subtil, dass es einem entgeht, wenn man sich nicht voll auf das Werk konzentriert. Manchmal überfällt es einen so heftig wie auf einer Achterbahnfahrt. Das Erlebnis wird immer stärker, bis unsere Vorstellungen darüber, wo wir in der Welt stehen und was für Wesen wir in dieser Welt sind, sich schliesslich abrupt zerschlagen. Ich vermute, dass dieses Gefühl des Unheimlichen, dieses den Boden unter den Füssen Verlieren damit zusammenhängt, dass Kapoor die verwundbare Stelle entdeckt hat, an der er uns die normale körperliche Erfahrung unseres Selbstbildes oder Ich-Bildes entziehen kann: die Definition des Selbst durch sein Spiegelbild, deren massgebliche Darstellung sich nach wie vor in Lacans Essay über das Spiegelstadium findet.

Dort heisst es, dass das Ich sich selbst als ein solches erlebt durch die Identifikation mit seinem idealen Spiegelbild: Die Selbstwahrnehmung des Ich als Einheit wird bestimmt durch das Bild des Körpers, das andere von diesem haben. Es ist ein Blick von aussen auf den Körper, von einem im Wesentlichen äusseren Standpunkt; und trotz aller späteren Differenzierungen im sozialen Umfeld und im Erwachsenenleben bleibt dies die Art, wie das Ichgefühl aufrecht erhalten wird: Du bist, was sich als Bild für andere soziale Wesen ergibt, dieses Bild bist du.

Kapoors Arbeiten versperren uns im Moment oder in den Momenten des Schwindelgefühls den Zugang zu dieser bedingten und begrenzten Einheit; sie durchtrennen das Band zur Ich-Schablone, reissen uns davon los, brechen deren Bann. Für eine gewisse Zeit sind wir

NORMAN BRYSON ist zurzeit Professor für Kunstgeschichte an der University of California in San Diego.

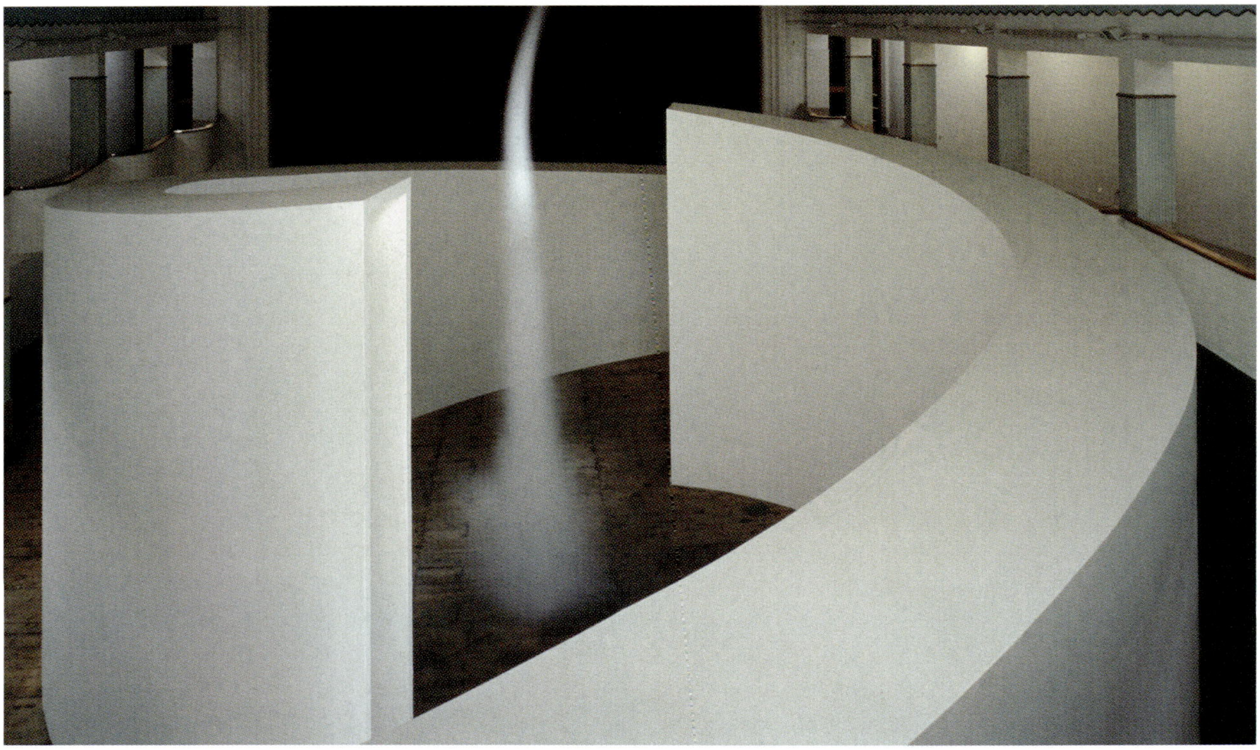

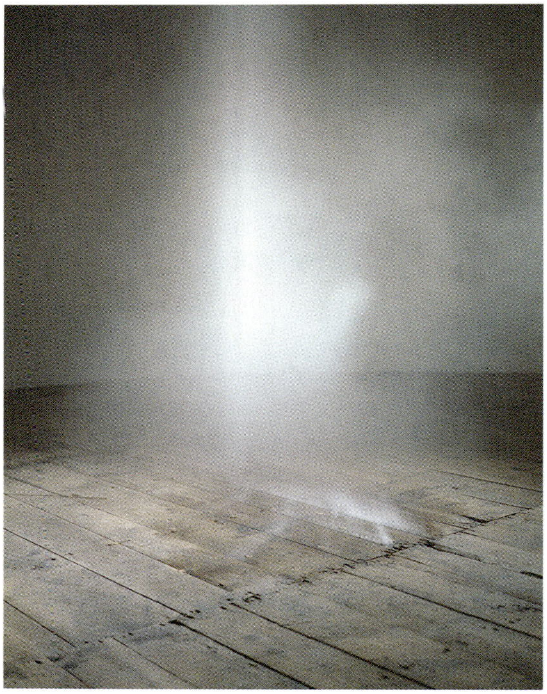

ANISH KAPOOR, ASCENSION, 2003, site specific room installation, mixed media, dimensions variable, Galleria Continua, San Gimignano, Italy / ortsbezogene Rauminstallation, diverse Materialien, Grösse variabel. (PHOTO: ELA BIALKOWSKA)

von diesem Standbild, diesem Monument, welches das Ich ausmacht, losgelöst. Wie geschieht das? Vielleicht wird Kapoors Vorgehen ein Stück weit verständlich, wenn wir analoge Momente betrachten, in denen die Grundkoordinaten, die unseren Platz in der Welt bestimmen, ins Wanken geraten: wenn sich, zum Beispiel – beim Abbiegen um eine Ecke oder nach einem anstrengenden Aufstieg –, unserem Blick plötzlich ein umfassendes Panorama eröffnet und der kleine Raumausschnitt, in dem wir uns normalerweise aufhalten, plötzlich aufreisst und sich bis zum Horizont ausweitet. Oder wenn sich in einem klassischen Steingarten in Kyoto diese kleinen Felsbrocken, die man zuerst sah, verändern und plötzlich zu Bergen, Tälern, Abgründen und Schluchten geworden sind, so dass man selbst nicht mehr die gewohnte Grösse hat, sondern gross ist wie ein Riese, oder aber winzig, ein Liliputaner – oder irgendwie beides zugleich. Das Schwindelgefühl bei Kapoor ist wie der Augenblick im Planetarium, wo die simulierte Dämmerung zur Dunkelheit wird, die Projektionsfläche an der Decke verschwindet und uns plötzlich auf allen Seiten das Himmelsgewölbe, das tiefe Schwarz der Galaxien umschliesst.

In unterschiedlicher Stärke stellt sich dieser Effekt bei Kapoor immer ein. Ich möchte das schrittweise aufzeigen: von den frühen Pigmentarbeiten bis zu den – ich würde sagen – «Portal»-Arbeiten der 90er Jahre und schliesslich den Kolossen der letzten Jahre, den riesigen polierten Spiegeln und der immensen Grösse von TARATANTARA (2000), Werke, die einen geradezu verschlingen zu wollen scheinen.

Schon in 1000 NAMES (1000 Namen, 1989–1990) wurde deutlich, dass die tatsächlich sichtbaren Formen mehr durch das wirkten, was sie verbargen, als durch das, was sie zeigten. «Bei den ersten Arbeiten mit Farbpulver wollte ich unter anderem etwas erreichen, das wie ‹nicht gemacht› wäre, so als manifestierte es sich selbst, als wäre es aus eigenem Willen da»; «das Pigment auf dem Boden bestimmt die Bodenfläche, und die Gegenstände wirken so, als würden sie aus dem Boden herausragen, wie Eisberge aus dem Wasser.»[2)] Das erste Aufbrechen des Galerieraumes geschieht wohl schon, wenn das Auge vergeblich versucht die Ebenen und Kurven, aus denen sich die Form der Arbeit ergibt, auszumachen, denn die leuchtend farbigen Staubteilchen widerstreben der Vorstellung einer festen, verbindlichen Gestalt von Grund auf: Das Pulver, aus festen Materialien gemahlen und doch voller Luftigkeit, beraubt die Formen ihrer idealen, platonischen Koordinaten und versieht sie mit unberechenbaren Rändern aus mikroskopisch kleinen Bergspitzen und Tälern, die schwerelos und wie entmaterialisiert erscheinen. Jede der Formen verweist auf eine Präsenz jenseits ihrer blossen Erscheinung, auf eine verborgene Existenz ganz anderer Grössenordnung jenseits der paar Zentimeter, die wir tatsächlich sehen können. Wir sehen etwa eine kleine pulverige Kegelform mit einer Mulde in der Mitte; aber es dauert nicht lange, bis die Wahrnehmung kippt und wir den Fudschiyama vor uns haben oder einen Mondkrater. Es ist ein kleines Häufchen Staub, zu Stufen geformt; aber jetzt ist es eine Mastaba oder eine Zikkurat; ähnliche Stufen, weniger als ein Meter hoch, werden zur Zeremonientreppe einer Pyramide.

Während die Formen ihre Grössenverwandlungen durchlaufen, setzt ein Kyoto-Garten-Effekt ein: Welche Grösse haben *wir*? Wir sind immer noch in der Galerie, in einem objektiven, perfekt ausgewogenen Raum; dennoch fühlt man, dass in anderen, virtuellen Dimensionen jede dieser Formen – und man selbst – ans Grenzenlose rührt. Das Gefühl ist sehr intensiv: Diese Pulverhaufen haben denselben exotischen Appeal wie Gewürze in einem Suk, wie Kurkuma, Chili oder Kajal. Unsere Sinne sind geschärft, aber irgendwie ist uns unser normales, begrenztes Körper-Ich, das wir im Spiegel sehen und das sich im Spiegel-

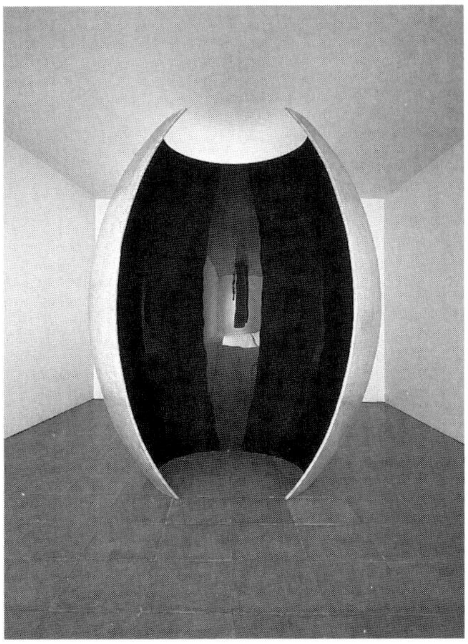

ANISH KAPOOR, ISHI'S LIGHT, 2003, *fiberglass and lacquer, 124' high, 98 1/2" in diameter /* ISHIS LICHT, *Fiberglas lackiert, 315 cm hoch, Durchmesser: 250 cm.*
(PHOTO: DAVE MORGAN, LONDON)

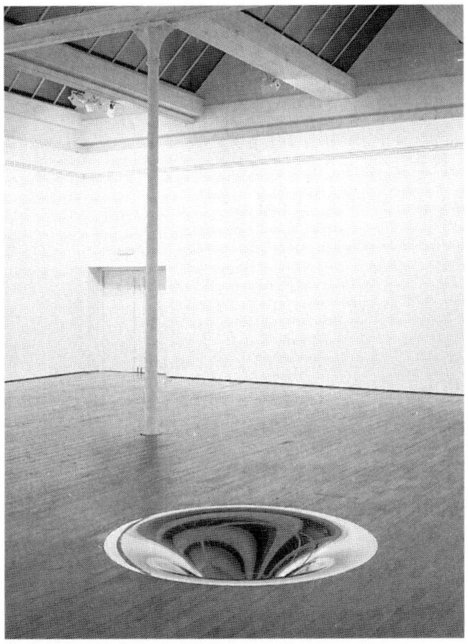

ANISH KAPOOR, TURNING THE WORLD INSIDE OUT II, *1995, chrome plated bronze, 57 x 72 13/16 x 72 13/16", Fondazione Prada, Milano /* DAS INNERE DER WELT NACH AUSSEN STÜLPEN II, *verchromte Bronze, 145 x 185 x 185 cm.*

stadium gebildet hat, im Lauf dieser Empfindungen entglitten. Wenn das Wort «anthropomorph» einen Prozess bezeichnet, in dem Dinge, die nicht menschlich sind, auf ein menschliches Mass reduziert werden, so ist dies das Gegenteil eines Anthropomorphismus: hier wird der Raum des Menschlichen, des vitruvischen Architektenmenschen, des «Masses aller Dinge», derart entleert, dass die Intensität der körperlichen Erfahrung – der Reiz der Farben, das Schwindelgefühl – zwar ihre Wirkung in uns entfaltet, aber jenseits unseres vitruvischen, gespiegelten Körpers. Man ist woanders und wird, wie Kapoor sagt, «hineingesogen» um alsbald sein «Ichgefühl zu verlieren».

Die Steigerung der Dynamik dieses Sogs hat Kapoors Arbeiten der letzten Jahre bestimmt; er hat in ihnen ein einmaliges Vokabular des nach innen gerichteten Wirbels entwickelt, ein magnetisches Feld, das einen nach innen zieht wie im Sog eines Wasserfalls. In den Arbeiten der 90er Jahre ist das Portal, das Sternentor, das Eingangstor zu einer dunklen Unendlichkeit ein oft wiederkehrendes Motiv. Man steht vor einem rauh behauenen Monolithen, UNTITLED (Ohne Titel, 1992), und schon beginnt man in einem anderen, geologischen Zeitrahmen zu denken: der Zeit der sich faltenden Felsformationen der Erdkruste, oder aber der Frühzeit des *Homo sapiens* und *Homo faber.* Das Genie Kapoors liegt darin, den «narrativen Gehalt» der Felsbrocken, die er behaut, zu aktivieren. Kapoors Kalkstein besteht aus Myriaden von Ablagerungen winziger Zellskelette, wo einst Meeresboden war; Kapoors Granit ist aus dem vulkanischen Feuer geboren, aus Magma unter demselben ungeheuren Druck aus dem Erdinneren, der auch die Diamanten erzeugte. In diesen Monolithen ist eine Öffnung geschlagen, eine Tür, die offensichtlich auf den Menschen und die Geschichte verweist: Was geschieht, wenn wir versuchen durch diese Tür zu gehen? Sobald unser Kopf sich dem Türsturz nähert oder ihn passiert, befinden wir uns auch schon mitten in dieser geologischen Geschichte. Wir finden uns als ein Wesen wieder, das seine Verbindung zum mineralischen Leben der Erde, aus dessen Elementen unser eigener organischer Körper letztlich entstanden ist, nie ganz abgebrochen hat. Wir sind ein werdender Fels, ein werdender Stein;

und das heisst präzis, dass wir unseren Ort innerhalb des begrenzten Körpers unseres Selbstbildes verlieren, da ein Teil von uns sich aus dem Körper entfernt, weit weg. Wir begegnen der Elastizität unseres Bewusstseins: Ja, wir sind noch immer in der realen Zeit und im realen Raum der Galerie oder des Museums, aber ein Teil von uns tanzt aus der Reihe, dreht ab in einen Daseinsbereich, von dem man gar nicht wusste, dass man dafür schon gerüstet war. Oder wir stehen vor IT IS MAN (Es ist der Mensch, 1989–1990), einer seltsamen Vertiefung, deren Magie darin besteht, dass man nicht weiss, w i e tief sie ist: Ist sie womöglich gar nicht tief, vielleicht nur ein paar Zentimeter? Reicht sie bis ans andere Ende des Blocks? Oder – und nun entfaltet sich die «Portal»-Wirkung – reicht sie womöglich über das andere Ende des Blocks hinaus und ist ein Tor zur dunklen Unendlichkeit, ein schwarzes Loch, dem nichts entfliehen kann, nicht einmal Licht – also auch wir nicht?

Daraus ergibt sich die aktuelle Richtung von Kapoors Arbeit: die zunehmende Steigerung der Kraft, die uns von unserem physischen Bild losreisst und uns als andersartige Wesen freisetzt. Nicht genug, dass TARATANTARA die grösste Skulptur ist, die wir je zu sehen bekommen werden (das ist sie allerdings auch): Sie zerstört den Massstab, mit dem wir das Mehr oder Weniger im Verhältnis zu unserem Körper zu messen pflegen. Unser Dasein dehnt sich bis zur Grösse des Universums aus oder schrumpft zu einem einzigen Quantenteilchen Lebensenergie. Und wenn wir vor Kapoors feurigen, gegossenen Spiegeln stehen, finden und verlieren wir uns gleich wieder im leuchtenden Glanz einer Oberfläche, die alles auf den Kopf stellt und am Ende negiert, was uns bisher jeder Spiegel gesagt hat: Dieses Bild bist du.

Wenn du das n i c h t bist, was bist du dann?

(Übersetzung: Suzanne Schmidt)

1) Anish Kapoor in: Claire Farrow, «Anish Kapoor: Theatre of Lightness, Space and Intimacy», *Art and Design* No. 33, 1993, S. 53.
2) «Anish Kapoor: Interview with Ameena Meer», *Bomb,* Winter 1990, S. 39.

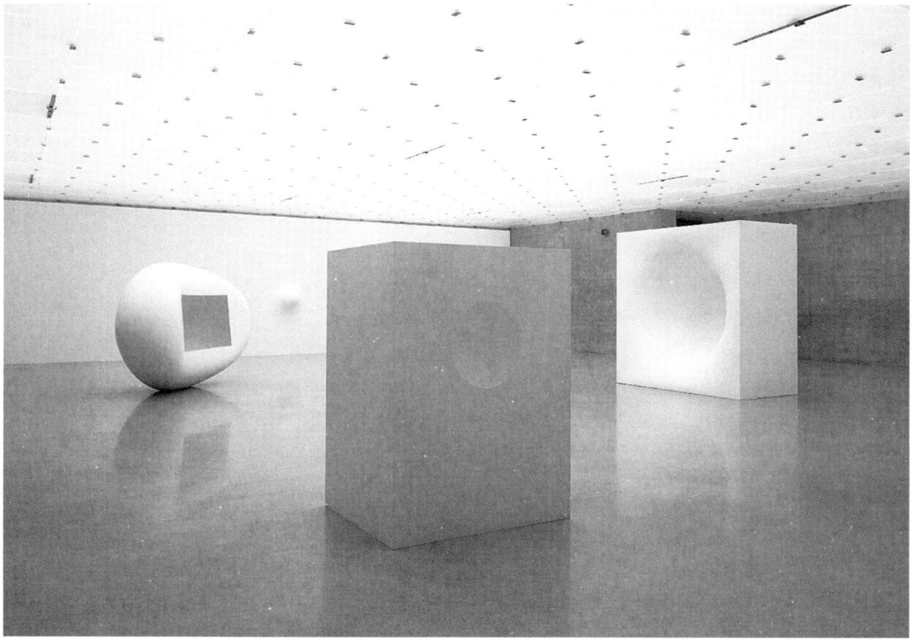

ANISH KAPOOR, UNTITLED, 1998, WHEN I AM PREGNANT, 1992, WHITE DARK III, 1995, WHITE DARK IV, 1998, installation view, "My Red Homeland," Kunsthaus Bregenz, 27 September – 16 November 2003 / OHNE TITEL, WENN ICH SCHWANGER BIN, WEISSES DUNKEL III, WEISSES DUNKEL IV. (PHOTO: NIC TENWIGGENHORN/KUNSTHAUS BREGENZ & LISSON GALLERY)

Ein Wort ins Ohr des Giganten

KURT W. FORSTER

Wir haben uns daran gewöhnt, dass die Skulptur vom Sockel gestiegen ist und sich breit gemacht hat. Schon die Land-Art eignete sich den Massstab der Landschaft und die Fernsicht an (und mochte deshalb auch auf Ansichten aus dem Flugzeug nicht verzichten). Heute betrachten wir Skulptur weder mit den Augen Alberto Giacomettis, der sie gleichsam von der Tiefe des Blicks verschlingen liess, noch mit denjenigen eines David Smith, der ihre Teile in tanzende Bewegung versetzte. Seit Jahren behauptet Skulptur ihren Platz mit freistehenden Stahlplatten von Richard Serra und vibrierenden Farbstelen von Dan Flavin. Der Kontrast zwischen tonnenschwerem Stahl und leuchtenden Gasmischungen, zwischen materieller Dichte und optischer Schwingung dreht sich nicht nur um die Ausmarchung der Bereiche, die Skulptur oder Bild eigen sind, sondern ruft auch Kontroversen über die Natur des Lichts – und die Mechanik seiner Wahrnehmung – in Erinnerung.

Gegen 1980 trat Anish Kapoor mit Skulpturen hervor, die dank der Konsistenz ihrer farbigen Oberflächen eine eigentümliche Wirkung ausüben. In den folgenden Jahren verlieh er ihnen Rundformen oder brachte Vertiefungen im Stein an, die manchmal spiegelglatt geschliffen oder mit Pigment eingefärbt sind. So absorbieren sie förmlich das Licht

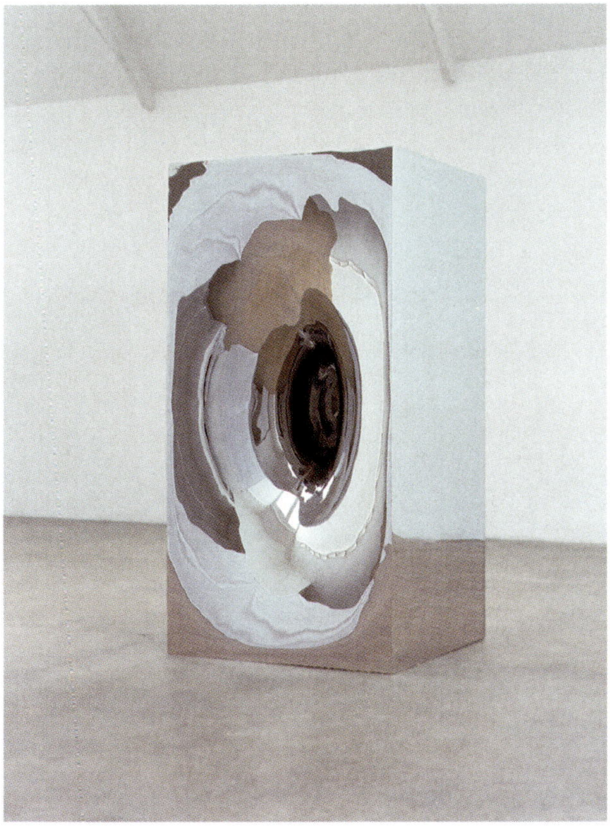

ANISH KAPOOR, UNTITLED, 1997, stainless steel, 77 3/4 x 39 3/16 x 39 3/16" / OHNE TITEL, Edelstahl, 197,5 x 99,5 x 99,5 cm. (PHOTO: STEPHEN WHITE, LONDON)

KURT W. FORSTER ist Gropius-Professor an der Bauhaus-Universität in Weimar und Direktor der Architektur-Biennale Venedig 2004, die unter dem Thema «Metamorphosen» steht.

oder werfen es schemenhaft wieder zurück. Trichterförmige Vertiefungen im Stein, in der Wand oder sogar im Boden durchdringen die konventionellen Schranken des Raumes und erweitern sich in ungeahnte Bereiche. Das Grau einer gewölbten Vertiefung und die Spiegelungen auf glänzendem Stahl erwecken in ihrer optischen Ambivalenz für Augenblicke den Eindruck, den Jean Cocteau in seinem Film *Orphée* (1950) durch das Auf- und Abtreten seiner Figuren durch wasserweiche Spiegelflächen erreichte. Doch die rätselhafte Natur von Kapoors Eintiefungen kommt ganz ohne die aufdringliche Suggestion Cocteaus aus und bezieht sich daher viel stärker auf die Skulpturen selbst. Die Leere um die Dinge und die denkbare Tiefe in ihnen prallen auf spiegelnden Oberflächen aufeinander, bedrängen das Auge und lösen beim Betrachten eine eigentümliche «Unruhe» aus.[1)] So hat Kapoor selbst sich Homi Bhabha gegenüber geäussert, dem er auch Stein als ein mit Zeit angereichertes Material schilderte, das dem Bildhauer gestattet in seine Geschichte einzudringen.[2)]

Bei Kapoor erscheinen die Oberflächen unstet, ihre konvexen Rundungen oder konkav eingewölbten Trichter erwecken den Eindruck, die Skulptur versinke in sich selbst. Die spiegelblanken Stahlkuben (UNTITLED, 1997), die wie hochgestellte Sarkophage den Betrachterinnen und Betrachtern entge-

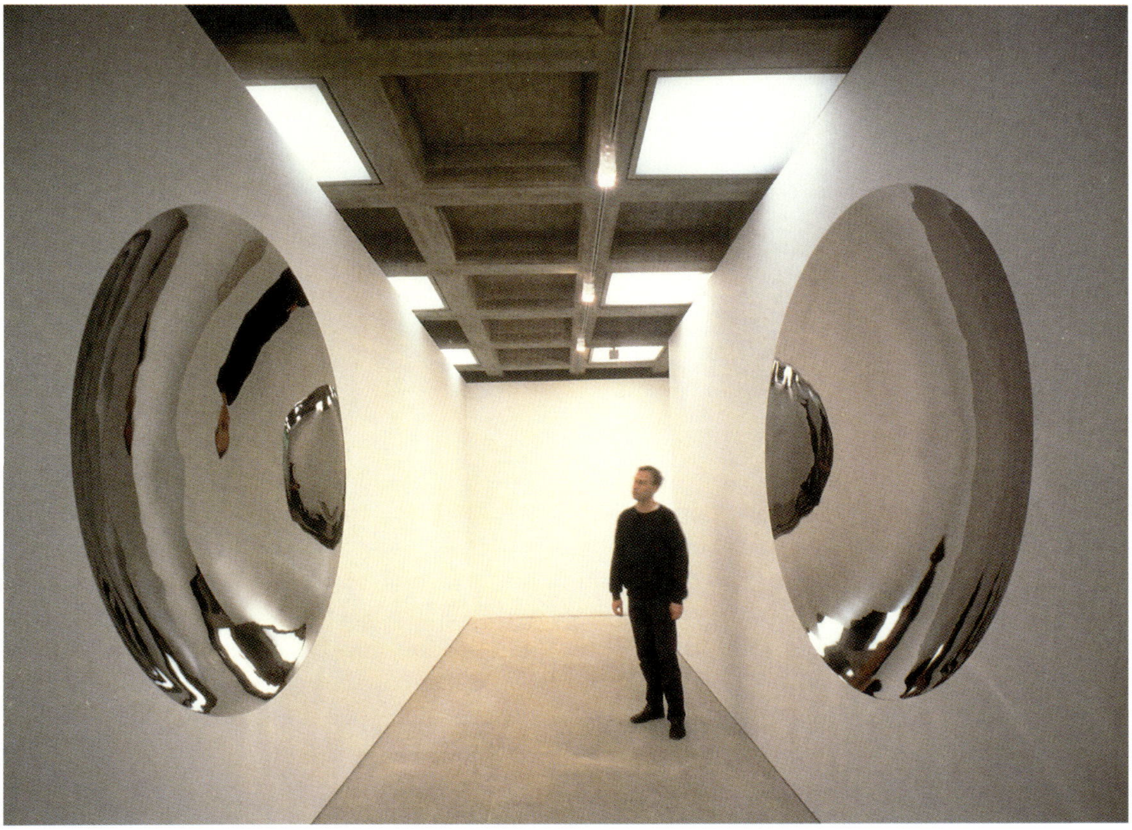

ANISH KAPOOR, DOUBLE MIRROR, 1997–1998, stainless steel, 2 parts, each 78¾" in diameter, Hayward Gallery, London / DOPPELSPIEGEL, Edelstahl, 2 Teile, Durchmesser je 200 cm. (PHOTO: JOHN RIDDY, LONDON)

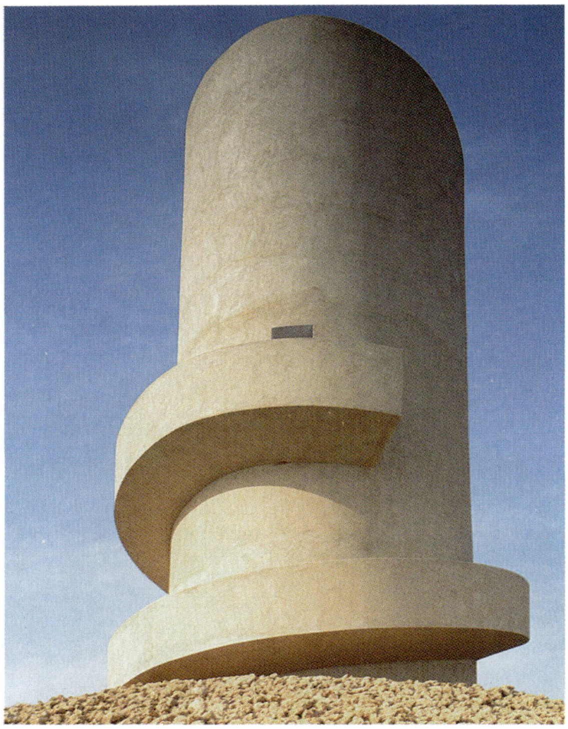

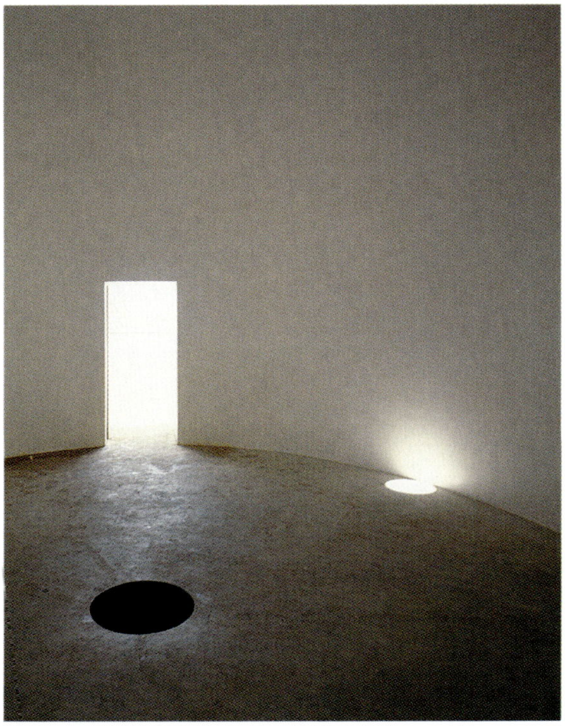

ANISH KAPOOR, BUILDING FOR A VOID, 1992, concrete and stucco, ca. 49¼' high, project for Expo 1992, Seville, Spain, exterior and interior view / GEBÄUDE FÜR EINEN LEEREN RAUM, Beton und Stuck, Höhe 15 m, Projekt für die Expo 1992 in Sevilla, Aussen- und Innenansicht. (PHOTO: JOHN EDWARD LINDEN, LONDON)

gentreten, zeigen anstelle einer optisch fassbaren Oberfläche ihr visuelles Versinken in sich selbst. Spontan, wie man es einem Versinkenden gegenüber täte, streckt man die Hand aus im vergeblichen Versuch sie festzuhalten. Aber die Gestalt der Skulptur ist dabei, in einem optischen Strudel zu verschwinden; hineingesogen in eine bewegte Oberfläche, entweicht sie in ihren eigenen Körper. Homi Bhabha erkannte, dass «das plötzliche Verschwinden der Fläche in einem tiefen, dunklen Loch uns in der Tat den Grund unter den Füssen entzieht».[3)]

Nun schafft aber diese unglaubliche Saugkraft, die aus den Skulpturen selber zu stammen und sie beinah zu verschlingen scheint, nicht etwa einen Ausnahmezustand, der sich nur bei bestimmten Oberflächen durch optische Effekte einstellte. Kapoors Objekte – diese neutrale Bezeichnung ist am ehesten geeignet, ihre Ambivalenz in einem Wort zu erfassen – finden ihre Eigenart gerade in diesem Verschlingen ihrer selbst. So spricht aus ihnen nicht nur die Idee der eigenen Tiefe, auch wo sie unsichtbar bleibt, sondern auch diejenige ihrer eigenen Zeit. Denn es braucht ganz einfach Zeit, sich ihrer Wirkung auszusetzen, ohne dass deshalb viel geschähe. Rein äusserlich passiert kaum etwas, aber im Laufe der Betrachtung gibt die Skulptur mehr und mehr von sich preis. Dabei entzieht sie den Betrachtenden etwas von jenem Grund, auf dem sie so fest zu stehen glauben, indem sie sich als eine eigentümlich in Raum und Zeit «gebogene» zu erkennen gibt. Diese Beugung – der Flächen, der Reflexionen, der Farben – bewirkt eben jenes Schweben, das uns verunsichern, ja beängstigen kann.

Man geht kaum fehl in der Annahme, dass diese Objekte ein anderes Verhältnis von Volumen und Oberfläche herstellen als unsere Schulweisheit uns träumen lässt. Statt das Volumen einer Skulptur ihrem Bild unterzuordnen oder ihren Körper lediglich als träge Erscheinungsform zu behandeln stellt Kapoor ein Spannungsverhältnis her. Seine Objekte stören gerade diejenige Relation, die den Nachweis von Substanz und Gestalt erbringt, nämlich die Relation von Oberfläche und Körper. Der Unterschied zwischen dem, was man nur mit den Augen abtasten und was man allein durch körperliches Erfassen begreifen kann, die Hypothese also, dass Skulptur ganz der Welt der Betrachtenden angehöre, wird von Kapoor schwer auf die Probe gestellt. In einem präzisen Sinne überführen die kontinuierlich gewölbten Flächen seiner Skulpturen das traditionelle Verhältnis von Fläche und Körper in ein Kontinuum. Aus ihrer Gegenüberstellung entsteht ein differenziales Zueinander. Deshalb sollte auch ihre weitere Anwendung immer mehr von Computerprogrammen abhängen, die imstande sind ein ganzes Bündel unterschiedlicher Algorithmen und ihre Interaktionen zu errechnen. Die Probe aufs Exempel lieferte dann Cecil Balmond, der leitende Kopf der Londoner Firma Ove Arup – Konstruktionslabor der zeitgenössischen Architektur par excellence –, mit seinen Berechnungsmodellen für die turmhohen Skulpturen Kapoors.

Ein Werk, das Kapoor im Jahr 2000 in einem ehemaligen Getreidelager des Hafens von Newcastle-upon-Tyne installierte, brachte seine Vorstellungen einen gewaltigen Schritt voran: TARATANTARA – ein Name wie ein Trompetenstoss – wurde in einem ausgekernten Hafensilo «aufgespannt». Richard Deacon beschrieb es folgendermassen: «Der Trichter aus rotem Plastikstoff erstreckte sich zwischen den stehen gebliebenen Längswänden von einem Ende des Gebäudes zum anderen und erweckte den Eindruck, eine Öffnung durchdränge sein Volumen. Von aussen schien das recht einfach; man sah das ausgespannte rote Material und machte sich eine Vorstellung von seiner Anbringung. Die fliessenden Flächen, die sich vom einen zum anderen Ende erstreckten – als eingefaltete Aussenhaut wirkten sie wie eine Art Windhose –, schufen einige Verwirrung, aber vereint mit den leuchtend roten, schwingenden Flächen des Plastikstoffes riefen sie einen überwältigenden Eindruck hervor.»[4] Das Überwältigende entspringt nicht nur den Dimensionen, die etwa einem zehn Stockwerke hohen Bau entsprechen, sondern vor allem der Verbindung von Innen und Aussen in Form eines phantastisch gedehnten Tunnels aus tiefrotem Plastikstoff. Hier erprobte Kapoor in gigantischem Massstab wieder die eigentümliche Kraft seiner Skulptur, die imstande scheint nicht nur ihr eigenes Volumen, sondern nun auch den Raum, in dem sie untergebracht ist, förmlich aufzuzehren. Kapoor selbst bemerkte dazu: «Die Verkürzung des Gebäudes, wenn man es von aussen durch die Form hindurch betrachtet, überrascht mich. Betrachtet man es von aussen, scheint das Gebäude nur halb so lang, als es tatsächlich ist. Von ausserhalb des Gebäudes kann man nur die Innenseite der Form erkennen. Im Inneren des Gebäudes erblickt man dagegen nur ihr Äusseres. Es scheint, als hätte sich der Innenraum des Gebäudes plötzlich erweitert, und was lediglich eine Öffnung war, nimmt nun Form an … Irgendwie verwandeln sich Innen und Aussen gegenseitig.»[5]

Auch die Wirkung dieser gigantischen Skulptur beruht auf dem Verhältnis von Nähe und Distanz, je nach Standpunkt der Betrachter und Beschaffenheit des Materials, das mit seiner paraboloiden Dehnung, der Farbe und ihren Effekten selbst Kapoor zu überraschen vermag. Im Rückblick erweisen sich diese Eigentümlichkeiten der Oberfläche als charakteristisch und nicht als beiläufig. Aus eben diesen Eigentümlichkeiten heraus entstanden die folgenden Werke, die sich immer deutlicher vom Massstab und der Materialität der früheren entfernen. In jüngster Zeit sind Werke aus Materialien entstanden, die der Skulptur lange fremd geblieben waren, zudem an Orten, die bereits von mächtigen Gebäuden beherrscht werden.

Einen vorläufigen Höhepunkt in Kapoors Anstrengungen, selbst die Architektur seiner Installationsorte zu überflügeln, setzt dabei die jüngste Arbeit in der Londoner Tate Modern, wo posaunenförmige Trichter beinah die gigantische Ausstellungshalle zu sprengen drohten. Sie führen räumlich vor, was man als visuelles Dröhnen bezeichnen könnte. Kapoor entwickelte die MARSYAS-Installation[6] des vergangenen Jahres aus einer Art Doppelhorn mit einer kuppelähnlichen Öffnung, die kraft der Elastizität des verwendeten Kunstfasermaterials über den Köpfen der Museumsbesucher schwebt. Die Entstehungsgeschichte dieser bisher gigantischsten Form, die den Versuch von Newcastle an Komplexität weit übertrifft, fasziniert durch ihre Mischung von visionärer Idee – eingefangen in kleinen Skizzen und Modellen – und raffiniertester Ingenieurtechnik. Der Ingenieur Cecil Balmond stimmte sich auf Kapoors Thema ein und enthüllt in seinem Katalogbeitrag «Die Häutung der Phantasie»[7], wie diese Riesenskulptur aus vierzig Tonnen Stahl und Stoff durch Verbindung von Zug, Elastizität und Last zu verwirklichen war. Mit der Installation in Newcastle hat sie zumindest eines gemeinsam: Skulptur verschlingt Architektur und stellt die festen Konturen und ausgezirkelten Räume in Frage. Was anfänglich als Tiefe im Stein bei aller Festigkeit als unermessliches Feld optischen Schwankens erschien, das dehnt und wölbt sich nun in den Trichtern und Tunnels aus farbigem Stoff und entzieht sich dem Zugriff der Betrachter. Kaum vorstellbar, dass Architektur mit und aus sich selbst zustande bringen könnte, was Kapoor mit seinen Installationen erreicht: Raum umzustülpen, einzufalten und auszuhöhlen. Dazu ist eine Vorstellungskraft nötig, wie sie die jüngere Astrophysik – also eine Beschäftigung mit den tatsächlich unerreichbar fernen und unvorstellbar alten Zeiträumen des Kosmos – vorführt, wenn sie unserer dreidimensionalen Alltagswelt die Vorstellung der sattelförmigen Räume der String-Theorie entgegenstellt, deren bildliche Darstellung, wie sie etwa auch Stephen Hawking[8] verwendet, abenteuerliche Affinitäten zu den von Kapoor angestrebten Raumtrichtern verrät. Was sich im Anblick von Kapoors Werken als etwas Ungreifbares und Unauflösliches anmeldet, hat zumindest eines gemeinsam mit der Notwendigkeit sich Dinge vorzustellen, die man nie sehen kann.

1) *Anish Kapoor,* Katalog der Ausstellung in der Hayward Gallery, London 1998, mit Beiträgen von Homi K. Bhabha und Pier Luigi Tazzi, University of California Press, Berkeley/Los Angeles/London 1998, S. 18: «... in that narrow passage [between the mirrors], paradoxically there is a restlessness, an unease ...»
2) Ebenda, S. 27: «There is a history in the stone and through the simple device of excavating the stone it's just as if a whole narrative sequence is suddenly there ...»
3) Ebenda, S. 24: «A sudden disappearance of surface in a deep, dark hole literally cuts the ground from under our feet ...»
4) Richard Deacon, «Baltic Anish», in: *Anish Kapoor, TARATANTARA,* ACTAR Verlag, Barcelona 2000, unpaginiert: «The tube of red vinyl stretched between the two remaining standing walls replaced the missing end walls and seemingly converted the building into a block with a hole through it. From the outside this was fairly simple, one saw the stretched red fabric and anticipated or imagined the mechanics of the installation. Although certainly the continuity of surface between the two ends—the effect of a folding of the outside into a vortex that swept through the building—caused some complications, and the glistening, vibrant surface of the vinyl gleamed with an awesome intensity.»
5) Ebenda, «Anish Kapoor in conversation with Sune Nordgren»: «The foreshortening of the building from the outside as one looks through the form is to me, surprising. The building appears to be only half as long as the impression one had of it from the external structure. From the outside of the building only the inside of the form is visible. From the inside of the building only the outside of the form is visible. It is as if the space inside the building had suddenly expanded and what was a hole became a form. [...] Inside and outside seem to be turning into each other.»
6) Vgl. den Ausstellungskatalog *Anish Kapoor, Marsyas,* Tate Publishing, London 2002.
7) Cecil Balmond, «Skinning the Imagination», in: *Anish Kapoor, Marsyas,* op. cit., S. 66–69.
8) Vgl. Stephen Hawking, *Das Universum in der Nussschale,* Hoffmann & Campe, Hamburg 2001.

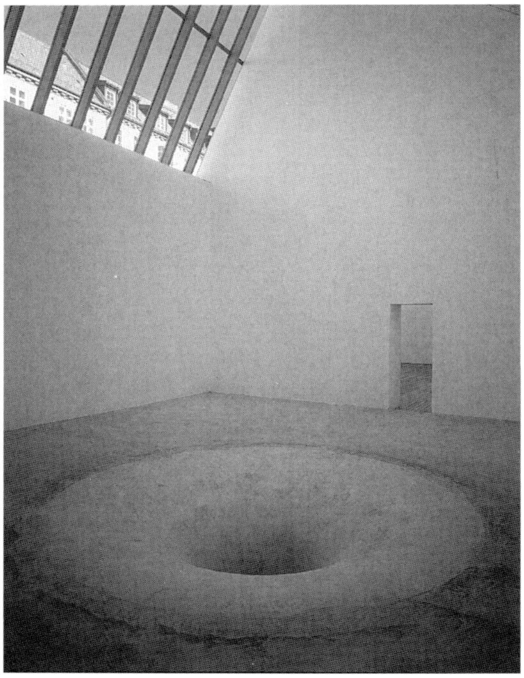

ANISH KAPOOR, UNTITLED, 1996, concrete, installation at Malmö Konsthall, Sweden, 9 November 1996 – 26 January 1997 / OHNE TITEL, Beton, Kunsthalle Malmö, Schweden. (PHOTO: GERRY JOHANSSON)

A Word in the Giant's Ear

KURT W. FORSTER

We have become accustomed to the fact that sculpture has climbed off its pedestal and spread about. Decades ago, Land Art appropriated the full-scale landscape and the long shot (for which reason it also insisted on the aerial view). Today we look at sculpture neither with the eyes of Alberto Giacometti, who you might say devoured it from the depths of the gaze, nor with those of David Smith, who set its parts into dancing motion. Sculpture has long since taken a firm stand with a spectrum ranging from Richard Serra's freestanding walls of steel to Dan Flavin's vibrant, colored stelae. The contrast between tons of heavy steel and luminous gases, between material density and optical wavelengths not only fuels the debate on the essence of sculpture versus image; it also recalls controversies about the nature of light and the mechanics of perception.

Around 1980, Anish Kapoor showed sculptures that produced a strange effect due to the texture of their colored surfaces. In the years that followed, he rounded their forms or carved hollows into stone. Sometimes polished to a high gloss or dyed a strong color, they absorb the light or refract it in diagrammatic form. Funnel-shaped recesses in stones, walls,

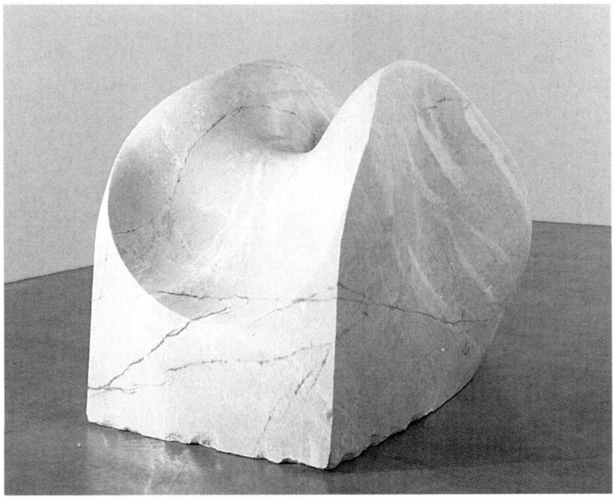

ANISH KAPOOR, UNTITLED, 2001, marble, 64 1/2 x 88 5/8 x 49 5/8", Barbara Gladstone Gallery, New York / OHNE TITEL, Marmor, 164 x 225,2 x 126,1 cm.

KURT W. FORSTER, holder of the Gropius chair at the Bauhaus University of Weimar, is director of next year's Architecture Biennale in Venice which will be dedicated to the theme of "Metamorphoses."

or even floors pierce the conventional limits of a room and reach out into unforeseeable territories. The gray of a curved recess and reflections on shiny steel yield an optical ambivalence that momentarily generates the same impression achieved by Jean Cocteau in his film *Orphée* (1950) when his figures enter and exit through the quicksilvery surface of mirrors. However, since Kapoor's enigmatic hollows share none of Cocteau's obtrusive suggestiveness, they refer much more intensely to the sculptures themselves.

The emptiness around things and the conceivable depth within them collide on reflecting surfaces, besiege the eyes and provoke a disturbing "unease," as Kapoor explains in conversation with Homi Bhabha.[1] He sees his stones as a substance enriched by time, whose history may be revealed in the process of sculpting.[2]

Kapoor's surfaces appear unstable; their convex curves or concave funnels make the sculpture look as if it were collapsing in on itself. The immaculate sheen of the steel cubes (UNTITLED, 1997) face viewers like upended sarcophagi with imploding surfaces that elude our visual grasp. Spontaneously we reach out in the vain attempt to rescue them from sinking, but the sculptural shape is in the process of vanishing into an optical maelstrom, as if sucked out of its own body and into a moving exterior. As Homi Bhabha describes it, "A sudden disappearance of surface in a deep, dark hole literally cuts the ground from under our feet."[3]

The extraordinary suction that emanates from these sculptures and seems almost to devour them is not a consequence of exceptional optical effects that occur only on certain surfaces. Kapoor's objects—this dispassionate designation is perhaps best qualified to capture their ambivalence in a single word—paradoxically find themselves in the act of self-consumption. They articulate the idea of their own depth, even where it remains invisible, but also the idea of their own time. It simply takes time to expose oneself to their impact and nothing much may actually happen. Very little does, in fact, happen externally, yet the longer we look, the more we learn from the sculpture. On the other hand, by showing itself to be curiously "curved" in space and time, it denies us some of the ground upon which we presume to be standing so firmly. The curvature—of surfaces, of reflections, of colors—causes a sense of suspension that is capable of disturbing and even frightening us.

We are certainly not off the mark in assuming that Kapoor's objects create a relation between volume and surface far different from anything we ever learned in school. Instead of subsuming a sculpture's volume to its image, or dulling its body into the appearance of a mere shape, he sets the two into an antagonistic relationship. His objects optically disrupt the relation that furnishes proof of substance and shape, namely the relation of surface to body. Kapoor effectively and literally undercuts the difference between what we explore only with our eyes and what we can grasp only through the physical sense of touch, that is, the hypothesis that sculpture belongs entirely to the world of the viewer. With utmost precision, the continuously curving surfaces of the sculptures transform the traditional relationship of surface and body into a continuum. Their juxtaposition gives rise to a differential linkage. For this reason, their further use should rely increasingly on computer programs capable of calculating an entire bundle of differing algorithms and their interaction. Cecil Balmond, director of the London firm Ove Arup—construction laboratory of contemporary architecture par excellence—put the rule to the test with his models for calculating Kapoor's towering sculptures.

In the year 2000, Kapoor took a giant step when he installed a work in a former flourmill in the port of Newcastle-upon-Tyne: TARATANTARA—a name like a flourish—was "hung" in the hollowed-out shell of a silo. Richard Deacon described it as follows: "The tube of red vinyl stretched between the two remaining standing walls replaced the missing end walls and seemingly converted the building into a block with a hole through it. From the outside, this was fairly simple; one saw the stretched red fabric and anticipated or imagined the mechanics of the installation. Although certainly the continuity of surface between the two ends—the effect of a folding of the outside into a vortex that swept through the building—caused some complications, and the glistening, vibrant surface of the vinyl gleamed with an awesome intensity."[4] We are overwhelmed not only

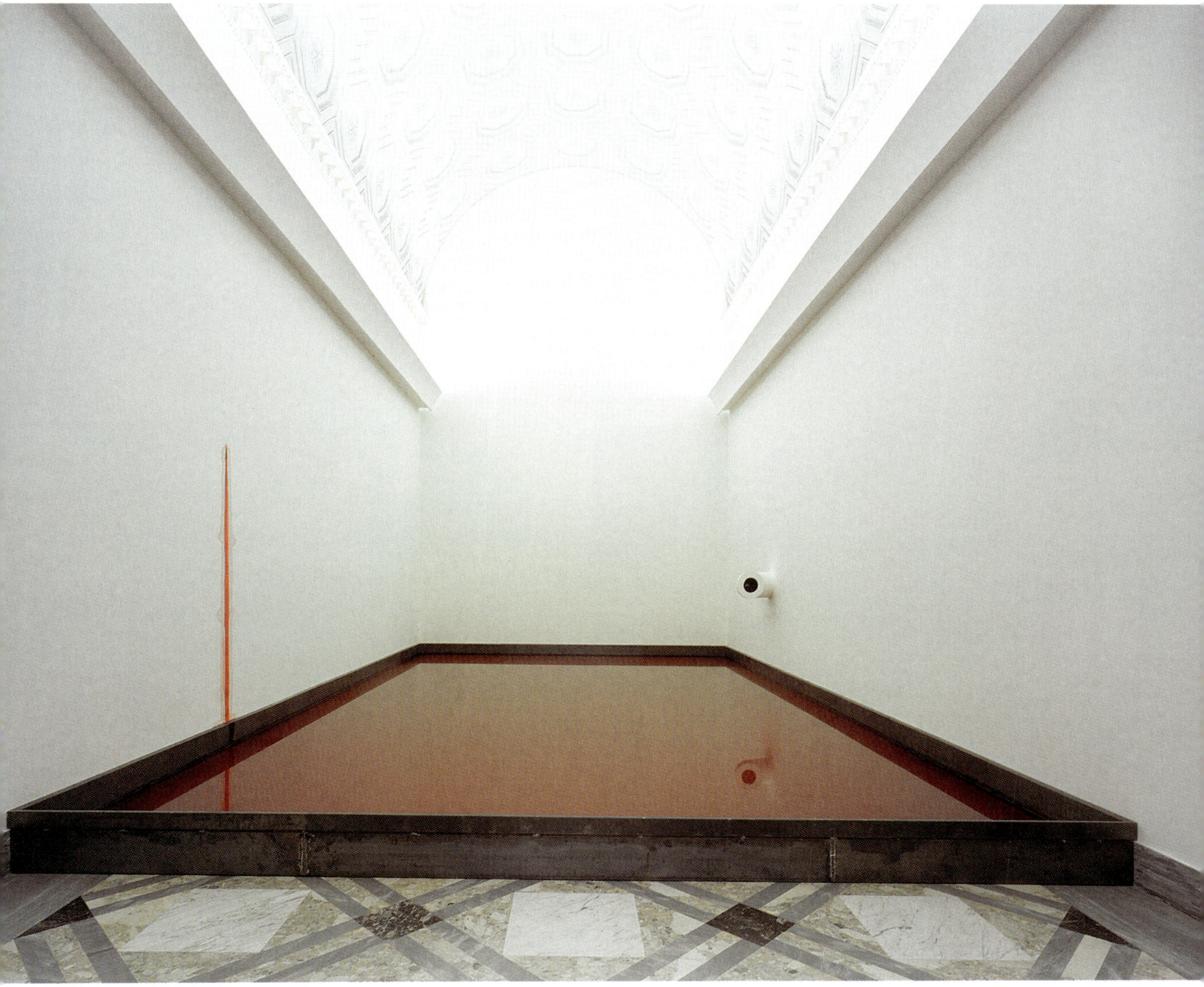

ANISH KAPOOR, UNTITLED, 2003, steel and water, dimensions variable, exhibition "Anish Kapoor," National Archaeological Museum, Naples, 25 October 2003 – 12 January 2004 / OHNE TITEL, Stahl und Wasser, Grösse variabel.

(PHOTO: PEPPE AVALLONE, NAPOLI)

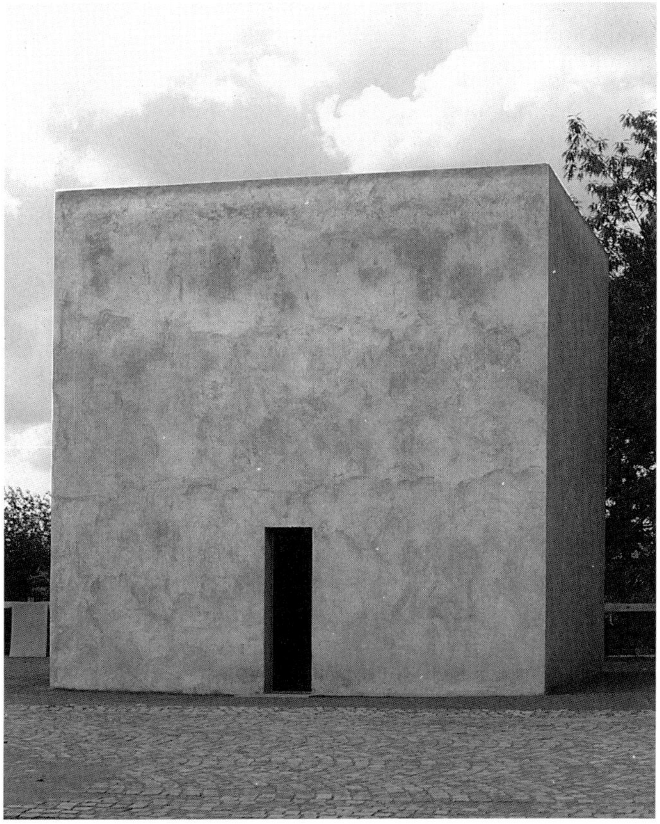

ANISH KAPOOR, DESCENT INTO LIMBO, 1992, concrete and stucco, 19 8/12 x 19 8/12 x 19 8/12", Documenta IX, Kassel, 1992, exterior view and interior detail /
EINSTIEG ZUR VORHÖLLE, Beton und Stuck, 6 x 6 x 6 m, Aussenansicht und Innenansicht.
(PHOTO: DIRK DE NEEF, GHENT)

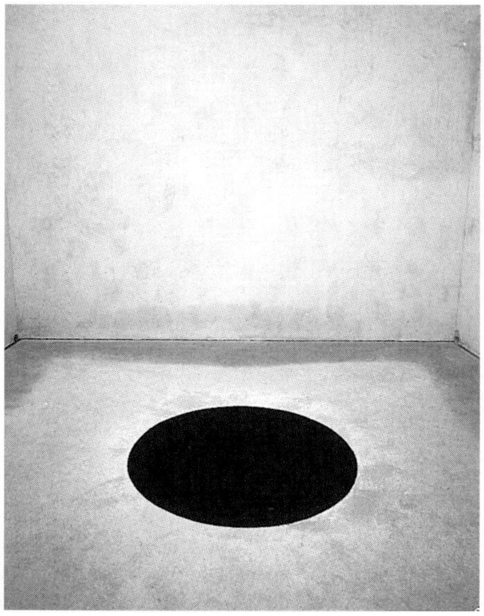

by the dimensions, corresponding approximately to a ten-storey building, but above all by the link between inside and outside in the form of a fantastically extended tunnel of deep red plastic fabric. Kapoor was again testing the curious power of sculpture that consumes its own volume as well as the room in which it is housed—but this time in gigantic scale. In his own words, "The foreshortening of the building from the outside as one looks through the form is to me, surprising. The building appears to be only half as long as the impression one had of it from the external structure. From the outside of the building, only the inside of the form is visible. From the inside of the building, only the outside of the form is visible. It is as if the space inside the building had suddenly expanded and what was a hole became a form ... Inside and outside seem to be turning into each other."[5)]

The effect of this gigantic sculpture also rests on the relation of closeness and distance, depending on the position of the viewer and the texture of the material, whose parabolic extension, colors, and effects even managed to surprise Kapoor himself. The surface properties of his materials proved in retrospect to be characteristic and not accidental. As such, they inspired work increasingly removed from the artist's earlier oeuvre in scale and material. Recently he has begun working with materials that were long alien to sculpture, and in places that are already dominated by mighty buildings.

A high point in Kapoors's efforts to exceed even the architecture of his sites was reached by the recent installation at London's Tate Modern, in which trumpet-shaped funnels threatened almost to burst the immense hall. Last year's MARSYAS installation[6)] is a spatial demonstration of what one might call a visual droning. Created as a kind of two-ended trumpet with a cupola-like opening, it floated above the heads of museum visitors thanks to the resistance of the synthetic material that Kapoor used. The evolution of the largest project to date, whose complexity utterly eclipses the experiment in Newcastle, shows a fascinating combination of visionary idea—captured in small sketches and models—and state-of-the-art, hi-tech engineering. Structural engineer Cecil Balmond tuned himself into Kapoor's agenda and in his catalogue essay "Skinning the Imagination,"[7)] he discloses how a highly sophisticated combination of pull, elasticity, and load made it possible to turn forty tons of steel and fabric into a giant sculpture. But MARSYAS does share one thing with the installation in Newcastle: both devour the architecture, calling into question the solid contours and encompassing spaces in the process. What once appeared as a fathomless, wavering field in the depths of the stone, hard as it may be, now deprives viewers of access as infinitely stretching, bending funnels and tunnels of colored fabric. It is inconceivable that architecture, with and of itself, could possibly ever bring about what Kapoor has achieved in his installations: turning space inside out, folding it in on itself and hollowing it out. Such an enterprise requires an imaginative approach of the kind manifested in recent astrophysics—a field concerned with the inaccessibly distant and inconceivably old time-spaces of the universe—by confronting our ordinary three-dimensional world with the idea of the saddle-shaped spaces of string theory. Their visual representation, as also used by Stephen Hawking,[8)] shows impressive affinities with the spatial funnels that Kapoor aspires to. We find comfort in discovering at least one bit of common ground between the incomprehensible, insoluble enigma of Kapoor's works and the necessity of imagining things we shall never be able to see.

(Translation: Catherine Schelbert)

1) *Anish Kapoor,* catalogue of the exhibition at the Hayward Gallery, London, 1998, with essays by Homi K. Bhabha and Pier Luigi Tazzi (Berkeley/Los Angeles/London: University of California Press, 1998), p. 18: "... in that narrow passage [between the mirrors], paradoxically there is a restlessness, an unease ..."
2) Ibid., p. 27: "There is a history in the stone and through the simple device of excavating the stone it's just as if a whole narrative sequence is suddenly there ..."
3) Ibid., p. 24.
4) Richard Deacon, "Baltic Anish," in *Anish Kapoor, TARATANTARA* (Barcelona: ACTAR Editorial, 2000), s.p.
5) Ibid., "Anish Kapoor in conversation with Sune Nordgren," s.p.
6) See *Anish Kapoor, Marsyas,* exh. cat. (London: Tate Publishing, 2002).
7) Cecil Balmond, "Skinning the Imagination," in *Anish Kapoor, Marsyas,* ibid., pp. 66–69.
8) Cf. Stephen Hawking, *The Universe in a Nutshell* (London: Bantam Press, 2002).

THE PERFORATE SELF OR NOUGHT IS NOT NAUGHT

MARINA WARNER

Why do you tear me from my self?

– Ovid, *Metamorphoses,* Book VI

Ovid tells the story of Marsyas, the satyr whom Apollo skinned alive, in the midst of a sequence of divine revenge killings; these follow one upon the other at a speed and pitch of intensity that make the reader gasp and shrink and grieve and cry out in protest.[1] Satyrs are a kind of Arcadian wild thing, part-goat, part-man, tall, erect, with furry thighs and cloven hooves, with a long bearded face, pointed nose, tufted ears and (sometimes) tufted, priapic penis; they run with Dionysus and Pan, and, like centaurs, have their own skills, wisdom, and powers. But they are always distinguished from the human order: they figure as uncivilized creatures of instinct and appetite who dance at drunken parties and peep at girls who have passed out, as in Bellini's THE FEAST OF THE GODS (1514–1529) and Titian's BACCHUS AND ARIADNE (1523–1524).

Something of this clash, between one kind of order and another, may reverberate beneath the story of Apollo's revenge on Marsyas. For, as Ovid tells the story, Marsyas picks up a pair of pipes made from bones and begins to play them so well that he attracts the admiration of everyone who hears him. It's almost always fatal to draw attention in myth (nobody is more jealous than a god or goddess), and when Apollo hears of Marsyas' growing fame, he challenges him to a contest. Midas, he of the golden touch (from another tale), is drafted as judge, and he gives out the satyr as the better musician. Whereupon, a furious Apollo turns his lyre upside down and plays it as deftly as before, then defies Marsyas to do likewise with his pipes. It is when Marsyas fails to do this that Apollo strings him up—also upside down—on a pine tree and has him skinned alive.

Marsyas' music sang the praises of the Mother, Pausanias wrote, and so there may be buried beneath the Ovidian story a much earlier account of the Olympian victory over older powers, with Apollo not only asserting Apollonian control over the demi-beast's Dionysian pleasure, but also quelling any nostalgia for the ancient Magna Mater. This relates to flayed bodies: Marsyas in his torment is butchered, reduced to meat on a hook, to the non-individualized raw flesh of form-before-form.[2] For Marsyas, time is being run backwards: hanged, he turns back

MARINA WARNER's most recent book is *Signs & Wonders,* a collection of essays. She is writing a book on the imagery and language of spirits, called *Castles in the Air: Figuring the Soul.*

ANISH KAPOOR, MARSYAS, 2002, PVC membrane, steel structure, installation at the Tate Modern Turbine Hall, Unilever Series, 10 October 2002 – 6 April 2003, detail / PVC-Membran, Stahlgerüst, Ausschnitt. (PHOTO: SAXON GROUP & TATE GALLERY, LONDON)

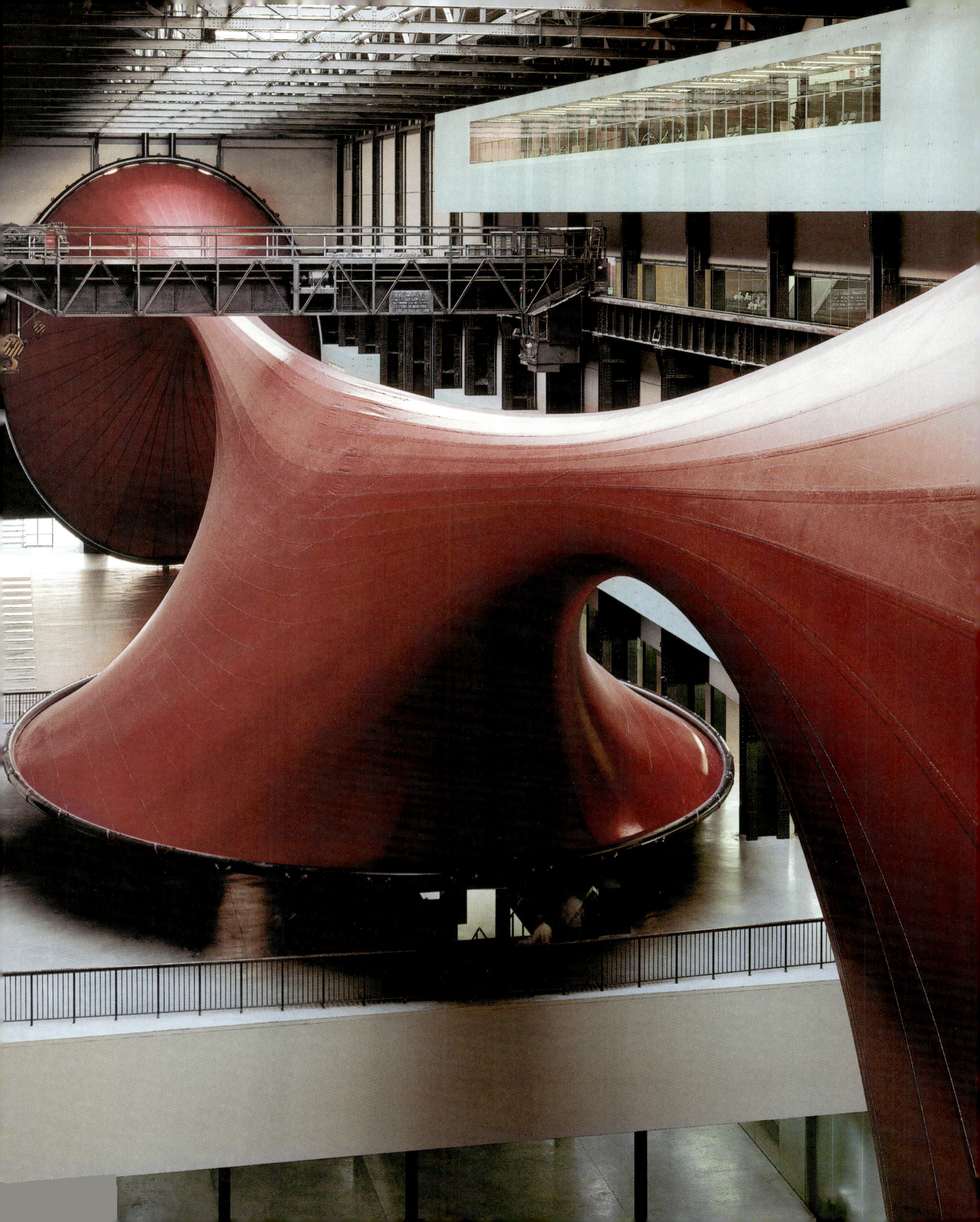

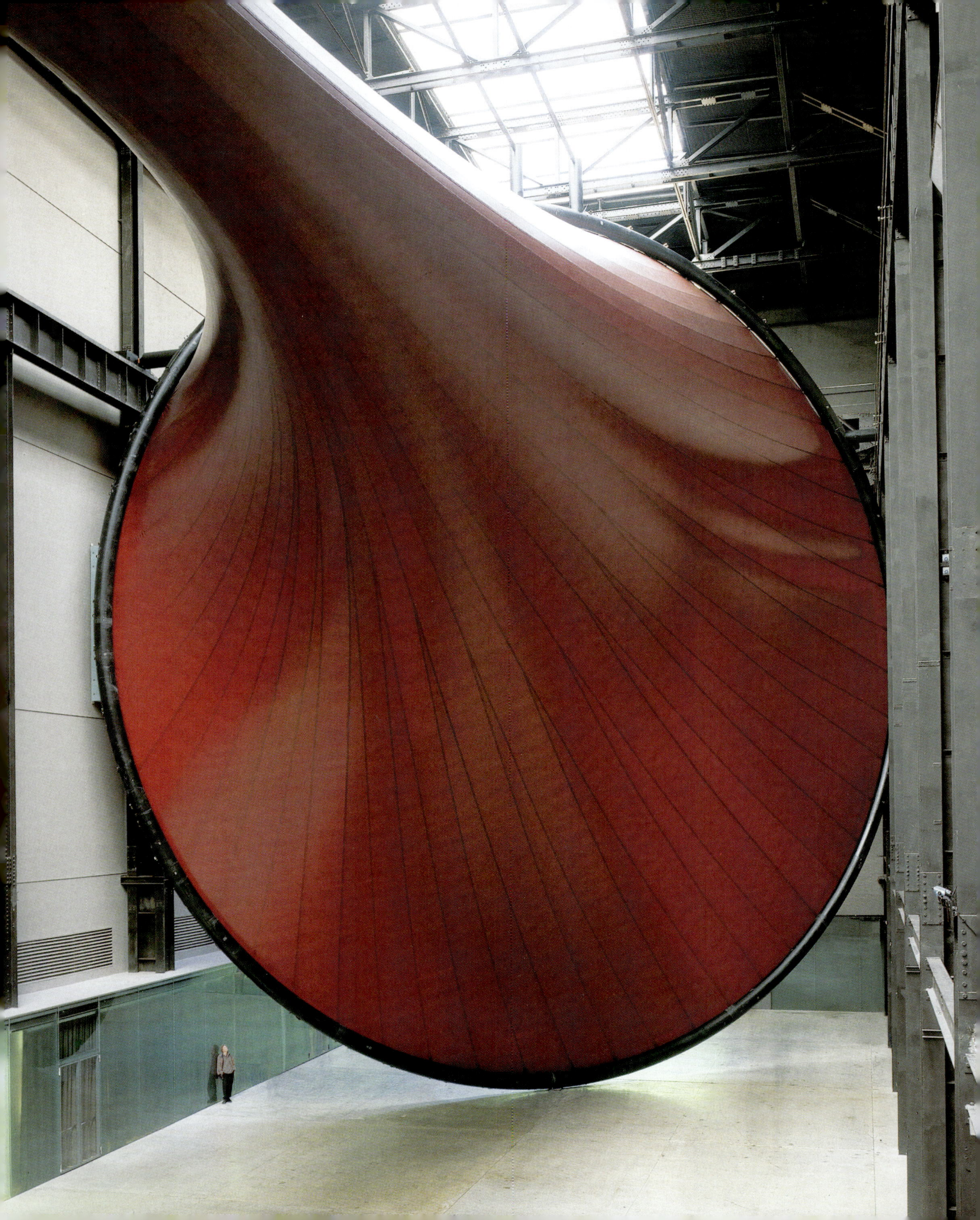

into a placental lump of origin, as the integument that holds his person—and his sexuality—is stripped from him.

Marsyas in agony also gives voice, in some ghastly mimicry of Apollo's lyre. So Ovid first sketches out one transformation, the satyr into a raw, bleeding, screaming carcass, before closing with the reprieve of Marsyas' natural metamorphosis into a river, fed by the tears of his mourners. The fifteen books of the *Metamorphoses* contain hundreds of such cruel just-so stories, providing every feature of the landscape with a mythological origin, and incorporating them into a continuing, generative cycle of energy, by whose strength and indestructibility, nothing and nobody are ever lost, ever extinguished. Ovid's impassioned narrative keeps his subjects—and himself—vivid, present, and alive. Metamorphosis, into a flower or a tree or a stream or a bird, offers a kind of hope—a reprieve from total annihilation. The last word of the poem is the defiant *vivam* (I shall live).

Marsyas was a frequent subject of classical art: the satyr who made music from a pair of bones embodied the possibility of human expression, of instinct, vigor, appetite changed wonderfully into song, into art. (The skin was exhibited, Herodotus reports, within historical memory: almost a *vera icon* or holy shroud of Turin.) The flaying cruelly represents an exchange of inner and outer: the *écorché* paradoxically shows forth the generic human body organs at the same time as symbolizing interiority unclothed, *nuda veritas.* Michelangelo paid tribute to Marsyas' potent ancestral ghost in his LAST JUDGMENT through the figure of St. Bartholomew holding his flayed skin, on which Michelangelo depicted his own features, stretched and distorted anamorphically in the folds of this fabric of flesh. There's a real comment on the illusion of art here, too, as painting flattens figures onto a plane, as flaying stretches the wrapped integument of a body on to a surface.

Anish Kapoor's narrative title (unusual in his work) recalls Titian's great late work, THE FLAYING OF MARSYAS (1575–1576), and the satyr's fate resonates with his longtime sculptural concerns.[3] Skin focuses his imagination as a sculptor: his work continues to obsessively explore the translation of forms from plane to volume, from line to surface, the tension between contour and space, and the boundary of inner and outer bodies. He allows materials' intrinsic heft to reveal the interdependency of bulk and membrane, and delights in the complexity of light's movements, giving play to reflection and refraction on surfaces until the sculptures themselves become etherealized and almost vanish from view. The myth of Marsyas is just one of the ways down into the mysteries that Kapoor plumbs with regard to this most polymorphous of the body's organs. He has said, "There's a kind of implied unreality about skin which I think is wonderful." Skin, unlike the eye or the tongue, resists visualization: it constitutes a boundary in itself, but existing only in extension, eludes delineating.

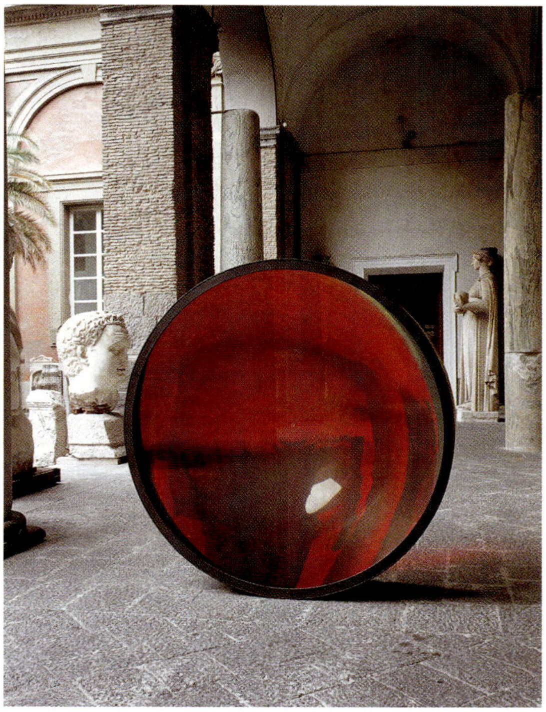

ANISH KAPOOR, BLOOD CINEMA, 2000, acrylic and steel, exhibition "Anish Kapoor," National Archaeological Museum, Naples, 25 October 2003 – 12 January 2004 / BLUTKINO, Acryl und Stahl.
(PHOTO: PEPPE AVALLONE, NAPOLI)

ANISH KAPOOR, MARSYAS, 2002, PVC membrane, steel structure, installation at the Tate Modern Turbine Hall, Unilever Series, 10 October 2002 – 6 April 2003, detail / PVC-Membran, Stahlgerüst, Ausschnitt. (PHOTO: SAXON GROUP & TATE GALLERY, LONDON)

The theme also engages with artists' meditations on meat: Kapoor himself has invoked Soutine's carcasses in association with his MARSYAS. Soutine was himself responding to both Rembrandt and to Rubens; in this tradition of heroic painting, massive expanses of living creatures, emblazoned in death, force a confrontation with the very limits on humans' humanity. Kapoor increasingly aligns himself with this painterly lineage: his recent exhibition at the Lisson Gallery, London, was called "Painting" (May–June 2003). Meat offers a metaphor for degree zero of survival, just as cannibalism appears whenever savagery or barbarians are at issue, while painted (or sculpted) meat performs a metamorphosis in itself of rawness into something other, changed by the act of imitation.

Anyone who looks at Titian's painting feels a terrible and eerie disquiet stirred by the lack of visible agony in this scene of torture. The artist clusters the cast of characters very close together and yet depicts no mutual interaction or even engaged eye lines; the paint strokes are scumbled, famously feathery and loose and tender; as the flesh of Marsyas is exposed, the satyr does not show agony and Apollo looks on, seraphically, while another angelic being plays a viol. It is possible that Titian's picture reconsiders the economy of Christian sacrifice (Christ's crucifixion), which ransoms human iniquity through atrocious and extreme suffering unto death, and instead affirms a pagan, Ovidian vision of continual organic transformation in which death cannot take place: his Marsyas escapes suffering because, as the poet writes, the soul lives on and nothing dies.

This would reverberate with Kapoor's inspiration from Indian aesthetics, drawing on Sanskrit myths of cyclical return and the eternity of forms. His work invokes for me the metaphysics of *svayamatrnna,* or "self-perforates," sacred ring-stones through which the breath of heaven flows. Coomaraswamy, the great aesthetic philosopher and curator (at Harvard), whom Kapoor reads, has written about this mystical idea of "doors in the sky." Votaries were passed through them in rituals of blessing and initiation. The three vast annular mouths of Kapoor's MARSYAS (2002), bonded to steel rings, indeed open funnels heavenwards, like one of John Martin's visionary vortices. Many other sculptures pierce cavities in stone, carve shapes in the void, and invite falling deep into matter. He refuses the idea of the void as empty in the figurative sense of hollow: for him, nought is laden, nought is not naught: this is the plenitude of the vacuum (as in quantum physics). Kapoor has trapped air in a cube of poured Perspex, watching for that wonder, the bubble that is nothing changed into form, "when space becomes an object."[4)]

Echoing classical thinking on the sublime, Kapoor declares he also wants to "turn the world inside out and upside down."[5)] (Where the sublime is present, wrote Longinus, "...the whole universe is turned upside down and torn apart."[6)]) Terror of a kind stirs when you find yourself plummeting into the depths of a mirror piece by Kapoor, or become disorientated by the play of reflections and detached from familiar moorings; the sheer scale of his works belittles you, while at the same time carrying you off in its oceanic embrace. When "the space within is bigger than the space as seemingly defined by the outside," the sense of your own corporeality changes and the contours of each observer's body may be undone: a kind of pleasurable dissolution of the container. Perhaps, even, a kind of flaying.

When encountering the work this sensation of terror does not call to mind Edmund Burke's "incomprehensible darkness," a horrific and engulfing chaos, but the vast unknowable made beautiful by form, an aesthetic principle that coheres with the Kantian sublime, turning away from the broken and horrifying body of chaos and meaninglessness into a pacific order where the hole is rendered whole and the void is dispelled, to be transformed into plenitude.[7)]

The dramatic, vast, raked hangar-like entrance to Herzog & de Meuron's interior of the Tate Modern has inspired dramatic and eloquent installations in the *Unilever Series* for the Turbine Hall, including Juan Muñoz's enigmatic and last major work DOUBLE BIND (2001). But Kapoor chose to emphasize the plunging length and extent of the space, not its height; he spanned it entirely with his MARSYAS stretched on three rings and suspended from cables. Looking at MARSYAS at Tate Modern was an experience that both amplified you and perforated you, that made you feel your human littleness and the grandeur of the world, while at the same time draw-

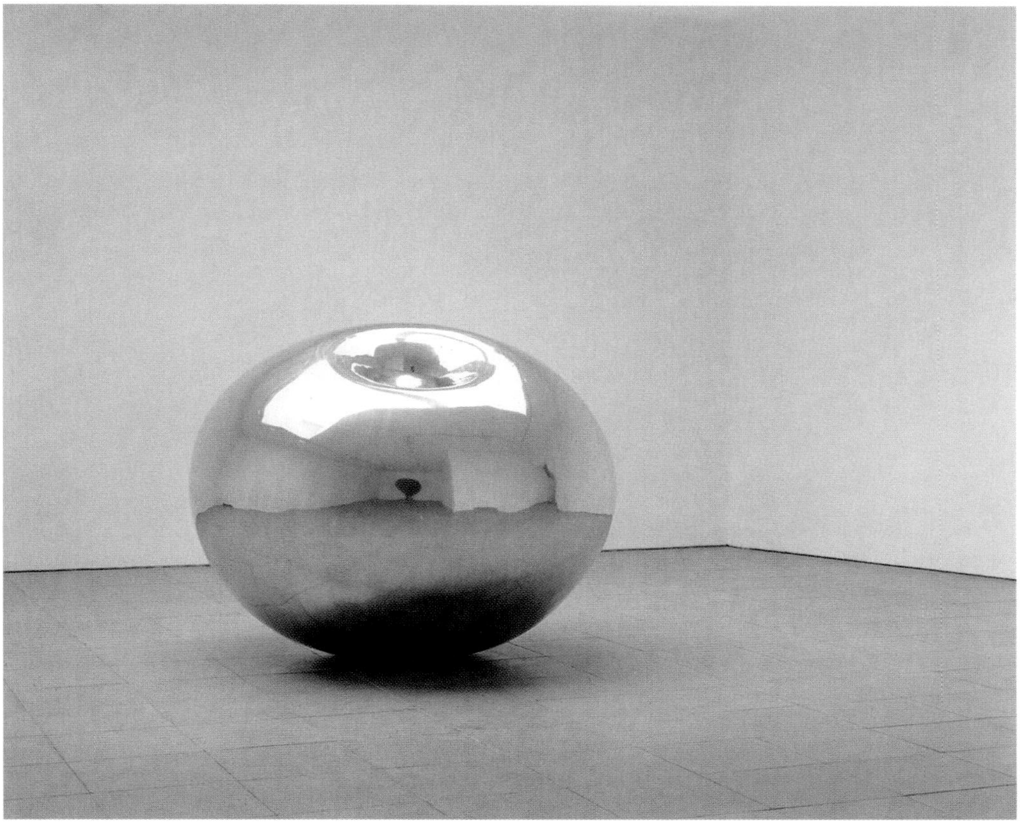

ANISH KAPOOR, TURNING THE WORLD INSIDE OUT, 1995, cast aluminum, $58\frac{1}{4}$ x $72\frac{1}{2}$ x 74", Lisson Gallery, London / DAS INNERE DER WELT NACH AUSSEN STÜLPEN, Aluminiumguss, 148 x 184 x 188 cm. (PHOTO: JOHN RIDDY, LONDON)

ing you up to soar and resound with it. In the act of identifying contemplation, you could feel your thought fall into its spaces, experience your body peeled away as it touched yielding here and resistance there, and the edges of consciousness moved through space according to those physical laws that Kapoor makes visible. Thomas McEvilley has savaged what he calls the "tamed sublime" in contemporary art, yet it still seems to me that the abstract containment of violence, as in Kapoor's MARSYAS and other pieces, performs a valuable move within the aesthetic of the sublime; it does not "tame" it or conceal its darkness from view, but offers it up to enrapturing metamorphosis. Kapoor has "forever wanted," he has memorably declared, "to turn the red of earth and body into sky"—and this most eloquent and inspired phrase touches the core of his achievement.

The visceral vibrations of Kapoor's aesthetic strike resonances with processes of emergence, with the enfleshment of all bodies, and above all with the maternal body as the vessel in which all bodies are formed and from which they make their entrance, often upside down, bloody, and howling. His alembic-like sculptures, highly satisfying swelling receptacles with narrow necks, closely resemble the alchemical flasks in which the Philosophical Child gestates. The deep, branching red trumpet cones of MARSYAS, asymmetrically lifting from a lower, central sphincter, open as a gullet and as whorled ears, but they also echo the arrangement of the birth canal and the fallopian tubes (this association arises even more strongly from Kapoor's working drawings). Redness also flows through paintings he has been making, using a medium for the pigment that allows the paint to drip, spotting the floor, while "wounds open" in the facture on the canvas. The colossal piece, MY RED HOMELAND (2003) (conceived especially for the exhibition at the Kunsthaus Bregenz, September 27

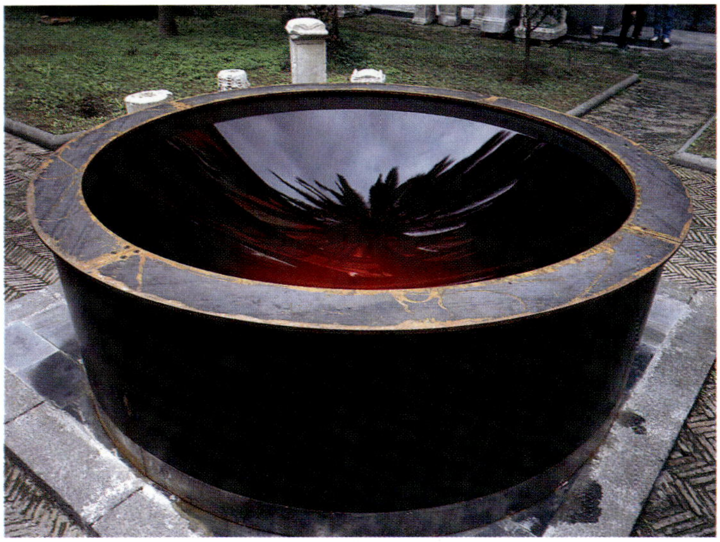

ANISH KAPOOR, TURNING WATER INTO MIRROR, BLOOD INTO SKY, 2003, steel, water, and motor, 68 1/8 x 118 1/8 x 118 1/8", exhibition "Anish Kapoor," National Archaeological Museum, Naples, 25 October 2003 – 12 January 2004 / WASSER ZUM SPIEGEL, BLUT ZUM HIMMEL MACHEN, Stahl, Wasser, Motor, 173 x 300 x 300 cm.
(PHOTO: PEPPE AVALLONE, NAPOLI)

to November 16, 2003), twelve meters in diameter, heaps more than twenty tons of viscous scarlet ooze on a circle like a threshing floor. This *informe* mass of fat and Vaseline, intentionally incarnadined like Lady Macbeth's bloody hands, is swept towards the edge by a revolving arm into squelchy heaps and folds and shapes which obey the materials' own intrinsic gravity and viscosity as their forms build and fall away. In this way, Kapoor allows form to make itself: "Somehow it is not enough that an object is made ... it's related to a very old aspect of Indian thinking that there are certain kinds of objects that are self manifest: they make themselves ... their mythology is that they are not made."[8]

Story translates into geometry: in MARSYAS, the satyr, embodying nature and art's relation, metamorphoses into the fundamental geometric law that straight lines threaded on a warp will form curves in space. This is what happens when "surface bends into structure." As the engineer Cecil Balmond wrote about the project, "The guessing game is between structure and metaphor."[9] Through the vast and passionate web of crimson skin, the skied body of Marsyas reveals to the viewer the invisible fabric of the world, the very impress of the impalpable forces that shape phenomena that vibrate and pulse in the air, fold and stratify mountains, stellate snowflakes, and cause waves to break in scalloped rills.

1) Some of the other episodes in Book VI tell the story of Philomel, raped and mutilated by Tereus, who is turned into a nightingale; Arachne who is punished by Minerva for her skills in weaving, and changed into a spider, and the massacre of Niobe and all fourteen of her children at the hands of Apollo and Diana.
2) Mary Jacobus, "Inside Out: Marion Milner, Psychic Space, and the Myth of Marsyas," paper delivered at the conference "Spaces & Places," Delphi, September 2003, and kindly lent by the author, Professor of English at Cambridge University, England, whom I thank very much indeed for giving it to me to read.
3) Titian's picture arrived in London from its home in the Czech Republic to hang in the National Gallery's show of Titian, just as Anish Kapoor's sculpture, MARSYAS, was about to be taken down in the Turbine Hall at Tate Modern: for a moment, the two works almost touched, as it were. Their fleeting passage in such proximity was totally unexpected and the synchronicity indeed seemed to Anish Kapoor a kind of wonderful blessing.
4) A. K. Coomaraswamy "Svayamatrnna: Ianua Coeli," in *The Door in the Sky: Coomaraswamy on Myth and Meaning,* ed. by Rama P. Coomaraswamy (Princeton, NJ: Princeton University Press, 1997), pp. 6–61. Interestingly, Courtney Love's band, Hole, responding to her husband Kurt Cobain's Nirvana, catches this strain in Indian mysticism.
5) This and subsequent quotes by Anish Kapoor are from a meeting between the author and the artist in 2003.
6) Longinus, *Peri Hypsous,* in: T.S. Dorsch, trans., *Classical Literary Criticism: Aristotle, On the Art of Poetry; Horace, On the Art of Poetry; Longinus, On the Sublime* (Baltimore: Penguin Books, 1965), p. 111. Quoted by Thomas McEvilley in "Turned Upside Down and Torn Apart," in *Sticky Sublime,* ed. by Bill Beckley (New York: Allworth Press, 2001), pp. 57–83.
7) See McEvilley, op. cit., pp. 57–83.
8) Anish Kapoor and Donna De Salvo, "A Conversation," in *Anish Kapoor, Marsyas* (London: Tate Publishing, 2002), p. 61.
9) Cecil Balmond, "Skinning the Imagination," in *Anish Kapoor, Marsyas,* op. cit., pp. 66–69.

DAS PERFORIERTE ICH ODER NULL IST NICHT NICHTS

MARINA WARNER

Warum ziehst du mich selber aus meiner Haut?
Ovid, *Metamorphosen,* Sechstes Buch

Ovid erzählt die Geschichte von Marsyas, jenem Satyr, den Apollo häutete, inmitten einer Serie von Rachemorden unter Göttern; diese Morde folgen einander mit derart atemraubender Geschwindigkeit und Heftigkeit, dass der Leser entsetzt nach Luft ringt und entrüstet protestiert.[1] Satyrn sind eine Art arkadische Wildwesen, halb Ziegenbock, halb Mensch, gross, aufrecht gehend, mit pelzigen Lenden und gespaltenen Hufen, einem lang gezogenen bärtigen Gesicht, spitzen büscheligen Ohren und (manchmal) ebensolchem erigiertem Glied; sie sind die Begleiter von Dionysos und Pan, und wie die Zentauren verfügen sie über eigene Fähigkeiten und Kräfte und besondere Weisheit. Aber immer sind sie klar von den Menschen zu unterscheiden: Sie treten als unzivilisierte, instinkt- und triebbestimmte Kreaturen auf, die auf rauschenden Festen tanzen und sich neugierig an besinnungslos gewordene Mädchen heranmachen, so etwa in Bellinis DAS FEST DER GÖTTER (1514–1529) oder Tizians BACCHUS UND ARIADNE (1523–1524).

MARINA WARNER arbeitet zurzeit an *Castles in the Air: Figuring the Soul,* einer Untersuchung von Sprache und Bildwelt der Geister. Zuletzt veröffentlichte sie den Essayband *Signs & Wonders.*

Etwas von diesem Zusammenprall unterschiedlicher Ordnungen mag in der Geschichte von Apollos Rache an Marsyas mitschwingen. Denn so wie Ovid die Geschichte erzählt, findet Marsyas zwei aus Gebeinen geschnitzte Flötenrohre und beginnt auf ihnen so schön zu spielen, dass er bei jedem, der ihn hört, Bewunderung weckt. In der antiken Sagenwelt ist es jedoch fast immer verhängnisvoll, Aufmerksamkeit zu erregen (denn niemand ist eifersüchtiger als die Götter und Göttinnen), und als Apollo von Marsyas' wachsendem Ruhme hört, fordert er ihn zum Wettstreit. Midas, durch dessen Berührung sich (in einer anderen Erzählung) alles zu Gold verwandelt, wird als Schiedsrichter beigezogen und erklärt den Satyr zum virtuoseren Musiker. Darauf stellt ein wutschnaubender Apollo seine Lyra auf den Kopf, spielt darauf genauso behend wie zuvor und fordert Marsyas auf, dasselbe mit seinen Flöten zu tun. Als dies Marsyas nicht gelingt, hängt Apollo ihn – ebenfalls kopfüber – an einer Pinie auf und häutet ihn bei lebendigem Leibe.

Marsyas' Musik erklang zum Lob der Mutter, schreibt Pausanias, deshalb liegt der Geschichte Ovids vielleicht eine viel frühere Schilderung des siegreichen Kampfs der olympischen Götter gegen ältere Mächte zugrunde, bei dem Apollo nicht nur den Sieg der apollinischen Beherrschtheit über die dionysische Lust des Mischwesens sicherstellt, son-

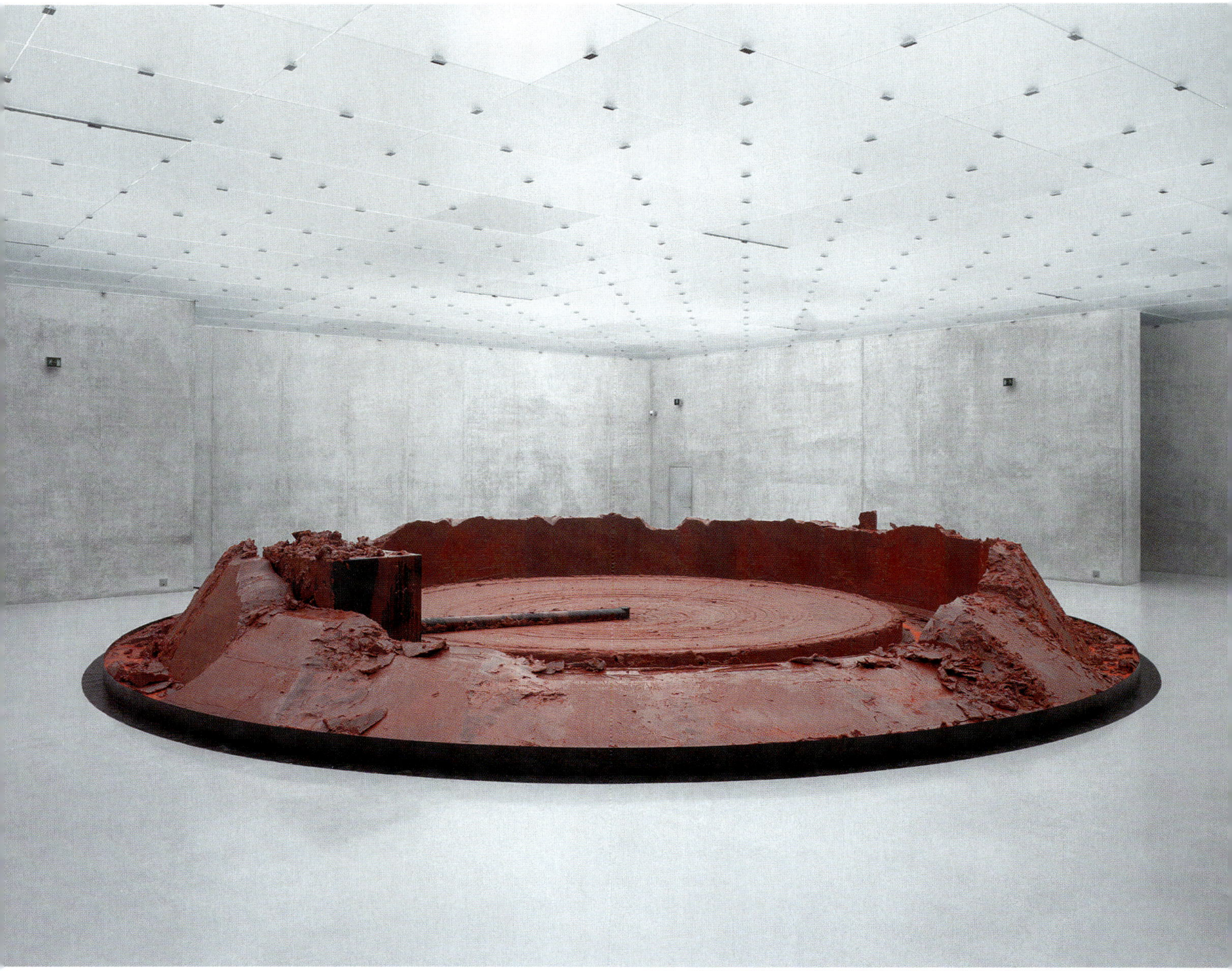

ANISH KAPOOR, MY RED HOMELAND, 2003, red vaseline, hydraulic motor, steel block, dimensions variable, exhibition "My Red Homeland," Kunsthaus Bregenz, 27 September – 16 November 2003 / MEIN ROTES HEIMATLAND, rote Vaseline, Hydraulikmotor, Stahlblock, Grösse variabel.
(PHOTO: NIC TENWIGGENHORN / KUNSTHAUS BREGENZ)

dern auch jedwede nostalgische Regung für die alte Magna Mater im Keim erstickt. Das passt zum gehäuteten Leib: Marsyas wird zur Strafe geschlachtet und auf ein Stück Fleisch am Haken reduziert, auf das unspezifische rohe Fleisch des «noch nicht Form Gewordenen».[2] Für Marsyas dreht sich damit das Rad der Zeit zurück: Aufgehängt wird er wieder zum ursprünglichen Plazentaklumpen, sobald ihm die Hülle, die seine Person – und Sexualität – birgt, abgezogen wird.

Im Todeskampf gibt Marsyas auch Laute von sich, ein furchtbares Echo der Lyra Apolls. So skizziert Ovid zunächst die Verwandlung des Satyrs zum rohen, blutenden, schreienden Kadaver, bevor die Gnade der natürlichen Metamorphose einsetzt: die Verwandlung des Marsyas in einen Fluss, gespiesen von den Tränen der ihn Beweinenden. Die fünfzehn Bücher der *Metamorphosen* enthalten Hunderte solch grausamer Recht-geschieht-ihm-Geschichten, die jedem Element der Landschaft einen mythologischen Ursprung geben und alles in einem kontinuierlich strömenden Energiekreislauf zusammenfassen, dank dessen Kraft und Unzerstörbarkeit nichts und niemand je verloren geht oder ausgelöscht wird. Dank Ovids leidenschaftlicher Erzählweise bleiben seine Figuren — und er selbst – aufs Lebhafteste präsent und lebendig. Die Metamorphose zu Blume oder Baum, Fluss oder Vogel lässt – dank dem Aufschieben der vollständigen Auslöschung – eine gewisse Hoffnung zu. Das letzte Wort der *Metamorphosen* ist denn auch ein trotziges *vivam* (ich werde leben).

Marsyas ist ein häufiges Motiv der klassischen Kunstgeschichte: Der Satyr, der auf Gebeinen Flöte spielt, steht für die menschliche Ausdrucksfähigkeit, für die Verwandlung von Instinkt, Kraft und Begehren in Gesang und Kunst. (Herodot schreibt, dass seine Haut geschichtlichen Berichten zufolge ausgestellt gewesen sei: beinah wie eine Veronika oder das heilige Leichentuch von Turin.) Die Häutung ist ein grausames Vertauschen von Innerem und Äusserem: Der Gehäutete gibt seine vitalen inneren Organe preis und ist zugleich ein Symbol entblösster Innerlichkeit, die «nackte Wahrheit» eben. Michelangelo zollte Marsyas' mächtigem Ahnengeist in seinem Deckenbild DAS JÜNGSTE GERICHT (in der Sixtinischen Kapelle) Tribut, und zwar in der Darstellung des Heiligen Bartholomäus, der seine abgezogene Haut in Händen hält, auf welcher Michelangelo seine eigenen Züge abbildet, verzerrt und sich anamorphisch in die Falten dieses menschlichen Gewebeteils schmiegend. Dahinter steckt auch ein echter Kommentar zum Illusionscharakter der Kunst, da auch die Malerei die menschliche Figur auf eine Fläche bannt, wie beim Häuten das bergende Gefäss des Körpers abgezogen und flach ausgebreitet wird.

Anish Kapoors narrativer, innerhalb seines Werks eher ungewöhnliche Titel ruft auch Tizians grossartiges Spätwerk DIE HÄUTUNG DES MARSYAS (1575–1576) in Erinnerung, wobei das Schicksal des Satyrs auch etwas aus Kapoors langjähriger Auseinandersetzung mit der Skulptur aufgreift.[3] Schon immer regte die Haut Kapoors bildhauerische Phantasie an: Sein Werk erforscht geradezu obsessiv die Übertragung von Formen aus der Ebene in den Raum und von der Linie zur Fläche, die Spannung zwischen

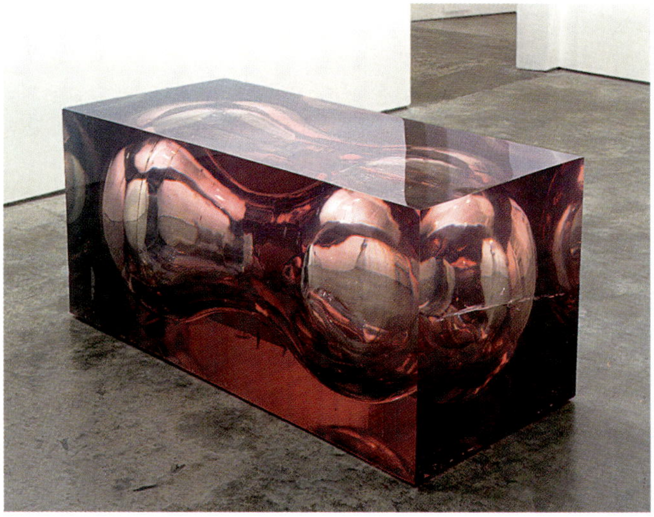

ANISH KAPOOR, RESIN, AIR, SPACE II, 2000, resin, 27 1/8 x 60 x 26 7/8" / KUNSTHARZ, LUFT, RAUM II, Kunstharz, 69 x 152,5 x 68,3 cm.

Umriss und Raum sowie die Grenze zwischen inneren und äusseren Körpern. Er lässt die Wechselbeziehung zwischen Wölbung und Membran durch das innere Gewicht der Materie sichtbar werden und freut sich am komplexen Spiel des Lichts, das sich auf den Oberflächen spiegelt und bricht und den Skulpturen eine ätherische Qualität verleiht, so dass sie sich beinah dem Blick entziehen. Die Sage von Marsyas ist nur einer von zahlreichen Wegen der Erforschung jener Geheimnisse, die Kapoor in Bezug auf dieses vielgestaltigste aller körperlichen Organe auslotet. Er meinte einmal: «Haut hat eine Art implizite Unwirklichkeit, die ich wunderbar finde.» Anders als das Auge oder die Zunge widersteht die Haut der Visualisierung: Sie stellt selbst eine Grenze dar, aber da sie nur in der Ausdehnung existiert, entzieht sie sich der zeichnerischen Darstellung.

Das Marsyas-Thema erinnert auch an künstlerische Auseinandersetzungen mit dem Thema «Fleisch»: Kapoor selbst assoziiert dazu Soutines Darstellungen blutiger Körper. Soutine wiederum bezieht sich auf Rembrandt und Rubens; in dieser Tradition der heroischen Malerei provozieren die riesigen, von im Tod verherrlichten, lebenden Kreaturen bedeckten Flächen eine Konfrontation mit den Grenzen der Menschlichkeit des Menschen selbst. Kapoor reiht sich in zunehmendem Masse in diese malerische Tradition ein: Seine jüngste Ausstellung in der Lisson Gallery in London trug den Titel «Painting» (Mai–Juni 2003). Fleisch ist auch eine Metapher für das nackte Überleben, während Kannibalismus immer mit Grausamkeit und Barbarei in Verbindung gebracht wird; gemaltes (oder modelliertes) Fleisch dagegen vollzieht in sich eine Metamorphose vom Rohen zu etwas anderem, eine Verwandlung, die durch den Akt der Nachahmung ausgelöst wird.

Jeder, der Tizians Bild betrachtet, empfindet eine entsetzliche, gespenstische Unruhe, die durch die Abwesenheit jedes sichtbaren Leidens in dieser Folterszene entsteht. Der Künstler drängt die Figuren sehr eng zusammen, zeigt jedoch keinerlei gegenseitige Interaktion, ja nicht einmal Blicke, die sich begegnen; die Pinselstriche sind verwischt, federleicht, locker und zart; wenn Marsyas' Fleisch blossgelegt wird, zeigt der Satyr keinen Schmerz und der zuschauende Apollo wirkt abgeklärt wie ein Seraphim, während ein anderes engelhaftes Wesen auf einer Viola spielt. Möglicherweise reflektiert Tizian in seinem Bild die Ökonomie des christlichen Opfers (der Kreuzigung, durch welche die menschliche Sündhaftigkeit durch das grausame Leiden und Sterben Christi gesühnt wird), indem er diesem die heidnische, Ovidsche Vision einer kontinuierlichen organischen Verwandlung gegenüberstellt, in welcher der Tod keinen Platz hat: Sein Marsyas entgeht dem Leiden, weil, wie der Dichter sagt, die Seele weiterlebt und nichts stirbt.

Das stünde im Einklang mit Kapoors Inspiration durch die indische Ästhetik, die sich auf Sanskrit-Mythen von der ewigen Wiederkehr der Dinge und der Ewigkeit der Formen stützt. Sein Werk erinnert mich an die Metaphysik des *Svayamatrnna* oder die «selbst-perforierten», heiligen Ringsteine, durch die der Himmelsatem fliesst. Coomaraswamy, der grosse ästhetische Theoretiker und Kurator (in Harvard), den auch Kapoor liest, hat über diese mystische Vorstellung von «Türen im Himmel» geschrieben. Im Rahmen von Segnungs- und Initiationsritualen mussten Personen, die ihr Leben Gott weihten, sich durch diese Steine hindurch begeben. Die drei riesigen, von Stahlringen gefassten, ringartigen Münder von Kapoors MARSYAS sind eigentlich offene, himmelwärts führende Trichter, vergleichbar mit John Martins visionären Strudeln. Andere Skulpturen weisen Höhlungen im Stein auf, zeichnen Formen in die Leere und laden dazu ein, sich tief in die Materie hineinfallen zu lassen. Kapoor lehnt die Idee der leeren Leere im Sinn des figurativ Hohlen ab: Für ihn ist das nicht Vorhandene aufgeladen, null ist nicht nichts, sondern die Fülle des Vakuums (wie in der Quantenphysik). Auf der Suche nach diesem Wunder, dass die Blase, die nichts ist, sich in Form verwandle und «Raum zum Objekt wird», hat Kapoor auch schon Luft in einen aus Perspex gegossenen Kubus gesperrt.[4)]

Kapoor nimmt Bezug auf die klassische Philosophie des Erhabenen, wenn er erklärt, er wolle ebenfalls «die Welt von innen nach aussen stülpen und auf den Kopf stellen».[5)] («Siehst du», schreibt Longinus, «wie die Erde in ihren Tiefen aufbirst, der Tartaros selbst sich entblösst, Aufruhr und Zwiespalt die ganze Welt ergreifen und alles zugleich, Himmel

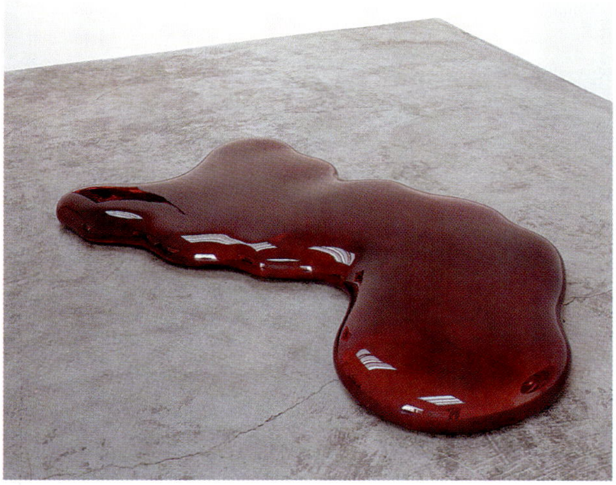

ANISH KAPOOR, BLOOD, 2000, fiberglass and lacquer, 90 15/16 x 48 x 5 15/16" / BLUT, Fiberglas lackiert, 231 x 122 x 15 cm. (PHOTO: REGEN PROJECTS, LOS ANGELES)

und Hölle, Sterbliches und Ewiges in der gerade tobenden Schlacht an Kampf und Gefahr teilnimmt?»[6]) Wenn man in die Tiefen eines Spiegels von Kapoor driftet oder durch das Spiel der Reflexionen die Orientierung und die vertrauten Bezugspunkte verliert, stellt sich eine Art Panik ein; allein schon die Dimensionen seiner Arbeiten lassen uns schrumpfen, während sie uns gleichzeitig in ihrer ozeanischen Umarmung davontragen. Wenn «der innere Raum grösser ist als der Raum, der durch das Aussen begrenzt zu werden scheint, verändert sich das eigene Körpergefühl und die Körperumrisse jedes Besuchers werden ungewiss: eine Art lustvolle Auflösung des Gefässes findet statt, vielleicht sogar eine Art Häutung.

Das Erschrecken in der Begegnung mit Kapoors Werken hat nichts zu tun mit Edmund Burkes «unverständlicher Dunkelheit», diesem entsetzlichen, alles verschlingenden Chaos, sondern eher mit dem ungeheuer grossen Unergründlichen, das durch Form schön geworden ist, ein ästhetisches Prinzip, zu Kants Idee des Erhabenen passend, das sich von der uneinheitlichen und schrecklichen Masse des Chaos und der Sinnlosigkeit abwendet und in einer friedlichen Ordnung aufgeht, in der die Höhlung ein Ganzes und die Leere vertrieben wird, um sich in Fülle zu verwandeln.[7])

Die dramatische Höhe der ausgeweideten Turbinenhalle, die ins Innere der von Herzog & de Meuron gestalteten Tate Modern führt, hat im Rahmen der *Unilever Series* einige äusserst wirkungsvolle und aussagekräftige Installationen gezeitigt, darunter auch Juan Muñoz' rätselhaftes, letztes grösseres Werk DOUBLE BIND (2001). Kapoor entschied sich jedoch dafür, anstelle der Höhe die enorme Länge und Tiefe des Raumes zu unterstreichen; er füllte den Raum in seiner vollen Länge und Breite mit seinem über drei Ringe gespannten und an Drahtseilen aufgehängten MARSYAS aus. Die Betrachtung der Installation in der Tate Modern war eine ebenso bereichernde wie eindringliche Erfahrung, die einen sowohl die menschliche Winzigkeit wie die Grossartigkeit der Welt spüren liess, während MARSYAS einen hinanzog, so dass man sich zugleich zu ihm empor- und mit ihm mitschwingen konnte. In diesem Akt einer sich identifizierenden Kontemplation spürte man, wie die eigenen Gedanken in seine Räume fielen, man fühlte seinen Körper von sich weggezogen, wenn er hier ein Nachgeben und dort einen Widerstand ertastete, und die Ränder des Bewusstseins bewegten sich im Raum gemäss den physikalischen Gesetzen, die Kapoor sichtbar macht.

Thomas McEvilley hat das, was er als das «gezähmte Erhabene» in der zeitgenössischen Kunst bezeichnet, aufs Heftigste kritisiert, dennoch scheint es mir, dass das abstrakte In-Schach-Halten der Gewalt in Kapoors MARSYAS und anderen Werken einen wertvollen Schritt in der Ästhetik des Erhabenen darstellt; weder zähmt es die Gewalt, noch entzieht es deren Dunkles unserem Blick, sondern es gibt sie zur Metamorphose frei. Kapoor hat «immer schon gewollt» und hat auch auf eindrückliche Art klar gemacht, «dass sich das Rote der Erde und des Körpers in Himmel verwandelt». Dieses äusserst aussagekräftige und geistreiche Votum trifft den Kern seines Werks und seiner Leistung.

In den viszeralen Vibrationen von Kapoors Ästhetik klingen Auftauch- und Wachstumsprozesse an, die Fleischwerdung aller Leiber und vor allem der mütterliche Leib als Vehikel, in dem alle Leiber Form annehmen und aus dem sie ins Leben treten, meist kopfüber, blutig und schreiend. Seine kolbenartigen Skulpturen, angenehm satt gewölbte Gefässe mit engen Hälsen, sehen den Flaschen der Alchemisten, in denen das Philosophische Kind gestikuliert, sehr ähnlich. Die tiefen, verzweigten roten Trompetentrichter von MARSYAS, die sich asymmetrisch aus einem tiefer liegenden zentralen Ringmuskel erheben, öffnen sich wie ein Schlund oder spiralig gewundene Ohren, aber sie erinnern auch an die Konstellation von Geburtskanal und Eileitern. (Diese Assoziation drängt sich vor allem angesichts von Kapoors Arbeitsskizzen auf.)

Das Rote fliesst auch in einigen seiner Bilder, wobei er das Pigment mit einem Malmittel vermischt, das die Farbe tropfen lässt, so dass Flecken auf dem Boden entstehen, während sich auf der Leinwand «Wunden öffnen». Das für die Ausstellung im Kunsthaus Bregenz (Herbst 2003) geschaffene Werk MY RED HOMELAND (2003) hat einen Durchmesser von zwölf Metern und versammelt über zwanzig Tonnen einer blutroten zähen Masse auf einer kreisförmigen Grundfläche wie auf einer Art Dreschboden. Die ungestalte Masse aus Fett und Vaseline, absichtlich blutrot eingefärbt wie Lady Macbeths blutige Hände, wurde im zähflüssigen Zustand durch einen rotierenden Hebelarm an den Rand gedrängt, wo sie, entsprechend der Gravität und Viskosität des Materials, zu klumpigen Haufen, Falten und Formen erstarrte. So erlaubte Kapoor der Form, sich selbst zu schaffen: «Irgendwie genügt es nicht, dass ein Objekt gemacht wird ... das hat mit einem sehr alten Aspekt indischer Philosophie zu tun, nämlich, dass es gewisse Arten von Objekten gibt, die sich selbst manifestieren: Sie schaffen sich selbst, ... ihre Mythologie besteht darin, dass sie nicht gemacht wurden.»[8]

Eine Geschichte in Geometrie übersetzt: In MARSYAS verwandelt sich der Satyr, Verkörperung der Beziehung zwischen Natur und Kunst, in das geometrische Grundgesetz, dass auf einer Wölbung befindliche Geraden Kurven im Raum bilden; genau dies geschieht, wenn sich eine Fläche zur Struktur krümmt, wie der Ingenieur Cecil Balmond zu diesem Projekt schrieb. Und er fuhr fort: «Es ist ein Ratespiel zwischen Struktur und Metapher.»[9] Durch das riesige und auf Anhieb beeindruckende Gewebe aus tiefroter Haut enthüllt der weit oben hängende Leib des Marsyas dem Betrachter den unsichtbaren Stoff, aus dem die Welt besteht, den Abdruck jener unfassbaren Urkräfte, die den Phänomenen ihre Gestalt geben, die in der Luft schwingen und pulsieren, die Berge falten und schichten, die Schneeflocken zu Sternen formen und die Wellen zu sich kräuselnden Rinnsalen brechen lassen.

(Übersetzung: Wilma Parker)

1) Weitere Episoden dieses sechsten Buches berichten, wie Philomela – von Tereus vergewaltigt und verstümmelt – in eine Nachtigall verwandelt wird; wie Minerva Arachne um ihrer Webkünste willen bestraft und in eine Spinne verwandelt; und wie Apollo und Diana die vierzehn Kinder Niobes niedermetzeln, so dass diese vor Schmerz zu Stein erstarrt.

2) Vgl. Mary Jacobus' Vortrag, «Inside Out: Marion Milner, Psychic Space, and the Myth of Marsyas», an der Konferenz «Spaces & Places», Delphi, September 2003, den mir die Autorin freundlicherweise zu lesen gab.

3) Tizians Bild wurde für die grosse Tizian-Ausstellung in der National Gallery aus Tschechien nach London geholt und traf dort ein, als Anish Kapoors MARSYAS in der Turbinenhalle der Tate Modern eben heruntergeholt wurde: Für einen Moment kamen die beiden Werke beinah miteinander in Berührung. Dieser fliessende Übergang, bei dem beide sich so nah kamen, war ganz unerwartet und das zeitliche Zusammentreffen erschien Kapoor als wunderbarer Zufall.

4) A. K. Coomaraswamy, «Svajamatrnna: Ianua Coeli», in: *The Door in the Sky: Coomaraswamy on Myth and Meaning,* hrsg. v. Rama P. Coomaraswamy, Princeton University Press, Princeton 1997, S. 6–61. Interessanterweise nimmt auch Courtney Loves Band, Hole, Bezug nehmend auf Nirvana, die Band ihres Ehemannes Kurt Cobain, diesen Zug indischer Mystik auf.

5) Diese und alle folgenden Aussagen von Anish Kapoor stammen aus einem Gespräch mit der Autorin im Sommer 2003.

6) Longinus, *Vom Erhabenen,* Kap. 9, Abs. 6 (hier zitiert nach der Übersetzung von Otto Schönberger, Reclam Verlag, Stuttgart 1997, S. 25).

7) Vgl. dazu Thomas McEvilley, «Turned Upside Down and Torn Apart», in: *Sticky Sublime,* hrsg. v. Bill Beckley, Allworth Press, New York 2001, S. 57–83.

8) Anish Kapoor und Donna De Salvo, «A Conversation», in: *Anish Kapoor, Marsyas,* Tate Publishing, London 2002, S. 61.

9) Cecil Balmond, «Skinning the Imagination», in: *Anish Kapoor, Marsyas,* op. cit., S. 66–69.

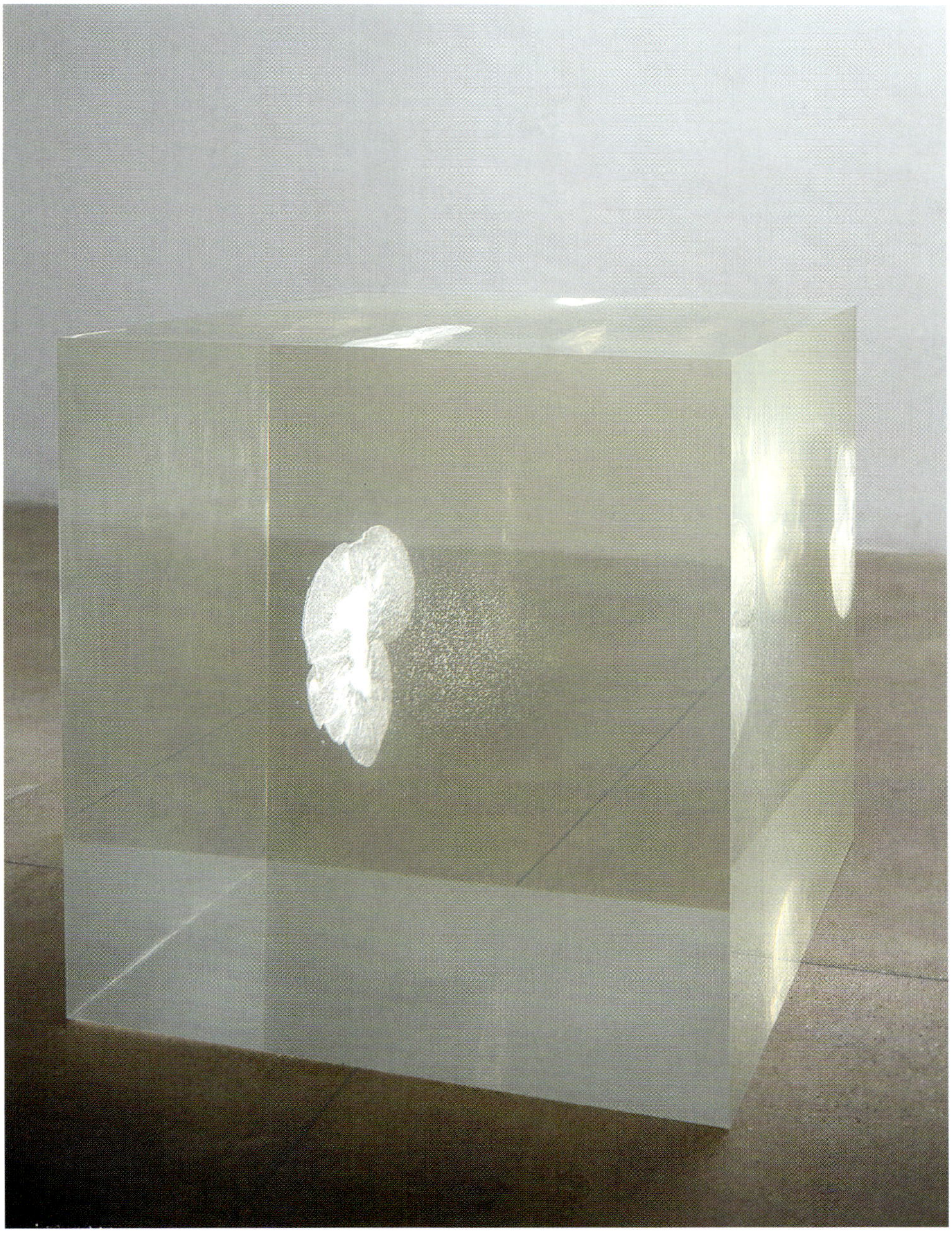

ANISH KAPOOR, SPACE AS OBJECT, 2003, acrylic, 31 7/8 x 31 7/8 x 31 7/8" /
RAUM ALS OBJEKT, Acryl, 81 x 81 x 81 cm. (PHOTO: DAVE MORGAN / LISSON GALLERY, LONDON)

EDITION FOR PARKETT

ANISH KAPOOR

UNTITLED, 2003

Perspex, handtinted stocking, paint,
10 1/4 x 10 1/4 x 15".
Edition of 60, signed and numbered certificate.

OHNE TITEL, 2003

Perspex, handgefärbter Strumpf, Farbe,
26 x 26 x 38 cm.
Auflage: 60, signiertes und nummeriertes Zertifikat.

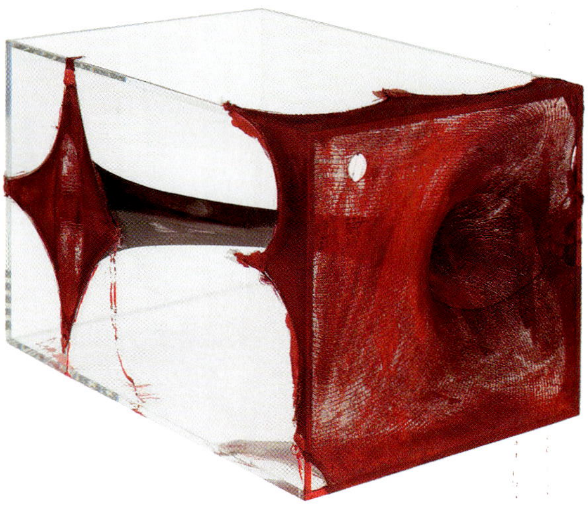

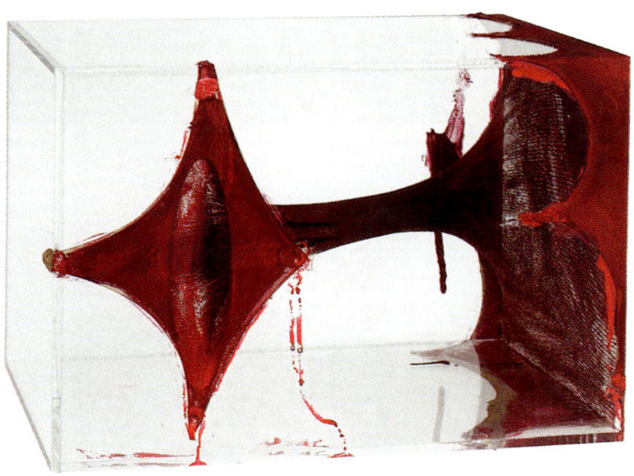

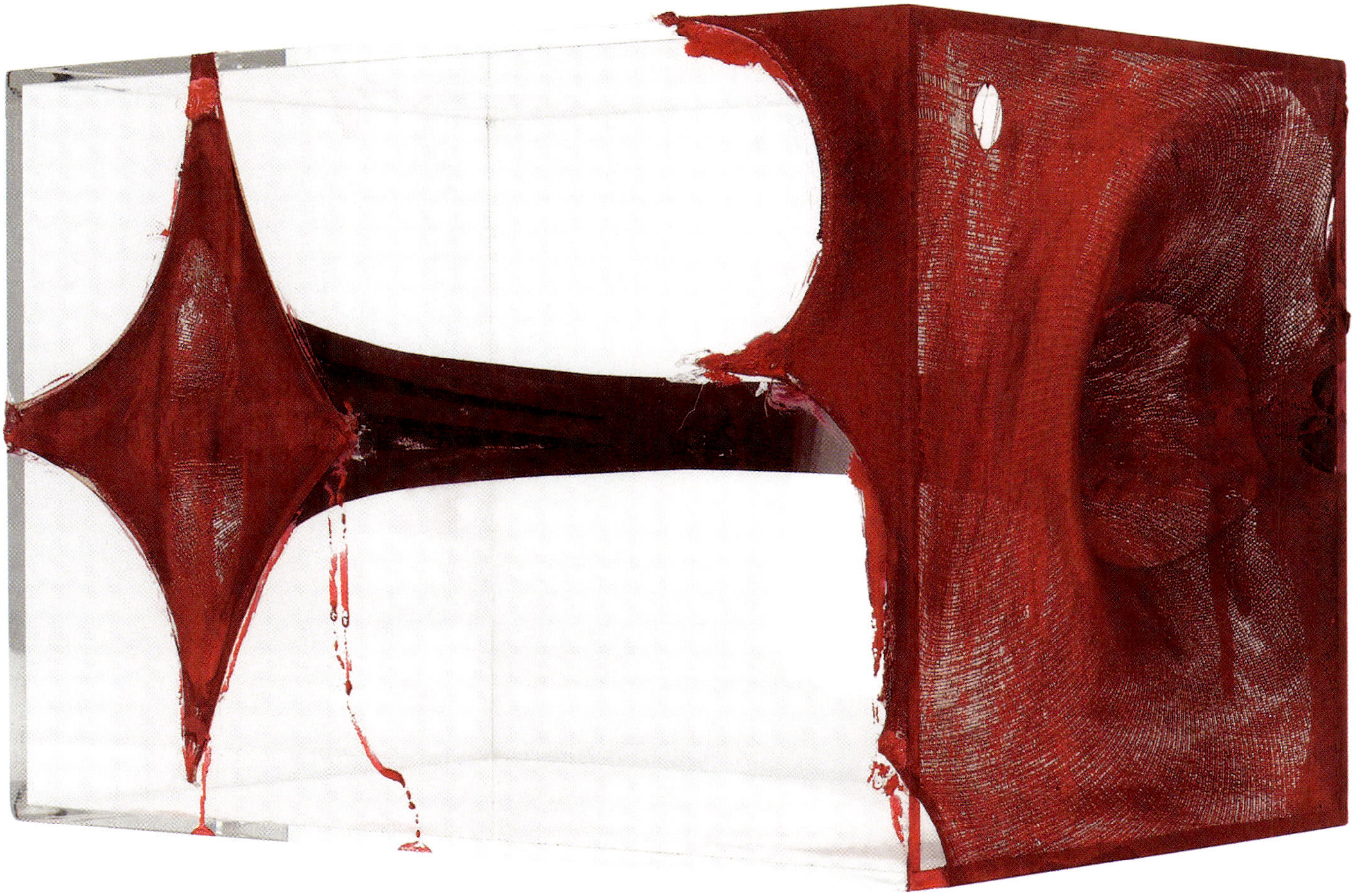

(PHOTO: MANCIA/BODMER, FBM STUDIO, ZÜRICH)

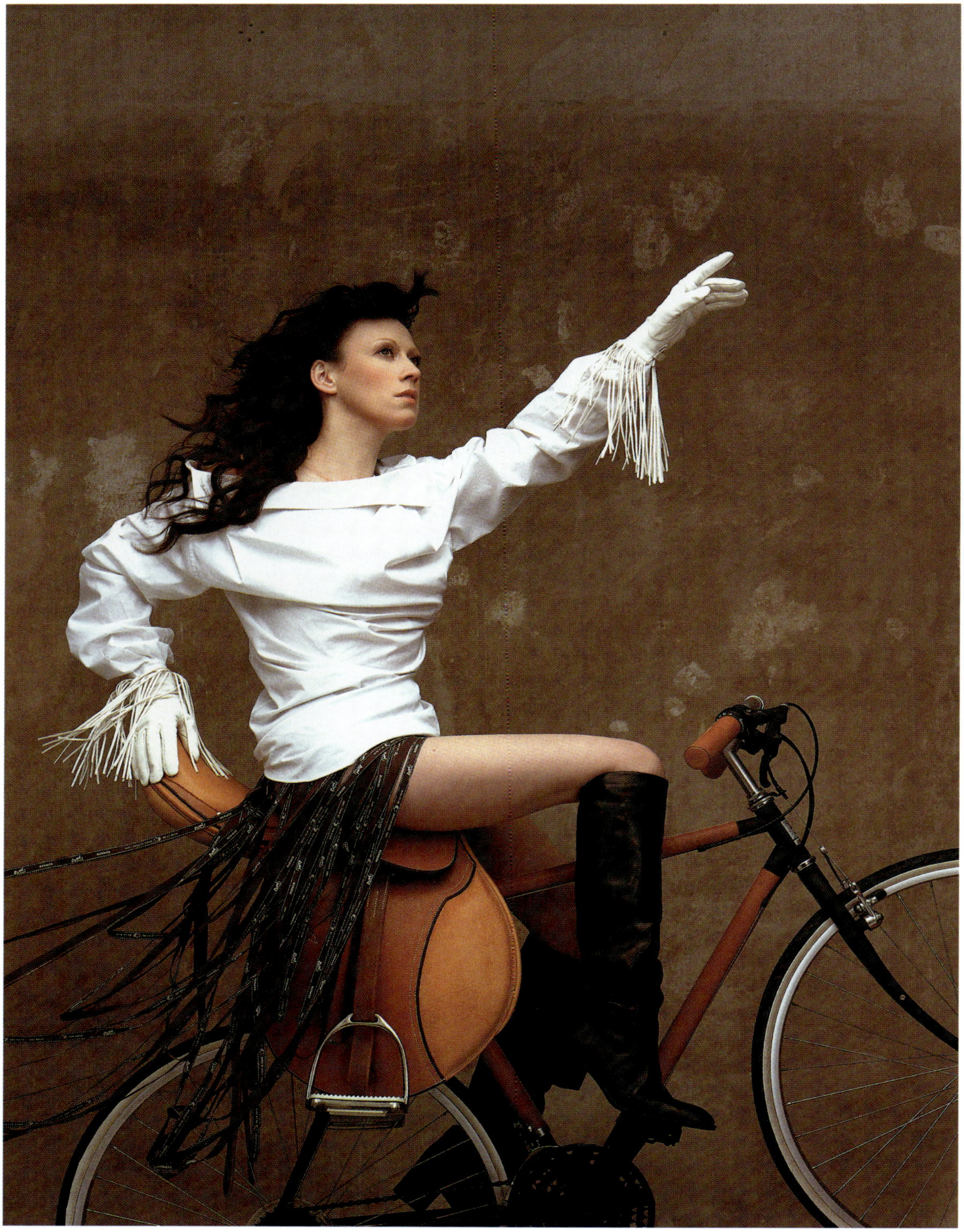

SWETLANA HEGER, PLAYTIME (SH & HERMÈS, PHOTOGRAPHED BY ALEXANDER GNAEDINGER), 2002.
(COURTESY: AIR DE PARIS, PARIS & !BID PROJECTS, LONDON)

STUART COMER

SWETLANA HEGER

Capitalist Neo-Realism

The recent work of Swetlana Heger presents a collage of economic relationships in which Heger performs as a carefully branded node within the current ecologies of marketing and cultural production. Since the mid nineties, Heger, born in the Czech Republic and currently based in Berlin, has worked along the porous boundaries between art, commerce and corporate patronage, teasing out the double bind that exists between these systems. PLAYTIME (2002–2003), an ongoing, long-term project originally hatched in the offices of a Frankfurt branding consultancy, inscribes Heger further into the paradox of these relationships by staging a series of "self-portraits" co-authored by a growing network of photographers, stylists and prominent luxury goods corporations. Each image that results from these collaborations seeks to establish Heger as a trademark product that can hold its own when communing with other major brands like Hermès, adidas, Levi's, New York Industries, and most recently Wolford AG.

Upon entering the Wolford web site, the visiting consumer is introduced to the luxury hosiery line by way of cascading phrases such as "Romantic and Soft," "Chic and Simple," "Elegant and Sexy." What then defines the Heger brand? "'Bohemian Bourgeois and New Mobiles,' which is more a way of life than a style," claims Heger.[1] Economist Jeremy Rifkin might shift the terminology to classify Heger as a "protean persona," a member of the emergent generation of "creative performers," who move "comfortably between scripts and sets as they act out the many dramas that make up the cultural marketplace."[2] It is precisely this fluid identity, rooted in a restless, access-based, post-ownership economy, that allows the Heger brand to reformulate itself continually, to co-inhabit the established brands with which she collaborates to exploit market opportunities.

During Heger's initial consultation with projects GmbH, the branding agency in Frankfurt, twelve dif-

STUART COMER is Curator for Events and Film at Tate Modern, London.

ferent marketing categories were identified in which to assert her trademarked identity as an artist: community, culture, design, economy, environment, family, food, individuality, mobility, publicity, sexuality, and technology. All integral components of daily, lived experience in Heger's market niche, these domains are not merely the set or stage depicted by Rifkin. They comprise a new set of commodities in which lived experience itself is circulated as capital. Heger's work is a sly negotiation of this emerging condition. The images she co-produces are not commissioned by the companies with which she interfaces. Rather, she absorbs their products into counterfeit mergers in which the rules of the game for both art and the market are recalibrated. She offers herself, her image, and her brand as a gateway into this slippery landscape of simulated desire. Her trademark is a specter that inhabits one label's identity and then another, segues from museum to market to magazine and back, collapsing her roles as artist, commodity, and catalyst.

In the new Wolford series, Heger worked with celebrated fashion photographer Bettina Komenda. Shot in Sorrento, Italy, the photographs cite the films of David Lynch, adding a noir spin to their coalition of fashion and flesh, artist and product. Against dark backdrops of lush tropical foliage, sharp lighting picks out the details of Heger's figure, wrapped in the slinky, saturated colors of Wolford's latest output. The clothes are tailor-made for the active body of a "New Mobile." Crouching in the grass or posing with a veil in a forest clearing, a black pageboy haircut frequently obscuring her face, Heger is both super model and Lynchian femme fatale. Her form also recalls models in the seventies' photographs of French photographer Guy Bourdin, who understood early on that the falsity of fashion photography facilitates a breakdown between the product and its image. Although some photographs in Heger's series depict her in strident poses, adorned in Technicolor stripes, the images in which she obscures and defers her face and identity point to the increasingly fugitive nature of branding.

In one particularly poignant image, she stands in the window of a hotel room, her chartreuse leggings of less interest to the viewer than the gaze with which she meets us and the right hand which she presses against the glass in an uncertain gesture. Is her stance one of dismissal, of outreach, or simply of reflective reverie? As in Lynch's films, the mystery remains unsolved, and Heger treads a fine line between phantom and flesh. Much like the Annlee manga character in Pierre Huyghe and Philippe Parreno's NO GHOST JUST A SHELL project (2002–2003), Heger seems poised to disappear at any moment, fading away from the kind of spectral encounter that Marx defines as the very basis of economic exchange.[3)] The reflection of the glass serves to remind us of our own investment in Heger's game; she activates commodity fetishism's anthropomorphic relationship with the viewer, a conversation between individuals and between commodities.

The issue of individuality and the constitution of the market-borne self are crucial to Heger's enterprise. She is often quick to quote the phrase "Individuality has become a mass phenomenon today," and this loss of autonomy in a networked society is the driving paradox of her position. The premium placed on individuality in a consumer-driven democracy has become entrenched in the continuing ascendance of "play" over "product." Adam Smith's model of self-interest—of accumulating capital to determine individual success—has given way to the hyper-connectivity and merger-mentality of current commercial relations. It is within this framework that Heger's work has emerged, and it comes as no surprise that she is frequently associated with a generation of artists engaged with what Nicholas Bourriaud famously termed "relational aesthetics."

Relational practices position the artist as a producer, a creative agent who fosters interactive, social experiences both within and outside the gallery by re-mixing the available forms and leitmotifs of the culture industry. Evolving from earlier appropriation strategies that sought to "de-author" artworks, artists such as Huyghe, Parreno, Rirkrit Tiravanija, Liam Gillick, Angela Bulloch, and progenitors such as Felix Gonzalez-Torres and Canadian collective General Idea court the entertainment industry model of "post-production"[4)] by re-formatting and fine-tuning cultural fragments already in circulation. Again, not unlike a Lynch script, these artists work in montage and mystery; they tend to diminish their presence in the work, operating like shadowy figures pulling the strings behind the scenes, encouraging all manner of networks to take place.

Heger's work can certainly lay claim to these tendencies, but its increasing emphasis on visualizing and branding the self sends the artist on a slight diversion from the established routes of post-production. The cover of a *Wired* magazine recently proclaimed the birth of the "Superproducer" in the music business. Whereas producers traditionally have lived "on the B-side of the music business: behind the scenes ..., while file-sharing hogs the headlines in music's digital evolution, there's been a quiet revolution in the studio."[5] Acts like The Neptunes have become major powerbrokers whose prestige now vies with the top acts with whom they collaborate. Their inter-brand relationships have evolved from a parasitic situation to a symbiotic one. "Their names have moved from the liner notes to the front of their own albums."[6] In a similar gesture, Heger's self-image foregrounds her recent work, sampling her own appearance as a brand and re-mixing it within the marketing architecture of the luxury sector. As a

SWETLANA HEGER, LIVE (SH & WOLFORD, PHOTOGRAPHED BY BETTINA KOMENDA), 2003.
(COURTESY: AIR DE PARIS, PARIS & IBID PROJECTS, LONDON)

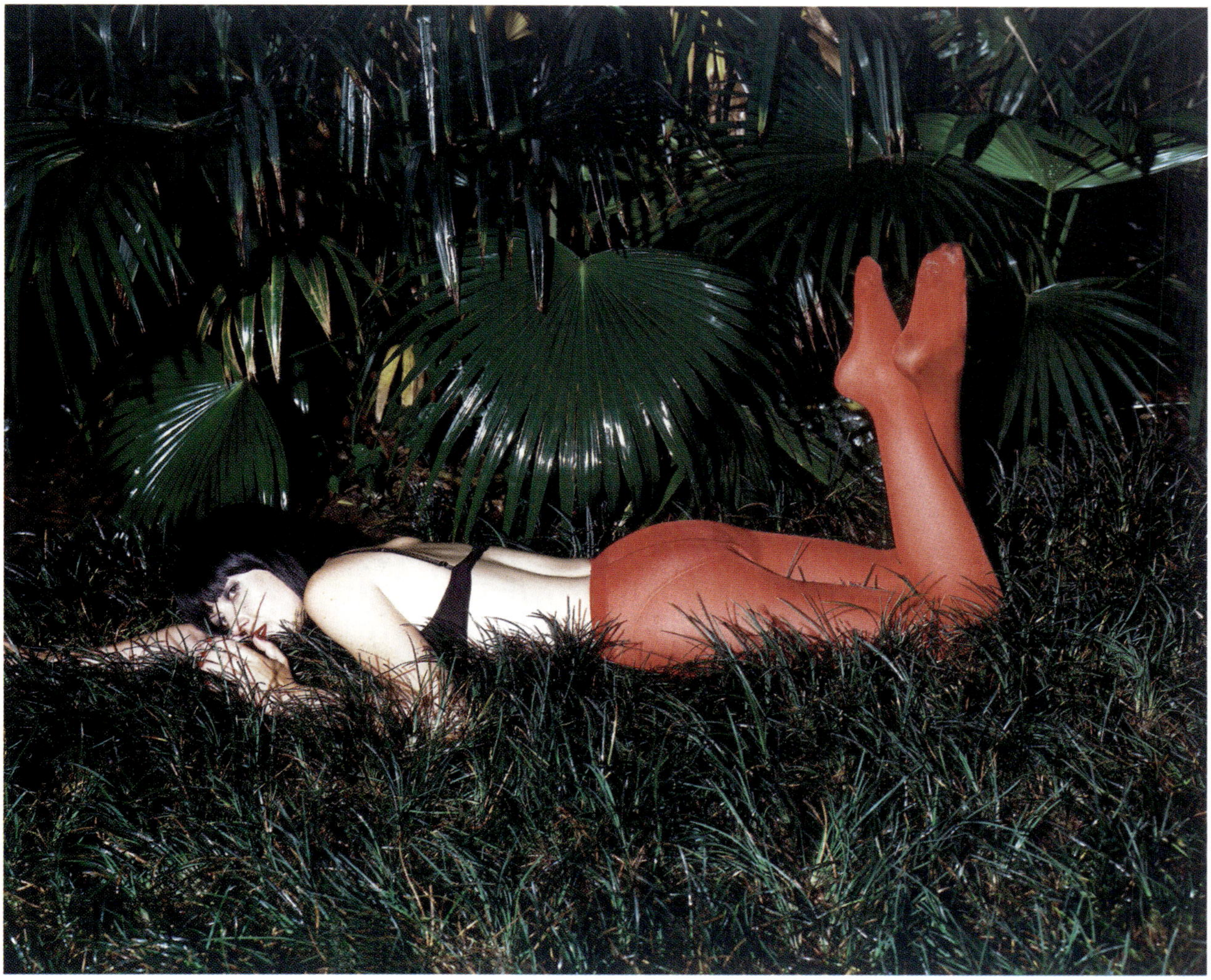

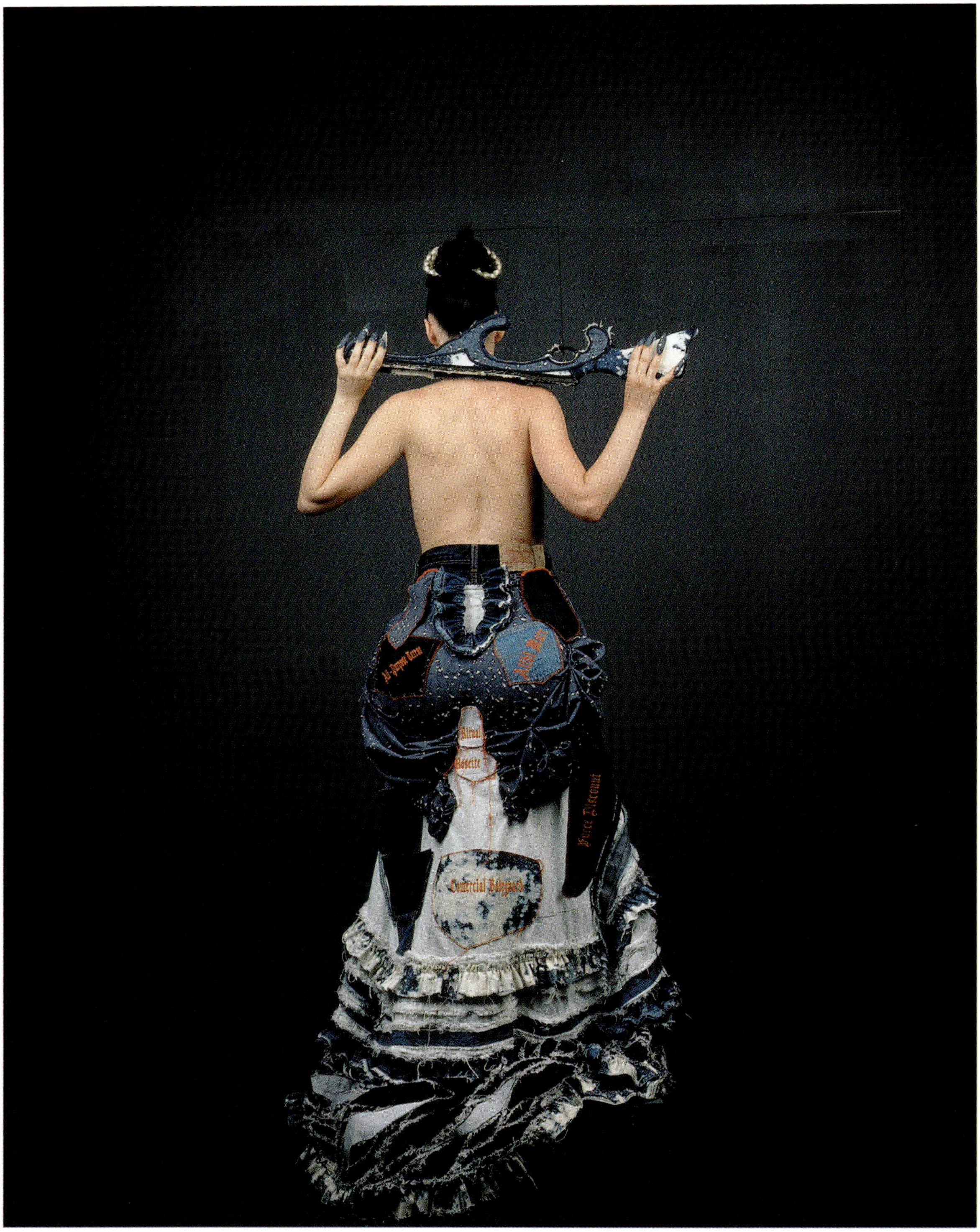

SWETLANA HEGER, LIVE (SH & LEVI'S, PHOTOGRAPHED BY ALI KEPENEK), 2002.

(COURTESY: AIR DE PARIS, PARIS & IBID PROJECTS, LONDON)

Superproducer, she facilitates the paradox of visibly manifesting her presence in the work just as her own authorship evaporates into a constellation of co-producers.

The priority Heger places on photography as the vehicle for her work also distinguishes it from the majority of relational practices, which tend to operate in installation formats to encourage the performativity of the viewer/participant. Placing collage, citation, and photography at the center of her branding ecosystem connects her directly to the historical origins of the appropriation and simulation strategies that she invokes in her work. Although the marketing systems she inhabits are as up to the minute as the industries with which she works, her images have a dialectical relationship with the deconstructive tactics of her cultural predecessors. By trafficking in fashion photography in particular, Heger hitches the hybrid intertextuality of her work's debt to the past to the rampant hunger for the new marked both by fashion and by the thriving economy of access.

Although Heger's open-ended use of self-portraiture recalls Cindy Sherman's early film stills, it resonates more directly with New York-based Dianne Blell's staged photographs from the late seventies. Citing images and poses from Arthur Elgort's then current fashion photography to Lucas Cranach and eighteenth-century painter Féréol de Bonnemaison, Blell also appeared in her work and coordinated her output through direct collaboration with stylists, make-up artists, and designers. Although the concept of interactive, networked collaboration has evolved dramatically since then, Blell nevertheless seems to have understood the complexities of abdicating exclusive agency in her work's production. Even more relevant, perhaps, to Heger's practice is the double entendre of Blell's photographs: they are both constructed image and performance document.

Heger's photographs must "perform" in their own right in corners of commerce that did not even exist in the seventies. Although they document the branding performances enacted in Heger's collaborations, their continued power lies in an ability to extend the Heger brand into and through multiple sites of culture and commerce, from galleries to web sites to exhibition catalogues and magazines. As "performers," they act out parodies of brand behavior, and it is this aspect that endows them with a critical function. To quote Benjamin Buchloh's discussion of the early Capitalist Realism of Sigmar Polke, "Parodistic appropriation reveals the divided situation of the individual in contemporary artistic practice." It "anticipates the failure of any attempt to subvert the ruling codification and allies itself, in advance, with the powers that will ultimately turn its deconstructive efforts into a cultural success." [7]

1) Susa Pop, "Swetlana Heger: Playtime," *Flash Art International*, vol. XXXIV, no. 224, May/June 2002, p. 93.
2) Jeremy Rifkin, *The Age of Access: The New Culture of Hypercapitalism, Where All of Life Is a Paid-For Experience* (New York: Jeremy P. Tarcher/Putnam, 2000), p. 201.
3) See Jacques Derrida, *Spectres of Marx* (New York and London Routledge, 1994), and Jan Verwoert, "Copyright, Ghosts and Commodity Fetishism," *Materials 03* (Cambridge, England: Institute of Visual Culture, 2002), pp. 8–11.
4) Nicolas Bourriaud, *Esthétique relationelle* (Paris: Les presses du réel,1998) and *Postproduction* (New York: Lukas & Steinberg, 2001).
5) Robert Levine and Bill Werde, "Superproducers," *Wired*, October 2003, p. 127.
6) Ibid.
7) Benjamin Buchloh, *Neo-Avantgarde and Culture Industry: Essays on European and American Art from 1955 to 1975*, October Books (Cambridge, MA and London: The MIT Press, 2001), pp. 350–351.

SWETLANA HEGER

Kapitalistischer Neorealismus

In ihren jüngsten Arbeiten präsentiert uns Swetlana Heger eine Collage von Wirtschaftsbeziehungen, in der die Künstlerin selbst sich sorgfältig zum Schnittpunkt der aktuellen Wechselbeziehungen zwischen Marketing und kultureller Produktion stilisiert. Die aus der tschechischen Republik stammende, zurzeit in Berlin wohnhafte Künstlerin hat sich seit Mitte der 90er Jahre mit den durchlässigen Grenzen zwischen Kunst, Kommerz und Sponsoring beschäftigt und die fatalen Verknüpfungen zwischen diesen Systemen ausgereizt. In PLAYTIME (2002–2003), einem auf längere Zeit angelegten Projekt, das ursprünglich in den Büros einer Frankfurter Imageberatungsfirma entwickelt worden war, bindet sich die Künstlerin noch enger ins Paradox dieser Beziehungen ein, indem sie eine Reihe von «Selbstporträts» inszeniert, an deren Entstehung ein ständig wachsendes Netzwerk von Photographen, Stilisten und bekannten Herstellern von Luxusprodukten beteiligt ist. Jedes in solcher Zusammenarbeit entstandene Bild ist darauf ausgerichtet, Heger als Markennamen zu etablieren, der sich auch gegenüber so grossen Namen wie Hermès, Adidas, Levi's, New York Industries oder neustens auch Wolford zu behaupten vermag.

STUART COMER ist Kurator für Veranstaltungen und Film in der Tate Modern, London.

Dem Besucher der Wolford-Website wird die Produktelinie der Luxusstrumpfwaren mit Wortkaskaden wie «romantisch und sanft», «schlicht und elegant», «sexy und raffiniert» vorgestellt. Was aber zeichnet Hegers Marke aus? «‹Bürgerliche Bohème und Neue Mobilität›, also eher eine Lebensweise als ein Stil», meint Heger.[1] Der Wirtschaftswissenschaftler Jeremy Rifkin würde die Terminologie vielleicht etwas abwandeln und Heger als «proteische Persönlichkeit», als Vertreterin einer neuen Generation «kreativer Persönlichkeiten» bezeichnen, die «sich sicher zwischen unterschiedlichen Inszenierungen des kulturellen Marktes» bewegen.[2] Genau diese fliessende Identität, die sich aus der rastlosen, eher über Zugang als Eigentum funktionierenden Wirtschaft ergibt, erlaubt es der Marke Heger, sich ständig neu zu formulieren, sich innerhalb bekannter Marken ein-

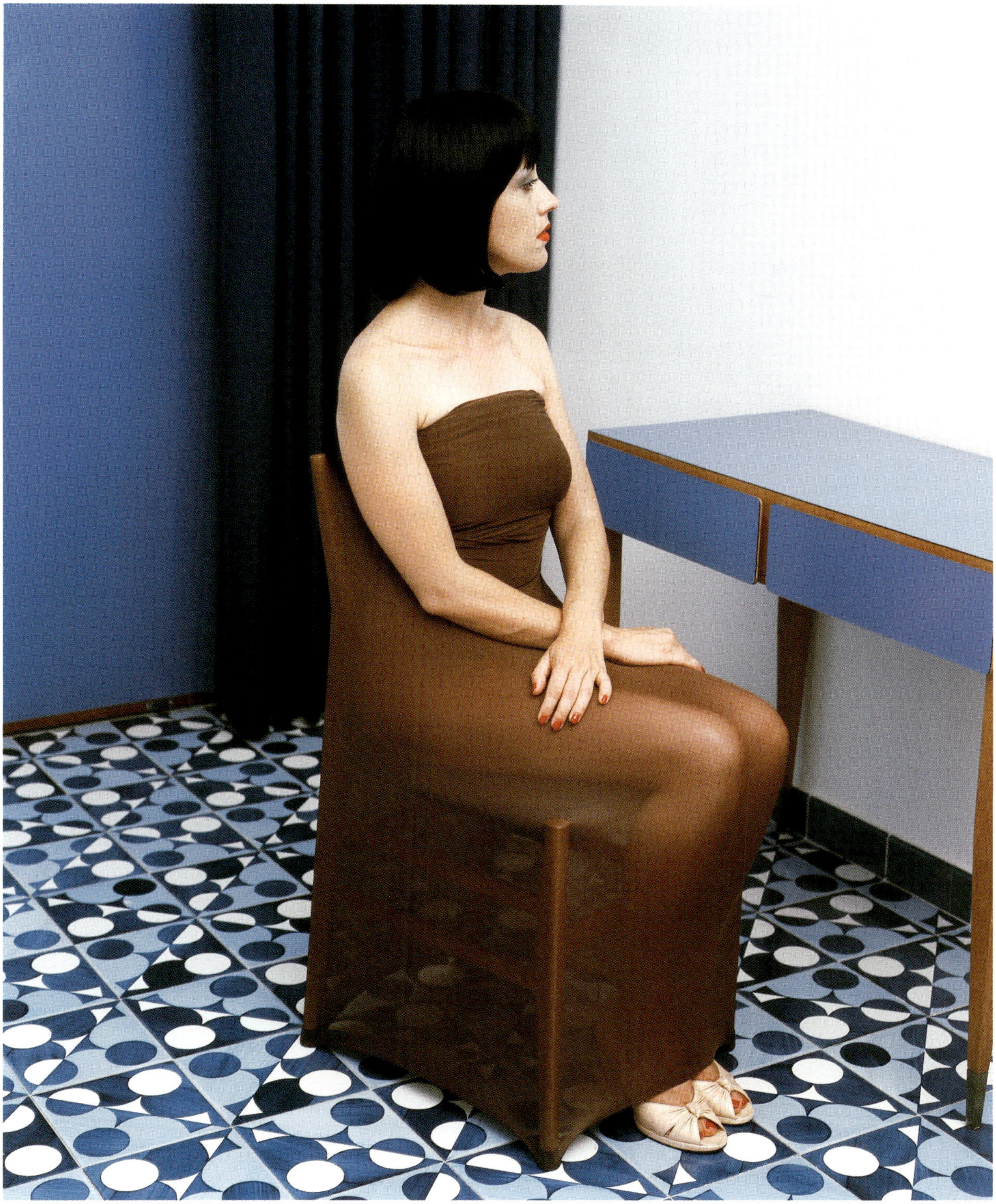

SWETLANA HEGER, LIVE (SH & WOLFORD, PHOTOGRAPHED BY BETTINA KOMENDA), 2003.

(COURTESY: AIR DE PARIS, PARIS & IBID PROJECTS, LONDON)

zunisten und in Zusammenarbeit mit diesen alle Möglichkeiten des Marktes auszuschöpfen.

Bei Hegers erstem Brainstorming mit der Frankfurter Beratungsfirma projects GmbH wurden zwölf für ihr Markenimage als Künstlerin wichtige Marketingkategorien ausgearbeitet: soziales Umfeld, Kultur, Design, Ökonomie, Umwelt, Familie, Nahrung, Individualität, Mobilität, Werbung, Sexualität und Technologie. Als integrale Bestandteile der täglich gelebten Erfahrung in Hegers Marktnische sind diese Bereiche nicht allein «Requisiten» oder verschiedene «Bühnen» im Sinne Rifkins. Sie umfassen ein völlig neues Warenangebot, innerhalb dessen selbst die gelebte Erfahrung als Kapital gehandelt wird. Hegers Werk nützt dieses neue Phänomen geschickt aus. Ihre in Koproduktion hergestellten Bilder entstehen nicht im Auftrag der Firmen, mit denen sie sich vernetzt. Vielmehr integriert sie deren Produkte in einem scheinbaren Gemeinschaftsprodukt, in dem jeweils die Spielregeln – sowohl für die Kunst wie für den Markt – völlig neu ausgelotet werden. Heger bietet sich selbst, ihr Image und ihren Markennamen als Eingangspforte zu dieser schlüpfrigen Region des simulierten Begehrens an. Ihr Markenzeichen ist ein Gespenst, das sich zuerst in einer, dann wieder in einer anderen Markenidentität einnistet, sich übergangslos vom Museum zum Markt zum Magazin und wieder zurück bewegt und so ihre Rollen als Künstlerin, Produkt und Katalysator unterläuft.

In der neuen Wolford-Reihe arbeitete Heger mit der berühmten Modephotographin Bettina Komenda zusammen. Die in Sorrent, Italien, entstandenen Photos zitieren Filme von David Lynch, was ihrer Kombination von Mode und Markt, Künstler und Produkt einen morbiden Touch verleiht. Vor einem dunklen Hintergrund aus üppigem tropischem Blattwerk sieht man grell beleuchtete, in die weichen, satten Farben der neuesten Wolford-Kreationen gehüllte Details von Hegers Figur. Die Kleider sind für den aktiven Körper einer Vertreterin der Neuen Mobilität massgeschneidert. Im Gras kauernd oder mit einem Schleier in einer Lichtung posierend, das Gesicht häufig unter einem schwarzen Pagenschnitt versteckt, ist Heger Supermodel und Femme fatale à la David Lynch zugleich. Ihre Gestalt erinnert aber auch an die Modelle auf den – in den 70er Jahren entstandenen – Aufnahmen des französischen Modephotographen Guy Bourdin, der bereits früh erkannt hatte, dass die Künstlichkeit der Modephotographie die Grenzen zwischen Produkt und Image verwischt. Auch wenn Heger auf manchen Photographien ihrer Serie bunt gestreift und in auffälligen Posen erscheint, so verweisen doch die Bilder, auf denen sie Gesicht und Identität kaschiert, auf die zunehmende Flüchtigkeit von Markenimages.

In einem besonders eindringlichen Bild steht sie am Fenster eines Hotelzimmers, wobei ihre grüngelben Leggings weit weniger interessant sind als der Blick, den sie uns zuwirft, oder die in einer vagen Geste gegen das Glas gepresste, rechte Hand. Ist ihre Haltung abweisend, einladend oder handelt es sich einfach nur um eine träumerische Pose? Wie in Lynchs Filmen bleibt das Rätsel ungelöst und Heger wandelt auf dem schmalen Grat zwischen Phantom und Wesen aus Fleisch und Blut. Wie die Mangafigur Annlee in Pierre Huyghes und Philippe Parrenos Gemeinschaftsprojekt NO GHOST JUST A SHELL (2002–2003) scheint sich Heger jeden Augenblick auflösen zu wollen; ihre Umrisse werden immer verschwommener im Lauf der geisterhaften Begegnung, die Marx als Grundvoraussetzung des Warentauschs betrachtet.[3)] Die Spiegelung im Glas erinnert an unsere eigene Beteiligung an Hegers Spiel; sie bringt die anthropomorphe Beziehung zwischen Warenfetischismus und Betrachter zum Spielen, einen Dialog zwischen Individuum und Ware.

Die Frage der Individualität und der Beschaffenheit des vom Markt erzeugten Ichs sind für Hegers Projekt von entscheidender Bedeutung. Der Satz «Individualität ist heute zu einem Massenphänomen geworden» kommt ihr sehr geläufig über die Lippen und dieser Autonomieverlust in der vernetzten Gesellschaft ist das dynamische Paradox ihrer Position. Der Bonus der Individualität in einer konsumabhängigen Demokratie ist verquickt mit dem unaufhaltsamen Siegeszug, den das «Spiel» gegenüber der «Ware» angetreten hat. An die Stelle von Adam Smiths «Eigennutz» – der Anhäufung von Kapital als Grundlage für persönlichen Erfolg – sind in der heutigen Wirtschaftswelt Hypervernetzung und Synergiedenken getreten. In diesem Rahmen hat sich auch Hegers Kunst entwickelt, und es ist nicht verwunderlich, wenn sie häufig einer Generation von Künstlern zugeordnet wird, die sich mit etwas beschäftigen, wofür Nicholas Bourriaud den bekannten Terminus «relationale Ästhetik» geprägt hat.

Relationale Strategien sehen im Künstler einen Produzenten und kreativen Vermittler, der sowohl innerhalb wie auch ausserhalb von Ausstellungsräumen interaktive, soziale Erfahrungen ermöglicht, indem er bereits vorhandene Formen und Leitmotive des Kulturbetriebs neu aufbereitet. Von früheren Aneignungsstrategien her kommend, die das Kunstwerk vom autoritativen Schöpfer zu befreien suchen, haben Künstler wie Huyghe, Parreno, Tiravanija, Gillick, Angela Bulloch oder Vorläufer wie Felix Gonzalez-Torres und das kanadische Kollektiv General Idea mit dem «Post-Produktions-Modell»[4] der Unterhaltungsindustrie geliebäugelt und bereits im Umlauf befindliche kulturelle Fragmente neu formatiert und ihren Zwecken angepasst. Ähnlich wie David Lynch lieben auch diese Künstler die Montage und das Rätsel; sie neigen dazu, sich selbst in ihren Arbeiten zurückzunehmen und wie graue Eminenzen hinter den Kulissen die Fäden zu ziehen, wobei sie jede Art von Vernetzung begrüssen.

All diese Tendenzen findet man auch in Hegers Werk, doch ihre Betonung von visueller Präsenz und Person als Marke lassen sie von den bereits etablierten Pfaden des «Postproduktiven» etwas abweichen. Auf der Titelseite einer neueren Ausgabe des Magazins *Wired* wurde die Geburt des «Superproduzenten» im Musikgeschäft gefeiert. Bisher waren die Produzenten gewöhnlich «auf der B-Seite des Musikgeschäfts anzutreffen: hinter den Kulissen ..., doch während das *file-sharing* in der digitalen Entwicklung der Musikindustrie die Schlagzeilen beherrschte, hat in den Studios heimlich, still und leise eine Revolution stattgefunden.»[5] Figuren wie The Neptunes wurden zu wichtigen Drahtziehern, die sich mit den Spitzenreitern, mit denen sie zusammenarbeiten, durchaus messen können. Ihre markenübergreifenden Beziehungen machten aus der ursprünglich parasitären eine symbiotische Situation. «Ihre Namen, vorher bloss auf der Rückseite des Plattencovers erwähnt, prangen jetzt auf ihren eigenen Alben.»[6]

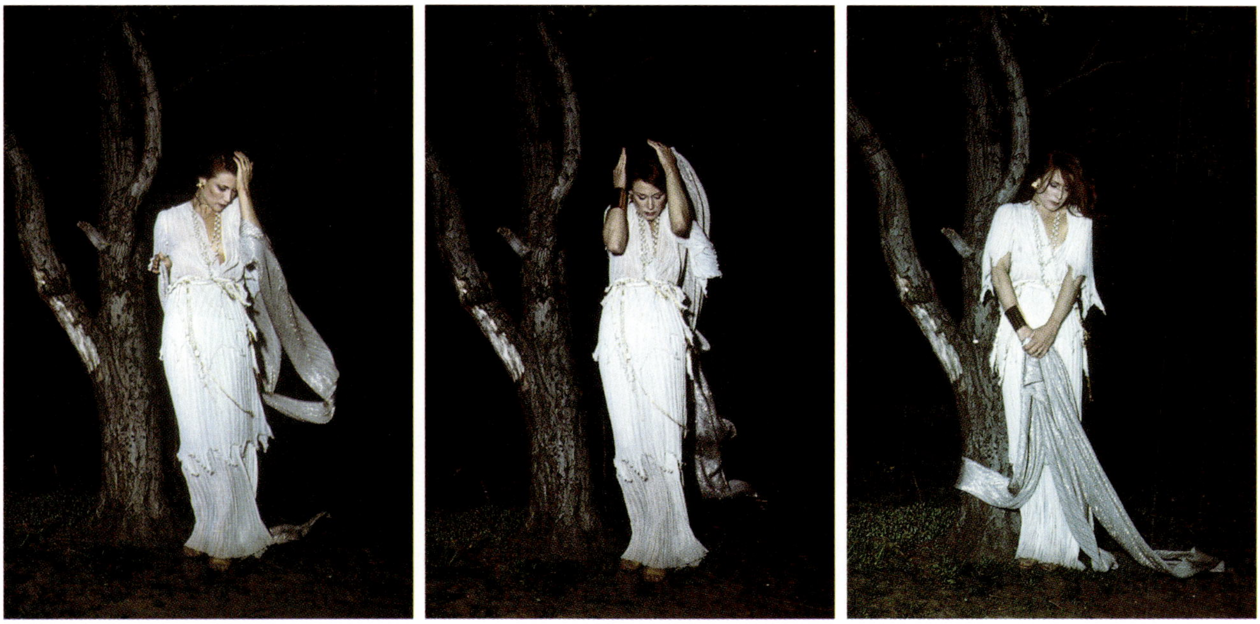

DIANNE BLELL, YOUNG WOMAN OVERTAKEN BY A STORM, 1979, triptych; modeling: Dianne Blell; design: Mary McFadden; photography: Edo; make-up & styling: Nikki Nichols / JUNGE FRAU, VOM STURM ÜBERRASCHT, Triptychon.

Ähnlich rückt auch Heger in ihren jüngsten Arbeiten ihr eigenes Image in den Vordergrund, indem sie ihre eigenen Auftritte sampelt und innerhalb der Marketingstrukturen der Luxusgüterbranche wieder aufbereitet. Als Superproduzentin sorgt sie paradoxerweise dafür, dass sie in ihren Arbeiten als Person sichtbar in Erscheinung tritt, während sie sich als Urheberin gleichzeitig in einer Konstellation von Co-Produzenten auflöst.

Durch die Vorrangstellung, die Heger der Photographie als Medium einräumt, unterscheidet sie sich von den meisten relational arbeitenden Künstlern, die eher Installationsformate bevorzugen um die performative Rolle der Betrachter/Teilnehmer zu stärken. Dass sie Collage, Zitat und Photographie in den Mittelpunkt ihrer Markenwelt rückt, verbindet Heger mit den historischen Ursprüngen der Appropriations- und Simulationsstrategien, die in ihren Arbeiten anklingen. Obwohl die Marketingsysteme, in denen sie sich eingenistet hat, ebenso hypermodern sind wie die Firmen und Produkte, mit denen sie arbeitet, haben ihre Bilder einen dialektischen Bezug zu den dekonstruktiven Strategien ihrer kulturellen Vorläufer. Durch die Tatsache, dass sie sich ausgerechnet der Modephotographie bedient, verquickt Heger die hybride Intertextualität der Verpflichtung ihres Werkes gegenüber der Vergangenheit mit dem Heisshunger auf das Neue, für das die Mode und die boomende Ökonomie des Zugangs stehen.

Zwar erinnert Hegers uneingeschränkte Selbstdarstellung an Cindy Shermans frühe Filmstills: Augenfälliger ist jedoch die Ähnlichkeit mit den gestellten Bildern der New Yorker Photographin Dianne Blell aus den späten 70er Jahren. Blell zitierte Bilder und Posen des damals aktuellen Modephotographen Arthur Elgort, aber auch Lucas Cranach oder den im 18. Jahrhundert lebenden Maler Féréol de Bonnemaison; sie ist auch selbst in ihrem Werk in Erscheinung getreten und hat in Zusammenarbeit mit Stilisten, Visagisten und Designern ihre Produktion koordiniert. Obwohl das Konzept der interaktiven, vernetzten Zusammenarbeit sich seither dramatisch verändert hat, scheint Blell schon damals erkannt zu haben, was es bedeutete, bei ihrer künstlerischen Produktion auf eine alleinige Urheberschaft zu verzichten. Für Hegers Arbeit wichtiger ist aber vermutlich der Doppelsinn von Blells Photographien: Es handelt sich sowohl um konstruierte Bilder als auch um Dokumente einer Performance.

Hegers Photographien müssen sich in kommerziellen Nischen behaupten, die es in den 70er Jahren noch gar nicht gab. Sie dokumentieren zwar, wie in Hegers Gemeinschaftsprojekten Markenbilder erzeugt werden, entfalten ihre volle Wirkung aber erst, indem sie es schaffen, die Marke Heger über unterschiedlichste kommerzielle und kulturelle Orte zu verbreiten, von Galerien über Websites zu Ausstellungskatalogen und Zeitschriften. Als «Performer» parodieren sie ein bestimmtes Markenverhalten und darin liegt auch ihre kritische Funktion. Wie Benjamin Buchloh in seiner Abhandlung über den frühen Kapitalistischen Realismus bei Polke meint: «Die parodistische Aneignung offenbart den Zwiespalt des Individuums in der zeitgenössischen Kunst.» Sie «nimmt das Scheitern jeglichen Versuchs, die herrschende Kodifizierung zu untergraben, vorweg und verbindet sich von vornherein mit jenen Kräften, welche die angestrebte Dekonstruktion schliesslich doch noch zum kulturellen Erfolg wenden.»[7]

(Übersetzung: Uta Goridis)

1) Susa Pop, «Swetlana Heger: Playtime», *Flash Art International,* vol. XXXIV, no. 224, Mai/Juni 2002, S. 93.

2) Jeremy Rifkin, *Access – das Verschwinden des Eigentums: warum wir weniger besitzen und mehr ausgeben werden,* Campus Verlag, Frankfurt am Main 2000, S. 270.

3) Vgl. Jacques Derrida, *Marx' Gespenster,* S. Fischer Verlag, Frankfurt am Main 1996, S. 15ff., sowie Jan Verwoert, «Copyright, Ghosts and Commodity Fetishism», *Materials 03,* Institute of Visual Culture, Cambridge 2002, S. 8–11.

4) Nicolas Bourriaud, *Esthétique relationelle,* Les Presses du Réel, Paris 1998, und *Postproduction,* Lukas & Steinberg, New York 2001.

5) Robert Levine und Bill Werde, «Superproducers», *Wired,* Oktober 2003, S. 127.

6) Ebenda.

7) Benjamin Buchloh, *Neo-Avantgarde and Culture Industry: Essays on European and American Art from 1955 to 1975,* (October Books), MIT Press, Cambridge MA/London 2001, S. 350–351. (Zitat aus dem Englischen übersetzt.)

HOW TO HAVE FUN WITH A

STRONG GIRL

I STAND BEFORE HER TREMBLING WITH ANTICIPATION AS SHE STRUTS AND PRANCES AROUND THE ROOM, BOLDLY DISPLAYING HER MAGNIFICENT PHYSIQUE. SHE'S FULL OF NARCISSISTIC PRIDE, AND IS OBVIOUSLY ENJOYING THE EFFECT SHE'S HAVING ON ME.

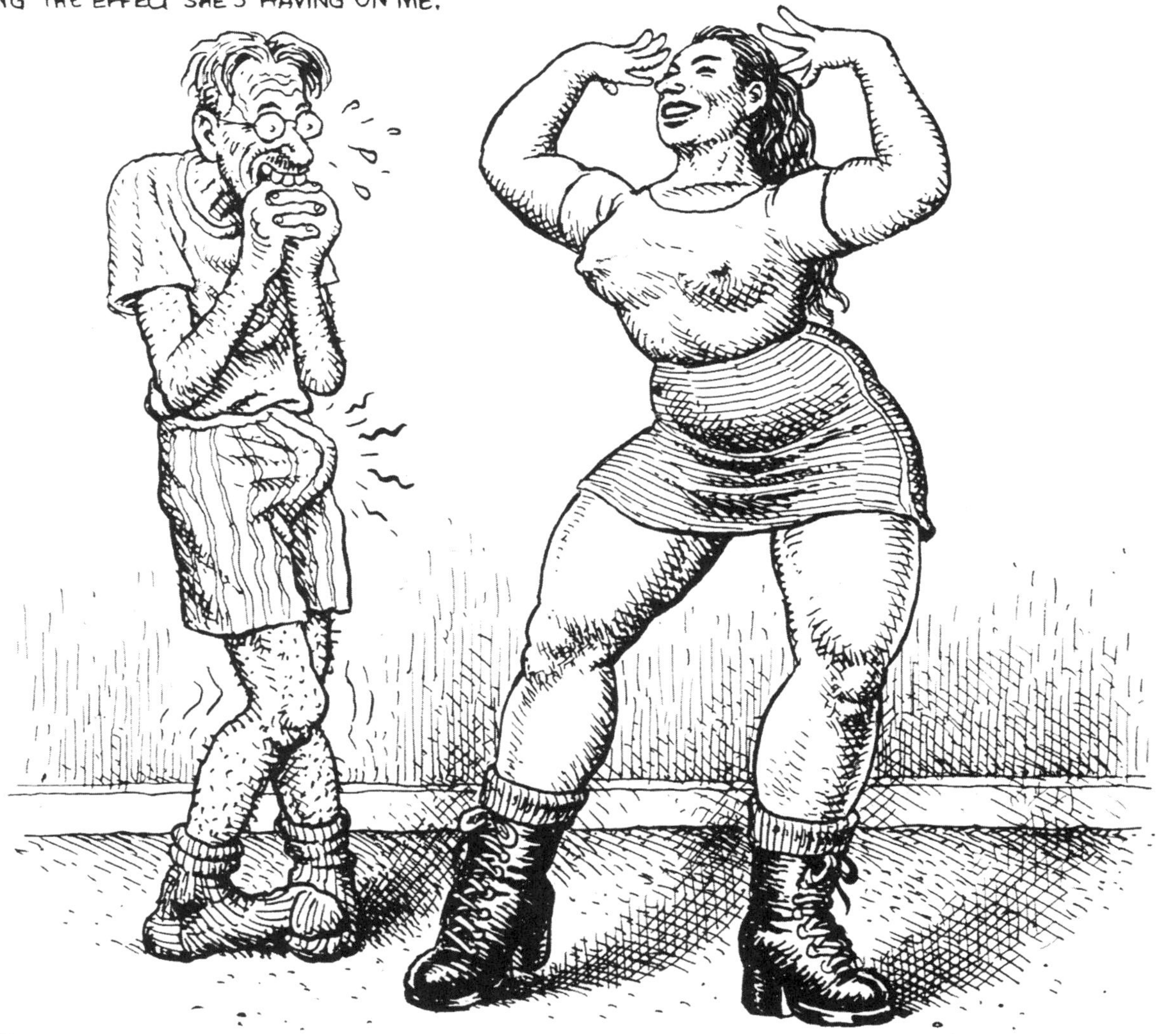

SHE IS BEAUTIFUL AND TERRIFYING AT THE SAME TIME, LIKE NATURE ITSELF! SHE'S GONNA GIVE ME A HARD TIME TOMORROW, BECAUSE BASICALLY SHE DOESNT LIKE ME, OR MEN IN GENERAL, VERY MUCH—AND WITH GOOD REASON. BUT SHE SEEMS TO ENJOY THE WORK-OUT I GIVE HER, SO TONIGHT I SHALL HAVE THE HIGH HONOR OF PUTTING THAT INCREDIBLE BODY OF HER'S THROUGH SOME PACES! OBOY OBOY!!

by R. Crumb
2002

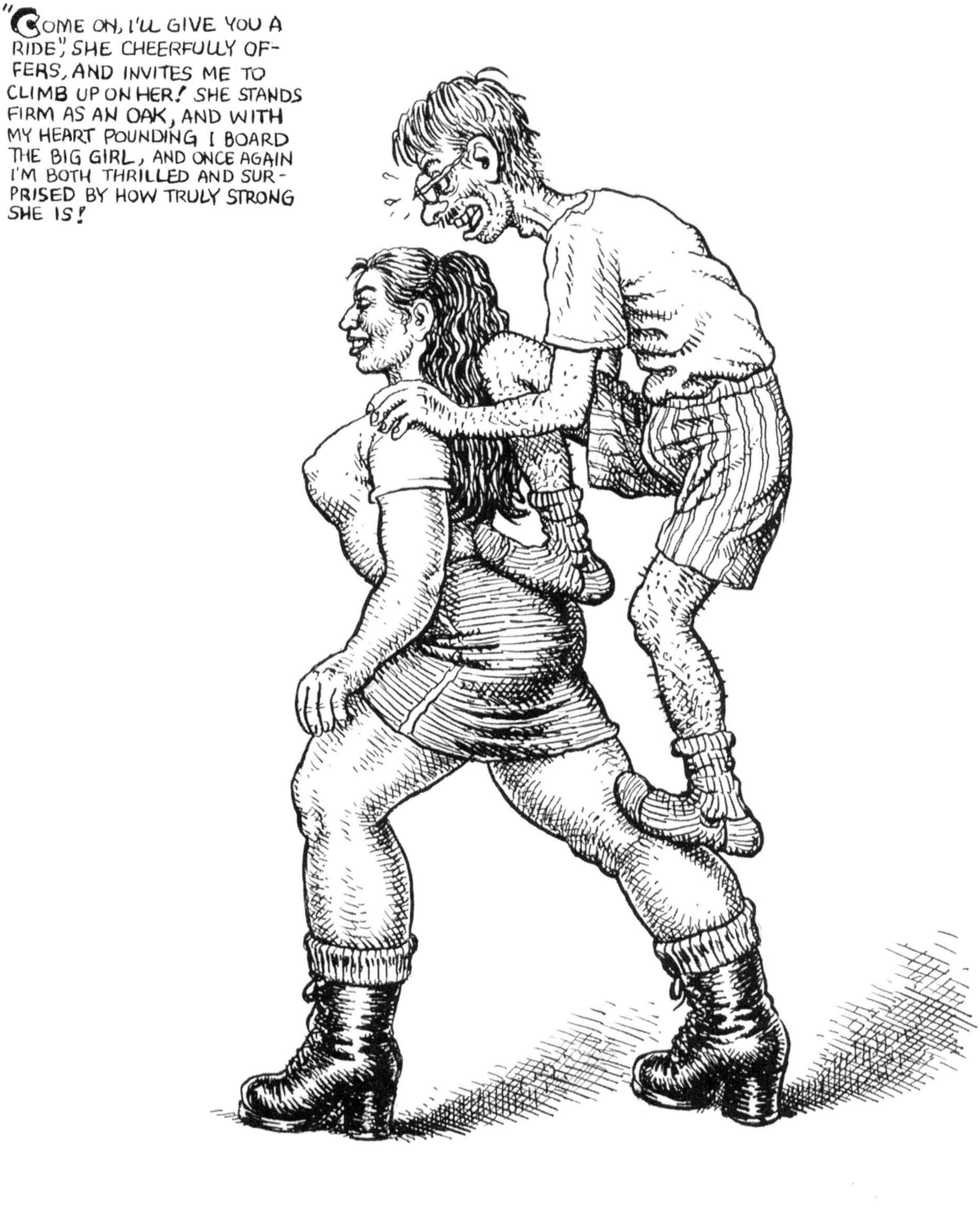
"COME ON, I'LL GIVE YOU A RIDE," SHE CHEERFULLY OFFERS, AND INVITES ME TO CLIMB UP ON HER! SHE STANDS FIRM AS AN OAK, AND WITH MY HEART POUNDING I BOARD THE BIG GIRL, AND ONCE AGAIN I'M BOTH THRILLED AND SURPRISED BY HOW TRULY STRONG SHE IS!

THE STRONG GIRL LOVES TO SHOW OFF HER PROWESS. SHE DANCES AROUND, LEAPING AND BOUNDING EFFORTLESSLY ON HER POWERFUL LEGS, WHILE I CLING ON TIGHTLY BACK THERE! I GET SO EXCITED THAT IT'S A SUPREME EFFORT OF WILL TO PREVENT A PREMATURE EJACULATION!

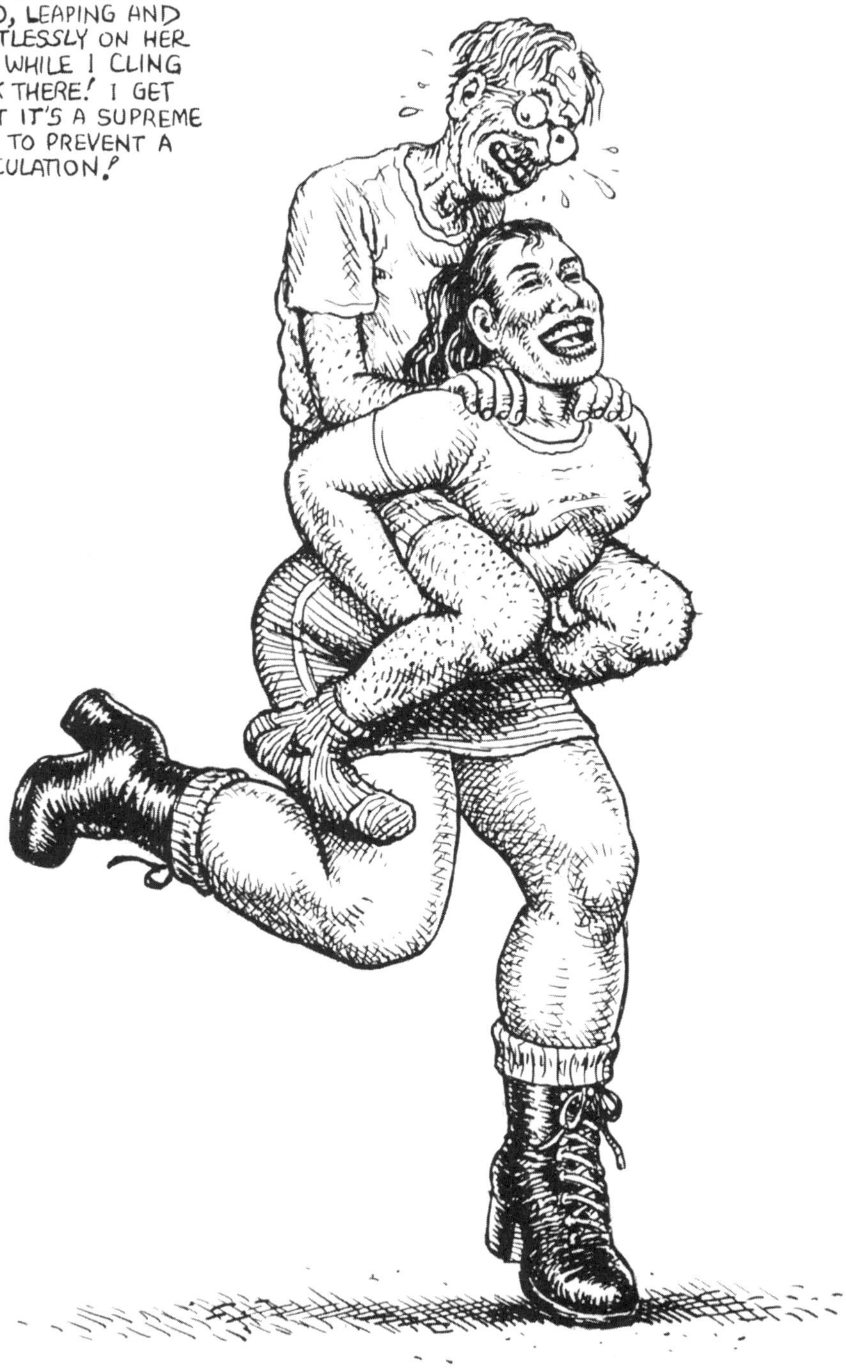

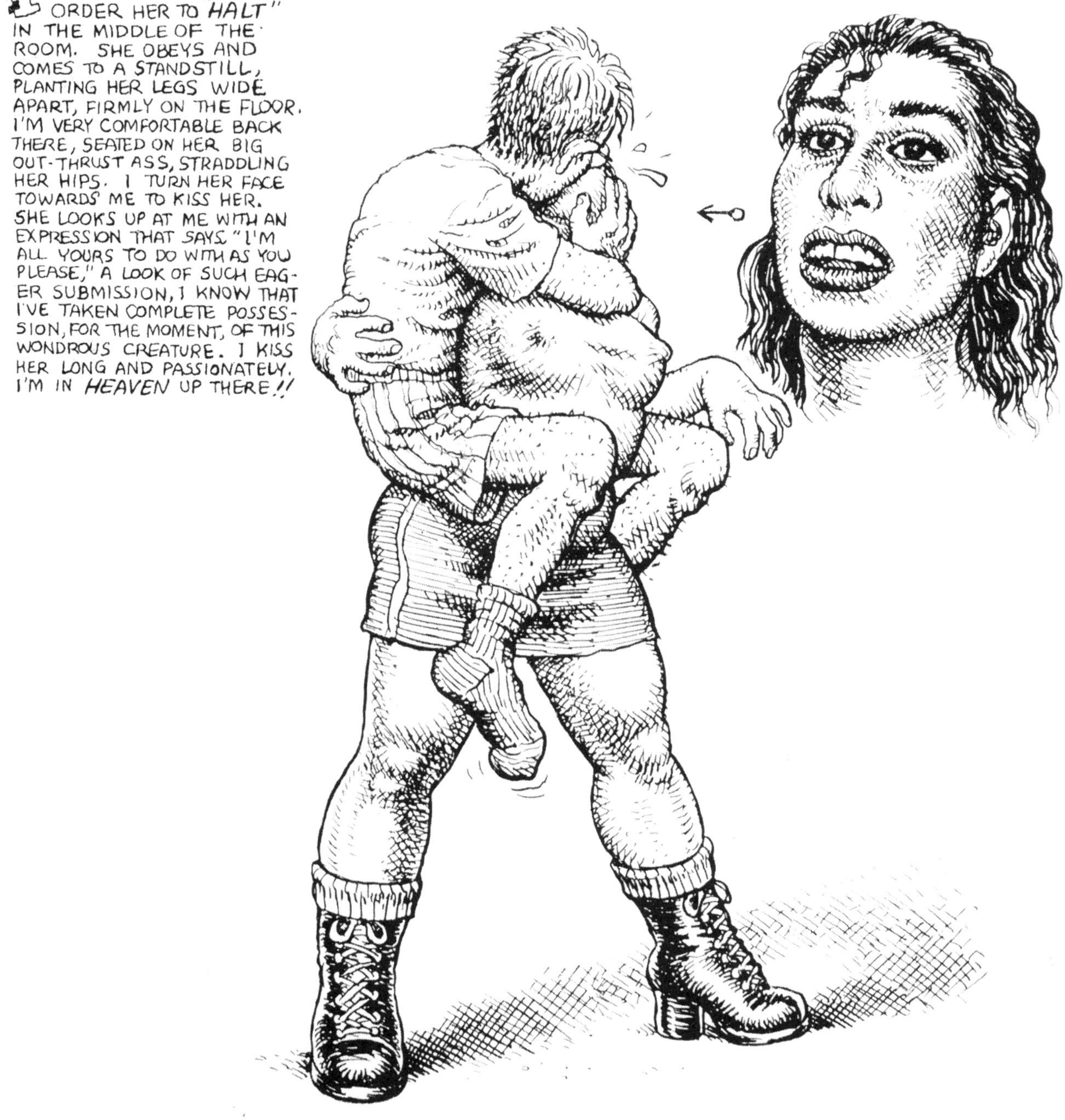
I ORDER HER TO "HALT" IN THE MIDDLE OF THE ROOM. SHE OBEYS AND COMES TO A STANDSTILL, PLANTING HER LEGS WIDE APART, FIRMLY ON THE FLOOR. I'M VERY COMFORTABLE BACK THERE, SEATED ON HER BIG OUT-THRUST ASS, STRADDLING HER HIPS. I TURN HER FACE TOWARDS ME TO KISS HER. SHE LOOKS UP AT ME WITH AN EXPRESSION THAT SAYS "I'M ALL YOURS TO DO WITH AS YOU PLEASE," A LOOK OF SUCH EAGER SUBMISSION, I KNOW THAT I'VE TAKEN COMPLETE POSSESSION, FOR THE MOMENT, OF THIS WONDROUS CREATURE. I KISS HER LONG AND PASSIONATELY. I'M IN HEAVEN UP THERE!!

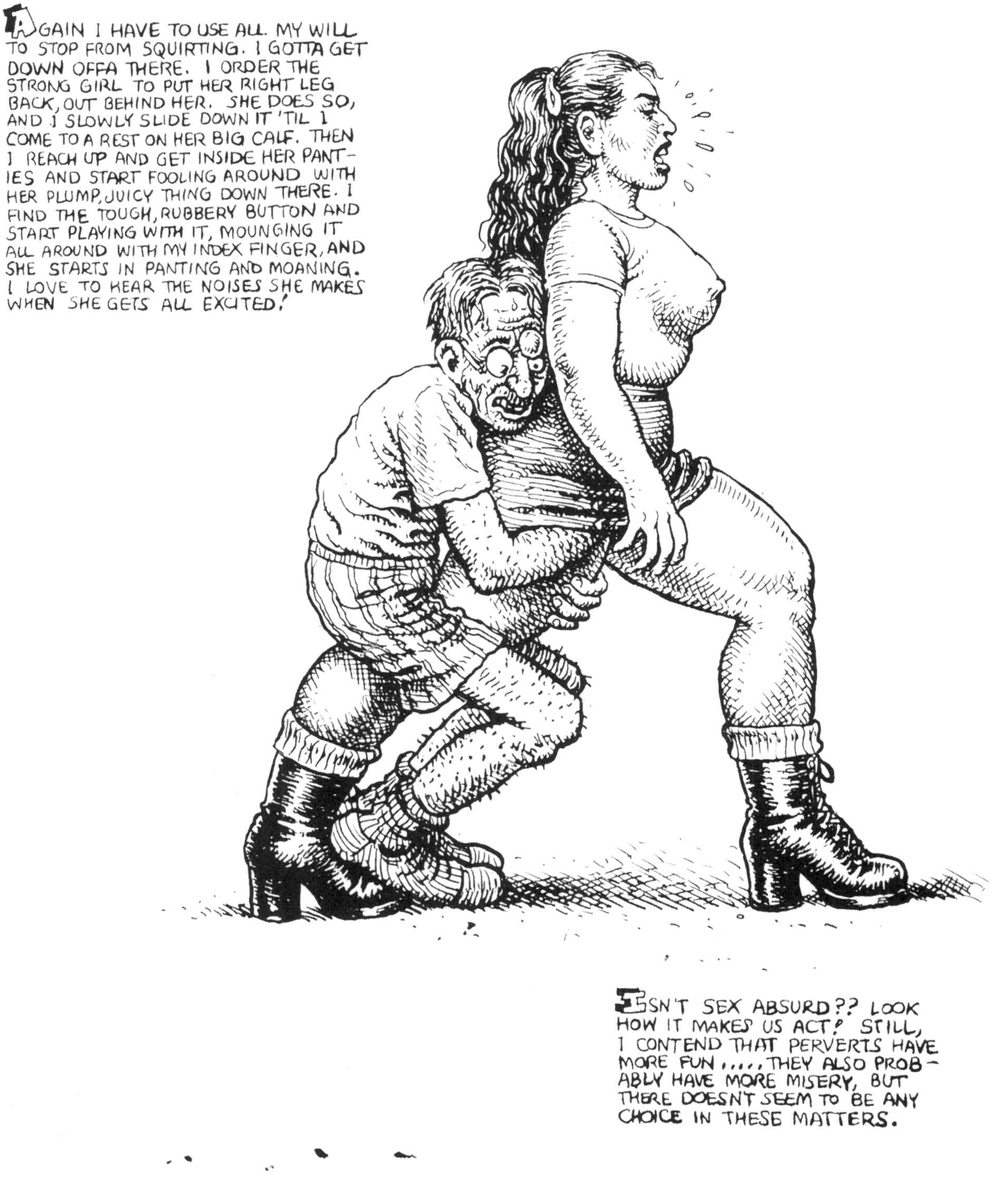
AGAIN I HAVE TO USE ALL MY WILL TO STOP FROM SQUIRTING. I GOTTA GET DOWN OFFA THERE. I ORDER THE STRONG GIRL TO PUT HER RIGHT LEG BACK, OUT BEHIND HER. SHE DOES SO, AND I SLOWLY SLIDE DOWN IT 'TIL I COME TO A REST ON HER BIG CALF. THEN I REACH UP AND GET INSIDE HER PANT-IES AND START FOOLING AROUND WITH HER PLUMP, JUICY THING DOWN THERE. I FIND THE TOUGH, RUBBERY BUTTON AND START PLAYING WITH IT, MOUNGING IT ALL AROUND WITH MY INDEX FINGER, AND SHE STARTS IN PANTING AND MOANING. I LOVE TO HEAR THE NOISES SHE MAKES WHEN SHE GETS ALL EXCITED!
ISN'T SEX ABSURD?? LOOK HOW IT MAKES US ACT! STILL, I CONTEND THAT PERVERTS HAVE MORE FUN.... THEY ALSO PROB-ABLY HAVE MORE MISERY, BUT THERE DOESN'T SEEM TO BE ANY CHOICE IN THESE MATTERS.

I KEEP ON NOODLING THAT THING AND *SLOWLY* THE *STRONG GIRL* BEGINS TO GO DOWN, WIMPERING AND PAINTING AND LETTING OUT LITTLE SOBS AND CRIES AS THAT LEG SLIDES FURTHER AND FURTHER BACK ALONG THE FLOOR. I KEEP AGITATING THE BUTTON UNTIL SHE'S ALL THE WAY DOWN TO THE FLOOR, AND FINALLY SHE JUST COLLAPSES, PANTING AND MOANING. I FIGURE SHE'S HAD ENOUGH, SO AT THAT POINT I TAKE MY HAND AWAY AND LET HER LAY THERE AND COOL DOWN A BIT.

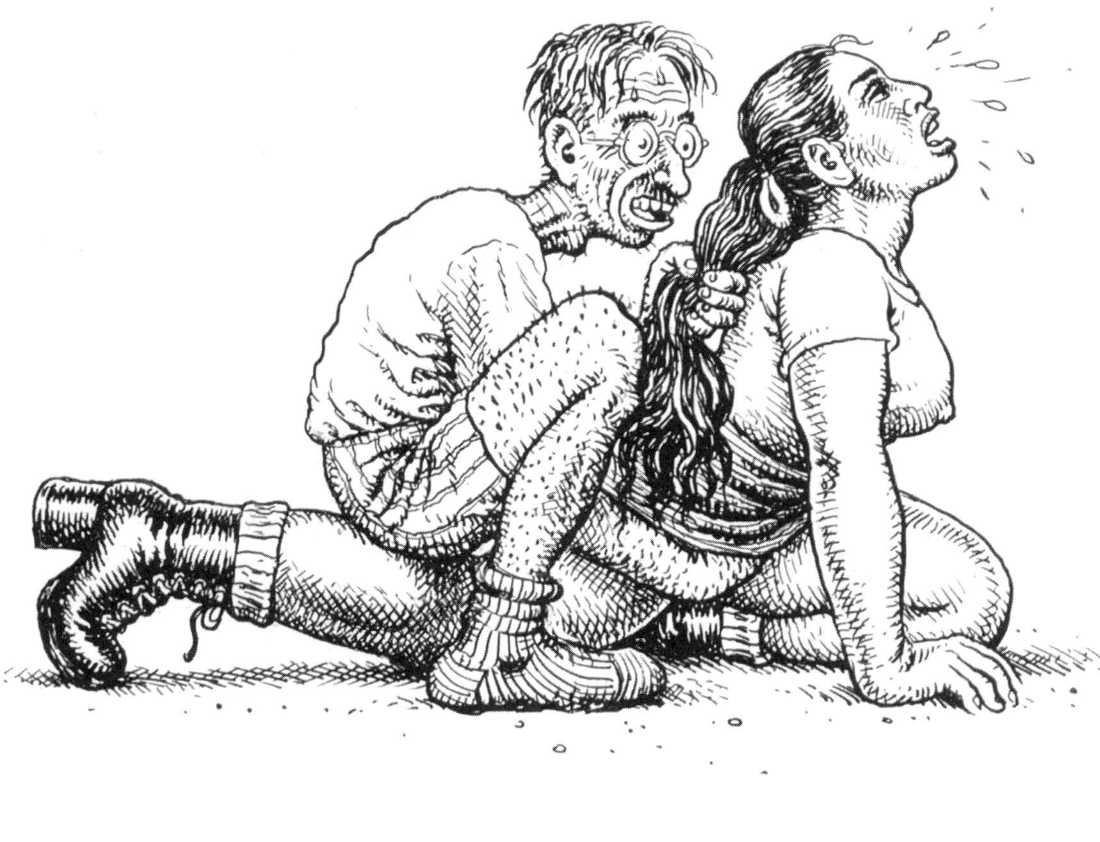

NOW THAT WE'RE DOWN ON THE FLOOR WE GET INTO SOME PLAYFUL ROUGH-HOUSING. THE STRONG GIRL COULD BREAK ME IN HALF IF SHE WANTED TO, BUT I CAN TELL SHE THINKS IT'S "CUTE" THE WAY I TRY TO "CONQUER" HER. SHE SAYS, "GO AHEAD, DO YOUR WORST," A BIG GRIN ON HER BEAUTIFUL FACE. I FOCUS MY EFFORTS ON ONE OF HER POWERFUL LEGS. I GET UP ON IT AND TRY TO BRING IT DOWN. THAT LEG COULD EASILY THROW ME OFF, BUT IT HUMORS ME AND LETS ME "WIN", SUCH A GOOD-NATURED BIG GIRL LEG IT IS! I'M THRILLED AS I MANAGE TO FORCE THAT SPLENDID LIMB OF HERS ALL THE WAY DOWN 'TIL IT'S RIGHT ABOVE THE STRONG GIRL'S HEAD AND CHEST!

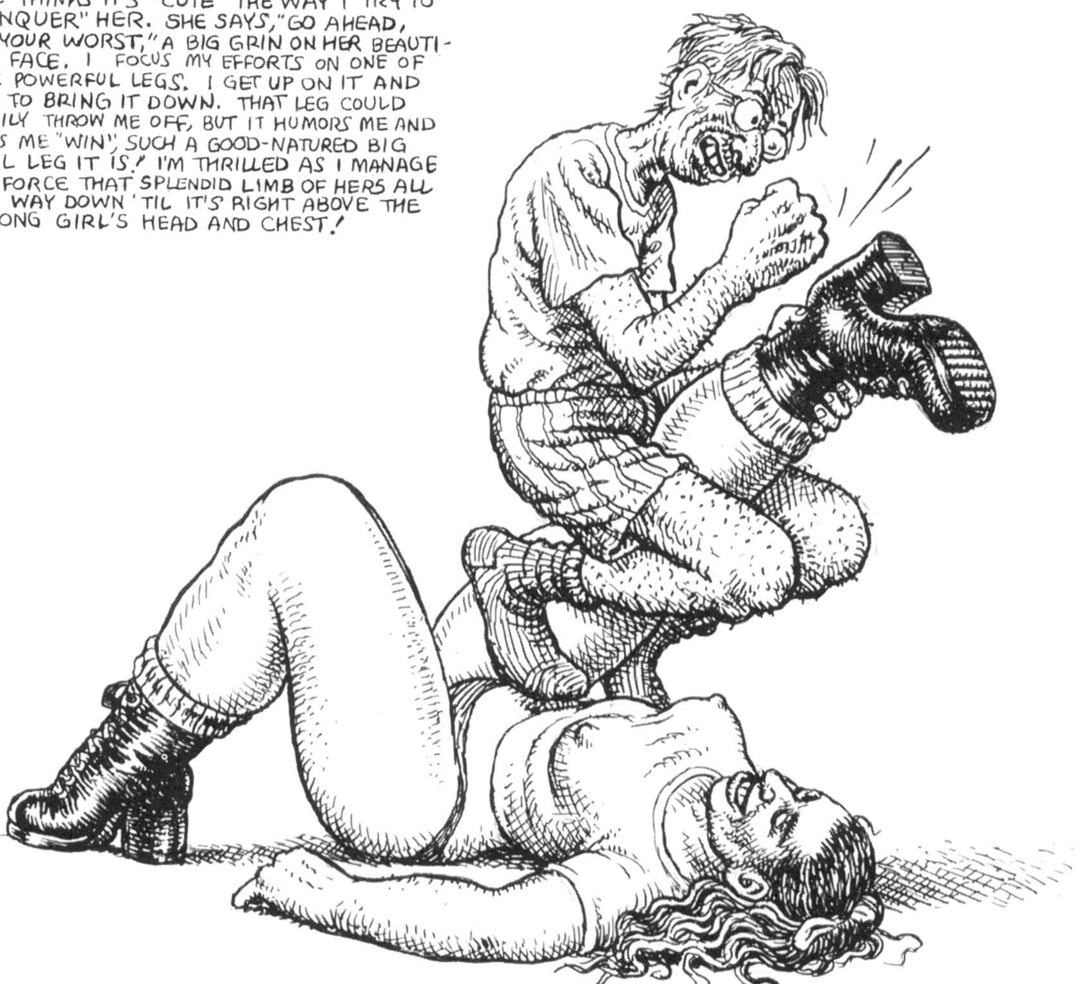

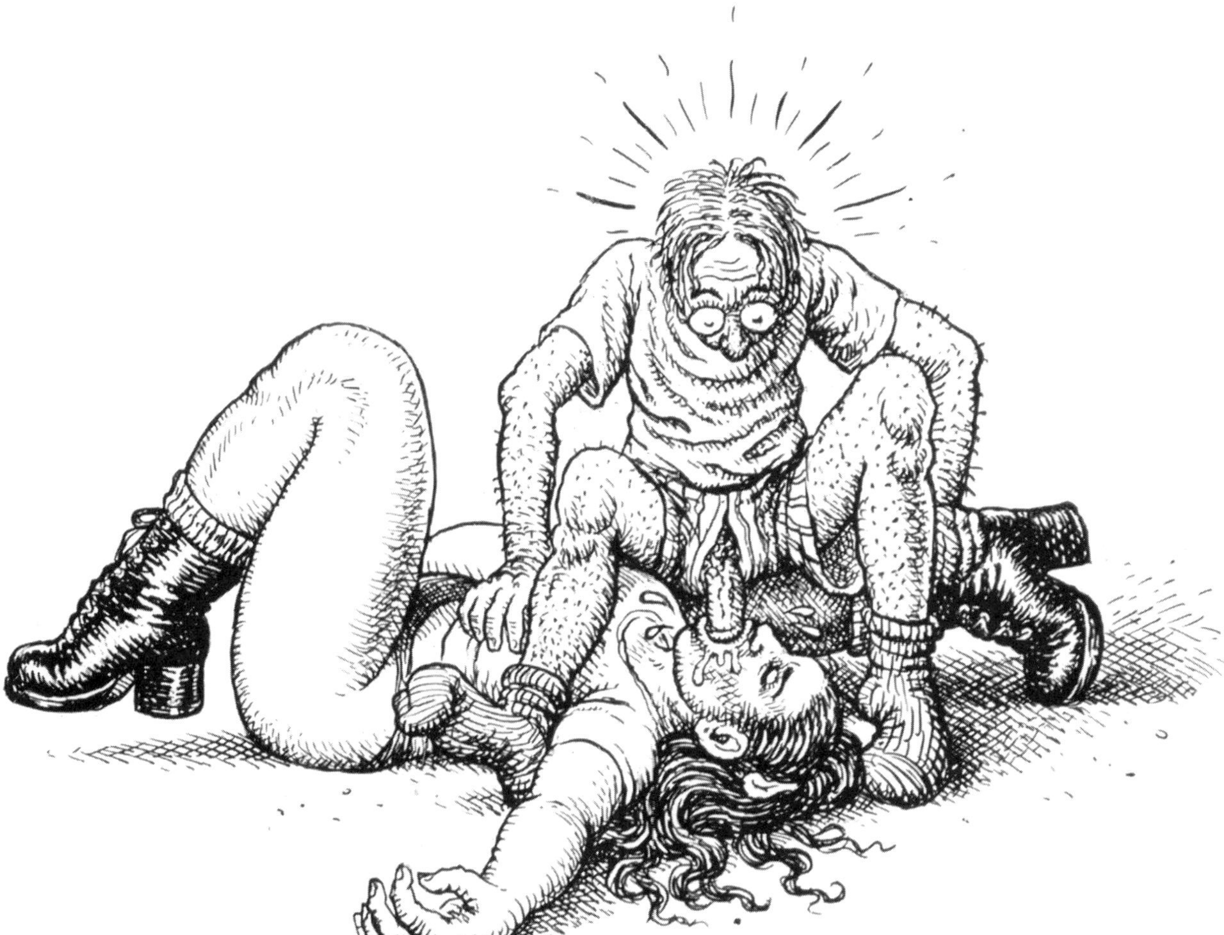

AND THEN — AND THEN — JUST AS THE TIP OF HER TOE TOUCHES THE FLOOR, SUDDENLY — *PLORP!* JUST LIKE THAT, MY HARD DICK, WHICH HAS POPPED OUT OF MY SHORTS , GOES RIGHT STRAIGHT INTO HER OPEN MOUTH, HER LIPS FORMING AN ACCOMODATING "O". THIS IS HEART-STOPPING ENOUGH, BUT THEN SHE STARTS BOUNCING ME UP AND DOWN ON HER LEG, MAKING MY DICK GO IN AND OUT, IN AND OUT! ONCE AGAIN, I CAN'T TAKE TOO MUCH OF *THIS* OR I'LL EXPLODE DOWN HER THROAT. I DON'T WANT TO BLOW IT OUT JUST YET, SO I PUT A STOP TO THIS BUSINESS AND JUMP OFF OF THAT LEG!

WE SIT THERE PANTING AND STARING AT EACH OTHER FOR A FEW MINUTES. SHE'S SITTING UP ON HER HAUNCHES, HER EYES ARE SWIMMING. SHE'S IN AN ALTERED STATE. I TAKE ADVANTAGE OF HER DELIRIUM AND GET UP IN FRONT OF HER AND AGAIN IM-POSE MY MEMBER INTO HER EAGER, OPEN MOUTH. THEN I BOLDLY STEP UP ONTO HER BIG THIGHS AND CLIMB RIGHT UP ONTO HER CHEST. SHE ARCHES BACK, LEANING ON HER HANDS. HER CHEST MAKES A BIG COMFORT-ABLE SHELF TO SIT ON, AND I HOLD ONTO HER HEAD WITH BOTH HANDS, GAZING INTO SPACE, AND THEN—*OH MY GOD*—SHE FORCES MY DICK TO PLUNGE DEEP DOWN HER THROAT BY ARCHING HER CHEST VIGOROUS-LY UP UNDER ME, UP AND DOWN... ONCE AGAIN I AM DEEPLY THRILLED BY THE STRONG GIRL'S ATHLETIC PROWESS!

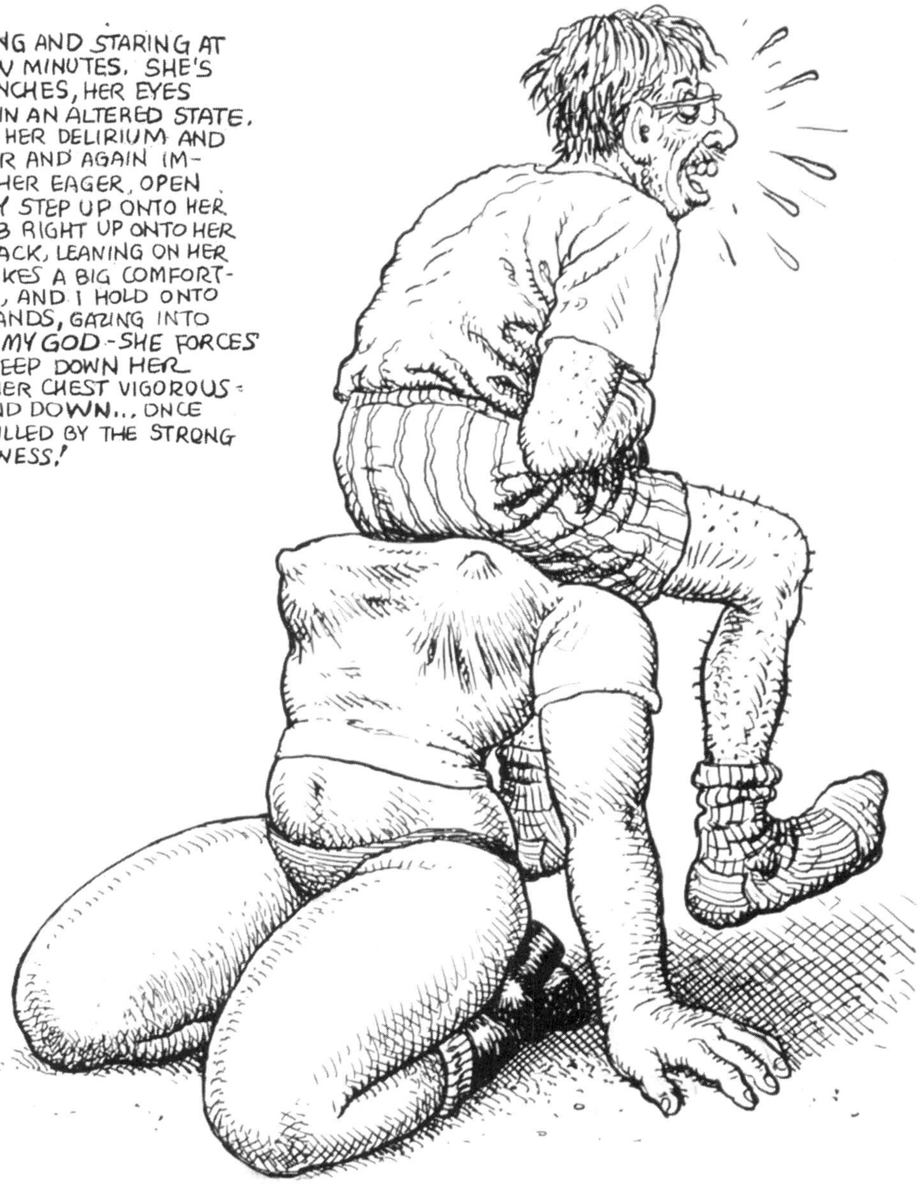

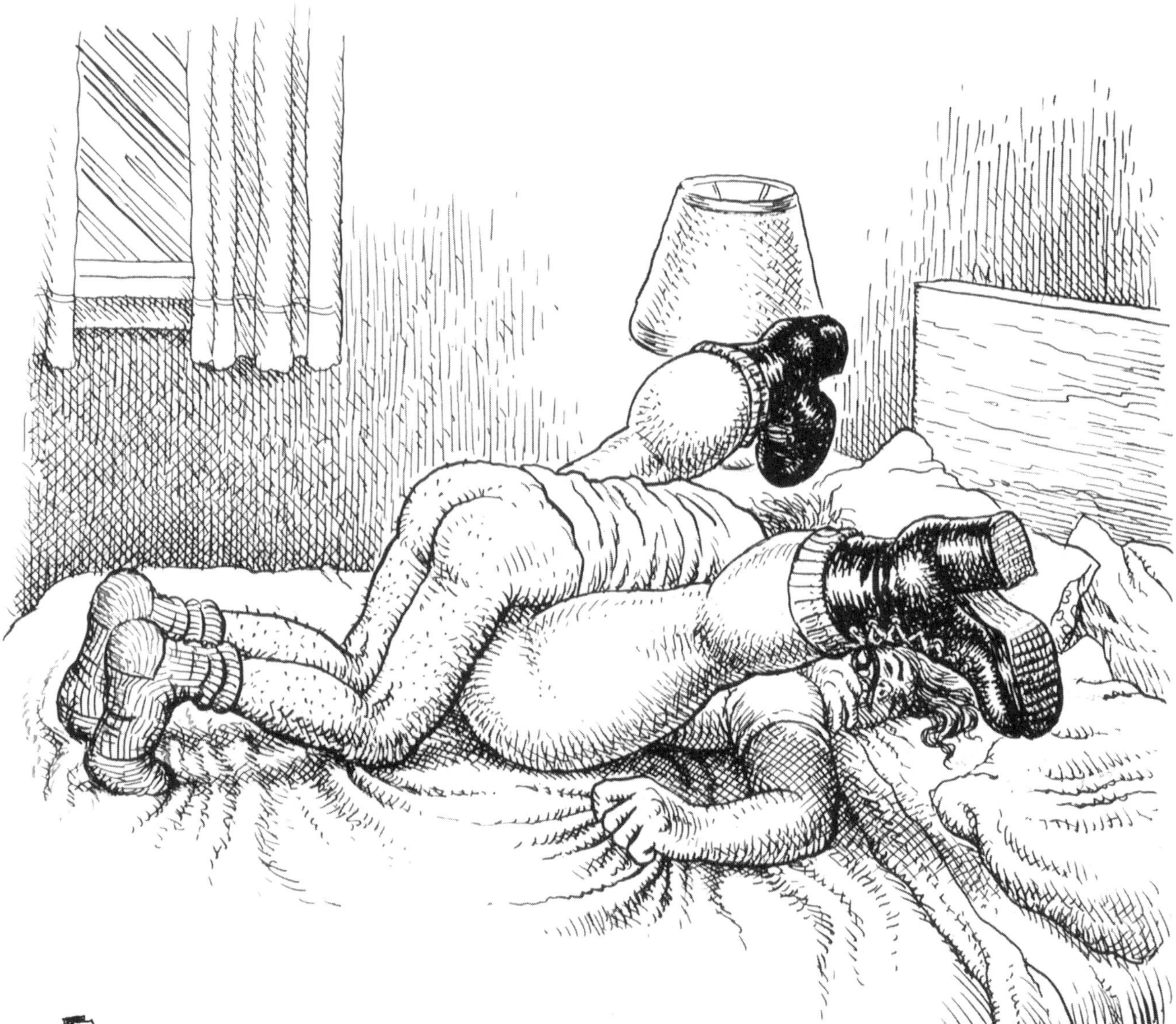

AGAIN I'M ABLE TO PRACTICE TANTRIC SEX YOGA AND STOP MYSELF FROM SHOOTING DOWN HER LOVELY THROAT, BUT I HAVE TO PUT A STOP TO HER INCREDIBLE ORAL CALISTHETICS. I TAKE HER BY THE HAND AND LEAD HER INTO THE BEDROOM. BY THIS TIME HER EYES ARE ROLLING UP IN HER HEAD. I TELL HER TO LIE ON HER BACK ON THE BED. SHE ASSUMES THE POSITION IMMEDIATELY, HER MAGNIFICENT LEGS SPREAD WIDE APART. WITH ECSTATIC JOY AND GRATITUDE I MOUNT THIS FINE, SUPERIOR WOMAN, AND WE HAVE A LEISURELY FACE-TO-FACE FUCK. HER RIGHT FOOT ACCIDENTLY KNOCKS THE LAMP OFF THE END TABLE BUT, OH WELL...WHO CARES!

I'M REAL PROUD OF MY SELF-CONTROL – I'VE STILL MANAGED TO KEEP FROM *UNLOADING* INTO HER. AFTER AWHILE I MAKE HER TURN OVER. SHE GETS UP ON HER HANDS AND KNEES AND I RAM MY DICK ALL THE WAY IN, THEN I CLIMB UP ON HER ASS. HER PELVIS IS ARCHED UP, MAKING IT EASY TO FUCK HER WHILE RIDING HER, BACK THERE ATOP THAT BIG BUTT! I HANG ON FOR DEAR LIFE AS SHE COMMENCES BUMPING AND GRINDING HER HIPS VIOLENTLY. I FEEL THE POWERFUL ASS MUSCLES FLEXING AND PULSING UNDER ME. SHE'S MAKING ALL SORTS OF WILD ANIMAL NOISES. I'M SO SUPREMELY THRILLED THAT HER VIOLENT UNDULATIONS BRING ME DANGEROUSLY CLOSE TO *LOSING* IT, AND SO I ORDER HER TO HOLD STILL. "DON'T MOVE A MUSCLE ON THIS THING, I'M WARNING YOU," I TELL HER. SHE STOPS MOVING, BUT THIS ONLY SEEMS TO EXCITE HER MORE. HER WHOLE BODY TREMBLES AND VIBRATES, AND SHE UTTERS STRANGE, UNEARTHLY NOISES. MAYBE SHE HAD A BIG ORGASM THEN, WHO KNOWS? SEEMED LIKE IT...

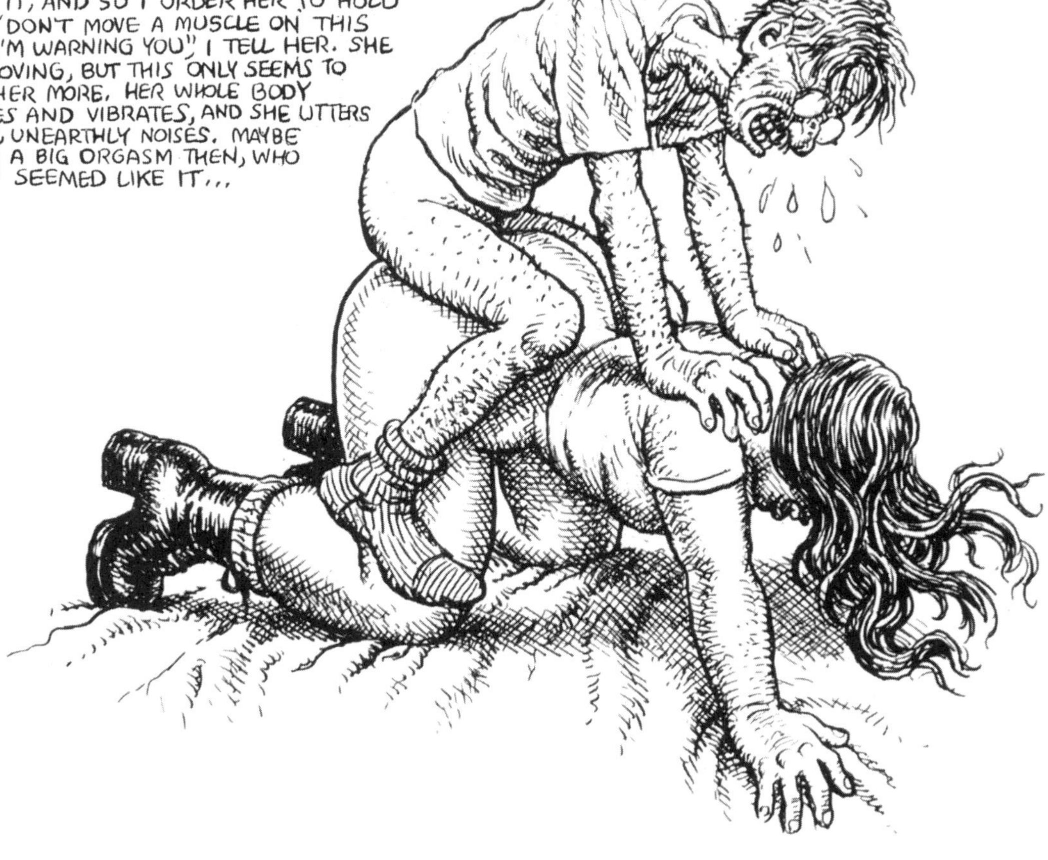

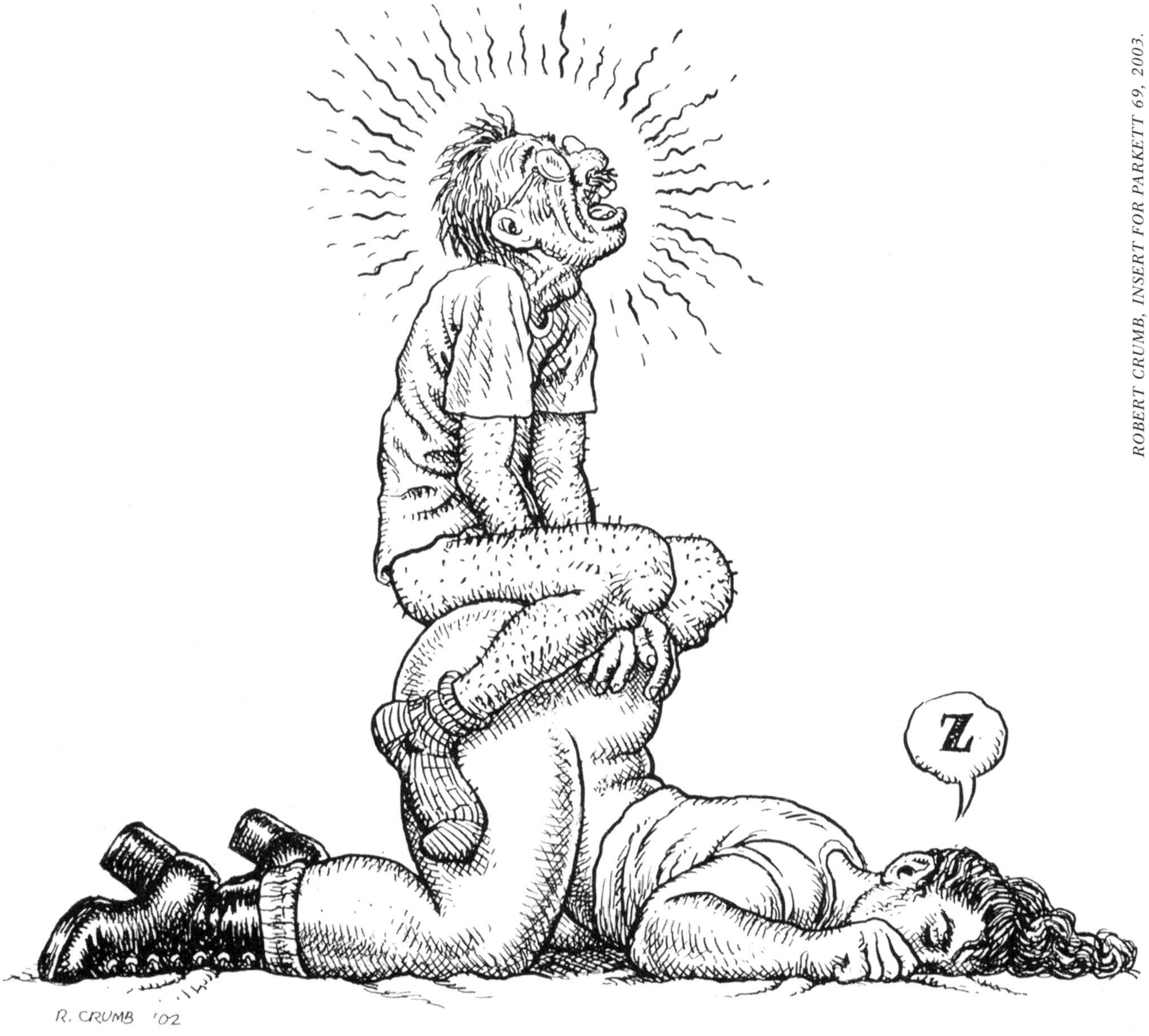

SHE LIES STILL, HER HEAD ON THE MATTRESS, HER BUTT TOWERING HIGH IN THE AIR. I LOVE BEING UP THERE WITH MY DICK DEEP IN HER CUNT. SOMETIMES I BOUNCE UP AND DOWN, THRUSTING INTO HER ALL THE WAY TO THE HILT. OTHER TIMES I JUST SIT THERE IN A DIZZYING STATE OF SEXUAL EUPHORIA. I NOTICE THAT SHE HASN'T MOVED FOR A LONG TIME. I LOOK DOWN AT HER HEAD FAR BELOW AND REALIZE THAT THE DEAR BIG GIRL HAS DRIFTED OFF TO DREAMLAND! WELL, SHE HAD A BUSY DAY, THE SWEET THING. I CONFESS THAT IT EXCITES ME GREATLY TO BE FUCKING HER WHILE SHE'S ASLEEP. IT'S LIKE SHE'S GONE AWAY AND LEFT ME IN CHARGE OF HER FABULOUS STRONG GIRL BODY! NOW I CAN'T HOLD IT BACK ANY LONGER... THIS IS IT... I HAVE A BRAIN-POPPING ORGASM UP THERE. THEN I GET DOWN, CURL UP NEXT TO HER AND GO TO SLEEP..

ROBERT CRUMB, INSERT FOR PARKETT 69, 2003.

MASSIMILIANO GIONI & ALI SUBOTNICK

THE ECONOMY OF ATTENTION

ART AND RADICAL THINKING IN TIMES OF STRATEGIC CONSENSUS

INQUIRY

In the past few years, politics, economics, and entertainment have increasingly been obsessed with reaching out to larger audiences. Consensus has become the new parameter by which decisions are made and actions evaluated. More importantly, consensus is no longer analyzed: it's rather constructed, built, and then presented as an undifferentiated, frontal entity—an extreme marketing tool.

In this context, expressing one's own beliefs is no longer an act of freedom or an exercise in critical analysis: the very moment we express our ideas, we are bound to surrender to the power of statistics. This logic seems to spread invariably to any field of contemporary life. In a blockbuster-oriented culture, quality itself often becomes a function, a Nielsen rating, while statistics are used as weapons to ensure a following to either a film or a president.

This attitude has invested the relatively new ground of contemporary art. Not only has contemporary art finally turned into a cultural industry, which—for better or for worse—can now compete with, and be compared to, other adjacent forms of infotainment such as the publishing and the film industries; it has also incorporated the strategies of marketing and consensus making in its own language. This attitude has resulted in a paradoxical situation, in which all the actors of the contemporary art game claim to be at once radical and innovative, and yet they aspire to being widely known, appreciated, and universally understood.

For this inquiry, we asked eight art professionals to provide in-depth statements: a wide and diverse representation of individuals operating in the field of contemporary art. This is a forum for different operators in the art field to openly discuss this topic and reply to questions such as: Which margins are still open to reconsider our roles and freedoms? How can we intervene on this vicious/virtuous circle that binds art to consensus and success? Is there still room for quantum leaps, innovation, and resistance? Is contemporary art bound to meet our expectations or to frustrate them? And what happens when the frustration itself is not only expected, but appreciated and therefore re-introduced in the process of consensual consumption?

MASSIMILIANO GIONI is artistic director of the Fondazione Nicola Trussardi and co-curator of Manifesta 5 (Donostia-San Sebastian, Spain, June 2004). ALI SUBOTNICK is former associate editor of *Parkett* and partner (with Massimiliano Gioni & Maurizio Cattelan) in The Wrong Gallery and *Charley* magazine.

RICHARD ARMSTRONG

The Henry J. Heinz II Director, Carnegie Museum of Art, Pittsburgh

This inquiry with its romantic questions sounds to me to be one of the plaintive cries from a late-nineteenth century Russian or Central European novel. There was a moment in eighteenth- to nineteenth-century France when the same questions were being posed, but between men and women in love. All the same, they are valid questions and the kinds of things that people are asking today as they look around in a contemporary culture where every mirror is from the carnival of consumerism.

I think there is such a thing as critical consensus and it's a function of access to media, proximity to information, and the proponent's ability not only to position him or herself, but also to articulate that position in a way that absorbs other people. To a large degree, responses to every kind of phenomenon (and aesthetic phenomena are not exempted from this) are conditioned, and it would be illogical and almost impossible to imagine completely original responses consistently coming from any one person. Therefore, people of like minds are frequently responding to things in comparable ways. You have to be able to flood the field around you with your point of view, so you have to figure out which responses are the richest and most active. Some people have truly forceful and accommodating responses to things; they're considered arbiters.

Contemporary art is its own project and operates on many fronts simultaneously: some avant-garde and some rear guard, and occasionally the two commingle. While we are something of an endangered species there is a predilection on the part of critical people—the population of the art world—to attack those nearest to them. Conversely, as people get a little older, a little fatter, and a little slower, they start recognizing that we should be protecting or at least allowing for one another. We don't reward eccentrics in the middle of their careers; we only reward them at the beginning and at the end. In the middle, it's people who stake out large territories and have the access to information, power, etc., who are in charge, and they're the ones variously demonstrating a consensus.

There are two ways you can add, or not, to the consensus from inside the museum. The most important one is through writing and communication, but collecting is also a crucial way for a consensus builder to demonstrate his or her leadership. The second one, which is incredibly satisfying at least to the person who is playing with the building blocks, is organizing and presenting exhibitions. This is a somewhat self-centered, relatively private enterprise, and it's highly ephemeral. Perhaps the last time that one saw such real cultural-shaping exercises was when Bill Rubin would hang The Museum of Modern Art's collection. Big survey shows like Venice or the Carnegie International only sometimes rise above the ten-week phenomenon, but they are crucial in light of building cultural compost and they allow for a first reconstruction of context. They're early and valiant attempts at putting together milieu and showing contrast—crucial to any consensus.

FRANCESCO BONAMI

Director, 50th International Art Exhibition, La Biennale di Venezia (2003), and Manilow Senior Curator at the Museum of Contemporary Art, Chicago

I think that the art world has lost its underground, a fundamental foundation of true innovation. We float on consensus or "dissensus." By "dissensus," I mean a form of negative consensus, i.e. the one that the recent Venice Biennale generated in quite staggering forms. I can't deny that I was quite shocked by the amount of consensus regarding the results of my direction of the last Biennale. The consensus/dissensus was mostly among colleagues and art critics, while the general audience delivered a completely different reaction. There are two different kinds of consensus in the world: the specialized consensus and the general consensus. As professionals, we lean to the former because it produces further professional opportunities, yet the general consensus defines the cultural mood and eventually the legacy of any artistic production.

I would like to (shyly) suggest that the Biennale brought back, inadvertently, some kind of underground attitude that these mega shows have lost along the way to becoming mega, and building up and capitalizing on consensus. But when did consensus become such a specific feature of the art world? And why has it been revisited with such force since the end of the nineties? Consensus exploded at the beginning of the eighties with the regressive Reaganite epidemic and the art-market boom, and it became not a goal, but a condition for an artist, dealer, critic, or curator to operate from. Anyone who did not generate consensus in one way or another was eventually excluded. Consensus created in the eighties became a sort of cultural or fashion apartheid. There were "consensus-only" galleries, restaurants, bars, discos, conversations, openings, etc. At a certain moment, consensus became a self-feeding mechanism, so if you didn't have consensus it was unlikely that you could in any way acquire it. Consensus produced consensus, and it was rare that you could lose consensus because once you got it, people assumed that you always had it. In the late eighties consensus faded slightly—bankruptcy may be the best antidote—and people disappeared from the art-world radar screen because they had no money left to fuel their consensus. Then, in the late nineties, consensus was revitalized, but in a different, possibly more dangerous form because devoid of any possible power; it was produced simply by hedonism and narcissistic attitudes. Cool is consensus. But to suggest, as we witness in the art world today, particularly in New York, that culture rests on consensus, reveals a profound misunderstanding of culture and society. Social structure, and art in particular, [rely on] differentiation; consensus is a form of mass suicide. There is no more funereal experience than to witness an event flooded with consensus, smiles on people's deformed faces while their voices blend in a cacophony of inconsequential acclamation of the event itself.

So the task is to produce "dissensus," to transform ourselves not into self-acclaimed walking corpses, but into sacrificial victims for a ritual devoted to the reestablishment of contradictory experiences, which is what culture should be about. Even now, with the game over and feeling like Michael Caine in the final sequence of John Houston's *The Man Who Would Be King*, a crippled figure, half blinded and deformed by a preposterous crucifixion, I still feel the energy produced in and by the critical realm around an event that departed from consensual premises and ended up in the squall of a dissenting, yet lively, mob. It is, after all, the severed head of the victim of consensus (Sean Connery) that Caine gifts, at the end of the movie, to his horrified listener.

AMY CAPPELLAZZO

International Specialist Head Contemporary Art, Christie's, New York

Consensus is a crux of the art world. Every generation has its leaders and tastemakers, whether they are curators, collectors, or advisors. I try to stay on top of new artists coming to the fore, and figure out when an artist is ready for auction. You can ruin a career at auction, but I love how auction brings transparency and democracy to an otherwise feudal market. When I accepted this job, many people scratched their heads; they saw it as a major departure from what I was doing as a curator of museum exhibitions and an advisor. I saw it as an essential next step. A curator has an influence on consensus and the market has an influence on consensus. Making an exhibition of an artist's work can bring about consensus; having a work at auction can measure another kind of consensus.

In the art market, collectors are the drivers of consensus: they have access to the most information; they're the great vortex of energy in the art world; and they are aggregators of inside information from dealers, curators, auction houses, and museum directors. It's the job of good dealers to create consensus by creating a market for their artists, particularly among influential collectors. It's about career building and making the artists' objects more desirable. It's based on the age-old economic theory of supply and demand, but not all buyers are created equal, so the idea is to sell to the collectors that can make a market.

Certainly selling your work is a plus, but many artists are more interested in their legacy. Usually artists sell their work while they're making their mark; the two go hand-in-hand. Then it is about sustaining it, and sustaining it is much harder than making it. This is about proximity and exposure. The consensus makers are much more critical once you've made it.

Although perceived as somewhat "corporate," there is definitely room for innovation and resistance in auction, both from artists and from arts professionals and collectors. The drive to be original—when it happens—always has an audience that responds to it, whether it's a curator who is a leader of the pack,

or a collector who is a tastemaker. There is room for innovation and individuality and the system rewards that. The art world is a bit insular but it's also very self-sustaining.
From a museological standpoint, consensus seems to be indicating that the art world probably has to move towards entertainment and a blockbuster mentality in order to survive. You can't be an expensive curiosity. In a museum, for example, if you're going to be the folly of a few, you have to be very well funded by those few. There are institutions that function like that and we love them. They are not dependent on consensus, but there is consensus about them because they're so special.

LYNNE COOKE

Curator, Dia Art Foundation

I don't think there is one art world any longer: it is now comprised of subgroups, which, like satellites, orbit around each other. There may be consensus within these various subgroups, but I don't think there is consensus across the whole system. The consensus that forms within any particular group depends, in part, on how that group is made up, on its infrastructure and dynamics. Consensus is built differently in each case and from moment to moment. For example, in the market, it's built around auction records, price structure, and a fostering of competitiveness among collectors, in short, via a careful stage-managing of careers. Certain young painters may command very high prices yet seldom appear in any of the major international exhibitions, and rarely are part of critical discourse. Nonetheless, they achieve a certain renown and have successful careers. By contrast, consensus in other subsets may be initially by means of curatorial and critical responses, as occurred with the recent focus on artists such as Pierre Huyghe or Douglas Gordon. The recognition they currently command evolved from the supportive interaction of certain coteries of curators, critics, institutions, and magazines.
In the main, consensus is temporary, like marketing and fashion trends. This is different from the consensus that ultimately codifies into an accord that enshrines an artist within a historical reading. That may be produced in various ways, not least by younger artists who, in looking back for inspiration, identify fertile forefathers or progenitors. Being artist-driven, such consensus may prove the most persuasive and enduring. But occasionally it is curators who resurrect an overlooked figure, recognizing something that seems prescient or timely in his or her work, some aspect or quality that hasn't been focused on previously. Occasionally even a book changes current thinking: an incisive articulate historian or critic can sometimes marshal that kind of sea change too.
In the case of institutions, the clearer the programmatic vision, the more possible it is to contribute to the forging of a substantive consensus. A scatter-shot program that simply follows trends will ultimately prove irrelevant. By having a coherent position, which need not imply an ideologically driven one, a program may initiate, foster, and develop a debate; by being partisan, polemical, and passionate, as Baudelaire demanded of critics, it may be possible to ground whatever consensus does ensue into something more sustained and enduring than mere fashion. There is no longer any one institution that determines taste and consensus in the way that Dorothy Miller's shows of the work of younger artists at the Museum of Modern Art in New York did in the fifties: no institution plays that kind of role any longer. The difficulty now is not the traditional one of surveying the enormous range and diversity of work, whether new or overlooked but ripe for reconsideration, but the fact that the playing field is so dispersed. It consequently becomes necessary to narrow one's focus, to define the arena or the legacies that one wishes to pursue and to follow those in detail and depth while acknowledging that much else will inevitably be left aside.

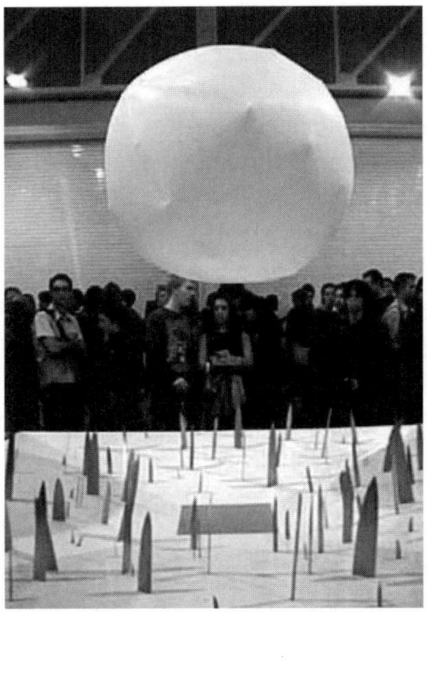

DAMIEN HIRST, BALLOON AND BLADES, 2003, opening at Gagosian Gallery, New York / BALLON UND KLINGEN, Ausstellungseröffnung.
(PHOTO: MARY BARONE)

BORIS GROYS

Professor for Philosophy and Media Theory at the Hochschule für Gestaltung in Karlsruhe, Germany; art critic and independent curator.

The art community is a place of conflict between different tastes, interests, and programs; it's a heterogeneous field; there's no common understanding of what it is and what it consists of. I don't think there is consensus in any aspect of the contemporary art world.

It is only possible to say that the people in the art world become interested from time to time in the discussion of certain topics and certain kinds of art that seem to them to be relevant and interesting. They react to the topics that stay in the center of common interest—not some kind of opinion or standard, but a notion, a movement, or an art phenomenon and this reaction is subject to fashion and trends. For example, an influential magazine may publish several contributions on the same topic, and it provokes others to think in the same direction and ask themselves, "What do I think about this?" or to write something about it. We have different approaches and opinions, but we also want to communicate, to write, and to take part in the discussions. The art press, curators, and critics are able to draw the attention of the art world to certain topics. For example, deconstructionism, multiculturalism, political art, Conceptual art, etc. were discussed for a certain time, and for each topic, there is an extensive amount of writing and an array of contributions. But in every case, after a certain amount of time has been spent discussing this topic, one year or one and a half years, you have a feeling that every substantial argument for or against it is already there and the discussion becomes exhausted and you don't want to participate anymore. It just dies. It's not that consensus has been achieved; it's simply that people get tired of the topic. But that's not bad, because as a result, some degree of clarity about this topic is achieved. At least at the end of every such discussion you know the standard arguments for and against it, and the standard attempts to mediate between them. You have a kind of discursive field, a strategy to catch the problem, classify it, and put it into perspective. In the end, you didn't solve the problem, but you're not interested in it any more. That's essentially what Wittgenstein said is the goal of philosophy, to kill the problem: not to solve it, but to make it completely uninteresting. That's precisely what the art world is doing.

YUKO HASEGAWA

Chief curator, 21st Century Museum of Contemporary Art, Kanazawa, and art critic

A broad consensus has been firmly established in the West and it is based on this premise that the mainstream contemporary art world is subject to ongoing development. The art world in the West is shifting from single-track Modernism, from the context of criticism and discourse, to an age of movements with prefixes such as "post" or "multi." There is a shared statement and history, shared information, that continues to undergo often-sudden changes.

In Japan new values and tastes are proposed only to be forgotten as just another passing trend; they do not accumulate and become the foundations of history. If any consensus exists at all, it would be that all values are leveled and equal. For example, both anime and Takashi Murakami's works are treated equally. The concept that nothing is more valuable than harmony—an idea emphasized by Shotoku Taishi in his Seventeen Article Constitution of the late sixth century—is still symbolic of Japan, a nation that represents the highest degree of consensus.

Apart from the situation in Japan, the issue of consensus is related to the phenomenon of mass dissemination and the socialization of contemporary art. Although there is obviously a market governed by the preferences of a few wealthy individual collectors, it isn't a simple reflection of their individual tastes, but is influenced by different social factors and mass culture.

There are two aspects to consensus: the positive aspect of compromise and the unavoidable aspect of staging that maintains, for the moment, the brisk business that is mainstream contemporary art. The latter resembles a business strategy, the aim of which is to produce a fictitious demand in order to push the consumer market. A new statement borrows the format of "the exhibition" by means of which it is repeatedly presented to the public. A budding curator may frequently put together exhibitions in a similar format, featuring the same artists, but no one criticizes this until the campaign extolling the newness of these exhibitions has fully penetrated the market. The art world needs someone to lay the illusionary carpet of a new consensus.

Thanks to economic globalism, the relationship between the fictitious nature of the consensus of the art world and politics and economics is becoming increasingly clear.

I propose (on an international level) that we move away from this illusion of consensus and seriously consider how we can make the shift towards a polyphonic context, even dismantling the origins of Modernism to create a separate context—a context in which multiple and different trends mutually stimulate each other to produce a rich melody, a situation in which we are freed from the hierarchy of values and genres. In the process of creating a new art museum, I want to devise ways of presenting and explaining twenty-first century art to people for whom Picasso is the only recent artist they are aware of. I want the community to take ownership of the art, to consume it, to taste it, and to think about it. And this is a process that should take place without having to mention names such as Marcel Duchamp or Joseph Beuys. A new statement is then created during this process that is neither an extension nor an application of an existing statement. By linking the issue of consensus that exists today to an extremely domestic issue, I address the magnetic field of polyphonic and multiple modes of consensus as an extremely interesting course of action.

TAKASHI MURAKAMI
Artist

Think Maurizio Cattelan. The artistic activities of this unwonted Italian genius in the contemporary art world always illuminate the direction I follow. His works are humorous, ironic, and never fail to tickle the noses of art historians with a few drops of aphrodisiac. He sporadically, but steadily releases such works at the rate of a movie director, who produces one film a year. Cattelan's oeuvre will no doubt continue to entertain art enthusiasts until his death and beyond, just as Marcel Duchamp's still does. He and his works can be appreciated with a promise of the future in mind, and his stability has been proven in the art market as well. Cattelan knows how to maintain a proper distance from the salons: he is the conscience of the contemporary art world and is an impeccable artist of our time.

Now I think about myself. I am Japanese, based in Japan, I do not speak English well, and above all, I do not know how to maintain a proper distance from the contemporary art industry. I unscrupulously create and release works, and there are numerous unsuccessful works sleeping in the back of my warehouse. If the core of contemporary art is defined as "a visualization of the artist's honest mind," my interest doesn't lie in the very center of art, but rather in the immature entertainment industry. Instead of considering art historians' reactions when I develop my work, I concentrate solely on satisfying myself as a severe critic as I watch documentaries about nature on the Discovery Channel, Hollywood action movies, and Japanese animations. Nevertheless, my admiration for Cattelan signifies that a thirst for art still lurks in a corner of my immature mind; the spirit of an artist trying to withstand the test of time lies at my core.

The credibility of an artist and his or her work is ultimately determined by the artist's frame of mind as an individual, re-

Art Basel, 2003.

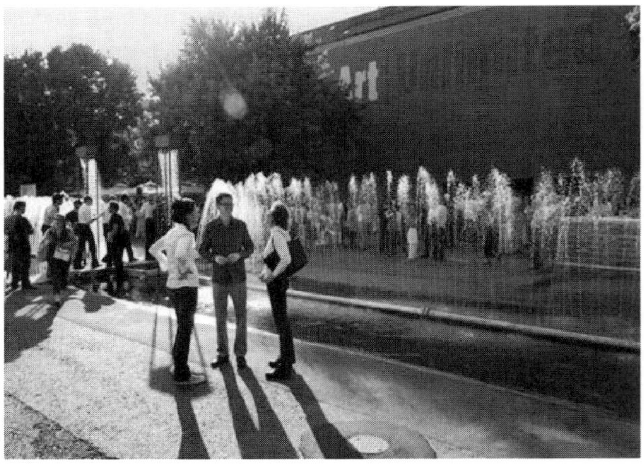

gardless of whether he or she is in the middle of a mass consumer society or in the world of noble contemporary art where works are valued for their rarity. Artists in the film industry like Walt Disney, George Lucas, and Steven Spielberg work hard to withstand the test of time: they thoroughly organize the marketing, presentation methods, and, of course, the images created in their studios. They create their own brands, protect their copyrights, and have the power to change the law itself. They are successful in exhibiting their film props in museums worldwide, in developing new technology, and in prolonging their lives as creators at the same time.

Maurizio Cattelan, Marcel Duchamp.

George Lucas, Walt Disney.

The future pursued by my heroes is too complex to predict, but its essence has already been sown here and there: We have to do everything we can to survive the test of time. I am now in the process of making the survival juice, which is a mixture of that essence. It may not be to everyone's taste, but I have a conviction that it will eventually become a necessity for artists. When the juice becomes easier to drink over the years, I believe that the future that I pursue will no longer cause conflicts among those concerned, and will be understood one hundred percent.

VICENTE TODOLI

Director Tate Modern, London

I don't think that there is consensus in the contemporary art world today and I hope there never will be! Consensus can be healthy to a certain degree, but absolute consensus kills the edges; it opens the way for standardization, which is exactly what art is not about, what art stands against. Art is an individual statement closer to dissent than consent. I believe in respect for individuality, one of the major contributions of the art world.

Consensus in the market or on the international exhibition circuit is temporal. You have the "usual suspects" from time to time, but this is not a value judgment. You could call it consensus, you could call it *l'air du temps*, or you could call it a wish for a superficial weltanschauung. But that's just a surface effect, and sometimes, unjustifiably, it may provoke a counter-reaction. Like if someone says "I'm sick of seeing the same people over and over," and then suddenly ... they disappear. There are many things I don't agree with, but I respect them, and I expect that from others. I certainly don't expect visitors to kneel [down] in awe, and say, "Oh yes, he's so right." Critical eyes and minds are what we want, it's healthy.

We [directors and curators] are intermediaries between artists and audience. We share our readings of visual culture and that diversity of readings gives the art community a service rather than a consensus. The multiplicity of views is what's desirable; and then, within that, you can find many degrees of this mysterious consensus. There is a degree of consensus, but it originates from this critical position.

I don't think consensus should be an objective, as it is in the business world. Even in the museums that I've run, I haven't fought for consensus in the program. Sometimes curators have come to me with an exhibition idea that wasn't really my cup of tea, but I saw that it was something they deeply believed in, so I said O.K. I've always been in charge of the programs, I wanted some edge, it was a way of achieving that openness, of not having everything rounded out, and of respecting the people I work with. I wouldn't do a program consisting entirely of such initiatives. You have a certain kind of outlook, then you try to add to it and to incorporate other individual ideas, which don't necessarily fit with yours. It creates a balance, and it plays down the ego factor.

Even taste ... is temporary, it's superficial, it evaporates. We can say the same about success: I don't think it is very interesting because it is measured according to general parameters. For example, what is success? How many museum exhibitions you do? How many collections your work is in? The price? That doesn't have anything to do with the art, it's parallel. You have to act without having consensus or success in mind, it makes no difference. Success and consensus are secondary. I'm more interested in the nucleus of things, but that's always an interpretation, and that offers infinite readings, which is the exact opposite of consensus.

MASSIMILIANO GIONI & ALI SUBOTNICK

DIE ÖKONOMIE DER AUFMERKSAMKEIT

KUNST UND RADIKALES DENKEN IM ZEITALTER DES STRATEGISCHEN KONSENSUS

UMFRAGE

In den letzten Jahren zeigten sich Politik, Wirtschaft und Unterhaltungsindustrie immer stärker davon besessen, ein grösseres Publikum zu erreichen. Konsens wurde zum neuen Kriterium, das Entscheidungen bestimmt und nach dem Handlungen bewertet werden. Und wichtiger noch: Konsens wird nicht mehr analytisch ermittelt, sondern wird konstruiert, erzeugt und dann als undifferenzierte, blockhafte Einheit präsentiert – ein äusserst wirksames Marketinginstrument.

In diesem Kontext ist es nicht länger ein Akt der freien Meinungsäusserung oder kritischen Analyse, wenn man seine Überzeugungen kundtut: Im selben Moment, in dem wir unsere Gedanken laut werden lassen, unterliegen wir bereits der Macht der Statistik. Diese Logik beherrscht mittlerweile, wie es scheint, jeden Bereich unseres Lebens. In einer Kultur, die sich an Strassenfegern und Bestsellern orientiert, wird Qualität leicht zu einer mathematischen Funktion, einem Nielsen-Rating, und Statistiken werden zu Waffen, die dazu dienen, die Anhängerschaft für einen Film oder einen Präsidenten zu sichern.

Diese Haltung hat auch das relativ junge Gebiet der zeitgenössischen Kunst erfasst. Die zeitgenössische Kunst ist letztlich nicht nur zu einer Kulturindustrie geworden, die nun – zu ihrem Glück oder Unglück – mit anderen Formen des Infotainment wie der Verlags- oder Filmindustrie wettstreiten und verglichen werden kann, nein, die zeitgenössische Kunst hat auch die Strategien des Marketing und der Konsensbildung in ihr eigenes Vokabular aufgenommen. Dies hat zu der paradoxen Situation geführt, dass alle Akteure des Spiels «Zeitgenössische Kunst» zwar behaupten radikal und innovativ zu sein, aber gleichzeitig Ruhm und Anerkennung suchen und von allen verstanden werden wollen.

In dieser Umfrage haben wir acht Leute, die beruflich mit Kunst zu tun haben, nach ihrer begründeten Meinung gefragt: eine breite und vielseitige Auswahl von Persönlichkeiten, die im zeitgenössischen Kunstbetrieb tätig sind. Es soll ein Forum zur offenen Diskussion dieses Themas sein, um Antworten zu finden auf Fragen wie: Welche Marge haben wir überhaupt noch, um unsere Rolle und unsere Freiheiten zu überdenken? Wie können wir diesen Teufelskreis, der Kunst mit Konsens und Erfolg verknüpft, durchbrechen? Ist überhaupt noch Platz für Quantensprünge, Innovationen und Widerstand? Muss zeitgenössische Kunst unsere Erwartungen eher erfüllen oder enttäuschen? Und was passiert, wenn die Enttäuschung nicht nur erwartet, sondern sogar geschätzt und damit wieder dem Prozess des konsensabhängigen Konsums einverleibt wird?

MASSIMILIANO GIONI ist künstlerischer Leiter der Fondazione Nicola Trussardi und Co-Kurator der «Manifesta 5» (Donostia–San Sebastian, Spanien, Juni 2004). ALI SUBOTNICK war bis November 2003 redaktionelle Mitarbeiterin von *Parkett* in New York; sie ist Mitinitiantin des Projekts The Wrong Gallery und der Zeitschrift *Charley* (zusammen mit Massimiliano Gioni und Maurizio Cattelan).

RICHARD ARMSTRONG

Henry J. Heinz II Director, Carnegie Museum of Art, Pittsburgh

Diese Umfrage klingt für mich wie der Klageschrei aus einem russischen oder mitteleuropäischen Roman des späten neunzehnten Jahrhunderts. Seither sind diese romantischen Fragen immer wieder laut geworden. Im achtzehnten und neunzehnten Jahrhundert in Frankreich wurden dieselben Fragen gestellt, aber zwischen verliebten Paaren; dennoch sind es wichtige Fragen und genau diese Dinge fragen sich Menschen heute, wenn sie sich in der zeitgenössischen Kultur umschauen, wo jeder Spiegel Teil eines gigantischen Konsumkarnevals ist.

Ich glaube, dass es so etwas wie einen kritischen Konsens gibt und dass er abhängig ist vom Medienzugang, der Greifbarkeit von Informationen und von der Fähigkeit des Einzelnen, sich nicht nur zu positionieren, sondern seine Position auch auf eine Weise zu formulieren, dass sie andere Leute anspricht. Unsere Reaktionen auf irgendwelche Phänomene (ästhetische Phänomene bilden da keine Ausnahme) sind weitgehend konditioniert und es wäre unlogisch, ja fast unmöglich, sich vorzustellen, dass irgendjemand regelmässig völlig unbeeinflusst auf Dinge reagieren könnte. Deshalb reagieren ähnlich denkende Menschen oft ähnlich auf dieselben Dinge. Da man sein Umfeld von seinem Standpunkt überzeugen will, wird man die ergiebigsten und wirksamsten Reaktionsmöglichkeiten wählen. Manche Menschen verfügen über wirklich überzeugende und befriedigende Antworten; sie gelten als Sachverständige.

Die zeitgenössische Kunst hat sich selbst zum Gegenstand und kämpft an mehreren Fronten gleichzeitig; einige in der Avantgarde, andere in der Nachhut, und gelegentlich sind beide vermischt. Obwohl wir eine Art gefährdete Spezies darstellen, greifen kritische Leute – aus denen die Kunstwelt nun mal besteht – mit Vorliebe jene an, die ihnen am nächsten stehen. Andrerseits beginnen die Leute, je älter, dicker und langsamer sie werden, allmählich einzusehen, dass wir uns gegenseitig beschützen oder doch wenigstens leben lassen sollten. Wir belohnen Exzentriker nicht in der Mitte ihrer Karriere, sondern nur am Anfang und am Ende. Dazwischen bleibt diese Aufgabe Leuten überlassen, die die Territorien grosszügig abstecken und Zugang zu Information und Macht haben; sie sind es auch, die mehr oder weniger einen Konsens demonstrativ zur Schau tragen.

Wer im Museum tätig ist, kann auf zwei Wegen zum Konsensus beitragen, oder auch nicht. Der wichtigste ist durch Schreiben und Kommunikation, aber auch das Sammeln ist ein wichtiges Mittel für Konsensstifter um ihre Führungsrolle zu demonstrieren. Der zweite, der zeitlich beschränkt aber unglaublich befriedigend ist, zumindest für denjenigen, der mit den Bauklötzen spielen darf, ist die Organisation und Präsentation von Ausstellungen. Das ist zwar ein etwas egozentrisches und verhältnismässig privates Unternehmen, aber vor allem ist es eine höchst ephemere Angelegenheit. Bei Bill Rubins Hängung der Sammlung im Museum of Modern Art in New York dürfte dies zum letzten Mal eine wirklich kulturbildende Übung gewesen sein. Grosse Überblicksausstellungen wie die Biennale in Venedig oder die Carnegie International wachsen selten über das drei Monate dauernde Phänomen selbst hinaus, dennoch sind sie wichtig für die kulturelle Kompostierung und ermöglichen eine erste Rekonstruktion von Kontexten. Es sind frühe wertvolle Versuche, Milieus und Kontraste aufzuzeigen – und das ist die erste Voraussetzung für jede Konsensbildung.

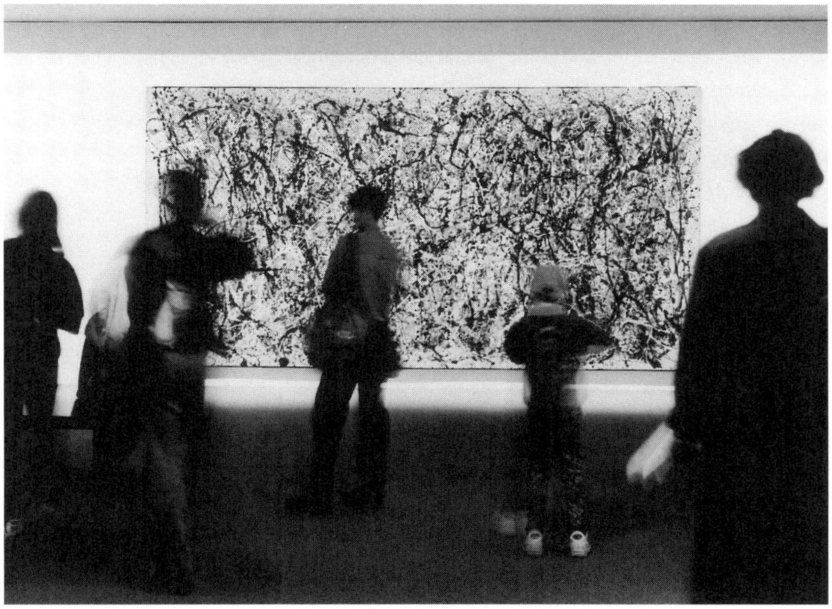

THOMAS STRUTH, MUSEUM OF MODERN ART I, 1994, c-print, 70 7/8 x 99 3/4" / C-Print, 180 x 238 cm. (COURTESY: MARIAN GOODMAN GALLERY, NEW YORK)

FRANCESCO BONAMI

Direktor der 50. Biennale von Venedig, 2003, und Manilow Senior Curator am Museum of Contemporary Art, Chicago

Ich glaube, dass die Kunstszene ihren Boden, ein festes Fundament echter Innovation, unter den Füssen verloren hat. Wir treiben auf einem Strom von Konsens oder Dissens dahin. Mit Dissens meine ich eine Art negativen Konsens, wie den, den die jüngste Biennale in Venedig in ziemlich verblüffenden Formen hervorgerufen hat. Ich kann nicht leugnen, ziemlich schockiert zu sein über das Ausmass an Konsens in Bezug auf das Resultat meiner Direktion der Biennale. Der Konsens/Dissens herrschte indes hauptsächlich unter Kollegen und Kunstkritikern, während das Publikum im Allgemeinen eine ganz andere Reaktion zeigte. Es gibt zwei verschiedene Arten von Konsens auf der Welt: den Konsens der Spezialisten und den der Allgemeinheit. Als Berufsleute orientieren wir uns eher am ersteren, da er neue berufliche Möglichkeiten eröffnet, dennoch ist es der allgemeine Konsens, der die kulturelle Stimmung und unter Umständen auch die Tragweite jeder künstlerischen Produktion bestimmt.

Ich möchte wagen zu behaupten, dass die Biennale unbemerkt eine Art Untergrundhaltung zurück ins Spiel gebracht hat, welche diese Megaausstellungen auf dem Weg ihres Megawachstums, ihrer Bildung von und ihres Bauens auf Konsens verloren haben. Doch wann ist Konsens eigentlich zum spezifischen Merkmal der Kunstwelt geworden? Und warum greift man seit Ende der 90er Jahre so vehement darauf zurück? Der Begriff Konsens gewann zu Beginn der 80er Jahre explosionsartig an Bedeutung mit der regressiven Ausbreitung des Reaganismus und dem Boom des Kunstmarktes; und er war nicht Ziel, sondern Voraussetzung für jeden Künstler, Händler, Kritiker oder Kurator. Jeder, der nicht auf die eine oder andere Weise konsensfähig war, wurde früher oder später ausgeschlossen. Der in den 80er Jahren gebildete Konsens wurde zu einer Art Kultur- oder Mode-Apartheid. Es gab Galerien, Restaurants, Bars, Diskotheken, Gesprächsrunden und Vernissagen, in die nur jene reinkamen, die am Konsens teilhatten. Zu einem bestimmten Zeitpunkt wurde der Konsens zum selbsterhaltenden Mechanismus, so dass es unwahrscheinlich war, je Konsens zu erfahren, sofern man nicht bereits zur Konsensgemeinde gehörte. Konsens erzeugte Konsens, und selten verlor jemand seinen Konsensstatus, denn hatte man diesen erst einmal erreicht, nahmen die Leute an, dass man ihn definitiv hatte. In den späten 80er Jahren verlor er etwas an Glanz – Bankrott ist vielleicht das beste Gegengift – und gewisse Leute verschwanden aus dem Radar der Kunstszene, weil sie kein Geld mehr hatten, um die Konsensmaschine zu ölen. Aber in den späten 90er Jahren lebte der Konsens wieder auf, allerdings in einer anderen, vielleicht noch gefährlicheren Form: Da keine Macht mehr dahinter steckte, wurde er lediglich durch Hedonismus und narzisstische Attitüden bestimmt. Das Coole ist ein Pendant zum Konsens. Aber zu sagen, wie man das in der Kunstwelt, vor allem in New York, heute hören kann, dass Kultur auf Konsens beruhe, enthüllt ein fundamentales Missverstehen dessen, was Kultur und Gesellschaft ausmacht. Gesellschaftliche Strukturen und insbesondere die Kunst beruhen auf Differenzierung; Konsens ist eine Art Massenselbstmord. Nirgends herrscht eine schlimmere Begräbnisstimmung als bei einer von Konsens triefenden Veranstaltung, dieses Lächeln auf den verzerrten Gesichtern von Leuten, die in die allgemeine Kakophonie des völlig irrelevanten Applauses für die Veranstaltung selbst einstimmen.

Es geht also darum, «Dissens» hervorzurufen, uns nicht in uns selbst beweihräuchernde Zombies zu verwandeln, sondern in potenzielle Opfer auf dem Altar der Wiedereinführung widersprüchlicher Erfahrungen, worum es in der Kultur ja eigentlich ginge. Auch jetzt noch, nachdem das Spiel aus ist und ich mich fühle wie Michael Caine in der Schlusssequenz von John Houstons *The Man Who Would Be King,* eine verkrüppelte Gestalt, halb blind und entstellt durch eine groteske Kreuzigung, spüre ich noch immer die Energie, die in und dank dem kritischen Umfeld eines Ereignisses erzeugt wurde, das von konsensbestimmten Vorgaben ausging und im Gewitterhagel einer nicht einverstandenen, aber lebendigen Meute endete. Immerhin ist es das abgetrennte Haupt eines Konsensopfers (Sean Connery), welches Caine gegen Ende des Films seinem entsetzten Zuhörer darbietet.

AMY CAPPELLAZZO

Leiterin der internationalen Abteilung für zeitgenössische Kunst bei Christie's, New York

Konsens ist die Crux des Kunstbetriebs. Jede Generation hat ihre Leader und Geschmacks-Trendsetter, seien das Kuratoren, Sammler oder Berater. Ich versuche über neu in Erscheinung tretende Künstler auf dem Laufenden zu bleiben und versuche herauszufinden, wann ein Künstler reif ist für eine Auktion. Eine Auktion kann eine Karriere zerstören, aber ich mag es, wie Auktionen Transparenz und Demokratie in einen sonst eher feudal strukturierten Markt bringen. Als ich diesen Job annahm, haben sich manche Leute gewundert; sie betrachteten es als Bruch mit meiner früheren Tätigkeit als Beraterin und Kuratorin von Museumsausstellungen. Ich sah es als entscheidenden nächsten Schritt. Ein Kurator beeinflusst den Konsens und auch der Markt beeinflusst den Konsens. Einen Künstler auszustellen kann einen Konsens bewirken, das Anbieten eines Werks auf einer Auktion macht eine andere Art von Konsens messbar.

Auf dem Kunstmarkt bestimmen die Sammler den Konsens: Sie haben Zugang zu den meisten Informationen; sie sind der grosse Energiestrudel im Kunstbetrieb; und sie sammeln Insiderinformationen von Händlern, Kuratoren, Auktionshäusern und Museumsdirektoren. Die Aufgabe eines guten Händlers ist es, einen Konsens zu erzielen, indem er einen Markt für seine Künstler schafft, insbesondere unter einflussreichen Sammlern. Es geht um den Aufbau von Karrieren und darum, die Objekte des Künstlers begehrenswerter zu machen. Dabei spielt das uralte Gesetz von Angebot und Nachfrage, aber nicht alle Käufer sind gleich mächtig, deshalb gilt es, an jene Sammler zu verkaufen, die den Markt bestimmen.

Gewiss, verkaufen ist gut, aber vielen Künstlern ist ihr Vermächtnis wichtiger. Gewöhnlich verkaufen Künstler ihre Werke, wenn sie sich einen Namen gemacht haben, das geht Hand in Hand. Danach geht es darum, auf der Höhe zu bleiben, und das ist viel schwieriger als der erste Erfolg. Nun geht es um Nähe und Ausgesetztsein; denn hat man es erst einmal geschafft, werden die Konsensmacher sehr viel kritischer.

Obwohl die Auktion als rein geschäftlicher Vorgang wahrgenommen wird, bietet sie durchaus Platz für Innovation und Widerstand, und zwar sowohl von Seiten der Künstler wie von Seiten der Sammler und derer, die sich beruflich mit Kunst befassen. Der Hang zur Originalität – wo vorhanden – findet immer ein dankbares Publikum, sei es ein Kurator, der eine Führungsrolle innehat, oder ein Sammler, der das Zeug zum Trendsetter hat. Es bleibt Raum für Innovation und Individualität und das System belohnt sie. Der Kunstbetrieb ist zwar eine Art Insel, aber er ist auch äusserst selbsterhaltend.

Vom museologischen Standpunkt aus, scheint der Konsens darauf hinzudeuten, dass der Kunstbetrieb sich wohl mehr der Unterhaltung und der Strassenfegermentaliät zuwenden muss, um zu überleben. Man kann keine teure Kuriosität sein wollen. Ein Museum etwa, das die Liebe einiger weniger sein will, muss von diesen wenigen mit sehr viel Geld unterstützt werden. Es gibt Institutionen, die so funktionieren, und wir lieben sie. Sie sind nicht vom Konsens abhängig, aber es gibt einen Konsens, was sie angeht, weil sie etwas so Besonderes sind.

LYNNE COOKE

Curator, Dia Art Foundation, New York

Ich glaube nicht, dass so etwas wie eine einheitliche Kunstszene noch existiert: Heute besteht die Szene aus Untergruppen, die einander wie Satelliten umkreisen. Innerhalb dieser diversen Gruppierungen mag es einen Konsens geben, aber ich glaube nicht, dass es einen gibt, der das ganze System umfasst. Der Konsens, der sich innerhalb einer Gruppe bildet, hängt davon ab, wie diese zusammengesetzt ist, von ihrer Infrastruktur und ihrer Dynamik. Konsens entsteht immer wieder anders und ist etwas Momentanes. Im Kunstmarkt etwa orientiert er sich an Auktionsrekorden, Preisstrukturen und der Pflege des Wettbewerbs unter Sammlern, kurz, über eine sorgfältige Inszenierung von Karrieren. Manche jungen Maler mögen sehr hohe Preise erzielen, obwohl sie selten an grösseren Ausstellungen in Erscheinung treten und kaum Gegenstand der kritischen Diskussion sind. Dennoch erreichen sie einen gewissen Bekanntheitsgrad und haben Erfolg. In einem anderen Teilbereich wiederum bildet sich ein Konsens zuerst dank den Reaktionen

von Kuratoren und Kritikern, so in jüngster Zeit im Fall des plötzlichen Interesses für Künstler wie Pierre Huyghe oder Douglas Gordon. Die Anerkennung, die beide heute geniessen, ist das Ergebnis eines fördernden Zusammenwirkens gewisser Kreise von Kuratoren, Kritikern, Institutionen und Zeitschriften.
Konsensus ist im Allgemeinen temporär, genau wie die Markt- und Modetrends. Etwas anderes ist jener Konsens, der in abschliessender Übereinstimmung einen Künstler einer bestimmten historischen Richtung zuordnet. Das mag auf verschiedene Weisen erfolgen, nicht zuletzt durch jüngere Künstler, die auf der Suche nach Inspiration fruchtbare Vorväter und Vorläufer ausmachen. Da er von Künstlern stammt, ist dieser Konsens vielleicht der überzeugendste und langlebigste. Aber gelegentlich sind es auch die Kuratoren, die einen vergessenen Künstler wieder hervorholen, da sie in seinem Werk etwas erkennen, was zeitgemäss oder seiner Zeit voraus ist, irgendeinen Aspekt oder eine Besonderheit, die man bisher nicht beachtet hatte. Manchmal kann sogar ein Buch die bestehende Meinung verändern: die klare Aussage eines Historikers oder Kritikers vermag gelegentlich eine solche Gezeitenwende herbeizuführen.
Im Falle der Institutionen ist es so, dass es desto wahrscheinlicher ist zu einer wesentlichen Konsensbildung beizutragen, je klarer die programmatische Sicht ist. Ein allzu beliebiges Programm, das lediglich gängigen Trends folgt, wird sich letztlich als irrelevant erweisen. Durch eine klare Position, die durchaus nicht ideologisch bestimmt sein muss, kann ein Programm eine Diskussion auslösen, pflegen und weiterführen; indem man polemisch und leidenschaftlich Partei ergreift, wie es Baudelaire von den Kritikern verlangte, lässt sich ein Konsens tiefer und dauerhafter begründen, als das bei einer blossen Mode der Fall ist. Es ist schon lange nicht mehr so, dass eine einzige Institution den Geschmack und den Konsens bestimmt, so wie das Dorothy Miller mit ihren Ausstellungen junger Künstler im Museum of Modern Art im New York der 50er Jahre tat: Keine Institution vermag mehr diese Rolle zu spielen. Die Schwierigkeit besteht heute nicht mehr darin, die enorme Bandbreite und Vielfalt der Werke zu überblicken – seien sie nun neu oder vergessen und wert, neu bewertet zu werden –, sondern in der Tatsache, dass das Betätigungsfeld so zersplittert ist. Man ist deshalb gezwungen sich zu beschränken, sich auf einen bestimmten Schauplatz oder auf bestimmte Künstler zu konzentrieren und diese genau und gründlich zu beobachten, im vollen Bewusstsein, dass vieles unweigerlich aussen vor bleiben muss.

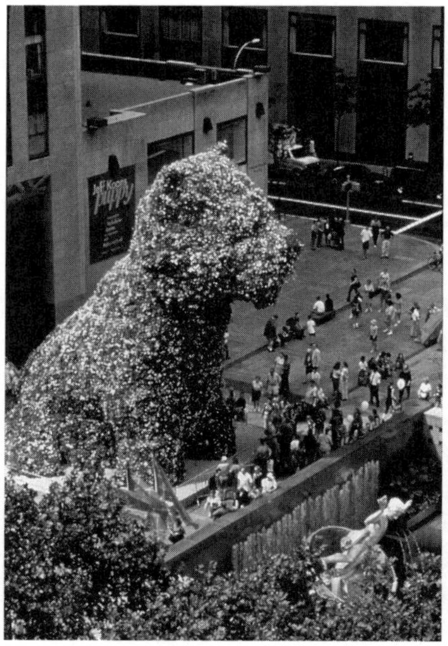

JEFF KOONS, PUPPY, 2000, Rockefeller Center, New York.
(PHOTO: BART BARLOW)

BORIS GROYS

Professor für Philosophie und Medientheorie an der Hochschule für Gestaltung Karlsruhe; Kunstkritiker und freier Kurator

Die Kunstwelt ist ein Ort der Auseinandersetzung zwischen unterschiedlichen Geschmäckern, Interessen und Programmen, kurz: ein heterogener Bereich; es gibt keine allgemeine Übereinkunft darüber, was sie ist oder wie sie sich zusammensetzt. Ich glaube nicht, dass es in irgendeinem Bereich der zeitgenössischen Kunst so etwas wie Konsens gibt.
Man kann höchstens sagen, dass die Leute, die sich in der Welt der Kunst bewegen, sich von Zeit zu Zeit für gewisse Themen und Kunstrichtungen interessieren, die ihnen wichtig und interessant erscheinen. Sie reagieren auf Themen, die im Zentrum des allgemeinen Interesses stehen – nicht auf irgendeine Meinung oder einen Standard, sondern auf einen Begriff, eine Bewegung oder ein Kunstphänomen –, und diese Reaktion unterliegt Moden und Trends. So kann zum Beispiel eine einflussreiche Zeitschrift mehrere Beiträge zum selben Thema publizieren und damit andere dazu bringen, sich Gedanken in derselben Richtung zu machen und sich zu fragen: «Was halte ich davon?», oder etwas darüber zu schreiben. Wir gehen verschieden vor und haben verschiedene Meinungen, aber

wir wollen auch kommunizieren, schreiben und an Diskussionen teilhaben. Kunstpublikationen, Kuratoren und Kritiker können die Aufmerksamkeit der Kunstwelt auf bestimmte Themen lenken. So wurden etwa Dekonstruktivismus, Multikulturalismus, politische Kunst, Konzeptkunst usw. eine Zeit lang diskutiert und zu jedem Thema entstanden eine Menge Texte und Beiträge. Aber immer, wenn ein Thema eine Zeit lang diskutiert worden ist, ein Jahr oder anderthalb Jahre, schleicht sich das Gefühl ein, dass eigentlich jedes wichtige Argument dafür oder dagegen bereits vorgebracht wurde; die Diskussion hat sich erschöpft und man mag sich nicht mehr daran beteiligen. Sie läuft sich einfach tot. Nicht, dass ein Konsens erreicht wäre; man ist einfach des Themas müde. Das ist jedoch nicht schlecht, denn am Ende hat man sich doch einen gewissen Grad von Klarheit über das Thema verschafft. Zumindest kennt man am Ende einer solchen Diskussion die Hauptargumente dafür und dagegen sowie die Standardansätze der Vermittlung zwischen den Positionen. Man verfügt über eine Art diskursiven Raum, eine Strategie um das Problem anzupacken, zu klassifizieren und in einen Zusammenhang zu stellen. Das Problem ist zwar nicht gelöst, aber es interessiert einen nicht mehr. Und das ist im Grunde genau das, was Wittgenstein als Ziel der Philosophie bezeichnet hat: das Problem zu erledigen, nicht es zu lösen, sondern es völlig uninteressant zu machen. Genau dies tut der Kunstbetrieb.

YUKO HASEGAWA

Kunstkritiker und Chefkurator des 21st Century Museum of Contemporary Art, Kanazawa, Japan

Im Westen hat sich ein breiter Konsens etabliert und auf dieser Basis entwickelt sich der Mainstream der zeitgenössischen Kunstszene. Im Westen ist ein Übergang vom einspurigen Modernismus, vom Kontext der Kritik und des Diskurses zu einer Form von Modernismus festzustellen, in der den verschiedenen Tendenzen Silben wie «Post» oder «Multi» vorangestellt werden. Es gibt e i n e Grundvoraussetzung – e i n e gemeinsame Aussage, Geschichte und Information –, die jedoch einem dauernden, oft brüsken Wandel unterliegt.

In Japan werden neue Werte und Vorlieben lediglich lanciert um sogleich als ein neuer Trend unter vielen wieder vergessen zu werden; die verschiedenen Trends werden nicht nebeneinander weiter gepflegt und bauen auch nicht aufeinander auf wie Elemente einer Geschichte. Wenn es überhaupt einen Konsens gäbe, dann den, dass alle Werte absolut gleich sind. So werden zum Beispiel *Anime*-Produkte und Takashi Murakamis Arbeiten gleich behandelt. Der Gedanke, dass es nichts Wertvolleres gibt als Harmonie – eine Idee, die Shotoku Taishi im sechsten Jahrhundert in seiner Verfassung zementiert hat –, ist noch immer ein Symbol für Japan, die Nation, die das Höchstmass an Konsens verkörpert.

Einmal abgesehen von der Situation in Japan hängt die Konsensfrage mit der Sozialisierung und massenhaften Verbreitung zeitgenössischer Kunst zusammen. Es gibt offensichtlich einen Markt, der durch die Vorlieben weniger reicher Privatsammler bestimmt wird. Dennoch spiegelt dieser Markt nicht nur deren persönlichen Geschmack wider, sondern wird von verschiedenen gesellschaftlichen Faktoren und von der Massenkultur beeinflusst.

Der Konsens hat zwei Seiten: den positiven Aspekt der Einigung auf etwas und den unvermeidlichen Aspekt einer Inszenierung, die momentan das harte Geschäft in Gang hält, das die zeitgenössische Mainstream-Kunst heute ist. Letzterer gleicht einer Geschäftsstrategie mit dem Ziel, eine künstliche Nachfrage aufrechtzuerhalten, damit der Markt nicht zusammenbricht. Ein neues Werturteil tritt unter dem Deckmantel einer «Ausstellung» auf und wird so dem Publikum gleich mehrmals präsentiert. Ein aufstrebender Kurator kann noch und noch Ausstellungen ähnlichen Formats zusammenstellen und dabei immer dieselben Künstler zeigen; niemand wird ihn deswegen kritisieren, bevor nicht die Jubelkampagne um die Novität dieser Ausstellungen auf den Markt durchgeschlagen hat, denn der Kunstbetrieb braucht jemanden, der den illusionären Teppich eines neuen Konsensus ausrollt.

Dank der wirtschaftlichen Globalisierung wird das Verhältnis zwischen dem fiktiven Charakter des Konsens im Kunstbetrieb auf der einen und Politik und Wirtschaft auf der anderen Seite zunehmend deutlicher.

Ich schlage vor, dass wir uns (auf internationaler Ebene) von diesem illusionären Konsens verabschieden und ernsthaft überlegen, wie wir zu einem polyphonen Kontext finden können, um die Anfänge der Moderne selbst zu demontieren und einen separaten Kontext zu schaffen – einen Kontext, in dem sich vielfältige und unterschiedliche Trends gegenseitig anregen und zusammen eine vielstimmige Melodie ergeben, eine Situation, in der wir von der Hierarchie der Werte und Gattungen befreit wären. Beim Aufbau eines neuen Kunstmuseums will ich Wege zeigen, wie man die Kunst des einundzwanzigsten Jahrhunderts Leuten näher bringen kann, für die Picasso der einzige und letzte zeitgenössische Künstler ist, von dem sie gehört haben. Ich will, dass die Gemeinschaft am Kunstbesitz teilhat, dass sie Kunst konsumiert, ausprobiert und über sie nachdenkt. Und dieser Prozess sollte stattfinden können, ohne dass Namen wie Marcel Duchamp oder Joseph Beuys ins Spiel gebracht werden. Dadurch ergibt sich eine Neubewertung, die weder blosse Erweiterung noch blosse Anwendung eines bereits bestehenden Urteils ist. Wenn ich die Konsensfrage, wie sie heute gestellt wird, mit meinem ganz persönlichen Anliegen in Verbindung bringe, gilt mein Interesse in erster Linie dieser polyphonen und vielfältigen Form von Konsens.

TAKASHI MURAKAMI

Künstler

Denk an Maurizio Cattelan. Die künstlerischen Aktivitäten, die dieses ungewöhnliche Genie aus Italien in der zeitgenössischen Kunstszene entfaltet, leuchten mir den Weg. Seine Arbeiten sind witzig, ironisch und versäumen nie, die Nase der Kunsthistoriker mit ein paar Tropfen Aphrodisiakum in Erregung zu versetzen. Solche Werke bringt er in gewissen zeitlichen Abständen, aber doch regelmässig hervor; sein Rhythmus gleicht dem eines Filmregisseurs, der jährlich einen Film produziert. Cattelans Werk wird ohne Zweifel bis zu seinem Tod und darüber hinaus fortfahren, die Kunstliebhaber zu entzücken, so wie das auch bei Marcel Duchamp noch immer der Fall ist. Er und seine Werke sind auch für die Zukunft viel versprechend und er hat auch im Kunstmarkt seinen stabilen Wert bewiesen. Cattelan weiss die richtige Distanz zu den Salons zu wahren; er ist das Gewissen der zeitgenössischen Kunstszene und ein unanfechtbarer Künstler unserer Zeit.

Nun aber zu mir. Ich bin Japaner, wohne in Japan, spreche nicht gut Englisch und, jetzt kommt es, ich verstehe es nicht, die richtige Distanz zum zeitgenössischen Kunstbetrieb zu wahren. Bedenkenlos schaffe ich Werke und trete damit an die Öffentlichkeit, und es gibt eine Menge erfolgloser Arbeiten, die zuhinterst in meinem Lager schlummern. Wenn der Kern der zeitgenössischen Kunst als «aufrichtige Visualisierung dessen, was der Künstler denkt», definiert wird, so gilt mein Interesse nicht dem eigentlichen Zentrum der Kunst, sondern eher der unreiferen Unterhaltungsindustrie. Während ich etwas entwickle, denke ich weniger an die mögliche Reaktion eines Kunsthistorikers, sondern konzentriere mich ganz darauf, mich selbst als strenger Kritiker auszuleben, indem ich Naturdokumentarfilme auf dem Discovery Channel anschaue, oder Hollywood-Actionfilme und japanische Trickfilme. Dennoch deutet meine Bewunderung für Cattelan darauf hin, dass in einem Winkel meines unreifen Hirns ein Bedürfnis nach Kunst besteht; in meinem Innersten verborgen steckt der Geist eines Künstlers, der die Prüfung seiner Zeit zu bestehen sucht.

Die Glaubwürdigkeit eines Künstlers und seines Werks hängt letztlich von seiner individuellen Denkweise ab, egal, ob er mitten in der Massenkonsumgesellschaft zuhause ist oder in der edleren Welt der zeitgenössischen Kunst, wo Werke wegen ihrer Rarität geschätzt werden. Der Versuch von Künstlern aus der Filmindustrie, wie Walt Disney, George Lucas und Steven Spielberg, die Prüfung der Zeit zu bestehen, macht ungeahnte Fortschritte: Ihre Marketing- und Präsentationsmethoden und natürlich die Bilder, die in ihren Studios entstehen, sind strikt durchorganisiert. Sie schaffen eigene Markenartikel, schützen ihre Rechte und sind mächtig genug, sogar das Gesetz zu ändern. Erfolgreich stellen sie ihre Filmkulissen in den Museen der Welt aus, entwickeln neue Technologien und verlängern zugleich ihr Leben als produktive Künstler.

Maurizio Cattelan, Marcel Duchamp.
George Lucas, Walt Disney.

Die Zukunft, auf die meine Helden zusteuern, ist zu komplex um vorhersagbar zu sein, aber der entscheidende Samen ist da und dort bereits gesät: Wir müssen tun, was wir können, um die Prüfung der Zeit zu bestehen. Ich bin gerade dabei, den Überlebenssaft zusammenzubrauen, eine Mischung aus diesen Grundessenzen. Er mag zwar nicht nach jedermanns Geschmack sein, aber ich bin überzeugt, dass er früher oder später für jeden Künstler unverzichtbar sein wird. Wenn der Saft mit den Jahren leichter hinuntergeht, glaube ich fest, dass die Zukunft, die ich anstrebe, keine Konflikte unter den Betroffenen mehr hervorruft und hundertprozentig verstanden wird.

VICENTE TODOLI

Direktor der Tate Modern, London

Ich denke nicht, dass es in der zeitgenössischen Kunstszene einen Konsens gibt, und ich hoffe, das wird nie der Fall sein! Bis zu einem gewissen Grad mag Konsens gesund sein, aber der totale Konsens tötet Randerscheinungen und öffnet die Schleusen für eine Standardisierung, also genau das, was Kunst nicht ist und wovon sie sich abhebt. Kunst ist ein individuelles Statement, das dem Dissens näher steht als dem Konsens. Ich glaube an die Respektierung des Individuums, eine der wichtigsten Leistungen der Kunstwelt.

Der Konsens ist der Markt oder im internationalen Ausstellungskreislauf etwas zeitlich Beschränktes. Von Zeit zu Zeit gibt es die «üblichen Verdächtigen», aber das ist noch kein Werturteil. Man kann es als Konsens bezeichnen oder als *l'air du temps* oder auch als Wunsch nach einer oberflächlichen Weltanschauung. Aber das ist nur eine Oberflächenwirkung und manchmal ruft diese eine nicht gerechtfertigte Gegenreaktion hervor. Wie wenn jemand sagt: «Ich habe es satt, immer wieder dieselben Leute zu sehen», und dann verschwinden sie plötzlich. Es gibt viele Dinge, mit denen ich nicht einverstanden bin, aber ich respektiere sie und erwarte das Gleiche von anderen. Gewiss erwarte ich von den Besuchern nicht, dass sie ehrfürchtig in die Knie gehen und sagen: «Ach, er hat ja so Recht.» Was wir uns wünschen, sind kritische Augen und Köpfe, das ist gesünder.

Wir – Direktoren und Kuratoren – sind Vermittler zwischen Künstlern und Publikum. Wir teilen unsere Interpretation visueller Kultur mit und die Vielfalt dieser Interpretationen erweist der Kunstgemeinschaft den besseren Dienst als ein Konsens. Die Vielfalt der Ansichten ist wünschenswert, denn innerhalb dieser Unterschiede findet man vielfach abgestuft diesen geheimnisvollen Konsens. Es gibt so etwas wie Konsens, aber er entsteht erst aus dieser kritischen Position heraus.

Ich glaube, Konsens sollte nicht unser Ziel sein, wie das in der Geschäftswelt der Fall ist. Selbst in den Museen, die ich leitete, habe ich mich nie um Konsens hinsichtlich des Programms bemüht. Manchmal sind Kuratoren mit Ausstellungsideen an mich herangetreten, die mir nicht wirklich gefielen, aber ich sah, dass sie selbst zutiefst davon überzeugt waren, also sagte ich ja. Ich habe immer Programme gestaltet und ich wollte Ecken und Kanten, also war das ein Weg, ebendies zu erreichen und gleichzeitig die Menschen mit denen ich zusammenarbeitete zu respektieren. Ich würde jedoch nie ein Programm machen, das sich durchgehend aus solchen Initiativen zusammensetzt. Man hat eine bestimmte Auffassung, dann beginnt man mit anderen zusammenzuarbeiten und versucht deren Ideen, die nicht unbedingt mit den eigenen harmonieren, zu integrieren. Das ergibt eine Balance, die den Ego-Faktor abschwächt.

Sogar Geschmack ist zeitlich bschränkt, er ist oberflächlich, verflüchtigt sich. Dasselbe gilt für den Erfolg: Ich glaube nicht, dass er sehr interessant ist, weil er an allgemeinen Parametern gemessen wird. Was heisst denn eigentlich Erfolg? Wie viele Museen einen ausstellen? In wie vielen Sammlungen ein Werk vertreten ist? Der Preis? All das hat nichts mit Kunst zu tun, es verläuft parallel dazu. Man muss handeln ohne an Konsens oder Erfolg zu denken, denn darauf kommt es nicht an. Erfolg und Konsens sind sekundär. Ich interessiere mich mehr für den Kern der Dinge, aber das ist immer eine Frage der Interpretation und erlaubt unendlich viele Deutungen, ist also das genaue Gegenteil von Konsens.

(Übersetzung: Wilma Parker)

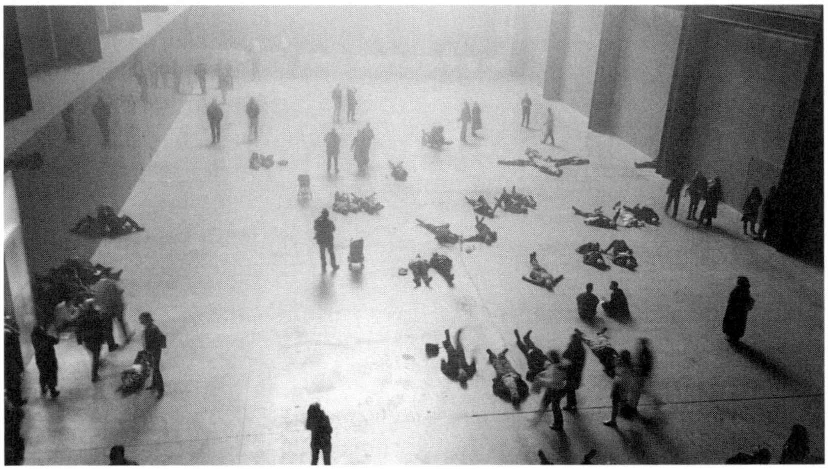

Tate Modern Turbine Hall, London, during Olafur Eliasson's installation THE WEATHER PROJECT, 16 October 2003–21 March 2004, Unilever Series / Blick in die Turbinenhalle während Olafur Eliassons Installation. (PHOTO: FLAVIA VOGEL)

CUMULUS

From America

IN EVERY EDITION OF PARKETT, TWO CUMULUS CLOUDS, ONE FROM AMERICA, THE OTHER FROM EUROPE, FLOAT OUT TO AN INTERESTED PUBLIC. THEY CONVEY INDIVIDUAL OPINIONS, ASSESSMENTS, AND MEMORABLE ENCOUNTERS—AS ENTIRELY PERSONAL PRESENTATIONS OF PROFESSIONAL ISSUES.

OUR CONTRIBUTORS TO THIS ISSUE ARE JESSE PEARSON, EDITOR OF "VICE" MAGAZINE, AND ERIC TRONCY, ART CIRITC, CO-DIRECTOR OF LE CONSORTIUM DIJON, AND CO-CURATOR OF THE LYON BIENNALE 2003.

I Do This, I Do That

THE PERSONALITY ARTIST AND HEAVY METAL DANDYISM

JESSE PEARSON

In Spencer Sweeney's drawing UNTITLED (2002), three nude male figures are cavorting in a wintry forest. The first, colored ice blue, has angel wings and is anally penetrating the second, who has green skin, four testicles, two penises, female breasts, red high heels, and a kingly mane and beard. The third figure, seen only from behind, wears a chef's hat and mysteriously wields a spatula. A discarded bottle, presumably drained of liquor, lies behind the angel/fucker. And, lest we forget, the king/fuckee is flashing the peace sign as if to say, "It's OK—I'm enjoying this."

At first glance, this appears to be the product of a perverted (albeit precocious) adolescent boy. The sex act and the genitals are drawn in loving detail and with considerable craft. The spitting up of subconscious fixations, melded with strange details that are too bizarre to be entirely subconscious, speaks volumes about Sweeney's method. He is one of the few young artists today to embrace a standpoint of simultaneously knowing, not knowing, and pretending not to know where his ideas come from.

There is a good degree of willfulness and negation in Sweeney's work—a paramount motivation for him is to "frustrate the audience and myself." Again, echoes of youth, when not-entirely-thought-out rebellion always seems like a good idea. But Sweeney is a grown-up. As for the sex acts he gleefully portrays in his work, he is fully allowed to go ahead and physically do those things whenever he wants (but, for the most part, he doesn't). This is because buggery outside of the paper, away from the drawn image, becomes something else entirely. Spencer seems to be more interested in depicting the act on a piece of paper and showing it to you than actually trying to do it to you for real.

This attitude is part of what places Spencer in a lineage of artist personality types that has fallen sadly by the wayside in our times. It is the notion of a rakish dilettante and dandy that Spencer lives out, updated to the present, when penises and heavy metal referents are as safe as milk, and you usually don't end up in jail (à la Oscar Wilde) for alleged sodomy. Sweeney's art (lately manifested mainly in paintings and drawings, but during his young career also including video, sculptural installations, and performance) cannot be fully appreciated until one has learned something of Sweeney's persona. His work and his reception lie in neither a retinal nor a cerebral place, but instead in an experiential and weirdly humanistic place. To know him is to love him.

For better or worse, artists who achieve a good degree of notice are granted leeway in their bad behavior. An extreme example of this is someone like Modigliani, who once threw a girlfriend out of his apartment window and then told the police who arrived to cart him off: "Hey, I'm an artist. I have different morals from people like you." There's also the drug infused "poor me"-ness of someone like Jean-Michel Basquiat. On the opposite end of this spectrum are artists who are permitted to be insufferably boring and academic. I'm thinking of the Neo-Geo painters as a fairly recent historical example of this. Some of these artists ruined the enjoyment of perfectly good geometrical paintings by indulging themselves in the cultural theory that was in vogue in the eighties, throwing around Baudrillard and Foucault the way their painting forebears threw around drunken punches.

The tradition of personality embraced by Spencer Sweeney is much

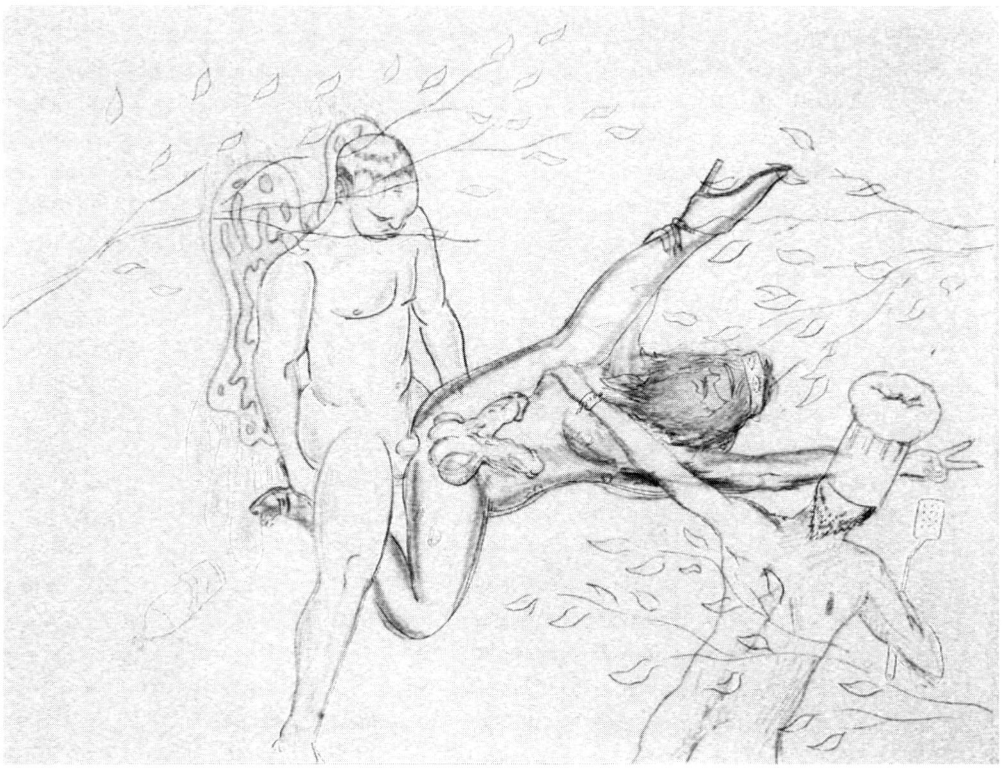

SPENCER SWEENEY, UNTITLED, 2003, colored pencil on paper, 11 x 13 1/2" / Farbstift auf Papier, 28 x 34,3 cm. (PHOTO: GBE [MODERN], NEW YORK)

more fun, inclusive, and sexy than all this. The true dandyish artists of at least the past thirty years are rock stars, whose life is art. Think of Marc Bolan, a sultry little elf covered in silk scarves, or David Bowie as Sweeney's forebears more than the artists who defined post-Pop Art as it slid into concepts and Minimalism. Figures further back in his lineage are Baudelaire, who saw the dandy and the *flaneur* as heroes of the modern world, and Tristan Tzara (after he founded Dada and before he ignobly retired to Surrealism and lyrical poetry). Baudelaire's enthusiastic take on city life and popular culture—that it's something we should let wash over us, picking and choosing stimuli as democratically as we like—greatly informs the personality category that Sweeney falls into in his everyday behavior and in his art, where his alphabet of signs is intensely personal and occluded—even though he uses things that we all know, from the Eiffel Tower to human skulls. This type of artist is expert at nothing but being himself, which includes going forth into the world, talking to people, staring at things, making drawings and paintings, eating at a restaurant, whatever. Like a rock star, who ostensibly has no time off, his art is h i m: the dabbler, the experiencer, the responder.

Who are his peers of the persona in today's art world? None I can think of, if thinking literally. Maurizio Cattelan seems to always be wearing a nicely tailored jacket, but he's an Italian, not a dandy. Toland Grinnell would look good in a cravat, but I've never seen him wear one. Roe Ethridge works the preppy thing to perfection but is less of a raconteur than he used to be, and too nice to fit the gadfly type discussed here.

Identifying the closest living relatives to Sweeney's social demeanor requires a broadening of the academy's view of what constitutes the art world and artistic practices. It seems that the creative people who most share this persona are not other painters, or even photographers. The punk rock/rap group A.R.E. Weapons (who used to be more of a performance art thing, with late nineties/early millennium shows at galleries like Pat Hearn and Gavin Brown's Enterprise) are very akin to Sweeney in their attitude and the projection of their creative acts. In their time in New York, they've morphed their aesthetic from the darker side of indie, to mustachioed sleaze ball, to their current and best-sounding incarnation, which lies somewhere between teenage metal head and Top 40 hip hop. All along, however, they have maintained a public artistic stance that mirrors Sweeney's and can best be described as sexy flippancy—very similar to the classic *boulevardier's* cynicism, which somehow maintained a human warmth. Also in this genus of dandified makers-of-things is the mega-fabulous fashion design quadrangle As Four. These four individuals, regardless of their sex, all look like Stevie Nicks dipped in a bucket of gypsy. They live together, are rumored to share a communal bed, and are a joy to see in public because they are the most extreme strata of person-about-town. It takes gumption, taste, and artful bravery to leave the house dressed like they do. Like the artist-personality Sweeney, they are onstage from the moment they wake up. It's twenty-four hour performance art.

Tristan Tzara's manifestos, equally informed by social belief and bombastic nihilism, were the cranky great-granddaddy of Actress, the performance group of which Sweeney was the token boy member. Actress cast a jagged and frustrating shadow on the downtown art world of the late nineties and early 2000. They were known for acerbic and petulant attitudes and infighting during interviews, as well as for exciting and confounding performances. In one, the members pounded blank canvases against their heads, exploding fake blood packets and becoming gory messes (shades of heavy metal head-banging, but we'll get to that a bit later). During another performance, Sweeney's contribution was to have his friend, the Japanese artist Taka Hiro Imamura, sing the Rolling Stones "Salt of the Earth" in his heavily accented English, accompanied on guitar by Sweeney. With its venomous attitude, Actress seems to have served as an image-cultivation finishing school for Sweeney. It was also perhaps a cautionary tale against all-out negativity, as he has since settled fully into the role of good-vibes-man-about-town-painter-DJ-professional Spencer. A little bit of this, a little bit of that.

As a dabbler, part of what an artist like Spencer does is act as surrogate fan for the things that excite him. To this end, Spencer is one of the most successful artists at championing heavy metal and punk in his art by utilizing motifs that are central to those genres of music. Metal has been mined by a range of artists with wildly varying degrees of success. On the Failure end of the heavy-metal-as-material-for-art scale is Matthew Barney's usage of it in his work, where it suffers from the cold stink of anthropology. On the Success end is Harmony Korine's use of black metal in the soundtrack to *Gummo.* Other artists have successfully integrated some of the language of metal—a singular mix of Norse and medieval

English historical references and novice Satanism—into their work. Banks Violette, an American artist who lives and works in New York, is particularly graceful with metal music symbols—a dash of demon warrior here, a touch of white pentagram there. Bjarne Melgaard (Australian born, lives and works in Oslo) is another artist who pulls off the synthesis of heavy metal ideas into his work, especially in his menacing ink drawings of lank-haired and made-up heavy metal boys.

Referring to heavy metal in art is a slippery proposition and one instance when the old adage "If you don't eat it, you can't shit it" holds great weight. Authenticity, the right to speak of something only if you're coming from a very particular standpoint with a particular voice, was a favorite weapon of hard line political correctness in the eighties and nineties. It tended to be a roadblock that prohibited dialogue and sanitized art. That being said, heavy metal is one lifestyle (punk rock is another) that shouldn't be engaged with if one doesn't have intimate experience with and abiding love for it. This is because the symbols of countercultural music are some of the most loaded and pure signs in human culture. When kids start to scribble band logos or doodle scenes inspired by their favorite bands, they are learning how to use symbols, those four black bars or a circle "A" can carry countless meanings, contexts, and variations. The doodling of metal and punk kids is as important in their development as when they learned the alphabet, and much more sophisticated. The lesson they learn is clear: pictures can be hugely provocative.

At the same time, punk and metal doodling is akin to automatic writing. Just as the brown paper cover on a teenager's *Algebra 2* textbook becomes covered in a mosaic of band names, symbols, drawings, and lyrics, so do the artists (who are these kids grown up) let their minds wander, throwing out cultural symbols haphazardly and looking for meaning afterwards (if at all). This is the crux between the gadfly artist and the specific references to metal in Sweeney's art, and it is where he finds his most successful works: the exemplification of Baudelaire's idea of the *flaneur,* Sweeney drifts and gathers ideas from his interactions with daily life. Since he personally tends to return like a prodigal son to metal and punk iconography, it bubbles into his drawings and paintings in an organic and exciting way.

A rallying cry amongst purists in the heavy metal music scene is "death to false metal." This motto, while reeking a bit too much of sober rules, is nonetheless helpful in defining what is metal orthodoxy. It keeps fans and bands constantly on the alert for suspect motivations and tourists. A similar instinct could be helpful in the art world. Categorical knowledge of the history of any subject isn't necessary to derive influence from it, but in the case of mining subcultures for ideas, it just may approach prerequisite to at least be a *flaneur* about it—to have it naturally cross the radar of your everyday life and to not be a butterfly collector for the academy.

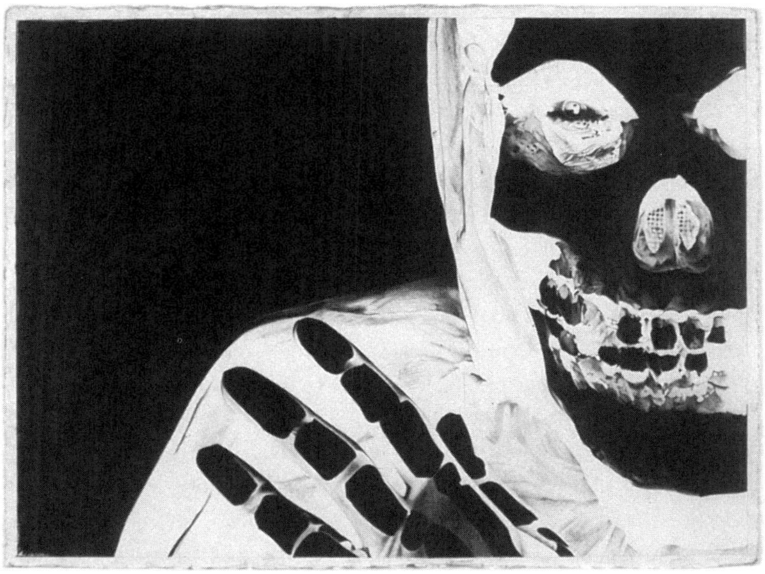

BANKS VIOLETTE, MISFITS (X-RAY), 2002, graphite on paper, 23 x 30" / Graphit auf Papier, 58,4 x 76,2 cm. (PHOTO: BRENDAN MAJEWSKI/TEAM GALLERY)

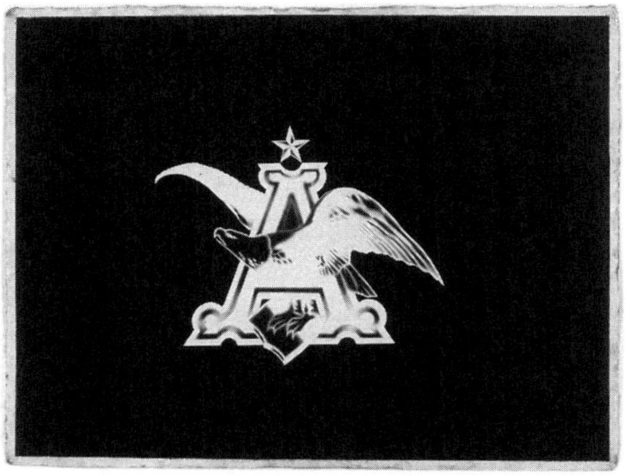

BANKS VIOLETTE, BUDWEISER (X-RAY), 2002,
graphite on paper, 23 x 30" / Graphit auf Papier, 58,4 x 76,2 cm.

Das eine tun und das andere nicht lassen

SELBSTDARSTELLUNGSKUNST UND HEAVYMETAL-DANDYTUM

JESSE PEARSON

Auf Spencer Sweeneys Zeichnung UNTITLED (2002) tollen drei nackte männliche Gestalten in einem winterlichen Wald herum. Die erste, stahlblau und mit Engelsflügeln, hat Analverkehr mit der zweiten, die von grüner Hautfarbe ist und vier Hoden, zwei Penisse, weibliche Brüste, hochhackige rote Pumps sowie eine königliche Mähne samt Bart aufweist. Die dritte, nur von hinten sichtbare Figur trägt eine Kochmütze und wedelt rätselhafterweise mit einem Pfannenheber herum. Hinter dem fickenden Engel liegt eine weggeworfene, wohl eben geleerte Schnapsflasche. Und nicht zu vergessen: Der gefickte König macht das *Peace*-Zeichen, als wolle er sagen: «Alles in Butter – ich hab meinen Spass.»

Auf den ersten Blick scheint dies das Produkt eines perversen (wenn auch frühreifen) Halbwüchsigen zu sein. Der sexuelle Akt und die Genitalien sind jedoch mit grosser Sorgfalt und beachtlichem Können in all ihren Einzelheiten wiedergegeben. Dieses Ausspucken unterbewusster Fixierungen in Verbindung mit seltsamen Details, die einfach zu grotesk sind, um ganz und gar unterbewusst zu sein, spricht Bände über Sweeneys Vorgehensweise. Er ist einer der ganz wenigen heutigen jungen Künstler, die einen Standpunkt einnehmen, der ihnen erlaubt, gleichzeitig zu wissen, nicht zu wissen und vorzugeben nicht zu wissen, woher ihre Ideen kommen.

Sweeneys Werk zeichnet sich durch eine tüchtige Portion Eigensinn und Verweigerung aus – so ist es für ihn ein sehr wichtiger Anreiz, «das Publikum und mich selbst zu frustrieren». Auch das erinnert an die Jugend – als jede Rebellion, auch wenn sie nicht wirklich durchdacht war, *a priori* als gute Idee galt. Doch Sweeney ist erwachsen. Und was die Sexualakte betrifft, die er in seinen Arbeiten mit geradezu diebischer Freude darstellt, so ist es ihm völlig freigestellt, all diese Dinge nach Belieben in die Tat umzusetzen, was er jedoch kaum tut. Denn Analverkehr, der nicht auf dem Papier, sondern jenseits des gezeichneten Bildes stattfindet, ist doch noch einmal etwas ganz anderes. Spencer findet es offensichtlich interessanter, den Akt auf einem Blatt Papier darzustellen und uns zu zeigen, als die Sache selbst durchzuexerzieren.

Auch dank dieser Haltung reiht sich Spencer in eine Tradition von Künstlerpersönlichkeiten ein, die heutzutage leider etwas auf der Strecke bleiben. Spencer verkörpert den draufgängerischen Dilettanten, den Dandy, allerdings der heutigen Zeit angepasst, in der Heavymetal- und Penissymbole runtergehen wie warme Milch, und in der man als mutmasslicher Sodomist gewöhnlich nicht im Gefängnis landet (wie noch Oscar Wilde). Sweeneys Werke (in letzter Zeit vor allem Bilder und Zeichnungen, zu Anfang seiner Karriere aber auch Videos, Installationen und Performance) weiss man erst richtig zu schätzen, wenn man die Person Sweeney etwas kennt. Seine Kunst und deren Rezeption finden weder über die Retina noch im Gehirn statt, sondern an einem experimentellen und seltsam menschlichen Ort. Sweeney kennen heisst Sweeney lieben.

Ob es gut ist oder nicht, für Künstler, die einen bestimmten Bekanntheitsgrad erreicht haben, gelten andere moralische Massstäbe. Ein extremes Beispiel hierfür ist Modigliani, der einst eine Freundin aus dem Fenster warf und dann der Polizei, die ihn abführen wollte, erklärte: «He, was soll das, ich bin Künstler. Ich hab andere Moralvorstellungen als ihr.» Daneben gibt es noch die unter Drogeneinfluss zustande gekommene «Ich-Ärmster»-Haltung eines Jean-Michel Basquiat. Am anderen Ende dieses Spektrums stehen jene Künstler, die es sich erlauben können, unerträglich langweilig und akademisch zu sein. Als Beispiel aus der jüngeren Vergangenheit fallen mir dazu die Neo-Geo-Maler ein. Manche dieser Künstler verleideten einem an sich gute geometrische Bilder, nur weil sie sich in endlosen kulturtheoretischen Erörterungen ergingen, die in den 80er Jahren gerade *en vogue* waren, und mit Baudrillard und Foucault ebenso aggressiv um sich schlugen, wie ihre malenden Vorfahren im Suff mit den Fäusten.

Die Tradition der Künstlerpersönlichkeit, die Spencer Sweeney verkörpert, ist ungleich viel amüsanter, geselliger und erotischer als all dies. Die wahren Künstlerdandys der letzten dreissig Jahre sind die Rockstars, deren ganzes Leben Kunst ist. Als Sweeneys Vorläufer kommen deshalb eher Marc Bolan, ein temperamentvoller, in Seide gehüllter Kobold, oder David Bowie in Frage als jene Künstler, welche im Übergang zu Konzeptkunst und Minimalismus die Post-Pop-Art erfanden. Verfolgt man diese Linie weiter zurück, stösst man auf Baudelaire, der im Dandy und Flaneur den Helden der modernen Welt erblickte, und auf Tristan Tzara (nach der Gründung der Dadabewegung und bevor er sich schändlicherweise hinter dem Surrealismus und der lyrischen Poesie verschanzte). Baudelaires Begeisterung für die Stadt und die Populärkultur – dass sie nämlich etwas sei, dem wir uns hingeben sollten, um uns unsere Kicks darin nach Belieben und ganz demokratisch zu holen – finden wir weitgehend bei der Art von Persönlichkeit wieder, die Sweeney im Alltag und in seiner Kunst zur Schau trägt, wobei er ein Zeichenalphabet verwendet, das sehr privat und schwer zu entschlüsseln ist, obwohl er – vom Eiffelturm bis zum Totenschädel — auf Elemente zurückgreift, die wir alle kennen. Dieser Künstlertypus versteht sich vor allem darauf, er selbst zu sein, und das heisst auch, in die Welt hinauszugehen, mit den Leuten zu reden, die Dinge genau anzuschauen, Zeichnungen und Bilder zu machen, in einem Restaurant zu essen und so weiter. Wie ein Rockstar, der offensichtlich nie frei hat, ist e r s e l b s t seine Kunst: er, der Dilettant, der Erlebnishungrige, der menschliche Radar.

Aber wo in der heutigen Kunstszene fände sich ein Mitstreiter im Zeichen der Persönlichkeit? Mir fällt buchstäblich keiner ein. Maurizio Cattelan trägt zwar immer ein gut geschnittenes Jackett, aber er ist eben ein Italiener, kein Dandy. Toland Grinnell sähe mit Krawatte gut aus, aber ich hab ihn noch nie eine tragen sehen. Roe Ethridge beherrscht die Studenten-Rolle zwar perfekt, aber er ist nicht mehr der Erzähler, der er einmal war, und ist schlicht zu nett für den Typus von Nervensäge, von dem hier die Rede ist.

Will man Sweeneys nächste lebende Verwandte in Sachen Sozialverhalten ausfindig machen, muss man die akademischen Vorstellungen über die Kunst und die Kunstszene etwas weiter fassen. Die Kreativen, die seiner Persönlichkeit am nächsten kommen, sind anscheinend weder Maler noch Photographen. Die Punkrock-/Rap-Band A.R.E Weapons (die früher der Performancekunst näher standen und Ende der 90er Jahre und um die Jahrtausendwende in Galerien wie Pat Hearn

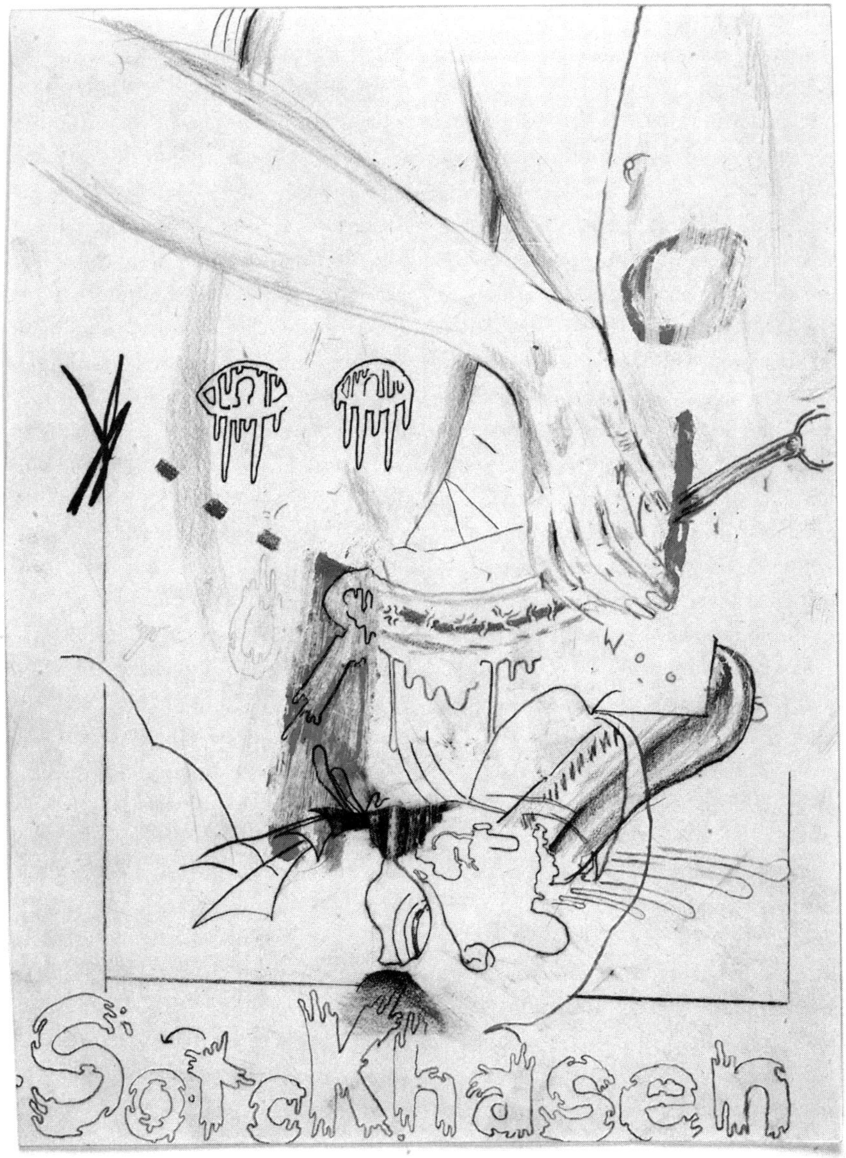

SPENCER SWEENEY, SOTCKHASEN, 2002, ink and colored pencil on paper, 10 x 7" / Tinte und Farbstift auf Papier, 25,4 x 17,8 cm. (PHOTO: GBE [MODERN], NEW YORK)

und Gavin Brown's Enterprise auftraten) kommt Sweeney, was den Stil und die Schubkraft ihrer Auftritte betrifft, schon näher. Während ihres Aufenthalts in New York hat sich ihre Ästhetik, von der dunkleren Seite des *Indie* her kommend über einen vulgären Schnurrbartstil schliesslich zur jetzigen, eindeutig bestklingenden Version entwickelt, die irgendwo zwischen *Teenage Metal Head* und *Top 40 Hip Hop* anzusiedeln ist. Dabei haben sie jedoch immer ein Künstlerimage gepflegt, das dem Sweeneys gleicht und sich am ehesten mit anzüglicher Schnoddrigkeit umschreiben liesse – nicht unähnlich dem Zynismus des klassischen Boulevardiers, der sich die menschliche Wärme irgendwie bewahrt hat. Zur selben Gattung der dandyhaften Macher gehört auch die supercoole Modedesigner-Viererbande As Four. Geschlechtsunabhängig sehen diese vier Individuen alle aus wie ein auf Zigeuner getrimmter Stevie Nicks. Sie leben zusammen, schlafen auch, so raunt man, alle in einem Bett, und ihre öffentlichen Auftritte sind eine wahre Augenweide, denn sie gehören zum Exzentrischsten, was die Stadt zu bieten hat. Es erfordert schon eine Menge Mumm, Geschmack und kunstvolle Unerschrockenheit, in einer solchen Aufmachung das Haus zu verlassen. Wie die Künstlerpersönlichkeit Sweeney stehen sie auf der Bühne, sobald sie die Augen aufschlagen. Ihr Leben ist ein einziger Performance-Akt rund um die Uhr.

Tristan Tzara mit seinen Manifesten, die sowohl von seinem gesellschaftlichen Credo als auch von bombastischem Nihilismus zeugen, fungiert als eine Art mürrischer Urgrosspapa der Performancegruppe Actress, in der Sweeney einst die Rolle des Alibi-Boys innehatte. Actress warf in den späten 90er und den ersten Jahren des neuen Jahrtausends einen wilden, frustrierenden Schatten auf die Kunstszene von *Downtown*-Manhattan. Sie waren bekannt für ihre aggressiv zickige Art und ihre internen Streitereien bei Interviews, aber auch für ihre aufregenden und erschütternden Auftritte. Einmal schlugen sich die Bandmitglieder leere Leinwände gegen die Köpfe und liessen dabei mit Theaterblut gefüllte Beutel platzen, bis sie sich in blutüberströmte Monster verwandelt hatten (die an Heavymetal-Keilereien erinnerten, aber dazu später mehr). In einer anderen Performance liess Sweeney seinen Freund, den japanischen Künstler Taka Hiro Imamura, in gebrochenem Englisch den Stones-Song «Salt of the Earth» singen und begleitete ihn auf der Gitarre. Es sieht ganz danach aus, dass Actress mit ihrer giftigen Boshaftigkeit Sweeney den letzten Schliff in Sachen Imagepflege gegeben haben. Vielleicht waren sie ihm auch eine Warnung vor zu viel Negativität, denn inzwischen ist er ganz und gar in die Rolle des Maler-DJ-Profis Spencer geschlüpft, der immer gut drauf und überall dabei ist. Das eine tun und das andere nicht lassen.

Als Amateur tritt ein Künstler wie Spencer durchaus auch mal als Fan von etwas auf, was ihn begeistert. So engagiert sich Spencer beispielsweise so erfolgreich wie kaum ein Künstler für Heavymetal und Punk, indem er in seiner Kunst Motive verwendet, die für diese Musikgenres von zentraler Bedeutung sind. Metal wurde nämlich von diversen Künstlern mit sehr unterschiedlichem Erfolg abgegrast. Am unteren Ende der Heavymetal-als-Rohstoff-für-Kunst-Skala steht Matthew Barneys Anwendungsversuch, der einen schalen Geruch von Anthropologie verbreitet. Am oberen Ende der Skala steht Harmony Korines Verwendung von Black Metal für den Soundtrack von *Gummo.* Auch andere Künstler haben Teile des Metal-Vokabulars – eine einzigartige Mischung aus altnordischen und mittelenglischen Elementen plus etwas Satanismus für Anfänger – erfolgreich in ihr Werk integriert. Besonders geschickt im Umgang mit musikalischen Metal-Symbolen erweist sich Banks Violette, eine amerikanische Künstlerin, die in New York lebt und arbeitet – ein Hauch dämonischer Krieger hier, eine Spur weisses Pentagramm da. Auch dem Künstler Bjarne Melgaard (ein Australier, der in Oslo lebt und arbeitet) gelingt es, Heavymetal-Ideen in sein Werk zu integrieren, vor allem in seinen Furcht einflössenden Tuschzeichnungen langhaariger Heavymetal-Typen in voller Kriegsbemalung.

Sich auf Heavymetal zu beziehen ist eine heikle Sache, und der alte Spruch «Wenn mans nicht isst, kann mans nicht scheissen» ist in diesem Zusammenhang besonders aufschlussreich. Authentizität – in dem Sinn, dass man von einer Sache nur sprechen darf, wenn man einen bestimmten Hintergrund hat und wirklich etwas dazu sagen kann – war in den 80er und 90er Jahren eine beliebte Waffe der Verfechter der *political correctness.* Der Begriff tendierte dahin, jeden Dialog und die reine Kunst sowieso von vornherein auszuschliessen. So viel dazu. Nun ist Heavymetal allerdings ein Lebensstil (Punk Rock wäre ein anderer), von dem man besser die Finger lässt, wenn man nicht wirklich damit vertraut ist und ihn über alles liebt.

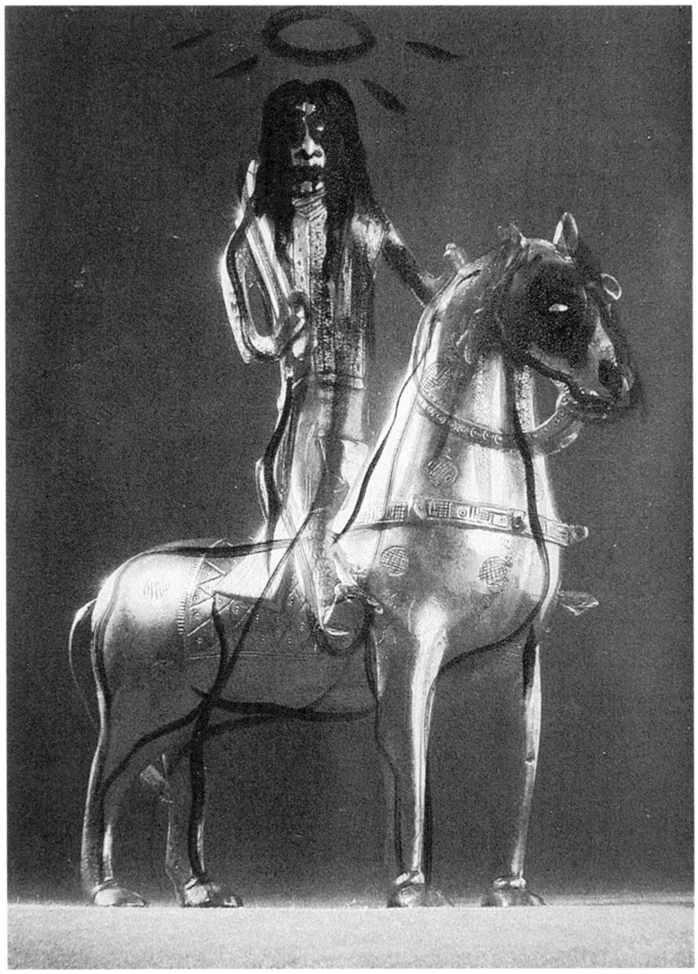

BJARNE MELGAARD, UNTITLED, 2001, oil on digital print on canvas, 27 9/16 x 19 11/16" / Öl auf Digitaldruck auf Leinwand, 70 x 50 cm. (PHOTO: GALERIE KRINZINGER, WIEN)

Denn die Symbole der alternativen Musikszene gehören zu den bedeutungsträchtigsten und reinsten Zeichen unserer Kultur. Wenn Kinder anfangen Band-Logos zu kritzeln oder von ihren Lieblingsbands inspirierte Szenen zu zeichnen, so lernen sie zugleich mit Symbolen umzugehen. Die vier schwarzen Balken oder das A im Kreis können unendlich viele Bedeutungen, Kontexte und Variationen beinhalten. Die Kritzeleien der Metal- und Punk-Kids sind für ihre Entwicklung ebenso wichtig wie das Lernen des Alphabets, nur weitaus komplexer. Die Lektion, die sie lernen, könnte klarer und deutlicher nicht sein: Bilder sind äusserst wirkungsvoll.

Gleichzeitig sind die Punk- und Metal-Zeichen mit dem automatischen Schreiben verwandt. Wie Teenager die braunen Papierumschläge ihrer Algebrabücher mit einem Mosaik aus Namen, Symbolen, Zeichnungen und Texten ihrer Lieblingsbands verzieren, lassen auch Künstler (dieselben Kinder, wenn sie erwachsen sind) ihre Gedanken schweifen und produzieren auf gut Glück kulturelle Symbole, für deren Bedeutung sie sich erst nachträglich interessieren (wenn überhaupt). Und genau dies ist der springende Punkt der Kunst Sweeneys. Zwischen seinem provokativen Dandytum und den klaren Rückgriffen auf Heavymetal findet er, was den Erfolg seiner Arbeiten ausmacht: die Umsetzung von Baudelaires Konzept des Flaneurs. Sweeney lässt sich treiben und sammelt seine Ideen in der Auseinandersetzung mit dem Alltäglichen. Und da er persönlich dazu neigt, wie der verlorene Sohn immer wieder zur Zeichensprache von Metal und Punk zurückzukehren, fliesst diese auf ganz natürliche Art in seine Zeichnungen und Bilder ein und sorgt für Spannung.

«Tod dem falschen Metal» lautet der Kampfruf der Puristen in der Heavymetal-Szene. Auch wenn es vielleicht etwas gar nach sturer Reglementierung riecht, ist dieses Motto doch hilfreich, um den «reinen Metal» zu definieren. Und es lässt Fans und Bands ständig auf der Hut sein vor verdächtigen Beweggründen und blossem «Tourismus». Dieser Selbsterhaltungstrieb könnte auch der Kunstszene nicht schaden. Um von einer Bewegung gewisse Einflüsse zu übernehmen muss man nicht ihre ganze Geschichte kennen. Durchforstet man jedoch eine Subkultur nach neuen Ideen, so wäre es keine schlechte Voraussetzung, zumindest als Flaneur auch in sie einzutauchen – man sollte sich in seinem Alltag ganz natürlich davon ansprechen und berühren lassen und nicht im Dienst der Wissenschaft mit dem Schmetterlingsnetz hinter besonders ausgefallenen Exemplaren herjagen.

(Übersetzung: U. Goridis/W. Parker)

BANKS VIOLETTE, GONE (JOSEPH, FIORELLA, JACOB DELASHMEUTT, ROYCE CASEY), 2001–2002, oil on canvas, 76 x 204" / Öl auf Leinwand, 193 x 518 cm. (PHOTO: BRENDAN MAJEWSKI/TEAM GALLERY)

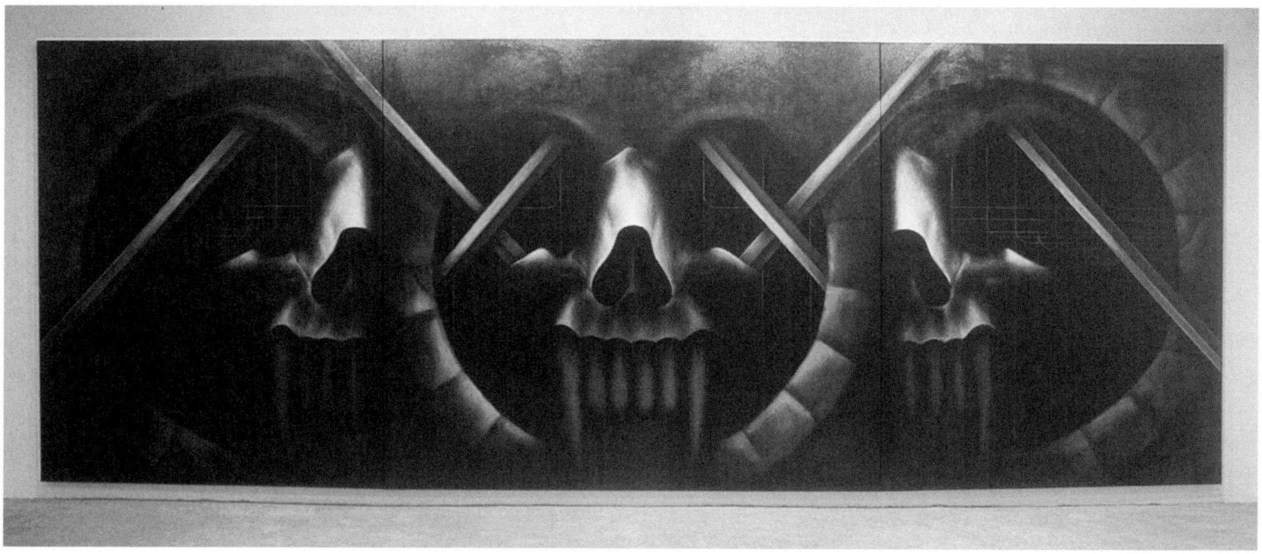

CUMULUS

Aus Europa

IN JEDER AUSGABE VON PARKETT PEILT EINE CUMULUS-WOLKE AUS AMERIKA UND EINE AUS EUROPA DIE INTERESSIERTEN KUNSTFREUNDE AN. SIE TRÄGT PERSÖNLICHE RÜCKBLICKE, BEURTEILUNGEN UND DENKWÜRDIGE BEGEGNUNGEN MIT SICH – ALS JEWEILS GANZ EIGENE DARSTELLUNG EINER BERUFSMÄSSIGEN AUSEINANDERSETZUNG.

IN DIESEM BAND ÄUSSERN SICH ERIC TRONCY, KRITIKER, CO-DIREKTOR DES CONSORTIUM DIJON UND CO-KURATOR DER BIENNALE LYON 2003, SOWIE «VICE»-REDAKTOR JESSE PEARSON AUS NEW YORK.

Eine Zukunft, die man gerne noch etwas hinauszögern möchte...

ERIC TRONCY

Seit rund zehn Jahren haben sich die Biennalen als quasi einzige Gelegenheit für Ausstellungen mit etwas weiterem Horizont durchgesetzt: Man kann nicht umhin festzustellen, dass ihre Vervielfachung Hand in Hand geht mit der zunehmenden Seltenheit grosser Ausstellungen, wie man sie noch bis in die 80er Jahre hinein kannte. Natürlich hat diese Veränderung zahlreiche Gründe, dazu gehört auch die Entwicklung des Kunstbereichs zu einer Industrie von Akteuren, die ihrerseits immer zahlreicher werden, und die Tatsache, dass der Avantgardegedanke selbst zunehmend eine kulturelle, touristische oder ereignisorientierte, aber selten künstlerische Alibifunktion hat. So rechtfertigte Lewis Biggs (der die Direktion der Tate Liverpool, die er seit 1990 innehatte, zugunsten der Direktion der Biennale Liverpool aufgab) die Einführung der Biennale von Liverpool 1999 – anlässlich eines internationalen Kolloquiums im Musée de Lyon im Jahr 2001[1] – ganz schön dreist, aber mit entwaffnender Aufrichtigkeit mit dem einfachen Satz: «Die Presse ist träge und die Kollegen haben keine Zeit.» In erster Linie sind die Biennalen touristische Ereignisse: Sie werden zur Hauptsache von den Gaststädten finanziert, um ihre kulturelle und wirtschaftliche Anziehungskraft aufzubessern. Einige unter ihnen, wie etwa Venedig, haben auch eine

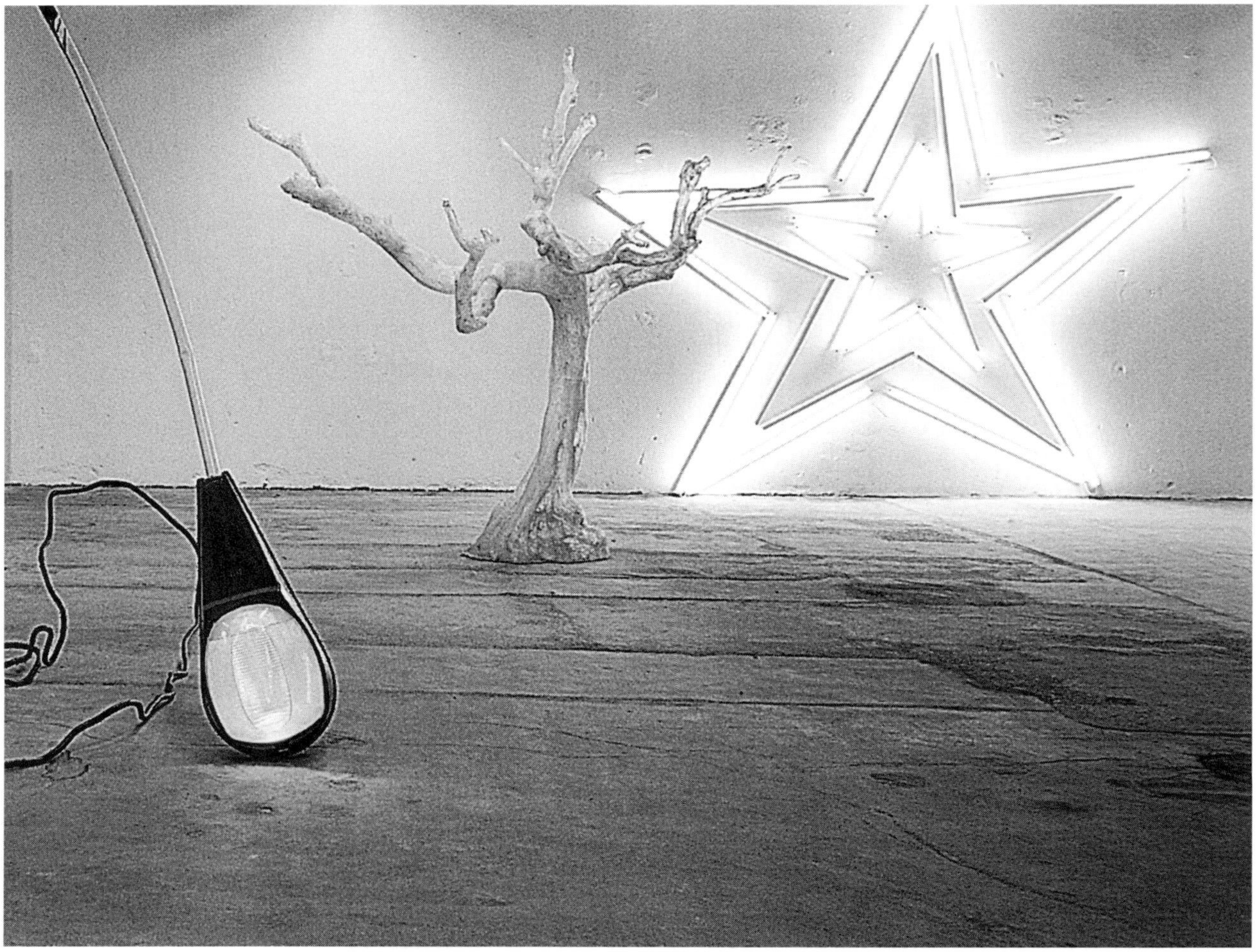

Biennale de Lyon 2003, exhibition view with works by /
Ausstellungsansicht mit Arbeiten von MARK HANDFORTH und UGO RONDINONE.

ganz alltägliche Funktion im protokollarisch vorgeschriebenen Länderwettstreit; andere schliesslich haben sich eher psychoanalytisch motivierte Aufgaben gestellt, im Rahmen eines komplexen Prozesses der Wiedergutmachung und des Abtragens der eingestandenen Schuld der reichen Länder in einer liberalen Weltwirtschaft. Aber wie dem auch sei, alle interessiert nur das Eine: die Besucherquote. Man registriert die Besucher und behandelt sie als ein Publikum, womit dem Verschwinden des Individuums in der Masse Vorschub geleistet wird – eine Zielsetzung, die man eigentlich in der Kunst nicht für möglich gehalten hätte. In einer Art Spiegelung dieser gewollten Aufblähung zur undifferenzierten Publikumsmasse hat sich wie von selbst auch ein inflationärer Anstieg der Zahl der Künstler zur gesichtslosen Masse ergeben. Und das in einem Mass, dass eine der ersten Fragen, die jedem Leiter einer Biennale unweigerlich gestellt wird, jene nach der Zahl der teilnehmenden Künstler ist, als wäre Quantität in diesem Zahlenspiel als unabdingbares Gegenstück auch ein Garant für die – bekanntlich immer fragliche – Qualität.

Dass die uns früher vertrauten, klar strukturierten Kunstströmungen (die in der Regel national geprägt waren: von den Konkreten in der Schweiz über die italienische Transavantgarde, die im

Wesentlichen amerikanische Neo-Geo-Bewegung, die deutschen Neoexpressionisten, die französische *Figuration libre,* bis hin zur *Young British Art,* deren nationaler Charakter sogar im Titel aufscheint) in den 90er Jahren verschwunden sind, hat natürlich zunehmend Ausstellungen vereitelt, die eine klare Ausrichtung hatten und entweder eine Gruppe von Künstlern vorstellten, von klaren theoretischen Voraussetzungen ausgingen, oder aber eine erkennbare Intention des Ausstellungsmachers zum Ausdruck brachten, wie etwa noch im Fall von «Westkunst», «Les Immatériaux», «A Forest of Signs», oder sogar noch «Les Magiciens de la Terre». Man kann nicht umhin festzustellen, dass die Durchsetzung des «jungen Künstlers» als sich selbst genügende Kategorie mittlerweile diese Leerstelle besetzt hat, um des weiteren festzustellen, dass es genau diese Kategorie ist, die, wenn nicht als Alibi, so doch als theoretische Grundlage für nicht wenige Biennalen herhalten musste.

Es gibt einen fundamentalen Unterschied zwischen einer Ausstellung (im Sinne der oben genannten Ausstellungen) und einer Biennale. Wenn die Ausstellung ein Text ist, den der Autor später publizieren möchte, so gleicht die Biennale eher der Rubrik in einer Zeitschrift, die jeden Monat oder jede Woche auf Teufel komm raus gefüllt werden muss. Die Ausstellung ist ein Text, die Biennale dagegen lediglich ein Vorwand. Während Donna Tartt oder Jeffrey Eugenides ohne weiteres zehn Jahre zwischen ihrem ersten und zweiten Roman verstreichen lassen können[2] und Blondie zwischen zwei Alben eine Pause von fünfzehn Jahren einlegen kann, kehrt die Biennale mit unerschütterlicher Regelmässigkeit wieder, aus dem einfachen Grund, dass sie vor jeder Idee und jeder künstlerischen Begründung einfach ein Format ist, das gefüllt werden muss. Denn, egal wie kulturell hochstehend ihre Zielsetzungen sein mögen, die Biennale oder Triennale muss unabhängig von der künstlerischen Realität der jeweiligen Epoche einfach stattfinden: Die Co-Kuratorin der letzten Manifesta, Stéphanie Moisdon-Trembley, hat schnell begriffen, dass sie bei ihrer «Goldsuche» in Europa in den Fussstapfen ihrer Vorgänger wandeln würde und dass nach drei Jahren nicht schon wieder wirklich neue künstlerische Positionen in Erscheinung treten können. Denn in der Logik der Biennalen hat die Ausschau nach dem Neuen rasch den Platz der theoretischen Argumentation eingenommen; der Kurator ist zum Entdecker geworden und die geographische Ausweitung seines Forschungsfeldes scheint seit «Les Magiciens de la Terre» ebenfalls als Fortschritt zu gelten.

War das Format erst einmal da, musste natürlich auch ein sinnvoller Inhalt dafür gefunden werden. Und – etwas vereinfacht gesagt – war man sich ohne bewusst darüber nachzudenken rasch einig, dass es die Aufgabe der Biennalen sei, sich mit der Gegenwart zu befassen. Das Fehlen theoretisch begründeter Bewegungen in der Kunst, gepaart mit den eher kulturellen denn künstlerischen Zielsetzungen des Formats «Biennale», haben die Organisatoren der Biennalen fatalerweise dazu verführt, zu denken, dass diese Gegenwart eher jene der Welt als die der Kunst sein müsse. Es ist weder besonders dreist noch originell, zu behaupten, dass die letzte «documenta» sich in erster Linie als quasi umfassendes Panorama des gegenwärtigen Elends dieser Welt präsentierte und weniger als Begegnung mit der Geschichte künstlerischer Formen in der Gegenwart.

All diese Überlegungen haben dazu geführt, dass wir die Biennale von Lyon 2003 nicht als Biennale angehen wollten, sondern als Ausstellung. Von Anfang an war uns klar, dass unser Ansprechpartner nicht das Publikum sein würde, sondern der Betrachter, und dass unser Interesse nicht der gegenwärtigen Welt gelten sollte, sondern der gegenwärtigen Kunst. Es war auch rasch klar, dass, wollten wir dieses Ziel in seiner ganzen Aktualität erfassen, die «jungen Künstler» gegenüber ihren älteren Kollegen nicht unbedingt bevorzugt würden – eines der perversen Resultate der Biennalen war nämlich, dass alle Künstler, deren Geburtsdatum die bedingungslose Hinwendung zur Gegenwart hätte in Zweifel ziehen können, von diesen Ausstellungsmöglichkeiten ausgeschlossen wurden. So erschien uns die Malerei von Christopher Wool ausserordentlich aktuell, desgleichen die Arbeiten

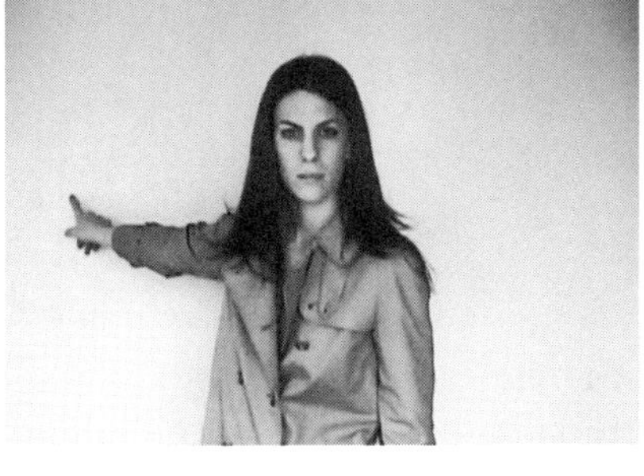

TRISHA DONNELLY, CANADIAN RAIN, 2002, video projection, Lyon 2003 / Videoprojektion.

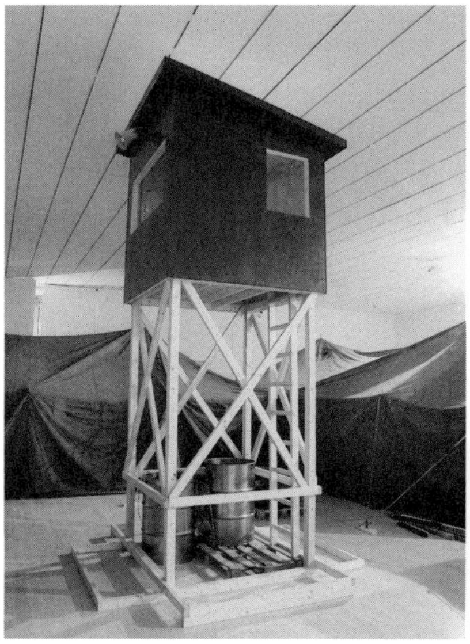

von Robert Grosvenor oder Gustav Metzger. Und statt die dritte Generation von Plagiatoren Larry Clarks zu präsentieren, schien es uns angebrachter, das Werk von Larry Clark selbst auf seine innovative Kraft hin zu untersuchen. So war es nur logisch und legitim, eher Yayoi Kusama als irgendjemand anderen einzuladen, um zu zeigen, wie Obsession zur Form wird – und nebenbei zu begreifen, dass das Formenuniversum dieser Künstler alle wesentlichen Elemente für die Entstehung der künstlerischen Sprachenvielfalt der aktuellen Kunst beinhaltet. Am Anfang dieser Ausstellung stand eine Grundüberzeugung: jene der Kontinuität der Kunst als einer eigenen Sprache. Wir vertrauten der sprachlichen Ausdruckskraft der Kunst noch immer und mehr denn je, in ihrer ganzen Eigenart und ohne jede Abstützung auf andere Ausdrucksformen. Vielleicht war es eines unserer Ziele, die Formen der Kunst ohne nostalgischen Rückgriff auf den Formalismus zu zeigen – selbst wenn paradoxerweise einige jüngere Künstler (Gary Webb, Dan Coombs, Mark Handforth) dazu tendieren, den Formalismus mit den Waffen unserer Zeit erneut ins Auge zu fassen. Schliesslich versteht es sich von selbst, dass wir diese Ausstellung ohne jede Einschränkung hinsichtlich nationaler Zugehörigkeit oder bezüglich Gattung, Stil oder Medien in Angriff nahmen: Was hat das schon mit Kunst zu tun?

Auch die Suche nach dem Neuen war kein Beweggrund für die Konzeption dieser Ausstellung: Wir haben uns keinerlei Reisen auferlegt, jede Art von Tourismus lag uns fern. Dass Katharina Fritsch uns einige von Postkarten inspirierte Werke vorlegte, hat uns gefreut, wirken doch so viele an Biennalen präsentierte Werke wie Postkarten ihrer Kuratoren.

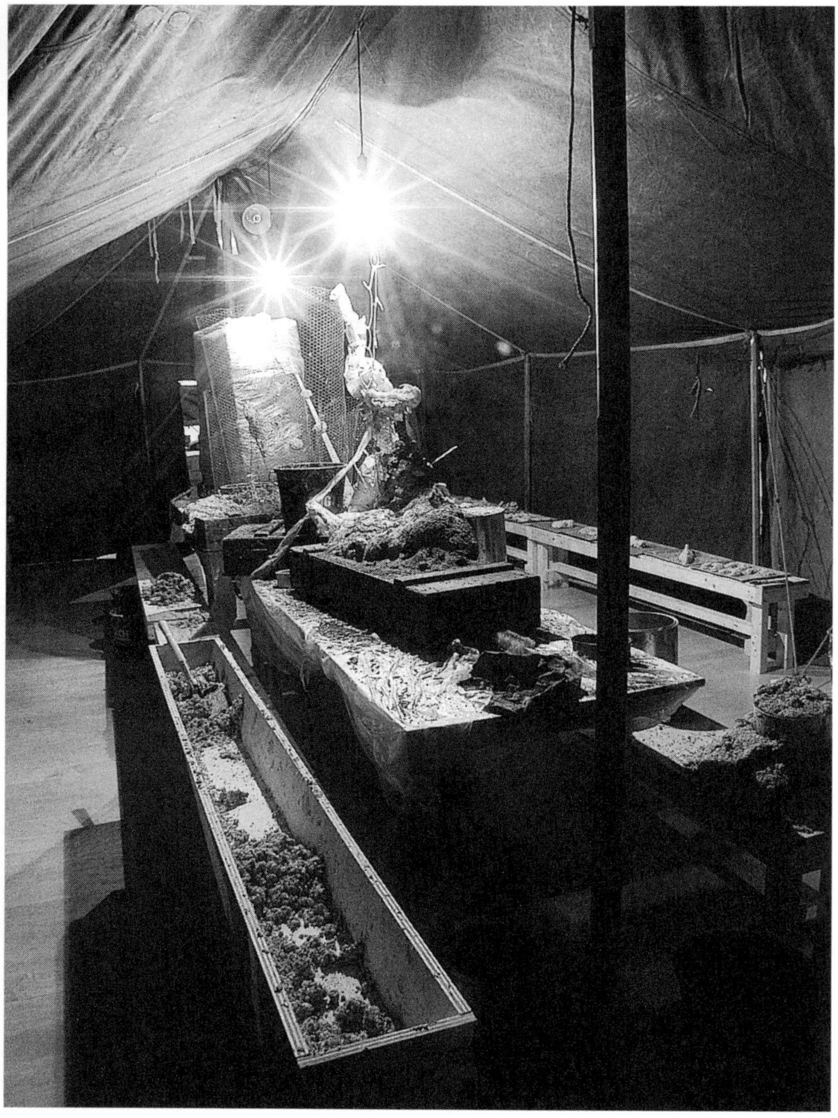

PAUL McCARTHY & MIKE KELLEY, SOD AND SODIE SOCK COMP. O.S.O., 1998, installation view, Biennale de Lyon 2003 / Installationsansicht.

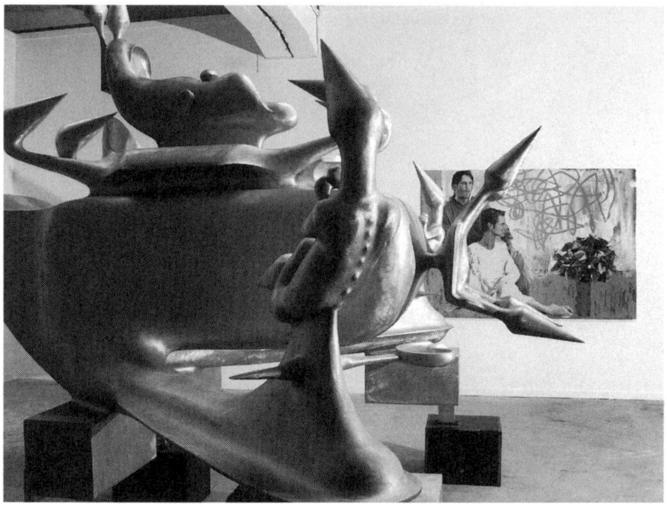

Exhibition view with works by / Ausstellungsansicht mit Werken von BRUNO GIRONCOLI und FRANZ WEST, Biennale de Lyon 2003.

Dagegen entstand diese Ausstellung auf der Basis unentwegter Diskussionen – an ihrem Anfang stand eher das Wort als die Bewegung. Schliesslich wurde der Präsentation der Werke in den Ausstellungsräumen ebenso viel Wichtigkeit beigemessen wie der Auswahl der Künstler, der «Teilnahmen» müsste man eher sagen, denn es schien uns für eine solche Ausstellung absolut nicht notwendig, irgendjemandem eine *Carte Blanche* zu erteilen. Dass SOD AND SODIE SOCK COMP O.S.O. (1998) von Paul McCarthy und Mike Kelley vor einigen Jahren bereits in der Wiener Sezession gezeigt wurde, hielt uns nicht davon ab, das aussergewöhnlich Treffsichere dieser Arbeit noch einmal aufzuzeigen.

Es wäre ideal gewesen, wenn wir der Ausstellung ihren Titel erst hätten geben können, als sie bereits stand, aber die Kommunikationsstrategie der Auftraggeber hat diese Absicht im Keim erstickt. Wir haben den Titel einem Film aus der Hollywood-Ära des französischen Cinéasten René Clair entlehnt: *C'est arrivé demain* (Es geschah morgen, 1944). Der Film (weit davon entfernt, ein Meisterwerk zu sein) schildert die Abenteuer eines Journalisten, der auf wunderbare Weise jeweils die morgige Zeitung schon am Abend zuvor erhält, und dies ausnützt, um seine Kollegen auf die Schippe zu nehmen und auszustechen – bis zu dem Tag, als er seine eigene Todesanzeige in der Zeitung liest. Während der Titel einerseits auf einen Zeitkollaps hindeutet, der durchaus einen Bezug zur Ausstellung selbst hat, schien uns dieses Szenario andrerseits auch erstaunlich genau auf den Kunstbetrieb im Allgemeinen und die Biennalen im Besonderen zuzutreffen. Ist es möglich, die vorbestimmte Zukunft zu verhindern? Diese Frage, die der Film sehr fein ausarbeitet, scheint sich uns auch im Hinblick auf den heutigen Kunstbetrieb zu stellen. Denn es ist unverkennbar, dass all die Abwege, die wir mittlerweile nur allzu gut kennen – vom Kunstobjekt zum Spekulationsobjekt, vom Gedanken zum Produkt, vom noch raffinierteren Gedanken zur noch raffinierteren Produktion, von der Kunst zur Kultur und zur Unterhaltung, von der Kritik zum Kommentar, vom Singulären zum Alltäglichen, vom Individuum zur Masse und so fort –, dass dies alles unser einstiges Tätigkeitsfeld, das inzwischen zur Industrie geworden ist, nur in eine Zukunft führen kann, die man gerne noch etwas hinauszögern möchte.

(Übersetzung aus dem Französischen: Suzanne Schmidt)

1) «L'exposition d'art contemporain», 17–18 September 2001, Musée d'art contemporain de Lyon. Organisiert von der Association des Conservateurs d'art contemporain (CAC40). Obwohl im Programm angekündigt, machten sich weder Saskia Bos noch Catherine David oder Kasper König die Mühe zu erscheinen.
2) Donna Tartt, *The Secret History* (1992) und *The Little Friend* (2002); Jeffrey Eugenides, *The Virgin Suicides* (1993) und *Middlesex* (2002).

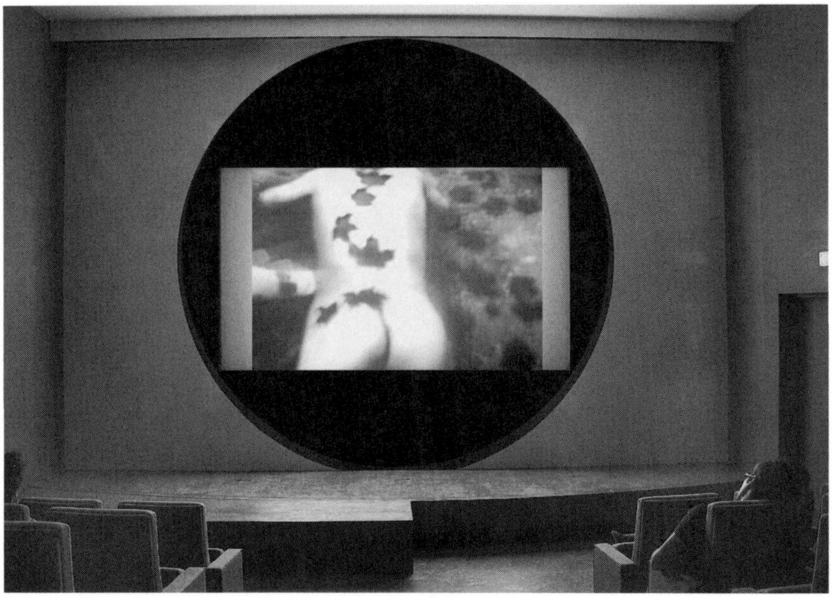

Reconstruction of Frederick Kiesler's movie screen (New York, 1929) for the presentation of artists' films at the Biennale de Lyon / Rekonstruktion der Kinoleinwand von Frederick Kiesler (New York, 1929) für die Biennale de Lyon.

A Future One Would Like to Be Able to Defer...

ERIC TRONCY

In the last decade, biennials have emerged by and large as the only occasions for large-scale exhibitions. Their proliferation, evidently, is in direct relation to the scarcity of wide-ranging exhibitions such as the ones one might have seen up until the eighties. There are, of course, many reasons for this proliferation: one might point out the transformation of the artistic field into an industry (whose actors are themselves in constant growth), as well as the evolution of the very notion of avant-garde into an alibi in the service of culture, of tourism, or of an event—but rarely of art. Thus, during an "international colloquium"[1] at the Museum of Contemporary Art in Lyon in 2001, Lewis Biggs (who left the position he had held since 1990 as director of the Tate Liverpool to become the director of the Liverpool Biennial) was able to justify the creation of the Liverpool Biennial in 1999 with this simple statement: "The press is lazy and our colleagues are busy." Above anything else, biennials are touristy events: they are financed in major part by cities for their own cultural and economic prestige. Some of them, like the Venice Biennale, also take on the role of an ordinary occurrence within the game of international protocol; others, finally, have assigned themselves missions of a psychoanalytic bent, inscribing themselves within a complex redemptive processing of the guilt of dominant countries in the global liberal economy. Whatever is said and done, the single objective of all biennials is their attendance level. Thus, they register and precipitate the mutation of the viewer into "the public," accelerating the disappearance of the individual within the mass—a goal one would have thought far from the usual concerns of art. In a kind of mirror structure, this desired inflation of the public's undifferentiated mass naturally brought about the inflation of an undifferentiated mass of artists—so much so that the first question typically put to the curator of a biennial has to do with the number of participating artists, q u a n t i t y being, in this case, the indispensable counterpart of a notoriously hypothetical q u a l i t y.

The disappearance, during the nineties, of structured artistic movements such as those that had existed until then (and which were essentially national in nature: Swiss Concrete Art, Italian Transavanguardia, mostly American Neo-Geo, German Neo-Expressionism, French *Figuration Libre*, and even the Young British Art, whose name itself proclaims its national spirit) has without a doubt slowed down the production of sweeping exhibitions based on the promotion of a group of artists, a theoretical notion or a personal agenda, as was the case for "Westkunst," "Les Immatériaux," "A Forest of Signs," or even "Les Magiciens de la Terre." The rise of the "young artist" as a category in itself has worked as a counterpoint, filling the gap, and indeed being used, if not as an alibi, at least as a theoretical basis, for a number of biennials.

There is a fundamental difference between an exhibition (in the sense of the exhibitions mentioned above) and a biennial. An exhibition is like a text that an author would then attempt to publish; a biennial, by contrast, is like those magazine columns that must come out each week or each month, no matter what. An exhibition is a text, a biennial is a pretext. Whereas Donna Tartt or Jeffrey Eugenides may let ten years go by between their first and second novels,[2] whereas Blondie can justify a fifteen-year break between two albums, the biennial returns, with an inexorable regularity, for the simple reason that it is not the artistic proposal of an author, but a format waiting to be filled. As culturally noble as its mission might be, the biennial or triennial must occur in absolute indifference to the reality of artistic projects at a given moment: as co-curator of "Manifesta 4," Stéphanie Moisdon-Trembley soon understood that prospecting in Europe meant walking on the well-trodden path of her predecessors, and that two years had not sufficed to allow new artistic proposals to emerge. Indeed, as the logic of past biennials has shown, prospecting can readily play the role of theoretical underpinning, transforming the curator into a kind of investigator whose extended field of inquiry, ever since "Les Magiciens de la Terre," seems to be taken as a sign of progress.

Once the format was there, it was necessary to invent an object for it. Schematically speaking, the object of a biennial was agreed, almost unconsciously, to be the purview of the present. The absence of any theorized artistic movement, along with the cultural (rather than artistic) ambitions of the biennial format, naturally led biennial

CLAUDE LEVEQUE, VALSTAR BARBIE, 2003, installation view, Biennale de Lyon 2003 / Installationsansicht.

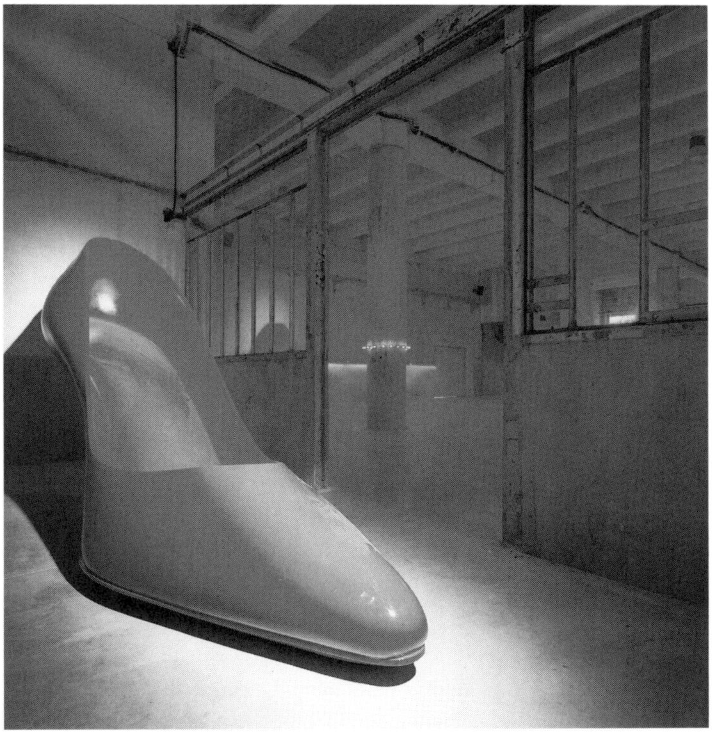

organizers to think that the present in question was that of the world, rather than that of art. It is neither impertinent nor original to state that "Documenta 11" presented itself, above anything else, as a quasi-exhaustive panorama of the world's woes at the present time, rather than as the convergence point of the present history of artistic forms.

These reflections led us to envisage the 2003 Lyon Biennial first and foremost as an exhibition and not as a biennial. It was clear to us from the start that our intended audience would be the viewer, not the public, and that the present of art, more than the present of the world, was our object. It soon became apparent as well that "young artists" were not necessarily better equipped than their elders to circumscribe this object in all its contemporaneity. One of the perverse effects of past biennials was to proscribe from their midst any artist whose birth date might have clouded the resolve to track down the present. Yet Christopher Wool's painting seemed extraordinarily contemporary to us; so did the work of Robert Grosvenor or Gustav Metzger. And instead of presenting the third generation of Larry Clark plagiarists, the work of Larry Clark seemed indeed the most apt to explore what it had itself invented. In the same line of thinking, it seemed more legitimate to invite Yayoi Kusama, rather than anyone else, once we set out to show how obsessions become form—and, on the whole, how the formal universes of these artists are essential elements in the development of the current diversity of artistic languages.

One conviction grounds the entire exhibition: that of the relevance of art as a language in itself. We still put faith in the enunciative power of art, now more than ever—an art taken in all its singularity, without its having to hang onto other forms of language. One of our ambitions is probably to show the forms of art without any nostalgia for formalism—even though, paradoxically, some younger artists (Gary Webb, Dan Coombs, Mark Handforth) seem to aspire to revisit formalism with the tools of our time. It goes without saying that we embarked on this exhibition without any constraints of nationality, genre, style, or medium: what does any of that have to do with art?

Prospecting was in no way a driving force: we didn't force ourselves to take trips, leaving tourism far from our concerns. We were even delighted by the fact that Katharina Fritsch presented a series of work based on postcards, particularly because so many works in biennials seem like postcards from their curators. Rather, the exhibition was built on the basis of countless conversations—speech, not motion, was its precursor. Finally, the display of works in the exhibition spaces was considered just as important as the choice of artists, or of "participations," to be more exact, for we deemed nothing in the structure of the exhibition to warrant that anyone be given carte blanche. The fact that SOD AND SODIE SOCK COMP O.S.O. (1998), by Paul McCarthy and Mike Kelley, was presented at the Vienna Secession a few years ago did not mean, in our opinion, that we had to abstain from showing the extraordinary relevance of this work today.

It would have been ideal to give the exhibition its title after it had been put together, but the public relations strategies of the biennial's patrons quickly defeated that ambition. We borrowed the title of the exhibition from a movie by the French filmmaker René Clair, from his Hollywood phase: *It Happened Tomorrow* (1944). The movie (which is far from a masterpiece) tells the story of a reporter who, every evening, miraculously receives the next day's newspaper, and is thus able to out-scoop all of his colleagues—until the day he sees the announcement of his own death on the obituary page. Not only does the title point to a temporal collapse, which is not without relevance for the exhibition itself, but the scenario also seemed remarkably pertinent to us, alluding as much to biennials in particular as to the art industry in general. "Is it possible to prevent the programmed future from happening?" the film asks, and the same question must be posed to the art industry today. For it is all too clear that the driftings we all know (without appearing to care)—of the art object toward the speculative object, of thought toward the product, of the sophistication of thought toward the sophistication of production, of art toward culture and entertainment, of criticism toward commentary, of singularity toward the ordinary, of the individual toward the mass—can only bring what was a field of activity and has become an industry toward a future one would like to be able to defer.

(Translated from the French by Anthony Allen)

1) "L'exposition d'art contemporain," 17–18 September, 2001, Museum of Contemporary Art, Lyon. Organized by the Association of Contemporary Art Curators (CAC40). Though mentioned on the program, neither Saskia Bos, nor Catherine David, nor Kasper König cared to attend.

2) Donna Tartt, *The Secret History* (1992) and *The Little Friend* (2002). Jeffrey Eugenides, *The Virgin Suicides* (1993) and *Middlesex* (2002).

SUNSET BOULEVARD

RODNEY GRAHAM'S RHEINMETALL/VICTORIA-8

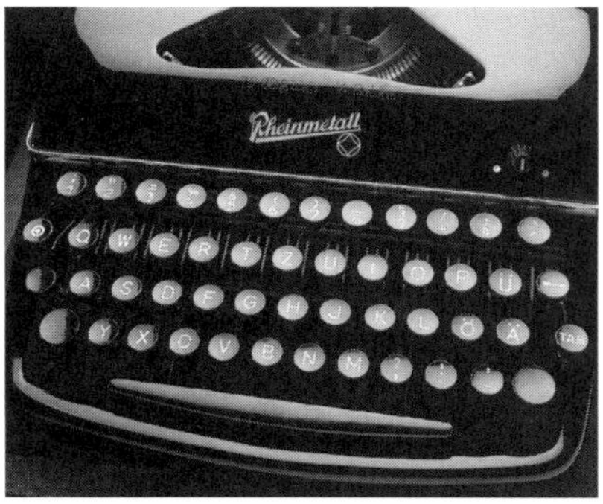

SERGIO RISALITI

Can one single object evoke an entire world, an entire civilization? That's the first question that comes to mind when facing one of Rodney Graham's most recent works, a film devoted exclusively to a typewriter made by Rheinmetall, Germany. The machine, found by the artist in a secondhand store in Vancouver, was produced between 1929 and 1935. It has obviously never been used although the owner's name, V. Balke, is engraved on it. We are mesmerized by it, as fascinated as we would be with an actor reciting a monologue on an otherwise empty stage. A Victoria-8 projector of the fifties also stands enthroned in the middle of the exhibition space.

Graham's 35-mm films are all short, formally perfect, sometimes ironic, and sometimes surreal. A decisive role is played by the paradoxical and bewildering twists that reveal inner mechanisms, drawing our attention to the set, that is to artificiality, or conversely, to the ambiguity and mysterious alchemy of the fiction. Graham's new installation possesses that same precise faculty for being both essential and poetic, both ironic and moving.

Given the complexity of the thoughts, references, and implications the film manages to conjure, it strikes the viewer as the very embodiment of art's evocative power. It is akin to pure poetry, in which Graham probably deliberately toys with the feelings of melancholy that he has elicited. His calculated direction and perfectly balanced doses of coldness and sentimentality appeal to us, although he never entirely reveals what it is that makes the

SERGIO RISALITI is a freelance curator in Florence.

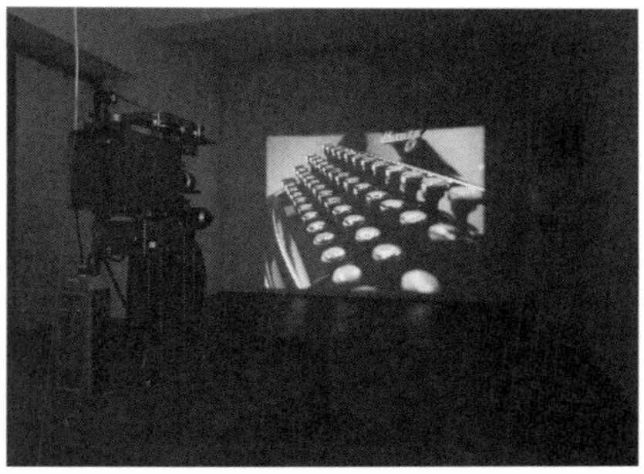

RODNEY GRAHAM, RHEINMETALL/VICTORIA-8, 2003, 35-mm-Farbfilmprojektion, Projektor, Endlosschlaufe, 10 Min. 50 Sek. Dauer, ohne Ton; Standaufnahme und Installationsansicht in der Galerie Hauser & Wirth, Zürich / 35-mm color-film projection, projector, loop of 10 mins. 50 secs., no sound; projection still and installation view. (PHOTOS: A. BURGER/HAUSER & WIRTH, ZURICH)

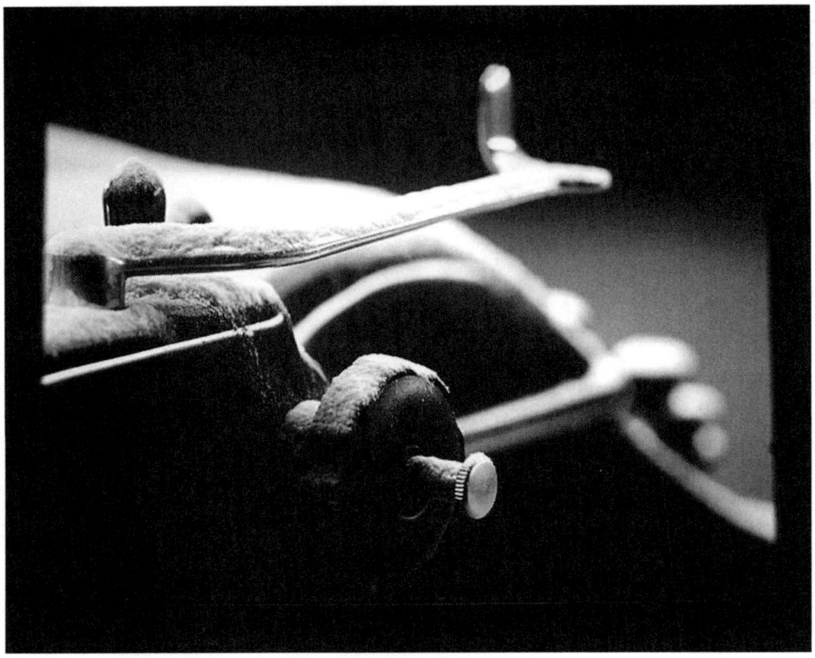

RODNEY GRAHAM, RHEINMETALL/VICTORIA-8, 2003,
35-mm color-film projection, projector, loop of 10 mins. 50 secs., no sound; projection still /
35-mm-Farbfilmprojektion, Projektor, Endlosschlaufe von 10 Min. 50 Sek. Dauer,
ohne Ton; Standaufnahme. (PHOTO: ICA VILLEURBANNE)

typewriter so seductive and lyrical or the projector so fascinating and sublime. When we watch the simple story, we seem to be watching the rise and fall of the universe or the flames and ashes of a love story.

Slowly the eye of the camera pans across the typewriter, caressing the surface as if it were naked skin: its forms, all the details, the keys and the hammers, even the reflections bouncing off the sparkling gold and silver logo.

Everything is geared toward celebrating the stylishness, the state-of-the-art elegance of the object. For a brief moment a ritual is enacted before our eyes: the bond between the projector—a valuable antique in its own right—and the typewriter as the fabulous, now obsolete invention that predated computers. And behind that glittering curtain of seduction and melancholy, we find film and literature, the gaze and history united in close proximity. *Ut pictura poesis,* as they call it in Latin. The enchanting beauty of the machine turns us into adoring admirers of the metal object upon which we gaze as we would upon a rose, an object of desire, or a fond memory. The typewriter evokes an age that braved the inaccessible frontiers of another world. Without showing them, the image suggests the white paper, the ink and the word, as well as their conquest of books and old libraries, of stories, novels, fairy tales, and adventures. The ceaseless rattling of the projector as the film reels off the eleven-minute loop inspires associations and generates an impression of time passing. Gradually, the atmosphere in the film changes dramatically. The picture of the typewriter magically mutates into a kind of landscape, for a blanket of snow slowly settles on top of it so that it appears to be aging until, finally, it is relegated to the past and to oblivion.

Wistfully we remember those *boules de neige,* showing scenes in little glass domes, which were buried under snow when you shook them. Whether the precipitation is snow or ashes or dust (Graham actually used flour), we are confronted with a disquieting slippage between the glistening, subtly erotic image and a vanitas representation. The poetry becomes a swan song. The eye of the projector is perhaps the eye of Klee's ANGELUS NOVUS (1920), who—at least as Walter Benjamin sees it—would like to gather and reassemble the wreckage of history, the rubble and the ruins, but is relentlessly driven back into the future by the wind.

(Translated from the German
by Catherine Schelbert)

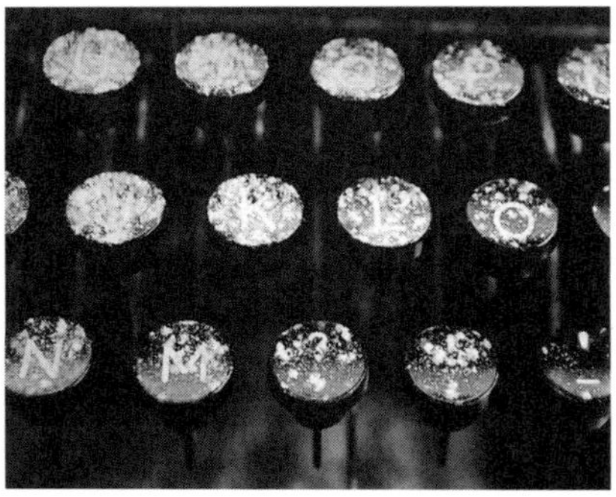

SUNSET BOULEVARD

RODNEY GRAHAMS RHEINMETALL/VICTORIA-8

SERGIO RISALITI

Kann ein einzelner Gegenstand eine ganze Welt evozieren, eine gesamte Zivilisation? Das ist die erste Frage, die sich vor einer der letzten Arbeiten Rodney Grahams stellt, einem Film, der einzig und allein einer Schreibmaschine der Marke Rheinmetall gewidmet ist. Der Künstler hat die Maschine, die zwischen 1929 und 1935 hergestellt und offensichtlich nie benutzt wurde, auf der jedoch der Besitzername V. Balke eingraviert ist, in einem Brockenhaus in Vancouver gefunden. Für einige Minuten bleiben wir fasziniert — wie vor einem Schauspieler, der einen Monolog auf leerer Bühne rezitiert – im Ausstellungsraum stehen, in dessen Mitte auch der Projektor Marke Victoria-8 aus den 50er Jahren thront.

Grahams 35-mm-Filme sind alle kurz, formal perfekt, manchmal ironisch, zuweilen surreal. Die entscheidende Rolle spielen jeweils paradoxe und verwirrende Wendungen, die einen inneren Mechanismus aufdecken, und das Set, also die Künstlichkeit, oder umgekehrt die Ambiguität und mysteriöse Alchemie der Fiktion hervorheben.

Auch diese neue Installation besitzt die präzise Qualität, ebenso essenziell wie poetisch zu sein, ebenso ironisch wie ergreifend.

Bedenkt man die Komplexität der Gedanken, Bezüge und Andeutungen, die der Film hervorzurufen vermag, so versichert er uns auch der evokativen Kraft der Kunst überhaupt. Er ist wie reine Dichtung und wahrscheinlich will Graham mit unseren Gefühlen, der in uns aufsteigenden Melancholie, spielen. Mit berechneter Regie und einer gerade richtigen Dosis Kälte und Sentimentalität reizt er uns, ohne gänzlich die Ursachen zu enthüllen, welche die Schreibmaschine so verführerisch und lyrisch, den Projektor so faszinie-

SERGIO RISALITI ist freier Kurator in Florenz.

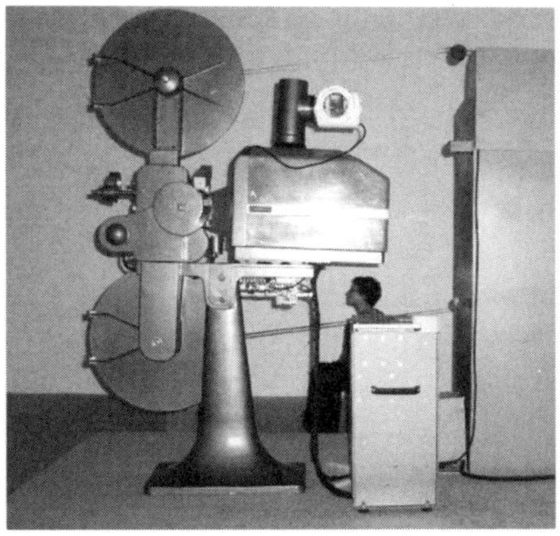

RODNEY GRAHAM, RHEINMETALL/VICTORIA-8, 2003, 35-mm color-film projection, projector, loop of 10 mins. 50 secs., no sound; projection still and view of the projector, Biennale de Lyon, 2003/ 35-mm-Farbfilmprojektion, Projektor, Endlosschlaufe, 10 Min. 50 Sek. Dauer, ohne Ton; Standaufnahme und Ansicht des Projektors. (PHOTOS: ICA VILLEURBANNE)

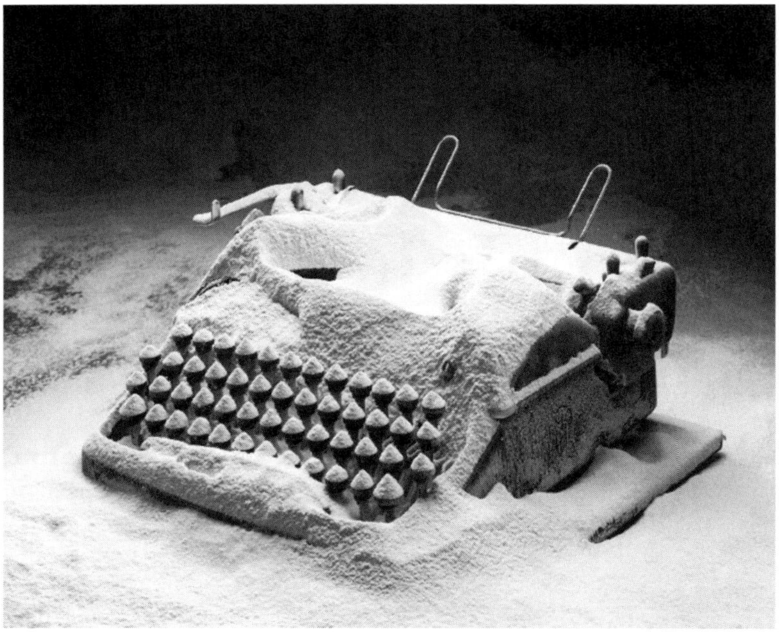

RODNEY GRAHAM,
RHEINMETALL/VICTORIA-8, 2003,
35-mm-Farbfilmprojektion, Projektor, Endlosschlaufe, 10 Min. 50 Sek. Dauer, ohne Ton, Standaufnahme. / 35-mm color-film projection, projector, loop of 10 mins. 50 secs., no sound; projection still.
(PHOTO: A. BURGER/HAUSER & WIRTH, ZURICH)

rend und sublim erscheinen lassen. Betrachten wir die schlichte Handlung, so ist es, als verfolgten wir Aufstieg und Fall einer Welt, Glanz und Asche einer Liebesgeschichte.

Langsam streift das Kameraauge über die Schreibmaschine, über ihre gesamte Oberfläche wie über nackte Haut: ihre Formen, alle Einzelheiten, Tasten und Hämmerchen werden untersucht, selbst das Logo mit seinen golden und silbern funkelnden Lichtreflexen.

Alles ist darauf angelegt, das Stilvolle des Objekts zu feiern, seine Eleganz und Modernität. Für einen Augenblick spielt sich vor unseren Augen ein Ritus ab: Die Verbindung von Projektor – auch bereits eine kostbare Antiquität – und Schreibmaschine, jener fabelhaften veralteten Erfindung aus der Vorzeit des Computers. Eigentlich geht es um die Vereinigung von Film und Literatur, von Blick und Geschichte, die sich hinter dem blitzenden Vorhang der Verführung und der Melancholie verbirgt. *Ut pictura poesis,* sagten die Lateiner. Die bezaubernde Schönheit der Maschine macht uns zu Verehrern eines metallenen Objekts, das wir wie eine Rose betrachten, wie ein Wunschobjekt, eine Erinnerung. Die Schreibmaschine evoziert eine Epoche, die unerreichbaren Grenzen einer anderen Welt. Ohne sie zu zeigen, suggeriert das Bild das weisse Blatt, die Tinte, das Wort und deren Ausbreitung in Büchern und alten Bibliotheken, Geschichten, Romanen, Märchen, Abenteuern. Das ununterbrochene Rattern des Projektors beim Abspulen des fast elf Minuten langen Loops regt zu Assoziationen an und vermittelt den Eindruck eines zeitlichen Ablaufs. Zusehends wird die Atmosphäre im Film eine ganz andere. Das Bild der Schreibmaschine verwandelt sich magisch in eine Art Landschaft, denn sie wird allmählich von einer Art Schneefall bedeckt, so dass sie zu altern scheint und langsam wie in die Vergangenheit, in die Vergessenheit gerückt wirkt.

Melancholisch erinnert man sich jener «Boules de neige», den kleinen Vitrinen mit Szenen, die sich in Schnee hüllen, wenn man sie schüttelt. Ob Schnee oder Asche oder Staub fällt (in Tat und Wahrheit ist es Mehl): Das glänzende, andeutungsweise erotische Bild verwandelt sich in eine *Vanitas*-Darstellung. Die Dichtung wird zum Schwanengesang. Und der Blick des Projektors ist vielleicht jener Blick des ANGELUS NOVUS (1920), des Engels von Klee, der sich – zumindest nach Walter Benjamins Interpretation – der Geschichte, den Trümmern und dem Zerschlagenen zuwendet und den ganzen Zauber wieder zusammenfügen möchte, jedoch vom Wind unerbittlich rückwärts in die Zukunft getrieben wird.

(Übersetzung aus dem Italienischen: Jacqueline Burckhardt)

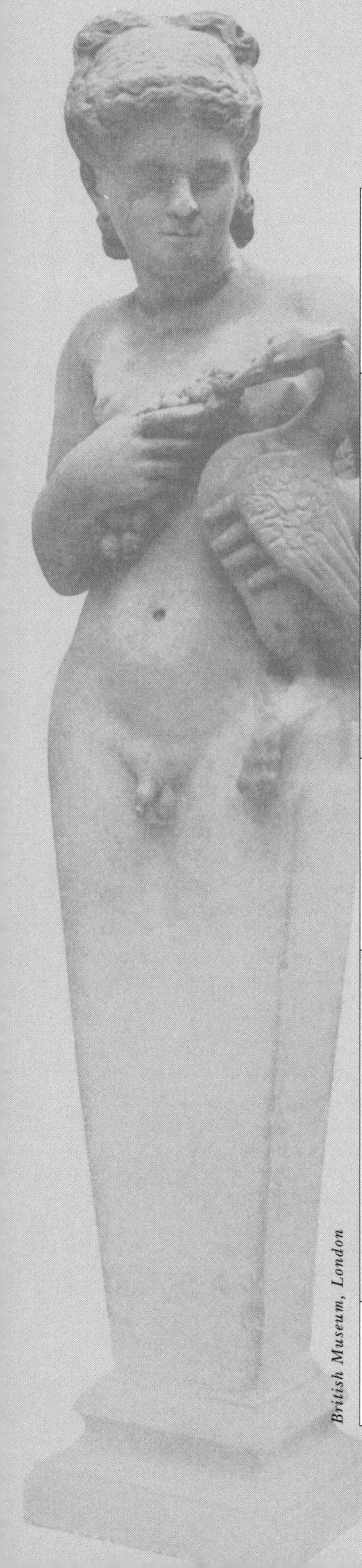
British Museum, London

Garderobe

'gär-,drōb

Literarische Weihen für Parkett!

Sagen Sie uns aus welchem Roman die folgende Passage stammt und gewinnen Sie ein Gratisabonnement unseres Jubiläumsjahrgangs (20 Jahre Parkett: Nr. 70–72/2004) – die ersten drei EinsenderInnen gewinnen!

«Da Wochenende war, versuchte ich, mich eher schlicht zu kleiden. Das fällt mir nicht leicht. Ich trug einen Kamelhaarrolli, einen Tweedblazer und Jeans. Und ein Paar handgefertigte Cordovan-Schuhe von Edward Green. Man nennt die Art auch Dundee. Sie wirken schick, bis man die Vibram-Sohle gesehen hat. Das Leder hat die doppelte Stärke. Der Dundee ist ein Schuh, der für Wanderungen übers Landgut bestimmt ist, für Krawattenträger, die durch den Dreck stapfen, und die Spaniels zotteln hinterher. Vier Monate hatte ich auf diese Schuhe warten müssen. Auf dem Schuhkarton steht: «Edward Green: Schuhmachermeister für die Wenigen.» Genau zu denen gehöre ich. Zu den Wenigen.
Ich holte Julie in einem gemieteten Mercedes ab, einem lärmenden Diesel. Sie hatte für die Fahrt ein paar Kassetten aufgenommen und Lesestoff mitgebracht: *The Guardian,* die zwei letzten Nummern von *Parkett.* Wir fuhren auf schmalen Alleen nach Nordosten.»

Parkett Enters Literary Hall of Fame!

Which novel contains the following passage? Be one of the first three to send us the correct answer and win a subscription to our three anniversary issues (20 years of Parkett, nos. 70–72/2004)!

"Since it was the weekend, I tried to dress down. It isn't easy for me. I wore a camel-hair turtleneck, tweed blazer, and jeans. And a pair of handmade cordovans by Edward Green. This particular style is called the Dundee. They look dressy until you notice the Vibram soles. The leather is of a double thickness. The Dundee is a shoe designed for touring the landed estates, for tromping through mud while wearing a tie, with your spaniels trailing behind. I had to wait four months for these shoes. On the shoebox it says: "Edward Green: Master Shoemakers to the Few." That's me exactly. The few.
I picked Julie up in a rented Mercedes, an unquiet diesel. She had made a bunch of tapes for the ride and had brought reading material: *The Guardian,* the last two issues of *Parkett.* We drove out the narrow, tree-lined roads to the northeast."

Send your postcard, fax, or e-mail to / Senden Sie die Lösung per Postkarte, Fax oder E-Mail an:
Parkett Publishers, Quellenstr. 27, CH-8001 Zurich, Fax ++41 1272 43 01
E-mail: s.schmidt@parkettart.com

Anzeigenbedingungen: Kauf eines Abonnements bzw. eines Geschenkabonnements bei Platzierung eines Inserates. / Advertising rates: Order of one (gift) subscription per ad.

COMPLETE YOUR PARKETT LIBRARY
VERVOLLSTÄNDIGEN SIE IHRE PARKETT-BIBLIOTHEK

OUT OF PRINT / VERGRIFFEN: **NO. 1** ENZO CUCCHI, **2** SIGMAR POLKE, **3** MARTIN DISLER, **4** MERET OPPENHEIM, **5** ERIC FISCHL, **6** JANNIS KOUNELLIS, **7** BRICE MARDEN, **8** MARKUS RAETZ, **9** FRANCESCO CLEMENTE, **10** BRUCE NAUMAN, **12** ANDY WARHOL, **13** REBECCA HORN, **16** ROBERT WILSON, **17** FISCHLI/WEISS, **19** JEFF KOONS, MARTIN KIPPENBERGER, **20** TIM ROLLINS&K.O.S., **22** CHRISTIAN BOLTANSKI, JEFF WALL, **25** KATHARINA FRITSCH, **26** GÜNTHER FÖRG, PHILIP TAAFFE, JAMES TURRELL, **27** LOUISE BOURGEOIS, ROBERT GOBER, **29** CINDY SHERMAN, JOHN BALDESSARI, **30** SIGMAR POLKE, **31** DAVID HAMMONS, MIKE KELLEY, **35** GERHARD RICHTER, **38** ROSS BLECKNER, MARLENE DUMAS, **45** MATTHEW BARNEY, SARAH LUCAS, ROMAN SIGNER

For out-of-print issues you can register your name and address with Parkett and you will be notified, if your issue(s) become(s) available on the secondary market / Für vergriffene Bände nimmt der Verlag gerne Ihren Suchauftrag entgegen und macht Ihnen bei allfälliger Verfügbarkeit im Handel ein Angebot.

COLLABORATIONS

CHRISTIAN MARCLAY
WILHELM SASNAL
GILLIAN WEARING

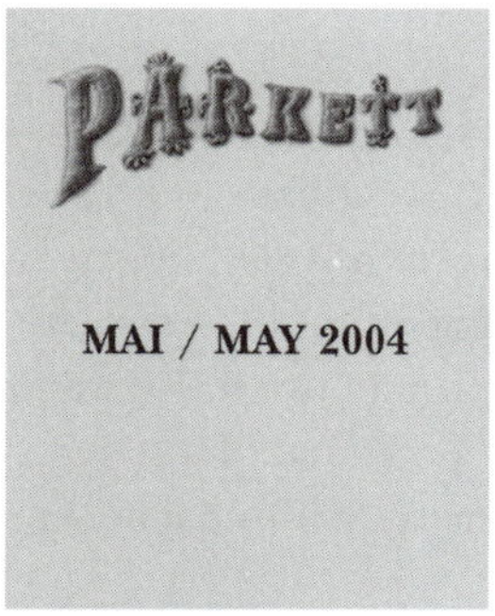

No. 70 - ISBN 3-907582-20-9

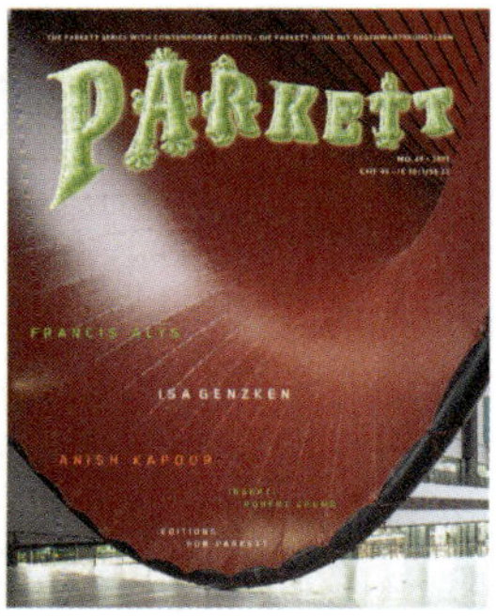

No. 69 - ISBN 3-907582-19-5

FRANCIS ALŸS
ISA GENZKEN
ANISH KAPOOR
SCOTT, ANTON, STORR, HEISER
LEE, KRAJEWSKI, BRYSON
FORSTER, WARNER
INSERT: **ROBERT CRUMB**
KAISER: **AMELIE VON WULFFEN**
COMER: **SWETLANA HEGER**
INQUIRY: CONSENSUS/KONSENS
CUMULUS AMERICA: J. PEARSON
CUMULUS EUROPE: E. TRONCY
BALKON: SERGIO RISALITI

FRANZ ACKERMANN
EIJA-LIISA AHTILA
DAN GRAHAM
FOGLE, DECTER, STANGE, ILES, ELFVING
KOCH, GUAGNINI/SCHNEIDER, MACDONALD
DI BARTOLOMEO, ROSENBERG MILLER
INSERT: **JONATHAN MONK**
D. KURJAKOVIC: **BOJAN SARCEVIC**
H. U. OBRIST: **BERNARD FRIZE**
G. JANSEN: **DIRK SKREBER**
LES INFOS: J. MURPHY
CUMULUS: C. RABINOWITZ, J. HOFFMANN
BALKON: HANS RUDOLF REUST

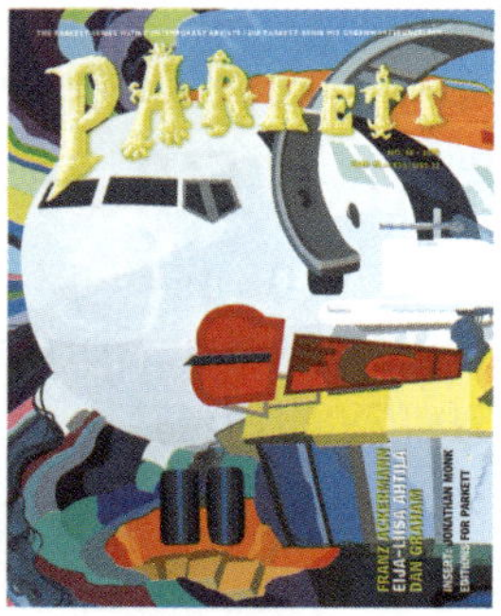

No. 68 - ISBN 3-907582-18-7

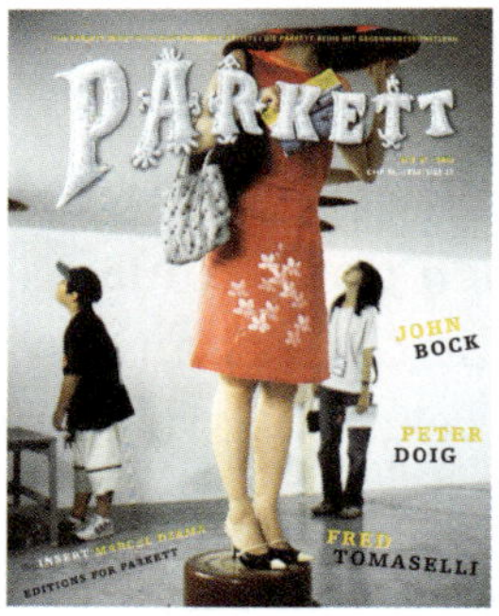

No. 67 - ISBN 3-907582-17-9

JOHN BOCK
PETER DOIG
FRED TOMASELLI
HOFFMANN, BIRNBAUM, AVGIKOS
BONAVENTURA, FUCHS, RUF
CAMERON, RONDEAU, PINCHBECK
INSERT: **MARCEL DZAMA**
T. SELVARATNAM: **SIMON STARLING**
S. OMLIN: **HANNE DARBOVEN**
VISCHER/HERZOG: SCHAULAGER BASEL
LES INFOS: H. BÖHME ON **WANG FU**
CUMULUS: FIRSTENBERG, KERSTING
BALKON: DANIELE MUSCIONICO

ANGELA BULLOCH
DANIEL BUREN
PIERRE HUYGHE
REBENTISCH, WILSON, PRINZHORN
RORIMER, GINGERAS, BUREN/HUYGHE
MILLAR, OBRIST, HOBBS
T. NICHOLS GOODEVE/G. BRUNO
E. DIMENDBERG: **ALLAN SEKULA**
LES INFOS: ROBERTO OHRT ON
MONICA BONVICINI
CUMULUS AMERICA: NATO THOMPSON
CUMULUS EUROPA: GREG HILTY

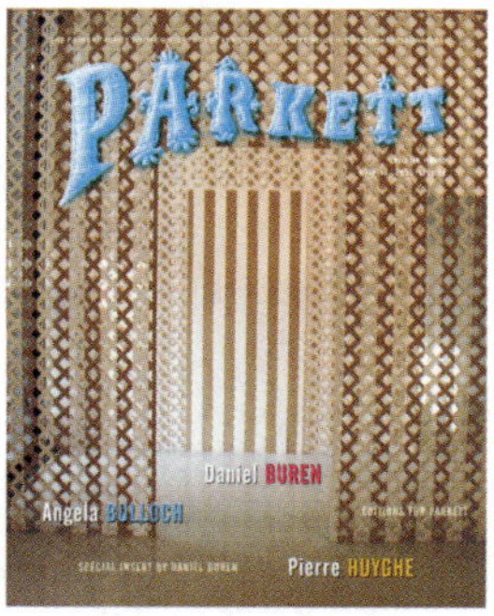

No. 66 - ISBN 3-907582-16-0

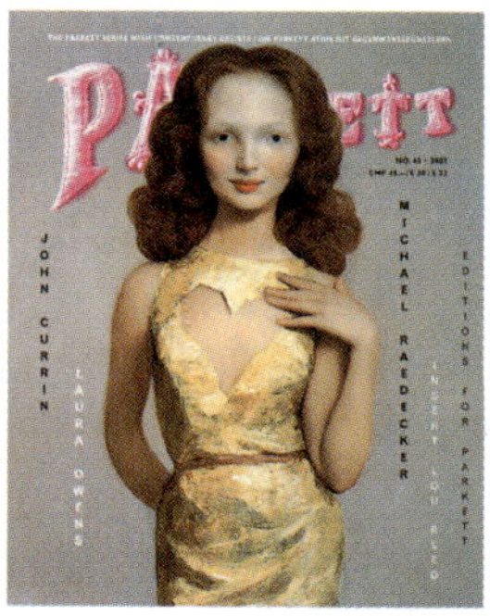

No. 65 - ISBN 3-907582-15-2

JOHN CURRIN
LAURA OWENS
MICHAEL RAEDECKER
SEWARD, VAN DE WALLE, BERG
FERGUSON, THOMSON, WEISSMAN
VERSCHAFFEL, MYERS, EGGERS
INSERT: **LOU REED**
KURT W. FORSTER: **JEFF WALL**
STORR: **DIETER ROTH & D. IANNONE**
K. BITTERLI: **HUBBARD/BIRCHLER**
LES INFOS: CHRISTINA VÉGH
CUMULUS: O. WESTPHALEN, T. HAHN
BALKON: SHEENA WAGSTAFF

OLAFUR ELIASSON
TOM FRIEDMAN
RODNEY GRAHAM
BLOM, MORGAN, CAMERON, MATSUI
WATERS/FRIEDMAN, COOKE, HALE
INSERT: **AMY SILLMAN**
VÉRONIQUE D'AUZAC:
XAVIER VEILHAN
INTERVIEW:
A.M. HOMES: **CHRIS VERENE**
HAKAN NILSSON: **ANNIKA LARSSON**
INQUIRY/UMFRAGE:
LEARNING FROM "DOCUMENTA"

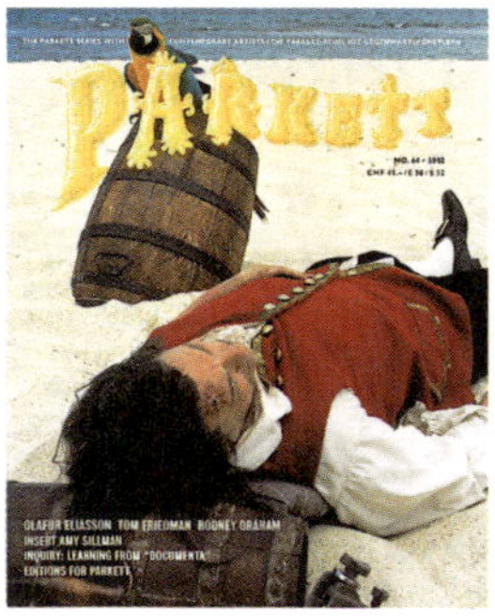

No. 64 - ISBN 3-907582-14-4

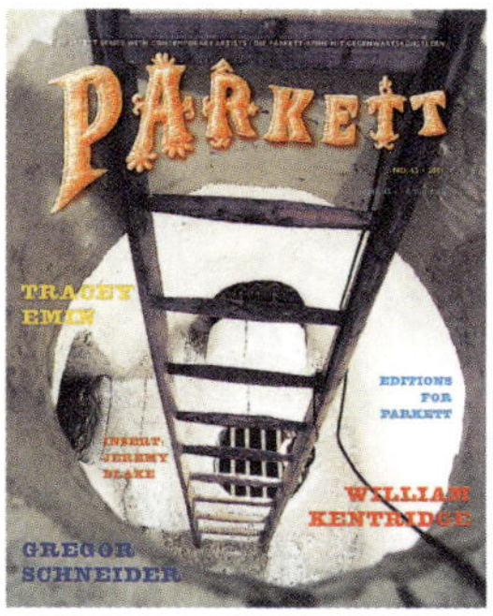

No. 63 - ISBN 3-907582-13-6

TRACEY EMIN
WILLIAM KENTRIDGE
GREGOR SCHNEIDER
BARBER, MUIR, PREECE
GUNNING, STEWART, GOLDBERG
PUVOGEL, LOOCK
INSERT: **JEREMY BLAKE**
CLAUDIA SPINELLI: **FABRICE GYGI**
RAINER FUCHS: **KATHARINA GROSSE**
ADRIAN DANNATT: **THE THREE**
CUMULUS: CHRISTIAN RATTEMEYER
DANIEL BIRNBAUM
BALKON: MICHAEL OPPITZ

JOHN WESLEY
TACITA DEAN
THOMAS DEMAND
MILLAR, CARABELL, SCHWARZ
NORDEN, KÖNIG/STOCKEBRAND
HAINLEY, SEARLE, RUBY, HEISER
INSERT: **G. STEINER & J. LENZLINGER**
PHILIP URSPRUNG: **ALLAN KAPROW**
RUSSELL FERGUSON: **GLEN WILSON**
EDWARD A. SCHEER: **MIKE PARR**
LES INFOS: DAVID GREENBERG
CUMULUS: G. CARMINE, S. DIETZ

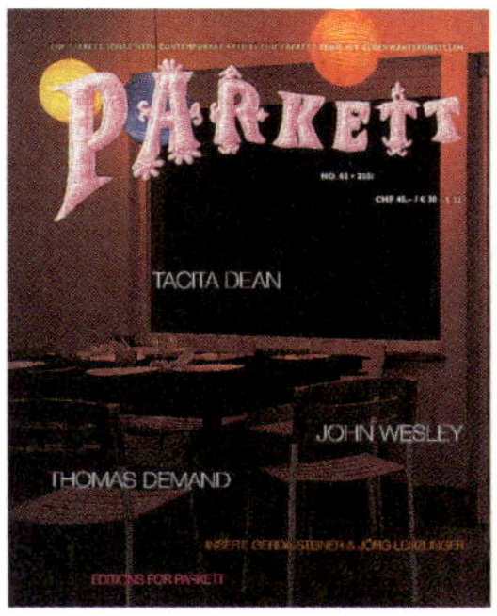

No. 62 - ISBN 3-907582-12-8

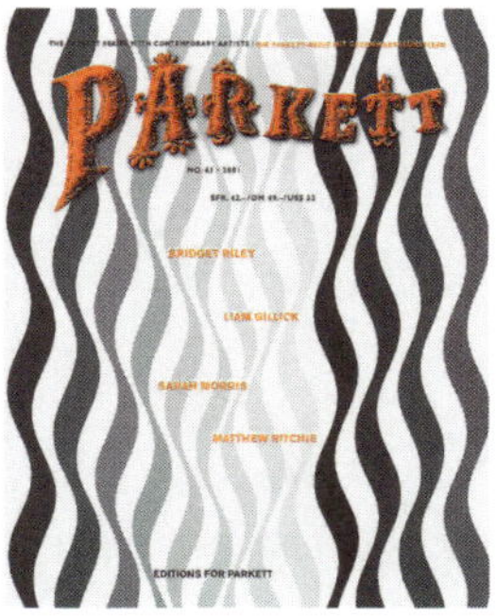

No. 61 - ISBN 3-907582-11-X

BRIDGET RILEY
LIAM GILLICK
SARAH MORRIS
MATTHEW RITCHIE
KUDIELKA, HICKEY
GILLICK, STEMMRICH, WOLLEN
NICHOLS GOODEVE, KLEIN
PRINZHORN, RABINOWITZ
GALISON/JONES, MARCUS
ELISABETH KLEY: **PAUL LINCOLN**
CUMULUS: O. ENWEZOR, M. WARNER
BALKON: STELLA ROLLIG

CHUCK CLOSE
DIANA THATER
LUC TUYMANS
PROSE, CLOSE/PEYTON, SHIFF
CLOSE/CURIGER, ARRHENIUS
HASLINGER, GILBERT-ROLFE
HOPTMAN, MOSQUERA, REUST
INSERT: **SHIRANA SHAHBAZI**
GREG HILTY: **JEREMY DELLER**
HOWARD SINGERMAN: **DAVID BUNN**
LES INFOS: T. DE DUVE—INTERVIEW
CUMULUS: F. WARD, H. U. RECK

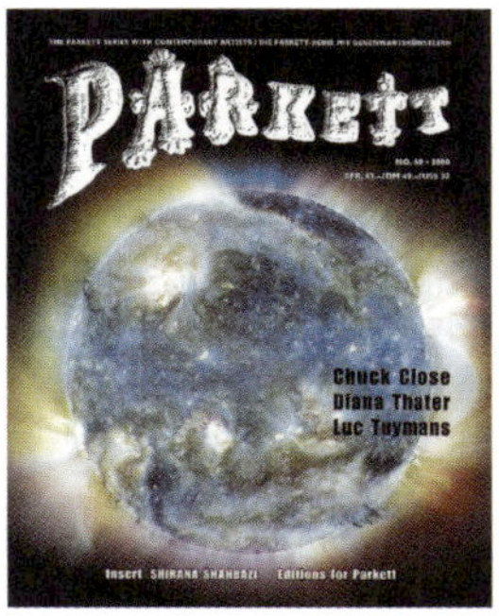

No. 60 - ISBN 3-907582-10-1

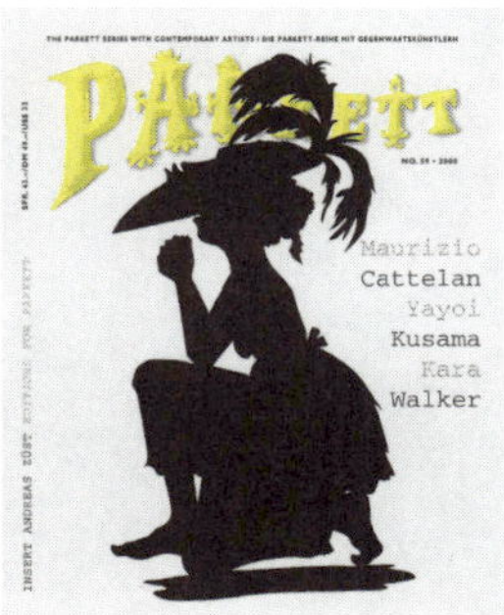

No. 59 - ISBN 3-907582-09-8

MAURIZIO CATTELAN
YAYOI KUSAMA
KARA WALKER
BOURRIAUD, GINGERAS, BONAMI
PANHANS-BÜHLER, MATSUI, POLLOCK
DUBOIS SHAW, JANUS, WALKER
INSERT: **ANDREAS ZÜST**
VINCENT KATZ
E. BRONFEN: **ANNETTE MESSAGER**
JAN AVGIKOS: **ANNA GASKELL**
LES INFOS: ALI SUBOTNICK
CUMULUS: M. ROWELL, L. FÖLDENYI
BALKON: MICHELLE NICOL

JAMES ROSENQUIST
SYLVIE FLEURY
JASON RHOADES
RUSSELL, KOONS/ROSENQUIST
HULTEN, FELIX, GLENN, LOBEL
DANNATT, RUF, KOETHER, FERGUSON
ORTH, SCHEIDEMANN/HERMANN
INSERT: **HENRY BOND**
G. WILLIAMS: **JANE & LOUISE WILSON**
S. ZIZEK, PAUL D. MILLER & CHRIS OFILI
LES INFOS: ANNA HELWING
CUMULUS: D. ROBBINS, H. TEERLINCK
BALKON: KNUT EBELING

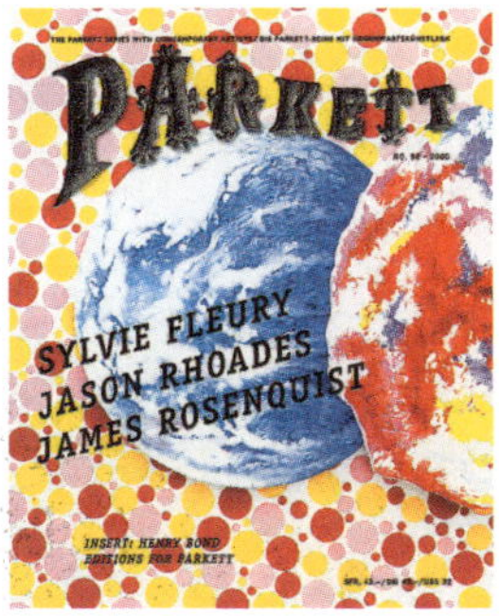

No. 58 - ISBN 3-907582-08-X

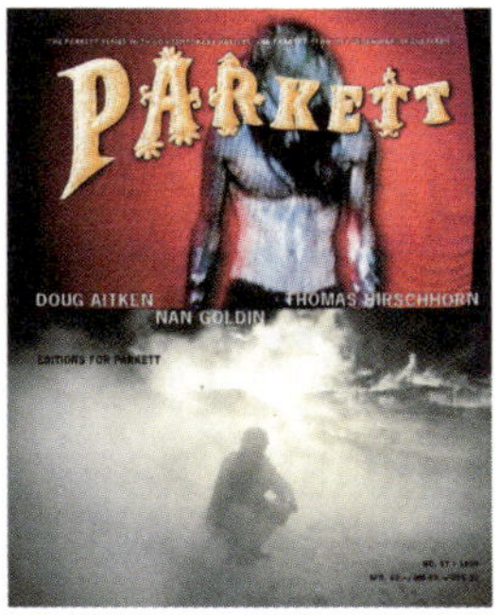

No. 57 - ISBN 3-907582-07-1

DOUG AITKEN
NAN GOLDIN
THOMAS HIRSCHHORN
ROBERTS, BONAMI, VAN ASSCHE
LEBOVICI, DANTO, LIEBMANN
FRIIS-HANSEN, HAKERT, EISENBERG
FLECK, GINGERAS, VERGNE, STEINWEG
D. GREENBERG: **DONALD BAECHLER**
ANDREA KROKSNES: **LOUISE LAWLER**
LIONEL BOVIER: **JOHN MILLER**
LES INFOS: RUDOLF SCHMITZ
CUMULUS: H.U. OBRIST, C. BUTLER
BALKON: J. STEINER/ANNELISE COSTE

ELLSWORTH KELLY
VANESSA BEECROFT
JORGE PARDO
KELLEIN, FER, MAURER, RIMANELLI
BRYSON, TAZZI, SEWARD, AVGIKOS
FERGUSON, VÉGH, VAN WINKEL
FRANGENBERG, BUSH
GREG HILTY: **CERITH WYN EVANS**
THOMAS Y. LEVIN: **CHRISTIAN MARCLAY**
LYNNE COOKE: **DIANA THATER**
LES INFOS: DIANE LEWIS
CUMULUS: A. DANNATT, P. NEDOMA

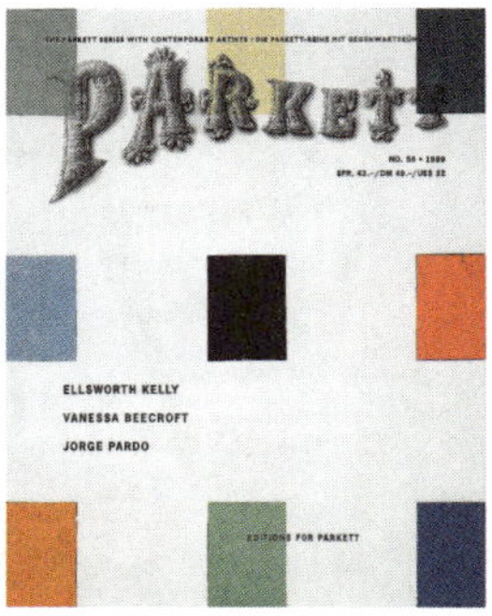

No. 56 - ISBN 3-907582-06-3

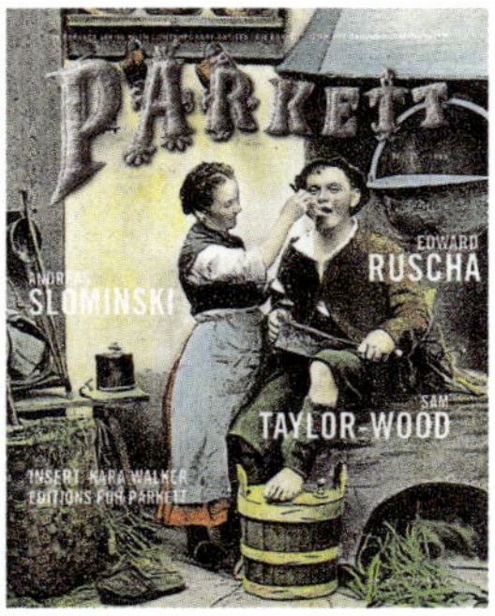

No. 55 - ISBN 3-907582-05-5

EDWARD RUSCHA
ANDREAS SLOMINSKI
SAM TAYLOR-WOOD
PERRONE, HIGGIE, SINGERMAN
SCHENKER, SCANLAN, SPECTOR, FREY
HEYNEN, GROYS/FUNCKE/HOFFMANN
BRONFEN, BONAMI, LAJER-BURCHARTH
INSERT: **KARA WALKER**
BORIS GROYS: **PAVEL PEPPERSTEIN**
RUDOLF SCHMITZ: **ALEXANDER KLUGE**
BEATRIX RUF: **EIJA-LIISA AHTILA**
CUMULUS: M. NICOL, S. ROLNIK

RONI HORN
MARIKO MORI
BEAT STREULI
SCHORR, GUNNARSSON, GOROVOY, LEWIS
SPECTOR, BRYSON, NAKAZAWA, NICHOLS
GOODEVE, STALS, DANTO, AMANO, SMITH
INSERT: **MATTHEW RITCHIE**
VINCENT KATZ: **ALEX KATZ**
H. BREDEKAMP: **STEPHAN VON HUENE**
PAUL D. MILLER: **SHIRIN NESHAT**
LES INFOS:
OKWUI ENWEZOR & WILLIAM KENTRIDGE
CUMULUS: VALÉRIA PICCOLI, MARIA LIND

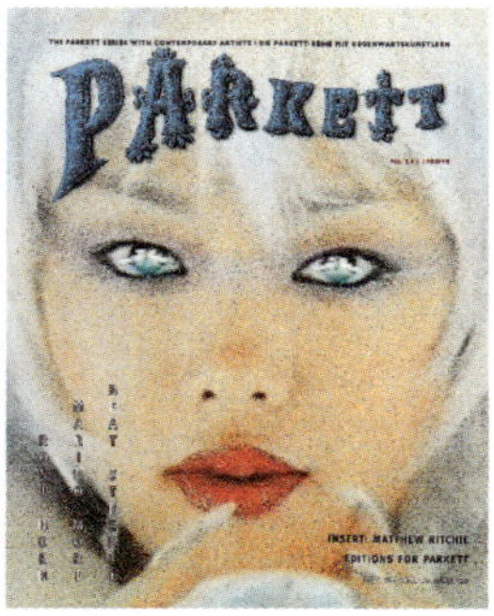

No. 54 - ISBN 3-907582-04-7

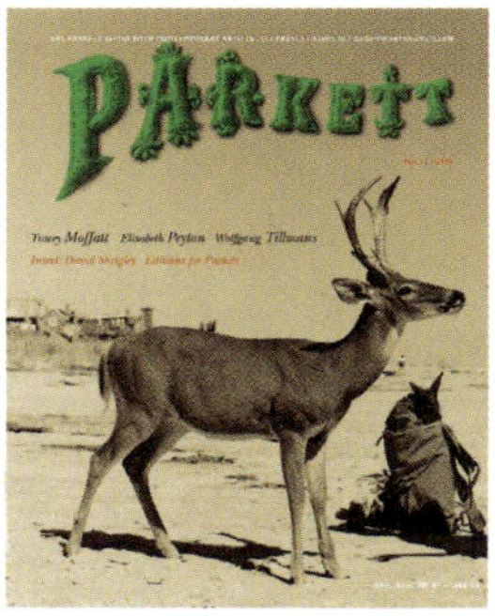

No. 53 - ISBN 3-907582-03-9

TRACEY MOFFATT
ELIZABETH PEYTON
WOLFGANG TILLMANS
MARTIN, LAJER-BURCHARTH, RIMANELLI
PILGRIM, URSPRUNG, LIEBMANN, MATSUI
WAKEFIELD, BUDNEY, NESBITT, ZIEGLER
INSERT: **DAVID SHRIGLEY**
C. BERNARD: **JOHAN GRIMONPREZ**
BERNARD MARCADÉ: **ROBERT GOBER**
LES INFOS DE L'ENFER: V. LIEBERMANN
CUMULUS: BLESSING, AUPETITALLOT
BALKON: STEINER/MAGNAGUAGNO

KAREN KILIMNIK
MALCOLM MORLEY
UGO RONDINONE
SCHORR, BÜRGI, JUNCOSA
MORLEY, LEBENSZTEJN, BONAMI
VERWOERT, HOPTMAN
INSERT: **THOMAS BAYRLE**
ED WHITE: **JEAN MICHEL OTHONIEL**
NEVILLE WAKEFIELD: **RICHARD SERRA**
GILDA WILLIAMS: **GILLIAN WEARING**
R. GRESKOVIC: **MERCE CUNNINGHAM**
CUMULUS: WALKER, KURZMEYER
BALKON: CECILIA VICUÑA

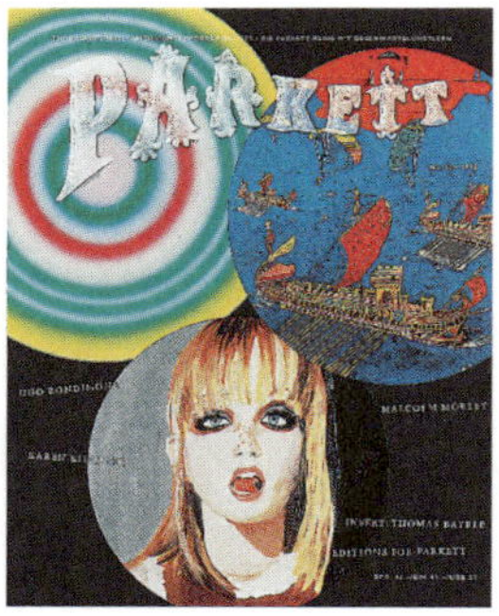

No. 52 - ISBN 3-907582-02-0

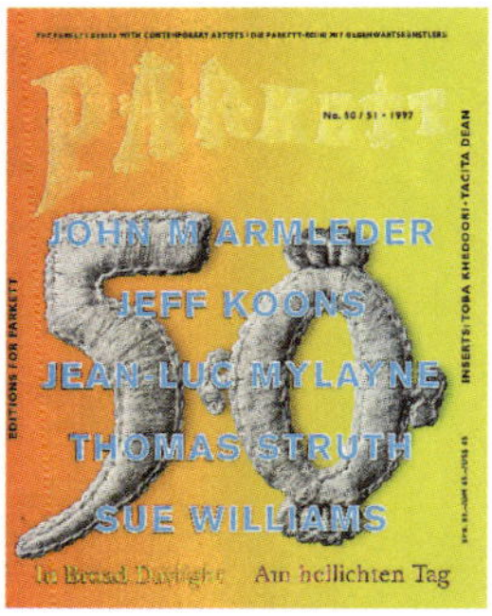

50/51 - ISBN 3-907582-00-4

JOHN M ARMLEDER, JEFF KOONS
JEAN-LUC MYLAYNE
THOMAS STRUTH, SUE WILLIAMS
DI PIETRANTONIO, BOVIER, MUNIZ
SEWARD, LOERS, NICHOLS GOODEVE
COOKE, DION, ARNAUDET, MYLAYNE
CURIGER, LINGWOOD,OKUTSU, BRYSON
SCHJELDAHL, NESBIT, DANNATT, CAMHI
INSERTS: **TOBA KHEDOORI, TACITA DEAN**
ONFRAY: **H. RIGAUD,** NICOL: **SAM SAMORE**
MURPHY, VAN DER WALLE, STEINER
KURT W. FORSTER: **FRANK GEHRY**
CUMULUS: COLEMAN, BIRNBAUM

LAURIE ANDERSON
DOUGLAS GORDON
JEFF WALL
FLOOD, BEZZOLA, FERGUSON
GILLICK/GORDON, BRYSON
PONTBRIAND, SCHORR, ANDERSON
BURCKHARDT, BUDNEY
INSERT: **SILVIA BÄCHLI**
COLIN DE LAND: **JOHN WATERS**
ROBERT STORR: **SEYDOU KEITA**
D. SALVIONI: **CLEGG & GUTTMANN**
CUMULUS: KITTELMANN, MEYER

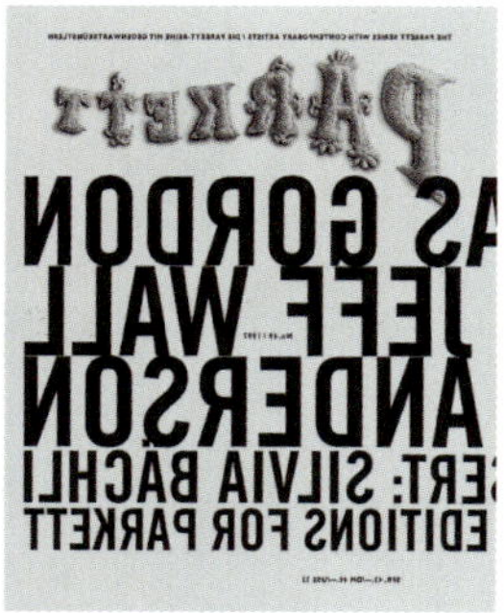

No. 49 - ISBN 3-907509-99-4

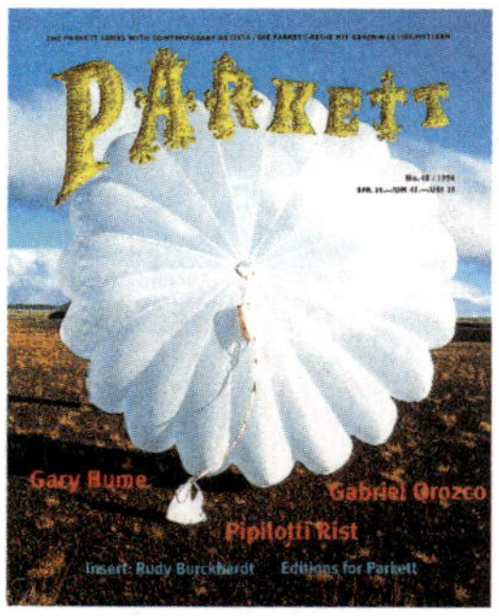

No. 48 - ISBN 3-907509-98-6

GARY HUME
GABRIEL OROZCO
PIPILOTTI RIST
BOVIER, MUIR, FOGLE, BONAMI
DE ZEGHER, SPECTOR, URSPRUNG
BABIAS, COLOMBO, ANDERSON
INSERT: **RUDY BURCKHARDT**
V. KATZ: **RUDY BURCKHARDT**
MARK VAN DER WALLE:
CHARLES LONG & STEREOLAB
FAYE HIRSCH: **BRUCE CONNER**
CH. DOSWALD: **IAN ANÜLL**
CUMULUS: LEGGAT, SCHNEIDER

TONY OURSLER
RAYMOND PETTIBON
THOMAS SCHÜTTE
COOKE, RICHARD, NERI
LEWIS, GROYS, ALS, RUGOFF
GOODEVE, SEARLE, MARI, REUST
WAKEFIELD, LOOCK, JANUS
INSERT: **ZOE LEONARD & CHERYL DUNYE**
JURI STEINER: **EMMA KUNZ**
M. WECHSLER: **CHRISTOPH RÜTIMANN**
SUSAN MORGAN: **DIANE ARBUS**
CUMULUS: PRINCENTHAL, BOVIER/CHERIX

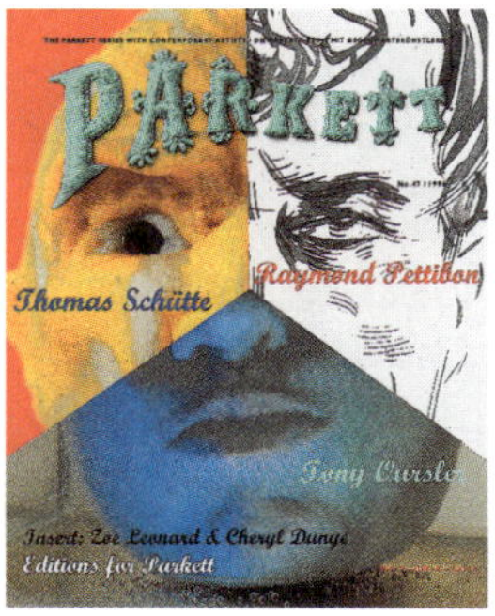

No. 47 - ISBN 3-907509-97-8

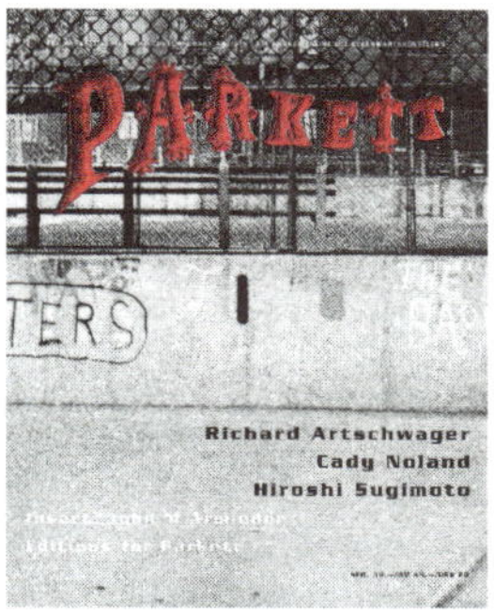

No. 46 - ISBN 3-907509-96-X

RICHARD ARTSCHWAGER
CADY NOLAND
HIROSHI SUGIMOTO
DEITCHER, SCHAFFNER, FORSTER
MUNIZ, ARMSTRONG, RELYEA
BOGDAN, GOODEVE, NICKAS
BRYSON, RUGOFF, DENSON
INSERT: **JOHN M ARMLEDER**
ROLAND WÄSPE: **ERWIN WURM**
D. BIRNBAUM: **ÖYVIND FAHLSTRÖM**
LES INFOS DU PARADIS: ROBERT FLECK
CUMULUS: MILLER, VETTESE
BALKON: MARTIN HELLER

VIJA CELMINS
ANDREAS GURSKY
RIRKRIT TIRAVANIJA
PRINCENTHAL, LEWIS, SILVERTHORNE
SHIFF, CRIQUI, BURCKHARDT, WAKEFIELD
SCHORR, MELO, GILLICK, FLOOD, STEINER
INSERT: **HANS DANUSER**
LES INFOS: LIAM GILLICK /DOUGLAS GORDON
LYNNE COOKE, DAVID DEITCHER
DANIEL KURJAKOVIC: **MARIE JOSÉ BURKI**
NAN GOLDIN: **PETER HUJAR**
NOEMI SMOLIK: **ANDREAS SLOMINSKI**
JASON SIMON: **MARK DION**
LUK LAMBRECHT: **MARK LUYTEN**

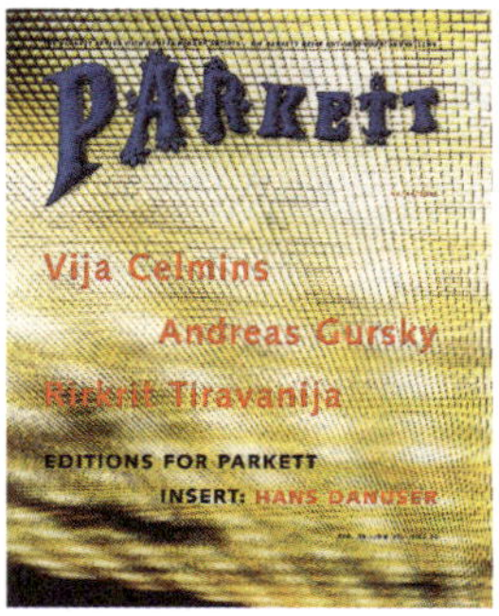

No. 44 - ISBN 3-907509-94-3

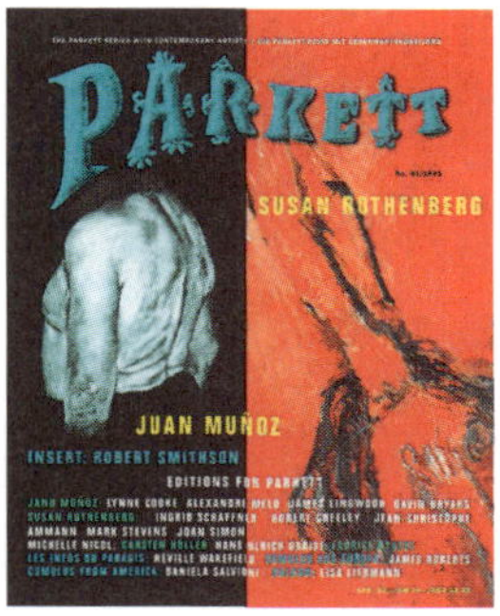

No. 43 - ISBN 3-907509-93-5

JUAN MUÑOZ
SUSAN ROTHENBERG
LYNNE COOKE, ALEXANDRE MELO
JAMES LINGWOOD, GAVIN BRYARS
ROBERT CREELEY, INGRID SCHAFFNER
JEAN-CHRISTOPHE AMMANN
MARK STEVENS, JOAN SIMON
INSERT: **ROBERT SMITHSON**
NEVILLE WAKEFIELD
MICHELLE NICOL: **CARSTEN HÖLLER**
H.U. OBRIST: **FABRICE HYBERT**

LAWRENCE WEINER
RACHEL WHITEREAD
B. ADAMS, F. RICHARD
D. SCHWARZ, D. SALVIONI
E. LEFFINGWELL, L. RELYEA
N. WAKEFIELD, R. SCHMITZ
T. FAIRBROTHER, S. WATNEY
INSERT: **NAN GOLDIN**
VINCE LEO: **ROBERT FRANK**
C. RITSCHARD: **MARKUS RAETZ**

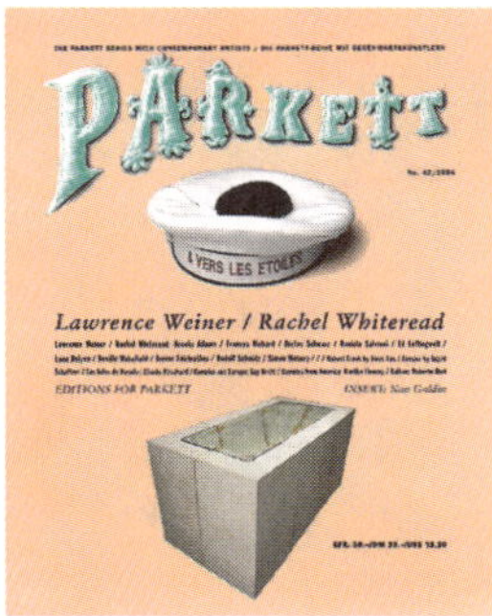

No. 42 - ISBN 3-907509-92-7

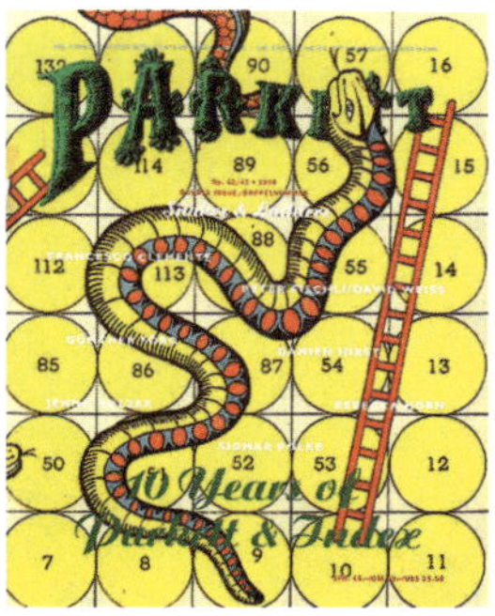

40/41 - ISBN 3-907509-90-0

FRANCESCO CLEMENTE
GÜNTHER FÖRG
PETER FISCHLI/DAVID WEISS
DAMIEN HIRST
JENNY HOLZER
REBECCA HORN
SIGMAR POLKE
HOLLAND COTTER, BORIS GROYS
MAX WECHSLER, DAVID RIMANELLI
JOAN SIMON, GORDON BURN
GILBERT LASCAULT, WERNER SPIES
BICE CURIGER, JEFF PERRONE
G. ROGER DENSON, VIK MUNIZ
DAVE HICKEY

CHARLES RAY
FRANZ WEST
K. KERTESS, CH. KNIGHT
P. SCHJELDAHL, R. STORR
J. AVGIKOS, A. HUBER
M. PRINZHORN, E. SCHLEBRÜGGE
HARALD SZEEMANN
D. ZACHAROPOULOS
INSERT: **PIPILOTTI RIST**
JEAN BAUDRILLARD
HANS RUDOLF REUST: **LUC TUYMANS**
PARKETT INQUIRY:
CHERCHEZ LA FEMME PEINTRE

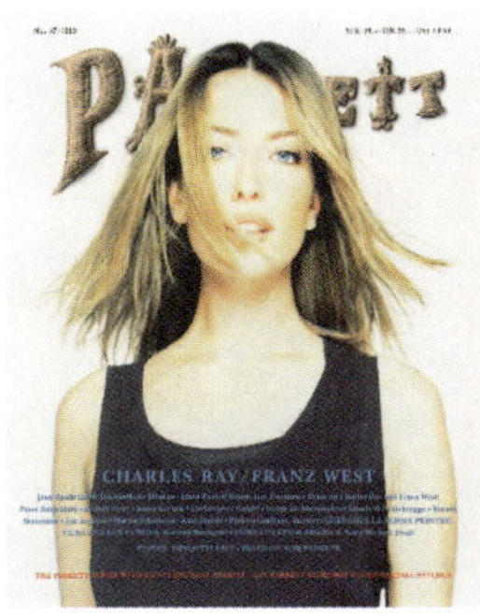

No. 37 - ISBN 3-907509-87-0

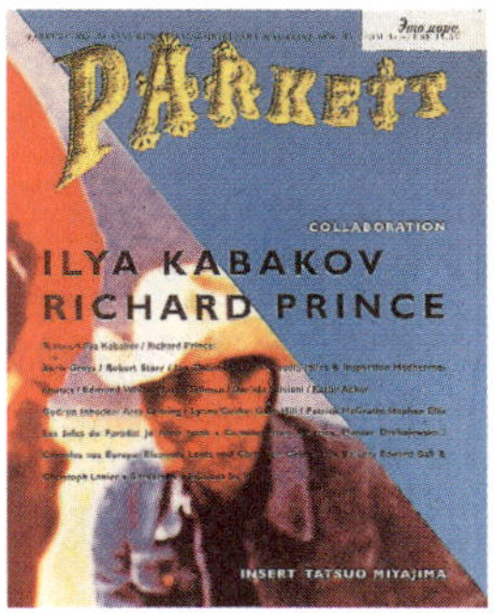

No. 34 - ISBN 3-907509-84-6

ILYA KABAKOV
RICHARD PRINCE
BORIS GROYS, ROBERT STORR
JAN THORN-PRIKKER
CLAUDIA JOLLES, EDMUND WHITE
SUSAN TALLMAN, DANIELA
SALVIONI, KATHY ACKER
INSERT: **TATSUO MIYAJIMA**
GUDRUN INBODEN: **ASTA GRÖTING**
LYNNE COOKE: **GARY HILL**
PATRICK McGRATH: **STEPHEN ELLIS**

IMI KNOEBEL
SHERRIE LEVINE
RUDOLF BUMILLER
RAINER CRONE/DAVID MOOS
LISA LIEBMANN, DANIELA SALVIONI
ERICH FRANZ, HOWARD SINGERMANN
INSERT: **DAMIEN HIRST**
SHEENA WAGSTAFF: **VIJA CELMINS**
JIM LEWIS: **LARRY CLARK**
LIAM GILLICK: **BETHAN HUWS**
THOMAS KELLEIN: **WALTER DE MARIA**

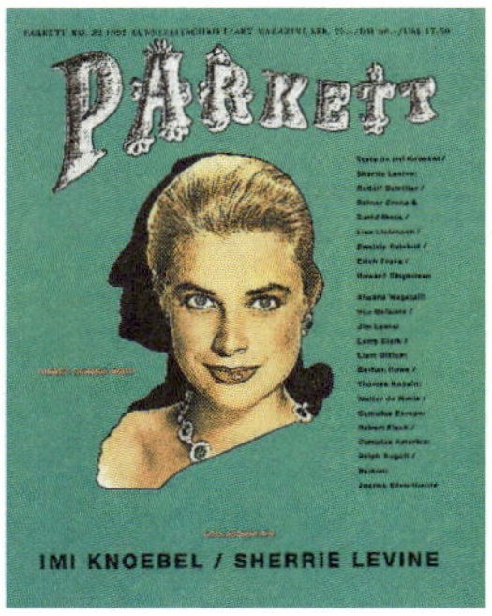

No. 32 - ISBN 3-907509-82-X

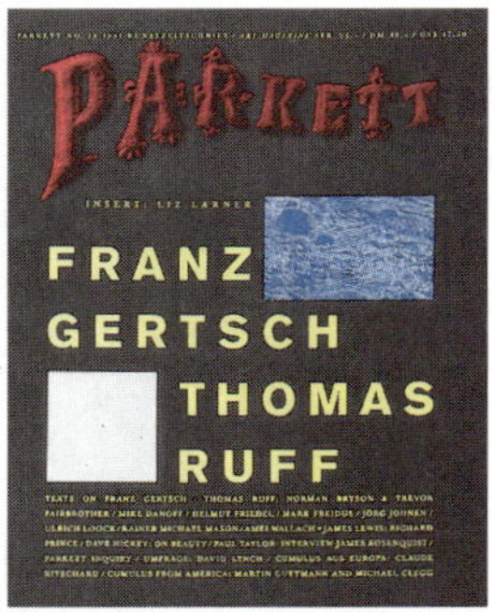

No. 28 - ISBN 3-907509-78-1

FRANZ GERTSCH
THOMAS RUFF
H. FRIEDEL, U. LOOCK
I. MICHAEL DANOFF
A. WALLACH. R. M. MASON
M. FREIDUS, J. JOHNEN
T. FAIRBROTHER/N. BRYSON
INSERT: **LIZ LARNER**
JAMES LEWIS: **RICHARD PRINCE**
DAVID HICKEY: **THE INVISIBLE DRAGON/DER UNSICHTBARE DRACHEN**
P. TAYLOR: **JAMES ROSENQUIST**

ALIGHIERO E BOETTI
JEAN-CHRISTOPHE AMMANN
GIOVAN BATTISTA SALERNO
RAINER CRONE & DAVID MOOS
FRIEDEMANN MALSCH
JEAN-PIERRE BORDAZ
ALAIN CUEFF
INSERT: **CINDY SHERMAN**
SHEENA WAGSTAFF: **SOPHIE CALLE**
HERBERT LACHMEYER/BRIGITTE FELDERER: **FRANZ WEST**
JUTTA KOETHER: **MIKE KELLEY**

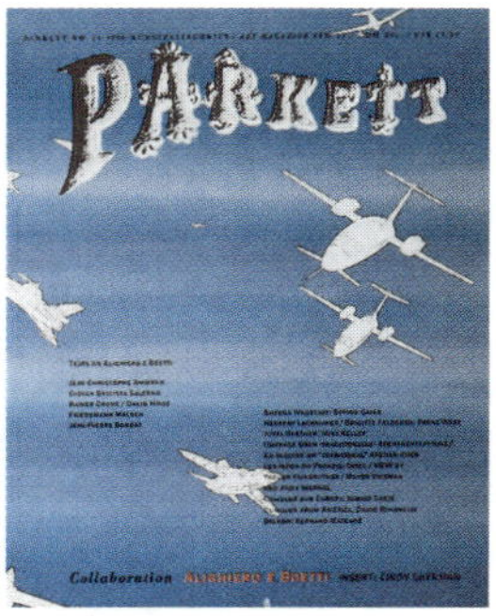

No. 24 - ISBN 3-907509-74-9

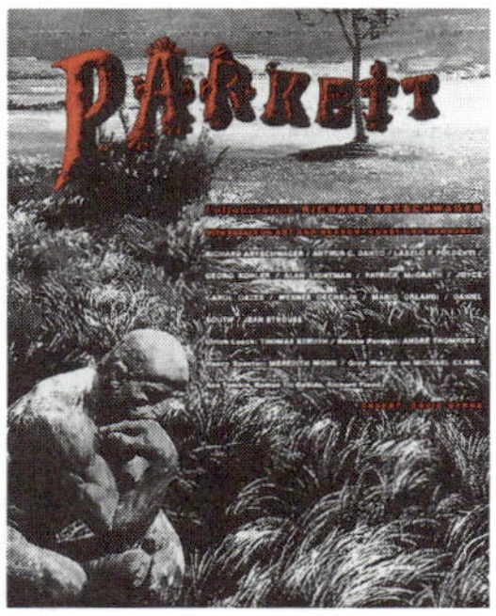

No. 23 - ISBN 3-907509-73-0

RICHARD ARTSCHWAGER
ARTHUR C. DANTO, GEORG KOHLER
MARIO A. ORLANDO
JOYCE CAROL OATES
WERNER OECHSLIN, ALAN LIGHTMAN, PATRICK McGRATH
DANIEL SOUTIF, LASZLO F. FÖLDENYI
JEAN STROUSE
INSERT: **DAVID BYRNE**
R.PUVOGEL: **ANDRÉ THOMKINS**
U. LOOCK: **THOMAS STRUTH**
N. SPECTOR: **MEREDITH MONK**

ALEX KATZ
JOHN RUSSELL, BROOKS ADAMS
DAVID RIMANELLI, FRANCESCO CLEMENTE, MICHAEL KRÜGER
RICHARD FLOOD, PATRICK FREY
CARL STIGLIANO, BICE CURIGER
GLENN O'BRIEN
INSERT: **WILLIAM WEGMAN**
LISA LIEBMAN: **ROBERT GOBER**
JACQUELINE BURCKHARDT: **GIULIO ROMANO**

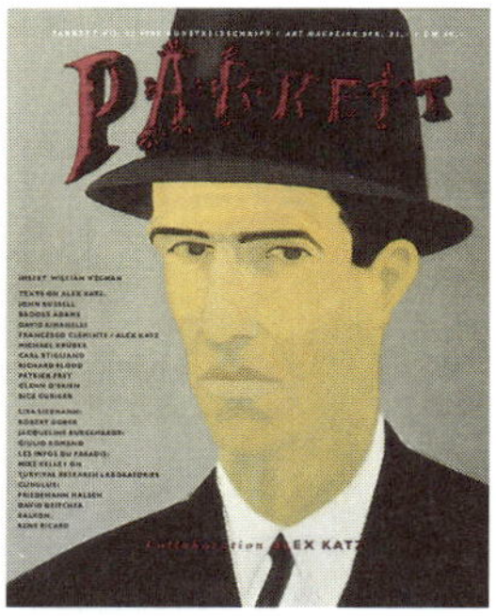

No. 21 - ISBN 3-907509-71-4

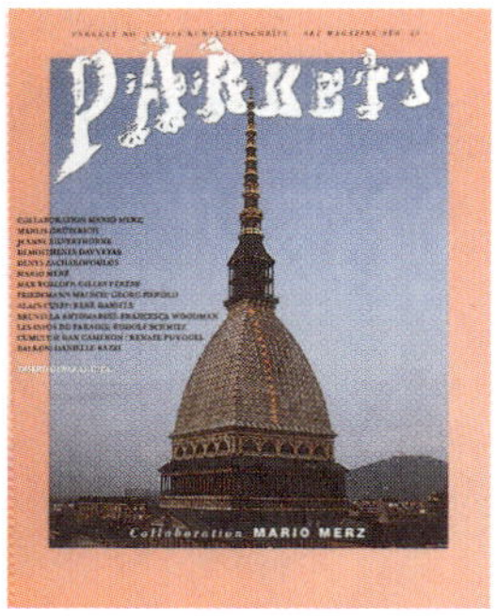

No. 15 - ISBN 3-907509-65-X

MARIO MERZ
MARLIS GRÜTERICH, JEANNE SILVERTHORNE, DEMOSTHENES DAVVETAS, HARALD SZEEMANN
DENYS ZACHAROPOULOS
INSERT: **GENERAL IDEA**
MAX KOZLOFF: **GILLES PERESS**
FRIEDEMANN MALSCH: **GEORG HEROLD**
BRUNELLA ANTOMARINI: **FRANCESCA WOODMAN**

GILBERT & GEORGE
DUNCAN FALLOWELL
MARIO CODOGNATO
JEREMY COOPER
DEMOSTHENES DAVVETAS
WOLF JAHN
INSERT: **ROSEMARIE TROCKEL**
ROBERT STORR: **NANCY SPERO**
HAIM STEINBACH: **MANIFESTO**
JÖRG ZUTTER: **THOMAS HUBER**

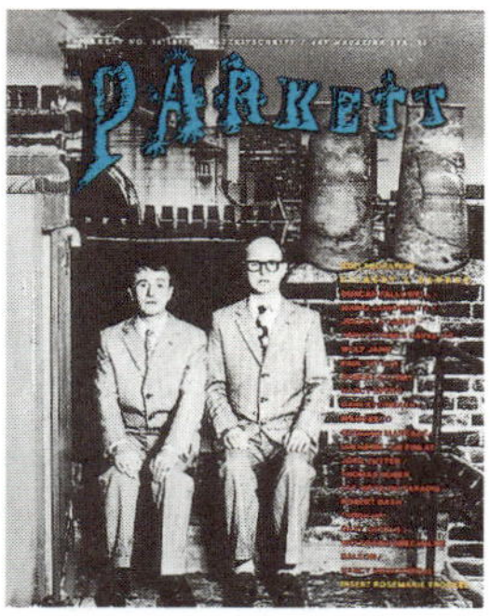

No. 14 - ISBN 3-907509-64-1

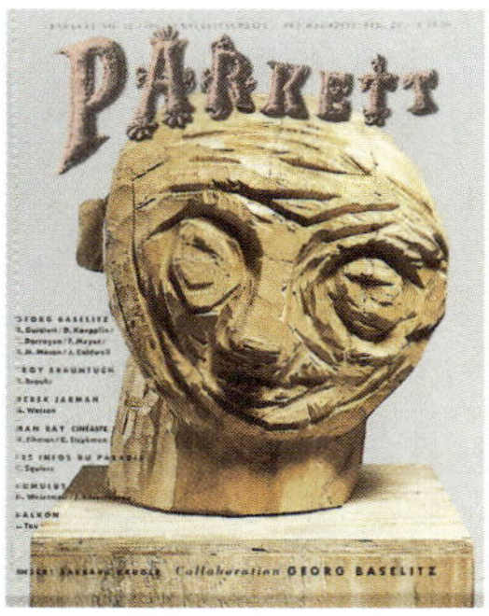

No. 11 - ISBN 3-907509-61-7

GEORG BASELITZ
REMO GUIDIERI
DIETER KOEPPLIN
ERIC DARRAGON
RAINER MICHAEL MASON
FRANZ MEYER, JOHN CALDWELL
INSERT: **BARBARA KRUGER**
GRAY WATSON: **DEREK JARMAN**
CAROL SQUIERS: **PHOTO OPPORTUNITY**
ROSETTA BROOKS: **TROY BRAUNTUCH**

Each volume of PARKETT is created in collaboration with artists, who contribute an original work specially made for the readers of PARKETT. The works are available in a signed and numbered Special Edition. Prices are subject to change. Postage is not included.

EDITIONS FOR PARKETT

Jeder PARKETT-Band entsteht in Collaboration mit Künstlern, die eigens für die Leser von PARKETT Originalbeiträge gestalten. Diese Vorzugsausgaben sind als nummerierte und signierte Editionen erhältlich. Preisänderungen vorbehalten. Versandkosten und MwSt. (Schweiz) nicht inbegriffen.

COLLECTOR OF URBAN DEBRIS:
THE ULTIMATE ACCESSORY FOR
EVERY POOCH-HAPPY FLANEUR.

BUNTER HUND: SINNBILD UND
UNVERZICHTBARES ACCESSOIRE
DES GLÜCKLICHEN FLANEURS.

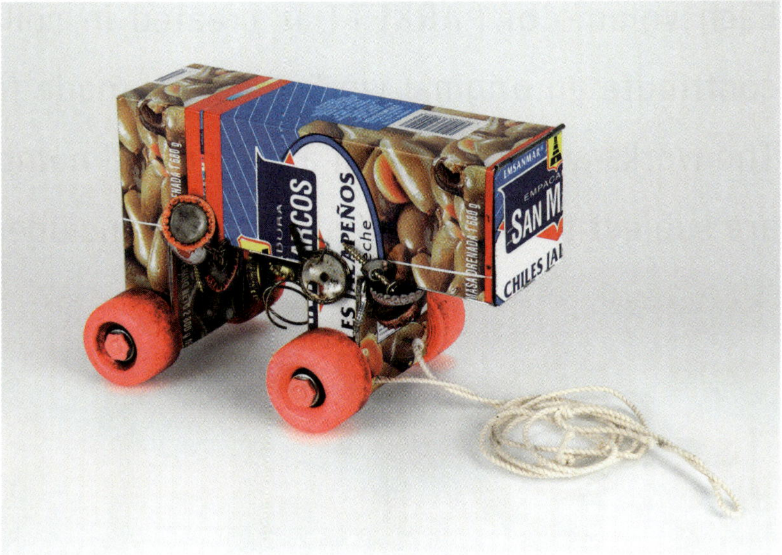

PARKETT 69

FRANCIS ALŸS

GHETTO COLLECTOR, 2003

Tin, magnets, plastic string, rubber wheels,
25 design variations, ca. 6 1/2 x 9 x 5".
Edition of 99, signed and numbered.
$ 1500 / € 1200

Blech, Magnete, Plastikschnur, Gummiräder,
25 Design-Variationen, ca. 16,5 x 23 x 12,5 cm.
Auflage: 99, signiert und nummeriert.
CHF 1900 / € 1200

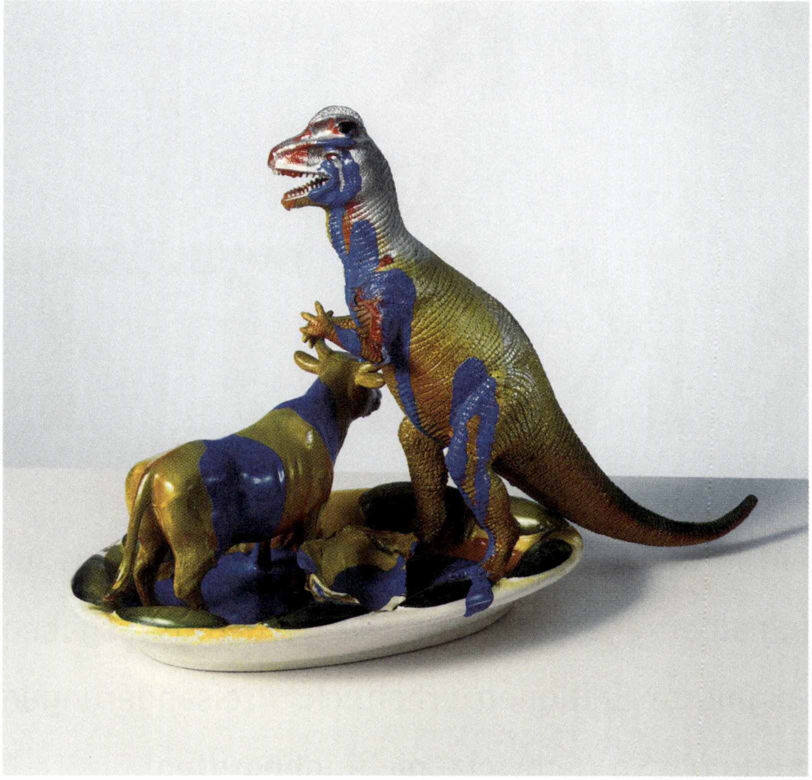

SURVIVAL OF THE TASTIEST:
EVOLUTION IN A NUTSHELL
DEMONSTRATED BY THE ODD COUPLE.

ZEIT ALS MAHLZEIT –
ODER DER EVOLUTIONÄRE TANZ
ALLEN FLEISCHES.

PARKETT 69

ISA GENZKEN

AL DENTE, 2003

Italienische Keramik, Lack, Kunststoff.
Je individuell von Hand gestalteter Teller
mit zwei Spielzeugfiguren (Kuh und Dinosaurier),
ca. 30 x 20 x 26 cm.
Auflage: 74, signiertes und nummeriertes Zertifikat.
$ 1200 / € 1000

Italian ceramic, lacquer, plastic.
Plate with two toy figures (cow and dinosaur),
each unique and handmade by the artist,
ca. 11 13/16 x 7 7/8 x 10 1/4".
Edition of 74, signed and numbered certificate.
CHF 1500 / € 1000

MINIATURE METAPHYSICAL MAELSTROM:
STRETCHED IN SPACE TO THE BREAKING POINT AND BEYOND.

IN DEN RAUM GESPANNT BIS ZUR SCHMERZGRENZE UND DARÜBER HINAUS:
EIN SINNLICHES GLEICHNIS DER EXISTENZ.

PARKETT 69

ANISH KAPOOR

UNTITLED, 2003

Perspex, handtinted stocking, paint,
10 1/4 x 10 1/4 x 15".
Edition of 60, signed and numbered certificate.
$ 1900 / € 1700

OHNE TITEL, 2003

Perspex, handgefärbter Strumpf, Farbe,
26 x 26 x 38 cm.
Auflage: 60, signiertes und nummeriertes Zertifikat.
CHF 2500 / € 1700

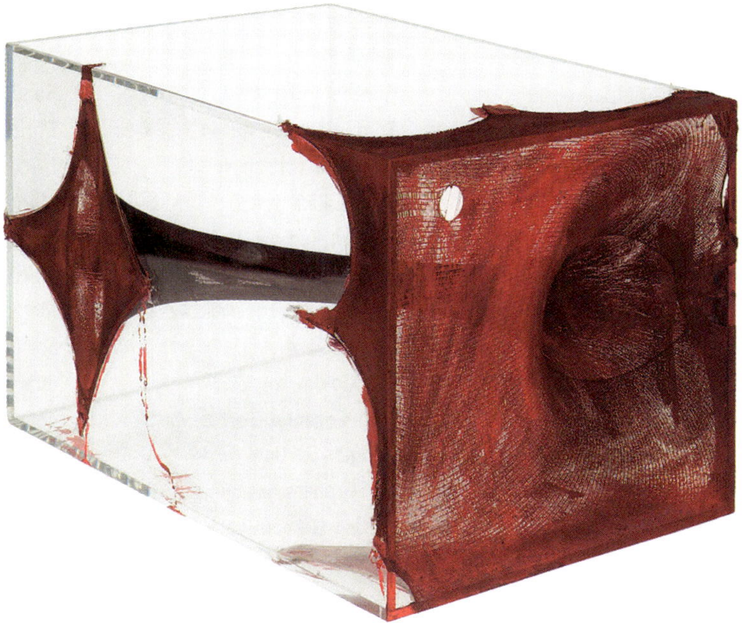

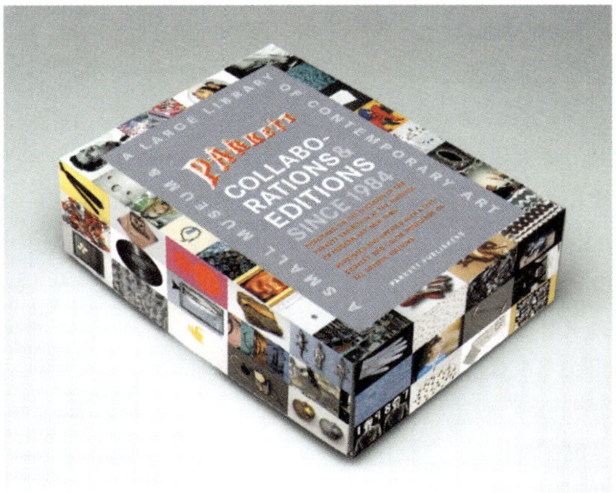

CHF 45 / $ 29 / € 30
ISBN 3-907582-23-3

PARKETT POSTCARD SET WITH TEXT BOOKLET ON MOMA SHOW

Featuring the artists' editions made for PARKETT since 1984
and a booklet with essays by Deborah Wye
(Chief Curator Illustrated Books and Prints at MoMA) and Susan Tallman.
128 color postcards, booklet with 2 texts, color reproductions of
64 PARKETT covers. 64 p., packed in a white box, 6 1/4 x 4 3/4 x 2 3/8".

PARKETT-POSTKARTEN-SET MIT TEXTBÜCHLEIN ZUR MOMA-AUSSTELLUNG

Mit Postkarten der seit 1984 von Künstlern für PARKETT geschaffenen Editionen.
Das Textbüchlein enthält 2 Essays zur Ausstellung im MoMA,
New York, von Deborah Wye (Chefkuratorin für illustrierte Bücher
und Grafik am MoMA) und Susan Tallman.
128 Farbpostkarten, Büchlein mit zwei Texten, Farbabb. von
64 PARKETT-Titelblättern u.a.m. 64 S., in weisser Schachtel, 16 x 12 x 6 cm.

PARKETT

ARTISTS' MONOGRAPHS & EDITIONS / KÜNSTLERMONOGRAPHIEN & EDITIONEN

FOR AVAILABILITY SEE NEXT PAGE / LIEFERBARKEIT SIEHE FOLGENDE SEITE

Franz Ackermann, vol. 68
Eija-Liisa Ahtila, vol. 68
Doug Aitken, vol. 57
Francis Alÿs, vol. 69
Laurie Anderson, vol. 49
John Armleder, vol. 50/51
Richard Artschwager, vol. 23, vol. 46
John Baldessari, vol. 29
Stephan Balkenhol, vol. 36
Matthew Barney, vol. 45
Georg Baselitz, vol. 11
Vanessa Beecroft, vol. 56
Ross Bleckner, vol. 38
John Bock, vol. 67
Alighiero e Boetti, vol. 24
Christian Boltanski, vol. 22
Louise Bourgeois, vol. 27
Angela Bulloch, vol. 66
Daniel Buren, vol. 66
Sophie Calle, vol. 36
Maurizio Cattelan, vol. 59
Vija Celmins, vol. 44
Francesco Clemente, vol. 9 & 40/41
Chuck Close, vol. 60
Enzo Cucchi, vol. 1
John Currin, vol. 65
Tacita Dean, vol. 62
Thomas Demand, vol. 62
Martin Disler, vol. 3
Peter Doig, vol. 67
Marlene Dumas, vol. 38
Olafur Eliasson, vol. 64
Tracey Emin, vol. 63
Eric Fischl, vol. 5
Peter Fischli /
David Weiss, vol.17, 40/41
Sylvie Fleury, vol. 58
Günther Förg, vol. 26 & 40/41
Tom Friedman, vol. 64
Katharina Fritsch, vol. 25
Liam Gillick, vol. 61
Isa Genzken, vol. 69
Franz Gertsch, vol. 28
Gilbert & George, vol. 14
Robert Gober, vol. 27
Nan Goldin, vol. 57
Felix Gonzalez-Torres, vol. 39
Douglas Gordon, vol. 49
Dan Graham, vol. 68
Rodney Graham, vol. 64
Andreas Gursky, vol. 44
David Hammons, vol. 31
Thomas Hirschhorn, vol. 57
Damien Hirst, vol. 40/41
Jenny Holzer, vol. 40/41
Rebecca Horn, vol. 13 & 40/41
Roni Horn, vol. 54
Pierre Huyghe, vol. 66
Gary Hume, vol. 48
Ilya Kabakov, vol. 34
Anish Kapoor, vol. 69
Alex Katz, vol. 21
Mike Kelley, vol. 31
Ellsworth Kelly, vol. 56
William Kentridge, vol. 63
Karen Kilimnik, vol. 52
Martin Kippenberger, vol. 19
Imi Knoebel, vol. 32
Jeff Koons, vol. 19, 50/51
Jannis Kounellis, vol. 6
Yayoi Kusama, vol. 59
Wolfgang Laib, vol. 39
Sherrie Levine, vol. 32
Sarah Lucas, vol. 45
Christian Marclay, vol. 70
Brice Marden, vol. 7
Mario Merz, vol. 15
Tracey Moffatt, vol. 53
Mariko Mori, vol. 54
Malcolm Morley, vol. 52
Sarah Morris, vol. 61
Juan Muñoz, vol. 43
Jean-Luc Mylayne, vol. 50/51
Bruce Nauman, vol. 10
Cady Noland, vol. 46
Meret Oppenheim, vol. 4
Gabriel Orozco, vol. 48
Tony Oursler, vol. 47
Laura Owens, vol. 65
Jorge Pardo, vol. 56
Raymond Pettibon, vol. 47
Elizabeth Peyton, vol. 53
Sigmar Polke, vol. 2, 30 & 40/41
Richard Prince, vol. 34
Michael Raedecker, vol. 65
Markus Raetz, vol. 8
Charles Ray, vol. 37
Jason Rhoades, vol. 58
Gerhard Richter, vol. 35
Bridget Riley, vol. 61
Pipilotti Rist, vol. 48
Matthew Ritchie, vol. 61
Tim Rollins & K.O.S., vol. 20
Ugo Rondinone, vol. 52
James Rosenquist, vol. 58
Susan Rothenberg, vol. 43
Thomas Ruff, vol. 28
Edward Ruscha, vol. 18 & 55
Gregor Schneider, vol. 63
Wilhelm Sasnal, vol. 70
Thomas Schütte, vol. 47
Cindy Sherman, vol. 29
Roman Signer, vol. 45
Andreas Slominski, vol. 55
Beat Streuli, vol. 54
Thomas Struth, vol. 50/51
Hiroshi Sugimoto, vol. 46
Philip Taaffe, vol. 26
Sam Taylor-Wood, vol. 55
Diana Thater, vol. 60
Wolfgang Tillmans, vol. 53
Rirkrit Tiravanija, vol. 44
Fred Tomaselli, vol. 67
Rosemarie Trockel, vol. 33
James Turrell, vol. 25
Luc Tuymans, vol. 60
Kara Walker, vol. 59
Jeff Wall, vol. 22 & 49
Andy Warhol, vol. 12
Gillian Wearing, vol. 70
Lawrence Weiner, vol. 42
John Wesley, vol. 62
Franz West, vol. 37
Rachel Whiteread, vol. 42
Sue Williams, vol 50/51
Robert Wilson, vol. 16
Christopher Wool, vol. 33

vol.	Collaboration		
70	Christian Marclay	m	e
	Wilhelm Sasnal	m	e
	Gillian Wearing	m	e
69	Francis Alÿs	m	e
	Isa Gentzken	m	e
	Anish Kapoor	m	e
68	Franz Ackermann	m	e
	Eija-Liisa Ahtila	m	e
	Dan Graham	m	e
67	John Bock	m	e
	Peter Doig	m	e
	Fred Tomaselli	m	e
66	Angela Bulloch	m	e
	Daniel Buren	m	e
	Pierre Huyghe	m	e
65	John Currin	m	
	Laura Owens	m	e
	Michael Raedecker	m	e
64	Olafur Eliasson	m	
	Tom Friedman	m	
	Rodney Graham	m	
63	Tracey Emin	m	e
	William Kentridge	m	e
	Gregor Schneider	m	
62	Tacita Dean	m	e
	Thomas Demand	m	
	John Wesley	m	e
61	Liam Gillick	m	
	Sarah Morris	m	e
	Bridget Riley	m	
	Matthew Ritchie	m	e
60	Chuck Close	m	
	Diana Thater	m	e
	Luc Tuymans	m	e
59	Maurizio Cattelan	m	
	Yayoi Kusama	m	e
	Kara Walker	m	
58	Sylvie Fleury	m	
	Jason Rhoades	m	e
	James Rosenquist	m	
57	Doug Aitken	m	e
	Nan Goldin	m	
	Thomas Hirschhorn	m	
56	Vanessa Beecroft	m	
	Ellsworth Kelly	m	
	Jorge Pardo	m	e
55	Edward Ruscha	m	
	Andreas Slominski	m	
	Sam Taylor-Wood	m	

vol.	Collaboration		
54	Roni Horn	m	e
	Mariko Mori	m	
	Beat Streuli	m	
53	Tracey Moffatt	m	
	Elizabeth Peyton	m	
	Wolfgang Tillmans	m	
52	Karen Kilimnik	m	e
	Malcolm Morley	m	e
	Ugo Rondinone	m	e
50/51	John Armleder	m	
	Jeff Koons	m	e
	Jean-Luc Mylayne	m	
	Thomas Struth	m	
	Sue Williams	m	
49	Laurie Anderson	m	e
	Douglas Gordon	m	
	Jeff Wall	m	
48	Gary Hume	m	
	Gabriel Orozco	m	
	Pipilotti Rist	m	
47	Tony Oursler	m	
	Raymond Pettibon	m	
	Thomas Schütte	m	e
46	Richard Artschwager	m	
	Cady Noland	m	
	Hiroshi Sugimoto	m	
45	Matthew Barney		
	Sarah Lucas		
	Roman Signer		e
44	Vija Celmins	m	
	Andreas Gursky	m	
	Rirkrit Tiravanija	m	e
43	Juan Muñoz	m	
	Susan Rothenberg	m	
42	Lawrence Weiner	m	e
	Rachel Whiteread	m	
40/41	Francesco Clemente	m	
	Fischli/Weiss	m	
	Günther Förg	m	
	Damien Hirst	m	
	Jenny Holzer	m	
	Rebecca Horn	m	
	Sigmar Polke	m	
39	Felix Gonzalez-Torres	m	
	Wolfgang Laib	m	
38	Ross Bleckner		
	Marlene Dumas		
37	Charles Ray	m	
	Franz West	m	e

vol.	Collaboration		
36	Stephan Balkenhol		
	Sophie Calle		
35	Gerhard Richter		
34	Ilya Kabakov	m	
	Richard Prince	m	
33	Rosemarie Trockel	m	
	Christopher Wool	m	
32	Imi Knoebel	m	
	Sherrie Levine	m	
31	David Hammons		
31	Mike Kelley		
30	Sigmar Polke		
29	John Baldessari		
29	Cindy Sherman		
28	Franz Gertsch	m	
	Thomas Ruff	m	
27	Louise Bourgeois		
	Robert Gober		
26	Günther Förg		
	Philip Taaffe		
25	Katharina Fritsch		e
	James Turrell		e
24	Alighiero e Boetti	m	
23	Richard Artschwager	m	
22	Christian Boltanski		
	Jeff Wall		
21	Alex Katz	m	
20	Tim Rollins + K.O.S.	m	
19	Martin Kippenberger		
	Jeff Koons		
18	Ed Ruscha	m	
17	Fischli/Weiss		
16	Robert Wilson		
15	Mario Merz	m	
14	Gilbert & George	m	
13	Rebecca Horn		
12	Andy Warhol		
11	Georg Baselitz	m	
10	Bruce Nauman		
9	Francesco Clemente		
8	Markus Raetz		
7	Brice Marden		
6	Jannis Kounellis		
5	Eric Fischl		
4	Meret Oppenheim		
3	Martin Disler		
2	Sigmar Polke		
1	Enzo Cucchi		

m = available monograph / erhältliche Monographie, e = available edition / erhältliche Edition
Delivery subject to availability at time of order / Lieferung solange Vorrat

PARKETT IN BOOKSHOPS (Selection)

PARKETT IS AVAILABLE IN 500 LEADING ART BOOKSHOPS AROUND THE WORLD. FOR FURTHER INFORMATION CONTACT:

PARKETT GIBT ES IN 500 FÜHRENDEN KUNSTBUCHHANDLUNGEN AUF DER GANZEN WELT. FÜR WEITERE INFORMATIONEN WENDEN SIE SICH BITTE AN:

PARKETT VERLAG, QUELLENSTRASSE 27, CH-8031 ZÜRICH, TEL. +41-1 271 81 40, FAX 272 43 01, WWW.PARKETTART.COM;

***PARKETT,** 155, AVENUE OF THE AMERICAS, 2ND FLOOR, NEW YORK, N.Y. 10013, PHONE +1 (212) 673-2660, FAX 271-0704, WWW.PARKETTART.COM*

NORTH & SOUTH AMERICA, ASIA, AUSTRALIA

DISTRIBUTOR / VERTRIEB
D.A.P. (DISTRIBUTED ART PUBLISHERS)
155 AVENUE OF THE AMERICAS, 2ND FLOOR,
NEW YORK, NY 10013

USA

AUSTIN, TX
BOOK PEOPLE
603 N. LAMAR

BERKELEY, CA
BERKELEY ART MUSEUM
2625 DURANT AVENUE
CODY'S BOOKS
2454 TELEGRAPHE AVENUE

BEVERLY HILLS, CA
RIZZOLI
9501 WILSHIRE BOULEVARD

BOSTON, MA
INSTITUTE OF CONTEMPORARY ART
955 BOYLSTON STREET
TRIDENT BOOKSELLERS
338 NEWBURY STREET

BUFFALO, NY
TALKING LEAVES
3158 MAIN STREET

CAMBRIDGE, MA
MIT PRESS BOOKSTORE
292 MAIN STREET

CHICAGO, IL
ART INSTITUTE OF CHICAGO
104 S. MICHIGAN
MUSEUM OF CONTEMPORARY ART
220 EAST CHICAGO AVENUE
QUIMBY'S
1854 W. NORTH AVENUE
SMART MUSEUM OF ART
5550 S. GREENWOOD AVENUE

CINCINNATI, OH
CONTEMPORARY ARTS CENTER
115 E. 5TH STREET

COLUMBUS, OH
COLUMBUS MUSEUM OF ART
372 COMMONS MALL
WEXNER CENTER BOOKSTORE
30 W. 15TH STREET

CORAL GABLES, FL
BOOKS & BOOKS
296 ARAGON ROAD

HOUSTON, TX
BRAZOS BOOKSTORE
2421 BISSONNET
CONTEMPORARY ARTS MUSEUM
5216 MONTROSE BOULEVARD
MENIL COLLECTION
1520 SUL ROSS

HUNTINGTON, WV
HUNTINGTON MUSEUM OF ART
2033 MCCOY ROAD

LOS ANGELES, CA
BOOKSOUP
8818 SUNSET BOULEVARD
MUSEUM OF CONTEMPORARY ART
250, S. GRAND
UCLA / ARMAND HAMMER MUSEUM OF ART
10899 WILSHIRE BOULEVARD

MIAMI, FL
BOOKS & BOOKS
296 ARAGON AVENUE, CORAL GABLES
MUSEUM OF CONTEMPORARY ART
770 N.E. 125TH STREET NORTH MIAMI

MINNEAPOLIS, MN
THE WALKER ART CENTER BOOKSTORE
VINELAND PLACE

NEW YORK, NY
GUGGENHEIM DOWNTOWN MUSEUM
575 BROADWAY
MUSEUM OF MODERN ART
11 W. 53RD STREET
NEW MUSEUM OF CONTEMPORARY ART
583 BROADWAY
RIZZOLI
454 WEST BROADWAY
SAINT MARK'S BOOKSTORE
31 3RD AVENUE

OAKLAND, CA
DIESEL, A BOOKSTORE
5433 COLLEGE AVENUE

OAK PARK, MI
BOOK BEAT LTD.
26010 GREENFIELD

OMAHA, NE
JOSLYN ART MUSEUM
2200 DODGE STREET

PHILADELPHIA, PA
AVRIL 50
3406 SANSOM STREET
WATERSTONE BOOKSELLERS
2191 HORNIG ROAD

PITTSBURGH, PA
CARNEGIE INSTITUTE
4400 FORBES AVENUE

PORTLAND, OR
POWELL'S BOOKS
7 NW 9TH STREET

PROVIDENCE, NY
ACCIDENT OR DESIGN
128 N. MAIN STREET
RHODE ISLAND SCHOOL OF DESIGN
2 COLLEGE STREET, 1765

SAN ANTONIO, TX
SLOAN / HALL SAN ANTONIO
5930 BROADWAY

SAN FRANCISCO, CA
A CLEAN WELL LIGHTED PLACE
601 VAN NESS AVENUE
CITY LIGHTS BOOKSHOP
261 COLUMBUS AVENUE
SAN FRANCISCO MUSEUM OF MODERN ART,
MUSEUMBOOKS
151 3RD STREET, 1ST FLOOR

ST. LOUIS, MO
LEFT BANK BOOKS
399 NORTH EUCLID

SANTA MONICA, CA
ARCANA
1229 3RD STREET PROMENADE
HENNESSEY & INGALLS BOOKS
1254 3RD STREET PROMENADE

ST. PAUL, MN
HUNGRY MIND BOOKSTORE
1648 GRAND AVENUE

SEATTLE, WA
UNIVERSITY BOOKSTORE
4326 UNIVERSITY WAY

WASHINGTON D.C.
NATIONAL GALLERY OF ART
6TH STREET & CONSTITUTION AVENUE, NW

CANADA / KANADA

CALGARY
TREPANIER BAER GALLERY
105 999 8TH STREET SW

MONTREAL
ARTEXTE
3575 STREET LAURENT
OLIVIERI LIBRAIRIE BOOKSTORE
185 STREET CATHERINE WEST

TORONTO
ART GALLERY OF ONTARIO
317 DUNDAS STREET WEST
ART METROPOLE
788 KING STREET WEST
DAVID MIRVISH BOOKS ON ART
596 MARKHAM STREET

VANCOUVER
VANCOUVER ART GALLERY
750 HORNBY STREET

AUSTRALIA / AUSTRALIEN

DARLINGHURST
EAST SYDNEY BOOKSTORE
THE DOME, THE ELAN BUILDING
1 KINGS CROSS ROAD

SYDNEY
MUSEUM OF CONTEMPORARY ART
140 GEORGE STREET, CIRCULAR QUAY NORTH
GLEE BOOKS
191 GLEBE POINT ROAD, GLEBE

NEW ZEALAND / NEUSEELAND

AUCKLAND
PROPAGANDA
2 CARR ROAD, MT ROSKILL

ASIA / ASIEN

JAPAN

TOKYO
AOYAMA BOOK CENTRE, SHIBUYA-KU
COSMOS AOYAMA GARDEN FLOOR B2F
5-53-97, JINGUMAE
ART & BOOKS
2-1-13-307
TAKANAWA, MINATO-KU
WATARI MUSEUM OF CONTEMPORARY ART,
ON SUNDAYS BOOKSHOP
376 JINGUMAE SHIBUYA-KU

SINGAPORE / SINGAPUR
PAGE ONE BOOKSTORE
20 KAKI BUKIT VIEW TECHPARK

GREAT BRITAIN / GROSSBRITANNIEN

DISTRIBUTOR / VERTRIEB
CENTRAL BOOKS
99, WALLIS ROAD
LONDON E9 5LN

BRISTOL
ARNOLFINI BOOKSHOP
16 NARROW QUAY

LONDON
BORDERS BOOKSHOP
120 CHARING CROSS ROAD

BORDERS BOOKSHOP
203–207 OXFORD STREET
CAMDEN ARTS CENTRE
ARKWRIGHT ROAD
HAYWARD GALLERY
SOUTH BANK
IAN SHIPLEY BOOKSHOP
70 CHARING CROSS ROAD
INSTITUTE OF CONTEMPORARY ARTS
12 CARLTON HOUSE TERRACE
THE MALL
SERPENTINE GALLERY
KENSINGTON GARDENS
TATE MODERN
BANKSIDE
ZWEMMER LTD. ART BOOKS
24 LITCHFIELD STREET

IRELAND / IRLAND

DUBLIN
DOUGLAS HYDE GALLERY
TRINITY COLLEGE

GERMANY / DEUTSCHLAND

DISTRIBUTOR / VERTRIEB
GVA VERLAGSSERVICE GÖTTINGEN
PF 2021
D-37010 GÖTTINGEN

BERLIN
BÜCHERBOGEN AM SAVIGNYPLATZ
STADTBAHNBOGEN 593
GALERIE 2000 KUNSTBUCHHANDLUNG
KNESEBECKSTRASSE 56/58
WALTHER KÖNIG BUCHHANDLUNG, MUSEUM FÜR GEGENWARTSKUNST
IM HAMBURGER BAHNHOF INVALIDENSTRASSE 50–51
WIENS LADEN & VERLAG
LINIENSTRASSE 158 (HOF)
WASMUTH GMBH & CO.
PFALZBURGERSTRASSE 43–44

BREMEN
BEIM STEINERNEN KREUZ GMBH
BEIM STEINERNEN KREUZ 1

DÜSSELDORF
LITERATUR BEI RUDOLF MÜLLER
NEUSTRASSE 38
WALTHER KÖNIG BUCHHANDLUNG
HEINRICH-HEINE-ALLEE 15

FRANKFURT
KUNST-BUCH, KUNSTHALLE SCHIRN
RÖMERBERG 7
WALTHER KÖNIG BUCHHANDLUNG
DOMSTRASSE 6

HAMBURG
HELMUT VON DER HÖH BUCHHANDLUNG
GROSSE BLEICHEN 21
SAUTTER + LACKMANN BUCHHANDLUNG
ADMIRALITÄTSTRASSE 71/72

HANNOVER
MERZ KUNSTBUCHHANDLUNG
KURT-SCHWITTERS-PLATZ

KARLSRUHE
HANS MENDE BUCHHANDLUNG
KARLSTRASSE 76

KÖLN
SCHADEN.COM BUCHHANDEL
BURGMAUER 10
WALTHER KÖNIG BUCHHANDLUNG
EHRENSTRASSE 4
KIOSK-BUCH-EVENT GMBH
IM MEDIAPARK 7

MÜNCHEN
HANS GOLTZ BUCHHANDLUNG
FÜR BILDENDE KUNST
TÜRKENSTRASSE 54
ILKA KÖNIG BUCHHANDLUNG
MAXIMILIANSTRASSE 35
L. WERNER BUCHHANDLUNG
RESIDENZSTRASSE 18

NÜRNBERG
WALTHER KÖNIG BUCHHANDLUNG
LUITPOLDSTRASSE 5

STUTTGART
LIMACHER BUCHHANDLUNG
KÖNIGSTRASSE 28 / KÖNIGSBAU

SPAIN / SPANIEN

BARCELONA
LAIE – CAIXAFÒRUM
MARQUES DE COMILLAS 6–8
LAIE – CCCB (CENTRE DE CULTURA CONTEMPORÀNIA DE BARCELONA)
MONTALEGRE 5

MADRID
MUSEO NACIONAL REINA SOFIA
C/ SANTA ISABEL, 52

FRANCE / FRANKREICH

PARIS
CENTRE POMPIDOU, FLAMMARION 4
26, RUE JACOB
GALERIE NATIONALE DU JEU DE PAUME
1, PLACE DE LA CONCORDE
LIBRAIRIE DU MUSÉE D'ART MODERNE
9, RUE GASTON DE SAINT-PAUL
CHRISTOPH DAVIET-THERY,
LIVRES & EDITIONS D'ARTISTES
10, RUE DUCHEFDELAVILLE
COLETTE
213, RUE SAINT-HONORÉ

ITALY / ITALIEN

MILANO
A&M BOOKSTORE
30, VIA TADINO

ROMA
GALLERIA NAZIONALE D'ARTE MODERNA
131, VIA DELLE BELLE ARTI
GALLERIA PRIMO PIANO
203, VIA PANISPERNA

NORWAY / NORWEGEN

OSLO
THE NATIONAL MUSEUM OF CONTEMPORARY ART
BANKPLASSEN 4 / SKATTEFOG

PORTUGAL

LISBOA
MODULO CENTRO DIFUSOR DE ARTE
CALÇADA DOS MESTRES 34 A–B

PORTO
MODULO CENTRO DIFUSOR DE ARTE
AV. BOAVISTA 854

SWEDEN / SCHWEDEN

STOCKHOLM
KULTURHUSET KONSTIG
MEDIA & KONSTBOKHANDEL
SERGELS TORG 3
MODERNA MUSEET
SKEPPSHOLMEN

GÖTEBORG
GÖTEBORGS KONSTMUSEUM
GÖTAPLATSEN / AVENYN

TURKEY / TÜRKEI

ISTANBUL
ROBINSON CRUSOE BOOKS PUSULA PRODUCTIONS
389 ISTIKAL CADDESI BEYOGLU

NETHERLANDS, BELGIUM AND LUXEMBURG

DISTRIBUTOR / VERTRIEB
IDEA BOOKS
NIEUWE HERENGRACHT 11
NL-1011 RK AMSTERDAM

NETHERLANDS / NIEDERLANDE

AMSTERDAM
ART BOOK
VAN BAERLESTRAAT 126
ATHENAEUM NIEUWSCENTRUM
SPUI 14–16
ROBERT PREMSELA BOOKSHOP
VAN BAERLESTRAAT 78

GRONINGEN
SCHOLTENS / WRISTERS BOOKSHOP
FULDENSTRAAT 20

ROTTERDAM
DONNER BOOKSHOP
LIJNBAAN 150

BELGIUM / BELGIEN

ANTWERPEN
F.N.A.C.
GROENPLAATS

BRUXELLES
TROPISMES LIBRAIRIES
GALERIE DES PRINCES 11

GENT
COPYRIGHT BOOKSHOP
JACOBIJNENSTRAAT 8

LUXEMBOURG / LUXEMBURG

LUXEMBOURG
CASINO LUXEMBOURG
41, RUE NOTRE-DAME

SWITZERLAND / SCHWEIZ

DISTRIBUTOR / VERTRIEB
SCHEIDEGGER & CO. C/O AVA
CENTRALWEG 16
CH-8910 AFFOLTERN A. A.

BASEL
FONDATION BEYELER
BASELSTRASSE 77, RIEHEN
GALERIE STAMPA
SPALENBERG 2
JÄGGI BUCHHANDLUNG
FREIE STRASSE 32
KUNSTHALLE BASEL
KLOSTERGASSE 5

BERN
STAUFFACHER BUCHHANDLUNG
IM KUNSTMUSEUM
HODLERSTR. 12

LUZERN
RÄBER BÜCHER AG
FRANKENSTRASSE 7-9

GENÈVE
LIBRAIRIE PAYOT
5, RUE DE CHANTEPOULET

MENDRISIO
GABRIELE CAPELLI LIBRERIA ARCHITETTURA
4, VIA NOBILI BOSIA

ST. GALLEN
RÖSSLITOR BÜCHER
WEBERGASSE 5

ZÜRICH
CALLIGRAMME BUCHHANDLUNG
HÄRINGSTRASSE 4
HOWEG BUCHHANDLUNG
WAFFENPLATZ 1
KUNSTGRIFF BUCHHANDLUNG
LIMMATSTRASSE 270
KUNSTHAUS ZÜRICH
HEIMPLATZ 1
KUNSTKIOSK
LIMMATQUAI 31
ORELL FÜSSLI KRAUTHAMMER
MARKTGASSE 12
ORELL FÜSSLI BUCHHANDLUNG
FÜSSLISTRASSE 4
SCALO BOOKS & LOOKS
WEINBERGSTRASSE 22 A
SEC 52 BUCHHANDLUNG
JOSEFSTRASSE 52

E X H I B I T I O N S

ZÜRICH

ARS FUTURA GALERIE AG	Bleicherweg 45 8002 Zürich Tel. 01 201 88 10 www.arsfutura.com info@arsfutura.com	MARIO SALA	**16.1.–6.3.2004**
DAROS EXHIBITIONS	Limmatstrasse 268 8005 Zürich Tel. 01 447 70 00 Fax 01 447 70 10 www.daros.ch	LOUISE BOURGEOIS	**13.3.–12.9.2004**
ELISABETH KAUFMANN	Müllerstrasse 57 8004 Zürich Tel./Fax 043 322 01 15 elkauf@yahoo.com	JAN FABRE "Wytte Hypnose"	**bis 25.1.2004**
		PAVEL PEPPERSTEIN	**Februar bis März 2004**
GALERIE LELONG	Utoquai 31 8008 Zürich Tel. 01 251 11 20 galerie.lelong@dplanet.ch	Artist books, Prints, Photography	**5.2.–27.3.2004**
		URSULA VON RYDINGSVARD "Outdoor – Indoor" – New Sculptures	**April bis Mai 2004**
MAI 36 GALERIE	Rämistrasse 37 8001 Zürich Tel. 01 261 68 80 www.artgalleries.ch/mai36 mai36@artgalleries.ch	MATT MULLICAN	**23.1.–28.2.2004**
		Arco Madrid	**12.2.–16.2.2004**
		Armory New York	**12.3.–15.3.2004**
MARK MÜLLER	Gessnerallee 36 8001 Zürich Tel. 01 211 81 55 www.markmueller.ch mark.mueller@dplanet.ch	JOACHIM BANDAU "Aquarelle und Skulpturen" Raum 3. FRANCIS BAUDEVIN	**10.1.–21.2.2004**
		Arco Madrid	**12.2.–16.2.2004**
		MARCIA HAFIF – "Paintings" Raum 3. STEFAN GRITSCH	**28.2.–10.4.2004**
		BEAT ZODERER	**17.4.–29.5.2004**
SEMINA RERUM IRÈNE PREISWERK	Cäcilienstrasse 3 8032 Zürich Tel. 01 251 26 39 www.seminarerum.ch ipreiswerk@bluewin.ch	CÉCILE WICK	**bis 31.1.2004**
		FLAVIO MICHELI	**5.2.–27.3.2004**
		SIMONE KAPPELER	**1.4.–27.5.2004**

E X H I B I T I O N S

BOB VAN ORSOUW	Limmatstrasse 270 8005 Zürich Tel. 01 273 11 00 mail@bobvanorsouw.ch	WALTER NIEDERMAYR NOBUYOSHI ARAKI Polaroids	**24.1.–13.3.2004** **20.3.–8.5.2004**
ANNEMARIE VERNA	Neptunstrasse 45 8032 Zürich Tel. 01 262 38 20 www.annemarie-verna.ch office@annemarie-verna.ch	FRED SANDBACK (1943–2003) In Memory SOL LE WITT Structure, Gouaches JERRY ZENIUK New Paintings	 **bis 31.1.2004** **10.2.–7.4.2004** **15.4.–29.5.2004**
JAMILEH WEBER	Waldmannstrasse 6 8001 Zürich Tel. 01 252 10 66 www.jamilehweber.com info@jamilehweber.com	KARL GERSTNER Bilder en Relief HANSPETER HOFMANN Fosbury Flop	**15.1.–28.2.2004** **5.3.–24.4.2004**
BRIGITTE WEISS	Müllerstrasse 67 8004 Zürich Tel. 01 241 83 35 www.likeyou.com/brigitteweiss brigitteweiss@bluewin.ch	IVES MAES (curated by Tom Nys) DAVID CHIEPPO	**9.1.–28.2. 2004** **5.3.–30.4.2004**

BASEL

NICOLAS KRUPP	Erlenstrasse 15 4058 Basel Tel. 061 683 32 65 www.nicolaskrupp.com nic@nicolaskrupp.com	HEIMO ZOBERNIG THOMAS BAUMANN ART Basel Miami Beach TUE GREENFORT JOHANNES WOHNSEIFER	**25.9.–15.11.2003** **20.11.–31.12.2003** **4.12.–7.12.2003** **8.1.–28.2.2004** **4.3.–24.4.2004**

ST. GALLEN

WILMA LOCK	Schmiedgasse 15 9000 St. Gallen Tel. 071 222 62 52 wilmalock@freesurf.ch	IMI KNOEBEL Neue Bilder	**25.2.–1.5.2004**

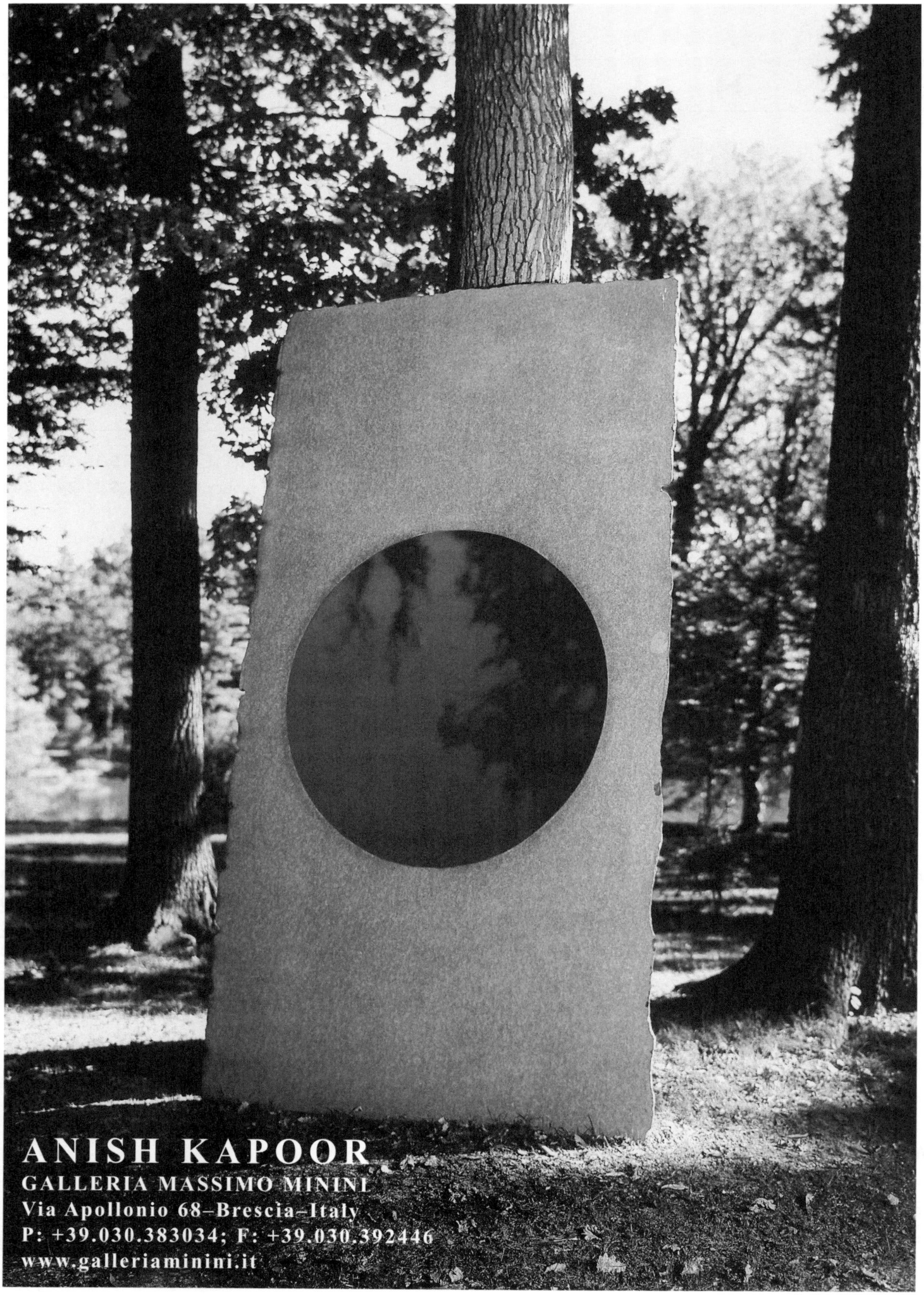

Photo: Paolo Mussat Sartor

important to me → as

My gallerists are as very friendly to all their employees (including cleaning people) as they are to their clients. They know a lot about art and its history and they love it with hair & body.
The extra-ordinary chief is funny & wise.
He thinks longterm as he is much more interested that I'm able to do (some) more good works than ~~tha~~ is to sell quickly.

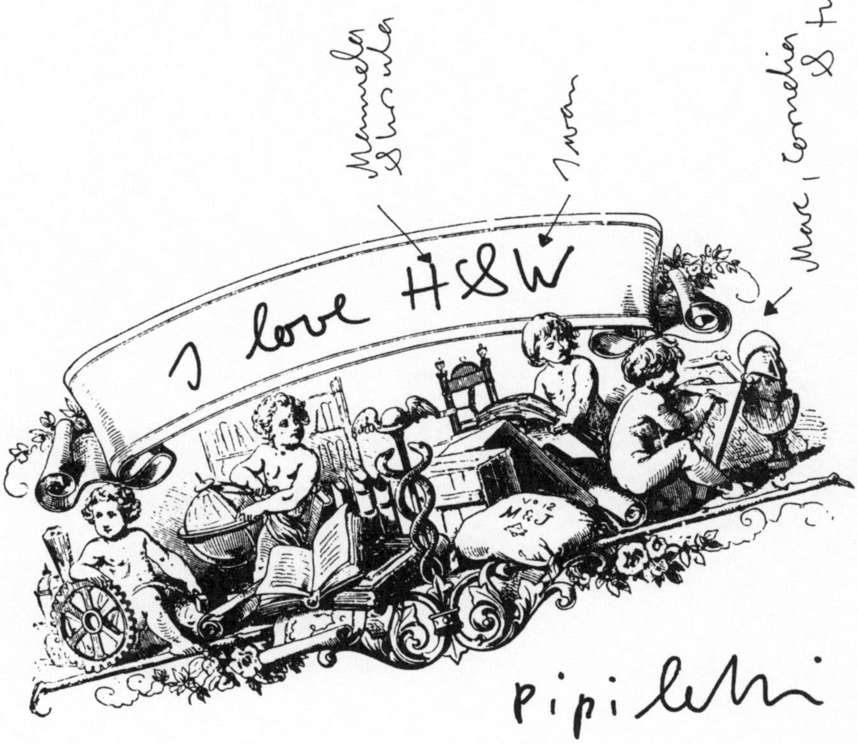

pipilotti

GEORG KARGL

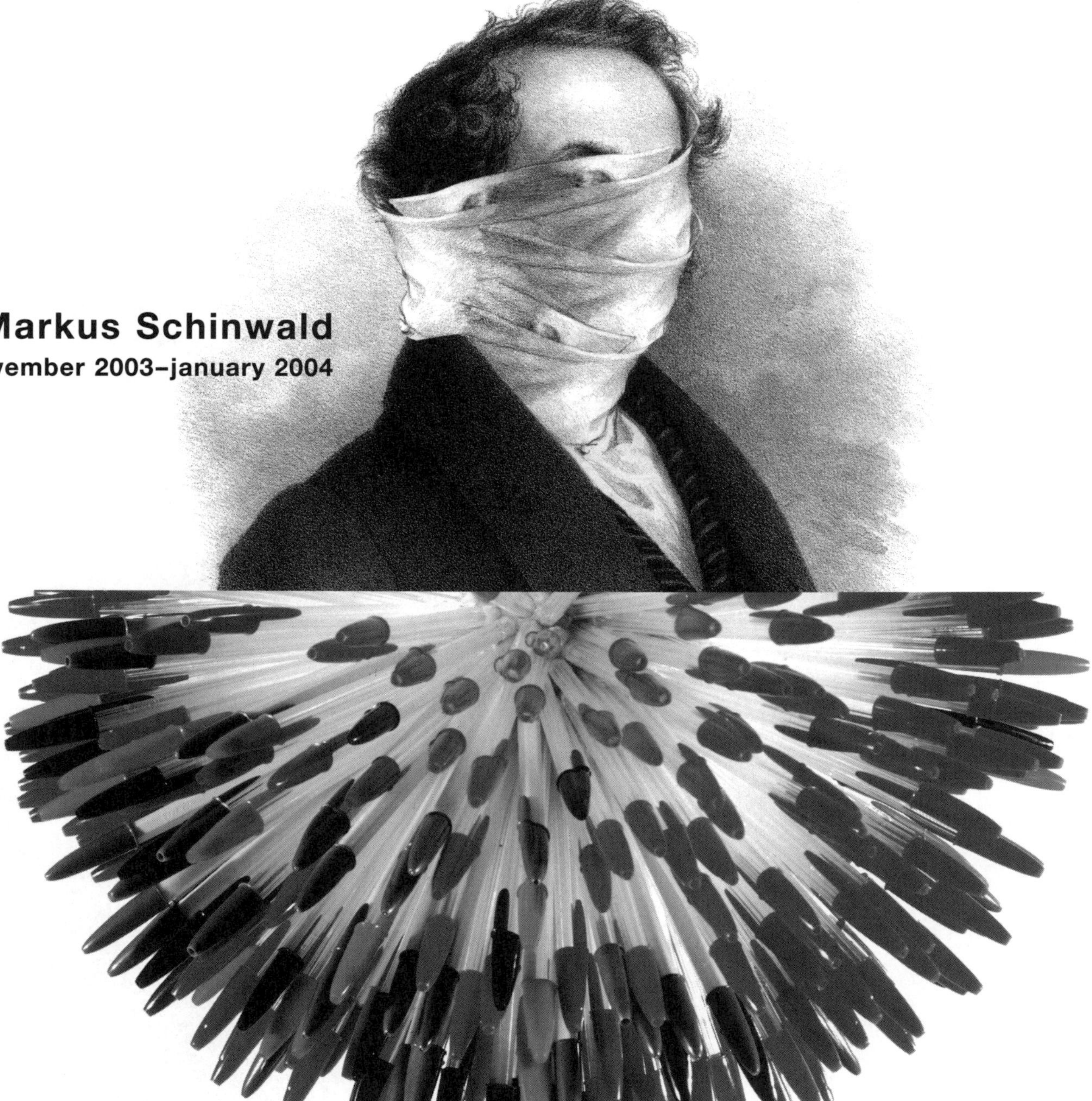

Markus Schinwald
november 2003–january 2004

Herbert Hinteregger
"Get the picture"
january 2004–march 2004

SCHLEIFMÜHLGASSE 5 WIEN 1040
TEL 5854199 FAX 58541999

WOLFGANG LAIB

DEZEMBER 2003 – FEBRUAR 2004

MAX BECKMAN

MÄRZ – MAI 2004

CARATSCH de PURY & LUXEMBOURG

LIMMATSTRASSE 264 CH-8005 ZÜRICH INFO@DPLZH.COM
T 41-1-276 80 20 F 41-1-276 80 21 MO–FR 10-6 SA 10-4

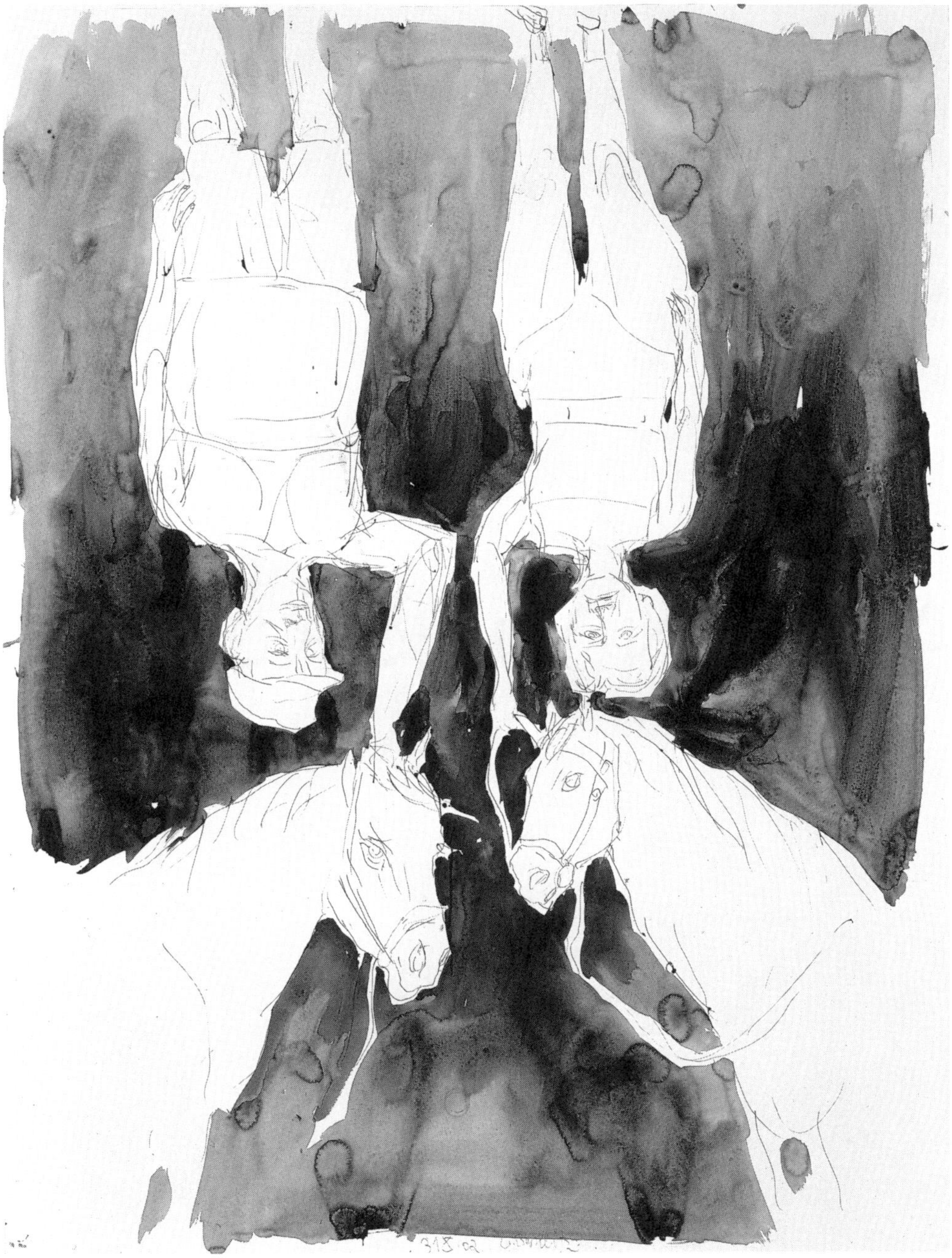

ANTON VIDOKLE

JANUARY 30 – MARCH 13, 2004

Massimo Audiello
526 West 26th Street, no 519 New York, NY 10001 t 212.675.9082 f 212.675.8680 email audiello@msn.com

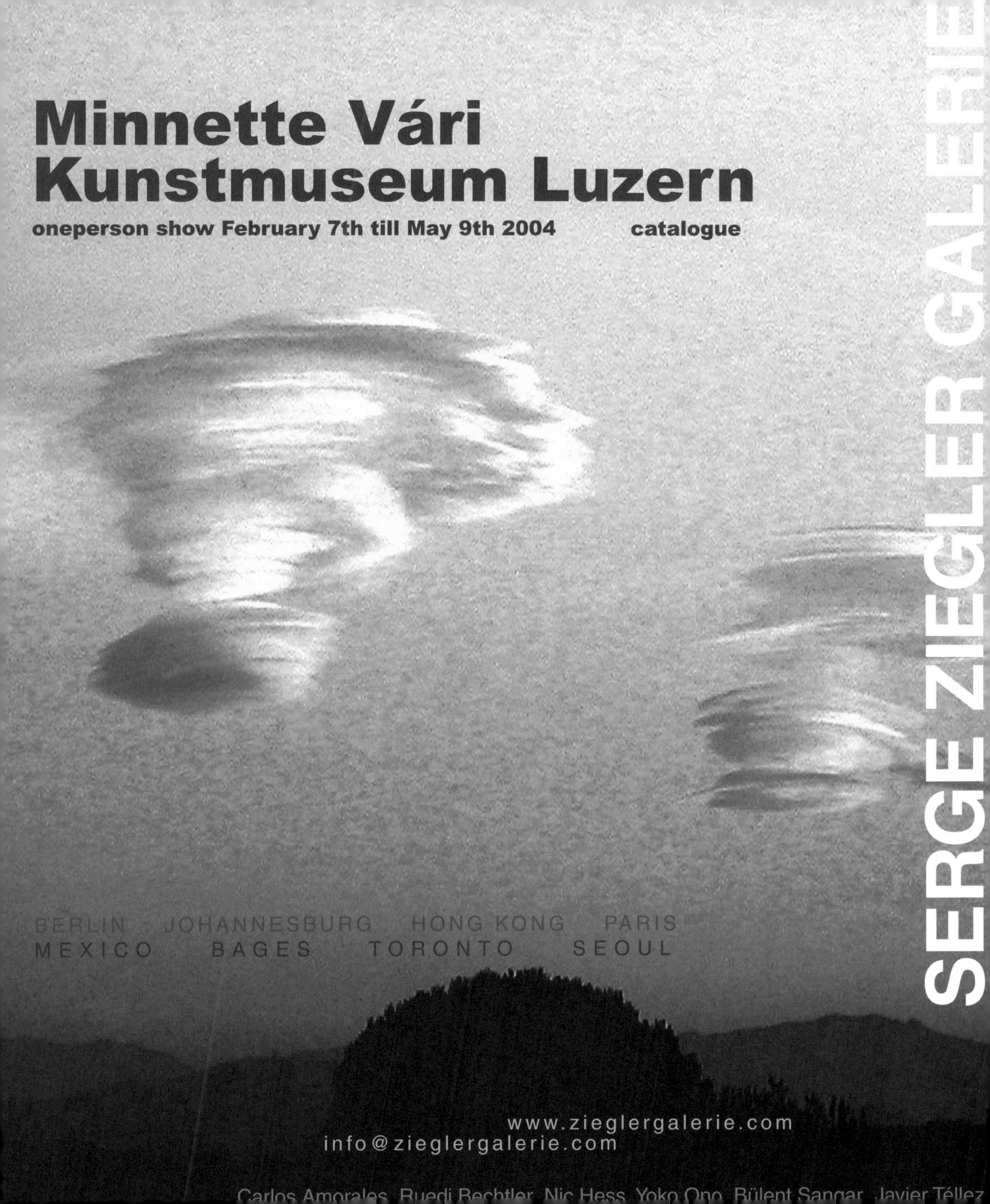
Minnette Vári
Kunstmuseum Luzern
oneperson show February 7th till May 9th 2004
catalogue
BERLIN JOHANNESBURG HONG KONG PARIS
MEXICO BAGES TORONTO SEOUL
SERGE ZIEGLER GALERIE
www.zieglergalerie.com
info@zieglergalerie.com
Carlos Amorales, Ruedi Bechtler, Nic Hess, Yoko Ono, Bülent Sangar, Javier Téllez

Dauer der Ausstellung: 22.01. bis 13.03.2004
contact@meyerkainer.at www.meyerkainer.com
T: +43 1 585 72 77 F: +43 1 585 75 39
A-1010 Wien, Eschenbachgasse 9
GALERIE MEYER KAINER
FRANZ WEST
erfahren (sie sind zu besitzen, sowohl taktil wie auch ~~eigentumsrechtlich~~) werden.
allerdings bisher nur in museen. jetzt endlich können sie auch in einer galerie
es ist keine idee, meine aussenskulpturen innen zu zeigen, sondern konvention,
GARTENMOEBEL

GARTENMOEBEL

es ist keine idee, meine aussenskulpturen innen zu zeigen, sondern konvention, allerdings bisher nur in museen. jetzt endlich können sie auch in einer galerie erfahren (sie sind zu besitzen, sowohl taktil wie auch ~~eigentumsrechtlich~~) werden.

FRANZ WEST

GALERIE MEYER KAINER

A-1010 Wien, Eschenbachgasse 9
T: +43 1 585 72 77 F: +43 1 585 75 39
contact@meyerkainer.at www.meyerkainer.com
Dauer der Ausstellung: 22.01. bis 13.03.2004

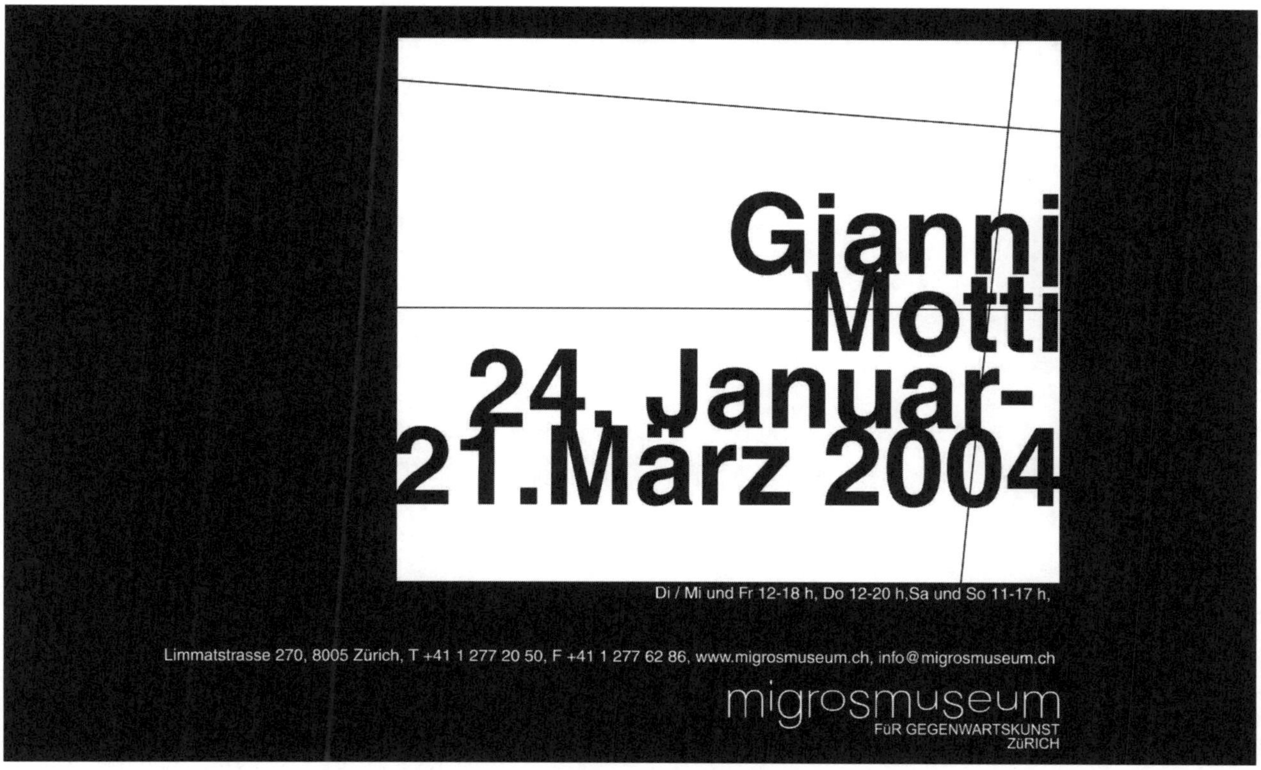

Gianni
Motti
24. Januar-
21.März 2004
Di / Mi und Fr 12-18 h, Do 12-20 h,Sa und So 11-17 h,
Limmatstrasse 270, 8005 Zürich, T +41 1 277 20 50, F +41 1 277 62 86, www.migrosmuseum.ch, info@migrosmuseum.ch
migrosmuseum
FüR GEGENWARTSKUNST
ZüRICH

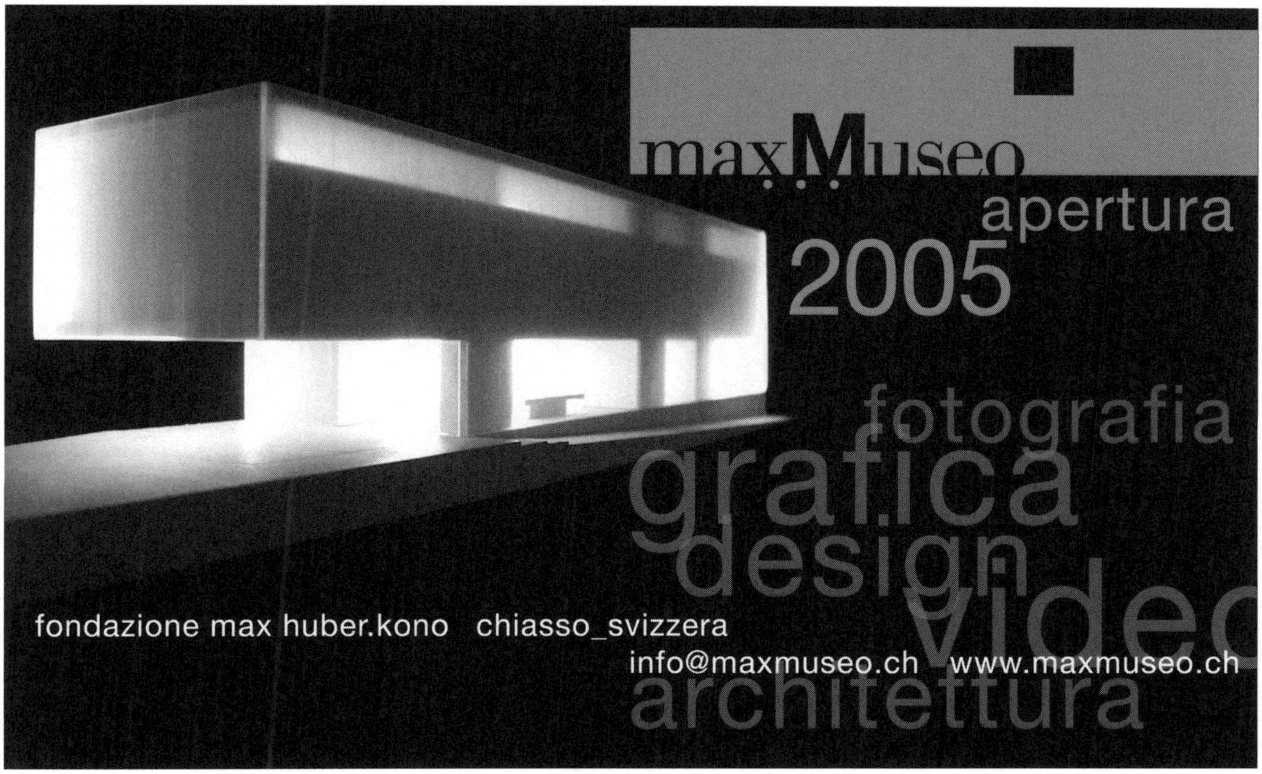

maxMuseo
apertura
2005
fotografia
grafica
design
video
architettura
fondazione max huber.kono chiasso_svizzera
info@maxmuseo.ch www.maxmuseo.ch

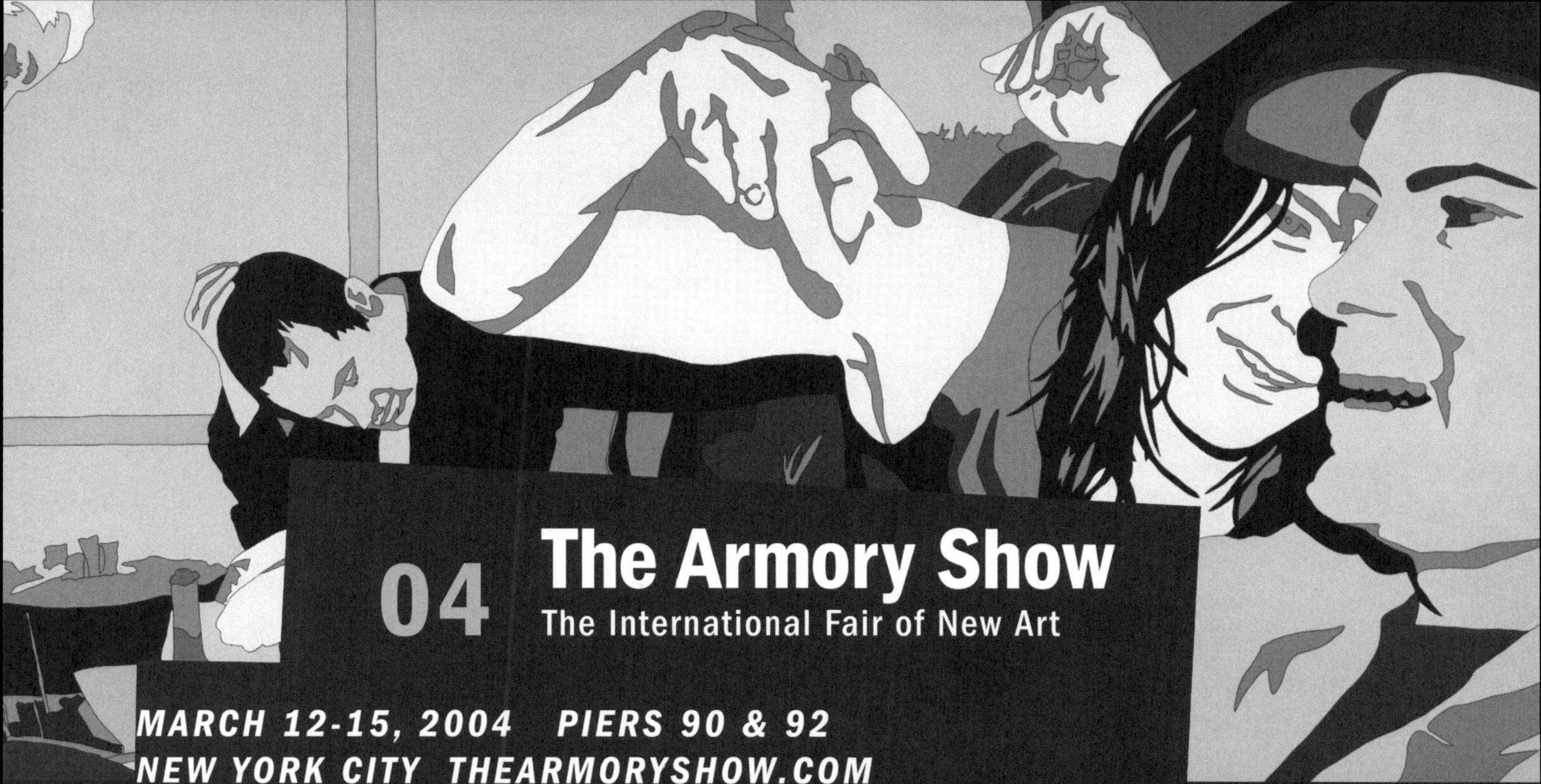

Lisa Ruyter, "Through A Glass Darkly", 2003, acrylic on canvas, 72 x 120 inches

04 The Armory Show

The International Fair of New Art

MARCH 12-15, 2004 PIERS 90 & 92
NEW YORK CITY THEARMORYSHOW.COM
Twelfth Avenue at 50th & 52nd Streets

» AACHEN » adamski/gallery for contemporary art » AMSTERDAM » Galerie Paul Andriesse » Annet Gelink Gallery » Torch Gallery » ANTWERP » Zeno X Gallery » BEIJING » Courtyard Gallery » BERLIN » Arndt & Partner » Galerie Ascan Crone, Andreas Osarek » Galerie Volker Diehl » Galerie EIGEN + ART » Kicken » Galerie NEU » Galerie Giti Nourbakhsch » Galerie Markus Richter » Galerie Thomas Schulte » Springer & Winckler Galerie » Galerie Barbara Thumm » BOSTON » Barbara Krakow Gallery » BROOKLYN » Bellwether » Pierogi » Roebling Hall » CHICAGO » Bodybuilder & Sportsman Gallery » Rhona Hoffman Gallery » Donald Young Gallery » COLOGNE » Buchmann Galerie » Galerie Ulrich Fiedler » Galerie Hammelehle und Ahrens » Michael Janssen Gallery » Galerie Christian Nagel » Galerie Aurel Scheibler » DRESDEN » Galerie Gebr. Lehmann » DUBLIN » Kerlin Gallery » DUSSELDORF » Sies + Höke Galerie » EDINBURGH » doggerfisher » FRANKFURT » L.A. Galerie-Lothar Albrecht » GLASGOW » The Modern Institute » HAMBURG » Jürgen Becker Galerie » Galerie Karin Guenther » Produzentengalerie » Galerie Sfeir-Semler » KARLSRUHE » Meyer Riegger Galerie » LONDON » The Approach » aspreyjacques » Sadie Coles HQ » Corvi-Mora » Entwistle » Stephen Friedman Gallery » Frith Street Gallery » greengrassi » Haunch of Venison » Lisson Gallery » Victoria Miro Gallery » Modern Art » Maureen Paley Interim Art » The Paragon Press » Timothy Taylor Gallery Ltd. » White Cube/Jay Jopling » Wilkinson Gallery » LOS ANGELES » Blum & Poe » China Art Objects Galleries » Marc Foxx » Mary Goldman Gallery » Michael Kohn Gallery » Richard Telles Fine Art » Susanne Vielmetter Los Angeles Projects » MADRID » Galería Marta Cervera » MEXICO CITY » Nina Menocal » Galería OMR » MILAN » Galleria Massimo De Carlo » MOSCOW » Aidan Gallery » NEW YORK » 303 Gallery » Brooke Alexander » Alexander and Bonin » American Fine Arts, Co. » Artemis Greenberg Van Doren Gallery » Peter Blum Gallery » Marianne Boesky Gallery » Tanya Bonakdar Gallery » Spencer Brownstone Gallery » Christine Burgin/Julie Sylvester » Clementine Gallery » James Cohan Gallery » Cohan and Leslie » CRG Gallery » D'Amelio Terras » Deitch Projects » Derek Eller Gallery » Feigen Contemporary » Ronald Feldman Fine Arts, Inc. » Fredericks Freiser Gallery » Klemens Gasser & Tanja Grunert, Inc. » GBE (Modern) » Sandra Gering Gallery » Barbara Gladstone Gallery » Marian Goodman Gallery » Gorney Bravin + Lee » Greene Naftali » I-20 » Susan Inglett » Casey Kaplan 10-6 » Paul Kasmin Gallery » Sean Kelly Gallery » Anton Kern Gallery » Nicole Klagsbrun Gallery » Leo Koenig, Inc. » Kravets/Wehby Gallery » Andrew Kreps Gallery » Lehmann Maupin » Galerie Lelong » LFL Gallery » Lombard-Freid Fine Arts » Luhring Augustine » Florence Lynch Gallery » maccarone inc. » Matthew Marks Gallery » Sara Meltzer Gallery » Metro Pictures » Robert Miller Gallery » Yossi Milo Gallery » Modern Culture » Paul Morris Gallery » Murray Guy » Carolina Nitsch » Nolan/Eckman Gallery » P·P·O·W » PaceWildenstein » Friedrich Petzel Gallery » Postmasters Gallery » The Project » Daniel Reich Gallery » Julie Saul Gallery » Kenny Schachter conTEMPorary » Jack Shainman Gallery » Brent Sikkema » Stux Gallery » Team Gallery » Jack Tilton Gallery » Leslie Tonkonow Artworks + Projects » Henry Urbach Architecture » David Zwirner » OSAKA » Kodama » OSLO » Galleri Wang » PARIS » Art : Concept » galerie cent8 – serge le borgne » Galerie Chantal Crousel » Galerie Anne de Villepoix » in SITU Fabienne Leclerc » Yvon Lambert » Galerie Nelson » Galerie Nathalie Obadia » Galerie Emmanuel Perrotin » Galerie Praz-Delavallade » Galerie Almine Rech » Galerie Thaddaeus Ropac » Galerie Georges-Philippe & Nathalie Vallois » SAN FRANCISCO » Rena Bransten Gallery » Jack Hanley Gallery » SAN GIMIGNANO » Galleria Continua » SAN JOSE (COSTA RICA) » Jacob Karpio Galería » SANTA MONICA CA » Angles Gallery » Rosamund Felsen Gallery » Richard Heller Gallery » SAO PAULO » Galeria Brito Cimino » Galeria Fortes Vilaça » SEOUL » Gallery Hyundai » SEVILLE » Galería Pepe Cobo » SHANGHAI » ShanghART » STOCKHOLM » Andréhn-Schiptjenko » Galleri Magnus Karlsson » SYDNEY » Roslyn Oxley9 Gallery » TEL AVIV » Dvir Gallery » Sommer Contemporary Art » TOKYO » Taka Ishii Gallery » Tomio Koyama Gallery » Mizuma Art Gallery Co., Ltd. » Ota Fine Arts » SCAI » Gallery Side 2 » TURIN » Galleria Franco Noero » TORONTO » Susan Hobbs Gallery » VIENNA » Kerstin Engholm Galerie » Georg Kargl » Galerie Krinzinger » Gabriele Senn Galerie » ZURICH » Galerie Hauser & Wirth » Mai 36 Galerie » Parkett Editions » Galerie Eva Presenhuber

» OPENING NIGHT PREVIEW PARTY TO BENEFIT THE EXHIBITION PROGRAM OF THE MUSEUM OF MODERN ART, NEW YORK THURSDAY MARCH 11, 2004 «
» FOR INFORMATION ABOUT THE OPENING NIGHT PREVIEW PARTY CALL 212.708.9680 OR EMAIL SPECIALEVENTS@MOMA.ORG «

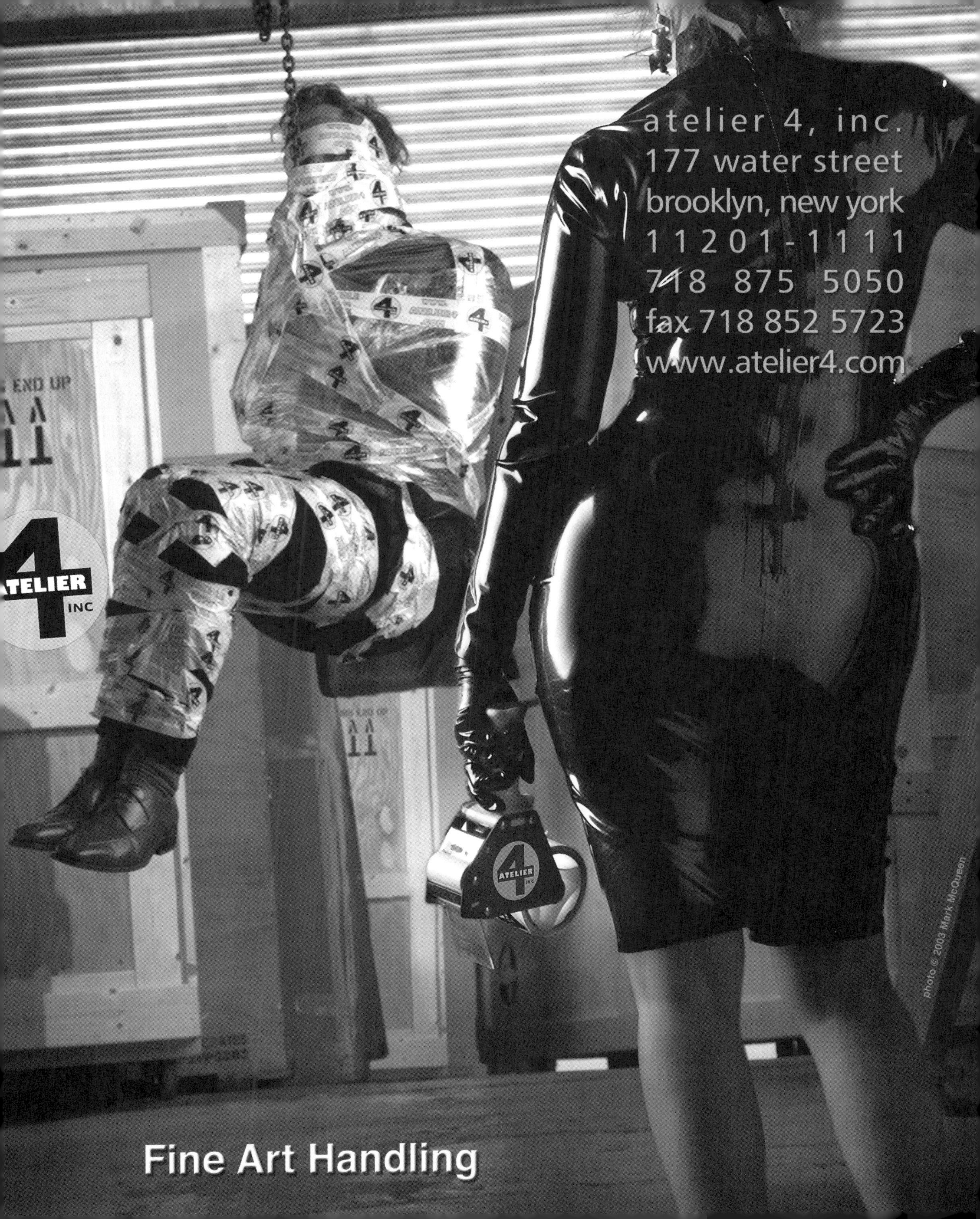
atelier 4, inc.
177 water street
brooklyn, new york
11201-1111
718 875 5050
fax 718 852 5723
www.atelier4.com
ATELIER 4 INC
photo © 2003 Mark McQueen
Fine Art Handling

design, communication and technology for on– and offline media

eyekon *on/offline media*

About us Eyekon is a full-service communication agency which has dealt with innovative, integrated communication in digital and analog media since it was founded in 1995. Our strength lies in establishing the interplay between design, communication and technology, or what can best be described as *"making sense"*. In our opinion, communication must not only make sense, it must also make use of all of the senses.

About our work Distinctiveness, originality and competent use of the possibilities electronic communication has to offer are integral components of our design. We not only pay particular attention to the visual aspects, we also delve below the surface, attaching a great deal of importance to organizing the information in logical and comprehensible structures. Our expertise encompasses all the wide-ranging facets of the media. We are experts at utilizing the potential of these diverse means of communication. Our concepts are clear-cut, and we have the knowledge and experience to realize our ideas not only visually, but also technically. Our consulting is geared towards sustainability and a design capable of meeting the future needs of our projects as regards concept, design and technology.

About our philosophy Our clients are our partners. Successful collaboration has been the key to maintaining long-term relations with them. By continually exchanging information with the clients and also accompanying them far beyond the actual projects, our consulting expertise contributes to lasting success. Moreover, clear structures in the projects guarantee efficient working processes and optimal results.

A selection of our references From the beginning, Eyekon has designed and managed projects for institutions and the cultural sector. A selection of our long-standing clients is provided below:

- Swiss National Library SLB
- University of Zurich
- Zürcher Hochschule Winterthur ZHW
- Verein Zürcher Museen
- Parkett Publishers

http://www.eyekon.ch

IT consulting, CMS, programming As a communication agency committed to long-term relations with our clients, we place great value on transparency and sustainability within the framework of IT consultation and the technical conception and realization of our solutions.

At present, the market for content management systems is still in the midst of a consolidation phase. Obtaining individual solutions from large and small providers is, therefore, still a high investment risk. In consideration of this fact, Eyekon uses proven well-established open source technologies. For complex projects we use the Zope open source applications server.

Zope has become one of the leading software platforms for content management systems, intranets and portal applications in recent years. There are countless modules available for extension, so that even the most unique problem (e.g., connection to existing information systems such as image data banks) can be solved efficiently. Zope, the international standard, has enabled us, as service providers of communication, to carry out complex projects with state-of-the-art features which have been custom tailored to meet the needs of the client, all the while maintaining a realistic budget.

A worldwide team of developers is involved, guaranteeing the future capacity of this standard as well as the sustainability of an investment in a solution based on this standard. The risk involved in being bound to one sole provider, which would probably require the addition of an assortment of individual programming solutions, is rendered entirely irrelevant with the decision to use Zope.

We have successfully implemented this standard in our complex projects for the Swiss Red Cross (SRK) (www.redcross.ch). Eyekon realized both the Web site and the intranet for the Swiss Red Cross.

Neither license fees for the application server nor a client license are required for Zope. Furthermore, the fact that there is an independent market providing support, that the hardware requirements are moderate, and that the Zope applications server is compatible with different platforms, e.g., Linux, Solaris and Windows, are additional advantages of this open source standard.

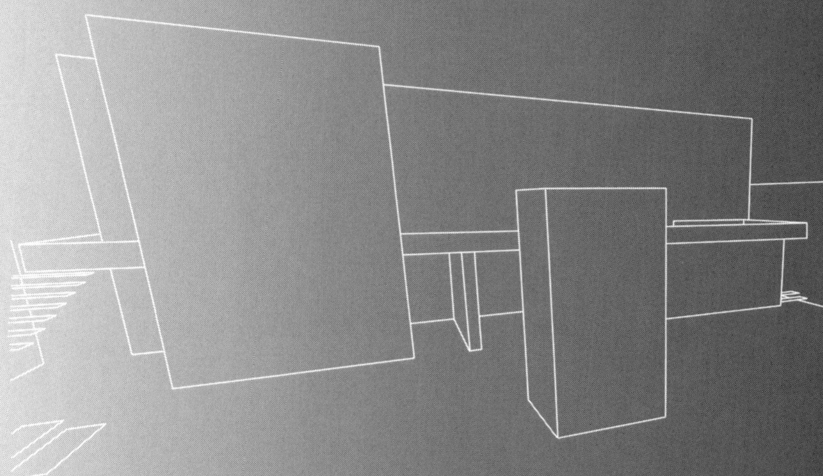

Gary Hume

24. Januar bis 21. März 2004

03. April bis 30. Mai 2004

Santiago Sierra

KUB

***Kunsthaus* Bregenz**
Karl Tizian Platz
A-6900 Bregenz

Telefon +43-(0)55 74-485 94-0
www.kunsthaus-bregenz.at

Dienstag – Sonntag 10 – 18 Uhr
Donnerstag 10 – 21 Uhr

SI WINTER + SPRING PROGRAM

ALEKSANDRA MIR / NAMING TOKYO PART II
JONATHAN MONK / TIME AND OR SPACE

OTHER EXHIBITIONS: DECLAN CLARKE / ISABELL HEIMERDINGER / SHIRANA SHAHBAZI

NOVEMBER 13 – DECEMBER 20 2003

MOMOYO TORIMITSU
NORMA JEANE

JANUARY 13 – FEBRUARY 20 2004

FIVE BILLION YEARS
GROUP SHOW WITH FRANÇOIS CURLET, PHILIPPE DECRAUZAT, SYLVIE FLEURY, TONY MATELLI, JONATHAN MONK AND MANY MORE TO BE ANNOUNCED

MARCH 10 – APRIL 30 2004

CHRISTOPH BÜCHEL

MAY 25 – AUGUST 7 2004

PLUS SI CURATOR TALKS 2003/4 BY

BEATRIX RUF (KUNSTHALLE ZÜRICH), THEODORA VISCHER (SCHAULAGER, BASEL), MASSIMILIANO GIONI (VENICE BIENNALE) AND OTHERS.

PREVIOUS SPEAKERS: HARALD SZEEMANN, JERÔME SANS AND NICOLAS BOURRIAU (PALAIS DE TOKYO, PARIS)

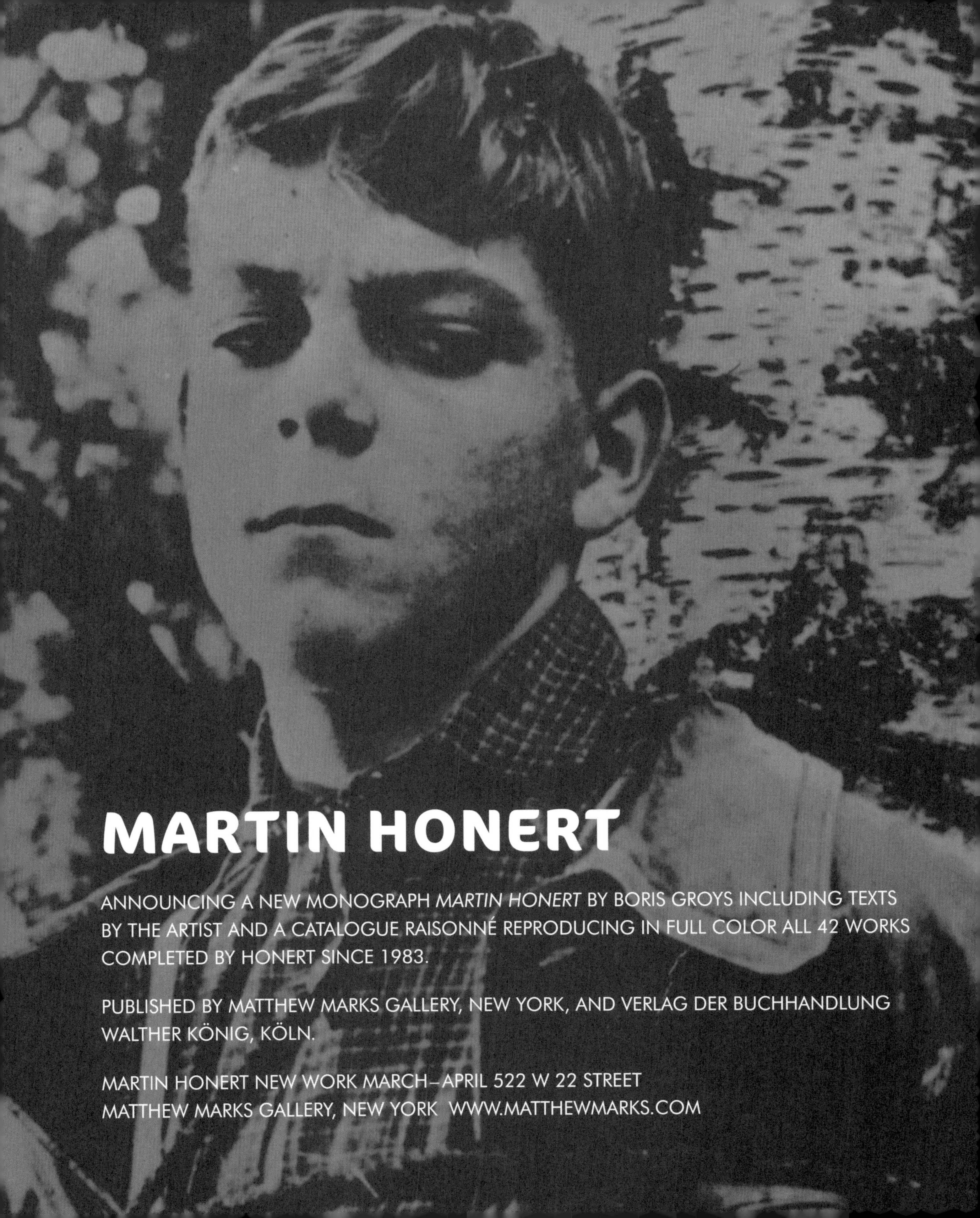
MARTIN HONERT
ANNOUNCING A NEW MONOGRAPH MARTIN HONERT BY BORIS GROYS INCLUDING TEXTS BY THE ARTIST AND A CATALOGUE RAISONNÉ REPRODUCING IN FULL COLOR ALL 42 WORKS COMPLETED BY HONERT SINCE 1983.
PUBLISHED BY MATTHEW MARKS GALLERY, NEW YORK, AND VERLAG DER BUCHHANDLUNG WALTHER KÖNIG, KÖLN.
MARTIN HONERT NEW WORK MARCH–APRIL 522 W 22 STREET
MATTHEW MARKS GALLERY, NEW YORK WWW.MATTHEWMARKS.COM

Arnie Zane: Photographs

In celebration of the 20th anniversary of
the Bill T. Jones / Arnie Zane Dance Company

January 8 – February 7

521 West 21st Street

Rudolf Stingel

February 14 – March 13

534 West 21st Street

Sophie Calle

March 20 – April 17

534 West 21st Street

Claes Oldenburg & Coosje van Bruggen

April 24 – May 29

534 West 21st Street

Paula Cooper Gallery

534 West 21st Street New York NY 10011 T 212 255 1105 F 212 255 5156

info@paulacoopergallery.com

karl gerstner

bilder en relief

15. januar – 28. februar 2004

hanspeter hofmann

fosbury flop

5. märz – 24. april 2004

galerie jamileh weber

waldmannstrasse 6
ch–8001 zürich
telefon +41 1 252 10 66
telefax +41 1 252 11 32
www.jamilehweber.com
info@jamilehweber.com
di-fr 11–18h, sa 10–16h

COLLECTOR OF URBAN DEBRIS:
THE ULTIMATE ACCESSORY FOR
EVERY POOCH-HAPPY FLANEUR.

BUNTER HUND: SINNBILD UND
UNVERZICHTBARES ACCESSOIRE
DES GLÜCKLICHEN FLANEURS.

PARKETT 69

FRANCIS ALŸS

GHETTO COLLECTOR, 2003

Tin, magnets, plastic string, rubber wheels,
25 design variations, ca. 6 1/2 x 9 x 5".
Edition of 99, signed and numbered.
$ 1500 / € 1200

Blech, Magnete, Plastikschnur, Gummiräder,
25 Design-Variationen, ca. 16,5 x 23 x 12,5 cm.
Auflage: 99, signiert und nummeriert.
CHF 1900 / € 1200

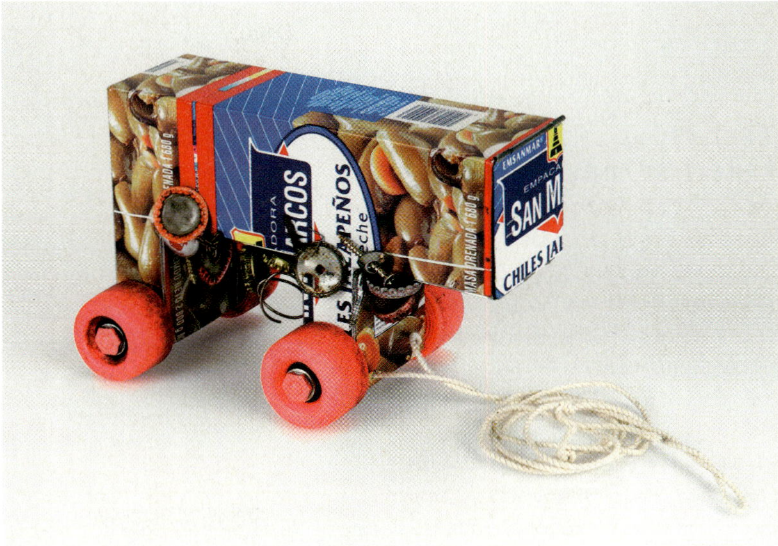

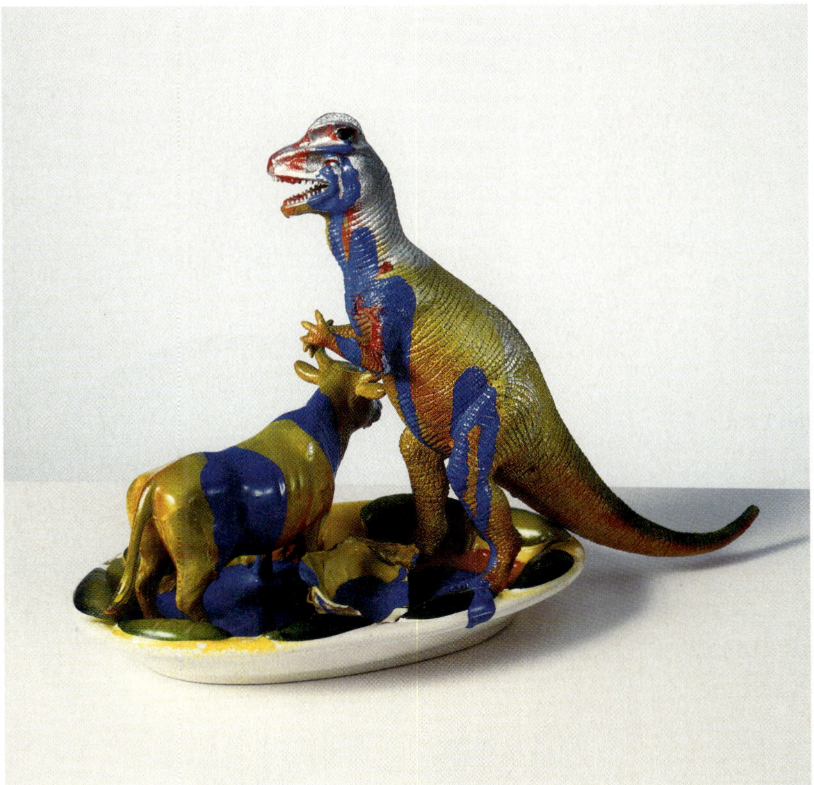

SURVIVAL OF THE TASTIEST:
EVOLUTION IN A NUTSHELL
DEMONSTRATED BY THE ODD COUPLE.

ZEIT ALS MAHLZEIT –
ODER DER EVOLUTIONÄRE TANZ
ALLEN FLEISCHES.

PARKETT 69

ISA GENZKEN

AL DENTE, 2003

Italienische Keramik, Lack, Kunststoff.
Je individuell von Hand gestalteter Teller
mit zwei Spielzeugfiguren (Kuh und Dinosaurier),
ca. 30 x 20 x 26 cm.
Auflage: 74, signiertes und nummeriertes Zertifikat.
$ 1200 / € 1000

Italian ceramic, lacquer, plastic.
Plate with two toy figures (cow and dinosaur),
each unique and handmade by the artist,
ca. 11 13/16 x 7 7/8 x 10 1/4".
Edition of 74, signed and numbered certificate.
CHF 1500 / € 1000

THE WRITING ON THE WALL AS UNIVERSAL PATTERN.

DIE SCHRIFT AN DER WAND ALS WINDROSE DES UNIVERSUMS.

PARKETT 61

MATTHEW RITCHIE

THE BAD NEED, 2001

Adhesive-backed vinyl, ca. 36 1/4 x 40 1/4",
to be installed at a height of 41 1/2" o.c. on a wall surface
(with a minimum size of 96 x 72") painted with the
eggshell acrylic paint supplied as part of the edition.
Accompanied by an annotated artist's book.
Edition of 70, signed and numbered, **$ 1380 / € 1270**

Vinylfolie mit Haftbeschichtung, ca. 91 x 101 cm, zur
festen Installation auf einer Höhe von 105 cm (Bildmitte) auf einer (mindestens 244 cm hohen und 183 cm breiten)
eierschalenfarben gestrichenen Wand. Die Acrylfarbe ist
Bestandteil der Edition.
Begleitbuch mit Anmerkungen des Künstlers.
Auflage: 70, signiert und nummeriert, **CHF 1950.– / € 1270**

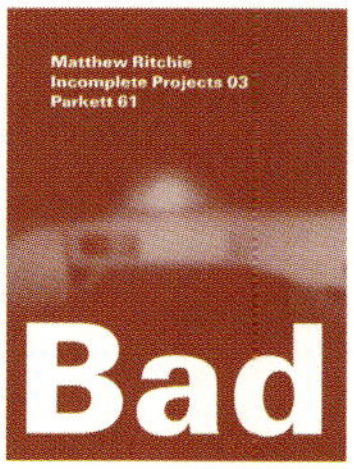

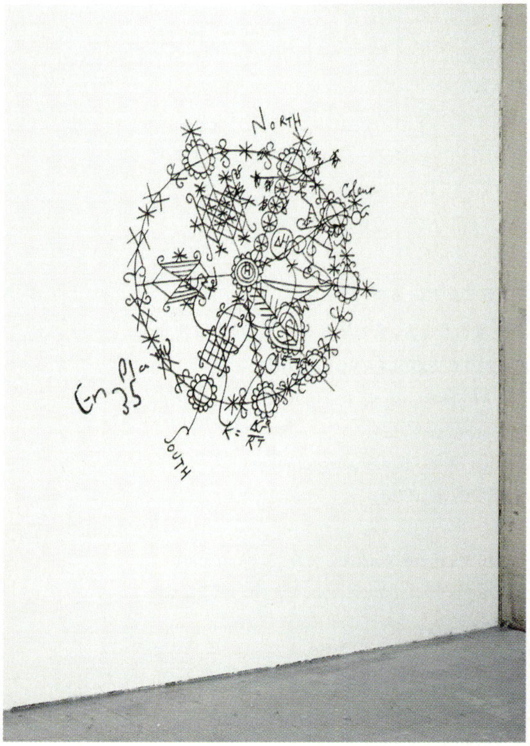

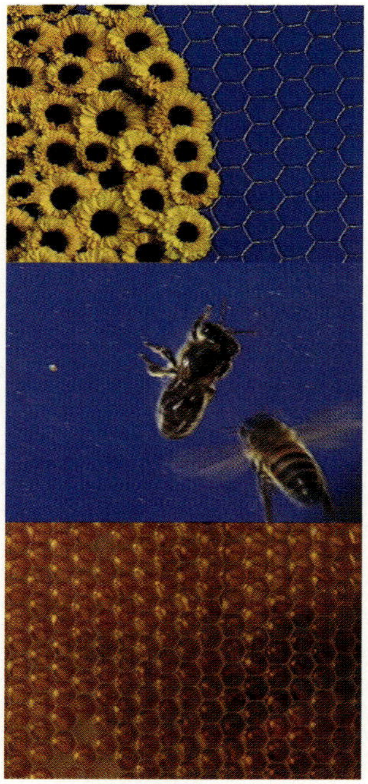

BEES IN HEXAGONS, ROOMS FILMED, BRIGHTNESS OF SHADOWS,
AND QUANTUM PHYSICS.

BIENEN, SECHSECKE, HELLE, SCHATTIGE RÄUME UND QUANTENPHYSIK.

PARKETT 60

DIANA THATER

UNTITLED, 2000

DVD (Digital Video Disc)
with endless loop.
Edition of 150,
signed and numbered, **$ 430 / € 390**

OHNE TITEL, 2000

DVD (Digital Video Disc),
Endlos-Schlaufe.
Auflage: 150,
signiert und nummeriert, **CHF 600.– / € 390**

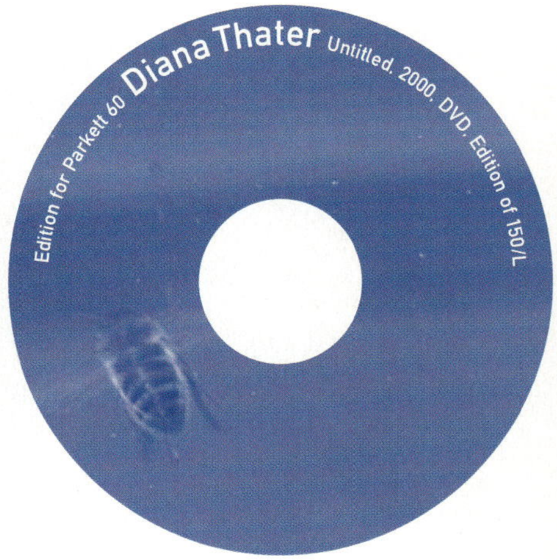

HAIRLINE, COASTLINE: A MENTAL AND PHYSICAL TOPOGRAPHY.

JORDAN, STYX ODER HARMLOSER WEEKEND-PLAUSCH AM SEE?

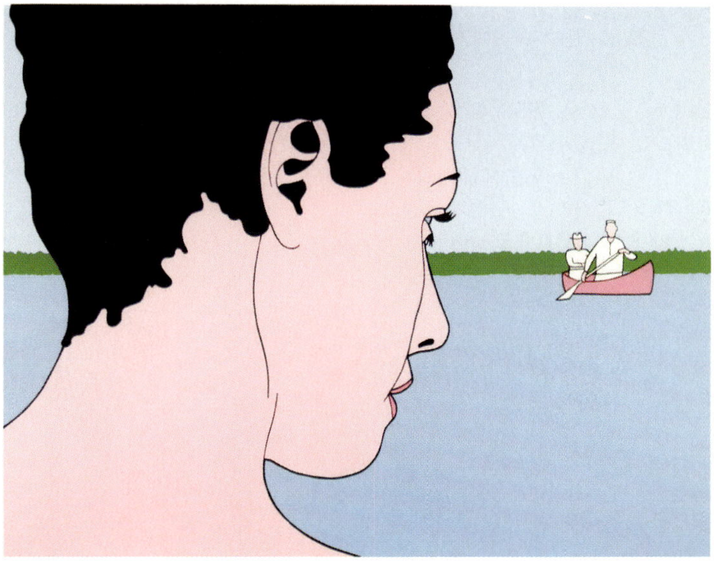

PARKETT 62

JOHN WESLEY

BOYFRIENDS, 2001

6-color silkscreen on Coventry 290 gm^2;
paper size 31 x 38", image size 28 x 35".
Printed by Bob Blanton, Brand X Editions, New York
Edition of 70, signed and numbered, **$ 1050 / € 980**

Siebdruck (6 Farben) auf Coventry 290 gm^2;
Papierformat 87,7 x 96,5 cm; Bild 71 x 89 cm.
Gedruckt von Bob Blanton, Brand X Editions, New York
Auflage: 70, signiert und nummeriert, **CHF 1500.– / € 980**

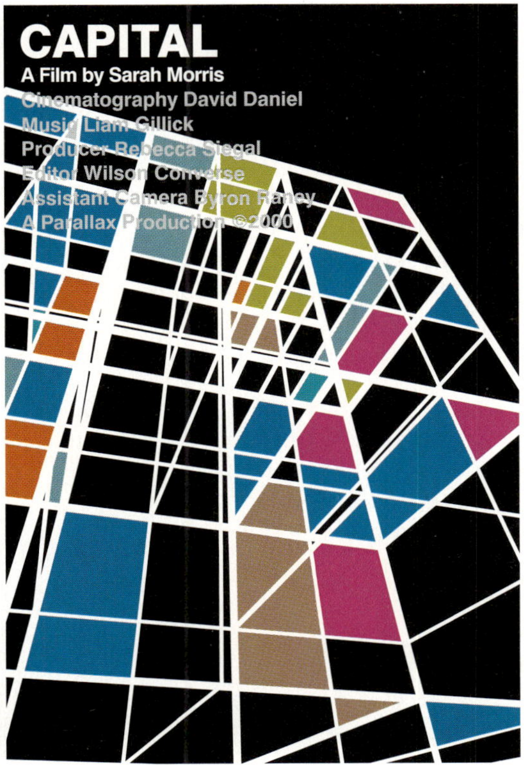

IN AND OUT OF LINE: LOOK UP, LOOK THROUGH, LOOK INTO THE DECEPTIVE TRANSPARENCE OF STRUCTURE.

KAPITALE ERFAHRUNG: DIE TRÜGERISCHE TRANSPARENZ DER STRUKTUR AUF SICH WIRKEN LASSEN.

PARKETT 61

SARAH MORRIS

CAPITAL (A FILM BY SARAH MORRIS), 2001

8-color silkscreen on 300 gm^2 Somerset satin, 60 x 40".
Designed by Sarah Morris/Peter Saville, printed by Coriander Studio Ltd., London.
Edition of 70, signed and numbered, **$ 1380 / € 1270**

Siebdruck (8 Farben) auf 300 gm^2 Somerset-Satin, 150 x 100 cm.
Design Sarah Morris/Peter Saville, gedruckt bei Coriander Studio Ltd., London.
Auflage: 70, signiert und nummeriert, **CHF 1950.– / € 1270**

MINIATURE METAPHYSICAL MAELSTROM:
STRETCHED IN SPACE TO THE BREAKING POINT AND BEYOND.

IN DEN RAUM GESPANNT BIS ZUR SCHMERZGRENZE UND DARÜBER HINAUS:
EIN SINNLICHES GLEICHNIS DER EXISTENZ.

PARKETT 69

ANISH KAPOOR

UNTITLED, 2003

Perspex, handtinted stocking, paint,

10 ¹/₄ x 10 ¹/₄ x 15".

Edition of 60, signed and numbered certificate.

$ 1900 / € 1700

OHNE TITEL, 2003

Perspex, handgefärbter Strumpf, Farbe,

26 x 26 x 38 cm.

Auflage: 60, signiertes und nummeriertes Zertifikat.

CHF 2500 / € 1700

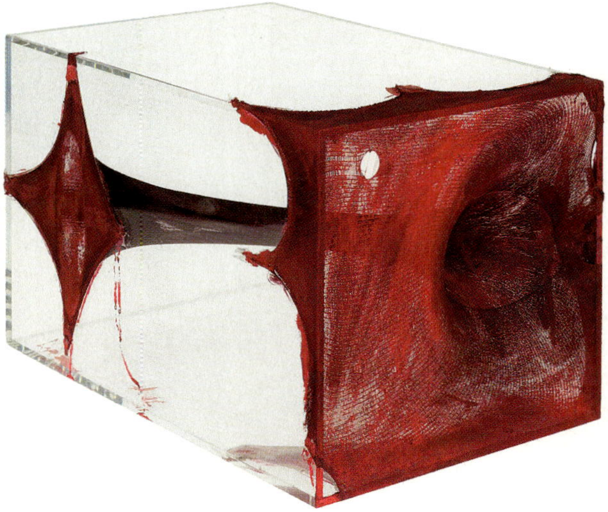

IGNORANCE IS THE MIRROR OF KNOWLEDGE
KNOWLEDGE IS THE MIRROR OF IGNORANCE

UNWISSEN IST DER SPIEGEL DES WISSENS
WISSEN IST DER SPIEGEL DES UNWISSENS

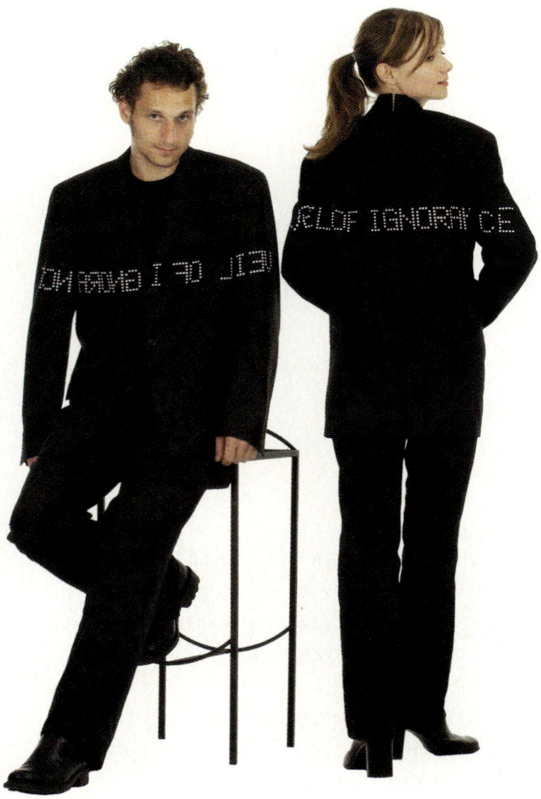

PARKETT 68

EIJA-LIISA AHTILA,

VEIL OF IGNORANCE, 2003

Pure wool jacket with text printed on front (mirror-inverted) and back.

Handprinted silkscreen lettering by Atelier für Siebdruck Lorenz Boegli, Zurich.

Available in 5 sizes (see size table below). Edition of 70, signed certificate.

$ 1400 / € 1200

Reines Wolljackett mit aufgedrucktem Text vorn und hinten (vorne spiegelverkehrt).

Handbedruckt bei Atelier für Siebdruck Lorenz Boegli, Zürich.

Erhältlich in 5 Grössen (siehe untenstehende Tabelle).

Auflage: 70, signiertes Zertifikat. **CHF 1800 / € 1200**

Measurements in cm / Masse in cm:

Men's Sizes / Herrengrössen: Continental European	US/UK	shoulder width / Schulter-breite	back width/ Rücken-breite	back length Rücken-länge	sleeve length / Ärmel-länge	chest measurement Brust-umfang /
48	38	62	48	77	65	110
C 96	38 short	62	48	75	63	114
50	40	64	49	79	66	114.5
C 100	40 short	64	49	76	64	116.5
52	42	66	51	81	67	117

INSTRUMENT DER GESCHÄRFTEN WAHRNEHMUNG. VIELLEICHT EIN SELBSTPORTRÄT ODER EIN BILD DER ROLLE DES KÜNSTLERS, DER ALLTÄGLICHE ABLÄUFE, DIE IN DER UNSCHÄRFE DER ROUTINE VERSCHWINDEN, IN DEN BRENNPUNKT ZURÜCKHOLT.

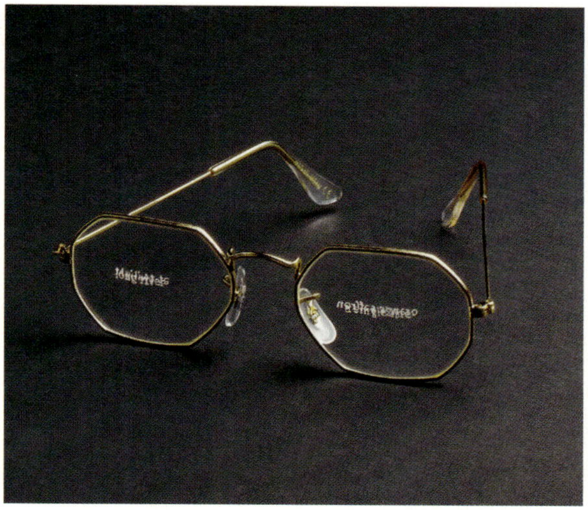

PARKETT 44

RIRKRIT TIRAVANIJA

UNTITLED, 1995 (450/375)

Gold-rimmed Ray Ban glasses with engraving on the lenses:
LONG RIVER A SINGLE LINE
ORANGE SAFFRON AT TWILIGHT
Ed. 80, numbered, with signed certificate, **$ 530 / € 490**

OHNE TITEL, 1995 (450/375)

Metallbrille Ray Ban mit Gravur auf den Gläsern:
LONG RIVER A SINGLE LINE
ORANGE SAFFRON AT TWILIGHT
Ed. 80, nummeriert, mit signiertem Zertifikat, **CHF 750.– / € 490**

INSTRUMENT OF HEIGHTENED PERCEPTION. A SELF-PORTRAIT PERHAPS OR A PICTURE OF THE PART PLAYED BY THE ARTIST AS HE BRINGS INTO FOCUS THE DAILY CHORES BLURRED BY HABIT.

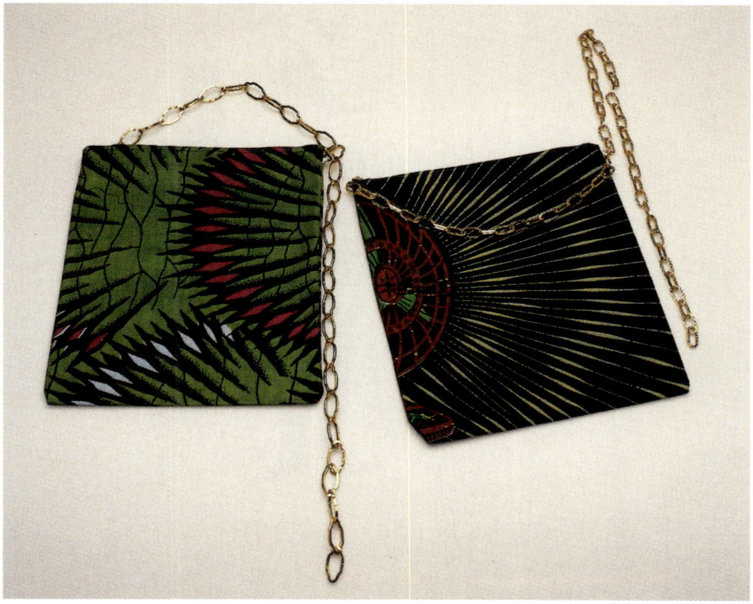

FRANZ WESTS SACKERL BIETET EINEN HINTERSINNIGEN KOMMENTAR ZUM EUROAMERIKANISCHEN ZENTRISMUS VON PARKETT.

TOTEM TOTE. A PARKETT-SIZED POUCH FASHIONED FROM HAND-PRINTED AFRICAN FABRIC IS A USEFUL ARTICLE FOR A SPECIFIC PURPOSE.

PARKETT 37

FRANZ WEST

ETUI FÜR PARKETT, 1993

Bedruckte afrikanische Baumwollstoffe, Kette,
Ed. 180, signiert und nummeriert, **CHF 250.– / € 160**

POUCH FOR PARKETT, 1993

Printed African fabric, chain, Ed. 180,
signed and numbered, **$ 180 / € 160**

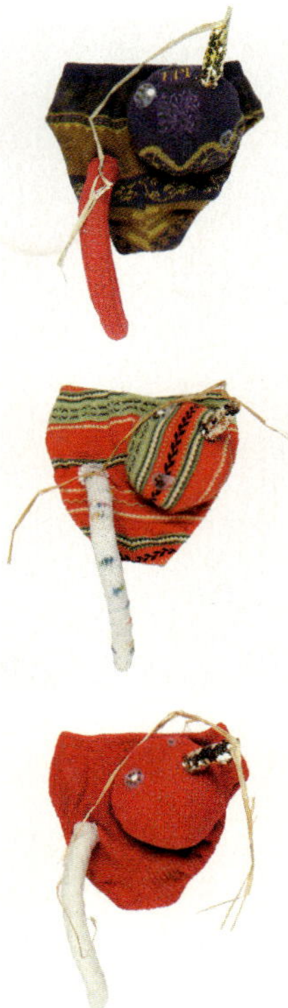

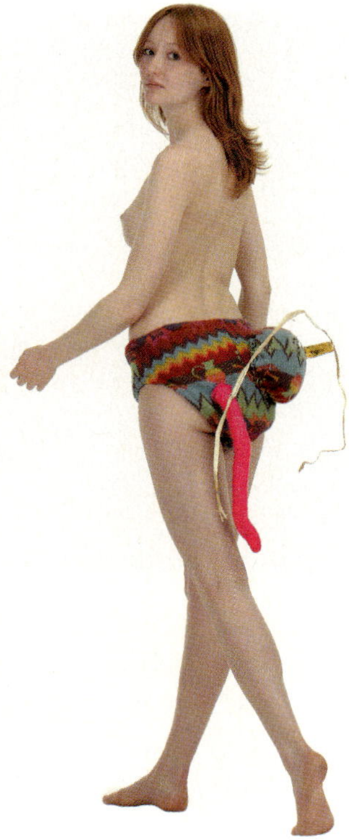

ANTI-BUNNY-KOSTÜM ODER KALTE KRATZHOSE:
DAS IDEALE NAHKAMPFTENÜ SAMT MIGRÄNETABLETTE
UND LETZTEM STROHHALM ZUM KLAMMERN.

ANTI-BUNNY COSTUME: THE IDEAL GET-UP FOR CLOSE
COMBAT, ALL-INCLUSIVE WITH HEADACHE PROTECTION
AND THE LAST STRAW.

PARKETT 67

JOHN BOCK

GEOMETRISCHER ORT DER 2 MIO. $ KNÖDELKNIK-KERBOCKERMIGRÄNEHITSHITBITSSOUFFLÉVISAGE, DRIN STROHMULMIGE ISOQUANTE TOUCHIERT GOLDENE BILANZREGEL + INSOLVENZSNOB, 2003

Unikat-Unterhose, Strickmaterial, Goldpailletten, Strohhalm, Silikon, Hasenkötel, Migränetablette.
Auflage: 60, signiertes und nummeriertes Zertifikat.
CHF 1400.– / € 920

Unique underpants, knitted fabric, gold sequins, straw, silicone, bunny droppings, migraine pill.
Edition of 60, signed and numbered certificate.
$ 1000 / € 920

PARKETT 67

PETER DOIG

GASTHOF, 2003

7-color etching with aquatint, 26 x 22",
on Hahnemühle 300 gm², natural white, 31 x 26".
Printed by Hope Sufferance Press, London.
Edition of 70, signed and numbered.
$ 1300 / € 1200

Radierung und Aquatinta (7 Farben), 66 x 55,5 cm,
auf Hahnemühle 300 gm², naturweiss, 73 x 63 cm.
Gedruckt bei Hope Sufferance Press, London.
Auflage: 70, signiert und nummeriert.
CHF 1800.–/ € 1200

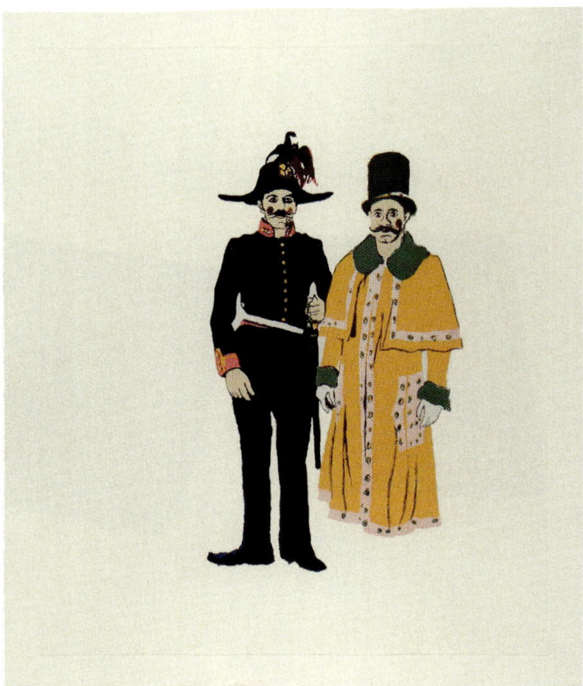

LAW AND ORDER? TWO CHARACTERS NO LONGER IN
SEARCH OF A MASTER.

RECHT UND ORDNUNG? ZWEI DIENER, DIE KEINEN HERRN
MEHR SUCHEN.

PARKETT 67

FRED TOMASELLI

CYCLOPTICON, 2003

Surface-mounted pigment print on Plexiglas, 12 x 12".
Printed by David Adamson, Adamson Editions, Washington, D.C.
Edition of 60, signed and numbered.
$ 1400 / € 1300

Pigmentdruck hinter Plexiglas aufgezogen, 30,5 x 30,5 cm.
Gedruckt bei David Adamson, Adamson Editions, Washington, D.C.
Auflage: 60, signiert und nummeriert.
CHF 1900.– / € 1300

THE ANATOMY OF A MIND SPEWING A TIDY UNIVERSE OF CHAOTIC INVENTION.

SYSTEM UND AUFLÖSUNG IM ZYKLOPENBLICK MENSCHLICHER WAHRNEHMUNG.

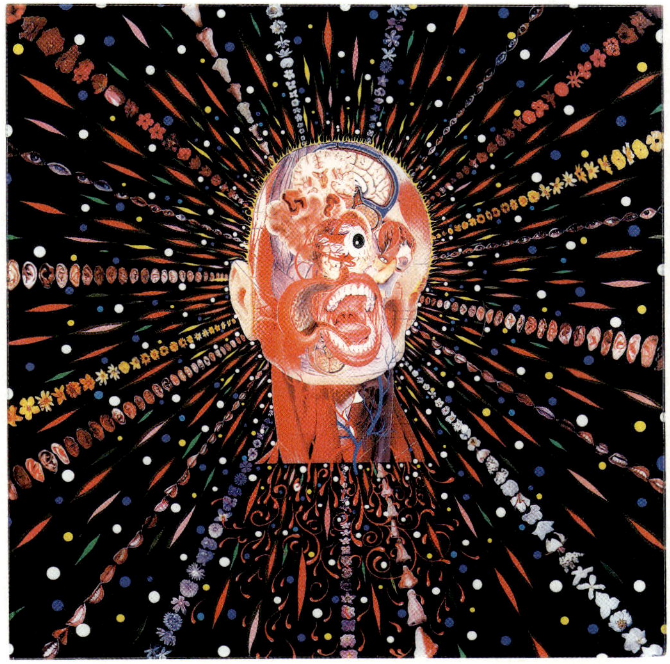

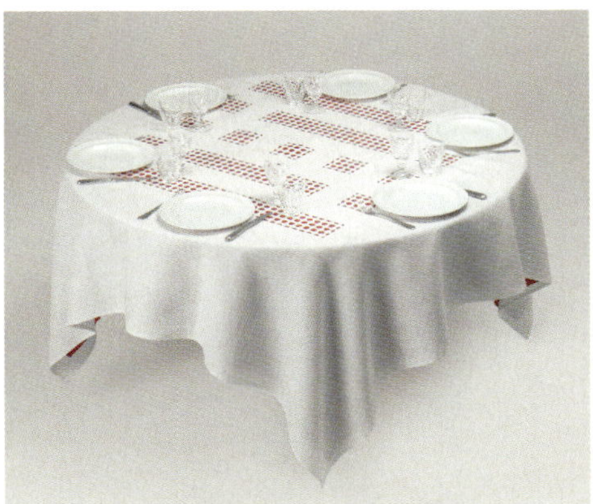

1A 2A 3A

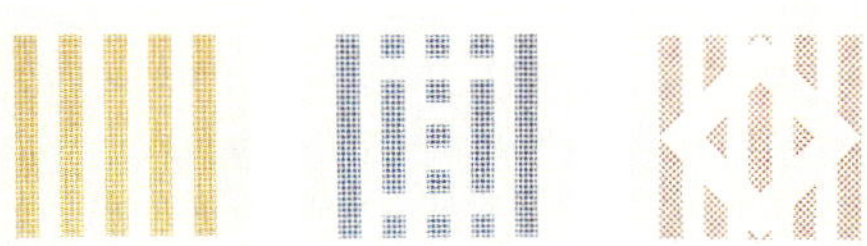

CLARITY OF FORM AND STATE-OF-THE-ART TECHNOLOGY CONJURE THE BAROQUE SPLENDOR OF HANDMADE LACE.

PER ASPERA AD ASTRA: MIT FORMALER STRENGE UND MODERNSTER TECHNIK ZU BAROCKER PRACHTENTFALTUNG.

PARKETT 66

DANIEL BUREN

UNIQUE TABLECLOTH WITH LASER-CUT LACE (OBJECT TO BE SITUATED ON TABLE), 2002

Two-layered tablecloth: off-white laser-cut design on monochrome underlayer.
Each tablecloth has a unique combination of design and color. Top layer 70 7/8 x 70 7/8"; bottom layer 67 x 67"; design 30 11/16 x 30 11/16"; width of stripes 8.7 cm
Washable polyester, laser-cut and produced by Jakob Schläpfer AG, St. Gallen
Edition of 78 unique versions (design versions 1A–3A: 13 each on different colors; diagonal design versions 1B–3B : 13 each on different colors),
stamped and numbered certificate, **$ 1560 / € 1440**
Special price for 3 tablecloths in 3 different designs **$ 3400 / € 3100**

UNIKAT-TISCHTUCH MIT LASERSPITZE (AUF TISCH ZU PLATZIERENDES OBJEKT), 2002

Weisses Tischtuch mit Laserschnittdesign und farbigem Untertischtuch.
Die Kombination von Muster und Farbe ist bei jedem Tischtuch anders.
Grösse 180 x 180 cm; Untertischtuch 170 x 170 cm; Muster 78 x 78 cm,
Breite des Streifenelements 8,7 cm
Polyester, waschbar, Laserschnitt und Herstellung: Jakob Schläpfer AG, St. Gallen
Auflage: 78 Unikate (Design-Versionen 1A–3A: je 13 auf verschiedenfarbigen Untertischtüchern; diagonale Design-Versionen 1B–3B: je 13 auf verschiedenfarbigen Untertischtüchern), gestempeltes, nummeriertes Zertifikat, **CHF 2200 / € 1440**
Spezialpreis für 3 Tischtücher in 3 verschiedenen Designs **CHF 4800 / € 3100**

TUNE IN TO THE MYSTERIOUS WORKINGS OF A LATE TWENTIETH CENTURY BAROQUE MIND.

EIN WISPERN IM OHR. WELLENWIRBEL IM STROM ZWISCHEN GESTERN UND MORGEN.

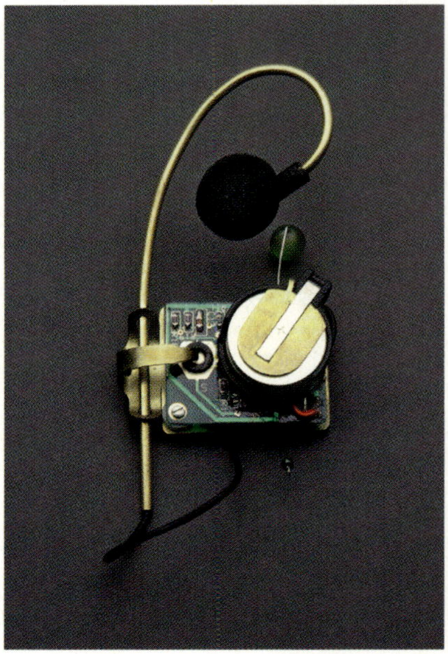

PARKETT 49

LAURIE ANDERSON

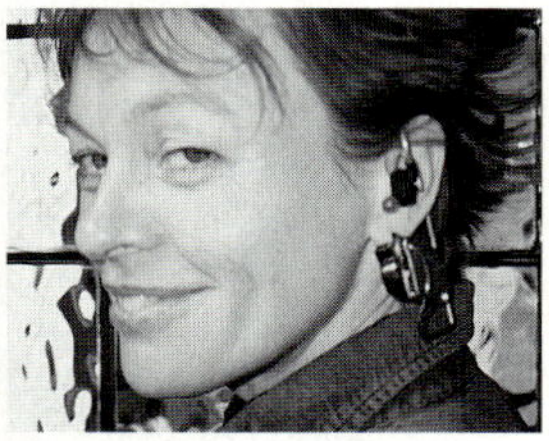

HEARRING, 1997

Earring with playable sound message
(approx. 20 sec.), brass, copper, circuit board,
loudspeaker, lithium battery,
plexiglas, wires, approx. size: 3 3/8 x 1 3/4 x 1".
Jewelry by Josiah Dearborn; engineering design Bob Bielecki.
Ed. 150, with monogram and numbered, **$ 430 / € 390**

HEARRING, 1997

Ohrring mit abspielbarem Tonstück (ca. 20 Sek.),
Messing, Kupfer, Chip, Lautsprecher, Lithiumbatterie, Plexiglas, Elektrodraht,
Grösse ca. 8,5 x 4,5 x 2,5 cm.
Juwelierarbeit: Josiah Dearborn. Technikdesign: Bob Bielecki.
Ed. 150, mit Monogramm und nummeriert, **CHF 600.– / € 390**

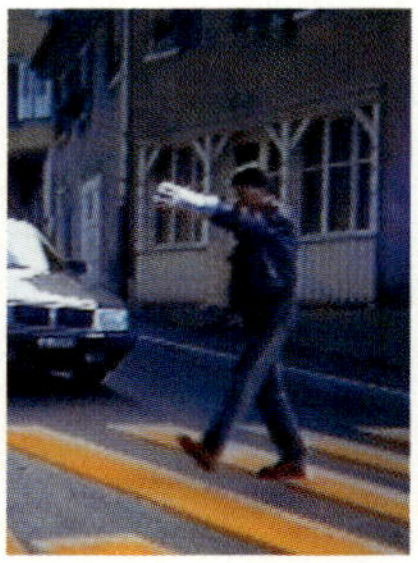

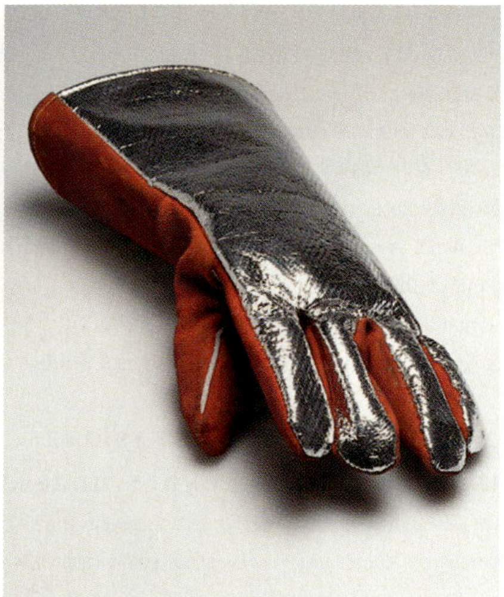

RED ALERT. A FIREMAN'S PROTECTIVE GLOVE PLAYS AN ACTIVE ROLE AS A MOCK TRAFFIC SIGNAL.

PARKETT 45

ROMAN SIGNER

FEUERWEHRHANDSCHUH MIT PHOTO, 1995

Handfläche aus hitzebeständigem Spezialspaltleder. Handrücken
aus hitzereflektierendem, aluminisiertem KEVLAR-Gewebe 550 g/m2,
isolierendes Wollfutter, Länge 35 cm,
Photographie aus einem Video von Aleksandra Signer, ca. 13 x 18 cm
Ed. 80, signiert und nummeriert, **CHF 750.– / € 490**

FIREMAN'S GLOVE WITH PHOTOGRAPH, 1995

Standard fireman's glove with heat-resistant red suede palm, heat-reflecting,
aluminized KEVLAR back, 550 g/m2, insulating woolen lining,
length 13 3/4", still from a video by Aleksandra Signer, approx. 5 1/8 x 7 1/8".
Ed. 80, signed and numbered, **$ 530 / € 490**

STOPP – EIN ROTSILBERNER HANDSCHUH. SCHUTZ VOR SIGNERS POETISCHEM FEUERREGEN? NEIN, KAMPFHANDSCHUH ZUM EINSATZ IM TÄGLICHEN STRASSENVERKEHR.

THIS TOO, TOO SOLID STONE: ALL THE WORLD LOCKED INTO THE TIMELESS EMBRACE OF THE AGES.

EINEN STEINWURF ENTFERNT VON DER EWIGKEIT: DER STOFF AUS DEM DAS UNIVERSUM IST.

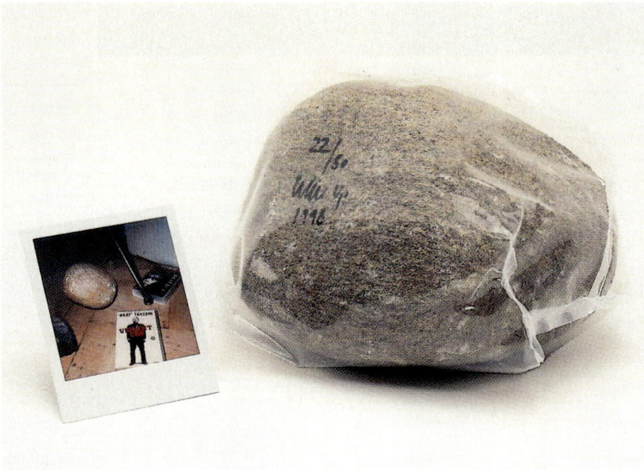

PARKETT 52

UGO RONDINONE

ALLE AUGENBLICKE HÖREN HIER AUF UND GEMEINSAM WERDEN WIR ZU JEDER ERINNERUNG, DIE ES JEMALS GEGEBEN HAT, 1998

Stein aus dem Maggiatal,
ca. 30 x 20 x 10 cm, Gewicht ca. 7 bis 10 kg,
Polaroidaufnahme des Steins durch den Künstler.
Auflage: 50, signiert und nummeriert, **CHF 750.– / € 490**

ALL MOMENTS STOP HERE AND TOGETHER WE BECOME EVERY MEMORY THAT HAS EVER BEEN, 1998

Stone from the Valle Maggia
(Ticino, Switzerland).
Approximate size 12 x 8 x 4'',
approximate weight 14 to 20 lbs.,
Polaroid photo of the stone by the artist.
Edition of 50, signed and numbered, **$ 530 / € 490**

MIRACULUM HELVUM MAGNUM.

PARKETT 50/51

JEFF KOONS

INFLATABLE BALLOON FLOWER (YELLOW), 1997

PVC, approx. 51 x 59 x 70''.
Manufactured by Schultes, Vienna.
Edition of 100, signed and numbered,
$ 3900 / € 3600

AUFBLASBARE BALLONBLUME (GELB), 1997

PVC, ca. 128 x 148 x 180 cm.
Hergestellt bei Schultes, Wien.
Auflage: 100, signiert und nummeriert,
CHF 5500.– / € 3600

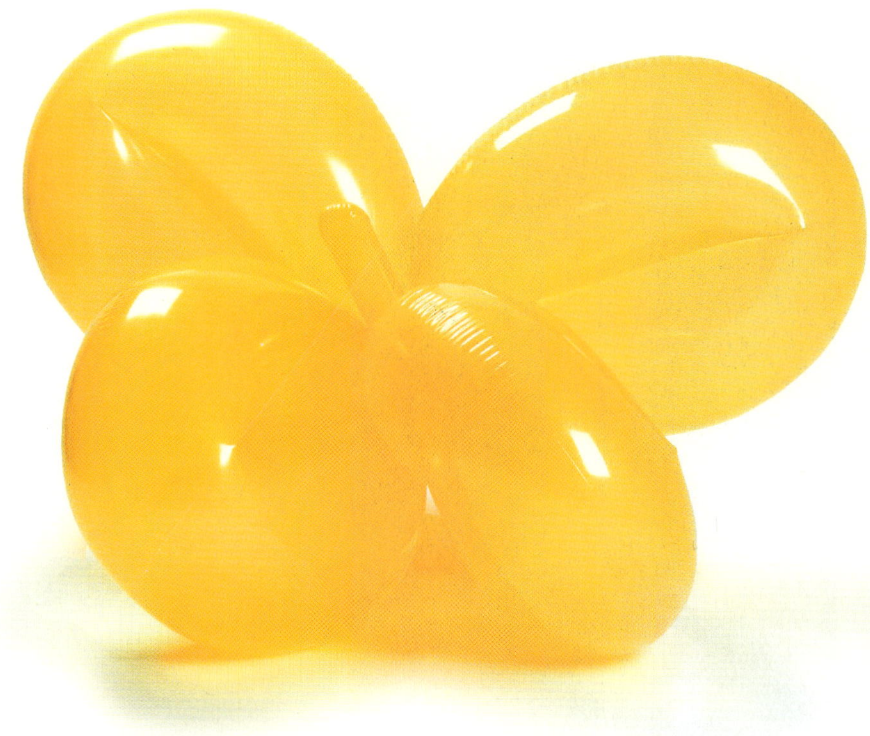

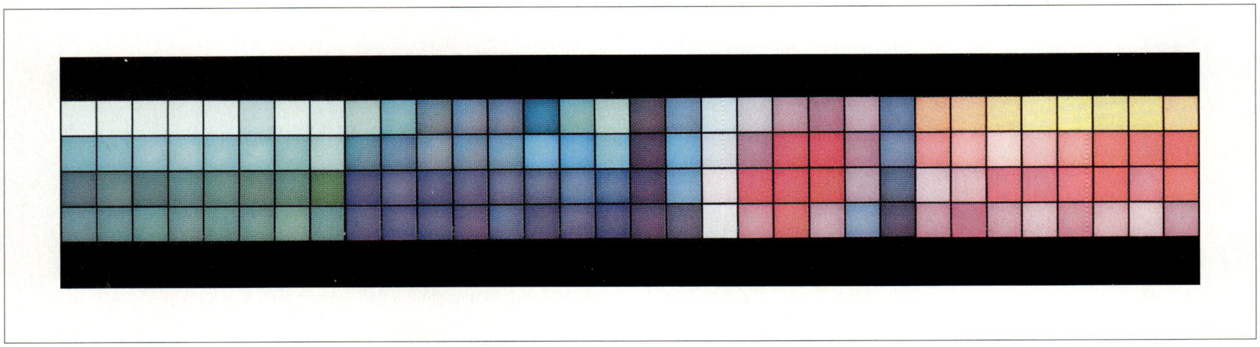

PARKETT 66

ANGELA BULLOCH

HORIZONTAL TECHNICOLOUR:

STILLS WITH NEGATIVE SPACE, 2002

C-print, 12 3/16 x 46" (image 8 7/16 x 42 7/16")
Printed by Philippe Laumont, Laumont Editions, New York
Edition of 80, signed and numbered, **$ 990 / € 920**

C-Print, 31 x 116, 8 cm (Bild 21,5 x 107,8 cm)
Produziert bei Philippe Laumont, Laumont Editions, New York
Auflage: 80, signiert und nummeriert, **CHF 1400 / € 920**

MOSAIC OF LIGHT: A COMPOSITION CULLED FROM THE VAST POTENTIAL OF UNTOLD SHADES OF COLOR.

LICHTMOSAIK: KOMPOSITION AUS MILLIONEN SCHLUMMERNDER MÖGLICHKEITEN.

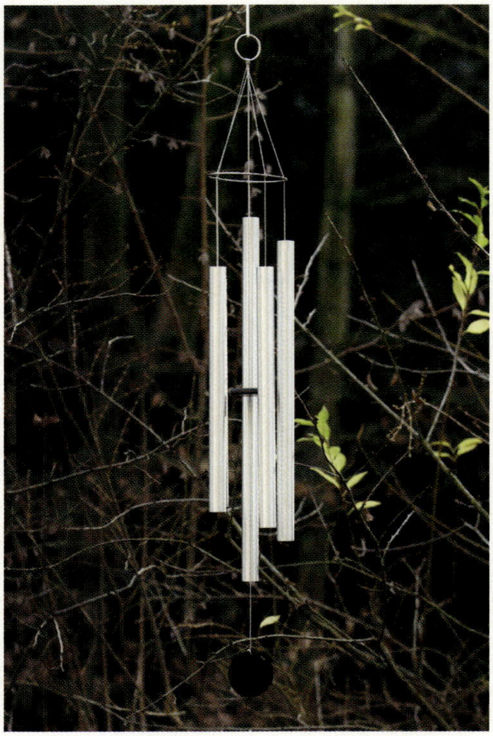

PARKETT 66

PIERRE HUYGHE

ALL BUT ONE, 2002

Windchime for outdoor use, 5 hand-tuned aluminum tubes, 1 3/8" diameter each; top hanging ring 2"; black cord, black wood striker, engraved aluminum wind plate, 4" diameter, overall length 55 1/8"; overall diameter 8"
Manufactured by Jeff Kile, Grace Note Windchimes, Mariposa, California
Edition of 70, signed and numbered certificate, **$ 1280 / € 1180**

ALLE AUSSER EINEM, 2002

Freiluft-Windglockenspiel , 5 handgestimmte Aluminiumrohre von je 3,5 cm Durchmesser; Aufhängering 5 cm Durchmesser, schwarze Kordelschnur, schwarze Holzscheibe als Klangklöppel, gravierte Windscheibe aus Aluminium, 10 cm Durchmesser, Gesamthöhe 140 cm; Gesamtdurchmesser 20,5 cm
Hergestellt von Jeff Kile, Grace Note Windchimes, Mariposa, California
Auflage: 70, signiertes und nummeriertes Zertifikat, **CHF 1800 / € 1180**

SPEAK, MEMORY: THE SERENDIPITY OF CAPRICIOUS WINDS GIVES THE FAMILIAR A NEW TWIST.

ERINNERUNG, SPRICH: WIND UND ZUFALL SPIELEN MIT UND LASSEN VERTRAUTES NEU ERSTEHEN.

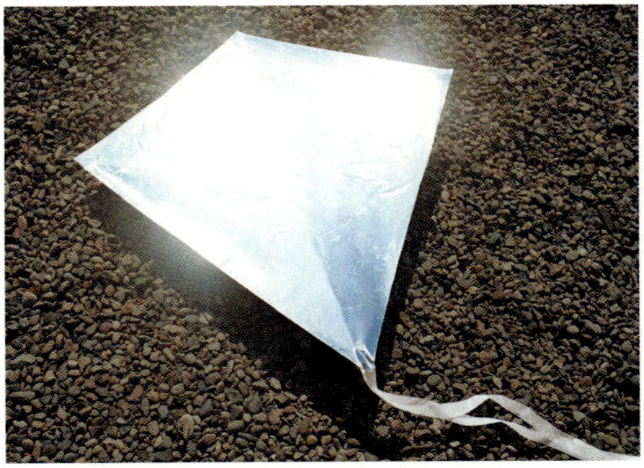

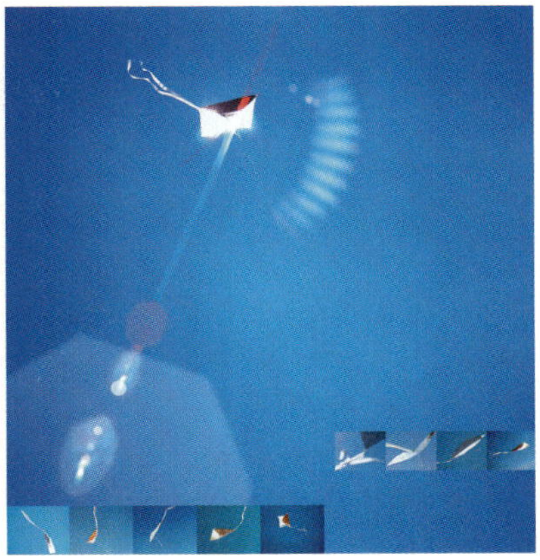

PARKETT 57

DOUG AITKEN

DECREASE THE MASS AND RUN LIKE HELL, 1999

Mirror kite, ca. 34 x $33\,^{1}/_{2}$", tail $37\,^{3}/_{8}$",
with poster of flying kite, ca. 20 x $15\,^{5}/_{8}$".
Edition of 60, stamped and numbered, **\$ 700 / € 650**

DIE MASSE VERKLEINERN UND RENNEN WIE DER TEUFEL, 1999

Spiegeldrachen, ca. 86,5 x 85 cm, Schwanz 95 cm,
und Plakat mit fliegendem Drachen, 51 x 39,6 cm.
Auflage 60, mit Prägestempel und nummeriert, **CHF 990.– / € 650**

FEATHER THE LIGHT AND CAST A SPELL: THIS KITE PREYS ON REFLECTION.

LICHTHUNGRIGER LUFTFLITZER HÄNGT SEINEN REFLEXIONEN NACH.

THE WEIGHTLESSNESS OF THE THIRD DIMENSION.

DIE SCHWERELOSIGKEIT DER DRITTEN DIMENSION.

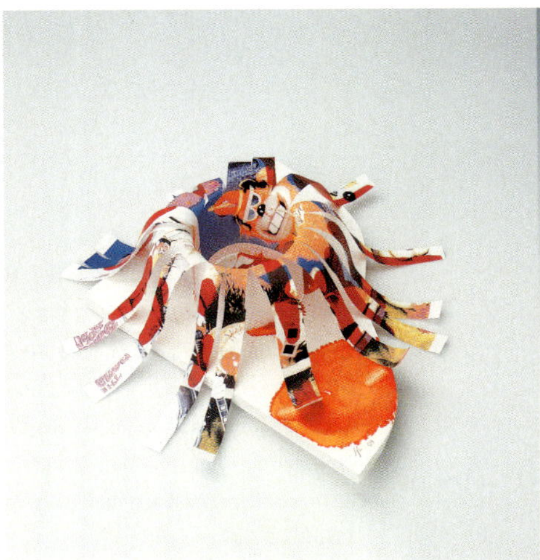

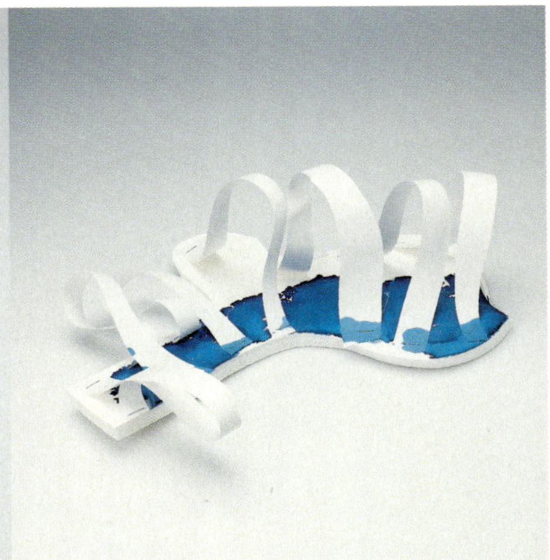

PARKETT 56

JORGE PARDO

UNTITLED, 1999

Unique sculpture, archival paper mounted on cardboard, colored pencil, ca. $9\,^{7}/_{8}$ x 4 x4"
Edition of 55, signed and numbered, **\$ 680 / € 620**

OHNE TITEL, 1999

Skulptur (Unikat), lichtbeständiges Papier auf Kartonsockel, Farbstift, ca. 25 x 10 x 10 cm
Auflage: 55, signiert und nummeriert, **CHF 950.– / € 620**

«BLUE MOON... AND THEN SUDDENLY APPEARED BEFORE ME THE ONLY ONE MY ARMS COULD EVER HOLD.»

BLAUER MOND –«ICH WÜRDE BIS ZUM KRANKEN MICH ZERGRÄMEN, VERLÖR' ICH DICH, DU TRAUTER NACHTKUMPAN!»

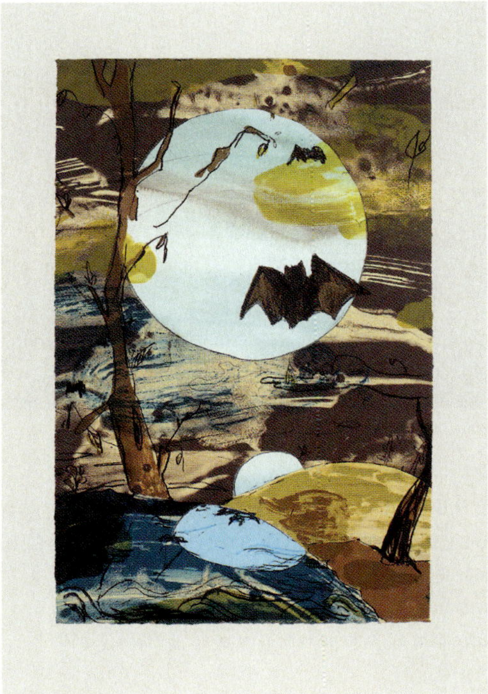

PARKETT 65

LAURA OWENS

UNTITLED, 2002

Handprinted 10-color lithograph on tan BFK Rives with three collage elements: one handpainted with watercolor on blue Magnani Pescia, two on white BFK Rives, the color of the moon will vary with each print, 18 x 12"
Printed by Ed Hamilton, Hamilton Press, Venice, California
Edition of 70, signed and numbered on the back, **$ 1350 / € 1250**

OHNE TITEL, 2002

Handgedruckte 10-Farben-Lithographie auf getöntem BFK Rives mit drei Collage-Elementen: eines handbemalt mit Wasserfarbe auf Magnani Pescia (Blau), zwei auf weissem BFK Rives, die Farbe des Mondes variiert von Blatt zu Blatt, 45,8 x 30,6 cm
Gedruckt bei Ed Hamilton, Hamilton Press, Venice, Kalifornien
Auflage: 70, rückseitig signiert und nummeriert, **CHF 1900.– / € 1250**

TWICE INCOMPLETE YIELDS COMPLETE PERFECTION: A HUMBLE SHACK THREADED IN REVERSE VISIBILITY AND REPRODUCED ON EXQUISITE SILK.

VERKEHRTE BILDWELT AUF SEIDE: EINE MEDITATION ÜBER GROB- UND FEINSTOFFLICHES.

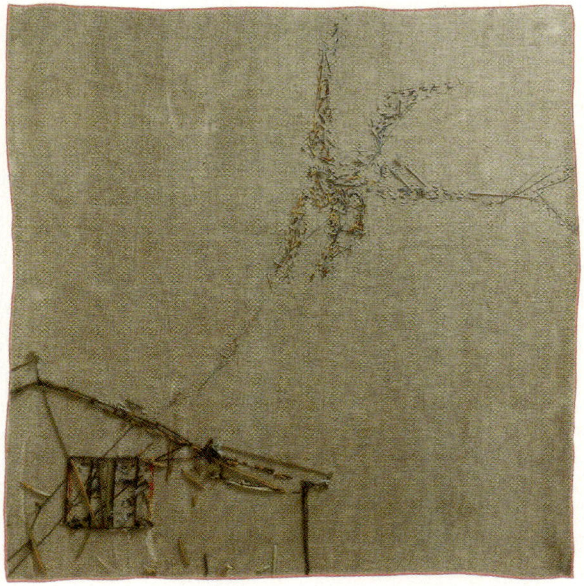

PARKETT 65

MICHAEL RAEDECKER

THE OTHER SIDE, 2002

13-color silkscreen print on pure silk satin scarf
with handrolled border, 33 1/2 x 33 1/2"
Detail from the back of the painting INCOMPLETE (2002)
Produced by Fabric Frontline, Zurich
Edition of 99, signed and numbered certificate,
$ 550 / € 500

13-Farben-Siebdruck auf Seidensatinfoulard,
handrouliert, 85 x 85 cm
Produktion: Fabric Frontline, Zürich
Ausschnitt der Rückansicht des Bildes INCOMPLETE (2002)
Auflage: 99, signiertes und nummeriertes Zertifikat,
CHF 770.– / € 500

BE YOUR OWN ARCHITECTURE:
REFLECT AND BE REFLECTED IN WALLS AND
ROOMS THAT ARE NONE.

ADDITION, SUBTRAKTION, MULTIPLIKATION,
DIVISION: DAS VERSPIE(GEL)LTE EINMALEINS
EINER MEHRDIMENSIONALEN ARCHITEKTUR.

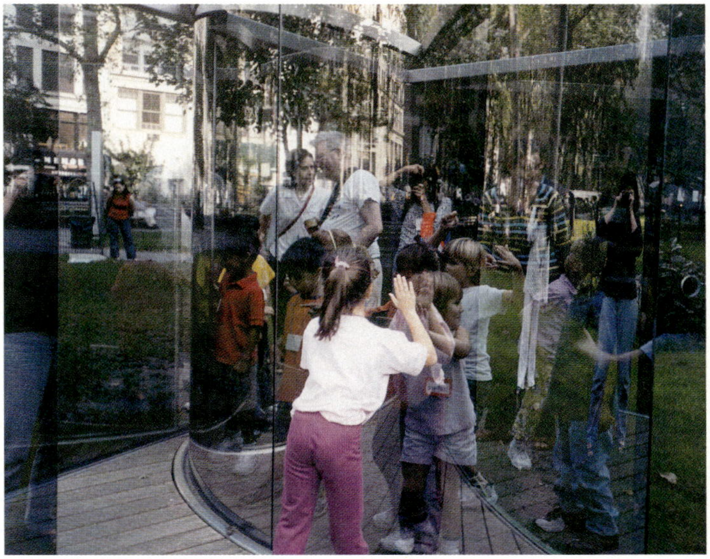

PARKETT 68

DAN GRAHAM

FUN FOR KIDS AT MY WORK IN A PARK IN MANHATTAN, 2003

Piezo Ultrachrome Pigment on Hahnemühle paper, 13 x 16 $^{1}/_{2}$".
Printed by Laumont Editions, New York.
Photograph by Rosalind Cutforth.
Edition of 60, signed and numbered on the reverse.
$ 1400 / € 1200

Piezo-Ultrachrome-Pigmentdruck auf Hahnemühle, 33 x 42 cm.
Gedruckt bei Laumont Editions, New York.
Photographie von Rosalind Cutforth.
Auflage: 60, auf der Rückseite signiert und nummeriert.
CHF 1800 / € 1200

SAISONALE GRAVITATION: INDIVIDUELLE SPUREN UND KRISTALLISATIONSPUNKTE
IM SOG DER MASSENNESTER DES GEKRÜMMTEN RAUMS.

SEASONAL GRAVITATION: INDIVIDUAL TRACES AND POINTS OF CRYSTALLIZATION
IN THE MAELSTROM OF MASS NESTING FROM PLACE TO PLACE.

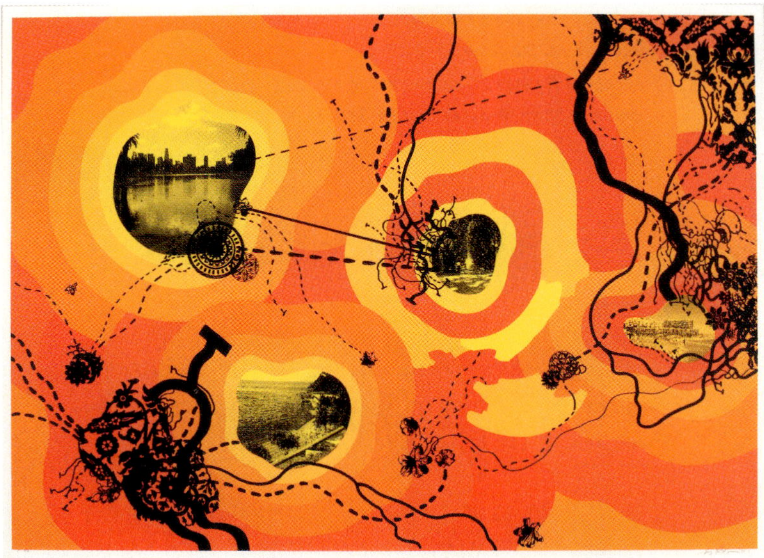

PARKETT 68

FRANZ ACKERMANN

PEAK SEASON, 2003

Siebdruck (10 Farben) auf Somerset 300 gm^2;
Blattformat 50 x 70 cm, Bildformat 48 x 68 cm.
Druck: Werkstatt für Kunstsiebdruck München.
Auflage: 70, signiert und nummeriert.
CHF 1700.– / € 1100

10-color silkscreen print on Somerset 300 gm^2;
paper size 19 $^{11}/_{16}$ x 27 $^{9}/_{16}$", image size 18 $^{7}/_{8}$ x 26 $^{3}/_{4}$".
Printed by Werkstatt für Kunstsiebdruck Munich.
Edition of 70, signed and numbered.
$ 1400 / € 1100

TRACEY, EIGHTY TIMES: THE FACES AND FACETTES OF UNQUALIFIED CANDOR.

ACHTZIG MAL TRACEY: ACHTZIG FACETTEN VON UNGEBÄNDIGTER OFFENHEIT.

PARKETT 63

TRACEY EMIN

SELF-PORTRAIT, 12.11.01

Unique color print from original Polaroid;
all images taken on the same day.
Image size 7 7/8 x 7 7/8", paper size 15 3/4 x 15 3/4".
Edition of 80, signed and numbered, **$ 990 / € 910**

SELBSTPORTRÄT, 12.11.01

Abzug einer Polaroidaufnahme, Unikat;
alle Aufnahmen entstanden am gleichen Tag.
Bildgrösse 20 x 20 cm, Papierformat 40 x 40 cm.
Auflage: 80, signiert und nummeriert, **CHF 1400.– / € 910**

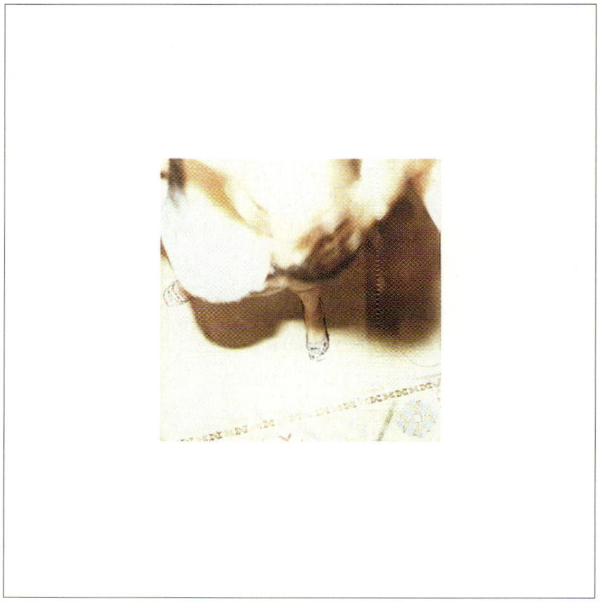

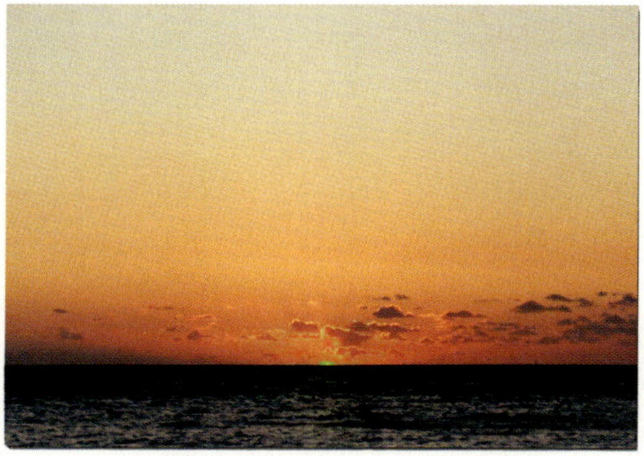

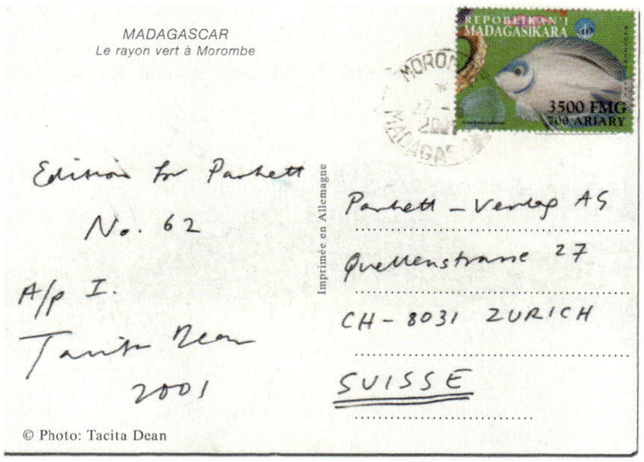

PARKETT 62

TACITA DEAN

THE GREEN RAY, 2001

Color postcard, 105 x 148,5 mm.
Printed by Steidl Verlag, Göttingen, Germany.
Edition of 100, signed, numbered, stamped, and posted in Morombe, Western Madagascar **$ 410 / € 380**

Farbpostkarte, 105 x 148,5 mm
Gedruckt bei Steidl Verlag, Göttingen.
Auflage: 100, signiert, nummeriert, mit Poststempel aufgegeben in Morombe, West-Madagaskar, **CHF 580.– / € 380**

THE ENCHANTMENT OF THE GREEN RAY HAS CAPTURED THE IMAGINATION OF JULES VERNE, MARCEL DUCHAMP, AND NOW TACITA DEAN.

DAS GRÜNE LEUCHTEN AM HORIZONT VERZAUBERTE JULES VERNE, MARCEL DUCHAMP UND AUCH TACITA DEAN.

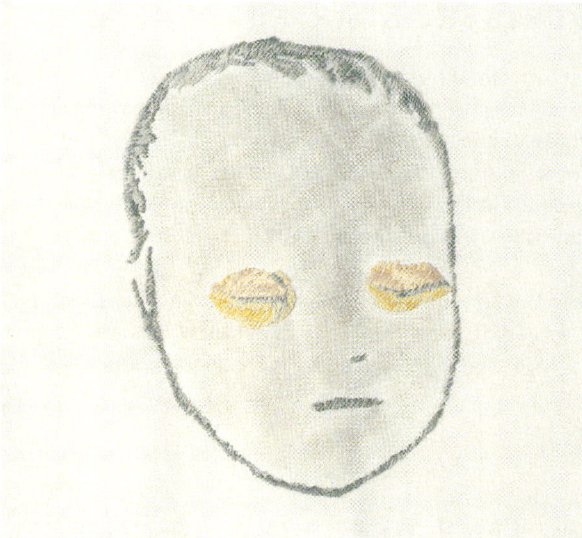

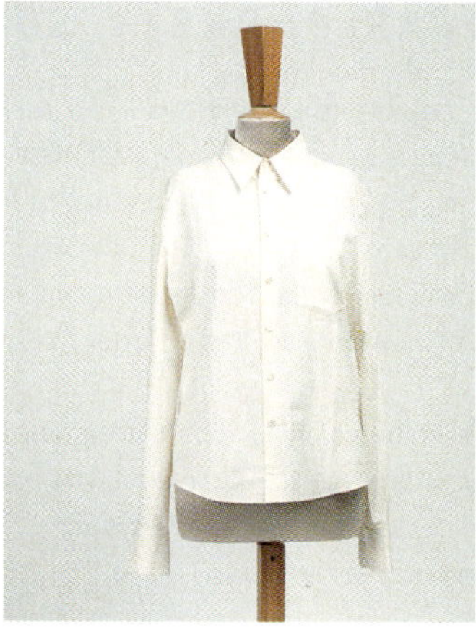

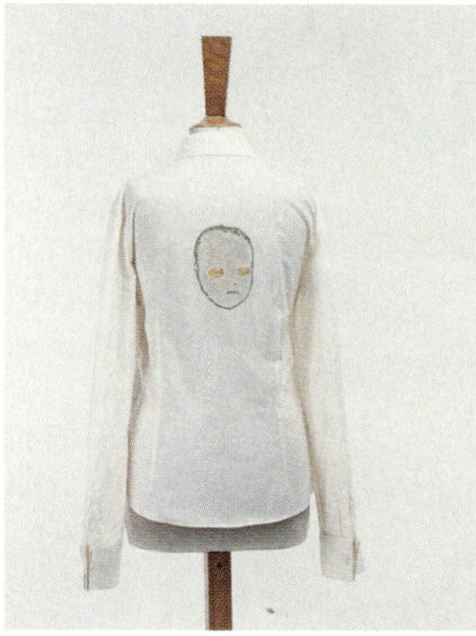

BORN TO WEAR: GIVE THIS CHILD A VOICE.

GEZEICHNETES KIND: MIT SORGFALT ZU TRAGEN.

PARKETT 60

LUC TUYMANS

SILENCE, 1990–2000

Men's cotton shirt with reproduction of the artist's painting SILENCE, 1991.
Shirt design by Walter van Beirendonck, 3 sizes (S, M, L).
Silkscreen version printed by Lorenz Boegli, Zurich.
Edition of 99, signed and numbered, **$ 570 / € 520**

STILLE, 1990–2000

Baumwoll-Herrenhemd mit Reproduktion des Bildes SILENCE, 1991.
Hemddesign Walter van Beirendonck, 3 Grössen (S, M, L).
Siebdruck-Version gedruckt bei Lorenz Boegli, Zürich.
Auflage: 99, signiert und nummeriert, **CHF 800.– / € 520**

NOSCE TE IPSUM. A FRAGMENTED WHOLE BECOMES ENMESHED IN REFLECTIONS ON INFINITY.

NOSCE TE IPSUM. TAUSEND SPLITTER IM SCHMETTERLINGS-NETZ DER REFLEXION.

PARKETT 59

YAYOI KUSAMA

INFINITY NETS, 2000

Silkscreen print on mirror, 10 x 8 1/4".
Edition of 70, signed and numbered on the back,
$ 950 / € 920

UNENDLICHKEITSNETZE, 2000

Siebdruck auf Spiegel, 25,5 x 21 cm.
Auflage: 70, auf der Rückseite signiert und nummeriert,
CHF 1400.– / € 920

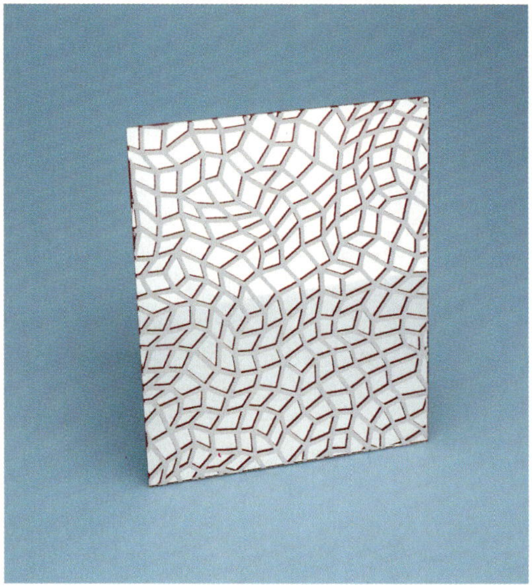

EDITIONS FOR PARKETT

DEAR PARKETT SUBSCRIBER, DEAR READER,

It gives us great pleasure to present this latest survey of currently available artists' editions. The Parkett exhibition at the Museum of Modern Art in New York (2001) was the most complete presentation of all the editions that artists have so far created especially for Parkett. The exhibition has traveled since to the Whitechapel Art Gallery, London, and to the Irish Museum of Modern Art, Dublin. The full documentation on all editions is available in a box containing color postcards of 128 editions and a text booklet with two essays on the MoMA show. Visit our website at www.parkettart.com, which includes among other features an extensive search engine on all artists and the 1000 Parkett texts published up to now.

Beatrice Fässler in Zurich or Ali Subotnick in New York will be happy to answer any questions you may have regarding Parkett's Musée en Appartement. Orders may be placed online (SSL secured) as well as by phone, fax or mail (see yellow order form in each issue). Prices are subject to change, postage and packaging are not included; orders will be filled on a first-come first-serve basis.

Yours sincerely,

SEHR GEEHRTE ABONNENTIN, SEHR GEEHRTER ABONNENT, LIEBE PARKETT-LESER,

Wir freuen uns sehr, Ihnen diesen neuesten Überblick über die zurzeit erhältlichen Künstlereditionen zu geben. Die Parkett-Ausstellung im Museum of Modern Art in New York (2001) war die bisher vollständigste Präsentation aller bis dahin von Künstlerinnen und Künstlern für Parkett geschaffenen Editionen. Inzwischen ist die Ausstellung auch in der Whitechapel Art Gallery, London, und im Irish Museum of Modern Art, Dublin, gezeigt worden. Eine Dokumentation aller Künstlereditionen bietet die handliche Postkartenbox mit 128 Farbpostkarten und einem Textbüchlein mit zwei Essays zur MoMA-Ausstellung. Besuchen Sie auch unsere Website, www.parkettart.com, wo u.a. eine Suchmaschine zu allen Künstlern und den über 1000 bis heute veröffentlichten Texten zur Verfügung steht.

Für alle Fragen zu Parketts Musée en Appartement steht Ihnen Beatrice Fässler in Zürich jederzeit gerne zur Verfügung. Ihre Bestellung können Sie uns online (Site ist SSL-zertifiziert), per Telefon, Fax oder Post (siehe gelben Antwortschein in jeder Ausgabe) zukommen lassen. Preisänderungen bleiben vorbehalten. Versand, Verpackungskosten und MWSt. (Schweiz) sind nicht inbegriffen. Die Lieferung erfolgt in der Reihenfolge des Bestelleingangs solange Vorrat.

Mit freundlichen Grüssen

Dieter von Graffenried
Publisher/Verleger

Bice Curiger
Editor-in-Chief/Chefredaktorin

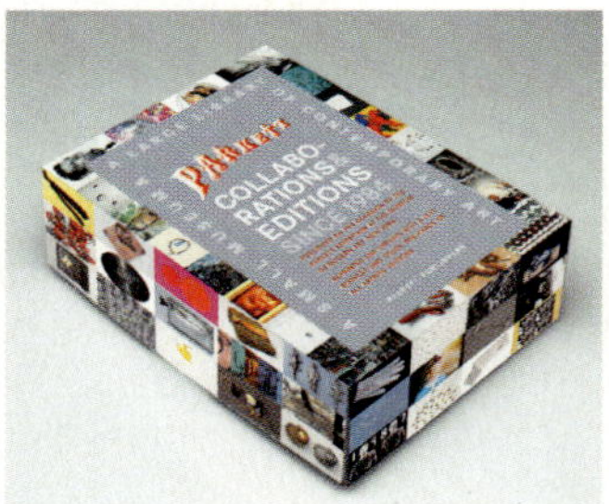

POSTCARD SET
WITH TEXT BOOKLET ON
MOMA SHOW
128 color postcards,
booklet of 64 pages,
colored box.
CHF 45.– / $ 29 / € 30
ISBN 3-907582-23-3

Parkett Verlag AG
Quellenstr. 27
8031 Zürich
Tel. +41-1-271 81 40
FAX +41-1-272 43 01

Parkett PUBLISHERS
155 AV. OF the americas
new york, ny 10013
phone (212)673-2660
FAX (212)271-0704
www.parkettart.com